The Economics
of Adjustment
and Growth

The Economics
of Adjustment
and Growth

Pierre-Richard Agénor
The World Bank
Washington, D.C.

ACADEMIC PRESS

A Harcourt Science and Technology Company

San Diego   San Francisco   New York   Boston   London   Sydney   Tokyo

Academic Press
A Harcourt Science and Technology Company
525 B Street, Suite 1900, San Diego, California 92101-4495, U.S.A.
http://www.academicpress.com

Academic Press
Harcourt Place, 32 Jamestown Road, London NW1 7BY, UK
http://www.hbuk.co.uk/ap/

Library of Congress Catalog Card Number: 99-69503

International Standard Book Number: 0-12-044555-7

PRINTED IN THE UNITED STATES OF AMERICA
00 01 02 03 04 05   EB 9 8 7 6 5 4 3 2 1

To my late mother, Rolande,
for her love, courage and devotion

CONTENTS

2 The Financial System, Money Demand, and Monetary Policy

3 Fiscal Deficits, Public Debt, and the Current Account

4 Exchange Rate Regimes

5 Inflation and Disinflation

6 Capital Inflows: Causes and Policy Responses

7 Currency Crises and Financial Volatility

12 Knowledge, Human Capital and Endogenous Growth

13 The Determinants of Economic Growth: An Empirical Overview

14 Structural Adjustment: Agriculture, Trade, and the Labor Market

15 Fiscal and Financial Sector Reforms

16 Adjustment and External Debt in Low-Income Countries

17 Sequencing, Gradualism, and the Political Economy of Adjustment

Annex A: The Informal Sector and The Urban Labor Market

Annex B: Informal Financial Markets

Annex C: Exchange Market Unification

Introduction and Overview

The process through which economic adjustment affects economic growth and standards of living remains at the forefront of the policy agenda in the developing world. In that regard, an important lesson of the past two decades is that macroeconomic and financial volatility may have adverse effects on growth rates and the level of income. Instability in relative prices and overall inflation may have a negative effect on the return to capital and the decision to invest; in turn, the lack of investment may hamper economic growth and raise the incidence of poverty. At the same time, it has been recognized that microeconomic rigidities may have sizable effects on macroeconomic imbalances. For instance, interest rate ceilings that result in negative real rates of interest have large effects on saving-investment balances and may therefore contribute to mounting balance-of-payments problems. Thus, attempts at macroeconomic stabilization may fail if they are not complemented with adequate microeconomic (and often institutional) reforms.

Although the intricate interactions between short- and medium-term adjustment policies are now well recognized by both economists and policymakers in developing countries, there have been only few systematic attempts to integrate them in a coherent framework. Most textbooks in the field of development economics have by and large maintained their focus on long-term growth, and continue to treat macroeconomic issues as a sideshow. My recent book with Peter Montiel, *Development Macroeconomics*, took the opposite position and focused almost exclusively on macroeconomic policy issues. However, the advanced nature of that book makes it more suitable for graduate students and technically oriented professional macroeconomists.

The purpose of this book is to fill the gap in the existing literature by providing a rigorous, but accessible, analysis of policy issues involved in both aspects of economic adjustment in developing countries—short-run macroeconomic management *and* structural adjustment policies aimed at fostering economic growth. As in my earlier work, the book continues to emphasize the need to take systematically into account important *structural features* of these countries for economic analysis. The underlying perspective is that structural economic characteristics play an important role in both the transmission of policy shocks and the response of the economy to adjustment policies. It is therefore essential to take into account the behavioral implications of these characteristics in designing stabilization and adjustment models aimed at guiding policy

1

decisions. As will become clear to the reader, an important analytical literature doing precisely that already exists; however, some of this literature has been available (often in compact form) only in professional economic journals. This book makes much of this material available in a coherent and, I hope, a relatively reader-friendly format.

The structure and contents of this book are likely to make it of interest to a variety of readers. A first group of readers is likely to be professional economists interested in a rigorous, but not overly mathematical, overview of recent developments in the economics of reform. It includes, in particular, economists in developing countries involved on a day-to-day basis with adjustment issues, economists working in international organizations dealing with development, and economists in private financial institutions. A second group of readers includes advanced undergraduate students pursuing a degree in economic management, or students specializing in political science or public affairs, with a basic knowledge of standard microeconomics and macroeconomics. Although the material covered in the book is dense, the relatively self-contained nature of most of the chapters provides considerable discretion to teachers in choosing the exact list of topics to be covered during, say, a full-semester course. Finally, parts of the book can also be used as supplementary readings for advanced undergraduate courses in development economics: macroeconomics (particularly Chapters 1 to 9), economic growth (Chapters 10 to 13), international economics (Chapters 6, 7, 14, and 16), and public economics (Chapters 3, 12, and 14).[1]

The book is organized as follows. Chapters 1 to 9 focus on policy issues related to short-run macroeconomic adjustment. Chapter 1 begins with a discussion of the determinants of consumption and saving in developing countries, including both standard theories (the permanent income hypothesis and the life-cycle model) and various extensions aimed at capturing factors that have been shown empirically to play an important role in developing economies, including income levels and income variability, intergenerational links, liquidity constraints, inflation and macroeconomic instability, government saving behavior, social security and pension systems, and changes in the terms of trade. The second part of the chapter focuses on the determinants of private investment and includes a brief review of standard models (which emphasize accelerator effects and the cost of capital) and a discussion of the role of uncertainty and irreversibility. As in the case of consumption and saving, several additional factors important in empirical studies related to developing countries are discussed, including credit rationing, changes in relative prices, public investment, macroeconomic instability, and the debt overhang. For both parts, a detailed review of the recent empirical evidence is provided.

Chapter 2 focuses on money demand, the structure of the financial system,

---

[1] It should be clear from this overview that there are a number of issues that normally figure prominently in textbooks in development economics but nevertheless are not addressed in this book. In particular, the rural economy is not discuss in any depth, despite its importance for the process of development. Basu (1997) provides a detailed discussion of many of the important topics in this area, including stagnation and backward agriculture, tenancy and efficiency, rural credit markets and interlinkages in rural markets.

and its implications for monetary policy. After reviewing the determinants of the demand for money in developing countries, it describes some of the main characteristics of the financial system in these countries—particularly the role of government restrictions and the role played by banks in the process of financial intermediation. The nature and operation of indirect instruments of monetary policy is taken up next, together with the sources of credit market imperfections and credit rationing. The last part focuses on the implications of a high degree of currency substitution (a situation in which agents use both domestic and foreign currencies as means of transactions and as stores of value) for monetary policy.

Chapter 3 examines various issues associated with fiscal policy in macroeconomic adjustment. It begins with a description of the composition of conventional sources of public revenue and expenditure in developing countries. Implicit sources of revenue and expenditure (such as seigniorage and the inflation tax, and contingent liabilities) are examined next, and their implications for the measurement of the quasi-fiscal deficit of the consolidated public sector are noted. The second part specifies the government budget constraint and describes various ways of measuring fiscal deficits. The third part presents a simple technique aimed at disentangling the short- and medium-term effects of fiscal policy. The next three parts examine the link between fiscal imbalances and current account deficits, and issues associated with public debt sustainability and public sector solvency. Finally, the chapter concludes with a discussion of the link between commodity price booms and fiscal deficits, and the link between fiscal adjustment, expectations, and economic activity.

Chapter 4 discusses various issues related to exchange rate management in developing countries. It begins by reviewing the recent evolution of exchange rate regimes in developing countries. It then considers the operation of currency board arrangements and exchange rate bands, two regimes that have regained some degree of popularity in recent years. The second part identifies the various criteria that may affect the choice of an exchange rate regime and highlights potential conflicts that may arise among them. Understanding the nature of these conflicts is important because, as recent exchange rate crises have demonstrated, policy challenges change over time; exchange rate arrangements must also be adapted to changing circumstances. The third part explores the role of credibility factors, as well as the implications of inconsistencies between fiscal and exchange rate policies for the viability of a fixed exchange rate regime. The links between exchange rates, competitiveness, and trade balance movements are examined in the fourth part, after a brief review of alternative measures of the real exchange rate. The last part examines the channels through which exchange rate adjustment may induce contractionary effects on output—an issue that remains controversial in the developing world.

The focus of Chapter 5 is on inflation and disinflation policies. The first part of the chapter discusses the sources of chronic inflation and hyperinflation. It begins with an examination of the link between fiscal deficits, seigniorage, and high inflation, and continues with a discussion of various other sources of high inflation, including wage inertia, exchange rate depreciations, terms-of-trade shocks, and the inflation bias associated with lack of credibility. The second part examines the factors affecting the choice of nominal anchors in disinflation programs, focusing notably on the macroeconomic dynamics associated with monetary- and exchange-rate-based stabilization programs. The third part focuses on the role of credibility in disinflation. It reviews sources of credibility problems and ways that policymakers can enhance (or, on the contrary, damage) credibility—including, in particular, central bank independence and price controls. The last part reviews two recent experiences with alternative types of adjustment programs: the case of Egypt (1992-97) where stabilization was based on a pegged exchange rate and Uganda (1987-95), where a money supply anchor was used. A key lesson of these experiences is the role played by fiscal adjustment.

Developing countries (and, to a lesser extent, economies in transition) have become an important force in the process of globalization and integration in trade, financial, and labor markets.[2] This acceleration marks a sharp break from past trends and reflects the adoption of outward-oriented reforms by a growing number of these countries. However, the trend toward globalization has not been without costs. The efficiency and risk-diversification gains associated with financial integration have been mitigated because it has raised the benefits of good policies and exacerbated the costs of policy mistakes. The recent financial crises in Mexico, East Asia, and Brazil have raised new concerns regarding the effects of large capital inflows in an environment in which financial institutions are weak. These issues are discussed in Chapters 6 and 7.

Chapter 6 focuses on the surge in capital inflows in the early 1990s and the policy responses they have elicited in the developing world. The first part of the chapter reviews overall trends in the evolution and geographical distribution of capital flows in the past two decades. The high degree of concentration of private capital flows to a small group of countries in Asia and Latin America is highlighted. The second part focuses on the factors underlying the surge in private capital flows since the early 1990s. It is shown that both domestic and external factors played a role, although their relative importance varied considerably across countries and regions. Examples of the first type of factors are the measures aimed at liberalizing capital movements taken in the late 1980s by a number of developing countries; an example of the second type is fluctuations in world interest rates. The third part reviews the recent evidence on the volatility of various components of capital inflows, whereas the fourth part discusses the macroeconomic effects of these flows—notably their effect on domestic liquidity and credit growth, the real exchange rate, and the balance of payments. The current account. The last part examines the policy responses to large capital inflows, including sterilization, nominal exchange rate flexibility, fiscal adjustment, and capital controls, and gives a detailed discussion of the nature and effectiveness of the type of restrictions put in place by Chile in recent years. Market failures, as any sensible economist will recognize, abound

---

[2]The share of trade (exports plus imports) in the gross domestic product of developing countries has risen from about one third in the mid-1980s to almost 45 percent in 1996; it could exceed 50 percent by the year 2005.

in the real world; they do not, however, necessarily make a case for government intervention—nor do they guarantee that government intervention, if it occurs, will be successful. Nevertheless, the experience of countries like Chile suggests that capital controls can be an effective means of limiting short-term speculative pressures and can be justified when these pressures are not warranted by underlying fundamentals, but instead result from rumors, contagion effects, and herding behavior.

As noted earlier, the incidence of financial crises seem to have increased in recent years, at the same time that global financial integration was increasing cross-border capital movements. Chapter 7 focuses on the determinants of financial crises. The first part reviews various types of models of currency crises, which emphasize both fundamentals and extraneous factors—such as changes in market sentiment. The second part reviews two recent currency crises, the Mexican peso crisis of December 1994, and the Thai baht crisis of July 1997. The third part examines the determinants of, and empirical evidence on, banking and currency crises. The final part attempts to identify factors affecting financial volatility on world capital markets (particularly the role of contagion and herding behavior) and ways through which the adverse effects of such volatility can be limited.

Chapter 8 focuses on aggregate accounts, flow and stock budget constraints, and their specification in macroeconomic models. The first three parts of the chapter discuss basic concepts of macroeconomic accounting, a summary format for current account and financial transactions, and various aggregate identities and key macroeconomic relationships, and show how they are related to the sectoral budget constraints. The fourth and fifth parts present two macroeconomic models: a static, three-good framework with imperfect capital mobility and a supply side-bank credit link, and a one-good, two-period intertemporal model of the current account which integrates both flow and stock budget constraints. Various extensions of these models are also discussed.

Chapter 9 focuses on tools for macroeconomic policy analysis. It begins by looking at ways of assessing macroeconomic fluctuations using cross-correlation techniques. A simple method for decomposing the effects of external shocks on the domestic economy is presented next. The third part focuses on the analytical foundations of financial programming—the basic approach underlying stabilization programs designed by the International Monetary Fund (IMF). Both simplified and more elaborate versions of the basic model are presented. The fourth part considers the medium-term programming framework of the World Bank, whereas the fifth part discusses various attempts aimed at merging the IMF and World Bank models by integrating medium-term, supply-side considerations (as in the Bank approach) in a financial programming framework. The resulting model, however, remains subject to a number of limitations, and several of them are identified. The sixth part discusses three-gap models. The final part presents a simple, three-good computable general equilibrium model which has proved to be particularly useful to assess the medium- and long-term effects of fiscal and trade policies on relative prices and resource allocation.

The question of what determines the rate of growth and how it can be influenced by economic policy has always been central to development economists. The second part of the book, which consists of Chapters 10 to 13, reviews the recent literature on economic growth and its determinants. Chapter 10 begins by summarizing the evidence on economic growth, focusing first on the long-run experience (over the period 1820-1992) of both industrial and developing countries and then more specifically on the post-World War II experience. The sharp divergence, in the developing world, of the performance of East Asian countries and sub-Saharan African countries is discussed in detail. The chapter concludes with a summary of the basic facts that appear to characterize the process of economic growth in developing countries. It discusses, in particular, the links between growth, saving, and investment, as well as the link between poverty, inequality, and economic growth. Chapter 11 presents and analyzes the standard, neoclassical model of economic growth (the Solow-Swan model) and assesses its ability to answer some of the basic facts identified in Chapter 10. Chapter 12 presents the new, endogenous growth theories. The first part of the chapter explores the sources of knowledge accumulation and the resulting effects on growth. The second part analyzes the role of human capital accumulation in the growth process, and the link between human capital, education and training, and public policy. The last part examines the effects of various other factors on growth, including fiscal policy, inflation and macroeconomic instability, trade openness, financial development, political factors, and income distribution. It also emphasizes the critical role played by institutions (a credible legal system for the enforcement of property rights, proper checks and balances to avoid corruption in the public sector, and the development of rent-seeking activities) for an efficient allocation of individual skills and talents. Establishing and maintaining the rule of law by improving the functioning of public institutions may indeed be one of the most important tasks of governments in the developing world today—although such reforms may raise serious political problems because of vested interests.

Developments in growth theory have been accompanied in the past few years by a flurry of empirical studies aimed at assessing the determinants of economic growth in developing countries. Chapter 13 reviews the recent empirical evidence on both "old" and "new" theories. It discusses studies based on both growth accounting techniques and econometric regressions; it also highlights some of the several methodological problems confronting many of the existing empirical studies. The growth accounting methodology, in particular, is used to analyze the controversy over the sources of growth in East Asia since the early 1950s. The overview of the empirical, cross-country growth literature focuses on recent studies, which provide a better treatment of issues such as measurement errors, time averaging, simultaneity bias, and omitted-variable problems. In line with the endogenous growth models provided in Chapter 12, it considers physical and human capital, fiscal policy, inflation and macroeconomic stability, the degree of openness, and political variables and income distribution. The last part of the chapter assesses the evidence on the speed of convergence (or lack thereof) in income per capita across countries.

In recent years, numerous developing countries (spurred in part by the early and apparent success of liberalizing economies in East Asia) have implemented large-scale structural adjustment programs, particularly in the fiscal, financial, and trade areas. The third part of the book, Chapters 14 to 17, reviews the recent literature and evidence on structural reforms, as well as the role of political factors in the design of reform programs. Chapter 14 focuses on structural adjustment policies that have a direct effect on the real sector—including price liberalization in agriculture, trade reform (which may have a substantial impact on growth and the labor market), regional integration and the role of preferential trading areas, and labor market reforms. The effect of trade liberalization on wage inequality and the role of labor market structure and flexibility—measures aimed at reducing labor costs and minimum wages, and at curtailing the power of trade unions in the wage bargaining process—have indeed attracted much attention in developing countries in recent years.

Chapter 15 focuses on fiscal and financial reforms. The first two parts of the chapter discuss the efficiency effects of tax reform and its links with trade liberalization, as well as measures aimed at enhancing control and management of public expenditure. Civil service downsizing, fiscal decentralization, and pension reform are discussed next. The third part studies the effects on saving, investment, and growth of a policy that has featured prominently in financial reform programs, interest rate liberalization. Both the rationales and risks associated with this policy are reviewed, in light of the recent experience of developing countries. The fourth part of the chapter explores analytically the issues involved in exchange market unification (a particularly important policy issue for countries faced with a severely distorted exchange rate regime) and provides evidence on some recent unification attempts. The last parts of the chapter focuses on the links between financial liberalization and financial fragility. It discusses, in particular, measures aimed at reforming and strengthening weak banking systems—a phenomenon made manifest, in many countries, by domestic financial liberalization and increased openness to world capital markets. The key message of this analysis is that, as demonstrated by the financial turmoil that accompanied the Asia crisis, developing countries must proceed cautiously in opening their capital account. Capital account liberalization cannot take place in isolation, without appropriate macroeconomic, exchange rate, and financial sector policies.

At the same time that a small group of developing countries was receiving massive inflows of capital, the debt burden of several low-income countries has become unsustainable. As noted earlier, private capital inflows have concentrated on a small group of (upper-income) developing countries; low-income countries, particularly those of sub-Saharan Africa, have by and large failed to attract private flows, in some cases despite significant market-based economic reforms. Chapter 16 begins by discussing the links between foreign borrowing and growth and the effects of a large burden of debt on investment incentives and growth. The third part considers practical issues involved in measuring the debt burden, and the fourth part the various agreements under which debt relief has been provided to low-income countries. The last part examines recent attempts to reduce multilateral official debt, as well as their limitations.

Finally, Chapter 17 focuses on the sequencing of policy reforms and the role of political factors in the design of reform programs. The first part considers the various channels through which macroeconomic stabilization and structural reforms may interact during the liberalization process. The second discusses the sequencing and speed of reforms—an issue that has returned to the forefront of the policy agenda in many countries. Whether reform should be implemented overnight, and whether there exists an optimal sequencing of liberalization policies, are both subject of intense debate. Analytical arguments as well as the empirical evidence on these questions are reviewed. For instance, the existence of *policy complementarities* suggests that the implementation of a broad and consistent set of reforms may minimize the risks of policy reversals by enhancing their credibility and sustainability. At the same time, in a country where *implementation capacity* is weak, structural adjustment programs cannot have unrealistic expectations about how fast adjustment will occur; otherwise, they may underestimate the (economic and political) costs of more rapid implementation.

The last part of the chapter focuses on the political dimension of adjustment programs. The role of political feasibility in the design of these programs, and whether political sustainability can be ensured by an adequate sequencing of reforms, are both examined in detail. Other issues that are discussed in the chapter include poverty-reducing policies and social safety nets (a feature that is increasingly found in adjustment programs), and the link between corruption and foreign aid—whether or not aid can play a signaling and credibility-enhancing role in an environment in which corruption is high.

Each chapter ends with a detailed summary of the issues covered. Many of them incorporate a technical appendix as well. Three annexes deal with some special topics: modeling issues associated with labor market segmentation and the determination of wages and employment in the presence of a large informal economy; the structure, functioning, and macroeconomic implications of informal markets for credit and foreign exchange; and the short-run dynamics of exchange market unification.

Acknowledgments

This book is the product of my many years of research on the analytical foundations of economic adjustment programs in developing countries. This research has been conducted most recently at the World Bank Institute, where I am now heading the Macroeconomic and Financial Management Program. Some of the material presented here was first used as background documents for the lectures that I have given all around the world in the context of the Program's activities; some of it also comes from the notes prepared for my graduate courses in the Economics Department at Georgetown University during the academic year 1997-98. I was very fortunate, throughout my professional carrier, to engage in joint research with a number of highly talented economists; my intellectual debt to many of them (especially Joshua Aizenman, Bob Flood, Alexander Hoffmaister, John McDermott, Peter Montiel, and Mark Taylor) is unmeasurable. I am also grateful to Joshua Aizenman (who derived the results presented in the appendix to Chapter 1), Svetlana Andrianova, Claude Bismut, Stijn Claessens, Cécile Daubrée, Panicos Demetriades, Bill Easterly, Bill Maloney, Gil Mehrez, Jos Verbeek, Zeinab Partow, and several anonymous referees contracted by Academic Press for commenting on a preliminary draft. Their reactions and suggestions led to considerable improvements to the initial typescript, although none of them should be held responsible for the final product. I am also very grateful to Brooks Calvo for the exceptional quality of the research assistance that she has provided me for the past ten years, and to Nihal Bayraktar, who has more recently begun to excel in what can be at times an arduous task. Brooks has now moved on to take up new challenges, but her dedication and work ethic will continue to be a source of inspiration. Finally, I would like to express my appreciation to the publishers of the *European Economic Review*, the *Handbook of International Macroeconomics*, the *Journal of Development Economics*, and the *IMF Staff Papers*, for permission to dwell on material contained in some of my earlier publications.

Chapter 1

Consumption, Saving, and Investment

Consumption expenditure accounts for a large fraction of private spending in developing countries; understanding its determinants is thus important for short- and long-run economic analysis. The fraction of income that is not spent, domestic saving, plays an essential role as well: it continues to finance a large share of domestic investment in most developing countries. As discussed in Chapter 10, saving and investment rates are strongly correlated over time and across countries with rates of economic growth. From a policy perspective, understanding the patterns and determinants of consumption, saving, and investment may thus be a crucial step in designing programs aimed at raising standards of living.

Figure 1.1 shows some basic facts about domestic saving and investment rates around the world. The data suggest that gross domestic saving rates in developing countries are generally higher than those observed in industrial countries (with the exception of Japan). Among developing regions, saving rates are the highest in Asia—exceeding 30 percent of gross domestic product (GDP) for the period 1992-97. A similar pattern is observed for gross domestic investment; whereas investment rates have remained more or less stable in Latin America and the Caribbean, sub-Saharan Africa, and the Middle East, they have risen quite substantially in Asia, averaging about 32 to 33 percent of GDP during the period 1992-97.[1] The difference between domestic saving and domestic investment, foreign saving, has been particularly large in sub-Saharan Africa.

The first part of this chapter focuses on the determinants of consumption and saving in developing countries. It begins by reviewing the permanent income hypothesis, as well as the life-cycle model and some of its extensions. It then considers various factors that empirical studies have identified as playing an important role in developing economies: income levels and income variabil-

---

[1] The figure also shows that both saving and investment rates have fallen quite dramatically in Africa since the mid-1970s. These phenomena have important implications for observed rates of economic growth, as discussed in subsequent chapters.

ity, intergenerational links, liquidity constraints (which stem from credit market imperfections), inflation and macroeconomic instability, government saving behavior, the external debt burden, social security and pension systems, changes in the terms of trade, and the effect of financial development. The empirical evidence on these various effects is then analyzed.

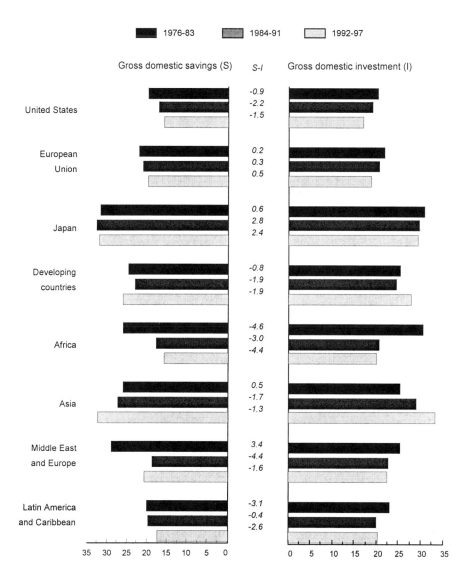

Figure 1.1. Saving and Investment Rates, 1976-97 (Percentage of GDP).
Source: International Monetary Fund.

The second part focuses on the determinants of private investment. Two standard effects are first reviewed: the flexible accelerator effect and the cost of capital. The more recent emphasis on the role of uncertainty and irreversibility is taken up next. As in the case of consumption and saving, several additional factors important in empirical studies are discussed: credit rationing and foreign exchange constraints, the real exchange rate, public investment, macroeconomic instability, and the external debt burden. Several recent empirical studies are then reviewed.

1.1 Consumption and Saving

The simplest approach to consumption and saving behavior is the so-called **Keynesian approach**, which assumes that current consumption, c, is a function of *disposable income*, $y - T$, where y is current income and T the level of taxes:

$$c = (1 - \theta)(y - T), \tag{1.1}$$

with $0 < \theta < 1$ denoting the marginal propensity to save.

The simple (and somewhat mechanical) approach described by Equation (1.1) has some merit, both as a first approximation in empirical macroeconomic models and, as discussed later, as a reflection of the behavior of consumers subject to **liquidity constraints**. However, decades of evidence on consumption and saving patterns in developing countries have highlighted the role of **intertemporal factors**, that is, the role played by households' choices between the present and the future.

1.1.1 The Permanent Income Hypothesis

The permanent income hypothesis (PIH), like the life-cycle model discussed in section 1.2, relates current consumption to a measure of **permanent** or **lifetime** disposable income. It was first proposed by Friedman (1957). To illustrate its implications, consider a simple framework in which consumers (or households) are identical and live for only two periods, 1 and 2. For simplicity, households are endowed with **perfect foresight**; thus, at period 1 they know with certainty the period-2 values of income, prices, and so on. Measured in nominal terms, the representative household's budget constraint for period 1 is given by

$$p_1 c_1 + p_1 A_1 = p_1(y_1 - T_1) + (1 + i_0)p_0 A_0, \tag{1.2}$$

where c_1 denotes consumption, A_0 the initial (end of previous period) stock of financial assets, A_1 assets at the end of period 1, y_1 factor income (or endowment), T_1 taxes, i_0 the nominal rate of return on assets held at the end of the previous period, and p_0 (p_1) the price index for the initial period (period 1).

Equation (1.2) can be rewritten as

$$p_1 A_1 - p_0 A_0 = i_0 p_0 A_0 + p_1(y_1 - T_1) - p_1 c_1,$$

which essentially states that the change in assets, $p_1 A_1 - p_0 A_0$, is equal to the sum of interest and noninterest income, $i_0 p_0 A_0 + p_1(y_1 - T_1)$, minus consumption spending, $p_1 c_1$.

Similarly, the budget constraint for period 2 is given by

$$p_2 c_2 + p_2 A_2 = p_2(y_2 - T_2) + (1 + i_1)p_1 A_1, \tag{1.3}$$

with y_2 in general different from y_1.

The household lives only two periods and leaves no net wealth to its heirs (that is, **no bequests**). Thus, $A_2 = 0$.[2] Suppose also that there is **no money illusion**; the period-by-period budget constraints of Equations (1.2) and (1.3) can thus be written in *real terms* by dividing, respectively, by p_1 and p_2. The first-period budget constraint becomes

$$c_1 + A_1 = y_1 - T_1 + (1 + r_0)A_0, \tag{1.4}$$

where r_0 is the real interest rate, defined as

$$1 + r_0 = (\frac{p_0}{p_1})(1 + i_0).$$

Similarly, the budget constraint for period 2, given that $A_2 = 0$, becomes

$$c_2 = y_2 - T_2 + (1 + r_1)A_1, \tag{1.5}$$

where now[3]

$$1 + r_1 = (\frac{p_1}{p_2})(1 + i_1). \tag{1.6}$$

Eliminating A_1 from Equation (1.4) by using Equation (1.5) yields the household's **intertemporal** or **life-time budget constraint**:

$$c_1 + \frac{c_2}{1 + r_1} = (1 + r_0)A_0 + (y_1 - T_1) + \frac{y_2 - T_2}{1 + r_1}. \tag{1.7}$$

In its simplest form, the PIH assumes that the household's objective is to maintain a *perfectly stable* (or *smooth*) consumption path ($c_1 = c_2$ in the present case) by dividing its lifetime resources equally among each period of life. The amount consumed by the household in each period is equal to its permanent income, y_P, which can be defined as the annuity value (in the sense of a regular, periodic payment) of the sum of assets held by the household and the discounted present value of (expected) future income. Formally, y_P is obtained as the level of income that gives the household the same present value of its lifetime

---

[2] For the condition $A_2 = 0$ to be optimal from the point of view of the household, it must be assumed that the marginal utility of consumption (as defined in section 1.2.1) in the second period is positive.

[3] Taking natural logarithms of Equation (1.6) yields $\ln(1 + r_1) = \ln(1 + i_1) - \ln(p_2/p_1)$. Using the approximation $\ln(1 + x) \simeq x$, for x small, yields $r_1 \simeq i_1 - \Delta \ln p_2$; that is, the real interest rate is approximately equal to the nominal rate of return minus the one-period-ahead inflation rate.

resources as that implied by its actual intertemporal budget constraint, that is, using (1.7):

$$y_P + \frac{y_P}{1 + r_1} = (1 + r_0)A_0 + (y_1 - T_1) + \frac{y_2 - T_2}{1 + r_1}. \tag{1.8}$$

In the particular case in which $r_0 = r_1 = r$, permanent income is

$$y_P = \left(\frac{1 + r}{2 + r}\right) \left\{ (1 + r)A_0 + (y_1 - T_1) + \frac{y_2 - T_2}{1 + r} \right\}.$$

If, in addition, the initial stock of assets is zero ($A_0 = 0$) and the interest rate is zero ($r = 0$), permanent income becomes an *exact average* of present and future disposable incomes:

$$y_P = [(y_1 - T_1) + (y_2 - T_2)]/2.$$

The difference between current and permanent income is generally defined as **transitory income**. Because $c_1 = y_P$, saving (which takes place only in period 1 in this simplified framework) is indeed nothing but the transitory component of current disposable income:

$$s_1 = (y_1 - T_1) - y_P. \tag{1.9}$$

The prediction that transitory income is entirely saved—or, more generally, that saving and borrowing are used solely for consumption-smoothing purposes—has formed the basis for a number of empirical tests of the PIH in developing countries, as discussed below.

1.1.2 The Life-Cycle Model

The life-cycle approach to consumption and saving behavior, first proposed by Modigliani and Brumberg (1954) and Ando and Modigliani (1963), postulates that individuals smooth consumption over time by taking into account anticipated changes in their **resources**, induced by **education** and **age**, as well as movements in the (expected) rate of return on savings. Figure 1.2 illustrates the stylized pattern of income, consumption, and savings predicted by the standard life-cycle model for a representative individual, under the assumptions of perfect credit markets. During the first part of his (or her) life, a typical individual earns relatively little and consumes a relatively large amount of goods; his consumption therefore exceeds his expenses, and he therefore borrows. Because income increases with education and age, the individual reaches a point where he no longer needs to borrow (point A); beyond that point, saving becomes positive. Income, however, begins to decline beyond a certain age; with consumption growing at a slower rate, saving continues to increase for a while but eventually also begins to fall. Once retirement is reached, income drops (by the distance BB') to a level below consumption. If the reduction in income is *unanticipated*, consumption falls abruptly upon retirement, from C to C'. If, on the contrary, the fall in resources is perfectly anticipated, consumption begins to decline smoothly before retirement age is reached with no discrete change at that point. In either case, the individual must *dissave* in order to maintain his consumption close to his needs, until his death.

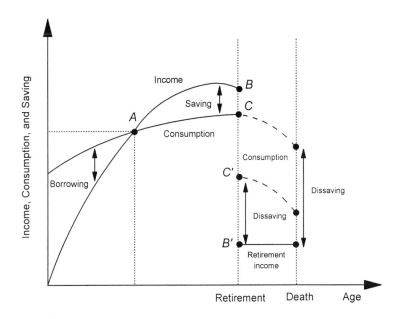

Figure 1.2. Income, Consumption, and Saving in the Life-Cycle Model. Source: Adapted from Deaton (1999, p. 42).

The Basic Framework

Analytically, the implications of the life-cycle approach can be illustrated in the same two-period framework presented above.[4] Suppose, as before, that the representative household leaves no bequests; thus, $A_2 = 0$. The household's **life-time budget constraint**, Equation (1.7), can be rewritten as

$$c_1 + \frac{c_2}{1 + r_1} = W_1, \tag{1.10}$$

where W_1 can be defined as **life-time wealth**. Note that W_1 depends directly on r_1; in particular, an increase in r_1 (for $y_2 - T_2$ given), lowers the present value of future income and therefore reduces W_1. Thus, $dW_1/dr_1 < 0$.

Suppose now that the household's preferences are **intertemporally additive**, that is, that its **lifetime utility**, U, is the sum of the utility of consumption derived in period 1, $u(c_1)$, plus the utility of consumption in period 2,

---

[4]The subsequent presentation draws in part on Muellbauer (1994).

$u(c_2)$—discounted at the subjective **rate of time preference**, $\rho > 0$. Formally,

$$U = u(c_1) + \frac{u(c_2)}{1 + \rho}, \tag{1.11}$$

where the **sub-utility function** $u(\cdot)$ is assumed to be increasing in c but at a decreasing rate—that is, $u' > 0$ and $u'' < 0$. The value of ρ measures the **degree of impatience**; the higher it is, the lower the utility provided by future consumption.

Maximizing (1.11) with respect to c_1 and c_2 subject to the life-time budget constraint (1.10) can be performed by forming the **Lagrangian expression**

$$L = u(c_1) + \frac{u(c_2)}{1 + \rho} - \lambda \left\{ c_1 + \frac{c_2}{1 + r_1} - W_1 \right\},$$

where λ is the **Lagrange multiplier** (see, for instance, Chiang, 1984, pp. 372-375). The first-order optimality conditions are given by

$$u'(c_1) = \lambda,$$

$$u'(c_2)/(1 + \rho) = \lambda/(1 + r_1).$$

Combining these two equations yields

$$u'(c_1) = \frac{1 + r_1}{1 + \rho} u'(c_2), \tag{1.12}$$

which is known as the **Euler equation**. Essentially, this equation states that the marginal utility of consumption at the current period must be equal to the marginal utility of consumption in the next period, weighted by the ratio of the market and subjective discount terms.[5]

In the special case in which the rate of time preference is equal to the real rate of return ($\rho = r_1$), Equation (1.12) becomes $u'(c_1) = u'(c_2)$, implying that

$$c_1 = c_2. \tag{1.13}$$

The household therefore maintains a completely smooth consumption path across periods, as in the simple form of the PIH discussed earlier.

For instance, with **logarithmic preferences**, lifetime utility is given by

$$U = \ln c_1 + \frac{\ln c_2}{1 + \rho},$$

and the Euler equation is

$$1/c_1 = \left(\frac{1 + r_1}{1 + \rho} \right)(1/c_2),$$

---

[5] The derivation treats r_1 and $y_2 - T_2$ as deterministic terms. Under more general assumptions, the Euler equation continues to have the form shown in Equation (1.12), but with the term $u'(c_2)$ on the right-hand side appearing in *expected* value form.

which again yields $c_1 = c_2$ if $\rho = r_1$.

Substituting Equation (1.13) in the life-cycle budget constraint (Equation (1.10)) yields

$$c_1 = \frac{W_1}{\kappa_1}, \quad \kappa_1 \equiv 1 + \frac{1}{1+r_1}, \tag{1.14}$$

where κ_1 is the inverse of the **marginal propensity to consume out of wealth**.[6]

Another specification is the case of preferences characterized by a **constant elasticity of substitution** (CES), in which lifetime utility is given by

$$U = \left\{ c_1^{-\alpha} + \frac{c_2^{-\alpha}}{1+\rho} \right\}^{-1/\alpha}, \tag{1.15}$$

where $\alpha > -1$. The **elasticity of substitution** between period-1 and period-2 consumption, σ, is given by[7]

$$\sigma = \frac{1}{1+\alpha}.$$

The Lagrangian expression is now

$$L = \left\{ c_1^{-\alpha} + \frac{c_2^{-\alpha}}{1+\rho} \right\}^{-1/\alpha} - \lambda \left\{ c_1 + \frac{c_2}{1+r_1} - W_1 \right\}.$$

The first-order optimality conditions are now given by

$$(c_1/U)^{-(1+\alpha)} = \lambda,$$

$$(c_2/U)^{-(1+\alpha)} = \lambda(1+\rho)/(1+r_1),$$

which can be rearranged to give the Euler equation as

$$c_1^{-1/\sigma} = \frac{(1+r_1)}{1+\rho} c_2^{-1/\sigma}. \tag{1.16}$$

Taking logarithms of both sides yields

$$\ln(\frac{c_2}{c_1}) = \ln\left[1 + \frac{(c_2 - c_1)}{c_1} \right] = \sigma \ln(\frac{1+r_1}{1+\rho}),$$

that is, using the approximation $\ln(1+x) \simeq x$:

$$\frac{(c_2 - c_1)}{c_1} \simeq \sigma(r_1 - \rho). \tag{1.17}$$

---

[6] As shown in Equation (1.14), κ_1 depends only on the real interest rate; in the presence of bequests, the marginal propensity to consume out of wealth (for, say, retired households) would generally be smaller.

[7] Formally, the elasticity of substitution between c_1 and c_2 is defined as the proportional change in the consumption ratio c_2/c_1 associated with a unit proportional change in the ratio of marginal utilities $u'(c_1)/u'(c_2)$, holding total utility constant.

Equation (1.17) shows that the elasticity of substitution measures the responsiveness of the change in consumption between the two periods to changes in **intertemporal prices**, that is, the real interest rate. The greater the elasticity of substitution is, the greater will be the reduction in current consumption (relative to future consumption) induced by a rise in the real interest rate.

Taking both terms in expression (1.16) to the power $-\sigma$ yields

$$c_2 = \left\{ \frac{1+r_1}{1+\rho} \right\}^{\sigma} c_1. \tag{1.18}$$

Combining this result with the lifetime budget constraint, Equation (1.10), yields an equation similar to (1.14),

$$c_1 = \frac{W_1}{\kappa_1},$$

but now with κ_1 given by

$$\kappa_1 = 1 + \left\{ \frac{1}{1+\rho} \right\}^{\sigma} \left\{ \frac{1}{1+r_1} \right\}^{1-\sigma}.$$

If the values of ρ and r_1 are sufficiently small, κ_1 can be approximated by[8]

$$\kappa_1 = 1 + \frac{1}{(1+\rho)^{\sigma}(1+r_1)^{1-\sigma}} \simeq 1 + \frac{1}{1+\sigma\rho + (1-\sigma)r_1}. \tag{1.19}$$

This expression has several implications.

- If the discount rate and the market interest rate are equal ($\rho = r_1$), changes in the elasticity of intertemporal substitution have *no effect* on κ_1 [which is thus equal to its value given in Equation (1.14), $1 + 1/(1+r_1)$].

- The sign of the effect of an increase in r_1 on κ_1 is

$$\mathrm{sg}(d\kappa_1/dr_1) = -\,\mathrm{sg}(1-\sigma),$$

which shows that

  - A change in the interest rate has *no* effect on κ_1 ($d\kappa_1/dr_1 = 0$) if σ is equal to *unity*.

  - In general, $d\kappa_1/dr_1$ is ambiguous; the effect of a change in the interest rate on saving is thus in general *indeterminate* because of conflicting **income** and **substitution effects.**[9]

---

[8] Let $x = (1+\rho)^{\sigma}(1+r_1)^{1-\sigma} - 1$; the second term on the right-hand side of the first expression is therefore $1/(1+x)$. Using the approximation $x \simeq \ln(1+x)$, for x small, implies that

$$x \simeq \ln(1+\rho)^{\sigma}(1+r_1)^{1-\sigma} \simeq \sigma\rho + (1-\sigma)r_1,$$

which can be substituted in the expression $1/(1+x)$ to give the result shown in the text.

[9] The overall effect is less likely to be positive with a low ratio of assets to income.

- If σ is *less than unity*, $d\kappa_1/dr_1 < 0$. Because, as shown earlier, dW_1/dr_1 is also negative, an increase in the interest rate in this case has an *ambiguous* overall effect on consumption and saving in the first period.

- If, on the contrary, σ is *greater than unity*, $d\kappa_1/dr_1 > 0$; and because $d\kappa_1/dW_1 < 0$, an increase in r_1 unambiguously *lowers consumption* $(dc_1/dr_1 < 0)$ and *raises saving*.

- The greater the degree of intertemporal substitution σ is, the larger the marginal effect on consumption and saving induced by a change in the interest rate will be $(\partial[d\kappa_1/dr_1]/\partial\sigma > 0)$.

- If the degree of intertemporal substitution σ is *zero* and disposable income in period 2 is equal to the period-1 level $(y_2 - T_2 = y_1 - T_1)$, then $\kappa_1 = 1 + 1/(1 + r_1)$ and

$$c_1 = \frac{W_1}{\kappa_1} = \frac{(1 + r_0)A_0}{1 + 1/(1 + r_1)} + (y_1 - T_1), \qquad (1.20)$$

which shows that an increase in the real interest rate, r_1, by increasing the return on the level of assets, raises current consumption.

- If the elasticity of substitution σ is *positive* and the initial level of assets zero $(A_0 = 0)$, and with disposable income in period 2 equal to the period-1 level,

$$c_1 = \kappa_1^{-1}\left[(y_1 - T_1) + \frac{y_2 - T_2}{1 + r_1}\right],$$

which implies that an increase in the interest rate has an unambiguously *negative* effect on consumption. By implication, large movements in the level of assets over time may make it difficult to use time-series techniques to detect a stable aggregate effect of real interest rates on saving.[10]

Age and the Dependency Ratio

The life-cycle model predicts that, in any given population, the *young* will save relatively little as they anticipate increases in their future incomes. *Middle-aged individuals*, who are nearing the peak of their earnings, tend to save the most, in anticipation of relatively low incomes after retirement. The *elderly* tend to have a low, or even negative, saving rate, although the desire to *leave a bequest* or to cover the *contingency of living longer* than expected could provide a motivation for saving even after retirement. Thus, the *aggregate saving rate* will tend to fall in response to an increase in either the **youth-dependency ratio** (that is, the ratio of under-20 age group to the 20-64 age group) or in the ratio of the elderly to the working age population.

---

[10] As discussed later, a small and unstable real interest rate effect is consistent with the evidence for developing countries.

To formally assess the influence of age in the life-cycle model described above, consider the case in which the household's horizon is $T > 2$. In addition to results similar to those derived earlier, it can be shown that the inverse marginal propensity to consume out of assets, κ_1, varies with the time horizon and so with age (Muellbauer, 1994). Suppose that the real interest rate is constant over time at r, and that the values of ρ and r are sufficiently small; in the case of the **CES utility function**, in particular, κ_1 is given not by Equation (1.19) but by

$$\kappa_1 = 1 + \mu + \mu^2 + ... + \mu^{T-1} = \frac{1 - \mu^T}{1 - \mu}, \tag{1.21}$$

where[11]

$$\mu = \frac{1}{(1+\rho)^\sigma (1+r_1)^{1-\sigma}} \simeq \frac{1}{1 + \sigma\rho + (1-\sigma)r}. \tag{1.22}$$

If the household earns the same income in both periods ($y_2 = y_1$), and if the rate of time preference and the interest rate are equal ($\rho = r$), consumption in period 1 will be given by

$$c_1 = \frac{W_1}{\kappa_1} = \frac{(1+r_0)A_0}{\kappa_1} + (y_1 - T_1).$$

In such conditions, the effect of age on consumption will operate entirely through κ_1. Suppose, for instance, that $\rho = r = 0.04$. Then, from Equation (1.22), $\mu = 1/(1+r) = 0.96$, and from Equation (1.21):

$$\kappa_1|_{T=10} = 8.5, \quad \kappa_1|_{T=20} = 14.2, \quad \kappa_1|_{T=40} = 20.7.$$

These results show that the inverse of the marginal propensity to consume out of wealth *increases* with the time horizon; put differently, younger agents, with their longer time horizons, have a lower propensity to consume out of assets than older generations.[12]

---

[11] Consider, for instance, the case where $T = 3$. The CES utility function, Eq. (1.15) can be written as

$$U = \left\{ c_1^{-\alpha} + \frac{c_2^{-\alpha}}{1+\rho} + \frac{c_3^{-\alpha}}{(1+\rho)^2} \right\}^{-1/\alpha},$$

and the lifetime budget constraint, Eq. (1.10) becomes

$$c_1 + \frac{c_2}{1+r_1} + \frac{c_3}{(1+r_1)^2} = W_1.$$

The first-order conditions are given by Eq. (1.18) together with

$$c_3 = [(1+r_1)/1+\rho]^{2\sigma} c_1.$$

Combining these results with the lifetime budget constraint above yields $c_1 = W_1/\kappa_1$, with now

$$\kappa_1 = 1 + \mu + \mu^2,$$

where μ is defined in Eq. (1.22). The last term in that expression is the approximation given before [see Eq. (1.19)]. Generalizing the above expressions to the case where $T > 3$ is straightforward.

[12] Note that the difference between the marginal propensities to consume of the old and young *rises* as the average discount rate falls.

This result is important because it implies that, at the aggregate level, the distribution of assets between the young, the middle-aged, and the elderly matters for consumption and saving patterns. This issue is central to the question of the effects of per capita real income growth on aggregate saving behavior. Everything else equal, the larger the share of total wealth held by the middle-aged households (those whose income is the highest) in any given country, the higher the saving rate, and the higher the *growth rate* of income (see Chapter 12). However, as discussed below, everything else is *not* equal in the presence of **borrowing constraints**. In addition, demographic factors such as the share of the working population relative to that of retired persons are likely to explain only the *long-term trends* in saving, not the short-term fluctuations in the propensity to save.

1.1.3   Other Determinants

The analytical and empirical literature on consumption and saving behavior in developing countries has highlighted various limitations of the standard permanent income and life-cycle models described in the previous sections and offered various extensions. This section reviews some of the most important additional factors that have been found to be of empirical relevance in understanding consumption and saving in developing countries.

Income Levels and Income Uncertainty

Recent empirical research has highlighted the fact that at low or *subsistence levels of income*, the saving rate is also low. As documented in Chapter 10, as the level of income increases, so does the saving rate. This result has two implications:

- In low-income countries the response of saving to changes in *real interest rates* is likely to be weak; a significant response of household saving tends to occur only at levels of income substantially above the subsistence level (Ogaki, Ostry and Reinhart, 1996). This result has important implications for policies aimed at stimulating financial saving through interest rate liberalization (see Chapter 15).

- Changes in *income distribution*, induced for instance by redistributive tax policies, can have important effects on measured saving rates at the aggregate level.

Many households in developing countries derive their incomes from agriculture; but in that sector, incomes can be subject to relatively large fluctuations resulting from variations in climatic conditions or changes in domestic and world prices of agricultural commodities. These sources of **income uncertainty** are often compounded by **macroeconomic instability** and vulnerability to external shocks.[13] In general, increased uncertainty regarding future income will en-

---

[13]The higher saving rates registered by the low-inflation countries in Asia, for instance, suggest the importance of a stable macroeconomic environment.

hance the **precautionary motive** for saving (see the appendix to this chapter; Caballero, 1990; and Deaton, 1992), although in a highly unstable macroeconomic environment, increased uncertainty may reduce saving through its effect on the variability of rates of return.

Intergenerational Links

Some authors, such as Gersovitz (1988), have argued that the greater importance of extended family arrangements may imply that **intergenerational links** are likely to be particularly strong in developing countries. There are two ways in which such links can affect consumption and saving behavior:

- They may affect **household preferences** by affecting, for instance, the degree to which the marginal utility of consumption declines with the level of consumption, or by increasing the **rate of time preference**.

- They may lengthen the **effective planning horizon** over which households make their consumption and saving decisions.

Liquidity Constraints

Intertemporal consumption smoothing requires well-functioning financial markets to allow agents to borrow and lend across periods. In many developing countries, however, well-developed financial markets either do not exist, or when they do, they do not function very well. In particular, households often have limited access to credit markets, and **credit rationing** may be pervasive (see Chapter 2). The existence of **liquidity constraints** affects the ability of households to transfer resources across time periods as well as across *uncertain states of nature* relative to income. As a result, consumption (and thus saving) tends to be highly correlated with *current income*, rather than permanent income or life-cycle wealth, as indicated earlier. Empirical evidence by Veidyanathan (1993) and Rossi (1988) suggests indeed that the incidence of liquidity constraints may be quite significant in a number of developing countries.

Formally, liquidity constraints can be introduced in the simple two-period model presented earlier (in which $A_2 = 0$) by requiring that real financial assets in period 1 be nonnegative:

$$A_1 \geq 0.$$

Assuming, in addition, that households are relatively impatient (that is, that the rate of time preference is greater than the real interest rate) and thus willing to consume today, Deaton (1992) showed that there are two possible outcomes in period 1:

- The household wants to borrow but cannot, in which case consumption is the sum of current holdings of assets and current income, there is no saving, and marginal utility is not equated across periods.

- The household does *not* want to borrow, in which case consumption is *less* than the sum of assets and income, saving is positive, and marginal utility is equated across periods—as predicted by the Euler equation, Equation (1.12).

As also shown by Deaton (1992), the exact form of the relationship between consumption and current resources (assets and income) depends on the parameters (mean and variance) characterizing the distribution of income, as well as the structure of the household's preferences. At low levels of resources, liquidity constraints are binding, and all resources are spent. Beyond a certain level of resources (which depends, in particular, on the parameters of the process driving income), liquidity constraints cease to bind, the marginal propensity to consume begins to fall, and saving becomes positive due to precautionary considerations (as discussed earlier).

In the presence of liquidity constraints, **financial liberalization** can have an adverse effect on saving rates. To the extent that the desire of households to smooth consumption over time is constrained by limited access to credit markets, increased access to these markets will allow individuals to bring forward their consumption (and thereby reduce saving) over their working life, through increased borrowing. For instance, greater availability of loans for purchases of *housing* and *consumer durables* may obviate the need for households to save in preparation for making large initial payments for such purchases.

Inflation and Macroeconomic Stability

Consumption and saving may also respond to changes in the *rate of inflation*. If households are net creditors, an increase in the inflation rate for instance may lower real value wealth—even if it is accompanied by a commensurate increase in the nominal interest rate. To offset this negative wealth effect, households may raise their saving rate. The *variability* of inflation, which is often used as a proxy for macroeconomic stability, may also affect saving, possibly in opposite directions:

- To the extent that it increases uncertainty about *future income*, a high degree of price variability may lead to an increase in the saving rate, as a result of the **precautionary motive** for saving discussed earlier.

- But to the extent that a highly variable rate of inflation is associated with higher uncertainty on the real rate of interest (or the return of saving), it may have a depressing effect on the propensity to save.

Government Saving

A key feature of the life-cycle model is that saving behavior is directly influenced by households' assessments of their *future pattern* of income and consumption. A key variable that affects these assessments is government policy, particularly *government saving* or *dissaving*.

The extent to which shifts in government saving induce offsetting changes in private saving has been a central issue in much of the modern literature in macroeconomics and public economics. Three major interpretations of this relationship have been offered in the literature.

- The **conventional view** assumes that a fall in government saving (resulting from a tax cut or a bond-financed increase in government spending) will tend to raise consumption and reduce saving by *myopic* households (that is, households who care solely about the present), by shifting the tax burden from present to *future* generations. As a result, a decline in government saving will lead to a decline in national saving.[14]

- The **Keynesian view** suggests that higher *temporary* government dissaving will raise consumption and income, in the presence of under-utilized production capacity, proportionally to the inverse of the marginal propensity to save, as predicted by the standard **multiplier effect**. In turn, higher income will raise private saving. Whether or not this increase in private saving is large enough to offset the initial decline in government saving (and thus lead to a rise in national saving) is a priori *ambiguous*.[15]

- The **Ricardian view** asserts that to the extent that individuals are rational and *far-sighted*, they will realize that a permanent rise in government spending today (or, equivalently, an increase in government dissaving) must be paid for either now or later. They, therefore, will increase saving by an equivalent amount—hence the term **Ricardian equivalence** (Barro, 1974, 1989).

Similarly, the Ricardian view predicts that a rise in the budget deficit (dissaving) resulting from a *tax cut* will have no effect on the national saving rate because private saving will rise by an equivalent amount in anticipation of future tax liabilities.[16] Put differently, for a given present value of government purchases, the timing of taxes does not influence household consumption behavior.

The Ricardian view has been subject to a number of criticisms, at both the analytical and empirical level. From an analytical point of view, it dwells on four unrealistically strict assumptions:

- consumers are *far-sighted*;

- successive generations are linked by *altruistically motivated bequests*;

---

[14] The reduction in private saving may be dampened by a rise in the real interest rate—although, as will be discussed, this effect is likely to be relatively small. In an open economy, the rise in the domestic interest rate may also attract foreign capital and lead to an increase in *foreign* saving.

[15] If the reduction in government saving is assumed to be *permanent* rather than temporary, the effect on private saving would be similar to the one predicted by the conventional view if households are short-sighted.

[16] Thus, taken to its extreme form, the Ricardian approach implies that the choice between debt financing and tax financing of fiscal deficits is irrelevant.

- consumers do not face *liquidity constraints*; and

- taxes are *nondistortionary*.

The empirical evidence in favor of the hypothesis of full Ricardian equivalence appears mixed for industrial countries (see Seater, 1993). For developing countries, however, the bulk of the evidence is against it. A key reason is that although individuals in such countries may form expectations about their future tax liabilities in a systematic way, **liquidity constraints** (which play a pervasive role in these countries, as discussed earlier) may prevent them from acting on these expectations by adjusting their consumption-saving behavior as would be predicted by the Ricardian equivalence proposition.

The Debt Burden and Taxation

Government saving and dissaving behavior can also affect private saving indirectly through changes in *anticipations of future taxes*. For instance, in a situation in which the public sector's foreign debt burden suddenly deteriorates (as a result, say, of an increase in debt service resulting from a rise in world interest rates), the private sector may anticipate a significant increase in taxation in the future. The **substitution effect** associated with such expectations will tend to favor current consumption at the expense of saving, whereas the **income effect** would tend to reduce consumption in all periods. Thus, a high level of debt may reduce the national saving rate.[17]

Social Security, Pensions, and Insurance

As discussed in Chapter 15, the availability of formal public pension and social security schemes has increased significantly in many developing countries. As implied by the life-cycle framework, the potential effect of these schemes may be to lower the private saving rate through three channels:

- by *redistributing income* to the elderly;

- by reducing the need to *save for retirement* (unless the introduction of these schemes is accompanied by a reduction of the retirement age);

- by curbing the need for *precautionary saving* to cover the contingency of living longer than expected.

The impact of increased social security benefits on national saving may thus depend on the effect that such changes have on *public saving*.[18] To the extent

---

[17]See Chapter 16 for a discussion of the longer-run effects of foreign indebtedness on saving and investment.

[18]Strictly speaking, as pointed out by Edwards (1996c, p. 25), what matters is the relation between contributions and *expected* social security benefits in the future. Whether agregate saving increases will depend, however, on what happens to government saving once the social security reform is implemented.

that the social security system is *unfunded*, public saving will not rise directly to offset any induced decline in private saving. In line with the Ricardian argument developed earlier, it could be argued that in this case private agents would not reduce their current saving because they would anticipate that taxes will eventually have to be raised to finance future pension outlays. Nevertheless, the empirical evidence suggests that increases in public pensions result in a decline in private and national savings, albeit by less than the full increase in pension benefits (Mackenzie, Gerson, and Cuervas, 1997).

Private pension plans have also been developed in many developing countries in recent years. In principle, individuals should view their contributions to *funded* private pensions as a perfect substitute for other forms of saving. But, in practice, individuals do not seem to fully take into account their pension contributions in determining their saving behavior. The result is that the introduction of private pension plans is often accompanied by an increase in national saving rates. This is for instance the conclusion reached by Holzmann (1997) in the case of *Chile* (see Chapter 15).

Finally, the increased availability of various kinds of *insurance*, such as health, liability, unemployment, personal loss, and liability, may also influence saving behavior. To the extent that insurance plans limit expected outlays for contingencies and emergencies, they tend to reduce income uncertainty and therefore the need for precautionary saving.

Changes in the Terms of Trade

Another factor affecting saving in an open economy is **terms-of-trade shocks**, that is, large movements in the relative price of a country's exports in terms of its imports. A key channel through which such shocks are deemed to operate is the **Harberger-Laursen-Metlzer** (HLM) effect, which posits a positive relationship between (transitory) changes in the terms of trade and saving, through their positive effect on *wealth* and *income*.[19] More specifically, the HLM effect predicts that an adverse *transitory* movement in the terms of trade will lead to a decrease in a country's current level of income that is larger than the decrease in its permanent income, causing, as discussed earlier, a fall in saving. On the contrary, a *permanent* deterioration in the terms of trade, to the extent that it leads to a concomitant reduction in both current income and permanent income, will have no effect on saving.

The consumption smoothing effect emphasized by the conventional HLM effect may be partly offset by two types of substitution effects: an **intertemporal substitution** (or **consumption tilting**) effect, and an **intratemporal substitution** effect. To understand how these two effects operate, note first that the conventional HLM effect is usually derived in a static setting in which the domestic economy and the rest of the world produce the same tradable

---

[19] The initial formulation of the argument by Harberger (1950) and Laursen and Meltzer (1950) relied on a Keneysian-type open economy framework. Extensions to an intertemporal setting were provided notably by Obstfeld (1982) and Svensson and Razin (1983). These contributions also clarified the distinction between permanent and transitory shocks.

good. Consider instead a small open economy where households consume both imported and nontraded goods.

Suppose for a moment that these two categories of goods are perfect substitutes, so that their relative price is constant. Movements in the terms of trade may nevertheless induce large changes in the *temporal pattern* of consumption. For instance, a temporary deterioration in the terms of trade (induced by, say, a rise in the price of imported goods) leads to a rise in the the **cost of living**, that is, the price of current consumption relative to the price of future imports and future consumption. The increase in the overall price level leads to a rise in the *consumption rate of interest* (that is, the real rate of interest measured in terms of the price of the *consumption basket*), thereby increasing the cost of current consumption relative to future consumption and inducing agents to shift consumption into the future and to save more today. This is the **consumption tilting** effect. The larger the **intertemporal elasticity of consumption** (as defined earlier) is, the larger the increase in current saving will be.

Suppose now that imported and nontraded goods are not perfect substitutes, as the evidence suggests. Movements in their *relative price* induced by changes in the terms of trade will therefore also affect saving decisions. The reason is that, in an economy where households consume both home and imported goods, changes in relative prices affect the cost of living and thus the consumption rate of interest. As a result, there is an **intratemporal substitution** effect associated with a terms-of-trade shock; this effect may be large enough to offset the conventional effect associated with consumption-smoothing considerations. For instance, to the extent that an adverse, transitory terms-of-trade shock leads to a temporary increase in the relative price of imported goods, the switch toward nontraded goods will raise their relative price and the consumption rate of interest; total expenditure will fall and saving will tend to increase. This effect may be large enough to offset the decline in private saving induced by consumption-smoothing considerations.

Overall, therefore, the net effect of terms-of-trade shocks on saving is theoretically ambiguous. The importance of the consumption smoothing effect relative to the two types of substitution effects identified above can only be assesed empirically.

Financial Deepening

Financial development may affect saving both directly and indirectly. To the extent that improved financial intermediation leads to a reduction in the *cost* of intermediation, it will increase the return to saving. At the same time, to the extent that increased efficiency in the process of financial intermediation leads to an expansion of *investment* and stimulates the *rate of economic growth* (as discussed in Chapter 12), the increase in income will also lead to an increase in saving. Figure 1.3 shows, for a group of about 30 developing countries, the correlation during the period 1980-95 between gross domestic saving rates and an indicator of financial deepening, the ratio of *quasi-money* (saving and term deposits) over the *broad money* stock—the sum of *narrow money* (currency and sight deposits) plus quasi-money. The figure does suggest a positive relationship between these two variables. As noted earlier, however, in cases where financial liberalization leads to a an increase in the supply of credit to previously credit-constrained households, private saving may fall.

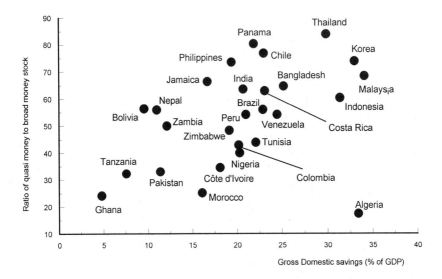

Figure 1.3. Financial Deepening and Saving Rates (Averages over 1980-95). Source: World Bank.

Household and Corporate Saving

Finally, it should be noted that the foregoing discussion focused only on saving by *households*. This focus is justified in the many developing countries where private saving rates are essentially determined by household behavior. In some others, however, *corporate saving* (in the form of, say, retained earnings) may also be significant and may respond to different variables than those affecting the decisions of households. Whether or not this distinction matters for understanding movements in the *aggregate* private saving rate depends on households' responses to higher corporate saving: if firms retain more earnings, households may save less by a corresponding amount. In such conditions, households *pierce the corporate veil* and aggregate private saving behavior will largely reflect household behavior. The study by López-Mejía and Ortega (1998) found indeed that in Colombia (as suggested in Figure 1.4) periods of high (low) corporate saving rates were accompanied by periods of low (high) household saving rates. Changes in dividends have no effect on private consumption (that is, affect only saving) because agents realize that changes in their income is offset by a decline of the same amount in the value of the firms that they hold.

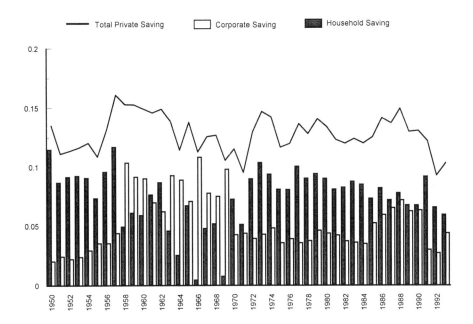

Figure 1.4. Colombia: Components of Private Saving, 1950-93 (Percent of GNP). Source: López-Mejía and Ortega (1998).

1.1.4   Empirical Evidence

It is important to note, at the outset, that data limitations make the empirical analysis of the determinants of consumption and saving behavior difficult in developing countries. In practice, saving is typically measured as a *residual* and is beset by classification, valuation, and measurement problems. For instance, *public saving* data for some countries include that of *public enterprises;* in other countries, public enterprise saving is included with that of the *private sector*. Nevertheless, the data suggest several regularities. In particular, saving rates vary considerably across regions in the developing world. Data compiled by Edwards (1996c) indicate that, for the period 1983-92, the private saving rate was 15.6 percent in Africa, 20.2 percent in Asia, and 13.8 percent in Latin America. For the sample period that Edwards considers, the saving rate was 21.3 percent for industrialized countries.

As noted earlier, a key implication of the PIH is that transitory income changes are (dis-)saved and permanent changes consumed. As discussed by Agénor and Montiel (1999, Chapter 3), there exists some evidence supporting this claim; several empirical studies found that the propensity to consume out of permanent income exceeds the propensity to consume out of current income. This is consistent with the PIH. At the same time, however, the elasticity of consumption with respect to permanent income is not typically found to be unity, nor is the propensity to consume out of transitory income found to be zero.

The more recent study by Loayza, Schmidt-Hebbel, and Servén (1999) confirmed these results. In particular, the evidence for both industrial and developing countries suggests that there exists a close correlation between actual income and consumption; the strict form of the PIH cannot explain this relationship.

Other recent studies of the determinants of saving in developing countries, in addition to Loayza, Schmidt-Hebbel, and Servén (1999), include those by Masson et al. (1995), Hadjimachael and Ghura (1995), Edwards (1996), and Dayal-Gulati and Thimann (1997). The study by Masson, Bayoumi, and Samiei (1995) covered 64 developing countries over the period 1970-93. Their results indicated that

- an increase in *public saving* tends to be associated with *higher national saving*, suggesting that Ricardian equivalence does not hold;

- a decrease in the **age dependency ratio** raises private saving substantially;

- increases in *per capita income* raises the private saving rate;

- changes in *real interest rates* had no significant effect on private or national saving;

- increases in *foreign saving* (as measured by the *current account deficit*) affected national saving negatively, but the offset was only partial (estimated to be between 40 and 50 percent), suggesting that an increased availability of external financing typically supports both higher consumption and higher investment;

- *terms-of-trade windfalls* are found to have a positive, but transitory, effect on national saving.

Hadjimachael and Ghura (1995) used a panel of 41 sub-Saharan African countries over the period 1986-92 to investigate the effectiveness of *public policies* in stimulating private saving and investment. They found that policies that kept inflation low, reduced *macroeconomic uncertainty*, promoted financial development, and increased public saving led to higher national saving rates. They also found that a reduction in the **external debt burden** significantly increased national saving—possibly because of a reduction in expectations of future taxation, as indicated earlier.

Edwards (1996c) studied the determinants of saving in a group of 25 developing countries and 11 industrialized countries over the period 1970-92. His results showed a significant effect on private saving rates of the following variables:

- the rate of growth of per capita income,

- the **monetization ratio**, which is similar to the indicator of financial deepening defined earlier;

- *foreign saving* (measured again by the current account deficit), with a negative coefficient less than unity—suggesting that the crowding out effect of foreign saving is less than one to one;

- *government saving*, with a negative effect that is less than one to one—in contrast to the Ricardian equivalence hypothesis;

- *social security* (as measured by the ratio of public expenditure on social security and welfare to total public spending), with a significantly negative coefficient.

The real interest rate (proxied by the ex post real bank deposit rate), the structure of the economy (as measured by the share of manufacturing, mining, and agriculture in output) and inflation variability were not significant. The age dependency ratio was also found to be insignificant for the group of developing countries as a whole, but results for Latin America only suggested that it had a significantly negative effect on saving.[20] Overall, the most important variables were the growth of per capita income, government saving, and the monetization ratio.

Dayal-Gulati and Thimann (1997) studied the determinants of private (personal and corporate) saving in a group of five Southeast Asian countries—Indonesia, Malaysia, Philippines, Singapore, and Thailand—and nine Latin American countries—Argentina, Brazil, Chile, Colombia, Mexico, Paraguay, Peru, Uruguay, and Venezuela—over the period 1975-95. They found evidence that terms-of-trade shocks have a positive effect on saving. Government saving only partially crowds out private saving, suggesting again a rejection of the strict form of the Ricardian equivalence proposition. Social security expenditures were associated with lower private saving and fully funded pension schemes had a positive effect. Macroeconomic stability (as measured by the deviation of inflation from an underlying moving average) and financial deepening (as measured by the ratio of broad money to output) also affected positively private saving and played an important role in explaining differences in saving patterns across the two regions. Per capita income also had a positive effect.

The study by Loayza, Schmidt-Hebbel, and Servén (1999) used an extensive cross-country database to study the determinants of saving. A novelty of the analysis was also their attempt to distinguish between short- and long-term determinants of saving rates—a distinction that appeared to be highly significant in their empirical results. Their analysis showed, in particular, that *macroeconomic uncertainty* (as measured by the variance of inflation) had a positive effect on private saving rates, consistent with the **precautionary motive** discussed earlier. *Public sector saving* had a negative but less than proportional effect on private saving, suggesting once again that Ricardian equivalence does not hold in strict terms. *Real interest rates* had no significant effect on saving, whereas *terms-of-trade improvements* were positively associated with private and national saving rates, although the effect was small.

---

[20] A negative correlation between saving and the age dependency ratio was also found by Cárdenas and Escobar (1998) in the case of Colombia.

Various other studies corroborated and complemented the findings described above. For instance, Ostry and Reinhart (1992) found that although intratemporal substitution between nontradables and importables may be a significant channel through which terms-of-trade shocks affect savings, overall their empirical results supported the view that transitory adverse movements in the terms of trade led to a reduction in private saving—as predicted by the HLM effect. In addition, Ghosh and Ostry (1994) found a positive correlation between the *variability* of the terms of trade and saving. Ogaki, Ostry and Reinhart (1996), in a detailed study covering a large number of developed and developing countries, found that saving rates tended to rise with per capita income levels, especially during the transition from low-income levels (where subsistence needs predominate) to middle-income levels. More specifically, the evidence suggested that saving rates tended to increase with the level of per capita income and to *level off* (or even decline) at very high levels of income—as illustrated notably by the experience of Canada, the United Kingdom, and the United States. This **inverted U-shape** pattern has been documented in other studies as well. Finally, Ogaki, Ostry, and Reinhart also found the **intertemporal elasticity of substitution**, even in middle-income countries, to be quite low—less than unity in most cases. For Tanzania, for instance, the estimated elasticity was 0.2, and for Chile and Brazil, it reached 0.6. These results imply, as shown earlier, that a rise in interest rates will in general have an ambiguous (or even negative) effect on consumption and saving—thereby mitigating the benefits of financial liberalization (see Chapter 15).

At the same time, however, there are several issues that are either inadequately addressed in the current literature or remain unresolved. One problem, for instance, is the evidence on the effect of foreign saving (as measured by the current account deficit) on domestic saving rates. As indicated earlier, Masson et al. (1995) and Edwards (1996) both found this effect to be significantly negative, with a coefficient of less than unity—a finding that suggests that foreign saving is a *substitute* , albeit a less than perfect one, for domestic saving. However, in the data that most researchers use, private saving is calculated *residually* as domestic investment plus the current account surplus minus public saving—a key *national accounts identity* that will be explicitly derived in Chapter 8. The implication, however, is that the use of the current account balance along with public saving as explanatory variables brings the regression equation close to being *overidentified*: the high significance levels on the current account balance could therefore be nothing but a statistical artifact.

Another important problem is the lack of robust empirical evidence on the effect of interest rates on saving. As shown earlier, the effect of a change in the real interest rate on saving is *theoretically ambiguous* as a result of conflicting **income** and **substitution effects**. The evidence (or the lack thereof) may thus be consistent with the view that these effects tend to *offset* each other, implying that the net effect is small and often cannot be adequately detected by the data. What this implies, as noted earlier, is that the direct effect of policies aimed at raising rates of return offered to savers may be largely ineffective. It should be noted, however, that several studies have used sample periods during which *regulated interest rates*, exhibiting little variation over time, were in place. Another problem is that the effect of interest rates on saving may be *nonlinear*: not only can it depend on the *level of income*, as shown by Ogaki et al. (1996), it may also be *stronger* at *positive real interest rates* than at the *negative real interest rates* often observed when nominal interest rates are subject to government controls (see Chapter 2). Along the same lines, it would be worth exploring to what extent terms-of-trade shocks tend to have *asymmetric effects* on aggregate saving rates, as a result, for instance, of the tendency of governments to increase spending excessively in good times (see Chapter 3).

1.2   Investment

Investment typically represents a much smaller component of aggregate demand than does consumption. But because it determines the rate at which physical capital is accumulated, it plays an essential role in the expansion of the economy's production capacity (see Chapters 11 and 12). This section reviews various models of investment behavior, based on both scale and relative price variables. It begins by describing the basic **flexible accelerator** model and then extends it to account for the **cost of capital**. Much of the recent analytical and empirical research on the determinants of investment has focused on the role of **uncertainty** and **irreversibility**; these issues are analyzed in the third part. The fourth part discusses various other factors that have been found to affect investment in developing countries.[21] The last part reviews some of the recent empirical evidence on the determinants of private investment in these countries.

1.2.1   The Flexible Accelerator

In its simplest form, the **flexible accelerator** model of investment is derived under the assumption that the production technology in the economy is characterized by a fixed relationship between the desired capital stock and the level of output. Formally, suppose that the *desired* stock of capital, $\tilde{K}$, is proportional to expected output, y^a:

$$\tilde{K} = \alpha y^a, \quad \alpha > 0. \tag{1.23}$$

Suppose that (because it takes time to build, plan, and install new equipment) the actual stock of capital adjusts to the difference between the desired stock at the current period and the actual stock in the previous period:

$$\Delta K = \kappa(\tilde{K} - K_{-1}), \quad 0 < \kappa < 1. \tag{1.24}$$

By definition, gross private investment, I^p, is given by

$$I^p = \Delta K + \delta K_{-1}, \quad 0 < \delta < 1, \tag{1.25}$$

---

[21] The *q-theory* of investment, which makes investment an increasing function of the ratio of the value of the firm to the cost of purchasing the firm's equipment and other capital goods, is not developed here because it has met with very limited empirical success in developing countries.

where δ is the rate of depreciation. Using the **lag operator** L (defined by $Lx = x_{-1}$), this equation can be rewritten as

$$I^P = [1 - (1 - \delta)L]K, \tag{1.26}$$

which implies also that $K_{-1} = I^P_{-1}/[1 - (1 - \delta)L]$. Combining this result with Equations (1.23) to (1.26) yields

$$I^P = \alpha\kappa[1 - (1 - \delta)L]y^a + (1 - \kappa)I^P_{-1}. \tag{1.27}$$

In the particular case where $\delta = 0$, $\kappa = 1$, and expected future output is well approximated by current output, the investment function becomes

$$I^P = \alpha\Delta y. \tag{1.28}$$

Equation (1.28) has a particularly simple form: it relates investment linearly to changes in current output. Variables such as profitability, uncertainty, and the cost of capital play no role. However, despite its simplicity (or perhaps because of it), Equation (1.28) continues to be used in practical applications (see Chapter 9).

1.2.2   The Cost of Capital

An alternative approach is to view investment as depending inversely on the **user cost of capital**, c_K, or equivalently the **flow price of capital services**, which consists of three components:

- an *opportunity cost*, which is measured by the interest that the firm would receive if it sold the capital and invested the proceeds. If i denotes the interest rate and P_K the price of one unit of capital (that is, the nominal market price of one unit of capital goods), this cost is iP_K;

- the cost resulting from the *depreciation* of the capital good; with δ denoting the rate of depreciation of capital, this cost (per unit time) is given by δP_K;

- the *capital loss* (or *gain*) resulting from the fact that the price of capital may be falling (rising), implying that the firm would obtain less (more) if it waits to sell the capital; this is measured by $-\Delta P_K$ per unit time.

Thus, the cost of capital is given by

$$c_K = P_K\left\{i + \delta - \frac{\Delta P_K}{P_K}\right\}, \tag{1.29}$$

where the quantity $i - \Delta P_K/P_K$ can be viewed as a real interest rate measured in terms of the price of capital goods.

In practical applications, the cost of capital is often combined with the flexible accelerator model described earlier. A simple way to do so is to write the *desired* capital stock as, instead of Equation (1.23), an inverse function of c_K in the form

$$\tilde{K} = \alpha y^a / c_K. \tag{1.30}$$

Using this specification simply leads to replacing y^a by y^a / c_K in Equation (1.27), implying therefore that investment is now inversely related to the cost of capital services. This extended model, however, continues to suffer from a major limitation: it does not account for the impact of *uncertainty* on the decision to invest.

1.2.3   Uncertainty and Irreversibility

An important insight of the recent literature on investment is that under uncertainty, private investment decisions may be significantly affected by **irreversibility effects** (Dixit and Pindyck, 1994). Such effects arise essentially from the fact that firm-specific investment typically involves **sunk costs** which can only be partially recuperated, because of the (generally large) discount that firms must face in valuing second-hand equipment. If the outcome of an irreversible investment turns out to be worse than expected, firms may get stuck with *excess capital* or *low returns*, whereas if prospects improve new entrants may compete away part of the gains. Because **downside risk** may increase without corresponding upside gain, *waiting* has value as it gives firms the opportunity to *process new information* before the decision to invest is actually taken.

To examine in a more formal manner the effects of uncertainty and irreversibility on investment, consider the following simple example from Servén (1997). Suppose that a *risk-neutral firm* must decide whether to invest in a project in which the initial cost is completely sunk at the purchase cost P_K at the beginning of period $t_0 = 0$.[22] It yields a known return of R_0 at the end of that period. But future demand for the good generated by the project is uncertain; as a result, the rate of return on the project in period $t = 1$ and beyond, denoted R, is also uncertain.

Given the information available at period 0, the expected value of the future return is $E_0 R$. The *net present value* of the *anticipated return stream of cash flows* associated with the project, V_0, is thus

$$V_0 \equiv -P_K + \frac{R_0}{1+i} + \left[\frac{1}{1+i}\right]^2 \sum_{h=0}^{\infty} (1+\rho)^{-h} E_0 R, \tag{1.31}$$

where i is the discount rate, taken to be equal to the rate of return on an alternative investment, such as riskless government bonds. The third term in this expression can be rewritten as

$$\frac{E_0 R}{(1+i)^2} \sum_{h=0}^{\infty} (1+i)^{-h} = \frac{E_0 R}{(1+i)^2} \left[1 + \frac{1}{1+i} + \frac{1}{(1+i)^2} + \dots\right]$$

---

[22] Risk neutrality in the present context means that the firm's utility is linear in realized profits; maximizing utility and maximizing profits are thus basically the same.

$$= \frac{E_0 R}{(1+i)^2} \left[\frac{1}{1 - 1/(1+i)} \right] = \frac{E_0 R}{i(1+i)}.$$

Using this result, Equation (1.31) can be rewritten as

$$V_0 \equiv -P_K + \frac{R_0 + E_0 R/i}{1 + i}. \tag{1.32}$$

The conventional **net present value criterion** suggests that the investment is profitable and thus should be made as long as $V_0 > 0$. Using Equation (1.32) and rearranging terms yields

$$R_0 - iP_K + \frac{E_0 R - iP_K}{i} > 0, \tag{1.33}$$

where the term iP_K can be interpreted as the user cost of capital in the case where the depreciation rate is zero [see Equation (1.29)]. With **full reversibility** of investment, the *future would not matter*; the optimal decision rule would thus be to invest today as long as

$$R_0 - iP_K > 0, \tag{1.34}$$

that is, as long as the current return exceeds the user cost of capital. The presence of irreversibility requires taking into account both the *difference* between the *expected return* and the user cost of capital, as shown in the last term of Equation (1.33).

But although Equation (1.33) must hold in an *ex ante* sense, it may not *ex post;* the reason is that there is a *nonzero probability* that at some period t in the future, the inequality (1.34) may be reversed, that is, $R - \rho P_K < 0$. The firm may thus be "locked" in an unprofitable investment. There is, therefore, an *incentive to delay* investment in order to learn more about the factors affecting future return—in the present case, about the state of market demand for the good produced by the firm.

To determine how uncertainty affects the decision rule (1.33), consider first the case where the firm knows for sure that uncertainty will completely vanish in period $t = 1$ and that the project's returns for $t = 2, ... \infty$ will remain constant at the level realized in the first period. Suppose then that the firm decides not to invest at all today and to invest next period if and only if the *realized return exceeds the user cost of capital*; in that case, the net present value of the anticipated stream of cash flows, V_1, will be given by

$$V_1 \equiv \Pr(R > iP_K) \left\{ \frac{-P_k}{1+i} + \left[\frac{1}{1+i} \right]^2 \sum_{h=0}^{\infty} (1+i)^{-h} E_0(R \mid R > iP_K) \right\},$$

where

- $\Pr(R > iP_K)$ is the probability that the *project's return exceeds the cost of capital;*

- $E_0(R \mid R > iP_K)$ is the *expected value* of R, *conditional on the project's return exceeding the cost of capital.*

Thus, in the particular case where $\Pr(R > iP_K) = 0$, one also has $V_1 = 0$. Comparing the above strategy with the previous case can be done by calculating

$$V_1 - V_0 = (\frac{1}{1+i}) \left\{ \Pr(R \le iP_K)\frac{E_0(iP_K - R \mid R \le iP_K)}{i} - (R_0 - iP_K) \right\},$$

an expression that is obtained by using the following result from basic statistics:

$$E_0 R = \Pr(R > iP_K)E_0(R \mid R > iP_K) + \Pr(R \le iP_K)E_0(R \mid R \le iP_K).$$

The firm is *better off investing today* if

$$V_1 - V_0 < 0,$$

a condition that can be rewritten as

$$R_0 - iP_K > \Pr(R \le iP_K)\frac{E_0(iP_K - R \mid R \le iP_K)}{i}. \qquad (1.35)$$

Condition (1.35) compares two expressions:

- the **cost of waiting**, as given by the net return foregone in period 0 by not investing, $R_0 - iP_K$;

- the **value of waiting**, given by the *irreversible mistake* that would be revealed tomorrow should future returns fall short of the user cost of capital ($R \le iP_K$). The *expected present value* of such mistake is measured by the right-hand side of Equation (1.35):

  - the mistake is made with probability $\Pr(R \le iP_K)$;
  - its expected per-period size, given today's information, is

  $$E_0(iP_K - R \mid R \le iP_K),$$

  - because it accrues every period into the indefinite future, it has to be multiplied by $1/i$ to transform it to present value terms.

Thus, condition (1.35) indicates that it is profitable to invest *immediately* only if the first-period return exceeds the conventionally measured user cost of capital by a margin that is large enough to compensate for the possibility of an irreversible mistake—that is, *if the cost of waiting outweighs the value of waiting.*

An important implication of Equation (1.35) is that the possibility that in the future R may exceed iP_K has no effect on the investment threshold and thus no effect on the decision to invest today. Intuitively, the reason for this asymmetry is that the option to wait has no value in those good states of nature in which investing would have been the right decision anyway—it is only valuable in those states in which investing today would have been, *ex post*, a bad decision. This **option value of waiting**, δ, is given by

$$\delta = \max\left(V_1 - V_0, 0\right).$$

If $V_1 - V_0 < 0$, the option has no value, and the optimal decision is to invest today (at period 0). In general, however, the option value of waiting can be large, especially in a highly uncertain environment. As a consequence, uncertainty can become a powerful deterrent to investment *even under risk neutrality*.[23] Such uncertainty may result from various domestic and external sources, including a high degree of volatility in aggregate demand, large movements in the terms of trade and relative prices, and incomplete credibility of adjustment policies (see Chapter 5).[24]

In the simple example considered here, an increase in the *spread* of the distribution of future returns—as a result, for instance, of increased **macroeconomic volatility**—that raises the likelihood of "bad" outcomes (that is, $R \leq iP_K$) will raise the critical threshold that the marginal productivity of capital must reach, and thus tend to depress investment. This result, however, does not always hold. If the opportunity cost of waiting, R_0, is uncertain rather than known—as would be the case for investment projects subject to completion lags—and the firm can abandon the project at a cost in the future (that is, investment is **partly reversible**), then higher uncertainty could *hasten* investment, by making extreme favorable realizations of R_0 more likely—even if at the same time extreme adverse realizations also become more likely. The reason is that the firm can now avoid the impact of negative outcomes on profitability by shutting down the project (Bar-Ilan and Strange, 1996). Thus, although both the value and the cost of waiting rise with higher uncertainty, the latter rises by a greater amount.

Nevertheless, the above setting implies that the higher the degree of irreversibility (that is, the higher the degree of asymmetry in investment adjustment costs), the more likely it is that uncertainty will have an adverse effect on capital formation. Recent research on the relation between uncertainty and investment has, however, emphasized the role of various other factors, such as market structure, the degree of risk aversion, and capital market imperfections. As shown by Caballero (1991), under asymmetric investment adjustment costs and with risk neutrality, uncertainty and investment tend to be positively related under perfect competition and constant returns to scale, whereas they tend to be negatively related under imperfect competition and decreasing returns to

---

[23]It is important to emphasize that these results do not depend on the existence of risk-averse firms or restrictions on the degree to which risks can be diversified. Even if firms are risk neutral, and even if risks are fully diversifiable, investment will still depend on the perceived degree of uncertainty.

[24]As noted for instance by Aizenman and Marion (1999), volatlity and uncertainty are in principle two different phenomena. Volatility (or variability) exists when a variable tends to fluctuate over time, whereas uncertainty exists when these fluctuations are unpredictable. In practice, however, volatile variables are often unpredictable as well.

scale.[25] Zeira (1990) also showed that with risk-averse agents, uncertainty has an ambiguous impact on investment. The higher the degree of risk aversion, the more likely it is that uncertainty will reduce investment. Finally, as shown by Aizenman and Marion (1999), a negative link between uncertainty (or volatility) and investment can result from the existence of a **credit ceiling** (see the discussion below). Such a ceiling may lead to a *nonlinearity* in the investor's intertemporal budget constraint. It may therefore hamper the expansion of investment in good times (that is, states in which the firm faces high and growing demand for its products) without mitigating the fall in bad times. This asymmetry may lead to a situation in which higher volatility reduces the average rate of investment.

The thrust of the preceding discussion is thus that, on purely theoretical grounds, the effect of uncertainty on private investment is in general ambiguous. Fundamentally this is because uncertainty affects investment through a variety of channels and, depending in particular on the degree of risk aversion, market structure, and the nature of adjustment costs, the relation between these variables can be either positive or negative. Empirical evidence (as discussed below) is therefore necessary to assess in what direction the net effect operates.

1.2.4   Other Determinants of Investment

In addition to the variables considered earlier, the decision to invest in developing economies has been shown to depend on a variety of other factors. These factors include most notably the degree of credit rationing, the availability of foreign exchange, movements in the real exchange rate, the level of public investment, the degree of macroeconomic volatility, and the existence of a large external debt.[26]

Credit Rationing

As discussed in more detail in Chapter 2, the lack of development of *equity markets* makes firms highly dependent on *bank credit* not only for **working capital needs** (associated with the need to pay workers and to buy raw materials, for instance) but also for the longer-term financing of capital accumulation. As also discussed in Chapter 2, in countries where interest rates are *highly regulated* (so that real interest rates are negative), excess demand for credit will typically exist, forcing banks to ration their loans. The fact that banks are imperfectly informed about the *quality* of the projects in which firms plan to invest may also lead to (endogenous) credit rationing. Both cases suggest that it is the *quantity*

---

[25] See Chapter 11 for a definition of constant, increasing, and decreasing returns to scale. Caballero's results clarified an early contribution by Abel (1983), who showed that in the absence of irreversibility and under risk neutrality, an increase in uncertainty (over the behavior of output prices) tends to increase the desired capital stock and thus investment.

[26] Income distribution, which is not discussed here, may also affect investment decisions through its effect on the profit rate, the level of aggregate demand, and social and political instability. Chapters 13 and 14 discuss the longer-run effects of income inequality.

of credit, rather than its price (the interest rate) that should be considered as a determinant of investment.

Foreign Exchange Constraint

Capital goods such as machines and equipment must often be imported in developing economies. In a country like Argentina, for instance, in the mid-1990s, more than 40 percent of merchandise imports consisted of capital goods and spare parts for these goods. Because the foreign exchange needed to pay for such imports may not be available—as a result of, say, balance-of-payments difficulties or because of higher-priority needs, such as external debt service—investment may be subject to a *foreign exchange constraint*.

The Real Exchange Rate

The real exchange rate (as measured by the price of nontraded goods relative to the price of traded goods) affects private investment through both demand- and supply-side channels:

- On the *demand side*, a real exchange rate depreciation resulting from a nominal depreciation lowers private sector real wealth and expenditure through its effect on domestic prices; the fall in domestic absorption may lead firms to revise their expectations of future demand and to lower investment outlays, through the accelerator effect.

- On the *supply side*, because a real exchange rate depreciation raises the price of traded goods (measured in domestic-currency terms) relative to the price of home goods, it may stimulate investment in the tradable sector and depress capital formation in the nontradable sector.

In general, if the price of domestic factors of production (wages and the price of capital goods) increases less than proportionately to the domestic-currency price of final output, a real depreciation will stimulate aggregate supply and raise private investment. However, to the extent that a real depreciation raises the real cost of **imported capital goods** (a likely outcome if the country is dependent on noncompetitive imported capital goods and intermediate goods), it will have an adverse effect on private investment by raising the user cost of capital (Buffie, 1986) or by dampening expectations of future output through the accelerator effect.

Public Investment

Public investment has in general an *ambiguous effect* on private investment as a result of two opposing factors:

- Public investment may, by increasing the fiscal deficit, **crowd out** private capital formation by reducing credit available to the private sector or by raising interest rates.

- Public investment in infrastructure projects (such as capital outlays in power, telecommunications, transport, health and education) may, at the same time, be *complementary* to private investment.

Figure 1.5, which draws on data compiled by Aizenman and Marion (1999), shows the correlation between the share of private investment in output and the share of public investment in output, averaged over the period 1970-92, for a large group of developing countries. The figure does not suggest any clear correlation pattern between the two variables, as theory suggests. As discussed below, however, more formal econometric studies (which control for various other determinants of private investment) are more conclusive.

Macroeconomic Instability

As noted earlier, in the presence of irreversibility and asymmetric adjustment costs, macroeconomic instability may have large (and possibly negative) effects on private capital formation. There are several other channels through which macroeconomic instability may affect private investment:

- An unstable macroeconomic environment is often characterized by a high *level of inflation*; in turn, a high inflation rate may lower investment by *distorting price signals* and the information content of relative price changes.

- Macroeconomic instability also translates into *high inflation variability*; in turn, a highly variable inflation rate may have an adverse effect on **expected profitability**; if firms are risk averse, their level of investment will fall.

More generally, an increase in policy uncertainty may cause risk-averse firms to reallocate resources away from risky activities, thereby lowering the desired stock of capital.[27] Through the accelerator effect identified above, this fall may translate into a reduction in private investment.

The Debt Burden Effect

A large ratio of foreign debt to output may have an adverse effect on private investment through various channels.

- Resources used to service the public debt may *crowd out* government investments in areas where large complementarities (as discussed above) exist between public and private capital outlays; this would tend to reduce private investment.

---

[27] Credit rationing may also intensify as uncertainty increases.

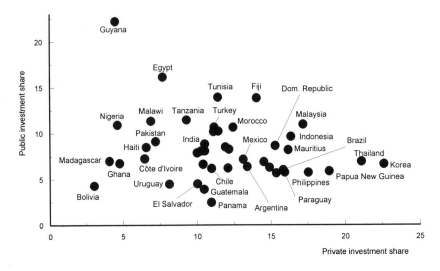

Figure 1.5. Private and Public Investment Shares (in percent of GDP).
Source: Aizenman and Marion (1999, pp. 173-74).
Note: Countries not identified in the figure are Peru, Paraguay, Bangladesh, Costa
Rica, Nepal, Colombia, Iran, Zimbabwe, Venezuela, Ecuador, Kenya, Sri Lanka, and
Mali.

- A high debt-to-output ratio (and a concomitantly high debt service ratio)
  may lead domestic agents to transfer funds abroad instead of saving domestically because of the *fear of future tax liabilities* to service this debt;
  this is similar to the effect alluded to earlier in the context of saving.
  It tends to lower private investment both directly and indirectly—in the
  latter case by raising the domestic cost of capital goods.[28]

- A high debt burden could discourage foreign direct investment by increasing the likelihood that the government may resort to the *imposition of
  restrictions* on external payment obligations—including on current payments on investment income. To the extent that foreign direct investment
  is complementary to domestic private investment, the latter will fall also.

- When firms hold a large stock of foreign-currency liabilities, they become
  highly vulnerable to exchange rate movements. A nominal depreciation,
  for instance, raises automatically the burden of debt and reduces the firm's
  net worth. The resulting increase in the risk of default may lead domestic
  banks to tighten credit restrictions (as discussed above) and may depress
  investment.

Figure 1.6 shows the correlation between the debt burden, as measured by
the ratio of debt service payments to GDP, and the share of private investment in

---

[28] In this sense, a large external debt burden constitutes an additional source of macroeconomic uncertainty.

GDP for a group of heavily indebted poor countries (as discussed in Chapter 16) during the period 1982-95.[29] The figure indeed suggests a *negative correlation* between the debt burden and private capital formation.

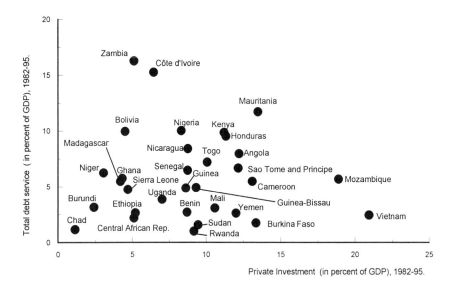

Figure 1.6. Heavily Indebted Poor Countries: Total Debt Service and Private Investment (In percent, 1982-1995).
Source: World Bank.

1.2.5   Empirical Evidence

The foregoing discussion suggests a general empirical formulation of a private investment function that encompasses many of the empirical specifications used in studies conducted in recent years for developing countries. With I^p/y denoting the ratio of private investment to output, this specification can be written as

$$\frac{I^p}{y} = H(\Delta y, c_K, \frac{L^p}{P}, R^*, I_G^I, I_G^O, z, \sigma_z, \pi, \sigma_\pi, \frac{D^*}{y}). \qquad (1.36)$$

This specification includes

- the **income accelerator** effect, as captured by changes in output, Δy;

- the **user cost of capital**, c_K, as defined in Equation (1.29);

- **credit rationing**, as captured by the real stock of bank credit to the private sector, L^p/P;

---

[29]In many studies, the debt service ratio performs better than the debt-to-output ratio as an indicator of the adverse impact of the external debt burden on private investment. This is the case in Oshikoya's (1994) study, which is discussed later.

- the **foreign exchange constraint**, as measured by the country's (average) level of foreign reserves, R^*;

- **public investment**, which consists of investment in infrastructure, I_G^I, and other investments, I_G^O, with the former variable expected to have a positive effect and the second an ambiguous effect;

- The **real exchange rate**, z, which has in general an ambiguous effect;

- **macroeconomic instability**, as captured by the variability of the real exchange rate, σ_z, the level of inflation, π, and the variability of inflation, σ_π;

- The **ratio of foreign debt to output**, as measured by D^*/y.

A detailed overview of the early empirical literature on investment in developing countries was provided by Rama (1993). Rama reviewed 31 studies of investment covering the period from the 1960s to the mid-1980s. Dynamics in many cases were captured by specifying a *partial adjustment process*, of the type shown in Equation (1.24). Such a process, however, does not account very well for the various lags that arise in practice between the moment the decision to invest is taken and actual investment—such as delays involved in choosing, receiving, and installing new capital goods. More importantly, most of these studies were plagued by **specification bias**, and possible **spurious correlation** results; the time-series properties of the endogenous and exogenous variables were often not properly assessed before estimation (see the appendix to Chapter 2).

Two more recent studies are those of Oshikoya (1994) and Hadjimichael and Ghura (1995) for sub-Saharan Africa. Oshikoya's study provided a detailed analysis of the determinants of private investment during the 1970s and 1980s in eight African countries: four *middle-income* countries (Cameroon, Morocco, Mauritius, and Tunisia) and four *low-income* countries (Malawi, Tanzania, Zimbabwe, and Kenya). For sub-Saharan Africa as a whole, real GDP per capita grew on average by only 0.4 percent per annum during 1973-80, and fell by 1.2 percent per annum during the period 1980-89. Investment also fell substantially during that period; the ratio of total domestic investment to GDP fell from 20.8 percent per annum during 1973-80 to 16.1 percent during 1980-89. In the sample of countries considered by Oshikoya, the private investment ratio fell in the early 1980s but increased in the late 1980s in middle-income countries; this ratio fell throughout the 1980s among the low-income countries. The share of private investment in total investment also fell, for the group as a whole, from 53 percent in 1970-79 to 51.4 percent during 1984-88. This overall result, however, reflects essentially the sharp increase in the public investment rate in low-income countries; middle-income countries were able to increase the share of private investment in total investment during the late 1980s.

Oshikoya estimated separate investment equations (with the lagged dependent variable as a regressor) on pooled data for the period 1970-88. His results indicated, in particular, the following points.

- *Changes in real output* (which capture the accelerator effect) had a significant and positive impact on private investment only in low-income countries.

- *Public investment* was positively related to private investment in both groups, with a stronger complementarity effect in middle-income countries.

- The impacts of the real exchange rate and inflation differed markedly across the two groups. The *real exchange rate* had a positive and significant effect on middle-income countries, but a negative (albeit statistically insignificant) effect in low-income countries. The *inflation rate* had a strong and unambiguously negative impact in the low-income countries but a positive and significant effect in the middle-income countries.

- The *debt service ratio* had a strong, negative effect on private investment in both country groups.

- Measures of *macroeconomic uncertainty* and *instability* (the coefficients of variation of real output growth and the real exchange rate) had a negative effect on investment during the 1980s.

Standardized regression coefficients, which are unit-free and measure the relative importance of the independent variables on the private investment rate, suggested that the debt service ratio, the domestic inflation rate, the public investment rate, and the real exchange rate had the largest effect on private investment in middle-income countries. Credit to the private sector, domestic inflation, the growth rate of output, and the debt service ratio had the largest effect on private investment in low-income countries. The importance of the accelerator effect in the latter group may be due to investors having myopic expectations or short planning horizons.

Another empirical study focusing on sub-Saharan Africa by Hadjimichael and Ghura (1995) reaches very similar conclusions.

- Public and private investment appear to be complementary.

- Policies aimed at fostering macroeconomic stability (lower inflation and real exchange rate variability) tend to promote private investment.

- A high debt burden (measured as the ratio of external debt to exports) has an adverse effect on investment.

Four recent studies, by Servén (1997, 1998), Pattillo (1998), and Aizenman and Marion (1999), provide further evidence on the adverse effect of uncertainty on private investment. Servén (1997) found evidence suggesting that uncertainty and macroeconomic volatility were key factors in explaining the low levels of investment observed in sub-Saharan Africa in the 1980s and 1990s. Pattillo (1998) pointed to the same phenomena in explaining the behavior of private investment in Ghana.

In a subsequent study, Servén (1998) focused on a large data set covering 94 developing countries over the period 1970-95. He first pointed out that simple measures of volatility (such as standard deviations of inflation or real exchange rates) may only *partially* capture the impact of policy uncertainty, and therefore make it quite difficult to test empirically its impact on capital formation. Instead, he constructed an alternative measure of uncertainty based on the dispersion of the **innovations** of macroeconomic variables—that is, the standard deviations of the *residuals* of an autoregressive forecasting equation for each variable. Specifically, five macroeconomic variables were considered in Servén's study: three related to the aggregate profitability of capital (output growth, inflation and the relative price of investment goods, the latter a proxy for the user cost of capital) and two more closely related to the relative profitability of different economic sectors (the terms of trade and the real exchange rate). These variables were entered both individually and in a composite form in the regressions. He controlled for some of the other determinants of investment discussed earlier—such as changes in output, the cost of capital (captured by the relative price of capital), the real interest rate, and credit to the private sector—and used alternative econometric procedures to allow for simultaneity, country-specific effects, and parameter heterogeneity across countries. The results indicated a robust negative effect of macroeconomic uncertainty on investment, particularly when such uncertainty was measured by the real exchange rate.

Finally, Aizenman and Marion (1999) also considered a large sample of developing countries (46 in all) over the period 1970-92. They measured macroeconomic volatility in several ways, including—like Servén (1998)—a specification based on the innovations of a set of aggregate variables (government consumption as a share of output, nominal money growth, and the real exchange rate). Figure 1.7 shows a scatter diagram relating money supply volatility and private investment in their sample, and is indeed suggestive of a negative relationship. The more formal econometric methods that Aizenman and Marion used confirmed a significant negative correlation between the alternative volatility measures that they constructed and private investment—even after allowing for various control variables suggested by the recent empirical literature on economic growth (see Chapter 13).[30]

Overall, therefore, most recent studies provide significant evidence of a negative link between uncertainty and private investment in developing countries—possibly reflecting, as noted previously, the role of irreversibility factors.

---

[30] It should be noted that Aizenman and Marion also found evidence that volatility negatively affected the rate of economic growth; this relationship provides an indirect channel (operating via the accelerator effect) through which uncertainty can affect private investment. They, however, did not include output growth as a regressor in their investment equations.

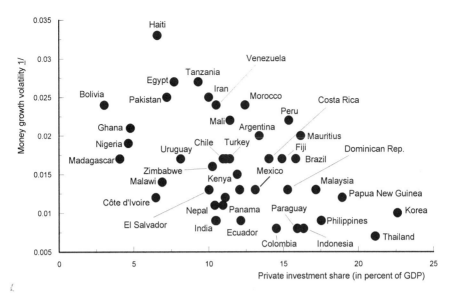

Figure 1.7. Private Investment Share and Money Growth Volatility.

Source: Aizenman and Marion (1999).

Note: The countries unidentified in the graph are Bangladesh, Guatemala, Nepal, and Sri Lanka.

1/ Money growth volatility is defined as the standard deviation of residuals from a first-order autoregressive process for the narrow money growth rate.

1.3   Summary

- Because of their ultimate effects on growth, understanding the patterns and determinants of consumption, saving, and investment is a crucial step in designing policies aimed at raising standards of living.

- The **permanent income hypothesis** postulates that individuals (or households) set consumption equal to their **permanent income**, defined as the annuity value of the sum of assets and the discounted present value of expected future disposable income. A key implication of this assumption is that transitory income changes are (dis-)saved and permanent changes consumed.

- The **life-cycle approach** to consumption and saving assumes that individuals have a finite horizon and attempt to smooth their consumption path on the basis of their (expected) life-cycle wealth or anticipated lifetime income. Saving is seen as providing for retirement and changes systematically over the individual's lifetime.

- Specifically, the life-cycle model predicts that the saving rate should decline as the *retired proportion* of the population increases; this result extends to those *below labor-force age* as well. Thus, the higher the **age dependency ratio**, the lower the saving rate will be.

Empirical studies have identified various other factors affecting consumption and saving in developing economies:

- **Income levels** and **income variability**: saving rates are low at low levels of income. Changes in **income distribution** therefore affect aggregate saving rates. High income variability tends to raise saving as a result of a **precautionary motive**.

- **Intergenerational links**, which affect both the effective planning horizon for consumption and saving decisions, and household preferences.

- **Liquidity constraints**, or restricted access to capital markets, which limit opportunities for households to borrow and lend and therefore the ability to smooth consumption intertemporally.

- **Inflation**, which may exert negative wealth effects, and **macroeconomic instability** (as captured by inflation variability), which may either raise saving (if it increases income uncertainty) or reduce it (if it increases uncertainty on the rate of return).

- **Government saving** behavior, which may have an ambiguous effect on private saving. **Ricardian equivalence**, in particular, postulates that deficits and taxes are equivalent in their effect on private consumption. This view, however, is subject to a number of criticisms at the analytical level and is not supported by the evidence for developing countries.

- The **debt burden**: a high level of debt may, through *anticipations of future taxes*, lower saving rates.

- **Social security, pension systems**, and **insurance**: the desire to accumulate assets for retirement or bequests depends on anticipated changes in income and wealth and the availability of pensions. The need to save for **contingencies** depends on the extent of **insurance** coverage.

- **Terms-of-trade** shocks: the **Harberger-Laursen-Metzler** effect predicts a negative relationship between adverse, *transitory* changes in the terms of trade and saving. However, If households consume both nontradables and importables, changes in their *relative price* induced by terms-of-trade shocks will also affect saving decisions through an **intratemporal substitution** effect, which may offset the conventional HLM effect.

- The degree of **financial development**: the need to save for large purchases of consumer goods depends on the extent to which households can borrow or not for these purposes. There is also an indirect effect through income, to the extent that increased efficiency in the financial intermediation process raises investment and the economy's growth rate.

Recent empirical evidence highlights the importance of public saving, the age dependency ratio (as predicted by the life-cycle model), the level of income per capita, and foreign saving. It also suggests that household saving is responsive to changes in interest rates only at levels of income *above the subsistence level*. The prediction of the permanent income hypothesis that transitory income changes are entirely saved is only partially supported by the evidence for developing countries.

Investment plays an important macroeconomic role because it determines the rate of growth of the physical capital stock and ultimately the growth rate of output. Models of investment behavior emphasize both quantity and relative price variables:

- The **flexible accelerator** assumes the existence of a fixed relationship between the desired capital stock and the *level* of output. In its simplest form, it generates a positive relationship between investment and *changes* in current output.

- The **user cost of capital,** which consists of an *opportunity cost*, a measure of the *depreciation rate of capital*, and the *capital loss* (or *gain*) induced by changes in the price of capital, has an adverse effect on investment.

- **Uncertainty** and **irreversibility** affect investment decisions because

  - most investments in fixed capital are partly or completely sunk; they cannot be fully recovered by selling the purchased capital goods once they have been put in place, and they cannot be used in a different activity without incurring a substantial cost;

  - investment decisions face uncertainty about their *future rewards*. Investors must consider various *possible* outcomes and attach probabilities to them.

- Because investors can control the *timing* of investment, they may postpone it in order to acquire more information about the future.

- Investment can thus be viewed as an *option* to purchase an asset at different points in time. The loss of this option, which is part of the opportunity cost of investment, is ignored in conventional net present-value calculations.

- The optimal investment policy is to balance the **value of waiting** for new information with the **cost of postponing** the investment in terms of foregone returns.

- The standard net present-value investment rule (invest when the anticipated return on the additional capital *equals* its purchase and installation costs) must therefore be modified: the anticipated return must *exceed* the purchase and installation cost by an amount equal to the value of keeping the option open.

- The volatile economic environment that characterizes most developing countries implies that uncertainty can have a strong effect on aggregate investment.

Other variables that have been found to affect investment in developing economies include:

- The degree of **credit rationing**, which results from the fact that, with limited or no equity financing, firms are highly dependent on bank credit not only for their working capital needs but also for the longer-term financing of capital outlays.

- **Foreign exchange constraints**, because capital goods are often imported.

- The **real exchange rate**, which affects private investment through both the demand side (as a result of *wealth* and *income effects*) and the supply side (notably through its effect on the domestic price of *imported capital goods*).

- **Public investment**, which can either **crowd out** private capital formation (by reducing credit available to the private sector) or increase it if it has a *complementary* nature, such as investment in **infrastructure** projects. The *composition* of public investment is thus important.

- **Macroeconomic instability**, as measured by a high and variable rate of inflation lowers investment by *a*) *distorting price signals* and the *information content* of relative price changes, and *b*) reducing *expected profitability*.

- The **debt burden**, which lowers private capital formation by reducing complementary investment, by raising the *fear of future tax liabilities* to cover debt service payments, and by discouraging complementary *foreign direct investment*.

- Recent empirical evidence for sub-Saharan Africa suggests, in particular, that public and private investment are complementary, that policies aimed at fostering macroeconomic stability (lower inflation and real exchange rate variability) tend to promote private investment, and that a high debt burden has an adverse effect on investment.

Appendix
Income Uncertainty and Precautionary Saving

The effects of income uncertainty on saving can be illustrated in a simple framework.[31] Consider the case of an economy in which the representative household lives two periods and faces the following budget constraints, in the absence of taxes ($T_1 = T_2 = 0$):

$$c_1 = y_1 - s_1, \quad c_2 = y_2 + (1+r)s_1, \tag{A1}$$

where c_h, y_h denote consumption and income, respectively, in period h, s_1 saving (in period 1), and r is the real interest rate. For simplicity, the household possesses no initial endowment. Income in the second period, y_2, is supposed to be stochastic; specifically, it is given by

$$y_2 = (1+\varepsilon)y_1, \tag{A2}$$

where ε is a random shock with zero mean and constant variance.

The household determines saving by maximizing the following intertemporal, time additive utility function:

$$U = u(y_1 - s_1) + E\left\{ \frac{u[(1+\varepsilon)y_1 + (1+r)s_1]}{1+\rho} \right\}, \tag{A3}$$

where ρ is the rate of time preference, and Equation (A2) is used to replace y_2. E is the mathematical expectations operator.

Let $r = \rho$; it can be established that saving is *proportional* to the variance of the shock ε:

$$s_1 = \frac{y_1}{2+r}\phi\sigma_\varepsilon^2, \quad \phi \equiv -\frac{u'''(y_1)y_1}{2u''(y_1)}. \tag{A4}$$

The above expression implies that saving is positively related to income uncertainty only if ϕ is positive. In turn, because $u'' < 0$, ϕ is positive only if $u''' > 0$, that is, only if **decreasing absolute risk aversion** prevails. In general, for a utility function $u(\cdot)$, the degree of absolute risk aversion, θ, is measured by (minus) the ratio of the second-order derivative to the first, that is, $-u''/u'$ (see Varian, 1992, pp. 177-178). Decreasing absolute risk aversion requires θ to fall as consumption increases, and this indeed requires the third-order derivative u''' to be positive. The term ϕ can be interpreted as (half) the elasticity measuring consumer's prudence—positive and higher values of this elasticity imply that an increase in uncertainty raises expected marginal utility, leading consumers to defer consumption, thereby increasing saving (see Leland, 1968; Sandmo, 1970).

To establish the above result, note that the first-order condition from Equation (A3) yields

$$u'(y_1 - s_1) = E\left\{ u'[y_1 + \varepsilon y_1 + (1+r)s_1] \right\}.$$

---

[31] The basic results of this appendix were derived by Joshua Aizenman.

It can be noted that

$$u'(y_1 - s_1) \simeq u'(y_1) - su''(y_1),$$

and that

$$u'[y_1 + \varepsilon y_1 + (1+r)s_1] \simeq u'(y_1) + u''(y_1)[\varepsilon y_1 + (1+r)s_1] + \frac{u'''(y_1)}{2}[\varepsilon y_1 + (1+r)s_1]^2,$$

which implies that

$$E\{u'[y_1 + \varepsilon y_1 + (1+r)s_1]\} \simeq u'(y_1) + u''(y_1)(1+r)s_1 + \frac{u'''(y_1)}{2}E(\varepsilon y_1)^2.$$

Using these results yields

$$-s_1 u''(y_1) \simeq u''(y_1)(1+r)s_1 + \frac{u'''(y_1)}{2}E(\varepsilon)^2 y_1^2,$$

which implies that

$$s_1(2+r) \simeq \sigma_\varepsilon^2 \frac{y_1^2}{2}\left(\frac{u'''}{-u''}\right).$$

This expression is simply Equation (A4), given the definition of ϕ. An implication of this result is that the elasticity of saving with respect to the (gross) interest rate, is negative and approximately equal to minus one half:

$$\frac{d \ln s_1}{d \ln(1+r)} = -\frac{1+r}{2+r} \simeq -0.5.$$

Chapter 2

The Financial System, Money Demand, and Monetary Policy

Key features of the financial system in many developing countries are the relatively low degree of institutional diversification, the limited availability of financial assets, and the importance of government intervention. Although informal finance continues to play a significant role in some countries (particularly in sub-Saharan Africa), commercial banks remain the dominant financial institutions. Assets available to savers are often limited to bank deposits and money market instruments. In some countries governments have attempted for years to control the flow of funds to various categories of agents, either directly through forced allocation of bank lending or by imposing various price and quantity restrictions on bank activities. Almost invariably, the result of these policies has been to limit credit availability and to create severe distortions and inefficiencies in the financial intermediation process, with adverse effects on saving, investment, and growth. Although financial liberalization has proceeded at a rapid pace in some countries (creating problems of its own, as discussed in Chapter 15), government intervention remains pervasive in many cases.

This chapter begins with a description of some of the main features of the financial system in developing countries, including the (still pervasive) importance of government restrictions and the role of banks in the process of financial intermediation. The second part examines the nature and operation of indirect instruments of monetary policy in countries where the financial structure is relatively diversified and asset prices tend be market-determined. Factors leading to endogenous forms of credit rationing are examined next. The fourth part focuses on issues posed by the simultaneous use of domestic and foreign currencies for the conduct of monetary policy. The last part reviews the determinants of the demand for money in developing countries.

2.1 The Financial System

There is great diversity in the degree of development of the financial system among developing countries. Figure 2.1 shows average values over the period 1980-95 for 44 developing countries and 15 industrial countries of two indicators of financial development: the ratio of narrow money to GDP, and the ratio of broad money to GDP. The latter measure can be viewed as indicative of the use of money and its close substitutes as means of payment. The second panel of the figure suggests that the depth of financial markets, as proxied by the broad money-to-output ratio, is higher in countries with relatively high income per capita.[1] At the same time, the evidence also suggests that means of payment and stores of wealth other than those included in the definition of broad money may be actively used in the more developed financial systems (see Mishkin, 1998).

In most developing countries, the financial system was for many years subject to a variety of government-imposed restrictions. Although financial deregulation has proceeded rapidly in the past decade or so, these restrictions remain pervasive today in many countries. The first part of this section examines the sources, and implications, of government restrictions on the functioning of the financial sector. The second discusses the role of commercial banks in the process of financial intermediation.

2.1.1 Financial Repression

In many developing countries, central banks continue to impose restrictions on the activity of commercial banks. In some cases, government intervention has the effect of keeping at very low (and often negative) levels the interest rate that domestic banks can offer to savers. In others, commercial banks have been compelled to hold short-term government securities at below-market rates, by imposing statutory **liquidity requirements**; at the same time, **required reserves** held by commercial banks at the central bank may be receiving below-market interest rates. All these restrictions are essentially *taxes* on the banking system and represent what McKinnon (1973) called, in a seminal contribution, **financial repression**.

More generally, a state of financial repression can be defined as a situation characterized by

- *ceilings on nominal interest rates*, which typically lead to negative real rates, with an adverse effect on financial savings and investment decisions;

- *quantitative controls* and *selective credit allocation* across production sectors, regions, or activities (often at preferential interest rates) considered by the government to be a "priority";

---

[1] Some studies have found, however, that this relationship may be *nonlinear* and may depend on the level of inflation—or, more generally, on the stability of the macroeconomic environment.

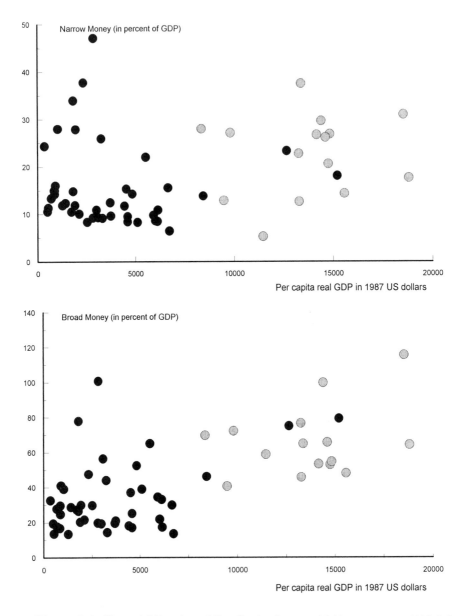

Figure 2.1. Financial Depth and Per Capita Income 1/ (Average over 1980-95).
Source: World Bank.

1/ 44 developing countries and 15 industrialized countries are included. A dark circle refers to developing countries and a lighter circle to industrial countries.

- high *minimum reserve requirements* on bank deposits, which may vary across financial instruments and financial institutions;

- direct control by the state of part of the banking system, with loan decisions guided more by political factors than by standard efficiency considerations;

- *forced allocation of assets* or loans to the public sector by private commercial banks. A common example is the use of **statutory liquidity ratios**, which require commercial banks to hold a given proportion of their assets in the form of government debt.

Interest rate ceilings that force rates to fall below market-clearing rates, in particular, may distort the economy through at least four channels (Fry, 1997, p. 755):

- Low interest rates tend to increase the preference of individuals for current consumption as opposed to future consumption (see Chapter 1); they tend therefore to *reduce savings* below the level that would be optimal from the point of view of society as a whole.

- Low interest rates on bank deposits relative to interest rates on informal financial markets may reduce the supply of funds through the banking system and promote *disintermediation* (see below).

- Bank borrowers who are able to obtain the funds they require at low rates of interest will tend to choose relatively more *capital-intensive projects*.

- The pool of potential borrowers typically contains entrepreneurs with *low-yielding projects*, who would not want to borrow at the higher market-clearing rate. To the extent that banks' selection processes contain an element of randomness, some investment projects that are financed will have yields below the threshold that would be self-imposed with market-clearing interest rates.

To a large extent, the motivation for financial repression is the *inability to raise taxes* through conventional means—either because of **administrative inefficiencies** (as discussed in the next chapter) or because of **political constraints**. By forcing commercial banks to lend to priority sectors, and by imposing large reserve and liquidity requirements on banks—thereby creating a captive demand for its own debt instruments—the government manipulates the financial system to promote its development goals.

Financial repression can yield substantial revenue to the government. One source of revenue from financial repression is the *implicit tax on financial intermediation* generated by high reserve requirement rates. A second source is the *implicit subsidy* from which the government benefits by obtaining access to central bank financing at below-market interest rates. Giovannini and De Melo (1993) estimated that during the period 1984-87, for instance, the Mexican government extracted about 6 percent of GDP (or about 40 percent of total conventional tax revenue) from controls on financial markets. On average, during the period that they considered, governments in their sample of developing countries extracted about 2 percent of GDP in revenue from financial repression. Fry, Goodhart, and Almeida (1996) provided estimates of the same order of magnitude.[2]

Although the acceleration of the process of financial liberalization in recent years has led to a sharp reduction in revenue from financial repression in many countries, commercial banking sectors continue to be heavily regulated in several cases. The implications of financial repression are twofold:

- *Severe inefficiencies*, which tend to restrict the development of financial intermediation, increase the spread between deposit and lending rates, and reduce saving and investment in the economy.

- *Informal modes of financial intermediation* tend to arise and flourish. The existence of such markets may alter substantially the transmission process of monetary policy (see Annex B).

2.1.2   Banks and Financial Intermediation

Whether or not they are subject to excessive government regulations, banks continue to dominate the financial system in most developing countries—low-income and middle-income countries alike. Other specialized institutions exist in many cases, but they typically account for only a very small portion of total financial intermediation in the economy. Bank deposits remain the most important form of household savings, and banks loans (together with retained earnings) are the most important source of finance for firms, both for working capital needs and investment in fixed capital. The overwhelming proportion of bank loans is, in fact, allocated to firms in many developing countries and is short term in nature.

As documented, for instance, by Rojas-Suárez and Weisbrod (1995), banks account for between 50 and 90 percent of the financing needs of firms in Latin American countries. In 1992, the share of commercial banks in total net credit to private sector allocated by banks and other financial institutions represented about 99 percent in Argentina, 94 percent in Bolivia, 62 percent in Brazil, 79 percent in Chile, 49 percent in Colombia, 67 percent in Ecuador, 91 percent in Mexico, 76 percent in Peru, and 85 percent in Venezuela (Rojas-Suárez and Weisbrod, 1995, p. 5). Similar figures can be found in Asia. Figure 2.2 shows the share of domestic credit provided by the banking sector in proportion to GDP for 1990 and 1995 for a group of developing economies. Although the ratio fell in several countries (most notably in sub-Saharan Africa), it increased in many others—particularly in Asia. In Malaysia and Thailand, for instance, the credit ratio increased dramatically and reached almost 140 percent in 1995. These figures are still low compared with those of Japan (266 percent in 1990 and 294 percent in 1995), but are similar in magnitude to those of Germany

---

[2] See Easterly and Schmidt-Hebbel (1994) for another set of estimates of government revenue from financial repression in a group of developing countries during the late 1970s and 1980s.

(110 percent in 1990 and 130 in 1995) and the United States (114 percent in 1990 and 129 percent in 1995).

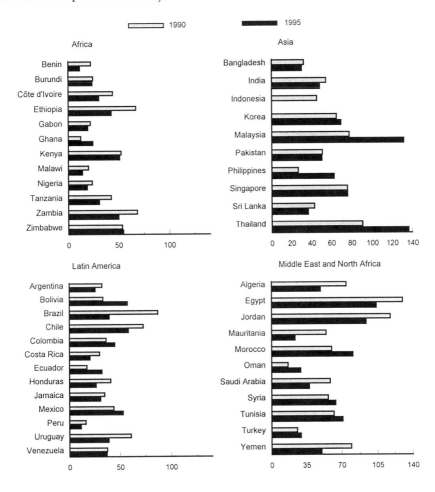

Figure 2.2. Domestic Credit Provided by Banking Sector (In percent of GDP). Source: World Bank.

Equity markets have increased in size in several developing countries in recent years. Figure 2.3 shows the dramatic increase in stock market capitalization (the value of all stocks quoted on the exchanges) in proportion of GDP in countries like Chile, Ghana, India, the Philippines, and Tunisia between 1990 and 1995.[3] In addition, capital market alternatives to bank loans have also become available on a wider scale. In Chile, for instance, a significant *corporate bond market* has developed since the early 1990s; and some of the larger and better-known

---

[3] Stock market capitalization remains nevertheless low compared with advanced industrial countries. In Japan, for instance, comparable numbers are 98 percent for 1990 and 71 percent for 1995; for the United States, these numbers are 55 percent for 1990 and 98 percent in 1995.

firms are now able to raise capital directly in the United States through *American depository receipts* (ADRs) and on Euromarkets through *global depository receipts* (GDRs).[4] Bond markets allow greater dispersion of risk and a more efficient allocation of resources (thereby lowering the cost of capital), as well as greater mobilization of savings—particularly the long-term resources needed to finance investments with long gestation periods. Active secondary markets in government debt are also necessary to conduct monetary policy through indirect instruments, as discussed below.

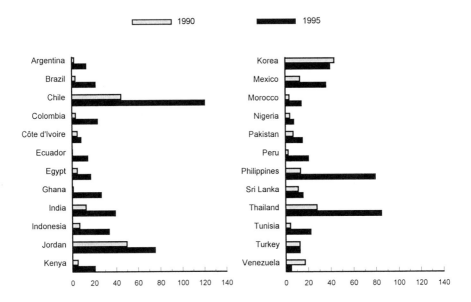

Figure 2.3. Stock Market Capitalization (In percent of GDP).
Source: World Bank.
Note: Stock market capitalization is the share price times the number of shares outstanding for all listed domestic companies.

Nevertheless, the role of equity markets and other sources of finance in the process of financial intermediation between households and firms remains limited in the developing world. Equity finance in many countries remains confined to the largest firms and has not yet become a significant competitor as an alternative to bank loans and retained earnings. In countries where corporate bond markets have developed (as in Chile), they remain quite narrow, concentrated, and relatively illiquid.

It is thus essential to understand the central role that banks play in the economy. In general, banks have three main functions:

---

[4]Foreign firms use ADRs to become listed on a U.S. stock exchange without being subject to the U.S. Security and Echange Commission's disclosure requirements. To issue ADRs, however, foreign firms must hold a deposit with a U.S. chartered bank to guarantee payment of dividends. Receipts verifying the existence of these deposits are the instruments that are actually traded.

- **transformation**-they transform the short-term, liquid deposits held by households (or asset holders) into illiquid liabilities issued by firms;

- **delegated screening and monitoring**-they screen potential borrowers and monitor actual borrowers on behalf of depositors;

- they **facilitate transactions** between agents (firms and workers, buyers and sellers) by providing *payment services.*

The legal, regulatory, and accounting structures within which banks operate in many developing countries remain weak and lack transparency. Inadequate **prudential supervision**, for instance, creates systemic fragility and may precipitate (or compound) bank runs and currency crises, as discussed in Chapter 7. The persistence of prudential problems also complicates the conduct of monetary policy. Weaknesses in the banking system distort the transmission process of monetary policy because banks that are less able to control their balance sheets will be *less responsive* to changes in the base money stock or interest rates. Moreover, banking problems may lead to pressure on the central bank to extend credit to *bail out* troubled banks, thereby reducing the scope for tightening liquidity and raising interest rates to fend off speculative attacks (see Chapters 7 and 15).[5]

2.2 Indirect Instruments of Monetary Policy

As indicated earlier, under financial repression central banks use **direct instruments** of monetary policy (such as controls on interest rates, credit ceilings, and directed lending) to regulate the price, quantity, or composition of credit in an attempt to generate the resources that governments cannot obtain through conventional taxation. The evidence suggests, however, that financial repression has often created severe inefficiencies in credit allocation and the financial intermediation process. Moreover, direct instruments tend to lose their effectiveness because agents find ways to circumvent them—by relying, for instance, on informal credit channels (see Annex B). As a result, many countries have in the past few years liberalized their financial systems and adopted indirect instruments of monetary management.

Indirect instruments of monetary policy are market based and operate essentially through interest rates. Their main purpose is to affect overall monetary and credit conditions through changes in the supply and demand for liquidity.[6] They include, first, **open-market operations**, which consist of the following elements:

---

[5] Information problems can prevent interest rates in the credit market itself from responding to changes in credit demand or central bank lending rates.

[6] For an analysis of the process of transition from direct to indirect instruments of monetary policy in developing countries, see Alexander, Baliño, and Enoch (1995). They emphasize the need to improve in parallel other features of the financial system, including bank supervision and the legal framework—a key issue in the current debate on financial liberalization (see Chapter 15).

- The direct sale or purchase of financial instruments (treasury bills or central bank paper), generally in the **secondary market** for securities. In countries where financial markets are not sufficiently developed, open-market type operations take place through central bank intervention in **primary markets** for securities. For instance, the central bank may hold regular **auctions** of treasury bills (or central bank credit) and vary the amount offered in order to influence the level of liquid reserves held by commercial banks.[7]

- **Repurchase agreements** (which entail the acquisition of financial instruments by the central bank under a contract stipulating an agreed date and a specified price for the resale of these instruments) and **reverse repurchase agreements** (the sale of financial instruments by the central bank under a contract stipulating an agreed date and a specified price for their repurchase), which are used to alter liquid reserves of commercial banks. In contrast with direct operations, such agreements are aimed at providing *temporary* financing of cash shortages and surpluses, but do not directly influence supply and demand in the instrument used as collateral.[8]

A second set of indirect instruments consists of **refinance** and **discount facilities** of the central bank, which are short-term lending operations that typically involve rediscounting high-quality financial assets (such as treasury bills). A third set consists of **reserve requirements**, which stipulate that commercial banks must hold a specified part of their assets in the form of reserves at the central bank. Despite their lack of flexibility as a policy instrument, reserve requirements can be an effective, one-off way of mopping up liquidity in the economy, particularly in periods of large capital inflows (see Chapter 6). However, *unremunerated* reserve requirements can be viewed as an implicit tax and may also lead to financial disintermediation.

The use of indirect instruments allows policymakers to exercise *greater flexibility* in implementing monetary policy. As documented for instance by Borio (1997), almost all industrial countries rely now on this type of instruments to control the behavior of monetary aggregates. Repurchase and reverse repurchase agreements, in particular, are often preferred to outright open-market operations because they do not require a liquid secondary market for securities, they have only an indirect impact on the price of the securities that are being temporarily transferred, and they require no link between the maturity date of these securities and that of the transaction (Borio (1997, p. 40)). Indirect instruments (particularly repurchase and reverse repurchase operations) are also becoming more widely used in the more advanced developing countries. In *Brazil*, for instance, the monetary authorities use both outright pur-

---

[7] Feldman and Mehra (1993) provide a general discussion of the applications of auction markets (including auctions of government securities, central bank credit, and foreign exchange) and bidding techniques.

[8] Short-term repurchase and reverse repurchase agreements are also useful instruments for offsetting large shifts in liquidity caused by a surge in capital inflows or sudden outflows, as discussed in Chapter 6.

chases and sales of treasury bills in the secondary market, as well as repurchase agreements through informal auctions (typically with overnight maturities), as instruments of monetary control. In the *Philippines*, reverse repurchase agreements are used to absorb excess liquid reserves; their maturities range from one week to a month, with a maximum of one year. More generally, as discussed in Chapter 15, the process of financial liberalization has been accompanied by increased reliance on the use of indirect instruments of monetary policy, particularly open-market operations (repurchase and reverse repurchase agreements). In *sub-Saharan Africa*, despite the embryonic nature of secondary markets for government debt in many countries, progress in that area has been notable during the early 1990s (Mehran et al., 1998).

Nevertheless, the transition away from a regime of direct instruments may create a variety of problems. In particular, the conduct of *open-market operations* may lead to two types of difficulties.

- The volume of central bank transactions may be large relative to the total volume of transactions in the secondary market. In such conditions, sales of government securities by the central bank to reduce liquidity may lead to a rise in interest rates on these securities—thereby raising the domestic *debt burden* of the government. Repurchase operations, based on the central bank's own securities, may in this case be preferable.

- A conflict may also arise between monetary management objectives and debt management objectives when monetary policy relies on **primary market sales** of government securities. For instance, the Treasury may be tempted to manipulate auctions in order to keep funding costs below market. More generally, when monetary management relies on primary market sales of government paper, a high frequency of auctions may hamper the development of an active secondary market.

2.3 Credit Rationing

A key feature that distinguishes the credit market from other markets for goods or financial assets is that the interest rate charged by a given bank on a loan contract to a given borrower typically differs from the return the bank *expects* to realize on the loan, which is equal to the product of the contractual interest rate and the *probability* that the borrower will actually repay the loan. Because of **imperfect** or **asymmetric information** between banks and their borrowers—that is, a situation in which borrowers have greater information about their own default risk than do banks—this probability is almost always less than unity. A seminal analysis by Stiglitz and Weiss (1981) showed that in the presence of asymmetric information **credit rationing** may emerge *endogenously*.

The key idea that underlies this result is that the probability of repayment may be negatively related to the contractual interest rate; that is, as the interest rate on the loan increases, the probability of repayment may decline. The repayment probability for some borrowers may actually fall by more than the increase in the contractual interest rate if the latter rises beyond a certain level—implying that the expected return to the bank on loans to these borrowers may actually diminish as a result of further increases in the contractual rate. Because the bank has no incentive to lend in such conditions, it will stop lending completely to these borrowers—even if they are willing to accept higher contractual interest rates. There is, therefore, **credit rationing**. This result is one of the key insights of the Stiglitz-Weiss analysis.

The Stiglitz-Weiss model can be described as follows. Consider an economy populated by a bank and a group of borrowers, each of whom has a single, one-period project in which he (or she) can invest. Each project requires a fixed amount of funds, L, and this is the amount that each borrower must obtain to implement the project.[9] Each borrower must pledge **collateral** in value $C < L$.

Assume also that each project requiring funding has a distribution of *gross payoffs*, $F(R, \theta)$, where R is the project's return (assumed constant across projects) and θ a parameter that measures the **riskiness** of the project. Projects yield either R (if they succeed) or 0 (if they fail); the borrower cannot, in any case, affect R. A higher value of θ is taken to represent an increase in risk. More precisely, an increase in θ captures an increase in the *variance* of the project's return, while leaving its mean constant. Shifts in θ are thus assumed to be *mean preserving*.[10]

The borrower receives the fixed amount of loans, L, at the contractual interest rate r and defaults on the loan if the project's return R plus the value of the collateral C are insufficient to repay the loan. The bank receives either the full contractual amount $(1 + r)L$ or the maximum possible, $R + C$. Assuming that lenders face no **collection** or **enforcement costs**—an assumption that will be further discussed below—the return to the bank is given by the smaller of these two values:

$$\min\{R + C; (1 + r)L\}.$$

Because the project yields a zero return if it fails, the return to the borrower is given by

$$\max\{R - (1 + r)L; -C\}.$$

Stiglitz and Weiss show that for a given contractual interest rate, r, there is a *critical value* of θ, say $\tilde{\theta}$, such that an agent will borrow to invest if, and only if, $\theta > \tilde{\theta}$; that is, the interest rate serves as a **screening device**. They also show also that an increase in the interest rate triggers two types of effects:

- an **adverse selection effect** (which translates into a rise in the threshold value $\tilde{\theta}$), resulting from the fact that by increasing the riskiness of the pool of applicants, less risky borrowers drop out of the market; and

- an **adverse incentive effect**, or **moral hazard effect**, which occurs because other borrowers are induced to choose projects for which the probability of default is higher—in turn because riskier projects are associated

---

[9] This assumption therefore rules out the possibility for the borrower to invest his or her *own funds* or to raise funds by other means—such as equity issues or promissory notes.

[10] See Varian (1992, p. 186) for a simple example of a mean-preserving distribution.

with higher expected returns. This has a negative effect on the lender's expected profit, which may dominate the positive effect of an increase in the contractual interest rate.[11]

The first result, $\partial\tilde{\theta}/\partial r > 0$, implies that the direct, positive effect of an increase in the contractual interest rate on the bank's expected (mean) rate of return on its loans, ρ (defined as the product of the contractual interest rate and the probability of repayment), may be partly offset by the negative effect due to the increase in the riskiness of the pool of borrowers. If the latter effect indeed dominates, the mean return to the lender ρ will not be monotonically related to r and *rationing* may incur in equilibrium.

The above results can be illustrated with the help of Figure 2.4. The northeast panel in the figure shows the demand for loans, L^d, and the supply of loanable funds, L^s, both as functions of the contractual loan rate, r. The demand for loans is depicted, in a standard fashion, as a negative function of the loan interest rate. By contrast, the supply of funds is taken to be positively related to the loan interest rate *only up to* a certain interest rate level, $\tilde{r}$. As indicated earlier, increases in the interest rate beyond the bank-optimal rate $\tilde{r}$ trigger **adverse selection** and **adverse incentive** effects, which, by reducing the expected rate of return to the bank, lead to decreasing amounts of credit offered to borrowers. Thus, the relationship between the interest rate and the supply of loanable funds turns negative, and the value of L^s decreases to the right of $\tilde{r}$. Put differently, the supply curve of loans has a *concave* shape.

As noted earlier, the expected rate of return to the bank, ρ, is the product of the contractual interest rate and the probability of repayment. Owing to the adverse selection and adverse incentive effects associated with a rise in the interest rate, the repayment probability declines *by more* than the increase in the interest rate beyond the threshold level of the contractual rate, $\tilde{r}$. The relationship between ρ and the contractual rate of interest is thus nonmonotonic, as illustrated by curve RR in the southeast panel of Figure 2.4. Moreover, RR has a more pronounced concave shape than L^s.

A higher expected rate of return raises the incentive to lend; there is, therefore, a positive relationship between ρ and the supply of loanable funds, as depicted in the Southwest panel of Figure 2.4. The northwest panel shows a 45-degree line mapping of the equilibrium loan amount and the supply curve of loans, L^s.

The value of the contractual interest rate that ensures equality between demand and supply of loans is obtained at point A in the northeast panel; however, the **credit-rationing equilibrium** (characterized by excess demand for loans) occurs at the interest rate $\tilde{r}$, where the expected return to the bank, ρ, is at its maximum level. Again, the market-clearing interest rate is *not optimal* for the bank, because at that level bank profits are less than at $\tilde{r}$. It is also *inefficient*, because borrowers with high repayment probabilities drop out and are replaced by those with high default risk. The non-market-clearing rate $\tilde{r}$ is

---

[11] The bank's expected profit may also decline if, for a fixed rate of interest rate, the collateral is increased; see Wette (1983).

both *optimal* and *efficient*, because bank profits are at a maximum level and risky borrowers are rationed out.[12]

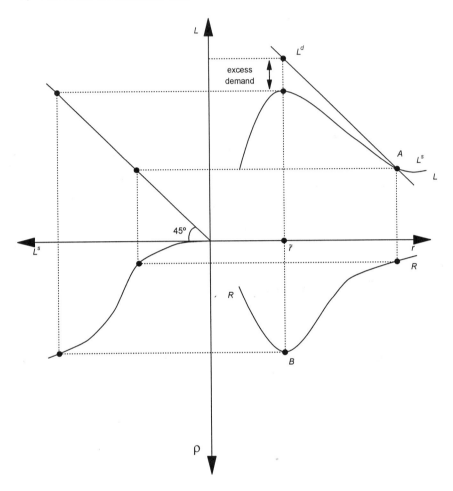

Figure 2.4. Interest Rate Determination in the Stiglitz-Weiss Credit Rationing Model.

Source: Adapted from Stiglitz and Weiss (1981, p. 397).

Thus, under imperfect information, lending rates that are below market-clearing levels can be observed even in competitive credit markets. Such non-market-clearing lending rates reflect an *efficient response* to profit opportunities. The implication of this analysis is that increases in interest rates, beyond a certain level, can be counterproductive. Even in a situation where there exists excess demand for loans, and even if there is some degree of competition

---

[12] Stiglitz and Weiss also show that it is possible to have, in a situation in which there are several groups of *observationally distinguishable* borrowers, complete exclusion of some groups from the credit market—despite the fact that the expected productivity of their investments may be *higher* than those of the groups that actually receive credit.

among banks, borrowers may face limits on their ability to borrow and banks may charge an interest rate below the level that would clear the market. It may be neither optimal nor efficient for the bank to raise interest rates to the market-clearing level, because at that rate the bank's expected profit is less than that achieved at the credit-rationing level, and borrowers with high repayment probabilities tend to drop out and are replaced by those with high default risks. The credit-rationing rate, however, is both optimal and efficient.

The Stiglitz-Weiss hypothesis of equilibrium credit rationing is helpful to understand why in some developing countries bank credit is severely rationed (in addition to the distortions in credit allocation induced by government regulations), with bank lending rates unresponsive to excess demand for credit. Kaufman (1996), for instance, used the Stiglitz-Weiss model to explain some of the aspects of Argentina's economic crisis of 1995-96 (see Chapter 7). Kaufman suggested that the degree of riskiness of projects (as measured by the coefficient θ above) can be *endogenously* related to the level of economic activity—which itself depends on the amount of loans available. This link creates a channel through which credit rationing can be exacerbated and may display persistence over time.

The Stiglitz-Weiss model may also be useful to explain the frequent incidence in developing countries of relatively high holdings of **excess reserves** (held not only in the form of cash but also short-term liquid assets in some countries) by commercial banks. In an environment in which the probability of default on loan commitments is high, excess reserves will also tend to be high. Figure 2.5, for instance, shows the evolution of excess liquid assets—calculated as the difference between total liquid assets and required liquid assets—held by deposit money banks in Thailand, before and after the financial and economic crisis that erupted in mid 1997 (see Chapter 7). The data show a very sharp increase in excess liquidity in the immediate aftermath of the crisis—a phenomenon that is consistent with a higher incidence of credit rationing (as a result, for instance, of a perceived increase in the risk of default) of the Stiglitz-Weiss variety. Of course, this increase could also be, at least in part, demand induced—as a result of the slowdown in economic activity. No definitive judgment has yet been reached on this issue. In general, nevertheless, the effectiveness of monetary policy actions depends importantly on whether banks are holding excess liquid reserves or not, the degree to which interest rates can be deemed sensitive to changes in excess reserves, and the degree to which bank lending decisions are influenced by the perceived riskiness of potential borrowers.

The Stiglitz-Weiss model suffers, however, from several limitations. The first is the assumption that lenders are completely unable to assess the degree of riskiness of potential borrowers. If interest rate increases do indeed lead to more risky projects being funded, banks have incentives to invest in **screening technologies** in order to acquire information about the risk characteristics of their customers. This is particularly plausible in a dynamic context, even though screening may be hampered somewhat by high-risk borrowers attempting to mimic low-risk borrowers.

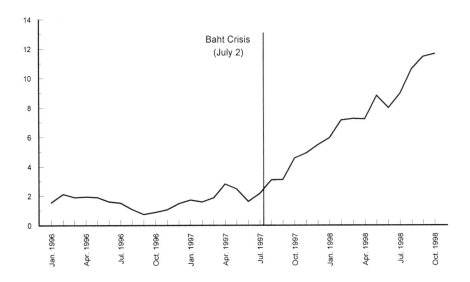

Figure 2.5. Thailand: Excess Liquid Assets, 1996-98 (in percent of total deposits in commercial banks).
Source: Bank of Thailand and International Monetary Fund.

A second issue relates to the role of collateral, C, in the model. Wette (1983) showed that adverse selection effects similar to those emphasized by Stiglitz and Weiss may result if lenders attempt to raise mean returns by increasing the collateral required from borrowers. Bester (1985) argued, however, that if lenders can vary *both* collateral requirements and the contractual loan rate to screen loan applicants, the possibility of a rationing equilibrium disappears. In a subsequent contribution, Stiglitz and Weiss (1992) argued that even if banks are able to manipulate interest rates and collateral, rationing may still emerge in equilibrium if borrowers are subject to **decreasing absolute risk aversion.**[13]

A third, and perhaps more important, issue relates to the role of **collection** and **verification costs.** As noted earlier, such costs are absent in the Stiglitz-Weiss model. The asymmetry of information is purely *ex ante*: although projects differ in their distributions of return before implementation, lenders can observe (costlessly) *actual* outcomes. An alternative approach, developed notably by S. Williamson (1986), is to assume that projects are *ex ante* identical but lenders must incur *ex post* **monitoring** and **enforcement costs** to a) verify the outcome of the project and b) legally enforce the terms of the loan contract (notably seizure of collateral) if the borrower chooses to default. As shown by S. Williamson (1986), in such conditions it is the positive relation-

---

[13] See the appendix to Chapter 1 for a definition of decreasing absolute risk aversion. It should be noted, however, that Stiglitz and Weiss (1992) consider only the case of a fixed collateral value. The extent to which their results carry over to the case in which the value of the collateral itself depends on whether the project succeeds or not *ex post* is not entirely clear.

ship between the contractual interest rate and *expected monitoring costs* that may generate a non-monotonic relationship between the expected return to the lender ρ and the loan rate r, thereby creating the possibility of credit rationing. This alternative approach to credit market imperfections may be particularly relevant for developing countries, where enforcement of loan contracts may be difficult due to the severe weaknesses in the legal system. It has recently been extended in a variety of directions and has proved fruitful to address, in particular, the role of the credit market in the transmission of exogenous shocks to the supply side.[14]

2.4   Monetary Policy in a Dollarized Economy

Dollarization (or **currency substitution**) refers to a situation in which a foreign currency is used as a unit of account, store of value, and a medium of exchange, concurrently with the domestic currency (Giovannini and Turtelboom, 1994). Figure 2.6 shows a common measure of the degree of dollarization, the proportion of foreign currency deposits held in the banking system relative to the domestic broad money stock for six developing countries: Bolivia, Chile, Mexico, Peru, Turkey, and Uruguay. The figure suggest that dollarization has been at times pervasive in these countries.[15] Moreover, it seems to be associated with periods of high inflation; this is particularly so for Bolivia, Chile, Mexico, and Peru. Figure 2.7, which displays a variety of macroeconomic indicators for Turkey during the period 1987-96, shows also that the dollarization ratio (measured now as a the share of foreign currency deposits in total bank deposits) grew significantly during the period, in line with the increase in inflation rates. Dollarization can thus be viewed as an endogenous response by domestic agents attempting to avoid the **inflation tax** and capital losses on assets denominated in domestic-currency terms (see Chapter 3). At the same time, of course, it responds to *portfolio diversification* needs—which may exist even at relatively low inflation rates.

The evidence also suggests that, even after sharp reductions in inflation, dollarization can remain relatively high. This is what apparently occurred in countries such as Bolivia, Uruguay, and Peru, as illustrated in Figure 2.6. Several explanations have been offered to explain the persistence of a high degree of dollarization in a low-inflation environment. Guidotti and Rodríguez (1992) suggested that **transactions costs** incurred in switching from one currency to the other—justified by the assumption of economies of scale in the use of a single currency—imply that there is a range of inflation rates within which the degree of dollarization is likely to remain unchanged. Along the same line, Uribe (1997b) argued that transactions costs incurred in switching currencies

---

[14] See Agénor and Aizenman (1999) and the discussion in Chapter 8.

[15] It should be noted that using foreign currency deposits to measure the degree of dollarization can seriously underestimate the pervasiveness of the problem; if the *risk of confiscation* of foreign-currency assets held in domestic banks is high, agents may hold their cash outside banks. Foreign currency deposits may also be held abroad and data on these deposits are limited.

may themselves depend on the degree of dollarization in the economy; put differently, from an individual's point of view, it is more costly to switch from the domestic currency to the foreign currency if the degree of currency substitution is low. Reducing the propensity to hold foreign currency balances therefore requires a very low inflation rate to induce individuals to regain skills in the use of the domestic currency.

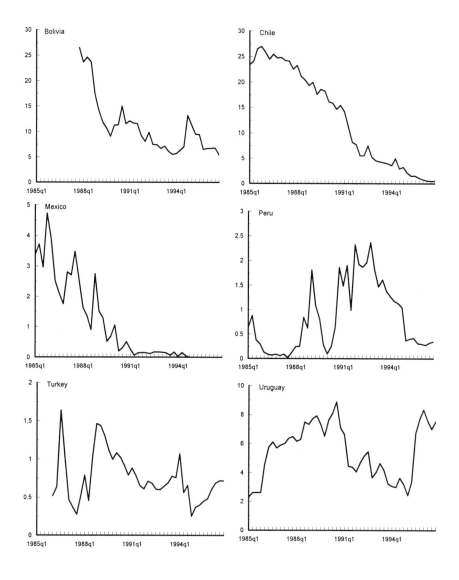

Figure 2.6. Foreign Currency Deposits Held in the Domestic Banking System (In proportion of the domestic broad money stock).
Source: International Monetary Fund.

An alternative explanation that does not rely on the existence of transactions costs in explaining the persistence of the dollarization process has been offered by McNelis and Rojas-Suárez (1996). They emphasized the fact that the degree of currency substitution depends not only on expectations of inflation and exchange rate depreciation, but also on the **risk** (or **volatility**) associated with these variables. Whereas during periods of high inflation the risk component tends to be dominated by the level of inflation itself, in periods of low inflation (or *poststabilization* episodes) risk factors become more important. Everything else equal, increased risk (or volatility) of prices and exchange rates would induce asset holders to switch away from domestic currency and toward foreign currency. Thus, reducing the degree of currency substitution requires not only a reduction in the levels of expected inflation and exchange rate depreciation, but also a reduction in the volatility of these variables. The empirical evidence for Bolivia and Peru (countries where, as indicated earlier, the degree of dollarization remained high even after inflation stabilization was achieved) provided by McNelis and Rojas-Suárez supports the view that **depreciation risk** is an important factor in explaining the persistence of dollarization.

To the extent that dollarization leads to an increase in the flow of funds into the banking system, it may be beneficial. A low degree of dollarization may merely reflect "normal" portfolio diversification needs. However, high degrees of dollarization may complicate significantly the conduct of monetary and exchange rate policies.

First, dollarization involves a **loss of seigniorage revenue** (as discussed in the next chapter), because the demand for domestic base money is lower than otherwise. This loss in revenue can lead to increased monetary financing and thus high inflation—which may in turn lead to a further reduction in holdings of domestic money balances (see Chapter 5). The outcome may be an **inflationary spiral**, with **full dollarization** as the ultimate outcome.

Second, dollarization affects the choice of assets that should be included in the *monetary aggregates* that are used by policymakers as indicators of monetary conditions or target variables. Aggregates including foreign currency cash and deposits are relevant if the use of foreign currency as a medium of exchange tends to distort the link between domestic money and inflation. There may be less reason to consider such aggregates if dollarization represents *asset diversification*, with no implications for aggregate demand and inflation.[16]

Third, dollarization (in the form of foreign currency deposits in domestic banks) essentially index bank deposits to the exchange rate. Because the domestic-currency value of foreign-currency deposits rises proportionately with exchange rate depreciation, monetary aggregates tend to *accommodate inflationary pressures*. To the extent that loans extended against foreign-currency deposits are denominated in domestic currency, the **currency mismatch** may weaken banks' balance sheets if the exchange rate depreciates and if lending rates cannot be adjusted to absorb the loss on loan principal measured in foreign-

---

[16] In practice, of course, dollarization reflects some combination of both motives, there is a case for considering aggregates both including and excluding foreign currency deposits when assessing monetary conditions.

currency terms. These weaknesses can force the central bank to intervene, and the increase in liquidity can exacerbate inflationary pressures.

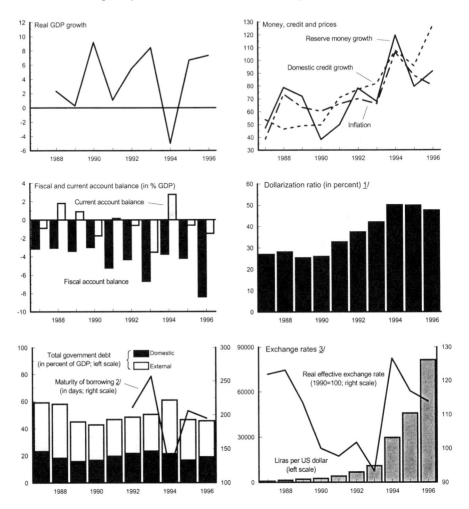

Figure 2.7. Turkey: Macroeconomic Indicators, 1987-96 (In percent per annum, unless otherwise indicated).

Source: International Monetary Fund and official estimates.

1/ Share of foreign currency deposits in total bank deposits.

2/ Newly issued debt.

3/ A rise is a depreciation.

Fourth, dollarization affects the choice of an *exchange rate regime* (as discussed in Chapter 4), because it implies short-term foreign-currency liabilities against which foreign exchange reserves of the banking system must be measured. Figure 2.8, which shows the ratio of foreign currency deposits held in the banking system relative to the foreign exchange reserves (excluding gold) held by the central bank for the six countries shown in Figure 2.6, suggests indeed that such ratios can be very high. In such conditions, an increase in foreign currency deposits held in domestic banks may increase the *vulnerability* of the banking system and the official exchange rate to abrupt reversals in market sentiment and capital flows (see Chapters 6 and 7).

Although the foregoing discussion suggests that dollarization may have adverse consequences for macroeconomic management, outright restrictions aimed at reducing holdings of foreign assets are likely to prove ineffective due to the ability of asset holders to evade them through informal currency markets (see Annex B). High degrees of dollarization are generally *not a cause*, but rather a *symptom*, of underlying financial imbalances and weaknesses.

2.5   The Demand for Money

The demand for money plays an important macroeconomic role. As discussed in Chapter 9, it is at the heart of several operational approaches to macroeconomic analysis, in particular the **financial programming** framework used by the International Monetary Fund. In general, of course, the stability of money demand is essential for the conduct of monetary policy.

Numerous studies of the determinants of money demand in developing countries have been conducted in recent years. Let m^d denote real money balances; a general expression that captures the variables most often used in empirical applications can be written as follows:

$$m^d = m^d(y, i, \pi, \varepsilon^a, \sigma_\pi), \tag{2.1}$$

where

- y is the **level of transactions** in the economy (measured either by real income or consumption expenditure), and is expected to have a positive effect;

- $i, \pi,$ and ε^a are, respectively, the domestic nominal rate of interest, the domestic inflation rate, and the rate of depreciation of the nominal exchange rate; these variables represent alternative measures of the **opportunity cost** of holding money, and are expected to have a negative effect on the demand for real money balances:

  - The interest rate captures substitution between domestic *interest-bearing assets* and money holdings;

  - the inflation rate captures substitution between *real assets* (such as durable goods and other valuables) and money holdings;

  - the rate of depreciation of the nominal exchange rate captures substitution between domestic money and foreign currency, that is, the degree of **dollarization** or **currency substitution**, as discussed earlier.

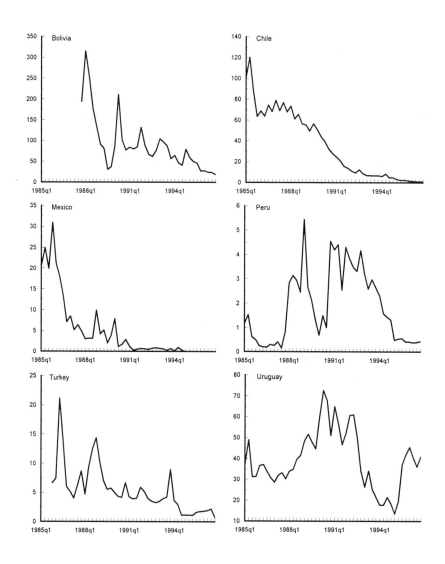

Figure 2.8. Foreign Currency Deposits in the Domestic Banking System (In proportion of total foreign reserves minus gold).
Source: International Monetary Fund.

- σ_π is the variability of inflation, which is often used as a proxy for *macroeconomic instability*; it tends to have a negative effect on holdings of money balances.

An example of a recent money demand study along the specification given in Equation (2.1) is the one by Choudhry (1995), which focuses on Argentina (August 1975-March 1987), Israel (April 1974-December 1988), and Mexico (January 1976-December 1987).[17] As documented by Agénor and Montiel (1999, Chapter 9), all three countries experienced high inflation, large current account imbalances, and drastic devaluations during the sample periods. Choudhry includes both the inflation rate and the rate of currency depreciation to measure the opportunity cost of holding domestic money. He finds evidence of a stable long-run money demand function in all three cases for both narrow and broad definitions of the money supply. Thus the evidence suggests significant currency substitution during the sample period. However, elasticity estimates suggest that the currency substitution effect, although statistically significant, is relatively small compared with the direct effect of inflation on money demand.

Various other variables have also been included as determinants of money demand in empirical studies. These include measures of *financial innovation* and *financial development*. As noted earlier, financial liberalization—interest rate deregulation and greater competition in banking markets, as well as the liberalization of restrictions on cross-border capital flows, as discussed in Chapters 6 and 15—may affect significantly the relation between money demand and its determinants and complicate the conduct of monetary policy.

2.6   Summary

- **Financial repression** refers to a situation in which the financial system is subject to *ceilings on interest rates, quantitative controls* and *selective credit allocation, high minimum reserve requirements* on bank deposits, *direct control* by the state of part of the banking system, and *forced allocation of assets* or loans to the public sector by private commercial banks.

- The source of financial repression is often the inability of governments to raise taxes through conventional means.

- Financial repression can yield substantial revenue to the government, notably through the *implicit tax* on financial intermediation generated by high reserve requirement rates. However, it entails also *severe inefficiencies* which tend to restrict the development of formal financial intermediation (and to encourage **informal modes of financial intermediation**), increase the spread between deposit and lending rates, and reduce saving and investment.

- Banks remain the dominant channel of financial intermediation in the developing world, despite the expansion of capital markets observed in recent years. In most Asian and Latin American countries, banks still account for more than 80 percent of financial intermediation. With few exceptions, *equity markets* play a relatively insignificant role. Market capitalization is

---

[17]Other studies include Ghartey (1998) on Ghana, and Price (1994) on Indonesia. All of these studies use *cointegration techniques* to distinguish between the short- and long-run determinants of money demand. See the appendix to this chapter for a brief description of the methodology.

usually much lower than in industrial countries, and turnover is generally low.

- A key function of banks as financial intermediaries is to alleviate the imperfections arising from the **maturity mismatch** between relatively liquid deposits and longer-term loans. Weaknesses in the legal and supervisory structure, however, make banks vulnerable to abrupt macroeconomic shocks and complicate the conduct of monetary policy.

- *Direct instruments* of monetary policy aim at regulating the price, quantity, or composition of domestic credit. However, they tend to generate inefficiencies in the intermediation process. *Indirect instruments*, by contrast, encourage intermediation through the formal financial system. They also permit *greater flexibility* in implementing monetary policy.

- **Credit rationing** in the Stiglitz-Weiss model arises *endogenously* in the presence of **imperfect** or **asymmetric information** between lenders and borrowers.

- Whereas moderate increases in the contractual lending interest rate tend to increase bank lending in the Stiglitz-Weiss model, rate increases beyond a certain level tend to lower the level of lending by changing adversely the *quality* of the pool of borrowers as a result of two effects:

  - safe—that is, the more creditworthy—borrowers are discouraged and drop out of the market (the **adverse selection effect**); and

  - other borrowers are induced to choose projects with a higher probability of default, because riskier projects are associated with higher expected profits (the **adverse incentive** or **moral hazard effect**).

- Thus, even in the presence of an *excess demand for loans*, the optimal response is to limit lending to potential borrowers and to charge an interest rate that maximizes the bank's *expected profits*, net of the cost of default. Raising the interest rate beyond this level would only lower the bank's overall return.

- **Dollarization** (or **currency substitution**) refers to a situation in which a foreign currency is used, concurrently with the domestic currency, as a unit of account, store of value, and a medium of exchange. It reflects *portfolio diversification* needs and, in high-inflation countries, an attempt by domestic agents to protect themselves from bouts of inflation and capital losses on assets denominated in domestic-currency terms.

- Dollarization tends to be *asymmetric*—it tends to remain high even after a reduction in inflation. This may reflect either large **transactions costs** incurred in switching from one currency to the other—costs that may themselves depend on the initial degree of dollarization. Alternatively, it may reflect the persistence of **depreciation risk**.

- A high degree of dollarization may complicate the conduct of monetary policy and exchange rate management because it involves a loss of **seigniorage revenue**, affects the definition of monetary aggregates, distorts the link between domestic money and inflation, and increases the vulnerability of commercial banks to *currency depreciation*.

- Outright restrictions aimed at reducing the degree of dollarization are unlikely to be effective because agents would typically *evade* them through informal currency markets. High degrees of dollarization are generally a *symptom* rather than *a cause* of underlying financial imbalances.

- The **demand for money** plays an important macroeconomic role. In addition to conventional transactions and opportunity cost variables, the substitution with real assets and foreign currency may be important. The degree of *inflation variability* and the pace of *financial innovation* may also play a significant role.

Appendix
Money Demand and Cointegration

Equation (2.1) can be viewed as describing a **long-run equilibrium** relationship. To determine if such a relationship holds in practice, economists have in recent years increasingly relied on **cointegration tests**.[18]

The main idea behind cointegration is a specification of models that include beliefs about the movements of variables relative to each other *in the long run*, such as the money demand function specified in the text. Intuitively, cointegration implies that in a long-run equilibrium relationship between different **nonstationary** variables, it is required that these variables should not move too far away from each other.[19] Individually these variables might drift apart in the short run, but in the long run they are constrained. More formally, two or more nonstationary time series are cointegrated if a linear combination of these variables is stationary, that is, converges to an equilibrium over time. Thus, if the money demand function describes a stationary long-run relationship among real money balances, a transactions variable and the opportunity cost of holding money (say, the domestic interest rate), it can be interpreted to mean that the stochastic trend in real money balances is related to the stochastic trends in real income and interest rates. In other words, if these variables are cointegrated they will be constrained to an equilibrium relationship in the long run. Deviations from the long-run equilibrium may occur in the short run, but they are **mean reverting**.

In practical terms, there are three steps involved in this methodology.

- Show that all the variables appearing in Equation (2.1) are nonstationary. A common test is the **Augmented Dickey-Fuller (ADF) test** (see Chapter 9).

- Show that a linear combination between these (nonstationary) variables is stationary. One way of doing so is to determine whether the residual term of the second-step regression is stationary, using also an ADF test.

- After confirming that Equation (2.1) represents a cointegrating (long-run) relationship, study the short-run dynamics of the relationship by specifying an **error-correction (EC) model**.

Formally, suppose that the opportunity cost of holding money consists only of the domestic interest rate. The EC model then takes the form:

$$\Delta m_t^d = \alpha_0 + \sum_{h=0}^{n} \alpha_{1h} \Delta i_{t-h} + \sum_{h=1}^{n} \beta_h \Delta m_{t-h} - \gamma ec_{t-1},$$

---

[18] See, for example, Greene (1997) for a detailed treatment of the cointegration methods discussed in this appendix.

[19] Let x_t, for $t = 1, ...T$, denote a stochastic process; x_t is (weakly) stationary if its mean is independent of t, its variance is constant and independent of t, and its covariance $Cov(x_t, x_s)$ is a function $t - s$ but not of t or s. If any of these conditions are violated, x_t is nonstationary.

which relates a change in real money balances in period t to current and lagged changes in real income, measures of the opportunity cost of holding money, lagged real money balances, and an **error-correction term** ec_{t-1} which is derived as the residual from the long-run relationship (2.1)—that is, the difference between the actual level of real money balances and its predicted value. This variable approximates deviations from long-run equilibrium values of real money balances and represents the *short-run response* necessary to move money demand toward its long-run equilibrium level. When the coefficient of the error correction-term, γ, is significant and positive, convergence is assured. If γ is less than unity in absolute value, the adjustment process is stable and m^d will adjust toward its long-run value. The closer γ is to unity, the faster the adjustment process will be.

An increasingly common approach to testing for the existence of a long-run relationship is the **Johansen method**. Essentially, the method applies the **maximum likelihood principle** to determine the presence of cointegrating relationships in nonstationary time series (see Greene (1997)). Such relationships are detected and tests of hypotheses regarding elements of the cointegrating relationships can be conducted. Two different tests are provided to determine the number of cointegrating relationships, the *trace test* and the *maximum eigenvalue test*. If a nonzero vector (or vectors) is indicated by these tests, a stationary long-run relationship is implied. An example of a money demand study using the Johansen technique is the one by Choudhry (1995), as discussed in the text.

Chapter 3

Fiscal Deficits, Public Debt, and the Current Account

Key constraints on fiscal policy and macroeconomic management in developing countries are an inadequate tax base, a limited ability to collect taxes, reliance on money financing, and (in some cases) high levels of public debt. Administrative (and sometimes political) constraints on the ability of tax authorities to collect revenue has often led to the imposition of high tax rates on a narrow tax base. The consequences have been endemic tax evasion and a growing informal economy (as discussed in Chapter 12). The high degree of reliance on monetary financing of fiscal deficits in some countries has often resulted in macroeconomic instability, capital flight, and currency crises (see Chapter 7). High and growing levels of public debt exert pressure on real interest rates and have also led to financial volatility and macroeconomic instability.

This chapter provides an overview of fiscal policy issues in developing countries. The first part reviews the structure of public finances in these countries, focusing first on conventional (or explicit) sources of revenue and expenditure, and subsequently on seigniorage and the inflation tax, and quasi-fiscal activities. The second part examines the government budget constraint and the various ways in which fiscal deficits can be measured. The third part discusses a simple technique that has proved useful for assessing the medium-term stance of fiscal policy. The link between fiscal deficits and current account deficits is studied in the fourth part. Issues of public debt sustainability and public sector solvency are examined in the fifth and sixth parts. The last two parts focus on two important policy issues: the link between commodity price booms and fiscal deficits, and the link between fiscal adjustment, expectations, and economic activity.

3.1 Structure of Public Finances

Three aspects of public finances in developing countries are discussed in this section. The first is the composition of conventional sources of revenue and expenditure and differences between industrial and developing countries. The second is the revenue from money creation (seigniorage). The third is the importance of quasi-fiscal activities and the role of contingent liabilities.

3.1.1 Conventional Sources of Revenue and Expenditure

Public revenue and expenditure patterns in developing countries vary considerably across developing countries, as shown in Figure 3.1. During the period 1990-95, for instance, revenue of the *central government* in Madagascar barely exceeded 9 percent of GDP, while expenditure reached almost 18 percent. By contrast, in Singapore, revenue (at more than 25 percent of GDP) exceeded expenditure by almost 5 percentage points.[1]

The general structure of conventional sources of revenue and expenditure differs significantly between industrial and developing countries. As discussed by Burgess and Stern (1993), the main differences are the following.

- The shares of *total tax revenue* and *total central government expenditure* in output are larger in industrial than in developing countries. As shown in Figure 3.2, which covers averages over the period 1980-95, both ratios tend to increase with the level of real income per capita.[2] Figure 3.3, which covers the period 1870-1996, shows indeed that for the six most advanced industrial countries the ratio of government expenditure to GDP has increased almost continuously—exceeding now 50 percent in a country like France. One possible explanation for this rise in the size of government is the increased need for *risk insurance* as the degree of openness and exposure to large external shocks increase (Rodrik, 1998*b*).

- The *composition* of spending also differs between the two groups of countries. *Developing countries* devote a substantially larger fraction of expenditures to *general public services, defense, education,* and other economic services (reflecting the role of government in production) than do industrial countries, whereas the latter spend somewhat more on *health*, but substantially more on *social security*.

---

[1] A more comprehensive definition of the government would be the *general government*, which includes central, state, provincial, local government institutions, as well as agencies such as social security boards—but excluding state-owned enterprises. A comprehensive view of the government is essential to understand notions such as public sector borrowing, fiscal deficits, and solvency conditions, as discussed later. Available data, however, often relate to the central government.

[2] Stotsky and WoldeMariam (1997) studied the determinants of the tax revenue-to-GDP ratio in a group of 43 sub-Saharan African countries during the period 1990-95. Their analysis showed that the share of agriculture in output had a negative effect, and that the export-to-GDP ratio and import-to-GDP ratio both had a positive effect on the tax revenue-to-GDP ratio. The level of per capita income, by contrast, was not significant.

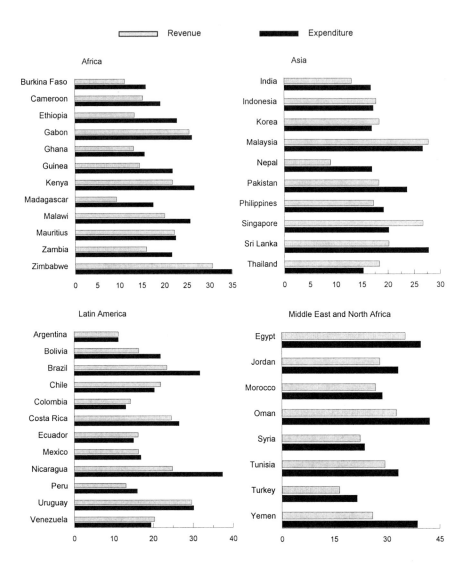

Figure 3.1. Central Government: Revenue and Expenditure (In percent of GDP, average over 1990-95).

Source: World Bank.

- The main source of *central government revenue* in both groups is *taxation*; however, the *share of nontax revenue* in total revenue (consisting, for instance, of transfers from public enterprises) is much higher in developing than in industrial countries.

- Within total tax revenue, the relative shares of *direct taxes, taxes on domestic goods and services*, and *taxes on foreign trade* vary considerably across developing countries and over time, as illustrated in Figure 3.4.[3] In industrial countries, income taxes account for the largest share of tax revenue, and taxes on foreign trade are negligible. The evidence suggests that there has been a gradual move away from trade taxes to taxes on domestic sales as economies develop and their domestic production and consumption bases expand.

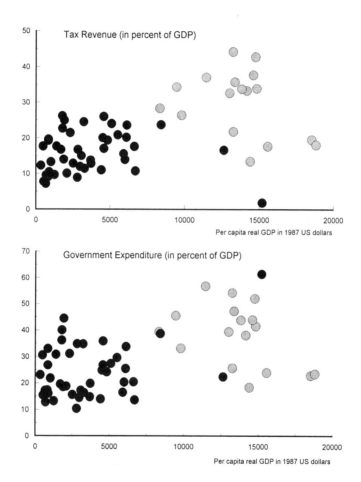

Figure 3.2. Tax Revenue, Government Expenditure, and Per Capita Real GDP 1/ (Average over 1980-95).

Source: World Bank.

1/ 44 developing countries and 17 industrialized countries are included. A dark circle refers to developing countries and a lighter circle to industrial countries.

---

[3] Trade taxes consist primarily of import rather than export duties in developing countries, and continue to be used quite extensively in some cases—although trade liberalization has led in most cases to a very significant reduction in tariffs in recent years (see Chapter 14).

- Within *direct taxes*, the share of tax revenue raised from *individual incomes* is much larger than that from *corporations* in developing countries, while the reverse is true in industrial countries.

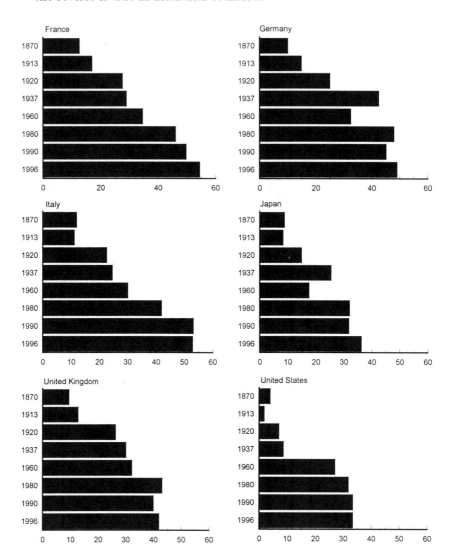

Figure 3.3. Industrial Countries: Government Spending, 1870-1996 (In percent of GDP).

Source: International Monetary Fund.

The need for revenue in developing countries is large. One reason, of course, is the need for the government to invest in infrastructure, foster the development of market institutions, and encourage employment creation in order to reduce poverty. Another reason may be related to a *deficit bias*, which is due to

the fact that although fiscal policy is decided collectively, the parties involved
(the different pressure groups and their representatives) do not fully recognize
the full social cost of the programs they support. This is known as the *commons problem*, and has been well studied in recent years in the context of Latin
America (see Grisanti, Stein, and Talvi, 1998).

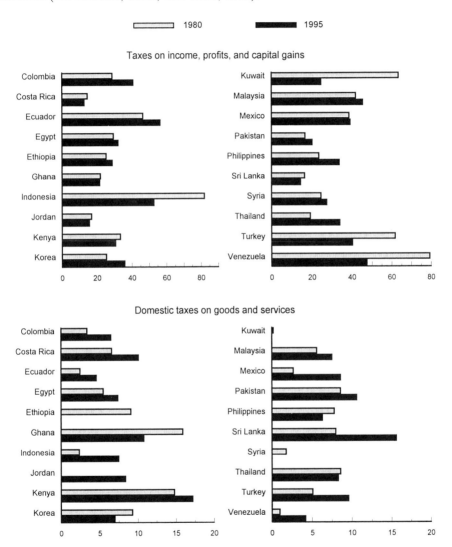

Figure 3.4. Direct and Indirect Taxes (In percent of total tax revenue).
Source: World Bank.

Despite high revenue needs, however, taxation systems in many developing
countries remain highly inefficient. A key reason has been the severe (administrative and sometimes political) constraints on the ability of tax authorities

to collect revenue. The consequences are that *direct taxation* plays a much more limited role in developing than in industrial countries (as documented by Burgess and Stern, 1993) and *high tax rates* tend to be levied on a *narrow base*— a policy that has encouraged tax evasion and led to a high degree of reliance on monetary financing.

3.1.2 Seigniorage and Inflationary Finance

Because, as indicated earlier, limited administrative capacity and political constraints hinder the collection of tax revenue in developing countries, and because many countries continue to have a limited scope for issuing of domestic debt (as a result of insufficiently developed capital markets, as noted in Chapter 2), developing countries tend to rely more on **seigniorage** than industrial countries. Seigniorage consists of the amount of real resources extracted by the government by means of *base money creation*. Denoting by M the nominal base money stock and P the price level, seigniorage revenue can be defined as the change in the nominal base money stock divided by the price level, $\Delta M/P$.[4] Equivalently, this expression can be rewritten as

$$\frac{\Delta M}{P} = \frac{M}{P} - (\frac{P_{-1}}{P})(\frac{M_{-1}}{P_{-1}}) = \Delta(\frac{M}{P}) + (1 - \frac{P_{-1}}{P})(\frac{M_{-1}}{P_{-1}}),$$

or,

$$\frac{\Delta M}{P} = \Delta(\frac{M}{P}) + (\frac{P - P_{-1}}{P_{-1}})(\frac{M_{-1}}{P}),$$

that is, with $m \equiv M/P$ denoting real money balances held by the public and $\pi \equiv \Delta P/P_{-1}$ the inflation rate:

$$\frac{\Delta M}{P} = \Delta m + \pi(\frac{P_{-1}}{P})m_{-1} = \Delta m + (\frac{\pi}{1+\pi})m_{-1}. \tag{3.1}$$

Equation (3.1) shows that seigniorage can also be defined as the sum of the *increase in the real stock of money*, Δm, and the change in the real money stock that would have occurred with a constant nominal stock because of inflation, $\pi m_{-1}/(1+\pi)$. The second term in that expression represents the **inflation tax**, with $\pi/(1+\pi)$ denoting the *tax rate* and m_{-1} the *tax base*. The determination of the *optimal* inflation tax is discussed in Chapter 5.

The above definitions also lead to the following observations.

- The last expression in Equation (3.1) implies that in a stationary state (with $\Delta m = 0$), seigniorage is equal to the inflation tax.

---

[4]The reason why the appropriate base for the inflation tax is not *broad money* but only *base money* is because the government extracts net resources from agents in the economy only to the extent that the erosion of the money stock resulting from inflation is not offset by inflationary gains that accrue to domestic borrowers. Only base money represents (central bank) liabilities that are not offset by private-sector debt owed to commercial banks.

- The monetary base in the above setting is implicitly treated as bearing no interest. This is not always the case; *required reserves* of commercial banks held with the central bank sometimes earn interest. In such conditions, the formulas in Equation (3.1) *overstate* seigniorage revenue and a correction must be made to obtain an appropriate measure.

A related concept to the conventional definition given above, also referred to as seigniorage, is the **interest burden foregone** (or interest savings) by the government through its ability to issue *non-interest-bearing liabilities*. The view here is that the private sector's revenue loss from foregone interest earnings (that is, the *opportunity cost of money*) corresponds to an equivalent revenue gain for the government from issuing money. It is measured in flow terms by iM/P, where i is the nominal short-term interest rate on, say, government bonds. As noted by Buiter (1997), the conventional measure of seigniorage, $\Delta M/P$, and the opportunity cost measure are related by the identity that equates the present discounted value of current and future seigniorage to the present discounted value of the current and future interest burden foregone (which corresponds approximately to the *operating profits* of the central bank), minus the initial base money stock. In practice, however, this concept is seldom used, because the choice of the relevant opportunity cost i is somewhat arbitrary.

During the 1980s, a number of developing countries, such as Zambia, relied heavily on seigniorage as a source of revenue to finance their budget deficits (see Adam, 1995). Figure 3.5 presents data on seigniorage for the more recent period of 1993-95 for a group of developing countries. The figure shows considerable differences across countries in the use of seigniorage—from almost 12 percent in Yemen to less than 1 percent in Tunisia. Figure 3.6 suggests that reliance on seigniorage tends to be associated with large fiscal deficits—an issue that will be explored further in Chapter 5.

3.1.3   Quasi-Fiscal Activities and Contingent Liabilities

Quasi-fiscal activities can be defined as operations whose effect can in principle be *duplicated* by budgetary measures in the form of an *explicit* tax, subsidy, or direct expenditure (McKenzie and Stella, 1996, p. 3). They are often carried out by the country's central bank, but sometimes also by public sector banks and other public financial institutions, such as development banks. They are motivated most of the time by the desire to hide what are essentially budgetary activities for political or other reasons.

Main examples of quasi-fiscal activities include:

- **Subsidized credit**, which involves most commonly lending at preferential rates by the central bank to the government or other public entities, or subsidized lending by specialized public sector financial institutions (such as agricultural or mortgage banks) to groups of borrowers from the private sector—often with inadequate collateral requirements.

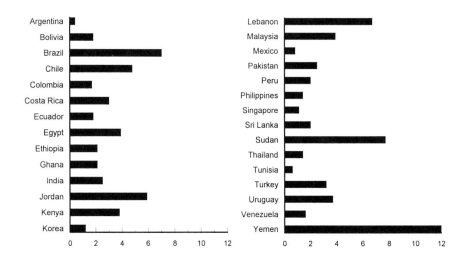

Figure 3.5. Seigniorage (In percent of GDP, average 1993-95).
Source: World Bank.
Note: Seigniorage is measured as the change in the base money stock divided by nominal GDP.

- Manipulation of **reserve** and **statutory liquidity requirements**, through, for instance, central bank regulations requiring commercial banks to hold large reserves (which then serve as a base for lending to the government at below-market rates) or a large share of their liquid assets in the form of government securities paying below-market interest rates. Both policies provide the government with captive sources of financing for its budget deficit.[5]

- **Multiple exchange rate practices**. This may take the form, for instance, of the central bank allowing access by the government to its foreign reserves at a more appreciated exchange rate to service its foreign debt or finance the purchase of imported goods by state-owned enterprises. Or, it may be a *surrender requirement* on export proceeds at a rate that is more appreciated than the market rate. This implicit tax on exports may have potentially large distortionary effects on trade flows and production patterns. Removing it—by unifying foreign exchange markets—also has potentially important implications for inflation (see Chapter 15).

- **Exchange rate guarantees** given by the central bank on the repayment of principal and interest on foreign-currency denominated debt of other public sector or private sector entities. For instance, the central bank may

---

[5] Note that if the central bank is at the same time required to remunerate liquid reserves at market-related rates, lending to the government at lower rates creates a quasi-fiscal expenditure.

guarantee to some privileged borrowers that the exchange rate at which debt-service payments are converted is the rate at which the loan was initially contracted. Such guarantees can entail a fairly sizable subsidy element.

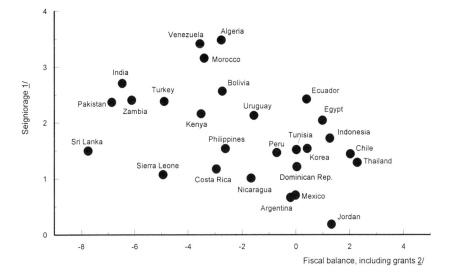

Figure 3.6. Fiscal Deficits and Seigniorage (In percent of GDP, average 1993-95). Source: World Bank.
1/ Seigniorage is the change in the base money stock divided by nominal GDP.
2/ Central government only.

- **Bailout** of **troubled commercial banks**, which occurs when the central bank provides an infusion of capital in troubled banks, or directly takes control of some of the nonperforming assets of problem banks.

- **Sterilization operations**, which essentially result from the central bank paying interest on its liabilities at a rate higher than the one earned on the foreign exchange reserves that it chose to accumulate, often as a counterpart to sustained capital inflows (see Chapter 7).

Exchange rate guarantees, in particular, are common operations for central banks; essentially, they imply that the *cost of borrowing* on a claim denominated in domestic currency is the rate of interest prevailing on world capital markets. If domestic interest rates are significantly higher than foreign rates, the implicit subsidy can be large and may lead to *overborrowing*. As long as the exchange rate remains at the level prevailing when the loan was contracted, the guarantee remains indeed implicit and has no effect on the profit-and-loss account of the central bank. However, if the nominal exchange rate *depreciates*, the Central Bank may face sizable losses. In Jamaica, central bank losses from exchange rate guarantees exceeded 5 percent of GDP in the early 1990s.

By shifting what are essentially taxes and subsidies from government accounts to the accounts of the central bank, quasi-fiscal activities can severely distort the measurement of revenues and expenditure not only of the government but of other public sector entities as well.[6] They may also render attempts to assess the stance of fiscal policy (on the basis, for instance, of an analysis of public debt sustainability, as discussed below) meaningless.

Examples of the importance of quasi-fiscal deficits (and how misleading conventional measures of fiscal deficits are as indicators of the fiscal policy stance) are provided by the experiences of Chile and Argentina. In the early 1980s, the monetary authorities in both countries extended emergency loans to financial institutions and suffered large losses from exchange rate guarantee programs. The central bank of Chile, in particular, suffered from large quasi-fiscal losses in the mid-1980s as a result of a guarantee on a foreign exchange resale scheme that it implemented during the period 1982-85 (McKenzie and Stella, 1996, p. 25). During that period, according to estimates provided by Easterly and Schmidt-Hebbel (1994), consolidated quasi-fiscal deficits averaged more than 10 percent of GDP a year in that country, more than double the size of conventionally measured deficits. According also to Easterly and Schmidt-Hebbel (1994), in Argentina, quasi-fiscal deficits of the consolidated public sector were roughly as large as conventionally-measured deficits during 1982-85; together they averaged 25 percent of GDP a year.

The foregoing discussion suggests that many quasi-fiscal activities lead to the creation of **contingent implicit liabilities**, which in general can be defined as obligations that the government is *expected* to fulfill, although the required outlays are typically uncertain before a failure (or some event) occurs. Important examples, as noted earlier, are the liabilities created by the need to support the financial system (when its stability appears to be at risk) and large enterprises (both private and state owned).

Governments in developing countries are also faced with various types of **contingent explicit fiscal liabilities**, which can be broadly defined as obligations that the government is legally compelled to honor if the entity that incurred them in the first place cannot (or chooses not to) do so; examples are state guarantees of borrowing by parastatal enterprises or local government entities (Polackova, 1998). Contingent liabilities, together with direct liabilities—both explicit and implicit, such as those assumed under pay-as-you-go social security schemes, and future recurrent costs of public investment projects)—have grown at a rapid pace in many developing countries in recent years. Because conventional measures of the fiscal stance (as discussed below) do not account properly for the expected future cost of all the contingent liabilities incurred by the government, they provide misleading indicators of its ability to pay and the sustainability of budget deficits.

Because of their potentially severe distortionary effects on the allocation of resources, eliminating or at least reducing the scope of quasi-fiscal activities

---

[6] The existence of large quasi-fiscal activities (as discussed later) may explain why, as shown in Figure 3.2, the ratio of government expenditure to GDP appears to be significantly lower in developing economies compared with industrial countries.

has become a key objective of macroeconomic management. The elimination of the implicit tax on exports, for instance, can be achieved through exchange market unification (see Chapter 15). For political and other reasons, however, the first-best solution may be difficult to achieve in the short term. It then becomes important to bring such operations into the budget, by first identifying and quantifying them, and subsequently transforming them into *explicit taxes* and *expenditures*. Appropriate accounting of explicit and implicit contingent liabilities is essential for assessing the stance of fiscal policy. However, this may be a very difficult task; as noted by Blejer and Cheasty (1991, p. 1667), the calculation of the expected cost of contingent liabilities may be complicated by **moral hazard** problems. The very fact that the government chooses to assume explicitly these liabilities may lead to changes in private sector behavior that may make the realization of the events against which liabilities are created more likely. Moreover, increasing fiscal transparency may encounter strong political resistance.

3.2   The Government Budget Constraint

In general, the budget constraint of the government can be written as

$$G - (T_T + T_N) + iB_{-1} + i^*EB^*_{g-1} = \Delta L^g + \Delta B + E\Delta B^*_g, \qquad (3.2)$$

where

- G is *public spending* on goods and services (including current and capital expenditure);

- T_T is *tax revenue* (net of transfer payments) and T_N non-tax revenue,

- B is the end-of-period stock of *domestic public debt*, which bears interest at the market-determined rate i;

- B^*_g is the end-of-period stock of *foreign-currency-denominated public debt*, which bears interest at the rate i^*;

- E is the *nominal exchange rate*;

- L^g is the nominal *stock of credit* allocated by the central bank.

The left-hand side of Equation (3.2) captures the components of the budget deficit: spending on goods and services and debt service, net of taxes. The right-hand side shows that the government can finance its budget deficit by either issuing domestic bonds, borrowing abroad, or borrowing from the central bank. For simplicity, the central bank is assumed not to charge interest on its loans to the government.

There are several points worth noting regarding Equation (3.2).

- It does not consider explicitly *foreign grants* or *revenues* derived from assets such as *natural resources* and *publicly owned capital*—components that may, in practice, be important in some countries. For simplicity, these items are subsumed in T_N.

- It excludes from public resources the *cash income* derived from *sales of public sector assets* (*privatization* of *public enterprises*). Receipts from privatization and the sale of other public sector assets are often counted as *revenues*; this practice tends to *underestimate* the level of the fiscal deficit. Privatization proceeds (resulting from the sale of government assets) are a *financing item* that normally belong *below the line*. They do not (or should not) affect the conventionally measured primary deficit.[7]

- It does not explicitly account for *extrabudgetary activities*. As recently as 1995, for instance, more than half of the countries in Latin America had special funds not included in the general government budget. In some countries these funds were not large, but in others (like El Salvador and Uruguay) they were quite substantial. In Uruguay, in particular, special funds amounted to close to 10 percent of the budget and were channeled to various decentralized agencies that had considerable latitude over the way they were spent.

The left-hand side of Equation (3.2) defines the **conventional fiscal balance**. Let $T = T_T + T_N$ denote total government revenue; the **primary** (or noninterest) **fiscal balance** can be defined as[8]

$$D = G - T.$$

Substituting this definition in Equation (3.2) yields

$$D + iB_{-1} + i^* E B^*_{g-1} = \Delta L^g + \Delta B + E \Delta B^*_g. \tag{3.3}$$

The conventional fiscal deficit can be very sensitive to *inflation*. The key reason is the effect of inflation on *nominal interest payments* on the public debt. Illustrative calculations by Tanzi, Blejer and Teijeiro (1993) show indeed that inflation can have a sizable effect on the conventional deficit when the domestic public debt (and thus the interest rate bill) is high. In such conditions, the conventional deficit does not provide a reliable measure of the increase in the government's real indebtedness. The inflation-induced part of the nominal interest bill is, in a sense, an **amortization payment** that compensates holders of government debt for the erosion of the real value of the debt stock; put

---

[7] Privatization proceeds do, however, affect the government's *net worth*; for instance, if the sale value of the public enterprise plus the present value of future taxes from the privatized entity exceeds the sum of the present value of future subsidies and future losses that the government would occur if it were to keep the enterprise, then the government's net worth will increase.

[8] In practice, as noted by Blejer and Cheasty (1991, p. 1655), the primary balance is often calculated by subtracting *total* interest payments from government expenditure; conceptually, however, only the *net* interest paid by the government should be taken out.

differently, some of the deficit dos not increase *real debt*, but effectively maintains it at its previous level. As a consequence, the conventional deficit suffers from two limitations.

- It is no longer a reliable indicator of the extent to which the fiscal stance is *sustainable*, in the sense that the issuance of public debt is occurring at a rate in excess of the growth rate of the resources available for eventual debt service (see below). For instance, the conventional deficit may increase sharply as a result of a sudden rise in inflation, without necessarily implying a deterioration in the longer-run sustainability of the fiscal stance.

- Changes in the conventional deficit no longer provide an adequate measure of *fiscal effort* by policymakers. The **primary balance** is in this case a more reliable measure—despite inadequately reflecting the financing implications of the policy stance.

Economists therefore often use an alternative concept to the conventional balance, the **operational balance**, which is calculated by netting out the inflationary component in nominal interest payments (and receipts) from the conventional balance, defined in real terms. To show the importance of this adjustment, suppose for simplicity that the government holds no external debt ($B^* = 0$). The government budget constraint, Equation (3.3), then becomes

$$D + iB_{-1} = \Delta L^g + \Delta B.$$

Dividing both sides of this expression by P yields

$$d + i(\frac{P_{-1}}{P})b_{-1} = \frac{\Delta L^g}{P} + (\frac{P_{-1}}{P})\frac{\Delta B}{P_{-1}}, \qquad (3.4)$$

where d is the real primary deficit and b the real stock of government bon .. The last term in this expression can be rewritten as

$$(\frac{P_{-1}}{P})\frac{\Delta B}{P_{-1}} = b - (\frac{P_{-1}}{P})b_{-1} = \Delta b + (1 - \frac{P_{-1}}{P})b_{-1},$$

or

$$(\frac{P_{-1}}{P})\frac{\Delta B}{P_{-1}} = \Delta b + \pi(\frac{P_{-1}}{P})b_{-1}.$$

Substituting this result in the government budget constraint gives

$$d + (i - \pi)(\frac{P_{-1}}{P})b_{-1} = \frac{\Delta L^g}{P} + \Delta b.$$

Because $P_{-1}/P = 1/(1 + \pi)$, the above expression can be rewritten as

$$d + (\frac{i - \pi}{1 + \pi})b_{-1} = \frac{\Delta L^g}{P} + \Delta b,$$

or equivalently

$$d + rb_{-1} = \frac{\Delta L^g}{P} + \Delta b, \tag{3.5}$$

where r is the real interest rate, defined by

$$r = \frac{1+i}{1+\pi} - 1.$$

The expression $d + rb_{-1}$ in Equation (3.5) measures the total deficit in real terms. It differs from the nominal deficit deflated by the price level P, which is given by the left-hand side of Equation (3.4), that is, $d + i(P_{-1}/P)b_{-1}$. Using the previous result $P_{-1}/P = 1/(1+\pi)$, this expression can be rewritten as

$$d + i(\frac{P_{-1}}{P})b_{-1} = d + (\frac{i}{1+\pi})b_{-1} = d + (r + \frac{\pi}{1+\pi})b_{-1}.$$

Comaring the last expression to (3.5) shows that simply deflating the conventional fiscal deficit by current prices leads to an *overestimation* of the real deficit, by the quantity

$$\frac{\pi}{1+\pi}b_{-1}, \tag{3.6}$$

which essentially represents the compensation to creditors for the falling real value of their claims on the government caused by inflation. Adjusting the conventional fiscal deficit by subtracting the quantity (3.6) is, again, particularly important when inflation is high. In Brazil, for instance, in 1988 the conventional deficit (or total borrowing requirement) of the *general government* (covering the federal government and states and municipalities) amounted to 27.3 percent of GDP, the operational deficit to 4.5 percent, and the primary deficit to -0.5 percent. Figure 3.7 shows the evolution of the operational and primary fiscal balances (together with interest payments) between 1985 and 1996; indeed, sharp differences between these two measures persisted throughout the period—particularly during the years of high inflation preceding the implementation of the **Real Plan** in July 1994 (see Agénor and Montiel, 1999).

The operational deficit becomes a problematic concept when inflation is *highly variable*, because of difficulties in measuring and interpreting real interest payments. Specifically, because interest rates are a function of *expected* inflation, the use of *actual* inflation rates (as shown in the formula above) to calculate the operational deficit can be misleading if large, unanticipated inflationary shocks occur during the period. For instance, expansionary fiscal policy (a rise in spending, say) could push actual inflation above the rate implied by the nominal interest rate (a scenario that is more likely to occur when debt is not recontracted very frequently), leading to *negative ex post real interest rates*, and thus a negative real interest bill. The operational balance may thus *improve* if this effect is large enough—although at the same time the primary balance is deteriorating.

Finally, it should be noted that inflation may also affect *noninterest expenditure* and *revenue*—and thus all three measures of fiscal deficits. For instance, inflation may increase spending on entitlement programs (such as *subsidies* and *transfers*) or lead to an increase in tax revenue if tax rates are progressive. It can also reduce real revenue in the presence of **collection lags**—an effect that has become known as the **Olivera-Tanzi effect**. The reason is because there is typically a lag between the time tax payments are *assessed* and the time they are *collected* by the fiscal authorities. In the case of indirect, *domestically based taxes* (such as turnover taxes), the collection lag is generally 4 to 6 weeks; for *direct taxes*, the lag is much longer, and may reach well over a year for personal income taxes. Even in the case of *customs duties*, where the assessed base is denominated in foreign currency, taxpayers are generally allowed several weeks to make payments to the tax administration. if n is the collection lag expressed in months, and π the monthly inflation rate, the amount by which real revenue drops is given by $(1 + \pi)^{-n} - 1$. For instance, with inflation running at 10 percent a month, real revenue collection would drop (relative to the case of zero inflation) by 9.1 percent if the collection lag is one month, 17.4 percent if the lag is 2 months, and 24.9 percent if the lag is three months. In practice, however, in a high-inflation environment, the effect of inflation on the interest bill tends to exceed its effect on spending and revenue.

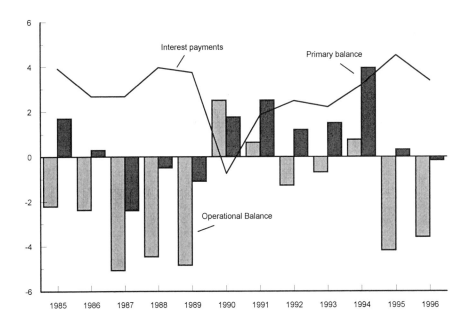

Figure 3.7. Brazil: Alternative Measures of the Fiscal Balance 1/ (In percent of GDP).

Source: Bevilaqua and Werneck (1997).

1/ General government only (Federal government and states and municipalities).

3.3   Assessing the Stance of Fiscal Policy

Useful tools for assessing the medium-term stance of fiscal policy are the *structural budget deficit* and the **fiscal impulse measure** developed by the International Monetary Fund and the Organization of Economic Cooperation and Development (see Blejer and Chu, 1988; and Heller, Haas, and Mansur, 1986). The key idea is that a proper assessment of medium-term fiscal strategies requires determining the extent to which changes in *actual* budget balances reflect *structural* factors, in particular *discretionary* fiscal policy action*s*, rather than *cyclical* movements.[9] This distinction is important because movements of the budget balance attributable to the business cycle (or short-term fluctuations in aggregate demand) can be viewed as essentially *self-correcting*, whereas changes in deficits owing to structural factors can be offset only through discretionary measures. Removing the self-correcting cyclical component from the observed budget balance, therefore, provides a more accurate indication of medium-term fiscal positions. The resulting indicator is the *structural budget balance*.

Calculations of structural budget balances are typically based on one of two alternative approaches.[10] In the first approach, budget elasticities are used to adjust revenues, T_S, and total expenditures, G_S, for movements in the cyclical *output gap*, GAP, defined as the difference between actual and *potential* (or *capacity) output*, in proportion of potential output, in order to generate directly an estimate of the *level* of the structural budget deficit, D_S:

$$D_S = G_S - T_S = G(1 - \eta_G GAP) - T(1 - \eta_T GAP),$$

where η_T and η_G are, respectively, the elasticities of revenue and expenditure with respect to output. Two remarks are worth making about η_T and η_G:

- The cyclical adjustment of government revenues may rely on *disaggregated estimates*—related, for instance, to personal income taxes, corporate income taxes, indirect taxes, social security contributions, and other revenues. An aggregate revenue elasticity η_T can then be formed as a *weighted average* of the disaggregated revenue component elasticities, by using as weights the average shares of the revenue component in total revenue during a given period.

- In most developing countries, unemployment benefits are low or nonexistent (see Chapter 14). Cyclical output movements would thus have typically a relatively weak effect on general government expenditures, implying that in most practical cases η_G is likely to be small.

The structural budget deficit indicator is generally measured in relative terms, in proportion of potential output, d_S. The cyclical budget deficit can

---

[9]Cyclical adjustments to the fiscal stance are also important to assess the dynamics associated with stabilization programs. Talvi (1997), for instance, estimates that in Uruguay during 1991-93, the cyclically adjusted budget deficit exceeded the actual deficit by a cumulative 9 percentage points of GDP.

[10]To simplify the exposition, lagged effects of the cyclical output gap on the budget are ignored.

then be estimated as the difference between the observed budget deficit and the structural budget deficit.

In the second approach (used by the International Monetary Fund), the cyclical revenue and expenditure components are expressed as ratios to GDP and directly estimated using parameters that describe the cyclical response of revenue and expenditure to movements in the cyclical output gap. The budget deficit as a percentage of GDP, d, is defined as the difference between the observed total expenditure-to-GDP ratio, g, and the revenue-GDP ratio, τ:

$$d = g - \tau.$$

Decomposing the revenue and expenditure ratios into *structural components* (τ_S and g_S) and *cyclical components* (τ_C and g_C) yields

$$d = (g_S + g_C) - (\tau_S + \tau_C).$$

The difference between the cyclical revenue and expenditure components measures the impact of cyclical effects on the budget deficit:

$$d_C = g_C - \tau_C = \alpha_G GAP - \alpha_T GAP,$$

where α_T and α_G denote, respectively, the cyclical response of the revenue and expenditure ratios to an increase of 1 percentage point in the cyclical output gap. The overall effect of the business cycle on the budget is given by the difference of the two cyclical response parameters ($\alpha_G - \alpha_T$). The *structural budget deficit, d_S,* is the difference between the actual and the cyclical budget deficits:

$$d_S = d - d_C.$$

The two approaches are basically equivalent, because the cyclical response parameters, α_T and α_G, and the revenue and expenditure elasticities, η_T and η_G, are related by

$$\alpha_T \simeq (\eta_T - 1)(\frac{T}{Y}), \quad \alpha_G \simeq (\eta_G - 1)(\frac{G}{Y}),$$

where T/Y and G/Y are revenue-to-GDP and expenditure-to-GDP ratios. However, presenting the estimates as ratios to GDP makes it easier to evaluate the *sensitivity* of estimates of structural budget balances to changes in assumptions about the cyclical output gap and the cyclical responsiveness of the budget.

A key aspect of the cyclical adjustment is the estimation of *potential output*. For industrial countries, a common approach is first to estimate a production function linking output to capital, labor, and total factor productivity. Potential output is then estimated as the level of output that is consistent with what is considered *normal capital utilization,* and with the *natural rate of unemployment*—the unemployment rate deemed consistent with stable nominal wage growth and inflation. These, in turn, are estimated by removing cyclical variations in labor market participation rates, total factor productivity, and unemployment. In developing countries, however, this approach is generally not feasible because of the lack of adequate and reliable data on variables such as the capital stock. Potential output is often approximated by trend output, which can be estimated for instance by the **Hodrick-Prescott filter** (see Chapter 9).

Calculating the **fiscal impulse measure** proceeds along the same lines as those involved in calculating the structural budget deficit.

- The first step is a decomposition of the actual budget deficit into a *cyclically neutral* component and a *fiscal stance* component. The cyclically neutral component is often defined by assuming that government expenditures increase proportionately to *potential* output and that government revenues increase proportionately to *actual* output. The fiscal stance is the residual between the cyclically neutral and the actual budget deficits.

- The second step is to calculate the fiscal impulse as the annual change in the fiscal stance measure, expressed as a share of output.

A negative value indicates a *contractionary* demand impulse emanating from fiscal policy, and a positive value an *expansionary* demand impulse.

A recent application of this methodology to developing economies is by Bevilaqua and Werneck (1997), which focused on Brazil and covered the period 1989-96. Their analysis corrected revenue and expenditure not only for changes in output but also for changes in inflation. It suggested, in particular, that the fiscal stance was significantly more expansionary than what conventional indicators (such as the primary deficit) indicated.

It is important to note, however, that there are several limitations associated with measures of structural budget deficits and fiscal impulse. One limitation is that movements in the structural components of revenues and expenditures cannot be viewed only as directly related either to discretionary fiscal policy measures or to the business cycle; other factors may matter as well.

- On the *revenue side*, such factors include changes in natural resource revenues, nonneutralities of the tax system with respect to inflation, and changes in the composition of the economy's tax base induced by economic growth.

- On the *expenditure side*, they include changes in interest rates, changes in the demographic composition of the population, and contingencies that lead to non-discretionary expenditures.

More generally, as noted by Chand (1993), fiscal impulse measures do not include the effect of **automatic stabilizers** on aggregate demand. In particular, the potentially different aggregate demand effects (multipliers) of individual expenditure and revenue components are typically not captured; neither are the effects of fiscal policy on *long-term interest rates* and the distortions associated with tax and transfer programs on the *supply side* of the economy.

3.4   Fiscal Imbalances and External Deficits

A key issue for policymakers in developing countries is the correlation between fiscal and external deficits. As derived in a detailed manner in Chapter 8, the link between fiscal accounts and the external balance can be expressed as

$$(I^p - S^p) + (G - T) = J - X - N_T, \tag{3.7}$$

where I^p is private investment, S^p private saving, G current government spending, T current government revenue, J (X) imports (exports) of goods and services, and N_T net current transfers from abroad. This equation is obtained simply by rearranging the accounting identities relating gross national income on an *expenditure basis* and an *income basis*. It indicates that the counterpart to the current account balance is the government fiscal deficit and the investment-saving balance of the private sector.

The implication of Equation (3.7) is that, as long as $I^p - S^p$ remains *stable*, changes in fiscal deficits will be closely associated with movements in current account deficits. In general, however, because fiscal deficits also affect the private sector's investment-saving balance, the correlation between fiscal and external deficits may not be a close one. Indeed, Figure 3.8, which shows the correlation between budget deficits and current account deficits for a group of developing countries for the period 1980-95, does not suggest any clear pattern.

Various factors may explain a low correlation between fiscal and external deficits. As discussed in Chapter 1, an increase in public expenditure may lead to a concomitant reduction of private investment (as a result of a *crowding out effect* through the credit market) with all other components unchanged; or, private saving may increase, as individuals anticipate the rise in *future taxes* that they may incur as a result of the need to service the higher level of public debt occurring today. Thus, the correlation between fiscal and external deficits depends on the effect of fiscal policy on the private sector's investment and saving decisions. In addition, fiscal deficits may *respond to*, rather than *cause*, changes in the current account. Both effects also suggest that the so-called **Lawson doctrine**—according to which large current account deficits resulting from excessive net private investment should not be a cause for concern—is in general misleading.

3.5   Consistency and Sustainability

An integrated framework for assessing the consistency between *fiscal policy* and *macroeconomic targets* (such as inflation, output growth, and real interest rates) has been proposed by Anand and van Wijnbergen (1989). This section begins by presenting a discrete-time version of their model and discussing its limitations. The analysis is then extended to consider *jointly* the issues of fiscal and external sustainability.

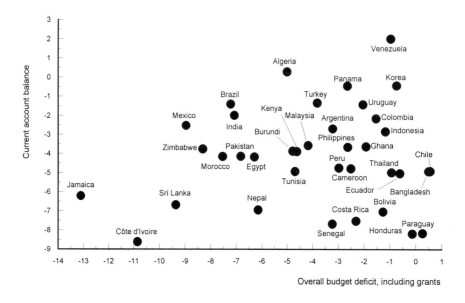

Figure 3.8. Budget Deficits and Current Account Deficits (In percent of GDP, average over 1980-95).
Source: World Bank.

3.5.1   A Consistency Framework

The consistency framework for fiscal and macroeconomic policy analysis proposed by Anand and van Wijnbergen (1989) essentially dwells on the government budget constraint presented above [Equation (3.2)]. It can be operated in two modes:

- the **deficit mode**, which allows the analyst to calculate a *financeable deficit*, given targets for inflation and other macroeconomic variables;

- the **inflation mode**, which allows the calculation of the *rate of inflation* consistent with given targets for the fiscal deficit and other macroeconomic variables.

As shown earlier, the government budget constraint states that the fiscal deficit (the sum of the primary deficit plus interest payments on domestic and external debt) must be financed by issuing either monetary liabilities, interest-bearing domestic bonds or by foreign borrowing. In the presence of various macroeconomic targets (such as a given rate of inflation), such sources of financing become *interdependent* and determine the level of the primary deficit that can be financed from *below the line*. To the extent that the actual deficit exceeds the level that can be financed (given the other policy targets), policymakers must either adjust their fiscal stance and/or revise their other objectives.

Consider the specification of the government budget constraint given in Equation (3.3), which is rewritten here for convenience:

$$D + iB_{-1} + i^* E B^*_{g-1} = \Delta B + E\Delta B^*_g + \Delta L^g, \qquad (3.8)$$

where D is again the non-interest primary deficit, B (B^*_g) the end-of-period stock of domestic (foreign) debt of the government, i (i^*) the interest rate on domestic (foreign) debt, L^g net credit from the central bank to the government, and E the nominal exchange rate.

The *first step* is to consolidate the balance sheets of the government and the central bank, to obtain a more comprehensive definition of the public sector and a more accurate measure of public sector expenditure and revenue. Adding and subtracting on the right-hand side of Equation (3.8) the quantity $E\Delta R^*$, the change in official reserves held by the central bank (measured in domestic-currency terms), yields

$$D + iB_{-1} + i^* E B^*_{g-1} = \Delta B + E(\Delta B^*_g - \Delta R^*) + (\Delta L^g + E\Delta R^*). \qquad (3.9)$$

As before, suppose that the central bank extends credit only to the government. Its balance sheet is given by

Assets	Liabilities	
L^g	C_U	
ER^*	RR	$\}M,$
	NW^{cb}	

where C_U is currency in circulation, RR reserves held at the central bank by commercial banks against their deposit liabilities, and NW^{cb} the central bank's accumulated profits or net worth. For simplicity, it is assumed that no interest is paid on required reserves.

The *monetary base*, M, is defined as the sum of *currency in circulation* and *required reserves* held by commercial banks at the central bank:

$$M = C_U + RR. \qquad (3.10)$$

The central bank's balance sheet and the above definition imply that the change in the monetary base, ΔM, is equal to the change in credit to the government, ΔL^g, plus the change in official reserves, $E\Delta R^*$, minus the change in the central bank's net worth, ΔNW^{cb}:

$$\Delta M = \Delta L^g + E\Delta R^* - \Delta NW^{cb}. \qquad (3.11)$$

From the profit-and-loss account of the central bank, and abstracting from other sources of revenue and expenditure, net profits consist of interest earnings on official reserves, $i^* E R^*_{-1}$, which have as a counterpart an increase in the central bank's net worth:

$$i^* E R^*_{-1} = \Delta NW^{cb}.$$

Subtracting central bank profits, $i^* E R^*_{-1}$, from the deficit on the left-hand side of Equation (3.9), and the central bank's increase in net worth, ΔNW^{cb}, from the public sector's increase in liabilities on the right-hand side and denoting by $B^* = B^*_g - R^*$ the public sector's net foreign debt yields

$$D + iB_{-1} + i^* E B^*_{-1} = \Delta B + E \Delta B^* + \Delta L^g + E \Delta R^* - \Delta NW^{cb},$$

where $\Delta B^* = \Delta B^*_g - \Delta R^*$. From the above definition of the change in the monetary base [Equation (3.11)], the last three terms of this equation are simply ΔM. Thus,

$$D + iB_{-1} + i^* E B^*_{-1} = \Delta B + E \Delta B^* + \Delta M, \tag{3.12}$$

Equation (3.12) consolidates the accounts of the government and the central bank. Two observations are useful at this stage.

- Because base money is considered a *liability* of the public sector, net foreign assets held by the central bank must also be subtracted from the government's foreign debt to calculate the net external liabilities of the public sector.

- The above derivations remain almost identical if the central bank lends to commercial banks and to the private sector. The definition of the base money stock needs to be adjusted to correspond to the central bank's net liabilities to the private sector. This is done by defining the *adjusted monetary base* as the sum of a) currency in circulation minus central bank credit to the private sector; and b) required reserves minus central bank loans to commercial banks.

To make explicit the links between deficits, money creation, and inflation, Equation (3.12) can be rewritten in real terms. Dividing each term by P, the domestic price level, yields

$$d + i(\frac{P_{-1}}{P})b_{-1} + i^* z(\frac{P^*_{-1}}{P^*})b^*_{-1} = \Delta B/P + E \Delta B^*/P + \Delta M/P, \tag{3.13}$$

where

- $d = D/P$ is the *real primary deficit*;

- $b = B/P$ the real value of the stock of domestic debt in terms of *domestic goods*;

- $b^* = B^*/P^*$ the real value of the *stock of foreign debt* in terms of *foreign goods*, with P^* denoting the foreign price level;

- $z = EP^*/P$ is the *real exchange rate*.

By definition,

$$\frac{\Delta B}{P} = b - (\frac{P_{-1}}{P})b_{-1} = \Delta b - \left[(\frac{P_{-1}}{P}) - 1\right]b_{-1}.$$

Again, let $\pi \equiv \Delta P/P_{-1}$ be the domestic inflation rate. As shown earlier, the above expression can be rewritten as

$$\frac{\Delta B}{P} = \Delta b + \pi(\frac{P_{-1}}{P})b_{-1}.$$

Similarly,

$$\frac{\Delta B^*}{P} = (\frac{P^*}{P})b^* - (\frac{P^*_{-1}}{P})b^*_{-1} = (\frac{P^*}{P})\Delta b^* - \left[(\frac{P^*_{-1}}{P}) - (\frac{P^*}{P})\right]b^*_{-1}.$$

that is, with π^* denoting the foreign rate of inflation:

$$\frac{\Delta B^*}{P} = (\frac{P^*}{P})\Delta b^* + (\frac{P^*}{P})(\frac{P^*_{-1}}{P^*})\pi^* b^*_{-1}.$$

Consequently,

$$\frac{E\Delta B^*}{P} = z\Delta b^* + z(\frac{P^*_{-1}}{P^*})\pi^* b^*_{-1}.$$

Using these results, and noting that

$$i(\frac{P_{-1}}{P}) = \frac{1+i}{1+\pi} - (\frac{P_{-1}}{P}), \quad i^*(\frac{P^*_{-1}}{P^*}) = \frac{1+i^*}{1+\pi^*} - (\frac{P^*_{-1}}{P^*}),$$

Equation (3.13) can be rewritten as

$$d + rb_{-1} + r^* z b^*_{-1} = \Delta b + z\Delta b^* + \Delta M/P, \tag{3.14}$$

where r and r^* denote *real interest rates* in terms of domestic and foreign goods, respectively, given by

$$1 + r = \frac{1+i}{1+\pi}, \quad 1 + r^* = \frac{1+i^*}{1+\pi^*}.$$

Equation (3.14) can be further rearranged to explicitly account for the effect of changes in the real exchange rate on the cost of servicing public debt. By definition,

$$\begin{aligned}
\Delta(zb^*) &= zb^* - z_{-1}b^*_{-1} = zb^* + z_{-1}(\Delta b^* - b^*), \\
&= zb^* + z_{-1}\Delta b^* - z_{-1}b^*,
\end{aligned}$$

that is,

$$\begin{aligned}
\Delta(zb^*) &= \Delta z b^* + z_{-1}\Delta b^* = \Delta z(\Delta b^* + b^*_{-1}) + z_{-1}\Delta b^* \\
&= \Delta z b^*_{-1} + z_{-1}\Delta b^* + \Delta z\Delta b^*.
\end{aligned}$$

Assuming that Δz and Δb^* are small implies that the last term can be ignored, so that

$$\Delta(zb^*) \simeq \Delta z b^*_{-1} + z_{-1}\Delta b^* = \hat{z}(\frac{z_{-1}}{z})zb^*_{-1} + (\frac{z_{-1}}{z})z\Delta b^*, \tag{3.15}$$

where $\hat{z} = \Delta z/z_{-1}$ is the *rate of depreciation* of the real exchange rate. Using this result to substitute for $z\Delta b^*$ in Equation (3.14) and rearranging yields

$$d + rb_{-1} + (r^* + \hat{z})zb^*_{-1} = \Delta b + (\frac{z}{z_{-1}})\Delta(zb^*) + \Delta M/P. \tag{3.16}$$

Equation (3.16) indicates that the real fiscal deficit of the consolidated public sector (defined as government and the central bank) must be equal to changes in the real values of domestic and foreign debt plus revenue from seigniorage.

From Equation (3.1), seigniorage revenue $\Delta M/P$ is given by $\Delta m + \pi m_{-1}/(1+\pi)$. The above equation can also be written as

$$d + rb_{-1} + (r^* + \hat{z})zb^*_{-1} = \Delta b + (\frac{z}{z_{-1}})\Delta(zb^*) + \Delta m + \frac{\pi}{1+\pi}m_{-1}. \tag{3.17}$$

Equation (3.17) can be used in various ways to ensure the consistency between fiscal policy and macroeconomic targets. Most importantly, it can generate two types of values for a given money demand function:

- the value of the *primary fiscal deficit* that is consistent with a given *total debt-to-output ratio* (for both domestic and foreign debt) and an inflation target;

- the value of the *inflation rate* (and thus seigniorage revenue), $\tilde{\pi}$, that is consistent with a given total debt-to-output ratio and a target for the primary fiscal deficit.

Consider the first mode. A simple possibility is to assume that both domestic and foreign debt ratios grow at the constant rate of growth of output, **g**:

$$\Delta b/b_{-1} = \mathbf{g}, \quad \Delta(zb^*)/z_{-1}b^*_{-1} = \mathbf{g}.$$

Measuring all variables in proportion of output yields therefore

$$\Delta b/y = \mathbf{g}(b_{-1}/y),$$

$$\frac{\Delta(zb^*)}{y} = \mathbf{g}(\frac{z_{-1}b^*_{-1}}{y}) = \mathbf{g}(\frac{zb^*_{-1}}{y})(\frac{z_{-1}}{z}).$$

Dividing each term in Equation (3.17) by output, and using the preceding results to substitute for $\Delta(zb^*)/y$ yields

$$\frac{d}{y} + \frac{rb_{-1}}{y} + (r^* + \hat{z})(\frac{zb^*_{-1}}{y}) = \mathbf{g}(\frac{b_{-1}}{y}) + \mathbf{g}(\frac{zb^*_{-1}}{y}) + \frac{\Delta m}{y} + (\frac{\tilde{\pi}}{1+\tilde{\pi}})\frac{m_{-1}}{y}. \tag{3.18}$$

Thus, for given values of the real domestic and foreign interest rate (r and r^*), the rate of depreciation of the real exchange rate, $\hat{z}$, a target rate of output growth, $\mathbf{g}$, an inflation target, $\tilde{\pi}$, and a properly specified money demand function (which allows calculation of revenue from the inflation tax at the target rate of inflation, $\tilde{\pi}m_{-1}(\tilde{\pi})/(1+\tilde{\pi})$, as well as Δm), Equation (3.18) allows the analyst to determine the **financeable primary deficit** (in proportion of output), $d/y|_f$. This value is given by

$$\left.\frac{d}{y}\right|_f = -(r-\mathbf{g})\frac{b_{-1}}{y} - (r^* + \hat{z} - \mathbf{g})(\frac{zb^*_{-1}}{y}) + \frac{\Delta m}{y} + (\frac{\tilde{\pi}}{1+\tilde{\pi}})\frac{m_{-1}}{y}.$$

Given the value of the financeable primary deficit the reduction in the *actual* deficit-to-output ratio, $d/y|_a$, required to achieve consistency can be calculated as

$$\left.\frac{d}{y}\right|_\Delta = \left.\frac{d}{y}\right|_a - \left.\frac{d}{y}\right|_f$$

Alternatively, for a given target value of $d/y|_f$, Equation (3.18) allows one to calculate the *consistent* (or *sustainable*) *rate of inflation*. In this case, however, **multiple solutions** for the sustainable inflation rate may arise if the money demand function is *nonlinearly* related to inflation and/or nominal interest rates—as occurs in the logarithmic example discussed below.[11]

In practice, estimates of base money demand [which are necessary to calculate the term $\tilde{\pi}m(\tilde{\pi})$ in Equation (3.18)] are derived by using a *complete model of portfolio choice* that includes not only the *demand for currency* but also the demand for *sight deposits, time deposits,* and (in countries where this is relevant) *foreign-currency deposits*, all as a function of income, inflation and interest rates (see, for instance, Anand and van Wijnbergen, 1989, for Turkey). The demand for reserves by commercial banks may also be estimated by using a simple portfolio model, taking into account existing legislation on reserve requirements. A major advantage of this extended approach is that it allows the investigator to assess the effects of *changes in financial regulations*—such as changes in reserve requirement rates or administered interest rates—on the financeable fiscal deficit or the sustainable rate of inflation.

In practical applications, it is common to use a two- or three-year moving average of actual real output growth rates and interest rates, and a constant real exchange rate ($\hat{z} = 0$), to generate an *ex ante* measure of sustainability. Two other considerations may also be important.

- Assessing the magnitude and likelihood of realization of **contingent liabilities**, such as *foreign exchange guarantees* (as discussed earlier), may be critical to adequately assess the fiscal stance and its sustainability (Towe, 1990). As much as possible, measures of the primary balance should include **quasi-fiscal losses**.

---

[11] In practice, analysts choose the lower of the two inflation rates.

- The degree of *concessionality of foreign debt* must be accounted for in assessing sustainability (see Cuddington, 1997). For many developing countries, foreign financing often contains a sizable *grant element*; the larger that element is, the higher will be the level of foreign indebtedness consistent with fiscal sustainability.[12] In effect, concessionality reduces the *effective real interest rate* on foreign borrowing.

To illustrate the functioning of the consistency framework described above, suppose that there are no commercial banks in the economy and thus no required reserves $(RR = 0)$; the monetary base consists therefore only of currency in circulation, C_U:

$$M = C_U.$$

Suppose that the demand for currency (or money, for short) takes the form[13]

$$\ln(C_U/y) = 0.1 - 1.5\ln(1 + \pi) - 2.1\ln(1 + i).$$

Suppose also that there is no foreign debt to begin with ($b^* = 0$, and therefore the path of the exchange rate does not need to be specified), that $\mathbf{g} = 0.02$, $\tilde{\pi} = 0.63$, $r = r^* = 0.04$, d/y is 0.04 initially, and that the targeted (domestic) debt-to-output ratio is 0.1. The financeable primary deficit can be calculated using Equation (3.18). The results are

$$d/y = 0.027, \text{ for } t = 1$$

$$d/y = 0.028, \text{ for } t = 2, ..., \ d/y = 0.030, \text{ for } t = 10.$$

Suppose now that the policymaker's objective is to find the inflation rate that is consistent with a primary deficit-output ratio constant at 0.03, beginning at $t = 1$. Similar calculations show that the *sustainable inflation rate* is

$$\pi = 73\%, \text{ for } t = 1$$

$$\pi = 71\%, \text{ for } t = 2$$

$$\pi = 58\%, \text{ for } t = 10.$$

The consistency framework described above cannot, of course, guarantee that all the objectives of macroeconomic policy will be achieved—it only ensures that the fiscal stance is consistent with these objectives. It remains, however, subject to two major limitations.

- It lacks a *simultaneous determination* of the primary deficit, output growth rates, and the real interest rate. A permanent reduction, say, in the primary deficit required for debt sustainability, brought about through a cut

---

[12] Foreign grants contain a 100 percent element of concessionality; they are, however, generally treated as an addition to *revenue*, not as a financing item.

[13] Alternatively, if the demand for broad money is known, the demand for base money can be obtained by assuming a constant multiplier. In practice, however, the money multiplier can display a high degree of variability and/or a significant trend.

in government expenditure for instance, would tend to *lower* real interest rates (by reducing the degree of **crowding out** in domestic capital markets), raise the rate of growth of output (by increasing *private investment*), and increase money demand (by reducing *inflationary expectations*).[14]

- To ensure a constant debt-to-output ratio, the sustainable primary deficit is calculated under the assumption that liabilities grow at the economy's rate of output growth. In this process, *lenders play no role*. As discussed below, the role of lenders is at the heart of the **solvency constraint**.

Accounting for the simultaneous determination of output growth, real interest rates, inflation, and the fiscal deficit requires extending the analysis to a *general equilibrium* setting. From an *operational* point of view, there is of course a *trade-off* between analytical rigor and the type of applied models that can be useful for practical policy purposes. As discussed in the next section, an attempt to develop a macroeconomic model that embeds the analysis of fiscal sustainability issues in a more comprehensive, but yet tractable, framework was made by Parker and Kastner (1993).

3.5.2   Fiscal and External Sustainability

The foregoing discussion focuses on the sustainability of the government fiscal stance—essentially the restrictions on fiscal policy that may result from restrictions on domestic and foreign borrowing. However, fiscal sustainability is neither *necessary* nor *sufficient* for **external sustainability**. The behavior of the *private sector* is a crucial link in explaining any divergences between fiscal and external sustainability. From the savings-investment identity given earlier [Equation (3.7)], any increase in government dissavings (the excess of government expenditure over revenue), given private savings and national investment behavior, will translate automatically into an increase in the current account deficit. However, a sustainable fiscal stance need not be sufficient for external sustainability if private sector behavior is such that its *net savings* (that is, gross savings minus gross investment) are highly negative and/or falling. Conversely, an unsustainable fiscal stance does not necessarily imply an unsustainable external position if net savings by the private sector are positive and/or growing.

The model developed by Parker and Kastner (1993) attempted to extend the Anand-van Wijnbergen framework to consider the links between fiscal and external sustainability. A key feature of their model is that net private savings, projected on the basis of estimated equations for consumption and investment, are added to net public savings to determine the current account balance. Real interest rates are also determined endogenously, and are specified as depending in part on the debt-output ratio. This specification captures the existence of a **risk premium**; the higher the level of public debt, the lower the probability

---

[14] As another example, it may be empirically important to allow for the feedback effect of inflation on the primary deficit—the Olivera-Tanzi effect discussed earlier. Different rates of inflation may affect not only the primary deficit but also the real interest rate and the rate of depreciation of the real exchange rate.

that debt will be sustainable, the higher the **risk of default**, and the higher the real interest rate—relative to the risk-free rate. Taxes are *exogenous*, but linking them to the growth rate of output is straightforward. Thus, for given targets for output growth (and thus fiscal revenue), inflation, and domestic and foreign borrowing, the model generates consistent estimates of *public spending*. The difference between *financeable* expenditure and *actual* expenditure provides the fiscal adjustment required to meet both fiscal and external targets. Conversely, given targets for output growth, domestic and foreign borrowing, and government spending, the model can generate consistent levels of inflation and interest rates. Thus, not only does the model attempt to capture explicitly the role of the private sector in assessing external sustainability, it also addresses another limitation of the basic consistency framework presented above—the need to account for general equilibrium interactions among macroeconomic variables. By introducing a risk premium in the determination of interest rates, the model also improves over the basic framework in which lenders play a completely passive role. It remains, however, far from a complete macroeconomic model.

3.6   Sustainability and the Solvency Constraint

The analysis of fiscal (and external) sustainability developed in the context of a consistency framework focuses generally on the *flow* budget constraint of the government, and tends to be essentially *static* in nature. It is now well recognized, however, that the government budget constraint has an *intertemporal* dimension as well. Associated with it is an **intertemporal solvency condition**, which is central to an evaluation of the medium- and long-run sustainability of fiscal deficits and public debt.

To derive the intertemporal budget constraint and the solvency condition that it implies, consider the flow budget constraint of the government, as given by Equation (3.2), and suppose for simplicity that there is *no foreign financing* of the deficit—an assumption that may accord particularly well with the situation of some of the smaller developing countries. It is straightforward to show that the budget constraint can be written in a form that represents a simplification of Equation (3.16),

$$d + rb_{-1} = \Delta b + \Delta M/P, \tag{3.19}$$

where d, b, and r are as defined above. Now, define

- **d** $= d/y$ as the **primary deficit** measured as a fraction of GDP;

- **b** $= b/y$ as the ratio of (end-of-period) government debt to GDP;

- $s = \Delta M/Py$ as seigniorage revenue as a fraction of GDP;

- **g** the rate of growth of real GDP.

Equation (3.19) can thus be rewritten as[15]

$$\Delta \mathbf{b} = \left(\frac{r - \mathbf{g}}{1 + \mathbf{g}} \right) \mathbf{b}_{-1} + \mathbf{d} - s. \tag{3.20}$$

Equation (3.20) indicates that if the domestic real interest rate, r, exceeds the rate of growth of output ($r > \mathbf{g}$), the debt-output ratio will increase *explosively* over time—unless seigniorage revenue exceeds the primary deficit by an amount that is sufficiently large.

Assuming constant values of r and $\mathbf{g}$ and solving Equation (3.20) *recursively forward* in time from period $t_0 = 0$ to period N yields[16]

$$\mathbf{b}_0 = \sum_{h=1}^{N} \left(\frac{1 + \mathbf{g}}{1 + r} \right)^h (s_h - \mathbf{d}_h) + \left(\frac{1 + \mathbf{g}}{1 + r} \right)^N \mathbf{b}_N, \tag{3.21}$$

which indicates that, at any point in time, the outstanding stock of domestic debt (in proportion of output) must be equal in value to the *present discounted value* of the future stream of seigniorage revenue, s_h, adjusted for the primary fiscal deficit, $\mathbf{d}_h$, between the current date and some terminal date N, plus the present discounted value of the debt held at that terminal future date.

Suppose that N is indeed the relevant terminal date for the government. The **solvency constraint** in this case requires that the outstanding level of debt at that date be *nonpositive*:

$$\mathbf{b}_N \leq 0. \tag{3.22}$$

Imposing this constraint to Equation (3.21) implies that the outstanding level of debt cannot exceed, for a solvent government, the present discounted value of future seigniorage revenue, adjusted for the primary fiscal deficit:

$$\mathbf{b}_0 \leq \sum_{h=1}^{N} \left(\frac{1 + \mathbf{g}}{1 + r} \right)^h (s_h - \mathbf{d}_h). \tag{3.23}$$

The current stance of fiscal policy is then deemed sustainable if its continuation through period N does not violate the solvency constraint (3.23).

In general, of course, although actual governments may have a limited term, they are not bound to repay debts contracted during their tenure at the end of their term. Thus, to the extent that future governments will honor the debts incurred today, the solvency constraint (3.22) is *overly restrictive*. All that is required to ensure solvency is that, eventually, the present discounted value of the *terminal debt* of the government goes to zero. Formally, the solvency

---

[15] As shown by Buiter (1997), in the general case in which the country borrows abroad and purchasing power parity does not hold, an equation similar to (3.20) can be derived by defining **d** as the *adjusted* primary deficit.

[16] The appendix to this chapter provides relevant formulas when r and $\mathbf{g}$ vary over time. In what follows perfect foresight is assumed to simplify notations.

constraint then takes the form of the **No-Ponzi scheme (NPS) condition**, given by

$$\lim_{N \to \infty} \left(\frac{1+g}{1+r}\right)^N \mathbf{b}_N \leq 0. \tag{3.24}$$

Given the NPS condition, as before, the value of the initial stock of debt must be equal to the present discounted value of the infinite flow of future seigniorage revenue adjusted for primary deficits:

$$\mathbf{b}_0 \leq \sum_{h=1}^{\infty} \left(\frac{1+g}{1+r}\right)^h (s_h - \mathbf{d}_h). \tag{3.25}$$

Clearly, the NPS condition matters only if the real interest rate on the public debt exceeds the long-run growth rate of GDP ($r > g$); otherwise, as implied by Equation (3.21), the debt will eventually *tend to zero* if the horizon N is sufficiently long.

The above framework can be used for various policy exercises. For instance, it can be used to calculate the magnitude of the (constant) primary deficit-output ratio that would be needed to get from an initial debt-output ratio $\mathbf{b}_0$, to a target future value of that ratio (say) H periods later, $\mathbf{b}_H$. This quantity, following Buiter (1997), can be called the *required* primary deficit-output ratio. By comparing the required ratio to the actual ratio (obtained by assuming, say, that current policies will remain unchanged) the **primary fiscal gap** can be obtained (Blanchard, 1993).[17] Specifically, let the required ratio be denoted as $\mathbf{d}_R^H(\mathbf{b}_0 - \mathbf{b}_H)$ and the actual H-period seigniorage-output ratio be s_A^H. By definition,

$$s_A^H = \left[\sum_{h=1}^{H} \left(\frac{1+g}{1+r}\right)\right]^{-h} \sum_{h=1}^{H} \left(\frac{1+g}{1+r}\right)^h s_h. \tag{3.26}$$

Thus, the required primary deficit-output ratio is

$$\mathbf{d}_R^H(\mathbf{b}_0 - \mathbf{b}_H) = \left[\sum_{h=1}^{H} \left(\frac{1+g}{1+r}\right)\right]^{-h} \left[\mathbf{b}_0 - \sum_{h=1}^{H} \left(\frac{1+g}{1+r}\right)^h \mathbf{b}_H - s_A^H\right].$$

The actual H-period primary deficit-output ratio can be defined as

$$\mathbf{d}_A^H = \left[\sum_{h=1}^{H} \left(\frac{1+g}{1+r}\right)\right]^{-h} \sum_{h=1}^{H} \left(\frac{1+g}{1+r}\right)^h \mathbf{d}_h.$$

The H-period primary gap is thus given by

$$\mathbf{G}^H(\mathbf{b}_0 - \mathbf{b}_H) = \mathbf{d}_R^H(\mathbf{b}_0 - \mathbf{b}_H) - \mathbf{d}_A^H. \tag{3.27}$$

---

[17] The sustainability index proposed by Blanchard (1993) is based on the difference between the actual tax rate and the *sustainable tax rate*, defined as the tax rate that is required to restore (for a given path of public spending and transfers) the level of the debt-ouput ratio to its initial level after a given number of years H.

For instance, the **one-period primary gap** that just stabilizes the debt-output ratio is given by the difference between the primary deficit that would just stabilize the debt-output ratio in period $t_1 = 1$ and the primary deficit that is expected to prevail at t_1. From Equation (3.27), this quantity is given by

$$\mathbf{G}^1(\mathbf{b}_0 - \mathbf{b}_1) = \left(\frac{r - \mathbf{g}}{1 + \mathbf{g}}\right)\mathbf{b}_0 + (\mathbf{d}_1 - s_1),$$

which is nothing but Equation (3.20) updated by one period.

Analyzing intertemporal solvency requirements is important to assess the stance of fiscal policy and its sustainability.[18] What the foregoing discussion implies, however, is that solvency is not *sufficient* to identify a unique fiscal stance. Suppose that for a given path of output growth and real interest rates there exists a given path of seigniorage, taxes, and recurrent spending that ensures solvency. Then, under the same assumptions, an increase in spending *today*, coupled with a sufficiently large reduction in spending *tomorrow*, will also ensure solvency. Similarly, a reduction in taxes today, associated with a sufficiently large increase tomorrow, will guarantee that the government is solvent. The reason is that what matters is the *present value* of government outlays and receipts. This *lack of uniqueness* implies that governments possess some degrees of freedom in the *selection* of fiscal policy instruments that they can manipulate to ensure solvency, as well as the *timing* of use of these instruments.

Governments also possess some degrees of freedom when current and expected policies imply that the *solvency constraint* is *violated*. The following are the main policy options that they may consider (individually or jointly) to close the solvency gap.

- Reduce current and future primary deficits, either by *cutting spending* or by *raising tax* and *nontax revenues*.

- *Increase* current and future *seigniorage revenues*. However, the scope for seigniorage to close the solvency gap is limited. If the economy is on the decreasing-yield segment of the **seigniorage Laffer curve**, an attempt to raise seigniorage revenue by increasing the growth rate of the nominal stock of base money will translate into higher inflation and a sharp fall in money demand, thereby *reducing* revenue (see Chapter 5).

- Declare an *outright default* or impose a *unilateral moratorium* on debt payments on the domestic and external public debt. However, by cutting access to capital markets and/or raising the **risk premium** embedded in domestic interest rates, such an option can *increase* the solvency gap.

In practice, solvency analysis is fraught with difficulties. Estimating the present values of seigniorage revenues and future primary deficits is difficult.[19]

---

[18] As discussed in Chapter 16, *external* solvency can be analyzed in a manner that is similar to the procedure used to assess fiscal solvency.

[19] An econometric assessment of the solvency constraint often takes the form of testing the *stationarity* of the debt-to-output ratio. See, for instance, Buiter and Patel (1992) and most importantly the critical discussion by Cuddington (1997).

Estimating the real rate of interest and the rate of output growth (in the more realistic case in which they vary over time) is also problematic for a sufficiently long horizon; the reason is that interactions (as discussed earlier) between these variables and the primary fiscal deficit must be taken into account to avoid biasing the results. Calculating the primary fiscal balance that ensures solvency does not address the question of whether the fiscal policy stance is consistent with growth and other policy targets. As pointed out by Zee (1988), once the endogeneity and interdependence of the primary fiscal balance, private savings and investment, interest rates, and output growth is recognized, government solvency as defined earlier is *not sufficient* for fiscal policies to be *sustainable*—in the sense that the level of public debt converges to a stable long-run equilibrium path consistent with the steady state of the economy.

Equally important, the solvency constraint [given either as Equation (3.22) or (3.24)] imposes only *weak restrictions* on fiscal policy. As indicated earlier, it has no meaning in an economy in which the real interest rate is lower than the growth rate of output. If $r < g$, a primary surplus is not necessary to achieve solvency—the government can run a primary deficit of *any size*, and this would be consistent with a sustainable debt-to-output ratio. In fact, the debt-to-output ratio may rise *without bound*, as long as the growth rate of the debt does not equal or exceed the real interest rate.

In practice, however, the size of the debt-to-output ratio may have an important influence on the private sector's *perception* of the government's *commitment* to meet its intertemporal budget constraint, as well as its *ability* to do so. As long as the private sector expects the government to generate a sequence of primary budget surpluses at some future period, the constraint imposed by either Equation (3.23) or (3.25) will be met. However, as the debt ratio continues to grow, private agents may become *skeptical* about the government's ability to meet its budget constraint; this *loss of credibility* may translate into *higher interest rates* (see below). Moreover, the larger the outstanding debt-to-output ratio is, and the longer appropriate policy actions are *postponed*, the greater will be the magnitude of the primary surplus needed to satisfy the solvency constraint. Because governments typically face a *limit* to the tax burden that they can impose on their citizens (notably because of adverse effects on incentives and income distribution), they face a **feasibility constraint** on the amount of revenue that they can raise (Spaventa, 1987). The result may be that a set of fiscal policies that initially met the solvency constraint may become inadequate over time.

3.7   Commodity Price Shocks and Fiscal Deficits

The root causes of fiscal deficits in developing countries are often found in the biases generated by inadequate political structures, such as those resulting from the *commons problem* discussed earlier, and political conflict (see Chapter 17). In addition, and particularly in the short run, *commodity price shocks* may also play a role. Many developing economies continue to depend heavily on primary commodities for the bulk of their export receipts. In sub-Saharan Africa, for instance, the share of primary commodities in total exports accounted on average for about three-fourths in 1997; in some cases it exceeded 90 percent. In many countries that are dependent on primary commodity exports, tax revenues are strongly affected by movements in commodity prices. When commodity prices rise, for instance, government revenues are boosted both *directly*, in countries where commodity-producing sectors are state owned, and *indirectly*, through increased revenues from trade and income taxes. As documented by Collier and Gunning (1996), governments in a number of commodity-exporting countries have often used these windfall gains to finance *procyclical expenditures* (instead of imposing a tax on export earnings) with the result that when commodity prices have declined, these countries have been left with large and unsustainable fiscal deficits. The reason, as noted by Cooper (1991, p. 87), is that

> Governments typically behave as if positive shocks are permanent, and negative shocks are temporary.

For instance, in coffee-producing countries such as *Kenya* and *Tanzania*, expansions induced by the coffee price booms of the late 1970s and early 1980s led to sharp increases in domestic and external debt burdens, largely because the windfall gains were used to fund public sector expenditures that yielded little or no return. The experience in many oil-exporting countries (such as Mexico, Nigeria, and Venezuela) was similar following the sharp rises in oil prices during the late 1970s. In many cases, the expansion of government spending induced by a transitory improvement in the terms of trade was accompanied not only by growing fiscal deficits but also by a sustained *real exchange rate appreciation*—a phenomenon known as the **Dutch disease** (see Corden, 1984)—which exerted an adverse effect on exports and sometimes led to severe balance-of-payments difficulties.[20]

Designing contingency mechanisms and institutional structures that are capable of ensuring that governments engage more in *expenditure smoothing* (by saving in good times and dissaving in bad times) in response to movements in primary commodity pricees and the terms of trade remains a key policy issue in many developing countries.

3.8   Public Debt and Fiscal Austerity

The conventional view of fiscal austerity (typically referred to as the **Keynesian view**) is that a cut in government spending will typically lower aggregate demand and reduce output. Some economists have argued, however, that the conventional view does not necessarily hold in countries where, to begin with, budgetary imbalances and the public debt are large. On the contrary, *fiscal austerity may be expansionary*. This possibility was referred to by Bertola and

---

[20] For a discussion of the sources of volatility in primary commodity prices, see Bleaney and Greenaway (1993), and Cuddington (1992).

Drazen (1993), in particular, as the case of the **negative fiscal multiplier**. Barry and Devereux (1994, 1995) also explored the implications of this view and reviewed some of the empirical evidence for industrial countries.

The idea of a negative fiscal multiplier rests essentially on the view that *expectations* about *future policy actions* may have a major effect on interest rates, depending on their *degree of credibility*—a notion that will receive more attention in the next two chapters. Consider, for instance, a country with a large and growing budget deficit and a high level of government debt. Suppose that the government announces its commitment to reduce the deficit within a given time frame, and begins its austerity program with an immediate cut in expenditure. To the extent that operators on financial market regard the (actual and future) policy measures as fully credible, interest rates may fall immediately. The reason is that a credible policy announcement may be viewed as reducing the risk of higher inflation, currency overvaluation, and possibly future financial instability (see Chapter 7). As a result, the **risk premium** in interest rates is likely to decline. In turn, the fall in interest rates and the associated reduction in the debt-service burden of households and firms may have expansionary effects on output through various channels:

- Via the *demand side*, by lowering the cost of capital (as discussed in Chapter 1) and thereby increasing investment, and by stimulating consumption of durables.

- Via the *supply side*, by reducing the cost of financing working capital needs for credit-dependent firms (see Chapters 2 and 8).

Reduced uncertainty about the sustainability of the budgetary situation may also help directly to improve confidence among firms and households. By reducing the **option value of waiting** (as discussed in Chapter 1), lower uncertainty may stimulate investment. Consumption and investment may also be stimulated if the reduction in public debt service payments translates into lower budgetary pressures and, at least to some extent, lower expected future tax rates.

In any particular setting, these various expansionary effects may well outweigh the conventional, negative short-term output effects associated with cuts in government spending or increases in tax rates. Although there is virtually no evidence on the importance of negative fiscal multiplier effects in developing countries, it is not an idea that can be dismissed lightly. It has important implications for the design of adjustment programs.

3.9   Summary

- The structure of *conventional sources* of revenue and expenditure differs significantly between industrial and developing countries.

- Shares of *tax revenue* and *government expenditure* in output are larger in industrial countries. Developing countries spend more on *general pub-*

lic services, *defense*, and *education*; industrial countries spend somewhat more on *social security* and *health*.

- Although the relative shares of *direct taxes, taxes on domestic goods and services*, and *taxes on foreign trade* vary considerably across developing countries, there has been a gradual move away from trade taxes to taxes on domestic sales. In industrial countries, *income taxes* account for the largest share of tax revenue, and *taxes on foreign trade* are negligible.

- Within *direct taxes*, the share of tax revenue raised from *individual incomes* is much larger than that from *corporations* in developing countries, while the reverse is true in industrial countries.

- The collection of **seigniorage** and **quasi-fiscal operations** are two important features of public finances in developing countries.

- **Seigniorage** consists of the **inflation tax** (the reduction in the purchasing power of private holdings of cash money balances due to inflation) and autonomous changes in the level of real money balances. To the extent that money creation causes inflation, thereby affecting the real value of nominal assets, seigniorage can be viewed as a tax on private agents' domestic currency holdings.

- Although there are considerable differences across countries in the use of inflationary finance, the evidence suggests that reliance on seigniorage is higher in countries with larger fiscal deficits.

- **Quasi-fiscal outlays** and **receipts** are operations (generally of the central bank) that are *functionally equivalent* to subsidies and taxes imposed by the government. Difficulties in raising tax revenue through conventional means often explain the importance of these operations.

- Examples of quasi-fiscal operations are *central bank loans* at subsidized rates of interest (equivalent to interest subsidies), losses associated with the purchase and sale of foreign exchange in a multiple exchange rate system (equivalent to *foreign exchange subsidies*), and the imposition on commercial banks of *reserve requirements* obliging them to hold central bank liabilities earning below-market rates of interest (equivalent to a *tax on deposits*).

- These quasi-fiscal operations are **contingent** (or **unfunded**) **fiscal liabilities** that should be recognized, estimated, and converted into their subsidy or tax equivalents in order to add them to the fiscal accounts, conventionally measured, of the consolidated public sector. Otherwise, changes in the government's fiscal balance may provide a misleading picture of the true situation of the public sector's overall financial position.

- Reductions in central government expenditures may simply reflect a shift to quasi-fiscal activities and implicit government liabilities, rather than real fiscal adjustment. In particular, when expenditure data do not account for the contingent or unfunded liabilities created by quasi-fiscal activities—such as the implicit subsidies provided in the form of government guarantees to public enterprises engaged in borrowing—the ratio of actual government expenditure to output may significantly *understate* the extent of public sector intervention in the economy.

- The **problem of the commons** arises dues to an important characteristic of many government programs: whereas they tend to generate benefits that are concentrated sectorally and or geographically, they are often financed from a common pool of resources. Under some institutional arrangements regarding the process of fiscal decision making, this can lead to overutilization of the common pool of resources, fiscal deficits, and overborrowing, because those who benefit from the programs fail to internalize their full cost.

- The conventional measure of the fiscal deficit derived from the **flow budget constraint** of the government can be very sensitive to inflation. A key reason is the effect of inflation on *nominal interest payments* on the public debt. Another reason is the **Olivera-Tanzi effect**, which refers to the erosion of the tax base by inflation due to the lag between the *assessment* and *collection* of taxes.

- In general, when inflation is high and variable, changes in the nominal interest bill can affect the usefulness of the conventional fiscal balance as a guide for policy assessment. More useful concepts are the **primary balance**, which excludes interest payments from expenditure, and the **operational balance**, calculated by netting out the inflationary component in net interest payments from the conventional balance.

- The **fiscal impulse measure** aims at capturing the effect of automatic stabilizers and discretionary changes in fiscal policy. It is calculated by first estimating the *cyclically neutral* component of the budget deficit (often under the assumption that government expenditures increase proportionately to *potential* output and that government revenues increase proportionately to *actual* output). The residual between the cyclically neutral and the actual budget deficits is called the *fiscal stance*. The fiscal impulse is the annual change in the fiscal stance measure, expressed as a share of output. Such measures, however, are subject to a number of limitations, due in part to their partial equilibrium nature.

- Macroeconomically, aggregate domestic investment must be financed by domestic savings, public and private, and foreign saving (the current account deficit). This identity is sometimes used to argue that if policies do not have any effect in improving either government or private sector savings, the external balance cannot be expected to improve.

- As long as the *net investment position* of the private sector remains *stable*, changes in fiscal deficits will be closely associated with movements in current account deficits. In general, however, because fiscal deficits also affect the private sector's investment-saving balance, the correlation between fiscal and external deficits may not be a close one.

- A **consistency framework** aims at ensuring that fiscal objectives are consistent with other macroeconomic policy targets, such as growth, inflation, real interest rates, and the external current account.

- The framework proposed by Anand and van Wijnbergen (1989) dwells on the flow budget constraint of the government and can be operated in two modes: the **deficit mode**, which gives the **financeable deficit**, given targets for inflation and other macroeconomic variables; and the **inflation mode**, which gives the rate of inflation consistent with given targets for the fiscal deficit and other macroeconomic variables. In both cases, to ensure a *constant debt-to-output ratio*, the sustainable primary deficit is calculated under the assumption that liabilities grow at the economy's rate of output growth.

- The Anand-van Wijnbergen framework remains, however, subject to several limitations. It lacks a *simultaneous determination* of the fiscal balance and other macroeconomic variables;[21] more complex models may be useful and may allow the analyst to assess the role of the investment-saving balance of the private sector in assessing external sustainability.

- Lenders, or holders of government liabilities, *play no direct role* in determining the sustainable debt-output ratio. Applications also rarely account properly for the contingent liabilities associated with quasi-fiscal activities; these may be important in assessing debt sustainability in the medium term.

- Assessing the sustainability of fiscal policy on the basis of aggregate public debt dynamics does not ensure a sustainable external current account. To do so requires taking into account also changes in *private* saving and investment behavior induced by predicted movements in output, debt, and interest rates.

- The government's **solvency constraint** (intertemporal, or present value constraint) indicates that the *discounted present value* of primary surpluses and seigniorage revenue (both in proportion of output) must be equal to the initial stock of the government debt-to-output ratio. The current stance of fiscal policy is *sustainable* if its continuation into the indefinite future does not violate the solvency constraint.

---

[21] Without a general equilibrium framework, it is possible that changes in macroeconomic policy that are intended to eliminate an *ex ante* inconsistency between the inflation target and the primary fiscal deficit will do so at the cost of increasing the degree of inconsistency between the inflation and deficit projections, on the one hand, and the assumed path of real output, the real interest rate, and the real exchange rate on the other.

- As long as the real interest rate is *lower* than the rate of growth of real output, this constraint does not bind. But if the real interest rate *exceeds* the rate of growth of real output, a policy aimed at maintaining a primary deficit that is expected to continue indefinitely may eventually lead to a violation of the solvency constraint *ex ante*. Satisfying the constraint *ex post* requires either a cut in the primary deficit, increased seigniorage revenue, or debt repudiation or restructuring.

- Solvency analysis, in practice, also lacks a *simultaneous determination* of macroeconomic aggregates.

- **Commodity price shocks** may have a significant impact on fiscal deficits. For countries that are heavily dependent on commodity exports, a rise in the price of these goods increases government revenues both *directly*, in countries where commodity-producing sectors are state owned, and *indirectly*, through increased revenues from trade and income taxes.

- Governments in a number of commodity-exporting countries have often used these *windfall gains* to finance *procyclical expenditures* with the result that once commodity prices started to decline, these countries were left with large and unsustainable fiscal deficits. Terms-of-trade shocks have also led to significant real appreciation (the **Dutch disease** phenomenon). Managing commodity price booms remains a key issue in fiscal policy.

- A cut in government spending is conventionally viewed as reducing aggregate demand and output. On the contrary, fiscal austerity may be *expansionary* if expectations about *future policy actions* affect interest rates. A credible commitment to reduce a large fiscal deficit, in particular, may lead to an immediate fall in interest rates (because of the perceived reduction in the risk of inflation), which may stimulate aggregate demand and output. There is, however, limited evidence on these effects in developing countries.

Appendix
The Generalized Solvency Constraint

Following Buiter (1997), this appendix derives the solvency constraint given in the text to account for variable output growth rates and interest rates. Solving Equation (3.20) recursively forward now gives, for $T > 0$.

$$\mathbf{b}_0 = \sum_{h=1}^{N} \Pi_{i=1}^{h} \left(\frac{1 + \mathbf{g}_Y^i}{1 + r_i} \right) (s_h - \mathbf{d}_h) + \Pi_{i=1}^{N} \left(\frac{1 + \mathbf{g}_Y^i}{1 + r_i} \right) \mathbf{b}_N, \qquad (A1)$$

so that, with the constraint $\mathbf{b}_N \leq 0$, the solvency condition (3.23) becomes

$$\mathbf{b}_0 \leq \sum_{h=1}^{N} \Pi_{i=1}^{h} \left(\frac{1 + \mathbf{g}_Y^i}{1 + r_i} \right) (s_h - \mathbf{d}_h). \qquad (A2)$$

With an infinite horizon, the solvency constraint (or **No-Ponzi scheme condition**) given by Equation (3.24) becomes

$$\lim_{N \to \infty} \Pi_{i=1}^{N} \left(\frac{1 + \mathbf{g}_Y^i}{1 + r_i} \right) \mathbf{b}_N \leq 0. \qquad (A3)$$

with Equation (3.25) now becoming

$$\mathbf{b}_0 \leq \sum_{h=1}^{\infty} \Pi_{i=1}^{h} \left(\frac{1 + \mathbf{g}_Y^i}{1 + r_i} \right) (s_h - \mathbf{d}_h). \qquad (A4)$$

The actual H-period seigniorage-output ratio, Equation (3.26), is now

$$s_A^H = \left[\sum_{h=1}^{H} \Pi_{i=1}^{h} \left(\frac{1 + \mathbf{g}_Y^i}{1 + r_i} \right) \right]^{-1} \sum_{h=1}^{H} \Pi_{i=1}^{h} \left(\frac{1 + \mathbf{g}_Y^i}{1 + r_i} \right) s_h,$$

and the required primary deficit-output ratio becomes

$$\mathbf{d}_R^H (\mathbf{b}_0 - \mathbf{b}_H) = \frac{\left[\mathbf{b}_{t_0} - \sum_{h=1}^{H} \Pi_{i=t_0+1}^{h} \left(\frac{1+\mathbf{g}_Y^i}{1+r_i} \right) \mathbf{b}_{t_0+H} - s_A^H \right]}{\left[\sum_{h=1}^{H} \Pi_{i=1}^{h} \left(\frac{1+\mathbf{g}_Y^i}{1+r_i} \right) \right]}.$$

Finally, the actual H-period primary deficit-output ratio is now given by

$$\mathbf{d}_A^H = \left[\sum_{h=1}^{H} \Pi_{i=1}^{h} \left(\frac{1 + \mathbf{g}_Y^i}{1 + r_i} \right) \right]^{-1} \sum_{h=1}^{H} \Pi_{i=1}^{h} \left(\frac{1 + \mathbf{g}_Y^i}{1 + r_i} \right) \mathbf{d}_h.$$

Chapter 4

Exchange Rate Regimes

Increased global financial integration and the growing incidence of currency crises in the developing world has led to renewed controversy over the role and performance of exchange rate regimes. The credibility effects of various types of exchange rate arrangements, for instance, have become important considerations in assessing the role of the various factors that may affect the choice of an exchange rate regime. At the same time, issues such as the effect of exchange rate changes on trade flows and output have also remained at the forefront of the policy debate, with notably the emphasis on the contractionary effects of exchange rate changes in the presence of imported intermediate inputs.

The first two parts of this chapter provide a typology of exchange rate regimes and an overview of the evolution of exchange rate regimes in developing countries. They also consider in detail the characteristics and functioning of two regimes that have regained some favor in recent years: currency board arrangements and exchange rate bands. The third part reviews the various factors that may affect the choice of an exchange rate regime and highlights the potential conflicts that may arise among them. The fourth part uses a simple illustrative model to emphasize the importance of *policy trade-offs* in affecting the degree of credibility of pegged exchange rate arrangements. The fifth part focuses on the effects of exchange rate changes on competitiveness and the trade balance. It begins by reviewing basic measures of competitiveness, and then considers the partial equilibrium approach to analyzing the effect of exchange rate changes on external accounts. The last part extends the analysis to consider a fully specified macroeconomic model that captures the role of imported inputs in the production process. The effects of exchange rate changes on both output and the trade balance are studied, and the limitations of the partial equilibrium approach are discussed.

4.1 The Nature of Exchange Rate Regimes

This section begins by presenting a general typology of exchange rate regimes. It then provides a more detailed discussion of currency boards and exchange rate bands. It concludes with a review of some recent evidence on the evolution of exchange rate arrangements in developing countries.

4.1.1 A Basic Typology

The array of exchange rate arrangements currently in operation in developing countries is wide and covers almost all types of regimes.

- **Pegged exchange rate regimes**, which come in several forms: **currency boards**, whereby the currency is irrevocably fixed against a foreign currency (see below); **adjustable pegs**, in which the currency is fixed against a foreign currency and is seldom changed; **crawling pegs**, whereby the currency is initially fixed but policymakers subsequently adjust the exchange rate at regular intervals to take into account changes in inflation differentials or the state of the trade balance.

- **Flexible exchange rate regimes**, in which the exchange rate is allowed to fluctuate in response to changes in demand and supply of foreign exchange. If the central bank does not intervene in the market for foreign exchange, the regime is a **free float**; otherwise, it is a **managed float**.

- **Band regimes**, which involve the announcement of a *central exchange rate* together with a **fluctuation band** (which may or may not be *symmetric*) around that rate. The central exchange rate is itself managed in some fashion—being, for instance, *fixed* or *crawling*. The implicit commitment of the central bank is to intervene actively at the *margins* of the band to prevent the exchange rate from moving outside the band. The implementation of a band also requires the adoption of a *set of rules* to guide foreign exchange market intervention, if any, within the band (see below).

- **Dual or multiple exchange rate regimes**, in which commercial transactions take place at fixed rates and financial transactions at a (generally more depreciated) floating rate.[1] In practice, such regimes have not worked well because of leakages among the various segments of the foreign exchange market. They are often adopted as transitory arrangements prior to fixing the exchange rate to an equilibrium value.

Under a *pure currency board*, the base money stock is fully backed by foreign reserves because the currency board only prints money against the reserve currency at a fixed exchange rate. Money issued by the currency board is also fully

---

[1] Dual exchange rate regimes may be *informal*, as happens when governments impose *foreign exchange restrictions* in an attempt to defend an overvalued pegged exchange rate; as discussed in Annex B, this typically leads to the emergence of a parallel market for foreign exchange.

convertible on demand (at the fixed exchange rate) into the reserve currency, and vice versa. By definition, the ratio of the base money stock to the stock of foreign currency reserves is given by the exchange rate between the domestic currency and the reserve currency. By contrast, deposits in private domestic banks are not backed by the currency board's foreign exchange reserves; these are liabilities of private banks. There is, in principle, no discount window and thus no possibility to offer lines of credit to private financial institutions experiencing short-term liquidity problems—a significant limitation of the system, as discussed below.

Floating exchange rate systems may be either an **interbank system** or an **auction system**, or a combination of these two systems.

- Under the *interbank system*, the exchange rate is negotiated in a market of commercial banks and authorized foreign exchange dealers. In theory, the exchange rate is allowed to fluctuate at any time. But, in practice, *minimum* and *maximum limits* are often imposed by the central bank on the commercial banks and dealers in order to prevent "cornering" of all the foreign exchange by any single member or group of dealers. This also prevents excessive exposure by commercial banks to **exchange rate risk**.

- In the *auction system*, export receipts are surrendered to the central bank at the prevailing exchange rate and the central bank, in turn, decides what amount of foreign exchange must be auctioned.

In practice, the two main variants of auction systems are the *Dutch auction system* and the *marginal price system* (see Feldman and Mehra, 1993). Under the former, each bidder whose bid is accepted must pay his or her bid price; a bidder may thus end up paying a significantly higher price if he or she incorrectly assesses the demand for foreign exchange. In the latter, a single rate called the *market-clearing price* is applicable to all bidders whose bids are accepted. Specifically, all bidders above the market-clearing price, that is, bids in excess of the highest bid which fully exhausts the available supply of foreign currency, are then allocated foreign exchange.

4.1.2 Currency Board Arrangements

In recent years there has been a revival of interest in currency boards, a popular exchange rate arrangement during the colonial era.[2] Such regimes are being advocated not only for small and highly open economies but also for large countries (see Baliño and Enoch, 1997). The case for a currency board is, first, similar to the case for a fixed exchange rate regime: by pegging the exchange rate, it constrains the scope for excessive monetary expansion.[3] This *monetary discipline* is likely to enhance confidence in the domestic currency and lead to lower

---

[2] Malaysia, for instance, established a currency board in 1897 and dismantled it in 1967. See Hanke ans Schuler (1994) for a discussion of currency boards during the colonial period.

[3] It is sometimes argued that adopting a currency board entails foregoing *seigniorage revenues*. As pointed out by Baliño and Enoch (1997), this is not quite correct because the central bank continues to earn interest on its foreign assets while paying none on its domestic

inflation for a given rate of monetary expansion. Two additional arguments, however, are put forward in favor of adopting currency boards.

- They may help solve the **devaluation bias** inherent in discretionary exchange rate policy induced by time inconsistency problems, as discussed later. By removing—or at least severely limiting—the scope for discretionary monetary policy, a currency board should result in even *greater discipline* and confidence than simply pegging the exchange rate.

- The additional *credibility gain* that a currency board provides may help deter *speculative attacks* and *currency crises*, as discussed in Chapter 7.

Of course, the difference between a currency board and a conventional fixed exchange rate regime is largely one of *degree*: a currency board can be abandoned just as a pegged exchange rate can. Institutional arrangements, however, typically make the abolition of a currency board considerably more difficult; this is precisely what provides the additional credibility of such regimes in the first place.

The additional credibility provided by a currency board, however, may come at a price.

- Compared to other pegged exchange rate regimes, currency boards are more constraining on monetary policy and on the ability of the authorities to alter the exchange rate peg. The cost associated with the *loss of flexibility* depends in general on how vulnerable the economy is to aggregate (domestic and external) shocks, and the availability of alternative policy instruments to offset the impact of these shocks.

- The credibility gain provided by a currency board to a country's economic policies may not be complete, because agents realize that such regimes can also be abandoned—even if doing so may be difficult. As a consequence, monetary authorities may not be able to completely eliminate the risk of devaluation and its impact on the **risk premium** faced by domestic borrowers on world capital markets.

- A currency board reduces the ability of the central bank to act as **lender of last resort** in the face of system-wide liquidity crunches. Because there is, in principle, no discount window, the central bank cannot offer lines of credit to private financial institutions experiencing short-term liquidity problems. Thus, countries with currency boards are *more prone to bank runs* and *financial panics* than countries with full-fledged central banks (see Chapter 15).

---

liabilities (the monetary base). Moreover, a central bank operating a conventional pegged exchange rate regime will also be limited in its ability to expand domestic credit, at least if it wants to sustain the peg for a sufficient duration. Thus seigniorage arguments are largely irrelevant in any comparison within the set of pegged exchange rate systems.

At the heart of this problem is the fact that private commercial banks usually hold just enough domestic currency to cover a *fraction* of their deposit liabilities. Under a currency board regime, commercial banks cannot rely on short-term borrowing from the central bank to finance transitory liquidity problems. As a result, a sudden loss of confidence by depositors can quickly turn into panic. The belief that a bank has become insolvent may trigger a run against that bank, as depositors try to withdraw funds before the bank runs out of cash. The bank's failure may create or exacerbate fears of other bank failures, thereby leading, through a **domino effect**, to a *full-blown financial crisis*. The *credit crunch* that may follow the crisis may have a large, adverse effect on output and employment, putting pressure on policymakers to abandon the currency board regime. By contrast, with a full-fledged central bank, an essentially *solvent bank* with short-term liquidity problems will not automatically go under as it would in a currency board system because it can have recourse to the discount window to cover the temporary cash shortage. Thus, currency boards face the same type of trade-off between credibility and flexibility that any other type of pegged exchange rate regime may face (see below).

4.1.3 Exchange Rate Bands

As indicated earlier, band regimes attempt to preserve some degree of exchange rate flexibility to promote relative price adjustment while retaining the role of the exchange rate as a **nominal anchor**. More specifically,

- relative to pegged exchange rate regimes, bands allow the exchange rate to adjust to *temporary* movements in relative prices and preserve some degree of **monetary autonomy**—the extent of which depends *positively* on the width of the band;

- relative to flexible exchange rate regimes, exchange rate bands, by constraining the range of fluctuation of the nominal exchange rate, continue to provide some nominal anchor for the domestic price level, depending now *negatively* on the width of the band (see Chapter 5).[4]

The extent to which a band regime succeeds in stabilizing the nominal exchange rate depends on its credibility. As formally demonstrated by Krugman (1991), in a perfectly credible band in which intervention takes place only at the upper and lower margins, the nominal exchange rate will be closer to the central rate than it would have been under flexible exchange rates—even without intervention. Thus, the mere presence of the announced band may be stabilizing. It is important to emphasize, however, that the extent to which the other alleged benefits will materialize or not depends crucially on how the band is managed.

---

[4]Another benefit of a band regime is that, as shown by Coles and Philippopoulos (1997), it would tend to stabilize the domestic inflation rate relative to what would happen under fixed exchange rates if inflation in partner countries is highly unstable.

- If the central bank intervenes so as to keep the exchange rate very close to the central rate, or allows it to remain continuously at the top or bottom of the band, the band regime will behave like a fixed exchange rate—providing therefore no scope for relative price adjustments and no monetary autonomy.

- If the central rate parity is determined so as to maintain the *real exchange rate* constant, for instance, the economy's nominal anchor will have to be provided by the *money supply*, as in the case of flexible rates (see Chapter 5).

4.2   Evidence on Exchange Rate Regimes

This section begins by reviewing the broad evolution of exchange rate regimes in developing countries since the early 1980s. It then focuses on the recent experience of some particular countries (including Brazil, Chile, Indonesia, and Israel) with exchange rate bands.

4.2.1   General Trends

In practice, a commonly used system to classify exchange rate regimes is the one introduced by the International Monetary Fund in 1982. It distinguishes between five categories: fixed to a single currency, fixed to a currency basket, limited flexibility (or quasi-peggers), managed flexibility, and independently floating. Figure 4.1 shows the evolution of the percentage of developing countries with pegged exchange rates based on the first two categories of this classification. The figure reveals a continuous fall in the number of pegged arrangements since the collapse of the **Bretton Woods** system of fixed but adjustable parities in the early 1970s. In the mid-1970s, 86 percent of developing countries had some type of pegged exchange rate regime. In 1996, fewer than half did. As illustrated by Figure 4.2, many of the countries that continue to peg their exchange rate are in sub-Saharan Africa and belong to the **CFA Franc Zone**.[5] Almost one-third of developing countries now claim to have independently floating rates.

In practice, however, exchange rate regimes are difficult to classify, for various reasons.

- The central bank may manage the exchange with considerable flexibility but set it daily or weekly on the basis of certain *indicators*—for instance,

---

[5] The CFA Franc Zone consists of two separate groups of sub-Saharan African countries and the Comoros. The first group includes the seven members of the West African Monetary Union (Benin, Burkina Faso, Côte d'Ivoire, Mali, Niger, Senegal, and Togo), whose central bank (the BCEAO) has responsibility for conducting a common monetary policy. The second group consists of the six members of another common central bank, the BEAC (Cameroon, the Central African Republic, Chad, the Congo, Equatorial Guinea, and Gabon). Each of the two groups and the Comoros maintain separate currencies, but these currencies are commonly referred to as the CFA franc, which was maintained at a fixed parity against the French franc from 1948 to January 1994.

inflation differentials, the current account or the overall balance of payments, or projected supply and demand conditions in the market for foreign exchange. In such conditions, however, the exchange rate cannot be deemed market determined or freely floating.

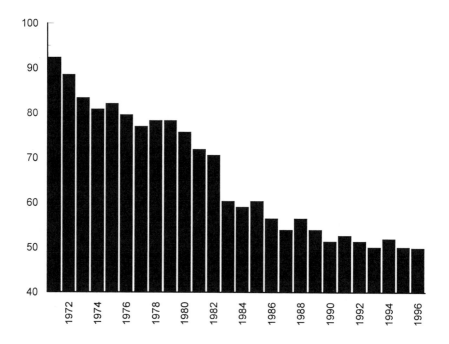

Figure 4.1. Developing Countries: Countries with Pegged Exchange Rates, 1970-96 (In percent of total number of countries).
Source: International Monetary Fund.

- In particular, **real exchange rate targeting** implies fluctuations in the nominal exchange rate to offset inflation differentials.[6] It is not clear whether an inflation-adjusted peg qualifies as a form of fixed exchange rate, or a form of arrangement whereby the exchange rate is flexibly managed.

- Determining how much foreign exchange market intervention is consistent with the category of *independently floating* regimes, for instance, requires assessing the degree to which intervention aims only at *smoothing* exchange rate movements—a difficult task in practice.

This last point is particularly important because it suggests that classification systems such as the one used by the International Monetary Fund are inadequate because they do not provide detailed enough information to determine

---

[6]For a discussion of real exchange rate targeting, see Lizondo (1993) and Montiel and Ostry (1991, 1992).

the *actual* degree of flexibility (that is the extent of central bank intervention) among countries adopting the more flexible regimes. In particular, many of the countries that now claim to have independently floating rates use official intervention to alter the exchange rate path and should be classified as managed floaters.

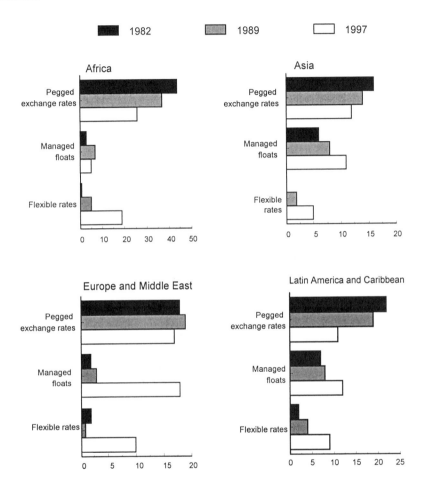

Figure 4.2. Developing Countries: Exchange Rate Arrangements 1/ (Number of countries).

Source: International Monetary Fund.

Note: Countries with pegged exchange rates are those countries classified by the IMF as pegged to a single currency, pegged to a basket of currencies or crawling peg. Countries with managed floats are those countries classified by the IMF as adjusting to a set of indicators and managed floating. Countries with flexible rates are the countries classified by the IMF as independently floating.

4.2.2 Exchange Rate Bands

In practice, and in line with the description provided earlier, the choice of an exchange rate band covers four dimensions:

- The definition of the *central rate*, which can be in reference to either a *single currency* or a *basket of currencies*.

- Whether the central rate should be *fixed, crawling*, or *realigned irregularly* by discrete amounts. The choice among these options depends in part on the differential between domestic inflation and the rate of inflation of major trading partners, and the extent to which *permanent shocks* to the real exchange rate should be accommodated or not.

- The *width* of the band, that is, the permitted range of fluctuation of the exchange rate around the central rate.

- The rules governing *foreign exchange market intervention* by the central bank inside the bands.

A growing number of developing countries have adopted exchange rate band regimes in the past few years, including Brazil (1995-99), Chile (1985), Colombia (1991), Ecuador (1994-99), Indonesia (1994-97), Israel (1989), and Mexico (1989-94).[7] The experience of these countries with respect to the four dimensions of implementation identified earlier has varied widely. Examples of (eventually) unsuccessful band regimes are those of Brazil and Indonesia, which are illustrated in Figure 4.3.

Exchange rate bands were introduced in Brazil in March 1995, in the aftermath of the Mexican peso crisis (see Chapter 7). The initial band was set at R$0.86-R$0.90 per U.S. dollar and was to be effective through May 1, 1995. However, because of the uncertainty about the exchange rate policy that would be adopted after that date, severe exchange market pressures developed. On March 10, 1995, the authorities set the band at R$0.88-R$0.93 per U.S. dollar and announced that it would be effective for an indefinite period. The band was subsequently modified on June 22, 1995, on January 30, 1996, and on February 18, 1997. The currency remained nevertheless subject to heavy speculative pressures. The central bank effectively used a *narrow trading band* of R$1.1975-R$1.2115 within a *maxi-band* of R$1.12-R$1.22 until January 13, 1999, at which point it decided to use only a maxi-band of R$1.20-R$1.32. On January 14, however, under renewed speculative pressures, the authorities abandoned the band regime, with the currency depreciating immediately from R$1.32 a day earlier to R$1.50.

A band regime was introduced in January 1994 in Indonesia, with an initial width of about 1 percent on either side of the central rate. The central rate of the rupiah was set with regard to an unannounced currency basket, and continued to

---

[7]The experience of Chile, Colombia, Indonesia, and Mexico is discussed by Agénor and Montiel (1999, Chapter 7).

be depreciated in accordance with inflation differentials, thereby continuing the policy of stabilizing the real effective exchange rate.[8] The intervention band was widened progressively over time. After the collapse of Thailand's currency on July 2, 1997 (see Chapter 7), the central bank widened further the trading band on July 11, 1997, but the currency depreciated to near the ceiling of the new band by July 21. Continued exchange market pressures forced the authorities to abandon the band altogether in August 1997.

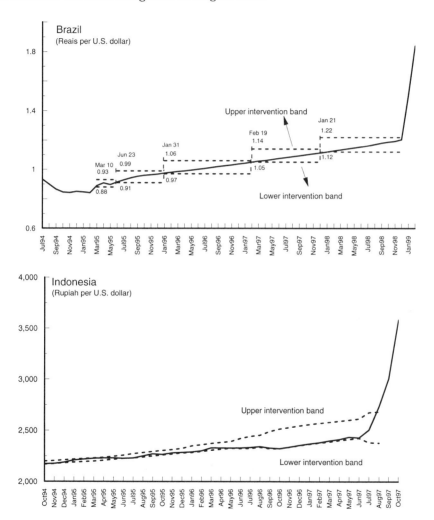

Figure 4.3. Brazil and Indonesia: Nominal Exchange Rate and Intervention Bands.

Source: International Monetary Fund.

---

[8] Between 1988 and 1994, Indonesia operated a crawling peg regime, whose main objective was to depreciate the nominal exchange rate in order to offset the inflation differential with the country's major trading partners and maintain a competitive real exchange rate.

From the case of Brazil, the review of the experience with exchange rate bands of Chile, Colombia, Indonesia, and Mexico provided by Agénor and Montiel (1999, Chapter 7), and the studies of Helpman, Leiderman, and Bufman (1994) and Leiderman and Bufman (1996), four major lessons appear to emerge:

- A band is a commitment to limited nominal exchange rate flexibility, not to a specific choice of nominal anchor. Bands are thus compatible with a variety of different weights that may be attached by the authorities to competitiveness and price stability objectives. Differences in such weights will be reflected in differences in the management of the *central rate*.

- There is no evidence suggesting that moving from a fixed rate to a band regime was associated with a significant increase in inflation. Thus, the greater flexibility that a band regime provides does not come necessarily at the expense of price stability. This finding suggests that some degree of *flexibility* can indeed *enhance credibility*.

- The adoption of a band regime, however, does not resolve credibility problems. The Brazilian, Chilean, Colombian, Mexican, and Israeli bands were all characterized by periods of high **expectations of realignment**, reflecting perceived misalignment of the real exchange rate.

- Active management of the central rate to keep the real exchange rate in line with its equilibrium level may thus be indispensable to ensure the viability of a bands regime under high capital mobility. If such adjustments are not implemented in a timely fashion, recurrent speculative pressures may lead to a regime collapse.

4.3   Choosing an Exchange Rate Regime

In part because of the increased incidence of currency crises during the past few years (see Chapter 7), the issue of exchange rate regime choice remains one of the most debated questions in macroeconomic management. This section begins with a review of the conceptual issues involved in choosing an exchange rate arrangement. It then examines some of the empirical evidence on the determinants of regime choice.

4.3.1   Some Conceptual Issues

In practice, the choice between fixed and floating exchange rates is not always clear-cut. The very notion, for instance, of a *freely floating* exchange rate regime may have little empirical content. As noted earlier, almost no country sets its monetary policy without paying at least some consideration to its exchange rate effects. In practice, the degree of exchange rate flexibility lies almost on a continuum, with exchange rate bands, crawling pegs, and managed floats of various kinds residing between the extremes of purely floating and fixed exchange rates.

Conventional arguments in favor of a *fixed exchange rate* are that it provides a **nominal anchor** to prices, has often been instrumental in helping to bring down inflation (as discussed in the next chapter), and that it may help *promote fiscal discipline* or contribute to maintaining it once achieved. Pegging to a low-inflation country can also help to signal the government's commitment to price stability discipline and generate credibility gains, in the form of lower expectations of inflation and devaluation (Agénor (1994)). However, there are also several arguments, against choosing a fixed exchange rate.

- The evidence on the disciplinary effect of a fixed exchange rate on fiscal policy appears inconclusive, as argued by Tornell and Velasco (1998).

- The credibility gain associated with pegging to a low-inflation country tends to be, in practice, limited (Svensson (1994)). Building credibility and establishing a firm commitment to price stability often requires significant *domestic* policy and institutional reforms, such as granting independence to the central bank (see Chapter 5).

- While nominal exchange rate stability is important, *flexibility* in the design of exchange rate policies is also necessary to avoid excessive real appreciation and offset the impact of destabilizing shocks.[9]

- Pegging may in fact prevent *real exchange rate adjustment* in response to large domestic and external shocks. Glick, Hutchison, and Moreno (1997), for instance, argued that the pegged exchange rate regimes in place until 1997 were not the explanation for low inflation in East Asia. On the contrary, pegging prevented real exchange rate adjustment in response to large external nominal shocks—most notably the sharp depreciation of the U.S. dollar against the yen and the deutschemark during 1985-87 and the fall in U.S. interest rates during 1989-93—and therefore complicated macroeconomic management.[10]

- A pegged exchange rate creates a **moral hazard problem**. By eliminating (or reducing the propensity to hedge) foreign **currency risk**, a credibly fixed exchange rate provides an *implicit guarantee* and encourages domestic firms and banks to borrow on world capital markets at rates of interest that are lower than those charged in the domestic market.[11] This

---

[9] An extensive analytical literature has analyzed the links between the *type of disturbances* that an economy is subject to (real and nominal shocks, for instance) and the optimal choice of an exchange rate system, as well as the optimal degree of exchange rate flexibility (or foreign exchange market intervention). However, as pointed out by Van Gompel (1994) in his extensive overview, there are very few robust results that emerge from it—in contrast to the claims made in the early literature.

[10] In their view, low inflation in the region until the mid-1990s was the result of an independent fiscal policy process.

[11] Moreover, with a pegged rate, agents know that the implicit guarantee of convertibility is limited by the availability of international reserves and the country's capacity to borrow abroad. Thus, when doubts arise as to the sustainability of its exchange rate arrangement, a country will attract mainly short-term, speculative capital inflows (see Chapter 6).

overborrowing (particularly when it is short-term in nature) increases the vulnerability of the economy to adverse shocks.

- In countries prone to large random shocks, monetary aggregates may fluctuate erratically.

The arguments in favor of a *flexible exchange rate* are that it gives national monetary authorities *greater independence* in choosing their inflation objective, and that it provides a (partial) solution to the moral hazard problem posed by a fixed exchange rate. By purposely leaving some scope for unexpected exchange rate movements and avoiding *implicit exchange rate guarantees*, policymakers can induce domestic borrowers to internalize (at least some of) the costs of failing to hedge appropriately their foreign-currency liabilities. Arguments *against* choosing a flexible exchange rate are that they may not prevent a *real exchange rate appreciation* (in periods of surges in capital inflows in particular, as discussed in Chapter 6) and they may be characterized by *excessive volatility* (possibly exacerbated by a high degree of **dollarization**, as noted in Chapter 2) with adverse real effects.

4.3.2 The Evidence

What does the evidence suggest regarding the determinants of regime choice and economic performance under the various regimes? Three recent studies help to shed some light on these issues. Collins (1996) studied the determinants of regime choice in Latin America and the Caribbean, using a group of 24 countries over the period 1978-92. Macroeconomic imbalances, as measured by current account deficits and moderate to high inflation, were found to be significantly associated with a move to more flexible exchange rate arrangements during the period 1978-86; these indicators, however, appeared to have mattered less during 1987-92. In both periods, smaller and less open economies appeared less likely to select a flexible rate arrangement. Collins also argued that the **endogeneity of regime choice** introduces sample **selection bias** and makes any attempt to associate exchange rate regimes and economic performance (as proxied by the rate of output growth) hazardous.

Ghosh, Gulde, Ostry, and Wolf (1997), using a sample consisting of a large group of industrial and developing countries covering the period 1960 to 1990, found that countries with some form of fixed exchange rate experienced generally lower and less variable inflation than countries with flexible exchange rate arrangements. The superior inflation performance, however, was found mainly in countries that adjusted their exchange rate peg infrequently or not at all. Countries that frequently changed their exchange rate parity did not derive anti-inflationary benefits from the peg: indeed, they experienced higher and more volatile inflation rates than countries with freely floating exchange rates. Viewed together with the recent decline in inflation in many flexible exchange rate countries to their lowest levels since the late 1950s, this evidence supports the argument that simply pegging the exchange rate does not necessarily deliver low inflation. Rather, it is the pursuit of appropriate macroeconomic policies that is important, whether in enabling an exchange rate peg to be maintained, or, in the case of flexible exchange rates, in ensuring adherence to a nominal anchor such as the money supply.

Along the same lines, the study by Ghosh, Gulde, and Wolf (1997) examined the inflation performance of countries operating a **currency board** during the period 1970-96. To avoid biasing the results of their study, they controlled for *regime choice endogeneity*, because countries with a lower inclination to tolerate high inflation may be more likely to adopt a currency board in the first place. They found that, on average, inflation under currency board arrangements was substantially *lower* than under other pegged exchange rate regimes. They argued that lower inflation was achieved in part through a *discipline effect*, which led to lower growth in the money supply. But the difference in money growth rates is not sufficient to explain fully the inflation differential, suggesting an additional *confidence effect* whereby higher money demand results in lower inflation, for a given money growth rate. The last effect appeared to be the main factor explaining the size of the differential. In addition, *fiscal deficits* and the *volatility of inflation* were also lower under currency board arrangements.

4.3.3 A Practical Guide

The foregoing discussion suggests that, in practice, there are a number of factors that policymakers should consider in choosing an exchange rate regime. As pointed out by Eichengreen and Masson (1998), these factors may be difficult to measure and may conflict with each other; the ultimate decision may thus depend on the *relative weight* attached to each of them in policymakers' preferences. In adition, these weights may change over time. Nevertheless, relevant factors to ponder in selecting an exchange rate arrangement in practice include:

- The **size** and **degree of openness** of the economy. The higher the share of trade in output, the higher the costs of exchange rate volatility. Thus, small, highly open economies should opt for a pegged exchange rate regime.

- The level of **inflation**. A country that maintains a rate of inflation that is higher than that of its trading partners needs to maintain a flexible exchange rate to prevent a loss in competitiveness.

- The degree of **price** and **wage flexibility**. The more rigid real wages are, the greater the need for exchange rate flexibility to respond to external shocks. In the absence of such flexibility, asymmetric real shocks that require real exchange rate adjustments may cause large drops in output in countries with rigid labor and product markets.

- The degree of **financial development**. In countries with thin and poorly developed financial markets, a flexible exchange rate regime may lead to large fluctuations in the exchange rate because of a limited number of transactions in the foreign exchange market.

- The degree of **credibility of policymakers.** The weaker is the **anti-inflation reputation** of the central bank, the stronger the case for pegging the exchange rate in order to build confidence that inflation will be controlled. Fixed exchange rates in many countries in Latin America and others like Egypt (as discussed in the next chapter) have helped economies to reduce inflation. In countries with a history of failed stabilization attempts, extreme forms of pegged exchange rate regimes (such as **currency boards**) may be the appropriate choice. However, the credibility gain may come at a high price; because of the loss in flexibility. Argentina is a case in point (see Chapter 7).

- The degree of **capital mobility.** The more open the economy is to capital movements, the more difficult it is to defend and maintain a fixed exchange rate regime. A fixed exchange rate, in a world of high capital mobility, is a target for speculators because it offers a *one-sided bet.* As noted earlier, it leads to *overborrowing* on world capital markets and to increases in spending and **speculative bubbles**—increases in asset prices (stock and property prices) that are unwarranted by the evolution of fundamentals. This weakens the financial sector, which may in turn lower confidence in the capacity of the authorities to defend the pegged rate regime.

The higher degree of capital mobility around the world (as discussed in Chapter 6) has indeed made pegged exchange rate regimes (adjustable or not) less credible and more difficult to sustain—even with sound economic fundamentals and a consistent policy mix. The vulnerability of such systems to abrupt changes in investor sentiment was well illustrated by some recent currency crises (see Chapter 7). As a result, economists like Obstfeld and Rogoff (1995) have argued that nowadays it may be preferable for countries to adopt either *permanently fixed* exchange rates (as in a monetary union) or *fully flexible* exchange rates.

More generally, the limitations that open capital markets and high capital mobility place on exchange rate management and monetary policy are well summed up by the notion of the **open-economy trilemma** emphasized by Obstfeld (1998): a country cannot simultaneously maintain fixed exchange rates and an open capital market while pursuing a monetary policy geared toward domestic economic objectives. Policymakers may choose only two of the above. If monetary policy is determined by domestic economic goals, either capital mobility or the exchange rate target must go. If a fixed exchange-rate regime and a highly open capital account are the primary policy goals, the goal of maintaining an autonomous monetary policy must be abandoned. Thus, the more important the exchange rate is as a policy goal, the more constrained monetary policy is in pursing other (domestic) policy objectives.

Finally, it is also important to emphasize that considerations affecting the choice of exchange rate regime (as well as policymakers' preferences) *may change over time.* When inflation is high, a pegged exchange rate may prove more effective at reducing it, at least in the short run (see Chapter 5). But when stabilization is achieved, countries should shift toward a more flexible regime. *Israel*'s exchange rate policy, for instance, entailed moving from a fixed exchange rate (imposed in the mid-1980s to stabilize from high inflation) to a currency band that was subsequently widened to prevent a *loss of competitiveness*. This **exit strategy** is particularly relevant when the resumption in economic activity is associated with inflationary pressures and in cases where large capital inflows are occurring. Under these circumstances, a more flexible exchange rate may help alleviate inflationary pressures and prevent an overvaluation of the real exchange rate (Eichengreen and Masson (1998)).

An exit strategy that may prove attractive is that of a **crawling band regime** (as discussed earlier) where the exchange rate is allowed to float within certain limits and the band itself is devalued according to a predefined path— determined on the basis of, say, the inflation differential between the domestic economy and its major trade partners. The aim of this regime is, as noted earlier, to get the best of both worlds: to give some anchor against inflationary expectations, but also to avoid overvaluation and restore the *two-way bet* for speculators by using sufficiently wide margins. Inflation is thus reduced more slowly, but as long as fiscal discipline is maintained the bands can be preserved. Without fiscal consolidation, however, this regime is no more successful than any other, as illustrated by Brazil's recent decision to abandon its band regime. Sustained fiscal imbalances lead to high domestic interest rates, attracting short-term capital inflows; an abrupt change in market sentiment may lead to unsustainable outflows—forcing the central bank to abandon the upper intervention rate and let the exchange rate float. From that perspective, the issue, then, is not one of *fixed versus floating rates*, but rather *good versus bad policies*.

4.4   Policy Trade-Offs and Exchange Rate Credibility

The underlying theme of most of the foregoing discussion is the notion that the use of the exchange rate as a policy instrument typically entails a *trade-off* among policy objectives. For instance, attempts to maintain a fixed exchange rate in the presence of high domestic inflation (which tends to reduce competitiveness) and a large and growing current account deficit is usually not viable if official reserves and the country's capacity to borrow on world capital markets are limited. Conversely, although a devaluation of the nominal exchange rate can lead to a depreciation of the real exchange rate and improve the trade balance (as discussed in the next section), it may lead to a rise in domestic prices—ultimately eroding the initial positive effect on competitiveness.

A key argument of the recent literature on exchange rate management is that a fixed exchange rate can lend *credibility* to a government's commitment to a stable monetary policy. By lowering inflationary expectations and thus interest rates, increased credibility can lead to higher output. The problem, however, is that the government's commitment to fixing the exchange rate may, itself, lack credibility. The reason is that, as indicated above, governments face **policy trade-offs** in choosing whether or not to fix the exchange rate. In particular, the government may be *tempted to renege* on its promise to keep the exchange rate fixed because of potentially high returns to an unexpected devaluation. Thus, unless the **cost of devaluation** (economic or political) is sufficiently high, a fixed exchange rate will almost never achieve full credibility.

A simple model that describes the type of policy trade-offs that governments face when choosing to fix the exchange rate was developed by Welch and McLeod (1993) and is presented here. The authorities face a trade-off in the following situation.

- On the one hand, a depreciation of the real exchange rate lowers imports and stimulates exports, thereby leading to the *accumulation of foreign exchange*. Foreign reserves, in turn, improve the supply of liquidity services for external transactions.[12]

- On the other, however, a nominal devaluation raises domestic prices through its effect on the price of imported (intermediate and final) goods.

To capture this policy trade-off between inflation and the accumulation of foreign reserves, suppose first that *unanticipated* depreciations of the domestic currency improve the balance of payments, that is, the change in the central bank's foreign reserves, ΔR:

$$\Delta R = \alpha(\varepsilon - \varepsilon^a) + u, \quad \alpha > 0, \tag{4.1}$$

where ε (ε^a) is the actual (anticipated) rate of depreciation of the nominal exchange rate, and u a random external shock with zero mean and variance σ_u^2. This equation can be viewed as a *quasi-reduced form* derived from a model in which output itself depends on unanticipated movements in prices. Indeed, assuming that the economy produces only a tradable good, that purchasing power parity holds continuously, and that world inflation is zero, the *actual* rate of inflation, π, is equal to the rate of depreciation, ε. Suppose that the *expected* inflation rate (or devaluation rate) by the private sector, π^a, is set *before* the government decides whether or not to alter the path of the exchange rate. π^a and π may in general differ; the private sector's loss function is thus a function of the difference $\pi - \pi^a$. But *on average*, inflation expectations must be correct. Thus, to minimize losses due to incorrect predictions, private agents will act so as to ensure that, *ex post*,

$$\pi^a = \mathrm{E}\pi, \text{ or } \varepsilon^a = \mathrm{E}\varepsilon. \tag{4.2}$$

The central bank's **loss function**, L, is assumed to be **quadratic** and is given by

$$L = \frac{\varepsilon^2}{2} + \frac{\beta}{2}(\Delta R - \Delta \tilde{R})^2, \quad \beta > 0, \tag{4.3}$$

---

[12] As noted by Welch and McLeod (1993), foreign reserves also have an *insurance value* that may be particularly high for those countries that do not have access to trade-contingent debt instruments issued on internatrional capital markets.

where $\Delta\tilde{R}$ denotes the *desired change* in reserves (assumed constant), and β a coefficient that measures the trade-off between inflation and international reserves; the higher β is, the higher the weight policymakers will attach to deviations of reserves from their target value.

Suppose that the central bank can react to shocks *faster* than the public, because prices are set before the shock is revealed. The central bank will then be able to cause *temporary deviations* from purchasing power parity by unexpectedly changing the nominal exchange rate. More specifically, suppose that the *timing of events* is as follows:

- The private sector sets its devaluation (or inflation) expectations and enters into contracts based on these expectations.

- The economy is hit by a random external shock (to the terms of trade or the world interest rate, for instance), u.

- The central bank sets the devaluation rate on the basis of the observed value of the shock.

Given this sequence, the equilibrium solutions are given as follows. Under **discretion**, or flexible exchange rate regime, the central bank chooses the rate of devaluation so as to minimize its policy loss. Formally, substituting Equation (4.1) in Equation (4.3) yields

$$L = \frac{\varepsilon^2}{2} + \frac{\beta}{2}[\alpha(\varepsilon - \varepsilon^a) + u - \Delta\tilde{R}]^2. \tag{4.4}$$

Minimizing this expression with respect to ε implies setting $\partial L/\partial\varepsilon = 0$, which yields

$$\varepsilon + \alpha\beta[\alpha(\varepsilon - \varepsilon^a) + u - \Delta\tilde{R}] = 0,$$

that is, with $\Omega = 1 + \alpha^2\beta$:

$$\varepsilon = \alpha\beta\frac{(\alpha\varepsilon^a - u + \Delta\tilde{R})}{1 + \alpha^2\beta} = \frac{\alpha^2\beta}{\Omega}\varepsilon^a + \frac{\alpha\beta(\Delta\tilde{R} - u)}{\Omega}. \tag{4.5}$$

Equation (4.5) represents the policymaker's **reaction function**, which takes the expected inflation-devaluation rate, ε^a, as given. In equilibrium, however, the value of ε^a must be consistent with the (expected) value of the devaluation rate set by the central bank, as given by its reaction function. Setting $\varepsilon^a = E\varepsilon$ in Equation (4.5), and noting that $Eu = 0$, this condition implies that

$$\varepsilon^a = \alpha\beta\Delta\tilde{R}. \tag{4.6}$$

Substituting this result back in Equation (4.5) yields

$$\varepsilon = \frac{\alpha\beta}{\Omega}(\Omega\Delta\tilde{R} - u) = \alpha\beta\Delta\tilde{R} - \frac{\alpha\beta}{\Omega}u, \tag{4.7}$$

which implies that

$$\varepsilon - \varepsilon^a = -\frac{\alpha\beta}{\Omega}u. \tag{4.8}$$

Substituting Equation (4.8) in Equation (4.1) implies that the actual change in reserves is

$$\Delta R = \alpha(-\frac{\alpha\beta}{\Omega})u + u = \frac{u}{\Omega}. \tag{4.9}$$

Because $\varepsilon^a = \mathrm{E}\varepsilon$, the private sector's expected loss is zero. Substituting Equations (4.6), (4.8), and (4.9) in (4.4) implies that

$$L = \frac{1}{2}\left\{\alpha\beta\Delta\tilde{R} - \frac{\alpha\beta}{\Omega}u\right\}^2 + \frac{\beta}{2}(\frac{u}{\Omega} - \Delta\tilde{R})^2.$$

Because u is uncorrelated with $\Delta\tilde{R}$, the *expected* loss of the central bank is

$$EL^D = \frac{(\alpha\beta)^2}{2}\Delta\tilde{R}^2 + (\frac{\alpha\beta}{\Omega})^2\frac{\sigma_u^2}{2} + \frac{\beta}{2}(\frac{\sigma_u^2}{\Omega^2} + \Delta\tilde{R}^2),$$

or equivalently

$$EL^D = \frac{\beta}{2}\left[\Omega\Delta\tilde{R}^2 + \frac{\sigma_u^2}{\Omega}\right]. \tag{4.10}$$

Under a **credible precommitment**, the central bank irrevocably fixes the exchange rate; the devaluation rate will thus be zero ($\varepsilon = 0$) and the private sector will also expect $\varepsilon^a = 0$. Setting $\varepsilon = \varepsilon^a = 0$ in Equation (4.1) implies that *actual* movements in reserves are given by

$$\Delta R = u. \tag{4.11}$$

Substituting this result in Equation (4.3), with $\varepsilon = 0$, yields

$$L^F = \beta(u - \Delta\tilde{R})^2/2.$$

Again, because $\varepsilon = \varepsilon^a$, the private sector's expected loss is zero. With u uncorrelated with $\Delta\tilde{R}$, the expected loss for the policymaker is simply

$$EL^F = \frac{\beta}{2}(\Delta\tilde{R}^2 + \sigma_u^2). \tag{4.12}$$

In the absence of a commitment mechanism that forces the central bank to maintain the fixed exchange rate, the best option (or *dominant strategy*) for the government is **discretion**, or a *flexible exchange rate*. The reason is that the payoff to the central bank when $\varepsilon > 0$ is *unambiguously larger* than when $\varepsilon = 0$. Knowing this, the private sector will always expect the central bank to opt for a flexible exchange rate regime. As a result, the **equilibrium outcome** will be the discretionary one.

On the contrary, suppose indeed that there is a commitment mechanism (such as legislation or membership in a **currency union**) that allows the central bank to precommit credibly to a fixed exchange rate. Is commitment always preferable? Consider first the case in which there are no random shocks to the economy, or equivalently here $\sigma_u^2 = 0$. From Equations (4.10) and (4.12),

$$\mathrm{EL}^D = \frac{\beta \Omega \Delta \tilde{R}^2}{2}, \quad \mathrm{EL}^F = \frac{\beta \Delta \tilde{R}^2}{2}, \tag{4.13}$$

which implies that, because $\Omega > 1$:

$$\mathrm{EL}^D > \mathrm{EL}^F.$$

Thus, the loss under discretion always exceeds the loss under commitment; a fixed exchange rate regime is always preferable.

Does this result continue to hold in the presence of random shocks, that is, $\sigma_u^2 \neq 0$? Subtracting the expression for EL^C given in Equation (4.12) from the expression for EL^D given in (4.10) yields

$$\mathrm{EL}^D - \mathrm{EL}^F = \frac{(\alpha\beta)^2}{2} \left[\Delta \tilde{R}^2 - \frac{\sigma_u^2}{\Omega} \right], \tag{4.14}$$

the sign of which is in general *ambiguous*. What this means is that even if there is indeed a commitment technology that allows the central bank to establish an irrevocably and fully credible fixed exchange rate, discretion may be preferable to precommitment. Specifically, as long as $\mathrm{EL}^D - \mathrm{EL}^F < 0$, the central bank is better off choosing discretion. It can be established that the effect of an increase in $\Delta \tilde{R}$ on the quantity $\mathrm{EL}^D - \mathrm{EL}^F$ is positive, that of σ_u^2 negative, and that of α and β ambiguous. For instance, the higher the degree of volatility of external shocks (the higher σ_u^2 is), the more likely it is that the central bank will choose a discretionary regime.

The foregoing analysis also indicates that fixed and flexible exchange rate regimes have different implications for inflation and reserves. If the central bank can credibly commit to the exchange rate rule that sets $\varepsilon = 0$, the equilibrium rates of exchange rate depreciation and inflation, ε, will be *zero*, whereas actual reserve fluctuations will completely accommodate external shocks [Equation (4.11)]. However, the higher the variance of the external shock u, or the larger the central bank's desired level of reserve accumulation, the higher will be its welfare loss.

One apparent possibility for the central bank to improve on the outcome associated with a policy of setting $\varepsilon = 0$ might involve **cheating**: the central bank may begin by announcing a fixed exchange rate and then choose to devalue. The reason is that *expected* inflation, upon announcement, *drops to zero*. Formally, maximizing Equation (4.4) with respect to ε with $\varepsilon^a = 0$ [or directly setting $\varepsilon^a = 0$ in the reaction function (4.5)] yields

$$\varepsilon = \frac{\alpha\beta(\Delta \tilde{R} - u)}{\Omega}. \tag{4.15}$$

Substituting this result in Equation (4.1) with $\varepsilon^a = 0$ implies that *actual* reserve accumulation under cheating will be

$$\Delta R = \alpha\varepsilon + u = \frac{\alpha^2 \beta \Delta \tilde{R}}{\Omega} + \frac{u}{\Omega}. \tag{4.16}$$

Substituting Equations (4.15) and (4.16) in (4.3) yields

$$L = \frac{1}{2}\left\{ \frac{\alpha\beta(\Delta\tilde{R} - u)}{\Omega} \right\}^2 + \frac{\beta}{2}[\frac{u}{\Omega} - (1 - \frac{\alpha^2\beta}{\Omega})\Delta\tilde{R}]^2.$$

The *expected* loss of the central bank is now

$$EL^C = (\frac{\alpha\beta}{\Omega})^2\frac{\Delta\tilde{R}^2}{2} + (\frac{\alpha\beta}{\Omega})^2\frac{\sigma_u^2}{2} + \frac{\beta}{2}(\frac{\sigma_u^2}{\Omega^2} + \frac{\Delta\tilde{R}^2}{\Omega^2}),$$

that is

$$EL^C = \left\{ (\frac{\alpha\beta}{\Omega})^2 + \frac{\beta}{\Omega^2} \right\}\left\{ \frac{\Delta\tilde{R}^2 + \sigma_u^2}{2} \right\}.$$

Because

$$(\frac{\alpha\beta}{\Omega})^2 + \frac{\beta}{\Omega^2} = \beta\frac{(1 + \alpha^2\beta)}{\Omega^2} = \frac{\beta}{\Omega},$$

EL^C can also be written as

$$EL^C = \frac{\beta}{\Omega}\left\{ \frac{\Delta\tilde{R}^2 + \sigma_u^2}{2} \right\}. \tag{4.17}$$

Suppose that $\sigma_u^2 = 0$. Using Equations (4.13) and (4.17), it can be shown that

$$EL^D > EL^F > EL^C.$$

Thus, although three regimes generate positive expected losses, the expected loss under cheating is lower than the expected loss obtained under commitment and discretion. Such a situation, however, is *not consistent*. The public would recognize the central bank's **incentive to cheat**, and the equilibrium outcome would revert to the discretionary flexible exchange rate case.[13] Rational individuals will recognize the policymaker's incentive to renege on its exchange rate announcement and will set expectations and prices to ensure that the *marginal cost* of devaluing is equal to the *marginal benefit* to the central bank.

The thrust of the foregoing analysis is that, in a setting in which both low inflation and accumulation of foreign exchange reserves are policy objectives, the possibility that the central bank can increase reserves by devaluing will hamper the credibility of a fixed exchange rate regime and lead to a **devaluation** or **inflation bias**—as long as the desired change in reserves is positive ($\Delta\tilde{R} > 0$), the central bank values reserve accumulation ($\beta > 0$), and exchange rate changes affect the balance of payments ($\alpha > 0$). Private agents, knowing that the central bank has an incentive to devalue to accumulate reserves, will expect a devaluation to occur. They will set prices accordingly, generating positive

---

[13] Also, once the public realizes that the government has cheated, it will lose *reputation*, which may be difficult to regain and will increase the policy loss over time. See Agénor (1994) and Cukierman (1992).

inflation regardless of the central bank's announced policy stance. Even if the central bank does not actually devalue when private agents expect it to happen, the economy will suffer from positive inflation.

Because $\Omega > 1$, the coefficient of the random variable u in the solution for reserves under discretion [Equation (4.9)] is *lower* than the corresponding coefficient under fixed exchange rates [Equation (4.11)]. The flexible exchange rate regime is thus better able to *dampen fluctuations* in foreign exchange reserves resulting from unexpected external shocks. Again, however, as in the case of a credibly fixed exchange rate, in equilibrium the central bank cannot affect the *expected* change (or *average* change) in foreign reserves.

The foregoing discussion is a useful illustration of how policy trade-offs affect the choice of an exchange rate regime. Although a credible commitment to a fixed exchange rate regime may eliminate the inflationary bias associated with the flexible rate regime, it also increases the economy's *vulnerability to external shocks*—as discussed above in relation to Equation (4.14). The choice of regime, therefore, depends on the relative importance the central bank attaches to each of these two policy objectives. More generally, whether a country should opt for a fixed exchange rate regime depends also on how much the central bank values reserves relative to inflation, β, how sensitive changes in reserve are to unexpected movements in the exchange rate, α, and the targeted change in reserves, $\Delta\tilde{R}$.

Other models that emphasize the trade-off that the use of the exchange rate as a policy instrument entails include those of Agénor (1994), Agénor and Masson (1999), and Devarajan and Rodrik (1992). Agénor (1994) emphasized the trade-off between the **competitiveness effect** (the fact that a nominal devaluation may lead to a real depreciation and an expansion of exports) and the **inflationary effect**, whereas Agénor and Masson focused on the trade-off between the **interest rate effect** and the **inflationary effect** in the presence of external shocks to the balance of payments and imperfect capital mobility. The interest rate effect results from the fact that an adverse shock to, say, capital flows lowers official reserves. In the absence of *complete sterilization* (as defined in Chapter 6), the fall in reserves translates into a fall in the money supply— which in turn puts upward pressure on domestic interest rates. Such movements in interest rates may have adverse effects on output—or, as discussed in more detail in Chapter 7, may exacerbate weaknesses in the banking system.

Devarajan and Rodrik (1992) considered a model in which the trade-off that policymakers face in managing the exchange rate involves

- the inflationary bias associated with exchange rate flexibility, as in the models discussed above;

- the fact that exchange rate changes can be used to reduce *output variability* by smoothing the consequences of *terms-of-trade shocks* on output.

In this model, as in the Welch-McLeod framework described earlier, it is not possible to rank *a priori* fixed and flexible (or discretionary) exchange rate regimes.

- For large terms-of-trade shocks flexible exchange rates are likely to be superior. Likewise, the more vulnerable the real economy is to these terms-of-trade shocks, the more desirable are flexible arrangements.

- The greater the policymaker's built-in inflationary (devaluation) bias, the greater is the temptation to implement a surprise devaluation, and the less desirable will a fixed arrangement be.

Finally, an important point conveyed by Agell, Calmfors, and Jonsson (1996) is the need to take into account not only the credibility problems that arise when the exchange rate *alone* is used as a policy instrument, but also the problems that may surface when *other instruments* are used at the *same time* by policymakers. Specifically, Agell, Calmfors and Jonsson (1996) considered the *interdependence* between exchange rate and *fiscal policies* in a small open economy, and its implications for the credibility of a peg. Their analysis uses a model in which the policymaker can use both exchange rate and fiscal policies to affect output and employment. They showed that the equilibrium under discretion involves both inflation (that is, a **devaluation bias**, as in the model described earlier) as well as *accumulation of public debt*. Under the commitment regime in which the exchange rate is credibly fixed, inflation is lower; but this does not unambiguously improve welfare. The reason is that in the absence of adequate restrictions on fiscal policy, the reduction in inflation is achieved at the expense of increased government deficits. Fiscal rules can, of course, be criticized. They often carry an arbitrary nature. More importantly, policymakers may need fiscal flexibility in the case of adverse shocks facing the economy. Nevertheless, the analysis by Agell, Calmfors, and Jonsson provides a crucial reminder of the importance of understanding the interactions between different policy instruments in the analysis of credibility issues.

4.5   Exchange Rates, Competitiveness, and the Trade Balance

Exchange rate adjustment has often figured prominently in adjustment programs implemented in countries suffering from chronically high current account deficits. The reason is that changes in nominal exchange rates can have significant effects on international competitiveness and trade flows, despite the fact that these effects can take a substantial amount of time to materialize. It is thus important to understand the mechanisms through which changes in nominal exchange rates affect imports and exports, and more generally economic activity. This section begins by describing some of the most commonly used measures of competitiveness. It then examines, using a partial equilibrium approach, the effect of devaluation on the trade balance. The next section will extend the analysis to consider a complete macroeconomic model and will study the effect of exchange rate changes not only on trade flows but also on real output.

4.5.1   Measuring Competitiveness

Measures of international competitiveness attempt to capture changes in the relative price of foreign tradable goods relative to domestic tradable goods; they are generally based on *real exchange rate indicators*.[14] As discussed by Marsh and Tokarick (1996), there are three widely used measures of international competitiveness for developing countries: those based, respectively, on *consumer prices, export unit values*, and *unit labor costs*.

The most frequently used measure of competitiveness is the real exchange rate based on consumer prices, z_C. This index is given by

$$z_C = E \cdot P_C^* / P_C, \tag{4.18}$$

where E is the nominal exchange rate (measured in units of domestic currency for one unit of foreign currency), and P_C (P_C^*) the domestic (foreign) consumer price index.[15] A rise in the domestic consumer price index relative to the foreign consumer price index would thus translate into an *appreciation* of the real exchange rate (a fall in z_C).

A major reason why the real exchange rate based on consumer prices, Equation (4.18), is often used in practice to assess competitiveness is because consumer price indices are *readily available* and published at *regular intervals*. However, there are also several drawbacks associated with the use of such indices in a developing-country context.

- Consumer price indices tend to exhibit *significant volatility* (due for instance to sharp changes in the price of nontraded agricultural goods), which may be unrelated to competitiveness.

- The domestic price index may be influenced by various types of *government interventions* (including *price controls* and *excise taxes*), which may affect its reliability.

- Changes in prices of *intermediate goods* (which account for a significant portion of foreign trade for many developing countries) are excluded from consumer price indices, thereby reducing their adequacy for measuring changes in competitiveness.

- Because consumer price indices include prices of *imported final goods*, they tend to reflect movements in the *nominal exchange rate*; as a result, they may understate changes in competitiveness. For instance, if the country's nominal exchange rate depreciates, the domestic-currency price of its imports will rise; and by raising consumer prices, the extent of the country's real depreciation will be reduced.

---

[14]Note that the real exchange rate here *does not* correspond to the relative price of tradable and nontradable goods *within* the country (that is, a measure of the terms of trade across production sectors), as used elsewhere in this book.

[15]For simplicity of exposition, the discussion assumes that the rest of the world consists of a single foreign country. In practice, all trading partners are weighted together to form a *composite* foreign country; the real exchange rate thus becomes a real *effective* exchange rate. For details, see, for instance, Bahmani-Oskooee (1995).

- Such indices often do not reflect accurately underlying developments in *factor costs*.

Another commonly used indicator of competitiveness is the real exchange rate index based on *export unit values* of manufacturing products, defined as

$$z_X = E \cdot P_{XV}^* / P_{XV}, \tag{4.19}$$

where P_{XV} is an index of export unit values of the home country, and P_{XV}^* a similar index for foreign competitors. This index, of course, is particularly relevant to explain the behavior of a country's exports. Although it does not contain any information relevant for assessing the performance of imports, it may be more appropriate than the index based on consumer prices (which includes the price of nontraded goods) to explain the behavior of the trade balance. A major drawback of this measure is that export unit values, being computed by dividing the nominal value of exports by the quantity exported, measure only the *average value* of exports per physical unit. They are thus *proxies* for the prices of exports, not the actual prices at which transactions take place. Changes in the index (4.19) are thus sensitive to changes in the composition of exports across countries—which can be themselves unrelated to changes in competitiveness per se.[16]

The third commonly-used indicator of competitiveness is based on *relative unit labor costs* in the manufacturing sector. For each country, the index of unit labor costs is defined as the ratio of an index of *hourly compensation per worker* in the manufacturing sector (obtained as total earnings of labor divided by employment) to an index of *value added per man-hour*, that is, *productivity*.[17] Formally, this indicator is defined as

$$z_L = \frac{E I_{ULC}^*}{I_{ULC}} = \frac{E w_M^* L_M^* / V_M^*}{w_M L_M / V_M}, \tag{4.20}$$

where w_M, L_M, and V_M (respectively, w_M^*, L_M^*, and V_M^*) are the wage rate, employment, and real value added—or real output—in the domestic (respectively foreign) manufacturing sector. This index is particularly useful as an indicator of competitiveness (and profitability) in manufacturing for countries where *wage costs* are an important component of production costs. However, it also has its limitations (Marsh and Tokarick, 1996).

- It becomes less useful where (as is the case in many developing countries) a variety of *intermediate inputs* are used in the production process and where *nonwage labor compensation* or capital costs are high.

- Unit labor costs are not always reliable and can be highly sensitive to *cyclical movements* in labor productivity.

---

[16] Export prices may also be heavily influenced by price strategies in the short run, such as *pricing to market*. See Marsh and Tokarick (1996).

[17] The index is also often calculated by using *normalized unit labor costs*, which are obtained by removing the cyclical movement in costs—using, for instance, the *Hodrick-Prescott filter* discussed in Chapter 9.

- Changes in unit labor costs may also reflect *substitution* among production factors rather than changes in competitiveness. For instance, an increase in *capital intensity* may raise the productivity of labor and lower unit labor costs without improving competitiveness, because capital now represents a higher share of unit production costs.

Cost- and price-based measures of competitiveness are related in a number of ways. To the extent, for instance, that the consumer price index is a (linear) function of the price of value added of each good produced in the economy (including manufacturing goods), and if each value-added price can be written as a function of labor costs and capital costs (profits), the real exchange rate indices based on consumer prices and unit labor costs are clearly related. However, to the extent that prices of intermediate goods or capital change over time, and to the extent that such changes are reflected in consumer prices, the behavior of the two indices can be markedly different.

Figure 4.4 compares, for a group of 20 developing countries for which data were available, the coefficient of variation—the ratio of the standard error to the mean—of the real effective exchange rate based on consumer prices and on unit labor costs, for the period 1979-95. Very few observations are actually located on or near the 45-degree line—a result that suggests that the two indices may provide very different pictures of real exchange rate fluctuations and thus changes in competitiveness. The implication of the above analysis is thus that although the consumer price-based real effective exchange rate remains the main index used for exchange rate analysis for the large majority of developing countries (principally because of data availability and comprehensiveness of coverage), it often does not necessarily provide an accurate measure of export competitiveness.

4.5.2   Devaluation and the Trade Balance

The effect of exchange rate changes on trade flows and the trade balance has been the subject of much debate in open-economy macroeconomics. The conventional analysis suggests that a nominal devaluation affects the economy through two types of channels:

- as an **expenditure-reducing** policy, it reduces private spending and aggregate demand by raising the *price level* and lowering *real money balances*—or, more generally, the real value of financial assets;

- as an **expenditure-switching** policy, it influences the composition of output and domestic absorption between traded goods (importables and exportables) and nontraded goods.

These supply- and demand-side effects of a nominal devaluation operate through its impact on relative prices and depend on various structural characteristics, including price and wage formation mechanisms in the nontradable sector. To the extent that prices of production inputs (labor and capital, say) rise *less than proportionately* to the increase in the domestic-currency price of output, a devaluation may lead to an expansion in activity—at least in the short run. The increase in the relative price of importables also tends to lower the demand for them and to increase demand for nontradables; this also tends to stimulate domestic output in the short run.

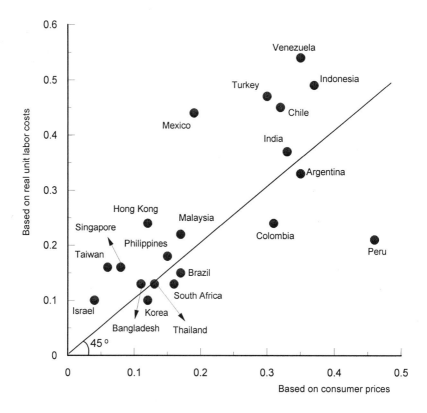

Figure 4.4. Coefficient of Variation of Real Effective Exchange Rates (Averages over 1979-95).

Source: International Monetary Fund.

Analysis of the effects of exchange rate changes on the trade balance is often performed in a *partial equilibrium* framework, that is, by analyzing solely the effects of parity changes on trade flows. For simplicity, suppose that the country considered produces only one good, which is used for both exports and domestic consumption. The price of the good, P, is fixed on domestic markets.[18] Let X and J denote the nominal values of exports and imports, respectively, defined as

---

[18] This assumption is not quite valid for most developing economies (export prices for these countries are usually set on world markets), but it will be adopted here, again, to simplify the presentation.

$X = PQ_X$ and $J = P_J Q_J$, where Q_X and Q_J are real exports and real imports. P_J is the price of imported goods measured in domestic-currency terms, that is, $P_J = E P_J^*$, with E the nominal exchange rate and P_J^* the world price. The trade balance in real terms (that is, in terms of the price of domestic goods) can be written as $b = Q_X - z Q_J$, where $z = P_J/P$ measures the relative price of imports in terms of domestic goods. The change in b is given by

$$\Delta b = \Delta Q_X - z \Delta Q_J - Q_J \Delta z,$$

which implies that

$$\frac{\Delta b}{\Delta z} = \frac{\Delta Q_X}{\Delta z} - z \left(\frac{\Delta Q_J}{\Delta z} \right) - Q_J,$$

or equivalently

$$\frac{\Delta b}{\Delta z} = \left(\frac{Q_X}{z} \right) \left\{ \left(\frac{\Delta Q_X}{Q_X} \right) \left(\frac{z}{\Delta z} \right) - z \left(\frac{\Delta Q_J}{\Delta z} \right) \left(\frac{z}{Q_X} \right) - \frac{z Q_J}{Q_X} \right\}.$$

Suppose that trade is balanced initially, so that $Q_X = z Q_J$. The above expression can be rewritten as

$$\frac{\Delta b}{\Delta z} = \left(\frac{Q_X}{z} \right) \left\{ \left(\frac{\Delta Q_X}{Q_X} \right) \left(\frac{z}{\Delta z} \right) - \left(\frac{\Delta Q_J}{\Delta z} \right) \left(\frac{z}{Q_J} \right) - 1 \right\}. \qquad (4.21)$$

Let $\eta_X \equiv (\Delta Q_X/Q_X)(z/\Delta z)$ be the relative price elasticity of the foreign demand for exports, and let $\eta_J \equiv -(\Delta Q_J/Q_J)(z/\Delta z)$ be (the absolute value of) the elasticity of the domestic demand for imports. Equation (4.21) then becomes

$$\frac{\Delta b}{\Delta z} = \left(\frac{Q_X}{z} \right) (\eta_X + \eta_J - 1),$$

or equivalently

$$\Delta b = \left(\frac{\Delta z}{z} \right) Q_X (\eta_X + \eta_J - 1). \qquad (4.22)$$

With given levels of domestic prices and the foreign-currency price of imports, $\Delta z/z = \Delta E/E$; an increase in the relative price z therefore reflects solely a nominal depreciation. Thus, Equation (4.22) requires, for the trade balance to improve ($\Delta b > 0$) following a devaluation, that

$$\eta_X + \eta_J > 1, \qquad (4.23)$$

which is known as the **Marshall-Lerner condition**: the sum of the elasticities of export supply and import demand must exceed unity for the trade balance to improve.[19]

The Marshall-Lerner condition suggests that a key step in assessing the effect of exchange rate changes on the trade balance is to assess the sensitivity

---

[19] The derivations given here assume that the supply elasticities of exports and imports are infinite. For a more detailed derivation of the Marshall-Lerner condition, see Södersten (1980, pp. 363-366).

of trade flows to changes in relative prices. In practice, such attempts take the form of estimating econometrically equations in which volumes of exports and imports are related to changes in relative prices and to changes in real activity either at home (for imports) or abroad (for exports). Such equations have consistently been used in policy work and macroeconomic models (see Chapter 9), although much of the early empirical work in this area lacked precision in the determination of real exchange rate elasticities. This lack of precision was associated with several factors.

- The use of *aggregate data* on trade flows, as is often the case in practice, may obscure differences in behavior across different *types of goods*, such as manufactured products and commodities. Figures 4.5 and 4.6 show the composition of merchandise exports and imports, respectively, in 1993 for a group of developing countries. The relative importance of food items, for instance, varies significantly across countries; price elasticities may also be very different.

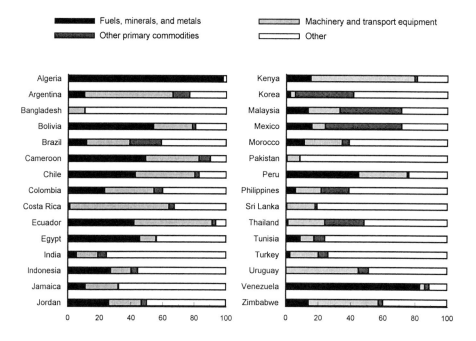

Figure 4.5. Composition of Merchandise Exports (Percent of total, 1993). Source: World Bank.

- Real exchange rate measures based on *consumer prices* have often been used in empirical studies because of their availability. As discussed earlier, however, such measures may not reflect adequately movements in the *price of tradable goods* because they also include prices of nontraded goods.

- Changes in the *trade policy regime* or shifts in the type of goods being traded over time may be important and are often inadequately captured in estimated regressions.

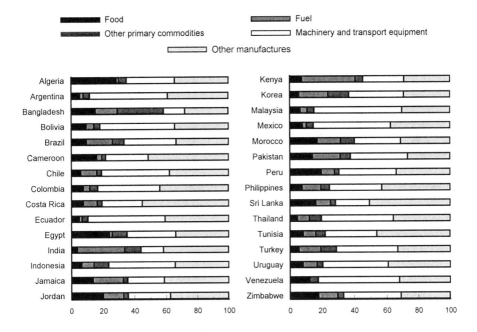

Figure 4.6. Composition of Merchandise Imports (Percent of total, 1993). Source: World Bank.

More recent studies continue to face some of these problems but have relied increasingly on **cointegration analysis** (as briefly described in the Appendix to Chapter 2) to achieve greater precision and determine short- and long-run elasticities. For instance, the empirical estimates of elasticities derived by Reinhart (1995) indicated a long-run price elasticity of import demand of -0.7 for Kenya, and a long-run price elasticity of export supply of 0.2, suggesting that the Marshall-Lerner condition is not satisfied. By contrast, the results for Colombia indicated a price elasticity of import demand of -1.4 and a price elasticity of export supply of 0.5, which ensured that a real depreciation would improve the trade balance. In general, empirical studies emphasize the importance of distinguishing between *short-* and *long-term* elasticities. For instance, the econometric results provided by Senhadji (1998, p. 264)—using again cointegration techniques—indicated that the short-term price elasticity for the real imports of goods and services of Nigeria was -0.3, whereas the long-term elasticity was -0.8.

Various other empirical studies confirm that there is a significant difference in the timing of the responses of trade volumes to activity and relative prices. Although the *real activity effect* occurs *almost immediately*, the response of trade volumes to changes in real exchange rates builds more gradually over time. Because a devaluation produces an unfavorable terms-of-trade response, with the domestic-currency value of import prices rising relative to export prices, the initial impact of a fall in the exchange rate on the nominal trade balance can be small or perverse. The expected effects of the exchange rate on the nominal trade balance may become apparent only in the medium term.

A possible explanation for this evidence is that apart from the price effects induced by a devaluation on the value of imports and exports, the response of *quantities* to these price changes may involve considerable time delays. If exports are invoiced in *local currency*, whereas imports are invoiced in *foreign currency*, the initial effect of the devaluation is to worsen the trade balance as the value of exports in foreign currency falls, while the dollar value of imports increases. Thus, as a result of a devaluation, the trade balance may get worse initially before it gets any better. This particular phenomenon gives rise to the so-called **J-curve effect**.

More generally, the literature focusing on the links between the exchange rate and the prices of internationally traded goods characterizes the **exchange rate pass-through**, or the degree to which exchange rate changes are reflected in the destination-country currency prices of traded goods, as consisting of the following phases (see Menon, 1995):

- An initial phase, the *currency contract* period, in which capital gains or losses on outstanding contracts are observed.

- A *pass-through* period, in which prices respond to the new exchange rate but quantities of trade are not yet affected.

- A *quantity adjustment* period, in which quantities and prices move toward a new equilibrium.

The trade balance can move in almost any direction in each of these subperiods, and the duration of the lags that are involved in the second and third phases—which depend, in particular, on product characteristics and whether **pricing-to-market behavior** (see Krugman, 1987; and Marsh and Tokarick, 1996) is present or not bears significantly on the overall outcome of the adjustment process. Put differently, a low pass-through would make it possible for trade flows to remain relatively insensitive to exchange rate changes, despite demand being highly elastic. Furthermore, if significant lags exist in the transmission of exchange rate changes to prices, and the subsequent lag in the response of trade volumes to the relative price change is also sizable, then the overall balance of payments adjustment process could be severely hampered.

Another important empirical issue is whether or not *supply terms* should also be included in export equations. Standard export volume equations only take account of *demand factors*, such as the growth of foreign income and relative prices, as indicated earlier. In a traditional demand and supply framework, the addition of a supply term involves relaxing the assumption that supply is *perfectly elastic*, which is used to identify the export equation. An alternative explanation, however, is the following. Suppose that all economies have the same underlying elasticities with respect to income. Then, with stable real exchange rates, *high-growth* economies should show a tendency for imports to *grow faster* than exports, whereas slow-growing economies should exhibit the opposite characteristic. Two factors may be responsible.

- As output expands, so does the *number of brands* produced by a country. Because consumers desire *diversity*, this increase in brands generates an increase in demand for exports (see Krugman, 1989a).

- The expansion of output supply may be correlated with the development of *higher-quality products* at prices that lead to an increase in the demand for exports.

This differential in the growth of exports and imports should be offset by an *appreciation* of the real exchange rate of faster-growing economies, as consumers are compensated for accepting more goods from these economies.[20] In practice, however, as discussed in Chapter 10, economies with high output growth rates also tend to have high growth rates of exports, with no significant evidence of real appreciation. Instead, there appears to be a one-to-one relationship between estimated foreign income elasticities of export demand and growth in domestic home output—a result that Krugman (1989a) referred to as the **45-degree rule**. Accounting for supply factors may thus be important in estimating export equations, in order to avoid misspecification bias. Export equations that include supply terms were estimated, for instance, by Muscatelli and Stevenson (1995) for a group of Asian countries, with generally significant results.

Two other issues are worth highlighting in assessing the effects of exchange rate changes on trade flows and the trade balance.

- Changes in the exchange rate may have *permanent effects* on the trade balance through the *fixed costs* of entering or leaving a market, as emphasized by Dixit (1989) and Baldwin and Krugman (1989)—the so-called **beachhead effect**.

- Several studies suggest that although the day-to-day *volatility* of exchange rates in flexible exchange rate regimes does not appear to affect trade flows, year-to-year fluctuations do seem to have a significant impact on these flows—although it may become apparent only after a year or two. Grobar (1993) has provided some evidence along these lines.

A more general problem relates to the *partial equilibrium* nature of the analysis on which the Marshall-Lerner condition is derived. In principle, a complete macroeconomic model must be used for assessing the *general equilibrium effects* of exchange rate changes on output, inflation, relative prices, the government budget, and the trade balance. The next section provides a simple setting of

---

[20] This discussion ignores the impact of differential productivity growth between traded and nontraded goods on the real exchange rate, the so-called *Balassa-Samuelson effect*.

this type in which *imported intermediated goods* play a role in the production process, as is often the case in developing countries. This model illustrates well the inadequacy of the partial equilibrium approach, and the importance of accounting for general equilibrium interactions.

4.6   Devaluation and Output with Imported Inputs

Imported intermediate goods play an important role in economic activity in developing countries. In some countries, the share of energy and non-energy intermediate imports can exceed three-fifths of total imports. Through the cost of imported intermediates, the nominal exchange rate may thus have important short-run *supply-side effects*, in addition to its standard demand-side effects. Intuitively, therefore, the real effects of devaluation will depend in general on the relative strength of the supply and demand responses.

A simple model highlighting the mechanisms through which a nominal devaluation influences output both through the cost of imported inputs on the supply side, and through trade flows and expenditure on the demand side, is the static framework proposed Gylfason and Schmidt (1983). To begin with, consider a small open economy operating a fixed exchange rate regime. Gross domestic output, q, is produced from two inputs, *labor*, n, and *imported oil*, v, so that[21]

$$q = q(n, v), \tag{4.24}$$

where the foreign-currency price of oil is fixed on world markets and normalized to unity. Assuming that the production function is *linearly homogeneous*, it may be expressed in terms of rates of change, so that[22]

$$\hat{q} = \theta\hat{v} + (1 - \theta)\hat{n}, \quad 0 < \theta < 1, \tag{4.25}$$

where θ and $1 - \theta$ are, respectively, the shares of oil and labor in output. The **elasticity of substitution** between the two factors is defined as

$$\sigma = -\frac{\hat{v} - \hat{n}}{\varepsilon - \hat{w}}, \tag{4.26}$$

where ε is the rate of devaluation of the nominal exchange rate (which is exogenous and equal to the domestic price of oil) and $\hat{w}$ is the rate of change of the nominal wage, and is taken as given.

The derived demand for oil may then be expressed in rate-of-change form as

$$\hat{v} = \hat{q} - (1 - \theta)\sigma(\varepsilon - \hat{w}). \tag{4.27}$$

---

[21] The analysis can be extended to the case in which output is also a function of capital; see Gylfason and Schmidt (1983).

[22] A function $f(x_1, ... x_n)$ is linearly homogeneous if, for a constant α, $f(\alpha x_1, ... \alpha x_n) = \alpha f(x_1, ... x_n)$. See Chiang, (1984, pp. 411-414)

Real national income, y, differs from gross output by the amount of oil imports:

$$y = q - (E/P)v,$$

where P is the price of domestic output. This equation can be rewritten as

$$\hat{y} = \frac{\hat{q}}{1-\theta} - \frac{\theta}{1-\theta}(\varepsilon - \pi + \hat{n}), \qquad (4.28)$$

where $\pi \equiv \dot{P}/P$. Assuming **marginal cost pricing** implies that

$$\pi = \theta\varepsilon + (1-\theta)\hat{w}. \qquad (4.29)$$

Combining Equations (4.27), (4.28), and (4.29) yields

$$\hat{y} = \hat{q} - \theta(1-\sigma)(\varepsilon - \hat{w}). \qquad (4.30)$$

Equation (4.30) shows that if the degree of substitutability between oil and labor is sufficiently small ($\sigma < 1$), a devaluation (an increase in ε) will reduce real income for a given level of domestic output and nominal wages.

Consider now the demand side. By definition, *gross national income, y,* equals the sum of real domestic expenditure, c, and exports, x, less imports of oil, v, and final goods, h, all measured in terms of the price of domestic output:

$$y = c + x - h - (E/P)v. \qquad (4.31)$$

Assuming that the trade balance is initially in equilibrium, that is,

$$x - h - (E/P)v = 0,$$

implies that Equation (4.31) can be rewritten as

$$\hat{y} = \hat{c} + \left\{\lambda + \frac{\theta}{1-\theta}\right\}[\hat{x} - (1-\beta)\hat{h} - \beta(\varepsilon - \pi + \hat{n})], \qquad (4.32)$$

where $0 < \lambda < 1$ and $\theta/(1-\theta)$ are the shares of final goods imports and oil imports, respectively, in national income and

$$\beta = \frac{\theta}{\lambda(1-\theta)+\theta}, \quad 0 < \beta < 1. \qquad (4.33)$$

β and $1-\beta$ are the shares of oil and final goods, respectively, in total imports.

Domestic absorption (in rate-of-change form) is assumed to be a linearly homogeneous function of (the rate of change of) income and real money balances:

$$\hat{c} = \gamma\hat{y} + (1-\gamma)(\mu - \pi), \quad 0 < \gamma < 1, \qquad (4.34)$$

where $\mu \equiv \dot{M}/M$ is the growth rate of the nominal money stock, M, and γ the short-run elasticity of expenditure with respect to income.

Exports are assumed to depend on the relative price of foreign goods (or the real exchange rate), E/P, so that, in rate-of-change form:

$$\hat{x} = \eta(\varepsilon - \pi), \tag{4.35}$$

where $\eta > 0$ is the absolute value of the price elasticity of export demand.

Imports of final goods, measured in terms of the price of domestic output, are assumed to depend on domestic spending and on the real exchange rate:

$$\hat{h} = \hat{c} - \delta(\varepsilon - \pi), \tag{4.36}$$

where $\delta > 0$ is the absolute value of the price elasticity of the demand for imports of final goods. For simplicity, the elasticity of the demand for final imports with respect to total expenditure is assumed to be unity.

Finally, the demand for oil (measured in units of domestic output) can be expressed as a function of income and the factor price ratio using Equations (4.27), (4.29), and (4.30):

$$\varepsilon + \hat{v} - \pi = \hat{y} + (1 - \sigma)(\varepsilon - \hat{w}). \tag{4.37}$$

Substituting Equations (4.34) to (4.37) into (4.32) yields the following expression for the effect of a devaluation (a rise in ε) on national income, for a given rate of growth of the money supply and nominal wages:

$$\hat{y}/\varepsilon = \{[\lambda(1 - \theta) + \theta]\Omega - \theta\Gamma\}/\Delta, \tag{4.38}$$

where

$$\Omega = \eta + (1 - \beta)\delta + \beta\sigma - 1,$$

$$\Delta = 1 - \gamma(1 - \theta)(1 - \lambda), \quad 0 < \Delta < 1,$$

$$\Gamma = \lambda(1 - \theta)(\eta + \delta - 1) + \theta\eta + (1 - \theta)(1 - \lambda)(1 - \gamma).$$

In the above expressions, the composite term Ω can be viewed as extending the traditional **Marshall-Lerner condition** [given earlier in Equation (4.23)] to the case of an oil-importing economy. Indeed, in the particular case in which $\theta = 0$, $\beta = 0$ and the term Ω becomes

$$\Omega = \eta + \delta - 1,$$

which is nothing but the Marshall-Lerner elasticity condition. The composite term Δ is the reciprocal of the multiplier of the model, and Γ/Δ can be viewed as representing the absolute value of the elasticity of y with respect to P in the income-expenditure Equation (4.32).

Thus, Equation (4.38) shows that, with μ and $\hat{w}$ given, the sign of $\hat{y}/\varepsilon$ cannot in general be ascertained a priori.

In the general case, $\hat{y}/\varepsilon$ is, for instance, positive if the numerator of the expression in the left-hand side of Equation (4.38) is positive, that is

$$[\lambda(1 - \theta) + \theta]\Omega - \theta\Gamma > 0,$$

or equivalently, given the definition of β given above [Equation (4.33)]:

$$\Omega - \beta\Gamma > 0.$$

More specifically, Equation (4.38) decomposes the effect of devaluation on real income into

- a **demand effect**, which is positive as long as the *extended* Marshall-Lerner condition is met, that is, $\Omega > 0$;

- a cost or **supply effect**, which is negative as long as the *traditional* Marshall-Lerner condition is met $(\eta + \delta > 1)$.

In more explicit terms, Equation (4.38) can be rewritten as

$$\hat{y}/\varepsilon = \{(1-\theta)[(1-\theta)\lambda(\eta+\delta-1) + \theta\eta - \theta(1-\lambda)(1-\gamma)] - \theta(1-\sigma)\}/\Delta.$$

In the above expression, the term $\theta(1-\sigma)$ captures the **factor substitution effect** of the devaluation. The higher (lower) the elasticity of substitution between oil and labor inputs, σ, the more likely it is that a devaluation will increase (reduce) real income. When, for instance, the domestic price of imported oil increases, firms would reduce their demand for oil and increase their demand for labor, thereby dampening the reduction in output and income, to an extent that depends on σ. The remaining terms represent the conventional effects occurring through the export and import price elasticities η and δ and the **real balance effect**, $1 - \gamma$. In particular, the higher (lower) the price elasticities of the demand for exports and final goods imports, the more likely it is that a devaluation will increase (reduce) real income.

Equation (4.38) also suggests additional results.

- Everything else equal, the smaller the real balance effect on domestic absorption (the higher γ), the more likely it is that the devaluation will raise income.

- In the particular case in which there is no imported oil, $\theta = \beta = 0$ and Equation (4.38) becomes

$$\frac{\hat{y}}{\varepsilon} = \frac{\lambda(\eta+\delta-1)}{1-\gamma(1-\lambda)},$$

  which shows that a devaluation raises real income ($\hat{y}/\varepsilon > 0$) as long as the conventional Marshall-Lerner condition is met.

In addition, the effect of a higher *share* of oil imports in gross output—and, equivalently, the weight of the exchange rate in the domestic price index—is in general ambiguous.

- On the one hand, an increase in θ raises both the *import cost* effect (provided that $\sigma < 1$) and the *real balance* effect of the devaluation. It also lowers the multiplier. Through both channels, a higher value of θ tends to increase the likelihood of a *negative* income effect.

- On the other, the interaction of θ with η and δ has an ambiguous effect on $\hat{y}/\varepsilon$.

Thus, to summarize, the smaller the degree of dependence of the economy on imported inputs (as reflected by a high value of σ), and the greater the expenditure-switching and expenditure-reducing effects (as captured by high values of η, δ, and γ), the less likely it is that the devaluation will exert a contractionary effect on income.

Because of the presence of imported inputs, income and *gross output* differ. It is thus useful to examine also the effect of the devaluation on gross output. Solving Equations (4.34)-(4.37) as before with μ and $\hat{w}$ constant yields

$$\hat{q}/\varepsilon = \hat{y}/\varepsilon + \theta(1 - \sigma),$$

which differs from the expression for $\hat{y}/\varepsilon$ given above by $\theta(1 - \sigma)$. Thus, a devaluation raises gross output more (or lowers it less) than real income as long as $\sigma < 1$, that is, as long as the real import bill for oil cannot be reduced proportionately in response to the exchange rate devaluation, owing to a low degree of substitutability between labor and oil in the production process.

The foregoing discussion has taken both the rates of growth of nominal money balances and nominal wages as given. Suppose, for instance, that both variables grow at the *same rate* as the rate of depreciation of the exchange rate ($\mu = \hat{w} = \varepsilon$). It can then be shown that

$$\hat{q}/\varepsilon = \hat{y}/\varepsilon = 0,$$

which essentially states that a devaluation has *no real effects* if it does not succeed in lowering real wages and the real money stock. This result is particularly important, given the long-run focus of the model.

More generally, suppose that nominal wages are *partially indexed* on the cost of living, so that

$$\hat{w} = \phi[(1 - \lambda)\pi + \lambda\varepsilon], \quad 0 < \phi \leq 1,$$

which implies that $0 < \hat{w}/\varepsilon \leq 1$. It can be shown that, for given μ,

$$\left.\frac{\hat{y}}{\varepsilon}\right|_{\phi>0} = \left.\frac{\hat{y}}{\varepsilon}\right|_{\phi=0} + \left\{\frac{\theta(1 - \sigma) - (1 - \theta)\Gamma}{\Delta}\right\}\frac{\hat{w}}{\varepsilon},$$

where the first term on the right-hand side corresponds to Equation (4.38). It can be established that the expression in braces on the right-hand side of this equation is *negative* and *larger*, in absolute value, than the first term. Thus, if nominal wages adjust fully to the devaluation (so that $\hat{w}/\varepsilon = 1$), then a devaluation will have a **contractionary effect** on output.

To establish the effects of a devaluation on the *trade balance*, define first the trade balance in real terms as

$$b = y - c.$$

Using Equation (4.34), and noting that $dx = \hat{x}x$ for any variable x, a change in b may be written as

$$db = dy - dc = (1 - \gamma)\hat{y}y + (1 - \gamma)\pi = (1 - \gamma)y(\hat{y} + \pi).$$

Assuming that wages are also given implies that $\pi/\varepsilon = \theta$, so that

$$\frac{db}{\varepsilon} = (1 - \gamma)y(\frac{\hat{y}}{\varepsilon} + \theta). \tag{4.39}$$

Thus, a *sufficient* condition for the devaluation to improve the trade balance is that it raises real income ($\hat{y}/\varepsilon > 0$). For the trade balance to deteriorate following a devaluation requires not only a **negative income effect** but also that the effect be *sufficiently large* to outweigh the unambiguously positive effect through θ—which reflects the expenditure-reducing effect of the devaluation through real balances. Equation (4.39) also shows that in the special case where $\theta = 0$ (that is, there are no imported inputs), and provided that $\gamma < 1$ (the normal case), a devaluation affects in the *same direction* income and the trade balance. In particular, as indicated earlier, both effects are *positive* if the conventional Marshall-Lerner condition holds ($\eta + \delta > 1$).

Two numerical examples considered by Gylfason and Schmidt (1983) are useful to illustrate the above results. Suppose for instance that nominal wage growth and nominal money growth are constant and that $\sigma = 0.3$, $\eta = 0.1$, $\delta = 1.7$, $\gamma = 0.7$, $\theta = 0.06$, $\lambda = 0.03$, and $\beta = 0.7$. In this case, the extended Marshall-Lerner condition is *not satisfied*, and a 10-percent devaluation has the following effects:

- a reduction in gross output by -0.5 percent;

- a reduction in income by -0.9 percent;

- a **deterioration** of the **trade balance** equivalent to -0.1 percent of GNP.

Thus, a devaluation has negative output and income effects. Suppose, by contrast, that σ, γ, and λ remain the same but that now $\eta = 0.5$, $\delta = 2.2$, $\theta = 0.03$, and $\beta = 0.5$. In this case, the extended Marshall-Lerner condition is satisfied and a 10-percent devaluation will raise gross output by 1.1 percent and income by 0.9 percent, and improve the trade balance by 0.4 percent of GNP. The important lesson of these simple experiments is that, once the supply-side effects of exchange rate changes are taken into account, whether or not a devaluation is contractionary can be fairly sensitive to some of the economy's structural parameters.

The literature on exchange rate management has identified various other channels through which a devaluation may affect the supply side. In particular, whereas the above analysis was developed in a *static* context, authors such as Risager (1988) emphasized the links between devaluation, nominal *wage inertia*, *profitability*, and *investment* in a *dynamic* setting. In Risager's model, firms produce one single good by means of labor and capital. The domestic good is an imperfect substitute for foreign goods; its price is thus determined endogenously by equating aggregate supply and demand. Nominal wages adjust to changes in the nominal exchange rate only with a lag. Firms are forward looking and investment is driven not only by the *current levels* of profits and interest rates, but also by the *expected future rate of return* on capital. In this setting, and provided that the Marshall-Lerner condition is met, a devaluation (a decline in the relative price of the domestic good relative to foreign goods) leads to an increase in net exports, a rise in aggregate demand, and thus an increase in the price of the domestic good. Because nominal wages do not change in the *short run*, the *product wage* (the nominal wage divided by the price of the domestic good) and real labor costs fall—thereby raising profitability and investment. In the *long run*, however, nominal wages and domestic prices adjust fully to the devaluation (thereby returning the product wage to its original level), and both the capital stock and domestic output increase. Of course, because firms are forward looking, the faster nominal wages are expected to adjust to the increase in prices, the lower the perceived increase in profitability—and thus the lower the initial increase in investment and output.

A nominal devaluation can have an adverse effect on output through various other channels, including through changes in interest rates, taxation, or the effect of the nominal depreciation on the domestic-currency value of external debt (as discussed by van Wijnbergen, 1986b).[23] The key lesson of the literature is that, far from being a curiosity, contractionary effects induced by nominal exchange rate changes can be significant; accounting for these effects may be important to ensure the sustainability of adjustment programs.

---

[23] Agénor and Montiel (1999, Chapter 8) provide an extensive discusssion of these various channels.

4.7   Summary

- Exchange rate arrangements in operation in developing countries cover
  pegged exchange rate regimes (including fixed rates, adjustable and
  crawling pegs, and **currency boards**), **flexible exchange rate regimes**
  (which include free floats and managed floats), and **band regimes**, which
  involve the announcement of a *central exchange rate* together with a *fluctuation band* around that rate. The central exchange rate is itself managed
  in some fashion—being, for instance, *fixed* or *crawling*. The central bank
  intervenes at the margins of the band, to prevent the exchange rate from
  moving outside it.

- **Pegged exchange-rate regimes** can cause distortions in the financial
  system. To the extent that the peg is considered an *implicit guarantee* that
  there will be no changes in the value of the currency, it is an incentive to
  borrow in foreign currencies and encourages the financial and business
  sectors to incur *excessive exchange risk*.

- The additional credibility gain provided by a **currency board**, compared
  with other pegged exchange rate regimes may be important for countries
  with a history of macroeconomic instability.

- However, currency boards are more constraining on monetary policy and
  on the ability of the authorities to alter the exchange rate peg. The cost
  associated with the *loss of flexibility* depends in general on the suscepti-
  bility of the economy to aggregate shocks, and whether alternative policy
  instruments are available. Because it reduces the ability of the central
  bank to act as **lender of last resort** in the face of economy-wide liquidity crunches, countries with currency boards are *more prone to bank runs*
  and *financial panics* than countries with full-fledged central banks.

- A **band regime** combines the advantages of both fixed and floating exchange rate regimes: it helps impose discipline on monetary policy, provides some degree of flexibility in response to external shocks (such as
  abrupt changes in capital flows, a rise in oil prices, or increase in world
  interest rates), helps limit exchange rate volatility, helps prevent overvaluation, and introduces some uncertainty about the path of the exchange
  rate—thereby lowering the incentives for foreign borrowing.

- The implementation of a credible band will, in and of itself, tend to have
  a stabilizing effect on exchange rate movements. However, in the presence
  of *fundamental policy inconsistencies*, a band regime is no more viable
  than a pegged rate regime.

- Although classifying exchange rate regimes can be difficult in practice, the
  evidence suggests that the number of pegged exchange-rate arrangements
  has fallen considerably since the early 1970s. At the same time, however,
  very few developing countries operate floating exchange rate regimes that
  are free from central bank intervention.

- The evidence suggests that countries with pegged exchange-rate regimes have experienced lower and less variable inflation than countries with flexible exchange rate arrangements. However, simply pegging the exchange rate does not necessarily lead to low inflation; overall consistency of the macroeconomic policy stance is needed for that purpose.

- In practice, factors that policymakers must take into account in choosing an exchange rate arrangement include the *size* and *degree of openness* of the economy, the level of *inflation*, the degree of *labor market flexibility*, the degree of *financial development*, the degree of *credibility of policymakers*, and the degree of *capital mobility*. In particular, a fixed exchange rate in a world of high capital mobility is a target for speculators because it offers a *one-sided bet*.

- The ability of a fixed exchange rate to lend *credibility* to a commitment to a stable monetary policy is limited by the fact that the commitment to fixing the exchange rate may, itself, lack credibility. The reason is that governments face **policy trade-offs** in choosing whether or not to fix the exchange rate. In particular, the government may be *tempted to renege* on its promise to keep the exchange rate fixed because of potentially high returns (in output terms) to an unexpected devaluation. Thus, unless the *cost of devaluation* (economic our political) is sufficiently high, a fixed exchange rate will almost never achieve full credibility.

- Measures of *international competitiveness* attempt to capture changes in the relative price of foreign tradable goods relative to domestic tradable goods; they are generally based on *real exchange rate indicators*. The three most widely used indicators for developing countries are those based on *consumer prices*, *export unit values*, and *unit labor costs*. They may, however, provide *conflicting signals* in practice.

- A nominal devaluation affects the economy through its **expenditure-reducing** effect (a reduction in aggregate demand stemming from a rise in prices and a fall in real wealth) and **expenditure-switching** effect (changes in the composition of output and domestic absorption between traded goods and nontraded goods).

- In a *partial equilibrium* framework, the condition for the trade balance to improve following a devaluation is the **Marshall-Lerner condition**, which requires the sum of the elasticities of export supply and import demand to exceed unity. However, even if the Marshall-Lerner condition is satisfied in the *long run*, *short-term* elasticities may be small enough to imply that an exchange rate adjustment will not lead *immediately* to an improvement in the trade balance.

- The **45-degree rule** refers to the fact that estimates of the elasticity of export demand to foreign income are high for high-growth economies and low for low-growth economies. The close correspondence between estimated activity elasticities for exports and real domestic growth suggests that terms measuring domestic supply should be incorporated in export equations to avoid mispecification.

- A nominal devaluation may have a short-run **contractionary effect** on output through its impact on the cost of *imported inputs*. Various other channels (operating through both the supply and demand sides) may also lead to an adverse output effect of exchange rate adjustment in the short run. Accounting for these adverse effects, if they are deemed large, may be important in the design of adjustment programs.

Chapter 5

Inflation and Disinflation

Assessing the sources of inflation and evaluating alternative strategies to disinflate have been for many years the focus of much research on stabilization issues in developing countries, particularly in Latin America. In part, of course, this results from the recognition of the substantial social costs imposed by high inflation. Although the days of very high inflation appear to have given way to more moderate inflation rates (at least for now) in Latin America and elsewhere, it is important to draw on the lessons of these experiences for macroeconomic management.

The first part of this chapter focuses on the sources of inflation. It begins by drawing a distinction between chronic inflation and hyperinflation, and discusses the sources of both phenomena: often large fiscal deficits, but also other proximate causes such as wage inflation, exchange rate depreciation and terms-of-trade shocks, changes in the frequency of price adjustment, supply-induced movements in food prices, and lack of credibility. The second part examines the factors affecting the choice of nominal anchors in disinflation programs, focusing notably on the macroeconomic dynamics associated with money- and exchange-rate-based stabilization programs. The third part examines the role of credibility in disinflation programs. It begins by reviewing the various sources of credibility problems and considers alternative options that have been suggested as ways to alleviate them—central bank independence, price and wage controls, and foreign assistance. The last part reviews two recent experiences with alternative types of adjustment programs: those of Egypt (1992-97) and Uganda (1987-95).

5.1 Sources of Inflation

In understanding the sources of inflation, a key distinction is between **hyperinflation** and **chronic inflation**.

5.1.1 Hyperinflation and Chronic Inflation

Hyperinflation is generally defined on the basis of **Cagan's criterion** as an inflation rate of at least 50 percent per month, or 12,975 percent per annum.[1] As argued by Végh (1992), there are three main features of hyperinflation:

- It typically has its origin in **large fiscal imbalances.**

- **Nominal inertia** tends to disappear. In the face of extreme rates of inflation, workers for instance refuse to engage in nominal wage contracts. Most wages and prices become indexed to a *foreign* currency—and many transactions are actually *conducted* in a foreign currency.

- It brings about such a *chaotic social and economic environment* that the public becomes convinced that the situation in untenable—eventually creating the political conditions for drastic policies aimed at attacking it at its roots.

A recent, and typical, example of hyperinflation in the 1990s is the former Zaire.[2] A deep and worsening political crisis during the period 1991-94 led to a drastic increase in government expenditure (including large rises in *government wages*). This increase, compounded by a drop in tax revenue, led to a worsening of the fiscal deficit, which was financed by money creation.[3] Inflation averaged 60 percent per annum during the 1980s, and surged to 4,500 percent in 1993 and 9,800 percent in 1994—an average monthly rate of 50 percent. For the 12-month period ending in September 1994, currency in circulation grew at a rate of several thousands percent, with inflation reaching an annual rate of 12,850 percent. At the peak of the hyperinflation process, in December 1993, inflation rose to almost 240 percent a month (Figure 5.1). Although monthly inflation fell substantially in 1995-96, it was not brought completely under control—in large part because of the inability of the government to reduce public expenditure and increase conventional tax revenue, in order to reduce its reliance on monetary financing of its fiscal deficit. During the whole period, domestic prices were increasingly set in *foreign currency* (U.S. dollars or Belgian francs). As shown in the lower panel in Figure 5.1, during the whole episode the monthly rate of depreciation of the *parallel exchange rate* remained closely correlated with the inflation rate.

The distinguishing features of **chronic inflation** stand in sharp contrast to those of hyperinflation.

- **Fiscal imbalances** are often *less acute* in the short run than those observed during episodes of hyperinflation. Consequently, it is often *more difficult* to mobilize political support for reform.

---

[1] A more modest threshold would be 20 percent per month, or 892 percent per annum.

[2] See Beaugrand (1997) for a discussion of Zaire's experience. Based on Cagan's criterion, Zaire's hyperinflation began in October 1991 and ended in September 1994.

[3] As argued by Beaugrand (1997), inflationary pressures were compounded by the *Olivera-Tanzi effect* (as discussed in Chapter 3) which lowered government revenue in real terms and led to increases in the real fiscal deficit.

- There is a high degree of **inflation inertia** resulting from widespread indexation of wages and financial assets.

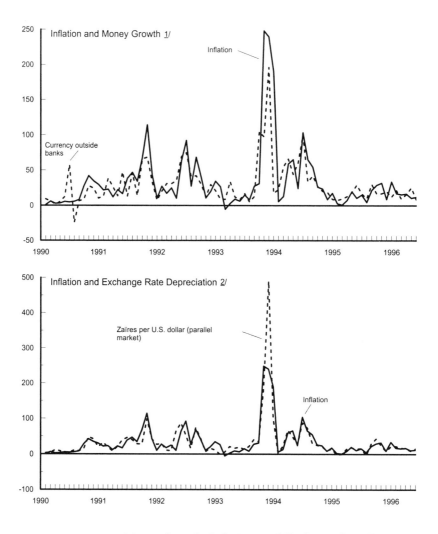

Figure 5.1. Zaire: Money Growth, Inflation, and Exchange Rate Depreciation, 1990-96.

Source: Beaugrand (1997).

1/ Monthly rate of change of the stock of currency outside banks.

2/ Parallel exchange rate in terms of old zaïres. The new zaïre was introduced in October 1993 at a parity of NZ=Z 3,000,000; later data have been rescaled accordingly.

- The public is often *skeptical* of new attempts to stop inflation, particularly when there is a history of *failed stabilization efforts*. This **lack of credibility** (as discussed below) can be a powerful source of inertia.

5.1.2 Fiscal Deficits, Seigniorage, and Inflation

The foregoing discussion suggests that, in countries where the tax collection system, capital markets, and institutions are underdeveloped, fiscal imbalances are often at the root of hyperinflation and chronic inflation; governments often have no other option but to monetize their budget deficits.

To analyze how monetary growth and fiscal deficits affect inflation, consider the following simple model, adapted from Bruno and Fischer (1990), which focuses on the *money market* and its dynamic adjustment process. Suppose that real money demand, m^d, is a function of the *expected* inflation rate, π^a. Under *perfect foresight* (that is, rational expectations in an environment with no uncertainty) expected and actual inflation rates are equal, so that $\pi^a = \pi$. Money demand is thus

$$m^d = m_0 \exp(-\alpha\pi). \tag{5.1}$$

Equilibrium of the money market requires equality between money supply and money demand, $m^d = m^s = m$, which in turn implies that

$$\pi = -\frac{\ln(m/m_0)}{\alpha}. \tag{5.2}$$

Equation (5.2) shows that, along an equilibrium path, inflation and real money balances are *negatively* related. It defines a *downward-sloping curve* in the π-m space, denoted MM (for money market equilibrium) in the upper panel of Figure 5.2. When $\pi \to 0$, m tends to m_0. At any given moment in time, the economy must be located along MM.

To examine the dynamics of the inflationary process, suppose that the real *fiscal deficit*, d, is given by

$$d = d_A + \phi\pi, \quad \phi > 0 \tag{5.3}$$

where d_A can be defined as the *autonomous component* of the deficit, and $\phi\pi$ a term measuring the **Olivera-Tanzi effect**—which, as discussed in Chapter 3, captures the fact that a rise in the inflation rate lowers the real value of tax revenue as a result of the lag involved in collecting taxes, thereby increasing the fiscal deficit.

The deficit must be financed by **seigniorage revenue**, that is

$$d = \mu m, \tag{5.4}$$

where $\mu \equiv \dot{M}/M$ is the rate of growth of the nominal money stock.[4]

The rate of change of real money balances is, by definition:

$$\dot{m}/m = \mu - \pi,$$

---

[4]This definition differs from the one given in Chapter 3 because of the continuous time nature of the present model. Defining seigniorage again as the change in the money base divided by the price level implies that $\dot{M}/P = (\dot{M}/M)m$, which is the definition given in the text.

which can be written as, using Equation (5.4):

$$\dot{m}/m = d/m - \pi. \tag{5.5}$$

Substituting Equation (5.3) in (5.5) therefore implies that in the steady state, with $\dot{m}/m = 0$, $\mu = \pi$ and

$$\pi = \frac{d_A}{m - \phi}, \tag{5.6}$$

which implies that inflation and real money balances are *negatively* related in equilibrium.[5] Equation (5.6) is shown as curve DD in the upper panel of Figure 5.2. When $\pi \rightarrow \infty$, m tends to ϕ, and when $m \rightarrow \infty$, π tends to zero. DD approaches therefore the horizontal axis asymptotically. Note that DD depicts only a *steady-state* relationship between m and π. The economy moves continuously along MM in the short run; MM must intersect DD only when the economy reaches its *long-run equilibrium position*, characterized by a constant level of real money balances.

In general, depending on the size of the autonomous component of the fiscal deficit, d_A, curves MM and DD may or may not intersect. The upper panel of Figure 5.2 illustrates three cases:

- the case in which there are *two equilibria*, corresponding to curve DD;

- the case in which there is *one equilibrium*, corresponding to curve $D'D'$;

- the case in which there is *no equilibrium* at all, corresponding to curve $D''D''$.

Under what conditions is the long-run equilibrium *unique*, as depicted by point A in the upper panel of Figure 5.2? Essentially, it depends on the size of the autonomous component of the fiscal deficit. Suppose, for simplicity, that $\phi = 0$. The steady-state relationship (5.6) is thus now given by $\pi m = d_A$. As noted earlier, when the rate of inflation approaches zero, real money balances tend to a finite value m_0; thus, the autonomous deficit must also be close to zero when inflation is very low. As the autonomous component of the deficit increases, steady-state seigniorage revenue (which is equal to the **inflation tax**) must increase as well.[6] But the relationship is *nonlinear* because as inflation rises, real money demand falls [Equation (5.1)]. More specifically, the *exponential form* of the money demand function implies that when inflation begins to rise, real money balances fall by relatively little, and revenue from the inflation tax increases at first. However, as inflation continues to rise, real money balances

---

[5] To ensure that the equilibrium inflation given by Eq. (5.6) is positive requires $m > \phi$. This condition can be rewritten in the form $\pi m/d > \eta_{d/\pi}$, where $\eta_{d/\pi}$ measures the *inflation elasticity* of the fiscal deficit. From Eq. (5.4), with $\mu = \pi$, $\pi m/d = 1$, the inflation elasticity of the deficit must therefore be less than unity to ensure that $m > \phi$.

[6] Again, note that the definition of the inflation tax given in Chapter 3, $\pi m/(1+\pi)$, becomes in continuous time πm, because $\dot{M}/P = \dot{m} + \pi m$, and $\dot{m} = 0$ in the steady state.

begin to fall at an accelerating rate, that is, at a rate *faster* than the rate at which inflation rises. Thus, after a phase during which πm increases (at a decreasing rate), it starts falling (at an increasing rate) and eventually tends to zero as π goes to infinity.

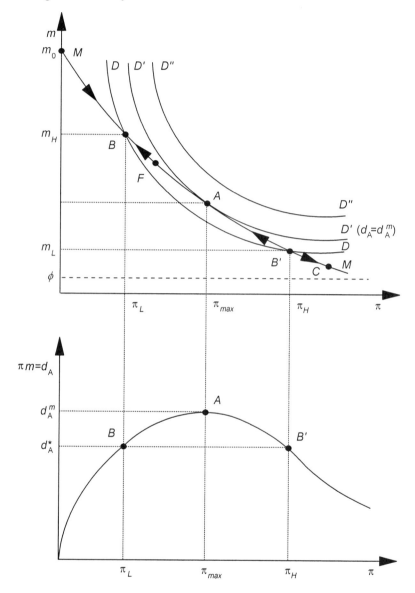

Figure 5.2. The Seignorage Laffer Curve and the High-Inflation Trap.

These results define a concave relationship, called the **seigniorage Laffer curve,** associating the (steady-state) inflation rate, π, and (steady-state) revenue from the inflation tax, $\pi m = d_A$. The curve is depicted in the lower panel of Figure 5.2. It shows that for a level of the autonomous deficit equal to, say, d_A^*, there are *two* corresponding rates of inflation, π_L and π_H, at points B and B'.[7] From the upper panel of Figure 5.2, the MM and DD curves in that case must intersect twice, at points B and B', corresponding again to π_L and π_H.

Uniqueness occurs only at the *optimal inflation rate*, π_{max}, which maximizes steady-state seigniorage; it is obtained by setting the derivative of πm with respect to π equal to zero:

$$\frac{d(\pi m)}{d\pi} = m + \pi\frac{dm}{d\pi} = 0, \tag{5.7}$$

which can be rewritten as

$$-\frac{dm/m}{d\pi/\pi} = \eta_{m/\pi} = 1.$$

This expression shows that the revenue-maximizing rate of inflation is reached when the elasticity of real money demand with respect to inflation, $\eta_{m/\pi}$, is exactly equal to unity.

Substituting Equation (5.1) in (5.7) yields

$$\frac{d}{d\pi}\left\{\pi\exp(-\alpha\pi)\right\} = 0,$$

which implies that

$$\exp(-\alpha\pi) - \alpha\pi\exp(-\alpha\pi) = 0.$$

Thus,

$$\pi_{max} = 1/\alpha, \tag{5.8}$$

which indicates that the optimal inflation rate is inversely related to the inflation elasticity of money demand.

Substituting Equation (5.8) in (5.1) and using Equation (5.6), the level of the autonomous deficit corresponding to π_{max}, d_A^m, is given by

$$d_A^m = \frac{m_0\exp(-1) - \phi}{\alpha}.$$

Both π_{max} and d_A^m are shown in the lower panel of Figure 5.2. Before point A, increases in inflation raise revenue from the inflation tax, so that $d(\pi m)/d\pi > 0$; equivalently, the elasticity of money demand, $\eta_{m/\pi}$, is *less* than unity for $\pi < \pi_{max}$. Beyond point A, by contrast, increases in inflation reduce revenue $(d(\pi m)/d\pi < 0)$ and $\eta_{m/\pi}$ is *greater* than unity.

The next question is to determine if the equilibrium, whether it is unique or not, is *stable*. This requires examining the *local stability* properties of the

---

[7]The same conclusion can be reached by depicting the inflation rate, π, against the *logarithm* of real money balances, $\ln m$. From Eq. (5.2), MM would now be a *straight line* with a negative slope, whereas from Eq. (5.6), given that $m = \exp(\ln m)$, DD would be a *downward-sloping curve*, convex toward the origin. Provided that the autonomous fiscal deficit is not too large, the model would again generate two equilibria.

model. As noted above, the dynamic path of the economy must always be along the MM curve, because money market equilibrium must hold continuously. Assuming that the level of the autonomous deficit is d_A^*, there are two possible long-run equilibrium inflation rates, as noted earlier. The issue, then, is whether the economy, starting from an arbitrary initial position on MM, will converge toward B or B' in the upper panel of Figure 5.2. Two cases must be considered.

- Suppose first that the economy's initial position is at point F on MM, with F located *above* DD. For a given level of inflation, real money balances are therefore *higher* than their steady-state level, given by π/d_A^* (see Equation (5.6) with $\phi = 0$). From Equation (5.5), $\dot{m}/m$ must then be *negative*. Thus, the adjustment process entails a *reduction* in m, an increase in inflation, and hence a move toward point B'.

- Suppose now that, on the contrary, the economy starts from an initial point on MM located *below* DD, at, say, C. In this case, for a given inflation rate, real money balances are *lower* than their steady-state value; and from (5.5), $\dot{m}/m$ must then be *positive*. Thus, the transitional dynamics entail now a *rise* in m and hence a move away from B.

The foregoing discussion suggests that point B, which is associated with a *lower* inflation rate, is *unstable*. Any disturbance or exogenous shock—such as a sudden increase in government spending, leading to a rise in the autonomous component of the fiscal deficit—will lead the economy away from B. On the contrary, point B', which exhibits *higher* inflation, is a stable equilibrium.[8] Put differently, given the nature of the adjustment process under perfect foresight, a country can be *stuck* in a situation in which inflation is persistently high—a situation characterized by Bruno and Fischer (1990) as being akin to an **inflation trap**.

Clearly, any equilibrium characterized by $\pi > \pi_{max}$ is *inefficient*: the same amount of revenue could be collected at a lower inflation rate. What can governments do to move the economy away from an inefficient position? The obvious answer is to change either the autonomous component of the fiscal deficit, d_A, or the rate of growth of the nominal money supply, μ, because both affect the position of the economy along the seigniorage Laffer curve. For instance, a *credible reduction* in the money growth rate may shift MM and DD in such a way that the MM curve will intersect the DD curve only once, as shown in the upper panel of Figure 5.2.

The view that countries can be stuck in an inflation trap is quite appealing because it appears to be consistent with a number of episodes of high and chronic inflation that were observed in Latin America during the 1970s and 1980s, as discussed for instance by Agénor and Montiel (1999, Chapter 9).[9] It is also of relevance for studying the dynamics of inflation in other developing countries

---

[8]However, as shown by Evans and Yarrow (1981), with *adaptive* (or *backward-looking*) expectations, point B would be stable whereas point B' would be unstable. See also Bruno (1991), Bruno and Fischer (1990), Dornbusch and Fischer (1986), and Lee and Ratti (1993).

[9]A problem with the above model, however, is that (as pointed out by Dornbusch,

where (as noted in Chapter 3) seigniorage accounts for a significant portion of fiscal revenues. Figure 5.3 shows the relation between inflation and seigniorage, and Figure 5.4 displays the relation between inflation and broad money growth. Both figures suggest a positive correlation between these variables, although the relation does not appear to be very close in either case. The evidence also suggests that the relationship between fiscal deficits and money growth is relatively weak, particularly in the *short run*. De Haan and Zelhorst (1990) and Karras (1994*b*) for instance investigated the link between monetary growth and budget deficits in developing countries. Both studies concluded that only in a small number of cases does a close, positive relationship exist between fiscal deficits and money growth. One possible explanation is the important role played by *expectations* about *future policy changes*, as emphasized by Kawai and Maccini (1990). A large budget deficit today, for instance, may be expected to be closed in the future through monetary or bond financing, which may raise expected and actual inflation immediately, or through a cut in government spending— which may lead to an *immediate fall* in the expected inflation rate. Because of the difficulty involved in measuring the stance of expectations, empirical studies of the links between fiscal deficits, money growth, and inflation are likely to lack robustness.

The conceptual basis for the public finance approach to inflation has also been subject to criticism. In an early contribution, Bailey (1956) questioned the use of the seigniorage approach as a positive theory of extreme inflation. Because taxation is an alternative to money creation and because the marginal cost of taxation is moderate relative to the welfare costs of extreme inflation, high money growth (and therefore high inflation) is not optimal. Moreover, the idea of a stable inflation trap may be of limited usefulness to understand episodes of very high inflation or hyperinflation. As aptly noted by Dornbusch, Sturzenegger, and Wolf (1990, p. 9), in such cases

> Inflation...reflects a state of fiscal chaos, rather than optimal public finance.

5.1.3   Other Sources of Chronic Inflation

In addition to fiscal deficits and money growth, there are several factors that can affect the inflationary process in the *short run*. These factors include wage inertia, exchange rate depreciation and changes in the terms of trade, the frequency of price adjustment, changes in food prices, and the inflation bias of monetary policy under imperfect credibility.

Sturzenegger, and Wolf, 1990) it is not entirely consistent with the evidence. An increase in the nominal money growth rate generally tends to *raise* initially real balances; *only later* does inflation increase and overshoots for a while. Evidence along these lines is also provided by Agénor and Hoffmaister (1997).

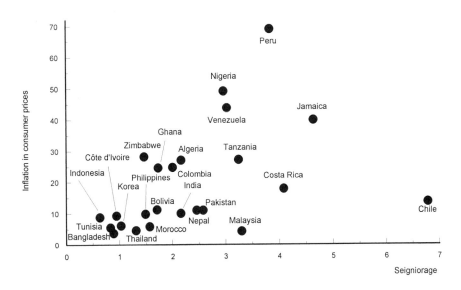

Figure 5.3. Inflation and Seigniorage (In percent of GDP, average 1990-95).
Source: World Bank.

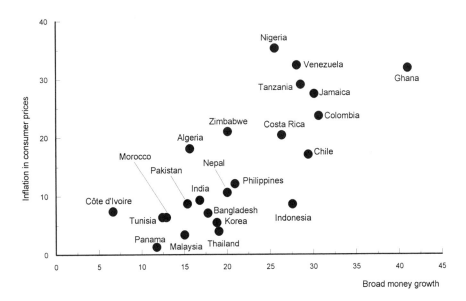

Figure 5.4. Inflation and Money Growth (In percent per annum, average over 1980-95).
Source: World Bank.

Wage Inertia

Backward-looking wage formation mechanisms—such as **wage indexation** on past inflation rates—can play an important role in inflation persistence, both directly and indirectly—in transmitting, as discussed below, exchange rate movements to domestic prices.[10]

Consider, for instance, the following simple model of an economy producing home goods and tradable goods. The inflation rate, π, is given by a *weighted average* of changes in prices of both categories of goods:

$$\pi = \delta \pi_N + (1 - \delta)(\varepsilon + \pi_T^*), \quad 0 < \delta < 1, \tag{5.9}$$

where δ is the share of home goods in the price index, π_N the rate of change in prices of home goods, π_T^* the rate of change in prices of tradables (in foreign-currency terms) and ε the devaluation rate. Changes in prices of home goods are set as a **mark-up** over nominal *wage growth*, $\hat{w}$, and the level of *excess demand* for home goods, d_N:

$$\pi_N = \hat{w} + \alpha d_N, \tag{5.10}$$

which implies that, in equilibrium (with $d_N = 0$), $\pi_N = \hat{w}$.

Nominal wage growth is determined through indexation on past inflation as follows:

$$\hat{w} = \gamma \pi_{-1}, \quad 0 < \gamma \leq 1, \tag{5.11}$$

with $\gamma = 1$ denoting full indexation. Combining Equations (5.9), (5.10), and (5.11) yields

$$\pi = \delta \gamma \pi_{-1} + \alpha \delta d_N + (1 - \delta)(\varepsilon + \pi_T^*), \tag{5.12}$$

which shows that inflation inertia exists as long as γ is positive. Empirical research on the experience of countries like Chile in the early 1980s and more recently Brazil has shown that backward-looking wage indexation can indeed contribute to inflation inertia (see Agénor and Montiel, 1999).

In addition, it has been observed in some countries that the *frequency* at which nominal wages are adjusted tends to increase with the inflationary pressures generated by exchange rate movements—thereby raising inflation itself. Exogenous shocks in the **wage bargaining process** could also exert independent impulse effects on inflation (see Chapter 14), which could persist over time in the presence of an accommodative monetary policy.

Exchange Rates and the Terms of Trade

A nominal exchange rate depreciation (resulting from, say, a devaluation) can exert direct effects on the *fiscal deficit* through two channels:

---

[10] As noted by Van Gompel (1994, p. 273), the absence, in practice, of *instantaneous indexation* is often the result of large costs associated with *a*) gathering and processing information on current movements in prices; *b*) renegotiating wage agreements; and *c*) increasing the frequency of wage payments.

- by affecting the domestic-currency value of *foreign exchange receipts* by the government (resulting, for instance, from surrender requirements on exports) and foreign exchange outlays, such as those associated with external debt service;

- by affecting the revenue derived from *ad valorem* taxes on *imports*. As discussed in Chapter 3, import taxes continue to represent an important source of revenue in many developing countries.

As a result, changes in the nominal exchange rate may affect the money supply and inflation. In addition, because exchange rate depreciation raises the prices of *import-competing goods* and *exportables*, it may exert pressure on wages as a result of its effect on the *cost of living*. This is particularly likely to occur in a setting in which (formal and informal) indexation mechanisms are pervasive, as indicated earlier.

Consider, for instance, a country facing a sharp deterioration in competitiveness and a large current account deficit, and suppose that policymakers decide to devalue the official exchange rate. The devaluation will increase both the domestic-currency price of imported *final goods* as well as *imported inputs* (such as oil, as noted in Chapter 4), thereby putting upward pressure on domestic prices. The increase in prices can be large enough to outweigh the effect of the initial devaluation on competitiveness—thereby prompting policymakers to devalue again. The process can therefore turn into a **devaluation-inflation spiral**. In addition, if wages are indexed on the cost of living, they will increase also, putting further upward pressure on prices of domestic goods. The rise in domestic prices will in turn further increase wages and contribute to inflation inertia. There is indeed evidence showing that exchange rate changes have a significant effect on inflation (see, for instance, Önis and Ozmucur, 1990 for Turkey; Alba and Papell, 1998, for Malaysia, the Philippines, and Singapore).

A similar process may be at play in countries where the official exchange rate is fixed but the *parallel market for foreign exchange* is large. A deterioration in external accounts may lead agents to expect a devaluation of the official exchange rate to restore competitiveness; such expectations will typically translate immediately into a depreciation of the parallel exchange rate. Because the parallel rate measures the *marginal cost* of foreign exchange, domestic prices will tend to increase. In turn, This increase in prices will further erode competitiveness, leading agents to expect an even larger devaluation of the official exchange rate—an expectation that may translate into a further depreciation of the parallel exchange rate.[11] The evidence suggests indeed a strong correlation between parallel exchange rate depreciation and inflation in many cases. This was the case for Zaire during the hyperinflationary episode discussed earlier (see Figure 5.1). Figure 5.5 shows that, although parallel exchange rates display a

---

[11] Again, wage indexation mechanisms may exacerbate the problem. Note that the increasing differential between the parallel and official exchange rates will typically lead to a diversion of exports from official channels (as noted in Annex B) and reserve losses, which may eventually force the authorities to abandon the official exchange rate (see Chapter 7).

higher degree of variability than prices, the correlation appears to be positive
in the case of Morocco and Nigeria during the 1980s and early 1990s.

Figure 5.5. Parallel Market Exchange Rate and Inflation (In percent).
Source: International Monetary Fund.

In countries where the government is directly involved in controlling exports
of a major primary commodity (as, for instance, with oil in Nigeria), there may
be a direct effect of changes in the *terms of trade* on the budget as well as an indirect effect through taxes on corporate profits and domestic sales—which may

be significant even if the government does not directly control exports. In such conditions, a deterioration in the terms of trade, for instance, would directly reduce government revenue and increase pressure for monetizing the fiscal deficit. Moreover, even an *improvement* in the terms of trade may lead to higher inflation in the future: as noted in Chapter 3, government spending has sometimes increased sharply in response to temporary **commodity price booms**; to the extent that such increases are difficult to reverse when commodity prices fall, the budget deficit may increase and inflationary finance may result.

The Frequency of Price Adjustment

In an environment in which high inflation is associated with highly variable inflation and uncertainty over the pricing horizon of price setters, the *frequency of price adjustment* becomes endogenous and tends to accelerate.[12] In turn, the shortening of the adjustment interval raises inflation, leading to a further shortening of the adjustment interval, and so on—with price setters more and more opting to denominate their prices in a foreign currency. Dornbusch, Sturzenegger, and Wolf (1990), in their analysis of inflationary episodes in Bolivia, Israel, Argentina, and Brazil, suggested indeed that there appears to be *increased synchronization* between domestic prices and the nominal exchange rate as inflation rises. Thus the shortening of price adjustment intervals may become another source of inflationary pressure, if the stance of monetary policy remains accommodative.

Food Prices

In many developing countries (particularly in sub-Saharan Africa) food items comprise the bulk of the goods included in consumer price indices. For instance, the consumer price index in Nigeria, which is a composite index for urban and rural areas, has food items representing 69 percent of the total basket. Consequently, supply-side factors affecting *food prices*—notably agroclimatic conditions—have an important effect on the behavior of prices. In an econometric analysis of inflation in Nigeria over the period 1960-93, Moser (1995) found that, indeed, *rainfall* had a significant effect on the rate of price increases—in addition to money growth and exchange rate changes. More generally, as shown in Figure 5.6, there is a close correlation between inflation in food prices and inflation in consumer prices. However, caution must be exercised in interpreting such a correlation as a causal relationship, because of the importance of food items in cost-of-living indices typically available in developing countries.

Time Inconsistency and the Inflation Bias

The discussion in the previous chapter suggested that imperfect credibility in the presence of policy trade-offs can generate a **devaluation bias** in exchange rate

---

[12] The existence of a positive relationship between the *level* and the *variability* of inflation is well documented in both developed and developing countries (see Dornbusch, Sturzenegger, and Wolf, 1990). Of course, high variability is not synonymous to high uncertainty.

management. In a similar manner, lack of credibility may impart an **inflation bias** to monetary policy. Lack of credibility may result again from the **time inconsistency** problem faced by policy announcements: a policy that is optimal *ex ante* may no longer be optimal *ex post*. The reason is that policymakers are typically not only concerned about inflation as a policy goal (even when it is initially high) but also with the fact that inflation (at least to the extent that it is unexpected) may carry benefits as well.

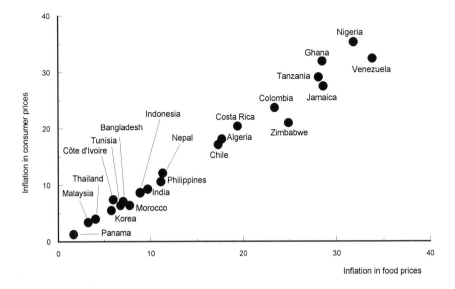

Figure 5.6. Inflation and Food Prices (In percent per annum, average over 1980-95).

Source: World Bank.

For instance, in the model first proposed by Barro and Gordon (1983), policymakers are concerned about both *inflation* and *unemployment*, with a **loss function** given by

$$L = \frac{1}{2}(y - \tilde{y})^2 + \frac{\theta}{2}(\pi - \tilde{\pi})^2, \quad \theta > 0, \tag{5.13}$$

where y is current output, $\tilde{y}$ its desired level, π actual inflation, and $\tilde{\pi}$ the desired inflation rate—which may be related to the need for revenue from the inflation tax.[13] The coefficient θ measures the relative importance of deviations of inflation from its target value in the loss function.

The economy is characterized by an **expectations-augmented Phillips**

---

[13] The idea that the policymakers' incentive to keep inflation high may be related to the need to maintain the revenue from seigniorage at high levels was emphasized by Barro (1983). Another reason may be the desire to reduce the real value of the nominal public debt.

curve given by

$$y = y_L + \alpha(\pi - \pi^a) + u, \quad \alpha > 0, \; y_L < \tilde{y}, \tag{5.14}$$

where y_L is the long-term (or capacity) level of output, π^a expected inflation, and u a disturbance term with zero mean and constant variance. The restriction $y_L < \tilde{y}$ ensures that the policymakers have an incentive to raise output above its long-run value.

Policymakers want private agents to expect low inflation, in order to exploit a favorable trade-off between inflation and output. But the mere *announcement* of a policy of low inflation is not credible. This is because once expectations are formed, policymakers have an **incentive to renege** on the announcement in order to increase output toward the desired level $\tilde{y}$ and reduce unemployment. Private agents understand the incentive to renege and therefore do not believe the policy announcement in the first place. As a result, inflation will in equilibrium be higher than it would be otherwise. Monetary policy (viewed here as consisting of direct control over the actual inflation rate) suffers therefore from an inflation bias.

Formally, substituting Equation (5.14) in (5.13) yields

$$L = \frac{1}{2} \{ y_L + \alpha(\pi - \pi^a) - \tilde{y} + u \}^2 + \frac{\theta}{2} (\pi - \tilde{\pi})^2. \tag{5.15}$$

With a binding commitment to low inflation, expected and actual inflation rates are equal ($\pi = \pi^a$); the loss function becomes

$$L = \frac{1}{2} (y_L - \tilde{y} + u)^2 + \frac{\theta}{2} (\pi - \tilde{\pi})^2,$$

and the value of π that minimizes the expected value of L is simply

$$\pi = \tilde{\pi}.$$

Under discretion, policymakers take expected inflation as given; the first-order condition for minimizing the expected value of Equation (5.15) with respect to π is thus

$$\alpha \left[y_L + \alpha(\pi - \pi^a) - \tilde{y} \right] + \theta(\pi - \tilde{\pi}) = 0,$$

which yields

$$\pi = \frac{\alpha^2 \pi^a + \theta \tilde{\pi} + \alpha(\tilde{y} - y_L)}{\theta + \alpha^2},$$

or equivalently

$$\pi = \tilde{\pi} + \frac{\alpha(\tilde{y} - y_L)}{\theta + \alpha^2} + \frac{\alpha^2(\pi^a - \tilde{\pi})}{\theta + \alpha^2}.$$

In equilibrium, expected and actual inflation must be equal; setting $\pi = \pi^a$ in the above expression yields

$$\pi = \tilde{\pi} + \frac{\alpha(\tilde{y} - y_L)}{\theta}, \tag{5.16}$$

In either case, because $\pi = \pi^a$, in equilibrium output can deviate from its capacity level only as a result of random shocks:

$$y = y_L + u. \tag{5.17}$$

Thus, under discretion, the equilibrium inflation rate will be higher than desired inflation (as shown in Equation (5.16)) because agents understand the policymakers' incentive to depart from a policy of low inflation once expectations are formed. The higher the difference between desired output and its capacity level $(\tilde{y} - y_L)$, the higher the slope of the Phillips curve, and the lower the relative importance of inflation in the loss function, the higher inflation will be.

As discussed earlier in the context of exchange rate management (Chapter 4), under most circumstances a **credible commitment** to a policy rule is *welfare enhancing* compared with a discretionary policy. In the above model, for instance, to the extent that policymakers can credibly commit themselves to low (or no) inflation, the economy will be better off: output will be the same as in the discretionary policy case [as shown by Equation (5.17), but inflation will be lower ($\pi = \tilde{\pi}$). The difficulty with this argument, of course, is that it is not easy for policymakers to announce credible commitments to noninflationary policies. Institutional mechanisms or arrangements through which policymakers can make credible commitments to noninflationary policies are discussed later. But in the absence of mechanisms that are capable of constraining policymakers' hands, announcements of a low-inflation policy will not be credible and the inflationary bias will persist.[14]

5.2   Nominal Anchors in Disinflation: Money vs. the Exchange Rate

One of the most debated issues in the analysis of disinflation policies is the relative merits of exchange-rate-based stabilization versus the targeting of money (or credit) growth in conjunction with exchange rate flexibility. This section reviews the main arguments for and against these two alternative approaches to inflation stabilization.

At the outset, it is worth noting that in an economy in which information is complete and no distortions or rigidities are present, exchange-rate targets or monetary targets are *equivalent* policies under perfect capital mobility. However, this equivalence need not hold in the presence of incomplete information, market distortions and rigidities, or imperfect capital mobility. Fischer (1986), for instance, showed that in an economy with **multiperiod nominal contracts**, in which policy fundamentals have been adjusted for disinflation purposes, exchange-rate targets dominate monetary targets under *some* configurations of the underlying parameters, but are dominated under some other

---

[14] As shown by Green (1996), a credible commitment to an explicit *inflation target* can mitigate the inflationary bias, but possibly at the expense of raising the *variability* of output.

configurations.[15] Agénor and Montiel (1999, Chapter 11) showed that, under imperfect capital mobility, disinflation through a reduction in the nominal deval-uation rate or a fall in the rate of growth of domestic credit are *not equivalent*; in the former case, the economy adjusts gradually to its long-run equilibrium position, whereas in the latter case there are no transitional dynamics.

In general, the choice between the exchange rate and the money supply as a nominal anchor can be viewed as depending on three main considerations:

- the *degree of controllability* and the effectiveness of the instrument in bringing down inflation;

- the *adjustment path* of the economy and the *relative costs* (measured in terms of output losses and lower employment) associated with each in-strument;

- the *degree of credibility* that each instrument commands, and its relation-ship with fiscal policy.

5.2.1   Controllability and Effectiveness

In general, policymakers cannot control directly the money supply, whereas fixing the exchange rate can be done relatively fast and without substantial costs. In addition, in an environment in which *money demand* is subject to large random shocks and *velocity* is unstable, the effectiveness of the money supply as an anchor is reduced, whereas an exchange rate peg will continue to anchor the price level through its direct impact on *prices of tradables*. On such grounds, then, fixing the exchange rate rather than the money stock may appear preferable. Moreover, because it is a clear, *monitorable target*, a pegged rate may bolster the government's commitment to the stabilization effort and help price- and wage-setters coordinate their price-setting decisions and expectations around a new, *low-inflation equilibrium* (Bruno, 1991). However, policymakers must also be able to *convince* private agents that they are willing and able to *defend* the fixed exchange rate. The discussion of policy trade-offs faced by exchange rate management in the previous chapter suggests that this may be difficult to achieve if the current account deficit is large or if official reserves are relatively low. If agents lack confidence in the authorities' ability to defend a fixed exchange rate, **speculative attacks** will occur, eventually forcing the abandonment of the fixed exchange rate (see Chapter 7).

5.2.2   Adjustment Paths and Relative Costs

In general, the dynamic adjustment paths of the economy associated with money-based and exchange-rate-based stabilization programs (and thus the rel-ative output costs associated with each instrument) tend to differ significantly.

---

[15] Although the robustness of Fischer's results remains an open issue (given the particular nature of the model that was used), the analysis illustrates a general point.

In the model of Calvo and Végh (1993), for instance, exchange-rate-based stabilization programs lead to an initial *expansion* and a *recession* later on, whereas money-based programs are characterized by an *initial contraction* in output. The former pattern has been dubbed the **boom-recession cycle** and is particularly marked in settings where the credibility of the stabilization program is low—in the sense of being perceived as *temporary*. Agents, in an attempt to take advantage of temporarily low prices of tradable goods, increase spending. The resulting current account deficit and real exchange rate appreciation (which is particularly marked if *nominal wage contracts* are **backward-looking** and prices are set as a *markup* over production costs) eventually undermine the program and validate expectations—by forcing the authorities eventually to abandon the attempt to fix the exchange rate. By contrast, an expected collapse of a money-based program does not lead to intertemporal expenditure switching because the central bank does not commit its reserves to support the exchange rate; there is, therefore, no anticipation of a currency crisis.

The evidence in favor of large **intertemporal substitution effects** is, however, relatively weak. In particular, the econometric study by Reinhart and Végh (1995) suggested that it can explain the behavior of consumption for some of the programs implemented in the 1980s, but not for the tablita experiments of the 1970s in Argentina, Chile, and Uruguay (see Agénor and Montiel, 1999). Essentially, the low intertemporal substitution parameters estimated for these countries suggest that nominal interest rates would have had to fall substantially more than they did to account for a sizable fraction of the consumption boom recorded in the data.

In a more detailed review of the empirical evidence, Agénor and Montiel (1999) also concluded that intertemporal effects were not large enough to explain the pattern of output, suggesting that other mechanisms may be at play. A particularly promising approach to understanding the behavior of consumption and output in exchange-rate-based stabilization emphasizes the interactions between monetary and *supply-side factors*. Such factors were analyzed, in particular, by Roldós (1995), in a dependent-economy model with capital (which plays a dual role as a financial asset and a production input), endogenous labor supply, and a **cash-in-advance constraint** on purchases of both consumption and capital goods. Roldós showed that, as a result of the cash-in-advance constraint, inflation creates a wedge between the real rate of return on foreign-currency-denominated assets and that of domestic-currency-denominated assets—which include money and capital. Thus, a stabilization program based on a permanent—and thus fully credible, in the Calvo-Végh sense—reduction in the devaluation rate (and ultimately the inflation rate) reduces the wedge and leads to an increase in the desired capital stock in the long run. In the short run, consumption and investment increase, causing a real appreciation, a current account deficit, and an increase in output of home goods. During the transition period, firms increase gradually their purchases of capital goods and their capital stock (which is constant on impact), drawing labor resources into the (capital-intensive) tradables sector, raising wages, and leading to further appreciation of the real exchange rate. Over time, the increase in output of tradable goods lowers the initial current account deficit generated on impact by the increase in aggregate demand.[16] Roldós' model does not predict a recession at a later stage; nevertheless, a comprehensive analysis of alternative models (based on simulation techniques) by Rebelo and Végh (1997) also emphasized the importance of supply-side factors (notably the role of *real wages*) in explaining the boom-recession cycle in exchange-rate-based programs.

Another important consideration is assessing how the relative costs of money-based and exchange-rate-based programs relate to their implications for *remonetization*. A pegged-exchange rate system provides a convenient way for households and enterprises to *rebuild their real money balances* after a period of high inflation.[17] The fall in inflationary expectations that a credible stabilization entails at the outset may lead agents to increase their desired holdings of real money balances. Under a pegged exchange rate, this increase is satisfied automatically through the *balance of payments*, as agents repatriate their capital held abroad and convert it costlessly into domestic currency. By contrast, under a money supply anchor (that is, a floating-rate regime), there is no automatic mechanism for agents to rebuild their real money balances, because the central bank does not have to purchase repatriated capital in return for domestic money—except perhaps for smoothing exchange rate movements. In principle, the central bank could support remonetization of the banking system by *expanding domestic credit* in line with rising demand for real money balances, but such a course of action is difficult to carry out, because domestic credit expansion by itself may undermine the credibility of the stabilization program. Therefore, many central banks refrain from domestic credit expansion, and the economy remains undermonetized, suffering from excessively high real interest rates and an overvalued currency. The result is that successful anti-inflation programs under a money supply target (and floating exchange rates) tend to be more contractionary than those carried out under pegged exchange rates.[18]

---

[16] In a related contribution, Roldós (1997a) showed that a gradual and permanent reduction in the nominal devaluation rate leads to an initial boom when the intertemporal elasticity of substitution in labor supply is larger than that in consumption. The expansion in output occurs in both the tradable and nontradable production sectors, as a result of a reduction in real wages. The reduction in the devaluation rate lowers inflation and raises the marginal value of wealth, thereby raising the opportunity cost of leisure and inducing an increase in labor supply in the initial phase of the program. The continued reduction over time in the rate of devaluation and the rate of inflation leads to further increases in the supply of labor and downward pressure on wages. By contrast, Roldós (1995) found that real wages increase during the transition (after falling on impact), whereas the long-run effect on labor supply is ambiguous.

[17] There exists considerable evidence showing a dramatic rise in velocity or demonetization in high-inflation economies.

[18] However, it should be noted that some recent research by Easterly (1995) and Gould (1996) suggested that money-based programs may *also* be characterized by an initial expansion of output.

5.2.3   Credibility, Fiscal Commitment, and Flexibility

The degree of credibility of the money supply and the exchange rate is an important consideration in choosing a nominal anchor. Credibility depends not only on the policymakers' ability to convey clear signals about their *policy preferences* (as discussed in more detail below) but also on the degree of controllability of policy instruments and the dynamic adjustment path of the economy, as discussed earlier. In particular, the public *observability* of the exchange rate at any point in time—as opposed to monetary and credit aggregates, which are only observable at substantial intervals, based on data that are usually supplied by the government—enhances the credibility of an exchange rate anchor. A money-based stabilization that is accompanied by an *immediate recession*, for instance, may lose credibility rapidly, if the short-term output and employment cost is high. Likewise, when the exchange rate is used as a nominal anchor, *residual inflation* in home goods prices may remain high (as a result, again, of backward-looking wage contracts); combined with the expansion of aggregate demand that often accompanies these programs, it may lead to a *real appreciation* that may immediately weaken the credibility of a policy aimed at fixing the exchange rate, because agents will anticipate future nominal devaluations aimed at realigning relative prices and prevent growing external imbalances.

In general, when lack of credibility is pervasive, the choice between money and the exchange rate may not matter a great deal; inflation will remain high regardless of the anchor.[19] An exchange-rate rule is, however, more successful in reducing inflation if there is *some* degree of credibility in the program; in this case, the initial expansion and the upward pressure on the real exchange rate will be dampened.

It has also been argued that an exchange rate anchor may induce a higher commitment to undertake the necessary accompanying stabilization measures, most importantly *fiscal adjustment*. The reason is that a loss in confidence (inducing large private capital outflows) threatens directly the program's anchor only in an exchange-rate-based stabilization plan. Because avoiding such a risk requires a high degree of confidence in the government's program, it may act as an incentive to stick to the targeted path of fiscal adjustment.[20] Thus, an exchange rate anchor is preferable whenever the underlying commitment of policymakers to fiscal discipline is presumed high.[21] Conversely, if there are doubts about the government's commitment to fiscal restraint, an exchange rate peg would also lack credibility and would be impossible to defend.

---

[19] The ppendix to this chapter shows that, in a setting in which wage contracts are staggered over time, the lower the degree of credibility, the higher will be the degree of inflation persistence.

[20] Note that this argument does not necessarily apply if the exchange stabilization is based on a *crawling peg*, because under such a regime a less stringent path of fiscal adjustment could be accomodated by designing appropriately the preannounced exchange rate depreciation schedule.

[21] The "underlying commitment of policymakers to fiscal discipline" refers to the exogenous preferences of policymakers, as opposed to their actual behavior, which is likely be endogenous to the choice of nominal anchor.

A good illustration of this last point is provided by Végh's (1992) review of ten exchange-rate-based programs (all of them in Latin America, except for the 1985 Israeli stabilization) aimed at stopping high chronic inflation. Seven of these programs were classified as failures, in the sense that the peg could not be sustained and initial reductions in inflation were subsequently reversed. In two cases the failure was attributed to a real appreciation of the currency following slow convergence of inflation, in spite of achieving fiscal balance (Chile and Uruguay, 1978). In the remaining five, however, *failure to implement a lasting fiscal adjustment* was the main factor. This evidence suggests therefore that the discipline induced by an exchange-rate anchor may not, in itself, be sufficient to ensure the fiscal adjustment necessary to sustain the peg.

5.2.4   The Flexibilization Stage

The foregoing discussion suggests that although a pegged exchange rate can be beneficial in stopping high inflation, maintaining it for too long can become problematic once inflation has stabilized at moderate (but not low) rates, with nominal rigidities (in price and wage formation) slowing further declines in inflation. With a fixed nominal exchange rate, continued inflation higher than that prevailing in trading partners implies an appreciation of the real exchange rate, which will erode external competitiveness and—unless matched by productivity gains in the traded goods sector—hinder export expansion.[22] In turn, a deteriorating trade performance may force the authorities to depreciate the exchange rate and reignite inflationary pressures. More generally, a shift toward a more flexible exchange rate regime (such as a *crawling peg* or a *band regime*, as discussed in the previous chapter) once macroeconomic stability is achieved, provides an important mechanism through which adjustment to internal and external shocks can occur.[23] At the same time, because switching away from a pegged rate may be perceived as a reduced commitment to low inflation, emphasis on fiscal and monetary discipline must be renewed to maintain credibility.

5.3   Disinflation Programs: The Role of Credibility

5.3.1   Sources of Credibility Problems

The current literature distinguishes among four different sources of credibility problems in disinflation programs:

---

[22] Note that a large devaluation at the outset of stabilization may lead to a large initial *undervaluation* of the real exchange rate. This strategy may provide a *cushion* to the system by allowing it, at least for a while, to absorb the real appreciation that may result from imposing a fixed exchange rate.

[23] As discussed in the next chapter, exchange rate flexibility may also be useful to facilitate the management of capital inflows. A relatively wide band of permissible currency fluctuations around a central rate, in particular, may help to deter short-term speculative movements.

- **Inconsistency** between the objective of disinflation and the policy instruments to achieve this objective, or the **sequencing** of policy measures in an overall reform program. For instance, if the main source of inflation is a large fiscal deficit and an expansion in money supply, a program that does not specify how fiscal discipline is to be restored will lack credibility.

- **Uncertainty** associated with the policy environment and exogenous shocks, which arises from the fact that the economy may be hit by shocks that are large enough to render the assumptions underlying an even well-designed (or internally consistent) program inadequate. If the *probability* of an adverse shock of this type is high, convincing private agents of the viability of the program targets (in the absence of **contingency mechanisms**) will be difficult and will adversely affect the degree of credibility of the stabilization effort. Examples of adverse shocks include external shocks, such as a deterioration in the country's terms of trade or a rise in interest rates on world capital markets.[24]

- **Time inconsistency** of policy announcements, which results from the fact that a program that is optimal *ex ante* may not be optimal *ex post*. As noted earlier, and as discussed in the previous chapter, time inconsistency leads to an **inflation bias** in monetary policy.

- **Incomplete** or **asymmetric information** about policymakers' preferences, which results from the fact that private agents may not know for sure how strong the commitment to a low-inflation strategy is, particularly at the inception of a stabilization program.

In fact, it is only *over time* that private agents will get to believe that policymakers are serious about their policy goal. This **learning process** will be slow in settings in which policymakers have a long tradition of **stop-and-go policies**, and the rotation of policymakers in office tends to be high—a situation that tends to create some degree of *confusion* regarding the true policy objectives and preferences of policymakers. **Imperfect monitoring capabilities** may also hamper the ability of private agents to detect policymakers' preferences. In particular, private agents may learn only gradually, through a **backward-induction process** (see, for instance, Cukierman, 1992). Under these conditions, policymakers can, in order to generate a temporary output gain, attempt to exploit their informational advantage. Nevertheless, imperfect monitoring capability makes *building reputation* by policymakers *more difficult*; and without a *reputation for seriousness*, policymakers will find it difficult to dampen inflationary expectations and reduce actual inflation.

---

[24] *Political uncertainty* may also affect credibility; the possibility that the government's majority base may collapse (because, for instance, it is built on a coalition of parties with different ideological orientations) may lead private agents to have doubts about the *political feasibility* of the stabilization program and to expect *policy reversals*—an issue that will be examined further in Chapter 17.

Direct and robust quantitative techniques for assessing the relative importance of these various sources of lack of credibility remains limited, and represents an important agenda for future research. At the present time, as discussed
by Agénor and Taylor (1992), there are two commonly used methods:

- Specify a model of the inflationary process in which lagged inflation appears, such as Equation (5.12), and estimate it with *recursive least-squares
  techniques*. Changes over time in the behavior of the coefficient of the
  lagged inflation rate (a measure of **inertia** or **persistence**) can then be
  used to assess changes in the degree of credibility. Increased credibility
  will translate into a lower coefficient. Edwards (1995), for instance, used
  this method to assess the credibility of macroeconomic policy in Venezuela
  during the mid-1970s and 1980s.[25]

- Study changes over time (possibly through *recursive least-squares techniques* as well) in the behavior of the coefficient of a variable measuring
  the opportunity cost of holding domestic money, such as the *expected* inflation rate (often proxied by the lagged actual inflation rate), the domestic
  interest rate, or the rate of depreciation of the (official or parallel) exchange
  rate, in a regression model of *money demand*. The assumption is that increased credibility will translate into not only a lower degree of persistence
  in the inflationary process (as argued earlier) but also in a shift toward
  domestic-currency-denominated assets—and in a lower weight attached to
  changes in the opportunity cost of holding domestic money balances.

5.3.2   Enhancing Credibility

Enhancing the degree of credibility of a disinflation program is important because it raises its probability of success. This subsection discusses four different
ways of doing so: the adoption of a drastic (big bang) program as a way to signal
the policymaker's commitment to disinflation, central bank independence, the
imposition of price controls, and conditional foreign assistance. The discussion
throughout focuses on countries where policymakers must deal with high inflation, rather than hyperinflation. Kiguel and Liviatan (1992b) have argued that
credibility is easier to establish in the latter case. In chronic-inflation countries,
where inertial mechanisms—such as staggered contracts, and implicit or explicit
indexation—are well developed, the public tends to view disinflation programs
as postponable, thus reducing their credibility. By contrast, as noted earlier,
the very nature of hyperinflation often leads private agents to believe that the
process is not sustainable.

---

[25] In Edwards' model of inflation, persistence is associated with both backward wage indexation and an exchange rate rule that relates the nominal devaluation rate to the (lagged)
inflation differential between the domestic economy and the rest of the world. Under full
wage indexation and full exchange rate indexation, inflation will exhibit a *unit root* and be
nonstationary.

Big Bang and Gradualism

A number of economists have advocated an early phase of *overadjustment* (that is, more stringent fiscal and monetary policies than would be otherwise necessary to attain the inflation objective) as a means to *signal* to skeptical agents the policymakers' commitment to inflation stabilization. Such measures may be easier to implement in countries where a new government with a broad anti-inflation mandate is just being put in place, because in such circumstances the public is often more willing to bear the costs that they entail. It has also been argued that the initial costs of a *big bang program* that brings inflation down quickly, although high, may be less than the costs associated with inflation continuing at a higher level for a long period of time.

However, instead of helping to alleviate the credibility problem, adopting an overly tight policy stance may exacerbate it—and lead to a complete abandonment of the stabilization program—because it may create expectations of *future policy reversals*. Such expectations may result from the conjunction of two factors:

- large short-run output and employment costs and a consequent loss of *political support*—particularly if, to begin with, a large political consensus was not established at the outset of the program;

- the fact that the future benefits of disinflation (in terms of a lower inflation tax and higher output) are *heavily discounted* by the public.

In such conditions, enhancing the credibility of a disinflation program may require not so much **shock therapy** but rather the implementation of measures that are regarded as politically and economically *sustainable* and viewed as difficult to reverse by future governments.

Central Bank Independence

An institutional mechanism through which the credibility of policymakers can be enhanced is to grant the central bank full independence in the conduct of monetary and exchange rate policies, with a clear mandate to maintain price stability. Such independence may be critical in countries where central bank financing of government budget deficits is often the main source of inflation. Countries where such reforms have been implemented in recent years include Chile, Mexico, Pakistan and Venezuela.

There are various factors, however, that may *mitigate* the credibility gain to monetary policy that central bank independence may provide.

- *Legal independence* does not guarantee the absence of freedom from *political interference* and *political pressure* on the central bank's policy decisions. In practice, most governments in developing countries retain some degree of influence on these decisions.

- Moreover, as pointed out by Blackburn and Christensen (1989), the government (which established the central bank's independence in the first place) often retains the ability to restructure (or abolish) independence should the central bank refuse to compromise its position (at least partly) on matters over which the government fundamentally disagrees. As a result, even an independent central bank may be willing to make concessions to the government in order to retain its autonomy.

- Adhering to a rigid anti-inflation policy stance implemented by an independent central bank may be suboptimal (compared with some degree of discretion or **contingent rules**) in an economy subject to adverse economic shocks.

- The credibility of monetary policy may depend on the *overall stance* of macroeconomic policy, rather than on the degree of central bank independence *per se*. For instance, if the *fiscal policy targets* adopted by the Treasury are inconsistent with the low-inflation target of the monetary authorities, and are perceived as such by the public, credibility will be impossible to achieve—even with a highly independent central bank.

More generally, independent monetary and fiscal authorities may adopt policies that generate *coordination problems* and generate costs that may outweigh the gain resulting from central bank autonomy alone. This point is well illustrated in the game-theoretic model of monetary and fiscal management built by Alesina and Tabellini (1990), in which inflation, public spending, and the level of *distortionary taxation* are all determined simultaneously from the *strategic interactions* between policymakers who possess conflicting objectives over inflation, employment, and public expenditure levels. The main insight of their analysis is the *ambiguity* of the net benefits from central bank precommitment to low inflation. The reason is that lower inflation reduces the revenue from inflationary finance (as discussed earlier) and forces the fiscal authority, in the presence of downward rigidity on public spending, to resort to a higher level of distortionary taxation.

Some early empirical studies, focusing mostly on *industrial* countries, concluded that countries where central banks had the highest degree of autonomy also had the lowest levels of inflation. Central bank independence in these studies was measured in terms of a variety of factors, including the appointment mechanisms for the governor and the board of directors, the turnover of central bank governors, the approval mechanism for conducting monetary policy (the extent to which the central bank is free from involvement with the government or parliament), statutory requirements of the central bank regarding its basic aim and financing of the budget deficit (including whether or not interest rates are levied on deficit financing), and the existence of a ceiling on total government borrowing from the central bank (see Cukierman, 1992).

However, a more recent review of the empirical literature by Forder (1998) found no robust association between central bank independence and inflation performance in industrial countries and highlighted several methodological problems in many of the early studies. The study by Sikken and De Haan (1998) for *developing* countries was also inconclusive. They measured central bank independence using various indicators:

- the **synthetic legal measure** reported by Cukierman (1992), which incorporates four sets of variables:

  - variables related to the appointment, dismissal, and term of office of the **governor** of the central bank;
  - variables related to the resolution of *conflicts* between the executive branch and the central bank over monetary policy and the participation of the central bank in the budgetary process;
  - **final objectives** of the central bank, as stated in its charter;
  - legal restrictions on the ability of the public sector to *borrow* from the central bank.

- the **turnover rate** of central bank governors, which attempts to capture *actual* (as opposed to legal) *independence*. As noted earlier, in developing countries measures of central bank independence based on legal statutes may be highly inadequate because *political instability* often means that the status of the central bank can be uncertain and/or subject to rapid changes.

- a **political vulnerability index**, defined as the fraction of political transitions that are followed within six months by a replacement of the central bank governor.

Using all four indicators and data for 30 developing countries for the period 1950-94, Sikken and de Haan found no evidence that central bank independence creates an incentive for governments to maintain low fiscal deficits. They also found that measures of independence are not clearly related to the degree of monetization of government budget deficits by the central bank. Thus, both analytical arguments and empirical evidence suggest that central bank independence may not have all the benefits that advocates tend to emphasize.

Price Controls

The case for using price controls has traditionally been viewed as resting on the argument that the inflationary process is characterized by substantial **inertia**, stemming from **explicit** or **implicit** indexation—a common feature, as discussed earlier, of economies suffering from chronically high inflation. Various economists have argued that, in such conditions, restrictive demand policies will be incapable of yielding a rapid fall in inflation.

There are also several arguments in favor of the *temporary* use of price controls which, as noted by Dornbusch, Sturzenegger, and Wolf (1990, pp. 51-52), can be summarized as follows:

- **A realignment device.** In economies in which pricing decisions are not instantaneous (as a result, for instance, of the existence of contracts that last a few months or longer), price controls may help *realign prices* quickly and *correct price distortions.*

- **A coordination device.** Adjusting to a new, low-inflation environment requires price setters to reset their prices. This resetting brings into play expectations about what other agents think; price controls help *coordinate expectations* toward a *low-inflation path.*

- **A fiscal device.** The reverse **Olivera-Tanzi effect** discussed earlier implied that the transition from high to low inflation yields an immediate gain in real revenue from taxation. This may lower the borrowing needs of the government from the central bank, helping to slow monetary expansion and thus overall inflation.

More recently, it has also been argued that price controls—despite the well-known microeconomic distortions that they entail—may help enhance credibility by serving as an *additional nominal anchor.*

Blejer and Liviatan (1987), for instance, considered a situation in which lack of credibility stems from **asymmetric information** between the public and the policymakers. In such conditions, as indicated earlier, the mere announcement of a low-inflation objective will not be fully believed. Private agents will adjust their expectations only gradually, after observing policy decisions. Price controls may give policymakers some *breathing room*—a period during which they can convince the public, by adopting, and sticking to appropriate monetary and fiscal policies, of their commitment to disinflate. By allowing a rapid reduction in inflation, the reverse **Olivera-Tanzi effect** will also lead to an improvement in the fiscal deficit in real terms (as mentioned above), adding credibility to the fiscal component of the program. Along the same lines, Persson and van Wijnbergen (1993) argued that price controls may help policymakers to reduce the **cost of signaling** their commitment to low inflation.

The most frequently cited example of a successful temporary application of price controls is the *Israeli stabilization* of 1985, during which all nominal variables, including the exchange rate, were frozen (see Bruno, 1991, and Kiguel and Liviatan, 1992*a*). Combined with a sharp fiscal contraction and a restrictive monetary policy, the temporary application of price controls led to a quick reduction in inflation and enhanced government credibility, without a severe economic contraction.

However, the use of price controls as a credibility-enhancing device have been criticized from various perspectives. At the conceptual level, at least two arguments make the argument in favor of such controls less than convincing.

- The use of price controls may actually be *counterproductive*—in contrast to the view adopted by Blejer and Liviatan (1987)—because they do not enable the public to learn whether sufficient fiscal restraint has been achieved, that is, whether inflation has really been stopped or has only been temporarily repressed. In fact, controls may *lengthen* the time required for expectations to adjust to a new equilibrium.

- The credibility-enhancing effect of price controls may vanish if policymakers are unwilling or unable to control all prices in the economy, and if *forward-looking price setters* in the *uncontrolled sector* understand the incentives to depart from a preannounced price control policy in an attempt to reduce the macroeconomic costs associated with a price freeze (see Agénor, 1995). Paradoxically, the imposition of price controls in such a framework may lead to **inflation inertia**.

At the practical level, there are also a number of problems associated with the use of price controls. The imposition, enforcement, and phasing out of such controls are often difficult from an administrative point of view. Most importantly, by suppressing some of the symptoms of inflation, price controls have often undermined governments' willingness to attack the disease at its roots. In fact, price controls have often been used as a *substitute*, rather than a *complement*, to fiscal and monetary adjustment. A case in point is Brazil, where three programs implemented in the late 1980s relied on price controls: the Cruzado Plan in 1986, the Bresser Plan in 1987, and the Verano Plan in 1989 (see Agénor and Montiel, 1999). However, because the price freeze was not accompanied by appropriate fiscal and monetary policies, inflation jumped to an even higher level in each case after a brief period of abatement. The repeated use of price controls diminished their effectiveness, as economic agents anticipated the price increases that would follow the flexibilization stage. Other experiences with price controls, as reviewed by Kiguel and Liviatan (1992*a*), lead to similar conclusions.

Aid as a Commitment Mechanism

It has recently been argued that countries engaged in disinflation programs may enhance their credibility and the probability of program success by subjecting themselves to an external enforcement agency whose commitment to low inflation is well established—such as a multilateral institution like the International Monetary Fund. Such an agency, in turn, provides foreign assistance *conditional* on attaining specific macroeconomic (and possibly structural) policy targets. Conditionality turns therefore the commitment mechanism into a *carrot-and-stick* one, which may strengthen the determination of the policymakers to enforce the terms of the agreement.

However, a variety of potential difficulties arise in judging the credibility-enhancing effect of foreign assistance.

- *Political considerations* often play a role in deciding whether particular countries should receive external financial assistance support. As a result, the public may be unwilling to accept an externally enforced program as a signal of the policymakers' commitment to low inflation.

- Conditionality is a *double-edged sword*. At the right level, it serves as an incentive to stick to the terms of the agreed program. However, if the degree of conditionality attached to foreign aid is perceived to be excessive (in the sense of being based on unreasonably tight policy targets), *uncertainty* about external support may rise, leading to a loss in political support, delays in stabilization and a higher possibility for the program to collapse (Orphanides, 1996).

5.4 Two Recent Stabilization Experiments

Episodes of chronically high inflation or outright hyperinflation have been common in the developing world for at least the past three decades.[26] A considerable literature (much of it summarized by Agénor and Montiel, 1999) has been devoted to the inflationary episodes of the 1980s and early 1990s, particularly those that brought chaos to several countries in Latin America. Instead of providing a detailed overview of this literature, this section focuses on two recent experiences: Egypt (1992-97) and Uganda (1987-95). These two cases illustrate well the main approaches to stabilize high inflation reviewed earlier. The Egyptian program is more akin to an exchange-rate-based stabilization whereas the Ugandan case is representative of a money-based approach. Both cases are also useful to emphasize the role of fiscal adjustment in stabilization programs.

5.4.1 Egypt, 1992-97

In the second half of the 1980s and early 1990s, Egypt faced large macroeconomic imbalances (see Figure 5.7).

- Although inflation, at an average rate of about 20 percent during the period 1985/86 to 1990/91, was not excessively high, the fiscal deficit reached an average of 15 percent of GDP during the same period, and annual rates of money growth averaged 18 percent.[27]

- The *dollarization ratio*, as measured by the share of foreign currency (U.S. dollar) deposits in total bank deposits, grew to about 40 percent in 1988 and 46 percent in 1990.

- Although a series of nominal devaluations, beginning in 1986, led to a depreciation of about 30 percent between 1986 and 1991 of the real effective exchange rate, the current account deficit reached about 8 percent of GDP in 1988/89 and almost 10 percent in 1990/91.

- Gross external debt increased substantially, amounting to about 147 percent of GDP during the period 1988/89-1990/91. Debt service, in proportion of exports of goods and services, exceeded 25 percent in 1989/90.

---

[26] There have also been episodes of chronic but moderate inflation; see Dornbusch and Fischer (1993) for a discussion of some of these cases.

[27] The fiscal year starts in July of the first year noted and ends in June of the following year.

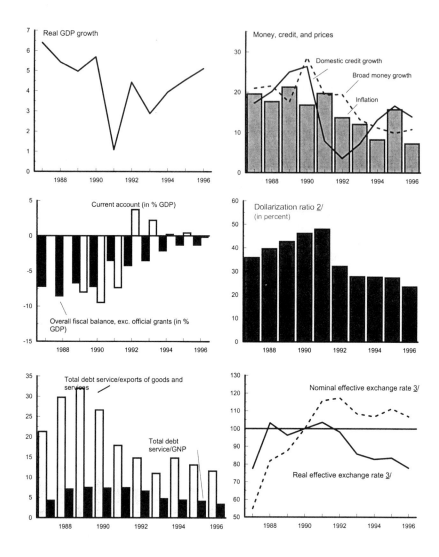

Figure 5.7. Egypt: Macroeconomic Indicators, 1987-96 (In percent per annum, unless otherwise indicated).

Source: International Monetary Fund.

1/ Data refer to the fiscal year (July 1-June 30), except for exchange rates. 1988, for instance, refers to 1987/88.

2/ U.S. dollar deposits in percent of total deposits.

3/ 1990=100; a rise is a depreciation.

Following several unsuccessful attempts at tackling these imbalances and liberalizing the economy, a program of macroeconomic stabilization and structural reform was implemented in 1991. Key features of the program were a combination of fiscal, monetary, and credit policies together with an exchange rate anchor policy which was viewed as a way of

- signaling the government's commitment to disinflate;

- limiting *pass-through effects* of nominal exchange rate changes on prices.

The program led to a substantial adjustment of fiscal accounts, through both increases in revenue and reductions in expenditure.

- A general sales tax was introduced in 1991, and a global income tax reform was implemented in 1993, with significant effects on revenue.

- The domestic-currency value of oil revenues and Suez Canal receipts as well as taxes on imports also increased substantially in early 1991, as a result of the depreciation of the exchange rate.

- Cuts in public expenditure amounted to about 7.5 percent of GDP. These cuts were largely concentrated on investment outlays; cuts in current expenditure affected mostly subsidies and transfers rather than wages.

- The debt forgiveness and rescheduling agreement that Egypt reached with its official creditors through the **Paris Club** in 1991 also led to a substantial reduction in interest payments on external foreign debt.[28] Interest payments as a percent of GDP fell from a peak of 9.5 percent in 1993/94, to 6.2 percent in 1996/97 (Handy et al.,1998, p. 16).

As a result of these measures, the overall deficit of the government declined sharply from about -8.6 percent of GDP in 1987/88 to -3.5 percent in 1992/93 and -1.3 in 1994/95. At the same time, the primary fiscal balance of the government improved from a deficit of about 9 percent of GDP in 1987/88 to a surplus of 5 percent in 1992/93 and 6.1 percent in 1994/95. Most of this adjustment took place during the first two years of the program. Gross domestic public debt fell from 70.5 percent of GDP in 1990/91 to 52 percent in 1996/97.[29]

Fiscal adjustment led to a sharp reduction in broad money growth, which fell from 28.7 percent in 1989/90 to 11.2 percent in 1993/94 and 10.5 percent in 1996/97. The rate of inflation declined from 16.8 percent in 1989/90 to 8.2 percent in 1993/94 and 6.2 percent in 1996/97. The intensified adjustment efforts from 1991 onward, combined with debt relief and a surge in capital inflows, also resulted in an improvement in external accounts and a substantial accumulation of foreign reserves. The current account improved from a deficit of about 9.5 percent in 1989/90 to a surplus of 1.1 percent on average for the period 1991/92-1996/97. Official reserves reached US\$ 28 billion in 1995/96. The ratio

---

[28] The Paris Club is an association of bilateral creditor countries (mostly industrial countries). See Chapter 16 for a discussion of its role in the context of debt rescheduling arrangements.

[29] During the same period Egypt also implemented a number of structural reforms aimed at liberalizing the trade system, eliminating input and consumer goods subsidies, and privatizing public sector enterprises.

of gross foreign debt to GDP fell from about 83 percent in 1990/91 to about 39 percent in 1996/97; the ratio of debt service to exports of goods and services fell from a peak of 26.6 percent in 1989/90 to 14.8 percent in 1993/94 and less than 13 percent in 1996/97. The improvement in external accounts occurred despite a significant appreciation of the real effective exchange rate (based on consumer prices), by about 30 percent between July 1991 and December 1996.[30]

The *dollarization ratio* fell from about 46 percent in 1989/90 to about 32 percent in 1991/92, 23 percent in 1995/96, and 20 percent in 1996/97. The de-dollarization process was accelerated by the large differential between interest rates on domestic assets and dollar deposits, which fell to 5 percent in 1994/95, compared with about 14 percent in 1991/92. In addition, the disinflation program appears to have gained credibility fairly rapidly, leading to a reduction in expectations of inflation and currency devaluation. Large capital inflows (a cumulative value of about US$ 5 billion, or 10.6 percent of GDP, between 1991/92 and 1993/94 alone) and the buildup of foreign reserves (which increased the central bank's ability to fend off speculative attacks) also enhanced the credibility of the exchange rate peg.[31]

The output cost of disinflation was a short-lived recession: real GDP growth dropped to 1.1 percent in 1990/91 (compared to 5.7 during the previous fiscal year) bur rebounded rapidly to 4.6 percent in 1994/95 and 5 percent on average for 1995/96-1996/97. This reflected two factors.

- Real credit growth to the nongovernment sector remained positive throughout the stabilization program, averaging 11 percent between 1992/93 and 1996/97. The share of domestic bank credit to the private sector reached 43 percent in January 1996, compared with 29 percent in 1990/91.

- Although interest rates were liberalized in early 1991 and jumped to relatively high levels at the inception of the program, they went down very quickly. Nominal interest rates on deposits reached 16 percent in 1991/92 but declined to 10 percent in 1995/96; during the same period, lending rates dropped from 19 percent to 14 percent. Real interest rates on deposits declined from 4.7 percent in 1991/92 to 2.9 percent in 1994/95 (Subramanian (1997)). This rapid decline in interest rates reflected both the rapid fall in inflation and the credibility gains, which dampened inflationary expectations; it avoided excessive financial pressure on weak firms and avoided a high default rate on their bank obligations.

---

[30] The dollar wage index computed by Subramanian (1997) suggests a real appreciation of about 25 percent between 1990/91 and 1995/96. The extent to which this appreciation reflected or not an *equilibrium* phenomenon, induced by productivity gains in the tradables sector, remains a matter of debate (see Subramanian, 1997).

[31] During the period 1991/92 to 1993/94, Egypt conducted massive *sterilization operations* to neutralize the effect of capital inflows on the monetary base (see Chapter 6). The *fiscal cost of sterilization*—calculated as the change in net domestic assets of the Central Bank of Egypt, which can be viewed as the counterpart to the capital inflows, times the interest rate differential between domestic and foreign assets—is estimated by Subramanian (1997) to have reached a cumulative value of 4 percent of output. See also Handy et al. (1998, pp. 26-33).

Key lessons of Egypt's stabilization experience are the importance of fiscal adjustment and the role of external factors. Debt reduction and write-offs (through their effect on debt service payments) contributed in significant ways to fiscal adjustment and improvements in the country's external accounts—despite an appreciating real exchange rate. Tighter policies, with a potentially higher output cost, would have been needed otherwise if the external constraint had been more severe. External assistance played an essential role in helping the program gain credibility rapidly, corroborating, to some extent, the potentially positive role of foreign aid highlighted earlier.

5.4.2   Uganda, 1987-95

Uganda faced a difficult economic situation in the mid-1980s, in part as a result of a civil war that started in the early 1980s and the economic devastation (notably in the transportation, power, and water facilities) that was associated with it. In 1986, per capita GDP was estimated to be at about 50 percent below the level of 1970, and inflation had risen to a yearly rate of 240 percent, from about 70 percent on average between 1978 and 1980. Domestic inflation combined with a fixed exchange rate regime led to a significant real appreciation and a loss of competitiveness. Foreign exchange shortages (despite increasing external payments arrears) led to a considerable spread between the official exchange rate and the parallel market exchange rate. The country also faced a significant and sustained deterioration in its terms of trade throughout the late 1980s and early 1990s; in part as a consequence of the collapse of the *International Coffee Agreement*, the price of coffee (Uganda's main export) declined steadily between 1985 and 1993. As a result, the country's terms of trade deteriorated every year from 1986 through 1992.

In 1987 the authorities launched a major stabilization effort in the context of a broad structural adjustment package, the *Economic Recovery Program*.[32] Stabilization took place through a tightening of monetary and fiscal policies. The Uganda shilling was devalued in May 1987 by 77 percent, with several smaller step devaluations initiated subsequently. The currency depreciation was accompanied by a substantial increase in producer prices, including a large rise in the coffee price paid to farmers. Import restrictions were also progressively removed.

GDP growth responded quickly to the adjustment measures, increasing in the first year of the program by about 8 percent over the previous year (Figure 5.8). But there was less success in achieving the program's stabilization objectives in the early years. Inflation remained high, reaching an annual rate of almost 200 percent in 1987/88.[33] The main factors behind this result were the insufficient effort to tighten fiscal policy, and the excessive growth of bank

---

[32] Other objectives of the program included substantial structural reforms in the areas of price liberalization, exchange and payment liberalization, public enterprise reform, financial sector reform, civil service reform, and army demobilization. See Sharer, De Zoysa, and McDonald (1995).

[33] The fiscal year starts in July of the first year noted and ends in June of the following year.

credit to the government. During the same period, broad money increased also by about 200 percent. Although both inflation and money supply growth fell significantly in 1988/89 (to about 100 percent and 75 percent, respectively) insufficient efforts to curb government spending led to a further increase in the fiscal deficit.

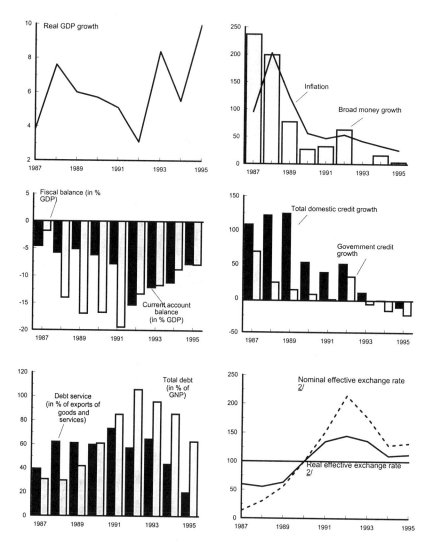

Figure 5.8. Uganda: Macroeconomic Indicators, 1987-95 1/ (In percent per annum, unless otherwise indicated).

Source: Sharer et al. (1995), International Monetary Fund and World Bank.

1/ Data refer to the fiscal year (July 1-June30) except for exchange rates. 1988, for instance, refers to 1987/88.

2/ 1990=100; a rise is a depreciation.

In addition to a lack of fiscal adjustment, the difficulties in achieving early price stabilization and an improvement in external accounts reflected also the maintenance of an *overvalued exchange rate*, and a difficult external environment. Indeed, Uganda faced a major deterioration in its *terms of trade* during the period 1987/88 to 1992/93. From a price of $2.05 per kilogram, coffee export prices fell steadily, reaching a low of $0.82 per kilogram in 1992/93—a decline of 60 percent. Accordingly, the value of export earnings dropped from $384 million in 1986/87 to $157 million in 1992/93. The lack of foreign exchange led to an accumulation of external arrears and an expansion of parallel currency markets.

Corrective actions were implemented during 1989/90 and 1990/91. The Uganda shilling was devalued by about 41 percent in late 1989, with further adjustments taking place in the ensuing periods. Government spending was cut and tax revenues increased. The improvement in the fiscal position led to a reduction in credit expansion and money supply growth. As a result, inflation dropped to slightly below 30 percent in 1990/91 (Figure 5.8). Continued efforts to liberalize domestic prices and the exchange system (through notably the adoption of a bureau market for foreign exchange receipts for noncoffee exports and private transfers) provided strong incentives to domestic producers and exporters of noncoffee products. Partly as result of these measures, the current account improved somewhat in 1991/92. However, because of weather-related supply factors and renewed pressure on domestic credit growth to the government (resulting from an increase in public sector spending), inflation rose to about 63 percent in that same year.

Fiscal and monetary discipline returned during the period 1992/93 to 1994/95.

- Strict expenditure control was accompanied with revenue measures and improved tax administration. Recurrent government expenditure dropped from 22.6 percent in 1991/92 to 18.7 percent in 1994/95, whereas total tax revenue rose to about 8 percent of GDP in 1992/93 and 10.5 percent in 1994/95, compared with 5.6 percent in 1988/89. The fiscal deficit dropped significantly from the peak reached in 1990/91.

- In November 1993, the foreign exchange market was unified with the introduction of an interbank market; all restrictions on current international transactions were also eliminated at the same time.[34] The removal of these restrictions not only provided strong investment incentives to exporters but also led to large private capital inflows.

Prices actually fell in 1992/93 by 0.6 percent, rose by 16 percent in 1993/94—in part as a result of adverse supply-side shocks—and by only 3.4 percent in 1994/95. The foreign exchange market was further liberalized. At the same time, real output growth reached 8.4 percent in 1992/93, 5.5 percent in 1993/94, and 10 percent in 1994/95. Broad money growth dropped to about 25 percent in 1994/95. The external current account deficit (including official grants) fell to -12.1 percent, -11.2 percent and -7.8 percent during the same period, compared

---

[34] Chapter 15 discusses policy issues associated with exchange market unification.

with -15.3 percent in 1991/92. The reduction in the external deficit in 1993/94 and 1994/95 was partly due to an improvement in the terms of trade, resulting from a recovery of world coffee prices and the substantial depreciation of the real effective exchange rate recorded over the previous years. However, debt and the external debt-service ratio remained high (see Chapter 16).

The experience of Egypt and Uganda shows that *fiscal adjustment* played a key role in the stabilization program. In Uganda such adjustment took not only the form of a reduction and reallocation of government expenditure (toward a rehabilitation of an infrastructure devastated by the civil war) but also a rise in revenue and a strengthening of tax administration. Fiscal adjustment (as well as financial sector reform, such as a restructuring of weak banks) allowed the authorities to maintain control over the money supply—and ultimately to tame inflation. The choice of a nominal anchor is by no means inconsequential, as discussed earlier, but without a significant reduction in fiscal imbalances, stabilization cannot last—regardless of the anchor chosen. A similar conclusion is reached by Ter-Minassian and Schwartz (1997) in a review of various stabilization programs implemented in Latin America since the early 1980s.[35]

At the same time, it is also important to emphasize that the *composition* of fiscal adjustment, or the way fiscal imbalances are reduced for stabilization purposes, also has important implications for growth that should be taken into account. The evidence for Latin America, in particular, suggests indeed that the initial brunt of expenditure cuts in stabilization programs often fell on public investment and/or operation and maintenance spending, as expenditures on wages and entitlement programs (such as social security payments, pensions, and transfers to various levels of government) are relatively inflexible in the short run (Ter-Minassian and Schwartz, 1997). It is also worth emphasizing that it does make a difference whether the fiscal deficit is reduced by cutting unproductive expenditure or by raising a tax that has strong disincentive effects—even though from the point of view of macroeconomic adjustment the result would appear to be similar. In particular, as discussed in Chapter 12, high rates of taxation levied on a narrow tax base foster tax evasion and may lead to an expansion of the *informal economy*, exacerbating fiscal constraints in the longer run.

5.5   Summary

- **Hyperinflation** (defined as an inflation rate of 50 percent per month or higher) is generally characterized by *large fiscal imbalances*, the disappearance of *nominal inertia* (with price setting and even transactions occurring in a foreign currency), and the perception that the process is unsustainable.

- **Chronic inflation** is characterized by less acute *fiscal imbalances* (which often makes it more difficult to mobilize political support for reform), a high degree of *inertia* resulting from widespread indexation of wages

---

[35] See also Agénor and Montiel (1999, Chapter 9).

and financial assets, and *lack of credibility* in the policymakers' ability to stabilize.

- Fiscal imbalances and pressures to monetize budget deficits may lead the economy to a *stable inflation equilibrium* or **high inflation trap**.

- Other sources of chronic inflation include nominal wage inertia (through implicit or explicit indexation), exchange rate depreciation and changes in the terms of trade (which may have direct and indirect effects on the budget), the frequency of price adjustment, changes in food prices, and the **inflation bias** of monetary policy, which results from the **time inconsistency** problem faced by **policy announcements**.

The choice between the exchange rate and the money supply as a **nominal anchor** depends on the *degree of controllability* and the effectiveness of the instrument in bringing down inflation, the *adjustment path* of the economy and the *relative costs* associated with each instrument, and the *degree of credibility* that each instrument commands.

- Whereas the money supply cannot be controlled directly, fixing the exchange rate entails essentially no costs. In addition, *instability in money demand* may preclude the adoption of a monetary target. Because it is an *easily monitored* target, a pegged rate is an attractive option in that it establishes an immediate *focal point* for coordinating price expectations and price setting.

- However, policymakers must also be able to *convince* agents of their ability to defend the pegged rate; this may be difficult if the current account deficit is large or if official reserves are deemed insufficient. In such conditions, **speculative attacks** may precipitate a currency collapse.

- The *adjustment paths* associated with money- and exchange-rate-based stabilization program (and thus the relative output costs associated with each instrument) tend to differ significantly. Exchange-rate stabilization programs are often characterized by a **boom-recession cycle**: an initial expansion in output and aggregate demand, and later on a recession.

- One explanation for the initial boom is related to the *lack of confidence* in the program's success: the perception that the program is likely to be *temporary* induces a boom in demand in anticipation of a collapse. The evidence on intertemporal substitution effects, however, does not suggest that such effects are large enough to explain the pattern of output. A more promising approach focuses on the *supply-side effects* of stabilization.

- The *degree of credibility* of the money supply and the exchange rate as nominal anchors depends in part on the policymakers' ability to signal its *policy preferences*, and in part also on the degree of controllability of policy instruments and the dynamic adjustment path. An exchange rate anchor may induce a higher commitment to undertake necessary fiscal adjustment measures.

- The main risk associated with a fixed exchange rate anchor comes from the side of inflation. Because prices often do not stop rising immediately after the nominal exchange rate is fixed, the *real* exchange rate becomes progressively overvalued. In turn, overvaluation creates expectations of devaluation.

- To avoid this problem, the exchange rate should be fixed at the outset, but once a significant reduction in inflation is achieved, a more flexible arrangement (a *crawling peg* or a *band regime*) should be adopted, in order to maintain a competitive real exchange rate.

- To the extent that the regime switch may increase inflationary pressures, fiscal policy may need to play a greater role in ensuring and maintaining macroeconomic stability.

Sources of *credibility problems* in disinflation programs include

- **inconsistency** between the disinflation goal and the policy instruments used to achieve this goal;

- **uncertainty,** in the absence of *contingency mechanisms*, associated with the policy environment and exogenous shocks;

- the **time-inconsistency** problem of policy announcements, which leads to an **inflation bias** in monetary policy;

- **incomplete** or **asymmetric information** about policymakers, which results from the fact that private agents may not know for sure how strong the commitment to a low-inflation strategy is.

The literature suggests four ways of *enhancing the degree of credibility* of a disinflation program:

- The adoption of a *drastic program* as a way to signal the policymaker's commitment to disinflation. However, an overly tight policy stance may exacerbate the credibility problem if it creates expectations of *future policy reversals*.

- Granting the central bank *full independence* in the conduct of monetary and exchange rate policies, with a clear mandate to maintain price stability.

    - However, *legal* independence does not guarantee the absence of freedom from *political interference* and *political pressure* on the central bank's policy decisions.

  – Moreover, adhering to a rigid anti-inflation policy may be suboptimal (compared with some degree of discretion) in an economy subject to adverse economic shocks. The credibility of monetary policy may also depend on the *overall stance* of macroeconomic policy, rather than on the degree of central bank independence.

- The temporary imposition of *price controls* as an additional nominal anchor, to help realign prices quickly and correct price distortions, coordinate expectations toward a low-inflation path, and increase real tax revenue (through a reverse **Olivera-Tanzi effect**). However, price controls may actually *lengthen* the time required for expectations to adjust to a new equilibrium, and may paradoxically lead to **inflation inertia**—if policymakers are unable to control all prices in the economy, and if price setters in the uncontrolled sector are forward looking. There are also a number of practical problems associated with the use of price controls.

- Recourse to *conditional foreign assistance* by an external enforcement agency whose commitment to low inflation is well established. However, an externally enforced program may be a noisy signal of the policymakers' commitment to low inflation due to political factors. Conditionality is also a double-edged sword. If the degree of conditionality attached to foreign aid is perceived to be excessive, it may increase uncertainty about its availability and lead to delays in stabilization.

- The experience of many developing countries (including Egypt and Uganda) suggest that, although the choice of a nominal anchor does matter, successful and lasting stabilization requires fiscal adjustment.

- But fiscal policy packages can differ significantly in terms of their (actual and perceived) degree of sustainability and can thus be associated with different patterns of behavior. Specifically, fiscal measures that are not perceived as being politically sustainable (such as a drastic cut in public sector wages) may lack credibility and may create expectations of future fiscal expansion and monetization.

Appendix
Inflation Persistence and Policy Credibility

This appendix presents a simple open-economy model, from Agénor and Taylor (1992), with overlapping wage contracts. The model demonstrates the link between the perceived degree of policy credibility and the degree of inflation persistence.

Let y_t, p_t, and e_t denote the logarithms of domestic output, prices, and the exchange rate (the domestic price of foreign currency), respectively. Output is demand determined and capacity output is normalized to zero. Foreign prices are held constant and also normalized to zero. Aggregate demand is assumed to be given by

$$y_t = \alpha(m_t - p_t) + \beta(e_t - p_t) + u_t, \tag{A1}$$

where u_t is a stochastic demand shock.

As in Taylor's (1980) model, wage setting is *staggered* so that optimal average current prices are an average of wages set in the current and the previous period, w_t and w_{t-1}, less any productivity shocks, s_t:

$$p_t = 0.5(w_t + w_{t-1}) - s_t. \tag{A2}$$

Wage contracts are set for half the labor force each period and last for two periods. Wage negotiators are assumed to attempt to maintain a constant real wage for the duration of the contract. If δ denotes the share of domestic goods in the consumption basket of workers, then the target wage is given by

$$w_t = 0.5[\delta p_t + (1 - \delta)e_t] \tag{A3}$$

$$+0.5[\delta E_t p_{t+1} + (1 - \delta)E_t e_{t+1}] + 0.5\gamma(y_t + E_t y_{t+1}),$$

where $\gamma > 0$ and E_t denotes the mathematical expectation operator conditional on information available to wage contract negotiators in period t. Equation (A3) thus represents both cost-push inflationary factors (the first two terms), as well as demand-pull inflationary factors (the last term).

Now, suppose that the exchange rate is fixed at $\bar{e}$ and that the monetary policy rule is such that

$$m_t = \phi p_t + v_t, \tag{A4}$$

where $0 < \phi < 1$ and v_t represents money supply shocks. The parameter ϕ measures the degree of monetary accommodation.

Solving Equations(A1) through (A4) for domestic prices, and setting $\bar{e} = 0$ for simplicity, yields the following difference equation:

$$p_t = \frac{\mu}{4}(p_t + E_t p_{t+1} + p_{t-1} + E_{t-1} p_t + \lambda_t - s_t), \tag{A5}$$

where

$$\mu = \delta + \alpha\gamma(1 - \phi) - \beta\gamma,$$

and

$$\lambda_t = \frac{\gamma}{4} \left[\alpha \{ u_t + E_t u_{t+1} + u_{t-1} + E_{t-1} u_t \} + v_t + E_t v_{t+1} + v_{t-1} + E_{t-1} v_t \right].$$

Solving Equation (A5) forward yields

$$E_{t-1} p_t = \kappa_1 p_{t-1} + \left(\frac{4}{\mu \kappa_2} \right) \sum_{i=0}^{\infty} \kappa_2^{-i} E_{t-1} (\lambda_{t+i} - s_{t+i}), \tag{A6}$$

where κ_1 and κ_2 are the roots of the system, $0 < \kappa_1 < 1 < \kappa_2$, and κ_1 is given by

$$\kappa_1 = \frac{2 - \mu}{\mu} - \frac{(2 - \mu)^2 - \mu^2}{\mu}.$$

If all stochastic shocks affecting aggregate demand, the money supply, and productivity are assumed to be simple **random walks** (so that, for instance, $E_{t-1} v_t = v_{t-1}$) then a closed-form solution for inflation may be derived from Equations (A5)and (A6):

$$\Delta p_t = \kappa_1 \Delta p_{t-1} + \psi_t, \tag{A7}$$

where ψ_t is a composite shock with $E_{t-1} \psi_t = 0$.

Thus, from Equation (A7), inflation will follow an $AR(1)$process with an autoregressive parameter κ_1. Moreover, from the above definitions of μ and κ_1, it can be shown that $\partial \kappa_1 / \partial \phi > 0$; the degree of inflation persistence rises with the degree of monetary accommodation. Indeed, with full monetary accommodation ($\phi = 1$), then $\kappa_1 = 1$, the inflation process contains a **unit root**, and the system is unstable.

To examine the effect of a lack of policy credibility on inflation persistence in the above framework, suppose that the authorities announce a nonaccomodative policy of the type $m_t = \bar{m}$, but agents attach a probability $0 < \rho < 1$ that the policy will actually be implemented. The probability that the accommodative policy rule (A4) will be followed instead is therefore $1 - \rho$. Solving the model as before, it is straightforward to verify that $\partial \kappa_1 / \partial \rho < 0$; the higher the credibility of the announced low inflation policy, the lower will be the degree of inflation persistence.

Chapter 6

Capital Inflows: Causes and Policy Responses

The degree of integration of financial markets around the world has increased dramatically in recent years. Measured in absolute terms, net capital flows to developing countries reached during 1993-96 their highest level since the debt crisis of the early 1980s. Private capital flows, in particular, have increased sharply since the early 1990s and have shifted from bank to nonbank sources, such as direct investment flows and portfolio investment (equities, bonds, and certificates of deposit). Such flows provide important potential benefits; in particular, they expand investors' opportunities for portfolio diversification and provide a potential for achieving higher risk-adjusted rates of return. The potential welfare gains resulting for international risk sharing can be large (Obstfeld (1994)). At the same time, however, the risk of abrupt reversals in capital flows has raised concerns among policymakers around the world. Such concerns were heightened by several recent financial crises—including (as discussed in the next chapter) the Mexican peso crisis of December 1994, the Asian crisis triggered by the collapse of the Thai baht in July 1997, and the Brazilian real crisis of January 1999. A key issue has been to identify the policy prerequisites that allow countries to exploit the gains, and minimize the risks, associated with financial integration.

This chapter provides an overview of the evidence on the determinants of, and policy issues associated with, the surge in capital flows. The first part discusses the recent behavior of capital flows, looking at both aggregate and individual-country data. The second part examines the factors (domestic and external) that account for the process of globalization of capital markets and the dramatic expansion of private capital flows since the early 1990s. The third part reviews the recent evidence on the volatility of various components of capital flows. The links between capital inflows, liquidity expansion, and movements in the real exchange rate are discussed in the fourth part. The last part examines the policy options that policymakers may have recourse to in order to limit the adverse short-term effects of capital flows on the economy. The analysis focuses, in particular, on sterilization policies, exchange rate flexibility, fiscal adjustment, as well as non-market-based approaches—including capital controls and changes in statutory reserve requirements.

6.1   The Surge in Capital Flows

Figure 6.1 illustrates the evolution of capital flows to developing countries during the period 1984-97. The figure shows that total *net* capital flows to develop-ing countries increased dramatically since 1989, particularly to Asia and Latin America. Annual inflows averaged more than $150 billion a year between 1990 and 1995, and exceeded $200 billion in 1996—an amount well above 2 percent of the combined GDP of developing countries.[1] The increase in *gross* flows since the mid-1980s has, in fact, been almost seven times as large as the increase in net flows. Figure 6.2 displays the behavior of total private capital flows in pro-portion of output for six countries in Asia and Latin America that accounted for the overwhelming proportion of total inflows to developing countries during the period 1982-97: Chile, Indonesia, Korea, Malaysia, Mexico, and Thailand. Again, the figure shows the dramatic increase in inflows in the early 1990s. Net inflows to some of these countries averaged 5 to 8 percent GDP over the period.[2] At the same time, *Africa* as a whole—with the exception of Nigeria and countries in North Africa (such as Tunisia and Morocco)—has attracted very little capital flows. This has reflected various factors, including most no-tably low growth prospects, political instability, and a volatile macroeconomic environment—all of which make returns on investments in many African coun-tries highly uncertain (see Bhattacharya, Montiel, and Sharma, 1997).

The data shown in Figure 6.1 also reveal a major change in the *composition of capital flows*. Indeed, much of the increase in capital inflows to developing countries since the early 1990s has taken the form of **portfolio investment** (including bonds, equities, and short-term instruments such as certificates of deposits and commercial paper), and **net direct investment**—particularly in Asia. *Short-term flows* (which include mostly interbank lending) have also increased significantly. By contrast, net *official flows* have fallen quite dramat-ically compared with the early 1980s in all regions. During the 1970s and early 1980s, most financing was indeed from commercial banks (to governments), and equity investment (both portfolio and direct) was a much smaller percentage than it is now.

Figures 6.3 and 6.4 show the behavior of total **foreign direct investment** (FDI) and **portfolio flows**, also in proportion of output, for the six Asian and Latin American countries shown in Figure 6.2. The data show that in recent years the composition of capital inflows to Asia has shifted significantly toward

---

[1] It should be noted, however, that as a percentage of exports, total aggregate resource flows to developing countries during the early 1990s, although much above their level in the mid-1980s, remained below their level in the mid- to late 1970s.

[2] As noted by Calvo and Reinhart (1996), several smaller countries in Latin America and elsewhere have also experienced large increases in capital inflows; when measured in proportion of GDP, these flows almost match those recorded by the larger countries.

portfolio investment. Equity flows to these countries, in particular, have taken the following forms:

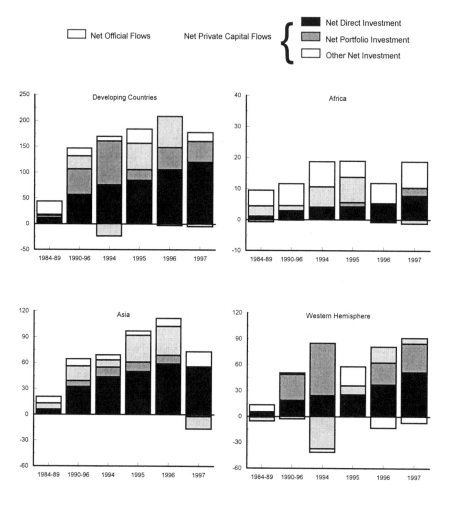

Figure 6.1. Net Capital Flows to Developing Countries, 1984-97 (In billions of US dollars).
Source: International Monetary Fund.

- **direct equity purchases** by foreign investors in domestic stock markets;

- investments through **open-end** (or **closed-end**) **country funds**, that is, mutual funds that allow (or prevent) shareholders to redeem (or from redeeming) their shares at any moment in time, at the prevailing market prices;

- **direct equity offerings**, that is, sales of new equity issues by direct placement with specific institutional investors;

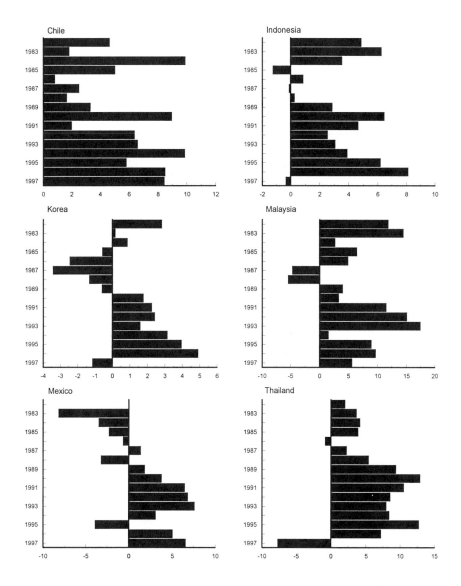

Figure 6.2. Selected Countries: Net Private Capital Flows, 1982-97 (In percent of GDP).

Source: International Monetary Fund.

- issues of rights on equities held by depository institutions in the form of **American Depository Receipts** (ADRs) and **Global Depository Receipts** (GDRs). ADRs and GDRs are receipts issued by financial intermediaries in industrial countries against shares held in custody by these intermediaries in the developing countries.

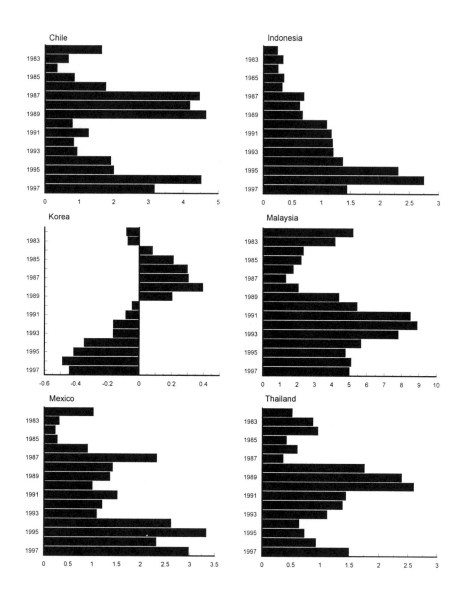

Figure 6.3. Selected Countries: Net Foreign Direct Investment, 1982-97 (In percent of GDP).

Source: International Monetary Fund.

The rising share of FDI has generally been considered to be one of the positive aspects of the surge in capital flows—in particular because it is generally taken to be determined by long-term profitability considerations (which makes these flows less subject to sudden shifts in market sentiment, as discussed in the next chapter) and often leads to the transfer of state-of-the-art technology. This latter aspect, as discussed in Chapter 12, is particularly important as a mechanism to foster economic growth.[3] However, there are several reasons why estimates of foreign direct investment flows, as measured by conventional balance-of-payments statistics, may *overstate* the actual importance of these flows (International Monetary Fund, 1997*a*, p. 64):

- FDI flows reported in Figure 6.3 include among other items new equity, retained earnings, intra-firm debt, and valuation adjustments. However, valuation adjustments largely reflect *currency fluctuations*; adding them to reported FDI flows distorts the data.

- The distinction between FDI and portfolio flows in balance-of-payments statistics is *arbitrary*. Foreign investment in the equity of a company above a critical proportion (usually 10 percent) of outstanding equity is classified as FDI, whereas that below the critical threshold is classified as portfolio investment. However, small differences above (below) the critical level do not necessarily represent any significant difference in the intentions of investors.

- If the foreign company undertaking the FDI borrows locally (from, say, a local bank) to finance its investment depending on the form of incorporation of the company locally, the setup of the plant may count as FDI while the bank lending could show up as a capital outflow, reducing the proportion of net bank lending in overall flows and raising the proportion of reported FDI flows.

- In some countries there may be tax or regulatory benefits from rechanneling domestic investment outlays through offshore instruments. As a result, FDI flows to the domestic economy may be overstated.

6.2   Domestic and External Factors

The process of globalization of capital markets and the surge in capital flows to developing countries have been the result of a variety of factors. Advances in *financial technology, information processing,* and *communications* have played an important role in explaining the increase in the speed of capital mobility. The dismantling of **capital controls** (as shown in Figure 6.5) and other barriers to financial transactions in many developing countries have also had a significant impact on the process of global financial integration. In particular, the removal of restrictions on repatriation of profits, and foreign ownership and participation in domestic stock markets, contributed to the expansion of equity flows to several developing countries.

---

[3] However, recent evidence also suggests that there is a threshold level of *income per capita* and *human capital* that needs to be crossed before FDI can make a significant contribution to overall growth performance. See Borensztein, De Gregorio, and Lee (1998).

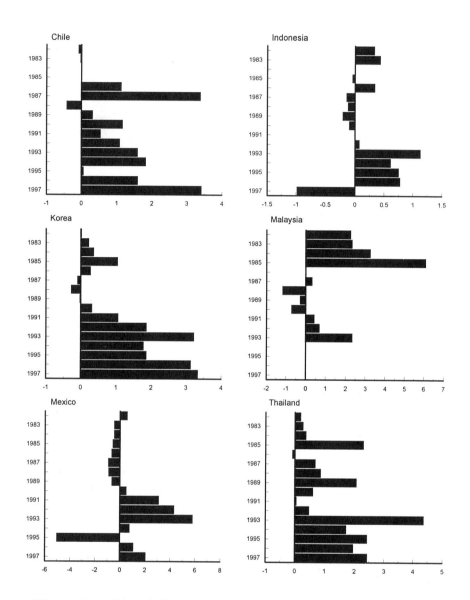

Figure 6.4. Selected Countries: Net Portfolio Flows, 1982-97 (In percent of GDP).

Source: International Monetary Fund.

In addition, as shown in several econometric studies, low interest rates prevailing in the United States and some other industrial countries in the early 1990s played an important role in explaining capital flows to developing countries in recent years. Frankel and Okongwu (1996), for instance, in an analysis of the determinants of portfolio capital flows in six Latin American and East Asian countries (Argentina, Chile, Mexico, the Philippines, Korea and Taiwan) using quarterly data covering the period 1987-94, found that U.S. interest rates had a major influence on these flows. As pointed out by Fernández-Arias (1996) and Fernández-Arias and Montiel (1996), this effect (also referred to as a **push factor**) may have been an *indirect* one: in addition to improving relative rate of returns in favor of developing economies, low world interest rates improved the *creditworthiness* of some debtor countries. Figure 6.6 illustrates the relationship between U.S. interest rates and net capital flows to Latin America during the period 1970-94. The figure suggests indeed that, since the early 1980s at least, the two variables have been inversely correlated.

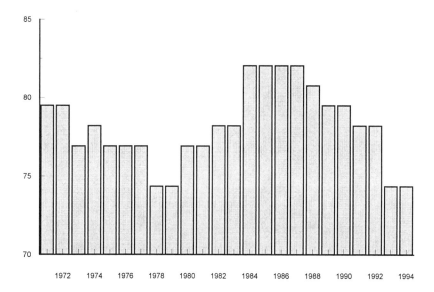

Figure 6.5. Developing Countries: Percentage of Countries with Capital Controls.

Source: International Monetary Fund.

However, the evidence also suggests that, in addition to world interest rates, domestic or **pull factors** (macroeconomic stabilization and structural reforms) have also played an important role in several countries. As noted earlier, capital account liberalization was an important component of structural adjustment in several developing countries. In several cases, *fiscal adjustment* (reductions in the share of government expenditure in output as well as lower budget deficits) played a key stabilizing role and was instrumental in attracting capital flows. In countries like Argentina, Thailand, Mexico, and Chile, significant reductions in fiscal deficits preceded the surge in capital inflows and were associated with important changes in public expenditure policies, reductions in government subsidies, and tax reform (see Corbo and Hernández, 1996). In Chile, the nonfinancial public sector balance was -0.4 percent of GDP three years prior to the inflow episode (which started in 1990), 3.6 percent two years before, and 5.3 percent a year before. In Thailand (where the inflow episode started in 1988), corresponding numbers are -6.3 percent, -4.8 percent, and -1.6 percent. Improved fiscal balances helped to lower inflationary expectations and conveyed a signal regarding the policymakers' commitment to achieve and maintain macroeconomic stability. Abdel-Motaal (1995), for instance, examined the determinants of capital movements in some Middle-Eastern countries (including Jordan, Egypt, Morocco, and Tunisia) and Asian countries (Bangladesh, India, Pakistan, and Sri Lanka). Motaal's analysis suggested that external factors (reductions in world interest rates) played a less important role in the increase in capital inflows to these countries; more important were internal factors (the momentum for reform), which led to improvements in the longer-term economic prospects of these countries. It should also be noted, however, that there are instances where it is large fiscal *imbalances*, coupled with a relatively tight monetary policy stance (and consequent upward pressures on domestic real interest rates), that have led to large inflows of short-term capital, defined broadly to include also portfolio flows. Notable examples are Brazil and Turkey (Agénor, McDermott, and Ucer, 1997).

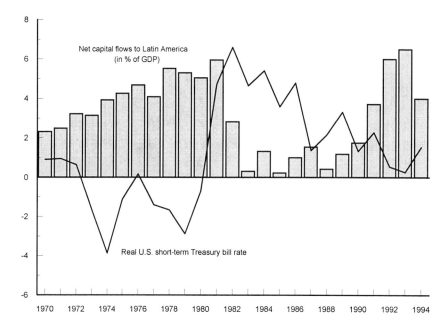

Figure 6.6. U.S. Interest Rates and Capital Flows to Latin America, 1970-94. Source: Inter-American Development Bank.

A possible way to reconcile the results of the various econometric studies cited above is to view the evolution of fundamentals and growing financial integration as determining the *long-term trend* in recent private capital flows, whereas cyclical movements in interest rates in industrial countries represent one of the main shorter-term factors affecting movements in capital flows around the long-term trend. At the individual country level, however, another important factor in the short term may be **herding behavior** or **contagion effects**, as discussed in more detail in the next chapter. Contagion effects, in particular, may arise because investors decide to temporarily withdraw from a country (or a group of countries) in order to reevaluate risks and returns following a crisis in a neighboring country. They may also arise as a result of technical factors—for instance, because **open-end mutual funds** must sell off assets to meet investor obligations. These effects tend to be short lived but they may also persist sufficiently to lead to a permanent reassessment of a country's fundamentals, thereby affecting longer-term flows of capital to that country.

The importance of distinguishing between the determinants of long- and short-term capital movements is well illustrated by the study by Larraín, Labán, and Chumacero (1997), which focused on private capital inflows to Chile during the period 1985-94. They found that each category of flows responds to different determinants.

- *Long-term* flows tended to respond to changes in economic fundamentals, such as the investment-output ratio and the external debt-output ratio (a proxy for **country risk**); short-term arbitrage conditions had no discernible impact.

- The behavior of *short-term* inflows varied depending on whether they were or not subject to **capital controls**—essentially an **unremunerated reserve requirement** introduced in June 1991, as discussed later.[4] Both categories of flows responded very significantly to interest rate differentials and arbitrage opportunities; in addition, short-term inflows that were subject to capital controls were significantly (and negatively) affected by changes in the reserve requirement rate.

Finally, among domestic factors, it is worth noting that there is evidence that the removal of **capital controls** on *outflows* may have led to an increase in *net inflows* of capital in several countries in the early 1990s, including Chile, Colombia, Egypt, and Thailand.[5] An analytical explanation of this apparent paradox was provided by Labán and Larraín (1997). They considered a model in which a policy aimed at liberalizing capital outflows takes the form of a reduction in the minimum period during which foreign investors must wait to repatriate the capital invested in the domestic country. This reduction is viewed as reducing the **degree of irreversibility** of the decision to invest domestically (see Chapter 1). This, in turn, lowers the **option value of waiting** until uncertainty about a possible change in the legislation that affects investment in domestic assets is resolved, because in this case nonresidents investing in the domestic economy will be stuck with the low-return asset for a shorter period of

---

[4]Inflows that are subject to capital controls consisted essentially of short-term loans to the Chilean private banking and non-banking sectors and (after 1991) changes in the stock of foreign currency deposits in the domestic banking system.

[5]Chile started to lift restrictions on capital outflows in February 1991, Colombia in January 1992, and Thailand in April 1991. See Corbo and Hernández (1996).

time. Thus, a reduction in the minimum repatriation period is likely to *increase*, not decrease, net capital inflows. Another explanation was offered by Drazen and Bartolini (1997); they argued that because controls on outflows are often imposed for fiscal purposes (namely, to maintain the base of the inflation tax, as discussed in Chapter 3), their removal can be interpreted by foreign investors as a *signal* that future capital taxation is less likely. This effect may be large enough to stimulate capital inflows.

6.3   How Volatile Are Capital Flows?

In 1996, five Asian countries—Indonesia, Malaysia, the Philippines, South Korea, and Thailand—received net private capital *inflows* of about $93 billion. In 1997, in the wake of the Thai baht crisis and its contagion effects (as discussed in the next chapter), they recorded an *outflow* of $12 billion—a turnaround of $105 billion (most of it in the second half of 1997), which was equivalent to about 10 percent of their combined GDP. Three of these countries (Indonesia, South Korea, and Thailand) experienced a deep recession and a sharp increase in unemployment.

Most of the reversal that occurred between 1996 and 1997 was accounted for by changes in bank lending and to a lesser extent portfolio flows; foreign direct investment remained essentially unchanged. Interbank lending to the crisis-stricken countries shifted in the second half of 1997 from an inflow of $40 billion to a net outflow of $30 billion. This evidence appears to be consistent with the conventional view on the degree of volatility of capital flows, which suggests that *short-term* flows (including again both portfolio investment and short-term bank lending) are inherently *more unstable* than longer-term flows (such as FDI and long-term bank lending). A study by Claessens, Dooley, and Warner (1995), however, using data for five developing countries and five industrial countries, found no significant differences between the time-series properties of short-term flows and long-term flows.[6] Portfolio flows, in particular, appeared to be no more volatile than other types of capital flows. They also found that because there is some substitution between the various flows, only an analysis of the aggregate capital account was meaningful. The implication of these results is that a program of capital controls aimed at discouraging a particular type of flow because of its (alleged) volatile behavior would not necessarily lead to more stable movements of capital (see below).

The results of Claessens, Dooley, and Warner (1995) were confirmed in a subsequent study by Chuhan, Perez-Quiros, and Popper (1996)—in a study of six developing countries (Argentina, Brazil, Indonesia, Korea, Mexico, and Pakistan) using quarterly data for the period 1985-94—but only in a **univariate** context. They found that short-term investment flows are sensitive to changes in all the other types of capital flows (including FDI), but that FDI is relatively

---

[6] For both individual and aggregate flows, they measured volatility by coefficients of variation, persistence by measures of serial dependence (autocorrelation functions), and predictability by time-series measures of forecasting performance.

insensitive to other flows—thereby supporting the conventional view that short-term capital flows are **hot money** whereas direct investment is not. They concluded that the composition of capital flows *does matter*; FDI may play a more prominent role in the determination of subsequent capital flows.

6.4   Macroeconomic Effects

The surge in capital flows has led in a number of countries to a **credit boom** and an expansion of domestic liquidity. The reason is that these flows (particularly those taking the form of short-term foreign-currency deposits) have often been intermediated directly by the banking system. Even in cases in which capital has flown into an economy through channels other than directly through banks, it may still increase the capacity of the banking system to lend. For instance, if foreign investors decide to acquire equity on domestic stock markets, they must exchange a foreign-currency deposit for a domestic-currency deposit to pay for their purchase. As a result, the local bank obtains foreign-currency funds that can be used to expand domestic lending. Figure 6.7 shows the ratio of credit to GDP in periods before and during episodes of capital inflows in a group of countries since the late 1970s. The data indicate that episodes of inflows were, in almost all cases, associated with a higher rate of credit expansion.

Another effect of capital inflows has been a real exchange rate *appreciation*, brought about through higher domestic inflation.[7] In general, whether capital inflows are inflationary or not depends on various factors. A key issue in this context is the nature of the *exchange rate regime*.

- Under *flexible* exchange rates, a capital inflow (regardless of its sources) will lead to an appreciation of the nominal exchange rate, a fall in the relative price of imported goods and a shift away from consumption of nontradables—all of which will reduce inflationary pressures. The higher the degree of exchange rate flexibility, the less likely it is that capital inflows will have an inflationary effect.

- Under *fixed* exchange rates, whether capital inflows increase inflationary pressures depends on whether they are driven by autonomous factors (such as changes in world interest rates) or are brought about by an increase in domestic money demand, resulting for instance, from lower inflation expectations. In the latter case, there will be no inflationary effect.

---

[7] This effect has in some cases reflected the relatively limited scope for market-based sterilization (as discussed below), itself resulting from the absence of well-developed financial markets and indirect monetary instruments.

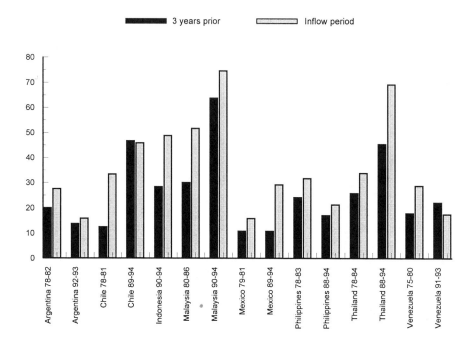

Figure 6.7. Capital Inflow Episodes and Bank Lending to the Private Sector (In percent of GDP).
Source: World Bank.

The impact of capital inflows on inflation under fixed exchange rates also depends on the *policy response* to these inflows, namely, whether intervention is sterilized or unsterilized.

- Under a regime of **unsterilized intervention** (in which the central bank exchanges domestic money for foreign-currency inflows), if capital inflows are an equilibrium response to an increase in money demand, they will not be inflationary because domestic interest rates are likely to rise. If capital inflows increase autonomously (as a result, say, of lower world interest rates), domestic interest rates will generally fall and inflationary pressures will increase.

- Under a regime of **sterilized intervention** (in which for instance the central bank exchanges directly bonds for inflows of foreign currency) an exogenous shift in money demand will lead to a larger increase in domestic interest rates than under unsterilized intervention, thus magnifying the downward pressure on prices exerted by capital inflows. By contrast, with an autonomous increase in capital inflows, domestic interest rates will not generally be affected: with a constant real money stock, agents would merely substitute interest-bearing domestic assets for foreign assets.

Thus, autonomous capital inflows under sterilized intervention will have little inflationary effect.

In practice, estimating the potential inflationary effect of capital inflows is difficult. The reason is that it is almost always impossible to attribute capital inflows solely to one type of shocks—movements in, say, world interest rates—at any particular moment in time. A common approach is to examine the sources of the macroeconomic imbalances that underlie the current account deficits that are being financed by capital inflows. The evidence provided by Calvo, Leiderman, and Reinhart (1996) and Corbo and Hernández (1996) suggests that in Latin America such deficits resulted mostly from increases in private *consumption*, rather than *investment*, as happened in Asia.[8] To the extent that consumption falls relatively more on nontraded goods, capital inflows will tend to raise inflationary pressures, generating exchange rate overvaluation and growing external deficits. The World Bank (1997*a*) found significant positive cross-country correlations during the inflow episode of the early 1990s between the extent of real appreciation and both increases in the current account deficit and in the share of consumption in domestic absorption. At a less formal level, the evolution of the real exchange rate shown in Figure 6.8 for a group of Asian and Latin American countries indicates indeed that in countries like Argentina and Brazil, a significant real appreciation occurred during the 1990s.[9]

An expansion in domestic liquidity and a real appreciation also characterized the experiences of *India* and *Turkey*. Figure 6.9 suggests a negative correlation between capital flows and the real exchange rate for Turkey, a country where the surge in inflows in the early 1990s occurred in the context of an inconsistent macroeconomic policy mix (a large and growing fiscal deficit, coupled with a tight monetary policy), which resulted in high domestic interest rates. In India, the increase in capital inflows in the early 1990s led to a rapid increase in domestic liquidity. The counterpart was an accumulation of international reserves as the central bank intervened to avoid an exchange rate appreciation. Reductions in domestic interest rates contributed to increased consumption, rising inflation, and an appreciation of the real exchange rate. Finally, as documented by Calvo and Reinhart (1996), a real appreciation also characterized the experience of some smaller Latin American countries (the Dominican Republic, Ecuador, El Salvador, and Uruguay) in the early 1990s with capital inflows, with the notable exception of Costa Rica.

The impact of capital inflows on the composition of aggregate demand and the real exchange rate depends also on the *composition* of these flows. As discussed earlier, a large proportion of capital inflows to Latin America in the past few years has taken the form of portfolio investment rather than foreign direct investment, in contrast with what occurred in some Asian countries. Because

---

[8] Corbo and Hernández (1996) compared the experiences of four Latin American countries (Argentina, Chile, Colombia, and Mexico) and five East Asian countries (Indonesia, Korea, Malaysia, the Philippines, and Thailand) with capital inflows.

[9] In addition, however, the lack of nominal exchange rate flexibility in both countries (Argentina after April 1991 and Brazil after February 1995) may have been a significant factor as well.

flows of foreign direct investment may involve less financial intermediation than portfolio investment, their impact on the real exchange rate may be more limited. It should be emphasized, however, that there is limited evidence on this particular conjecture.

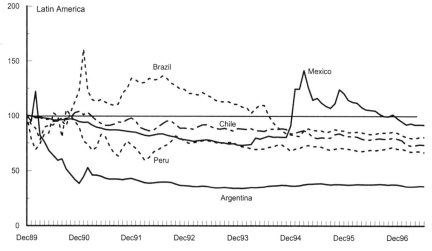

Figure 6.8. Real Exchange Rates in Asia and Latin America, December 1989-June 1997 1/ (December 1989 = 100).

Source: International Monetary Fund.

1/ An increase is a depreciation.

It is also important to note that capital inflows (as well as the policy responses to them, as discussed below) may imply contingent or **quasi-fiscal costs** because of their impact on the portfolio of assets held by the banking system. Intermediation of a surge in capital flows may weaken the *quality* of the banks' portfolios, increasing the vulnerability of the system to a sudden outflow of capital. This may be because of a **currency mismatch** (bank liabilities associated with capital inflows may be denominated in foreign currency, whereas loans are denominated in domestic currency) and a **maturity mismatch** (foreign-currency deposits by foreign investors may be short term, whereas loans are medium or long term). In such conditions, an exogenous shock (an abrupt change in foreign investors' sentiment) can force the central bank to intervene and bail out ailing banks in order to avoid contagious runs and further capital outflows. In addition, the increase in liquid liabilities may induce banks to engage in more risky lending behavior—possibly exacerbating the vulnerability created by the maturity mismatch. The cost of these contingent liabilities should be taken into account in any analysis of the macroeconomic effects of capital flows. At the same time, the risk of a systemic banking crisis also suggests that responding to a surge in inflows may require not only the implementation of short-term macroeconomic measures but also more fundamental improvements in **bank regulations** and **prudential requirements** (see Chapter 15).

6.5   Policy Responses

Countries facing a surge in capital inflows have used various *market-based-instruments,* such as sterilization, and some types of capital controls, as well as *non-market based instruments*, such as reserve and liquidity requirements. This section discusses the pros and cons of these instruments, and reviews some of the experiences in implementing them. At the outset, it should be emphasized that determining appropriate policy responses to capital inflows depends importantly on what motivates these inflows—in particular whether or not they are perceived as *temporary* or *permanent.* For instance, a capital inflow induced by a permanent increase in *money demand* (as a result of a remonetization phenomenon induced by lower inflation, as discussed in Chapter 5) is not a great source of concern from a macroeconomic point of view. It simply generates an accommodating increase in the money supply (through an expansion of the supply of credit intermediated by domestic banks), with limited inflationary pressures. In practice, however, determining to what extent capital inflows represent an endogenous response of this type is difficult. Data on **income velocity** as an indicator of money demand developments are not very reliable, because accurate estimates of movements in income are generally not available on a timely basis; they may, in any case, be hard to interpret because of the lags involved in the response of prices to changes in the money supply. The potential for shifts in money demand under unstable financial conditions or following financial reform makes an assessment of the monetary stance even more difficult. As a consequence, policymakers have often erred on the side of caution and used a range of instruments to respond to large capital inflows.

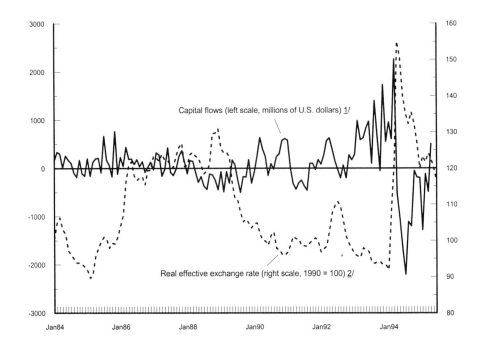

Figure 6.9. Turkey: Capital Inflows and the Real Exchange Rate, 1984-94.
Source: IMF and Central Bank of the Republic of Turkey.
1/ Calculated as the sum of net direct investment from abroad, net portfolio investment liabilities, other net investment liabilities, and net errors and omissions.
2/ An increase is a depreciation.

6.5.1   Sterilization

Central bank intervention in the foreign exchange market consists of any official sale or purchase of foreign assets against domestic assets. Intervention operations are typically financed using reserves, swaps or official borrowing. As indicated earlier, there are essentially two types of interventions:

- **nonsterilized** operations, which involve a change in the domestic monetary base. They are analogous to conventional **open-market operations** (see Chapter 2) except that foreign, rather than domestic, assets are bought or sold;

- **sterilized operations**, which involve an offsetting domestic asset transaction that restores the original size of the monetary base.[10] For instance,

---

[10] Some economists use a broader definition of sterilization that encompasses also changes in statutory reserve requirements and other measures that affect not only the monetary base but also the *money multiplier*. However, as discussed below, these different forms of limiting

an official nonsterilized purchase of foreign currency on the market for foreign exchange would result in an increase in the central bank's holdings of net foreign assets, R^*, and an expansion of the domestic monetary base, M. This operation can be sterilized by an offsetting sale of domestic bonds that reduces the central bank's net domestic assets, L, and returns the monetary base to its original level, that is

$$\Delta R^* + \Delta L = \Delta M = 0.$$

Sterilization was the first line of defense used by many countries facing large inflows in the early 1990s. The absorption of foreign exchange reserves by the central bank was viewed as a way to resist any tendency toward nominal appreciation; the simultaneous reduction in domestic credit was viewed as a way to resist the inflationary pressures associated with an expansion of the money supply.

For sterilization to be effective, capital mobility must be less than perfect; this is indeed what most of the evidence for developing countries suggests (see the appendix to this chapter). More generally, the ability to sterilize depends on the availability of instruments to sterilize, and the absorptive capacity of domestic financial markets. The *maturity* of the sterilization instruments is also important. To discourage speculative short-term capital flows, medium-term sterilization bonds are generally preferable to short-term securities. The reason is that they limit the vulnerability of the central bank to capital *outflows* when there is no guarantee (due to limited amounts of foreign exchange) that these bonds will be repaid on short notice—as might be necessary in case of a sudden shift in confidence. However, interest rates on longer-term bonds could increase commercial banks' exposure to capital outflows if they are required (as a result of central bank regulations) to hold a sizable share of their assets in such instruments. Thus, the maturity mix of the bonds can be chosen to reflect, in addition to fiscal considerations, factors such as the availability of foreign exchange, the need to strengthen the banking system, the duration of the inflows, and other factors affecting banks' reserves.

An important advantage of sterilization is that it can be implemented relatively quickly. It also provides some *breathing space* to policymakers, thereby allowing them to assess whether inflows are transitory or more likely to be permanent in nature. This may be particularly relevant in periods of unstable market conditions, during which policymakers may need to send clear signals about their monetary policy intentions. Moreover, the accumulation of reserves can provide some degree of cushion against a sudden reversal of inflows. In countries where the authorities do not have adequate prudential controls to ensure that banks maintain adequate quality of their asset portfolios (see Chapter 15), sterilization may help to insulate the domestic banking system from sudden reversals in inflows.

---

the expansion of monetary and credit aggregates have very different implications for variables such as the quasi-fiscal deficit and interest rates; a narrow definition is thus preferable.

The sharp increases in official reserves recorded by several countries that received large capital inflows since the early 1990s indicates that central banks intervened strongly in foreign exchange markets. In almost all cases the objectives were to prevent an expansion of liquidity and a nominal appreciation of the domestic currency. In the first few years of the capital inflow episode that began in 1988 in Thailand, for instance, the associated increases in net foreign assets were accompanied by declines in domestic credit (Glick, Hutchison, and Moreno, 1997). Overall, Thailand was relatively successful in limiting the impact of foreign reserve accumulation on monetary expansion. In general, it has been noted that East Asian countries were better able than Latin American countries to sterilize capital inflows in the early years of the inflow episode (Corbo and Hernández, 1996).[11]

An indicator of sterilization is the extent to which changes in net foreign assets held by the central bank, ΔR^*, are accompanied by offsetting changes in net domestic credit allocated by the central bank, ΔL. Such offsetting movements would indeed, leave the monetary base unaffected. More formally, the extent to which sterilization operations are neutralized by induced capital inflows is defined as the **offset coefficient**. This coefficient can be estimated empirically by regressing the change in the central bank's net domestic assets on the change in the central bank's net foreign assets, taking into account the *causality problem* of whether the decline in domestic credit is the cause of subsequent capital inflows, or an offset of previous inflows.[12] An alternative and indirect approach to assess the degree to which a country sterilizes is to study the evolution over time of the ratio of foreign reserves to the money supply. This indicator captures the purpose of sterilization operations, which is to control fluctuations in the supply of money by altering movements in domestic credit in response to purchases of foreign-currency assets by the central bank. Figure 6.10 presents ratios of foreign reserve assets held by the central bank to various definitions of the money supply (monetary base, narrow and broad money stocks) for the period 1989-97 for Chile.[13] The very sharp increase in these ratios suggests indeed that Chile sterilized aggressively between 1990 and 1993.

The experience of several developing countries in recent years shows, however, that sterilization can be difficult and may carry substantial costs.

---

[11] Part of the reason is that central banks in East Asia, unlike those in Latin America, were able to force public institutions, such as social security funds, state banks, and public enterprises, to hold government bonds. Thus because of the greater (or stricter) control that they exert over their financial markets and institutions, they were able to reduce liquidity without having to pay a large interest premium.

[12] See Kamas (1985) for a more elaborate application. Because perfect substitution between domestic and foreign assets implies a coefficient of minus unity in the regression, the simple regression framework suggested in the text has also been used to assess the degree of capital mobility; see the Appendix to this chapter.

[13] The indicator based on the monetary base can be sensitive to whether sterilization operations are accompanied or not by changes in *statutory reserve requirements*. Because reserve requirements are part of the monetary base, increases in statutory reserve ratios that occur at the same time that sterilization is being implemented through the direct issuance to the public of central bank liabilities (which are not part of the monetary base) may bias the indicator downward.

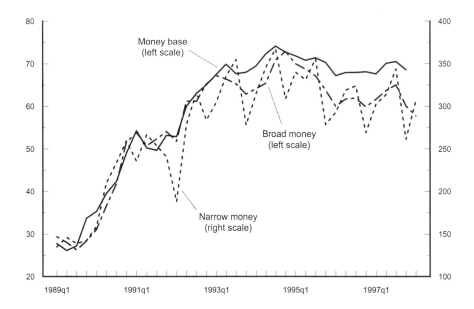

Figure 6.10. Chile: Impact of Sterilization on Monetary Aggregates 1/ (In percent).

Source: International Monetary Fund.

1/ Ratio of net foreign assets of the Central Bank of Chile, for various monetary aggregates.

- In countries where domestic markets in government securities are relatively *thin* and *illiquid*, the central bank's ability to sterilize may be limited because of the lack of adequate market-based instruments.

- Sterilization can lead to higher domestic interest rates if the bonds issued by the central bank for sterilization purposes are highly imperfect substitutes for the domestic assets (say, equities) that attracted capital inflows in the first place. In turn, high domestic interest rates make domestic assets *more attractive* to world investors than they would otherwise be, and may thus exacerbate capital inflows.[14] This is what occurred in Brazil, Chile, Colombia, and Malaysia in the early 1990s.

- When the central bank must offer interest rates on its sterilization bonds that are higher than the rates that it earns on the foreign reserve assets that it accumulates, sterilization becomes costly and may burden an

---

[14] Thus, unless the composition of domestic assets issued by the central bank for sterilization purposes matches that demanded by investors, changes in the structure of domestic asset returns are likely to occur. As a result, sterilization operations may be incapable of insulating aggregate demand from changes in capital flows.

already weak fiscal position (Calvo, 1991). It increases public debt or **quasi-fiscal deficits** by preventing a downward adjustment in domestic interest rates; it also prolongs capital inflows driven by expectations of short-term gains.

- In Chile, for instance, capital inflows averaged about 6-7 percent of GDP a year during the early to mid-1990s. The Central Bank initially tried to insulate domestic liquidity from the effects of these inflows by purchasing large quantities of foreign exchange, sterilized by issuing central bank paper. This policy, however, increased the central bank's already high **quasi-fiscal losses**. Net costs to the central bank were estimated to be around 0.8 percent of GDP in Chile and Colombia in 1991 (Kiguel and Leiderman, 1993) and 1.2 percent in Colombia in 1993 (Cárdenas and Barrera, 1997, p. 35).[15]

- The use of sterilization policies is constrained by the **maturity structure** of the public debt. The shorter the maturity of the liabilities issued by the central bank to conduct sterilization operations, the easier it is for investors to exchange the debt for foreign currency. Thus, the use of short-term domestic assets may facilitate a run on the banking system. It may also create roll-over difficulties for the central bank in the event of an abrupt reversal in capital flows.

Finally, whether the accumulation of foreign exchange reserves induced by sterilization operations is beneficial or not from the point of view of macroeconomic management is open to question. On the one hand, large official reserves create **moral hazard** because policymakers may be tempted to delay needed (and often more painful) adjustments, such as spending cuts aimed at reducing fiscal deficits and external imbalances. On the other hand, low reserves can undermine the credibility of an exchange rate target, leading to speculative pressures and, as discussed in the next chapter, to a currency crisis.

6.5.2 Exchange Rate Flexibility

Several countries have allowed their nominal exchange rate to appreciate in response to large capital inflows. This appreciation has taken place in the context of both flexible and pegged exchange rate arrangements—in the latter case through either a revaluation or a reduced rate of crawl of the central rate. Greater exchange rate flexibility, by introducing uncertainty or *exchange rate risk*, can discourage speculative short-term cross-border flows. Further, as discussed in Chapter 4, increased exchange rate flexibility provides a greater degree of independence in the conduct of monetary policy and allows more control over the behavior of monetary aggregates. Under a completely flexible exchange

---

[15] Cárdenas and Barrera also noted that interest rates in Colombia reached very high levels in December 1991—deposit rates stood at 38.5 percent, nearly 9 percentage points higher than in March of the same year. This is consistent with the argument mentioned earlier, which suggested that sterilization can lead to higher domestic interest rates.

rate, capital inflows lead to an appreciation of the nominal exchange rate and no change in official reserves or the money supply. Similarly, capital outflows translate into a nominal depreciation, with no effect on domestic liquidity. In *Chile*, for instance, a series of revaluations and changes in the width of the exchange rate band occurred during the period of large inflows, 1991-94 (see Corbo and Hernández, 1996). Specifically, the reference rate within the band was revalued by 0.7 percent in both April 1991 and May 1991, by 2 percent in June 1991, by 5 percent on January 23, 1992, and by 9.5 percent on November 30, 1994. In January 1992, the band itself was widened from 5 percent to 10 percent in either direction.[16]

To the extent that inflation is the main objective of macroeconomic management (as is the case for instance in the context of a disinflation program), allowing the nominal exchange rate to appreciate may be the optimal response to capital inflows. In the long run, movements in inflation induced by nominal exchange rate adjustments will depend on the extent to which a real appreciation leads to shifts in resource allocation from the tradable to the nontradable sector, and on the response of prices of nontraded goods to such shifts. A positive supply response will exert downward pressure on prices of nontraded goods, thereby reducing inflationary pressures. In the short run, a nominal exchange rate appreciation may affect inflation through three types of effects:

- A direct **price effect**, which stems from the impact of exchange rate movements on the domestic price of traded goods (prices of importable consumption goods and imported inputs) and indirect effects on the price of nontraded goods. In general, the extent to which a nominal exchange rate appreciation translates into lower domestic prices depends on the share of traded goods in total expenditure; the relative price elasticities of the demand and supply of nontradable goods; the price formation mechanism; and (implicit or explicit) wage indexation mechanisms.[17]

- A **wealth effect**, which results from the fact that a nominal exchange rate appreciation may put downward pressure on the overall price level. The increase in private agents' real wealth will raise aggregate demand; with a relatively inelastic supply of goods in the short run, inflationary pressures may increase, thus partly offsetting the downward effects of the initial appreciation on prices.

- An **expectations effect**, which depends on two related factors: the perceived structure of policy preferences, and the degree of credibility that

---

[16] In June 1998, in the face of large capital *outflows*, Chile narrowed the width of its exchange rate from ± 12.5 percent to ± 2.25 percent, in order to reduce exchange rate uncertainty. The band was widened again in September 1998 to ± 3.5 percent. Chile effectively introduced a floating exchange rate system in September 1999, when it suspended the trading bands around the peso.

[17] The short-run effect of a nominal exchange rate appreciation will also depend on the current phase of the economy's business cycle. Inflation response can be significantly influenced by the size of the output gap and the sensitivity of markups to excess demand.

agents attach to exchange rate appreciation. A real exchange rate appreciation brought about by a revaluation of the nominal rate, for instance, may dampen expectations of devaluation and inflation, thereby leading to a fall in domestic interest rates and an increase in money demand. The fall in interest rates may raise aggregate demand and increase inflationary pressures.

Policymakers, however, are generally concerned not only with inflation but also with the size of the current account deficit. When both objectives affect policy preferences, the benefits of real appreciation are less clear-cut and **trade-offs** in the use of the nominal exchange rate are likely to emerge (see Chapter 4). In general, whether a nominal appreciation has potentially adverse effects on exports or not depends on three factors:

- The extent to which the nominal appreciation translates into a real appreciation. In general, to the extent that a nominal appreciation tends to lower overall inflation, the associated real appreciation will be smaller than the nominal appreciation. The empirical evidence for developing countries suggests nevertheless that the real exchange rate responds significantly in the short run to nominal exchange rate adjustments (Reinhart, 1995). In the long run, a nominal appreciation has no effect on the real exchange rate—unless it is accompanied by permanent measures in the areas of fiscal, monetary, trade, and wage policies.

- The extent to which the real exchange rate has an impact on the supply of exports. This requires evaluating the short- and long-run price elasticities of exports. If the short-run elasticity is small and the exchange rate appreciation is perceived to be *temporary*, the impact will also be small.[18] The evidence reviewed in Chapter 4 suggests that long-run trade elasticities are often well below unity, implying that it would require large changes in relative prices to produce a sizable effect on exports.[19] Moreover, rather than the *level* of the real exchange rate, it may be its *volatility* that may have an adverse effect on exports, as some evidence for developing countries appears to suggest (Grobar, 1993).

- The extent to which the initial situation is one in which the real exchange rate is *undervalued* or not—as for instance at the inception of a disinflation program in which the nominal exchange rate is depreciated by a large amount before being fixed. A key consideration in this context is the rate of *productivity increase* in the exportables sector, relative to the rate of productivity increase in the nontradable sector. If the former is high—as

---

[18] If the exportables sector uses large quantitites of imported inputs, an appreciation of the exchange rate may even have a net positive effect on output (see Chapter 4).

[19] If countries possess some market power in their export markets, *pricing-to-market* behavior predicts that upward movements in the nominal exchange rate that are perceived to be temporary will have little effect on relative export prices, as producers absorb them by reducing their profit margins.

a result of, say, ongoing structural reforms—then some real appreciation may be an equilibrium outcome of the adjustment process.

In practice, determining the degree of initial undervaluation and therefore the *margin of flexibility* in letting the exchange rate appreciate can be a complicated process. To calculate the effects of a devaluation on the real exchange rate requires information on substitution elasticities between tradable and nontradable goods in consumption and production and on the share of tradable goods in total expenditure. This is the *first-round* or *impact* effect, which will be sustained (as noted earlier) only if appropriate monetary and fiscal policies are implemented concurrently. To determine the equilibrium level of the real exchange rate in the long run requires detailed information on these other policies; without such information, the path of the real exchange rate, following a nominal devaluation, cannot be predicted with any reasonable degree of precision. This source of uncertainty can significantly constrain the ability of policymakers to use nominal appreciation as a response to large capital inflows.

6.5.3 Fiscal Adjustment

By implementing cuts in government spending on nontradables, governments can lower aggregate demand and dampen the inflationary impact of capital inflows—thereby mitigating their effect on the real exchange rate. In addition, to the extent that it reduces the government's borrowing needs, a tighter fiscal stance can also lead to lower domestic interest rates and thus reduce incentives for short-term capital to flow into the country. In Thailand, for instance, current public expenditure was reduced from an average of 16.3 percent during the period 1985-87 to 15.3 percent in 1988 (the first year of the inflow episode), 13.6 percent in 1989, 12.9 percent in 1990, 12.3 percent in 1991, and 11.9 percent in 1992. Other countries where fiscal policy was tightened in response to capital inflows include Chile, Indonesia (1990-94), Malaysia (1988-92), and the Philippines during 1990-92 (World Bank (1997)). Corbo and Hernández (1996), who reviewed the experience with capital inflows of nine countries and evaluated the various mechanisms used to manage these inflows, concluded that aggregate demand measures (essentially fiscal contractions) were the most effective.

However, two possible difficulties may arise when using fiscal adjustment as a response to capital inflows:

- Cuts in government spending do not necessarily translate into lower fiscal deficits. They may lead, for instance, to a slowdown in activity in the nontradable sector, and a concomitant reduction in tax revenue. To the extent that the fiscal deficit remains high, persistent interest rate differentials may lead to continued inflows of short-term capital.

- Cuts in government expenditure often cannot be implemented on *short notice*. Fiscal policy is usually set on the basis of medium- or long-term considerations, rather than in response to what may turn out to be short-term fluctuations in international capital flows. Fiscal discipline thus lacks flexibility as a policy instrument to respond to capital movements.

6.5.4   Capital Controls

During the early 1990s, several countries introduced restrictions aimed at preventing or alleviating the disruptive effects of surges in capital inflows. In general, capital controls take the following forms (Mathieson and Rojas-Suárez, 1993):

- **Exchange controls**, or **quantitative restrictions**, on capital movements, comprising controls on external asset and liability positions of domestic financial institutions, especially banks;[20] domestic operations of foreign financial institutions; and external portfolio, real estate, and direct investments of nonbank residents.

- **Dual** or **multiple exchange rate arrangements**, that is, separate exchange rates for commercial and financial transactions. The commercial exchange rate is typically more depreciated than the financial exchange rate, in order to avoid adverse effects on competitiveness.

- **Taxes** on financial transactions and income to discourage or control capital flows, including *interest equalization taxes* to ensure that domestic (foreign) residents do not earn higher yields on foreign (domestic) financial instruments, and high *transaction taxes* to discourage short-term capital movements.

An example of the latter form of capital controls is the requirement that a sum related to the foreign-currency transaction be deposited, interest free, with the central bank for a period of time, thereby raising the *effective cost* of these foreign-currency transactions. This is the scheme that was used by Chile and Colombia, when the central bank imposed a reserve requirement on all new foreign loans (see below). Firms receiving foreign loans had to deposit a fraction of the loan, interest free, in the central bank. This reserve requirement operates *de facto* like an *implicit tax* on short-term foreign loans because borrowers had to pay interest on the full amount of the foreign credit but could use only part of it.

Formally, the derivation of the implicit tax associated with this scheme proceeds as follows.[21] Consider a situation in which a domestic agent wants to borrow on world capital markets. In the absence of any tax, the total cost of borrowing from the point of view of the domestic agent is

$$i^* DL, \tag{6.1}$$

---

[20] Such measures include limits on the share of foreign-currency liabilities of domestic commercial banks in their total liabilities. Although they are often presented as *prudential regulations* (see Chapter 15) these measures are tantamount to capital controls.

[21] The following derivations follow an unpublished appendix by Hernández and Schmidt-Hebbel (1999). A more complete derivation of formula (6.3) below is provided by De Gregorio, Edwards, and Valdés (1999).

where i^* is the foreign nominal interest rate (corresponding to the currency in which the reserve requirement is constituted, as discussed below), L the principal of the loan, and D its duration or maturity.

Suppose that the authorities impose a nonremunerated reserve requirement rate (which may or may not be a function of the maturity of the deposit), r, with a holding period of the required deposit at the central bank equal to T; the cost of borrowing is now

$$\left\{ \frac{i^*D}{1-r} - \frac{r}{1-r}i^*(D-T) \right\} L. \tag{6.2}$$

The first term on the right-hand side of this equation is the direct cost of lending applied to the quantity $L/(1-r)$, which is the fraction of the principal exempt from the reserve requirement. The second term is the implicit benefit (or cost) of the tax on lending, applied again to the fraction $L/(1-r)$, for the residual period by which maturity exceeds (falls short of) the holding period of the reserve requirement. As long as $T > D$, this second term represents an additional cost to domestic borrowers.

The additional cost associated with the reserve requirement is thus given by subtracting Equation (6.2) from (6.1), which gives

$$\frac{rTi^*}{1-r}L.$$

Measured per unit of foreign currency borrowed (that is, dividing by L) and per unit of time (that is, taking into account the duration of the loan), the implicit tax, ι, is therefore given by

$$\iota = (\frac{r}{1-r})(\frac{T}{D})i^*. \tag{6.3}$$

The amount by which the reserve requirement increases the cost of foreign borrowing for a domestic agent (or, conversely, reduces the rate of return for a foreign investor) depends on the level of international interest rates, the percentage of the reserve requirement, the duration of the investment, and the duration of the deposit. For instance, with a reserve requirement rate $r = 30$ percent, a cost of funds i^* equal to 7 percent, and a required holding period for the deposit of one year ($T = 1$), the tax rate is equal to 36 percent if the investment is for a duration of one month, 12 percent if the investment is for 3 months, 3 percent if the investment is for one year, 1 percent if the investment is for 3 years, 0.6 percent if the investment is for 5 years, and 0.3 percent if the investment has a 10-year maturity period.

In general, as noted by Dooley (1996), the use of capital controls has been justified on four grounds:

- to help limit fluctuations in foreign reserves (under a fixed-exchange rate regime) or exchange rates (under a floating rate regime) generated by volatile short-run capital flows;

- to ensure that domestic savings are used to finance domestic investment (by reducing the rate of return on foreign assets) and to limit foreign ownership of domestic factors of production and natural resources—an argument often made by nationalistic governments;

- to maintain the government's ability to tax domestic financial activities and income through both explicit and implicit tax instruments (such as the inflation tax, as discussed in the previous chapter);[22]

- to prevent capital flows from disrupting stabilization programs.

In a second-best world, the possibility that some capital account restrictions could be beneficial (because they help to offset the effect of preexisting distortions) cannot be excluded *a priori*. A classic example is the analysis of the effects of capital flows in the presence of trade distortions by Brecher and Díaz-Alejandro (1977). They considered the case of a small open economy with a relatively abundant labor endowment but nevertheless chooses to protect its capital-intensive industries. Because protection raises the rate of return to capital invested domestically, foreign capital will flow in, leading to an expansion of capital-intensive industries and a contraction of labor-intensive sectors. The misallocation of resources between production sectors is thus magnified, leading to a reduction in the value of domestic production at world prices. The free movement of capital is thus welfare-reducing in the presence of trade barriers on capital-intensive activities.

Another second-best argument for capital controls is that *implicit* or *explicit government guarantees* may distort capital flows. For instance, the perception that the government would assist private borrowers to service external debts during a crisis (in effect, bailing them out) creates **moral hazard** and can induce agents to borrow more than they would otherwise (McKinnon and Pill, 1996). In such conditions, imposing capital controls may be welfare improving if doing so reduces the risk that adverse shocks (such as a shift in market sentiment that leads investors to reduce abruptly their holdings of domestic assets) may translate into a full-blown financial crisis.

The first-best argument *against* capital controls is, of course, that instead of introducing additional distortions in the economy by restricting the movement of capital, a country may be better off eliminating the distortion that created the large inflows in the first place—in the two cases discussed above, by eliminating protection to capital-intensive industries (a sensible policy in a labor-abundant economy even in the absence of capital flows), and by reducing implicit or explicit government guarantees. Moreover, there are several practical difficulties associated with the implementation and enforcement of capital controls:

- By limiting access to world capital markets, capital controls may restrict competition in domestic financial markets. They may also actually encour-

---

[22]Razin and Sadka (1991), for instance, argued that empirical estimates of capital flight from developing countries suggest that governments cannot tax residents' income from foreign capital at the same rate at which they tax domestic capital income. As a result, it is optimal in their model for the government to restrict capital outflows.

age **capital flight** through informal markets (see Annex B). As a result, they create inefficiencies in the domestic financial system and inhibit risk diversification.

- Because they are inherently discriminatory, capital controls create rents that agents may try to capture through bribery, corruption, and abuse of political influence. Such **rent-seeking activities** may be an important source of *efficiency losses* and resource misallocation (see Alesina, Grilli, and Milesi-Ferretti (1994)).

- Capital controls are often used as a *substitute* to fundamental adjustments in the macroeconomic policy stance. Because the effectiveness of capital controls tends to deteriorate rather quickly over time, attempts to sustain inappropriate macroeconomic policies over a long horizon requires tigthtening these controls over time, thus leading to further distortions.

- The imposition of capital controls, even on a temporary basis, can reduce the credibility of a financial liberalization program, because agents may be led to believe that the government is backtracking. As noted in the previous chapter, the risk of *future policy reversals* can be a major impediment to credibility.

- The extent to which capital controls can be enforced effectively remains a matter of debate. There is evidence suggesting that controls on capital *outflows* have had little effectiveness.[23] While controls may be able to drive a wedge between domestic and foreign interest rates, the incentives to circumvent regulations (through informal currency markets, as discussed in Annex B) may be *larger* than the limited yield differential that controls generate. This is particularly the case in situations of financial market pressures and capital flight induced by macroeconomic imbalances.

Nevertheless, capital controls on *inflows* have received considerable attention over the past few years, most notably in light of Chile's experience. In June 1991, the Central Bank of Chile established a mandatory 20 percent **nonremunerated reserve requirement** on new foreign borrowing (excluding trade credits). This reserve requirement—which, as noted earlier, acts like an implicit tax on foreign borrowing—was later increased to 30 percent and extended to all liabilities to foreigners, including foreign-currency bank deposits, as well as to foreign investment in certain equities. The interest-free reserve requirement had to be kept at the central bank for one year, irrespective of the maturity of the loan or deposit, so that short-term inflows were taxed at a higher rate—thereby reducing their volume. The requirement rate was cut to 10 percent in June 1998

---

[23] The econometric study of Johnston and Ryan (1994), for instance, showed that capital controls in developing countries during the 1980s and early 1990s were not effective in insulating the capital account of their balance of payments from domestic and external shocks. However, the measurement of controls in that study (through the use of dummy variables) is problematic because it does not capture changes in the *intensity* of controls over time. Many other existing studies of the effectiveness of capital controls suffer from the same limitation.

and set to zero in September 1998—reflecting the effect of the Asian crisis on Chile (see the next chapter).

Other controls and regulations on foreign capital inflows imposed early on by Chile included a minimum one-year holding period for all foreign investment flows; minimum amount and minimum rating requirements for *American Depository Receipts* (as defined earlier) and bond issues; and some limitations on foreign investment abroad by Chilean banks and other domestic financial institutions such as pension funds and insurance companies. These limitations were progressively relaxed, and institutional investors (including pension funds) were subsequently authorized to invest part of their portfolio abroad. To this day, however, all foreign borrowing and investment flows remain subject to prior authorization by the central bank.

How successful was Chile's program of capital controls? As noted earlier, Larraín, Labán, and Chumacero (1997) found that the short-term inflows subject to capital controls were significantly (and negatively) affected by changes in the reserve requirement rate. Controls were also effective in increasing the *maturity* of inflows. Other studies attempting to assess the extent to which the nonremunerated reserve requirement on short-term borrowing used by Chile was successful in altering the level and composition of capital inflows have reached different conclusions. Hernández and Schmidt-Hebbel (1999) provided a detailed overview of the recent literature. Their analysis indicated that significant data problems and methodological shortcomings suggest caution in assessing the results of existing studies. Their own results indicated that the nonremunerated reserve requirement affected both the level and composition of capital inflows in the desired direction; these effects, however, were largely *temporary*.[24]

Other countries where capital controls have been used in recent years to regulate capital flows include Brazil and Colombia.[25] Both countries used various types of implicit (tax-like) and explicit controls, including, as in Chile, unremunerated reserve requirements. Colombia, in particular, adopted in September 1993 a one-year, 47 percent non-remunerated reserve requirement on all foreign loans with maturities inferior to 18 months; the reserve requirement was extended in March 1994 to loans with maturities of up to three years subject to differentiated rates—93 percent for one-year deposits, 64 percent for 18-month deposits and 53 percent for two years, regardless of the maturity of the loan. Borrowers were given the option to choose the desired holding period. In August 1994, the maximum maturity subject to the deposit requirement was extended to five years, and a new schedule of deposit rates (ranging from 140 percent for loans with a 30-day maturity, to 43 percent for loans with a five-year maturity period) was adopted. Empirical studies of the effectiveness of controls in these

---

[24] There is also some evidence suggesting that capital controls helped Chile avoid the *contagion effects* of the Mexican peso crisis (as discussed in the next chapter), by helping to limit and smooth out the impact of large and potentially destabilizing capital inflows on the economy.

[25] Malaysia introduced quantitative limits on capital inflows in January 1994; in particular, domestic residents were prohibited from selling short-term market instruments to foreigners, and controls were imposed on offshore borrowing and net foreign exchange positions of commercial banks (see World Bank (1997)).

two countries were provided by Cardoso and Goldfajn (1998) and Cárdenas and Barrera (1997). Cardoso and Goldfajn found that capital controls in Brazil were temporarily effective in altering both the level and the composition of capital flows. By contrast, Cárdenas and Barrera concluded that although withholding taxes was temporarily effective in reducing short-term capital flows to Colombia, they had no discernible effect on the total volume of capital inflows. These conclusions were by and large corroborated in a study by Montiel and Reinhart (1999), which analyzed (based on panel data techniques) the effectiveness of capital controls in a group of ten countries that experienced large capital inflows during the 1990s: Argentina, Brazil, Chile, Colombia, Costa Rica, Indonesia, Malaysia, Mexico, the Philippines, and Thailand. Montiel and Reinhart's analysis suggested that restrictions on capital inflows tended to reduce significantly the relative importance of short-term flows but had no discernible effect on the overall volume of capital flows.

In sum, the recent experience of countries like Brazil, Chile and Colombia suggests that, while not a substitute for fundamental adjustments in the macroeconomic policy stance in cases of large imbalances, controls on capital *inflows* may be a useful supplement, particularly if used on a temporary basis, to other policy measures aimed at discouraging short-term, speculative inflows. The evidence on controls on inflows (like controls on outflows) suggests that they may be subject to leakages over time and that their extended use produces important allocative distortions; unremunerated reserve requirements, for instance, were imposed not only on short-term inflows but also on foreign direct investment in some countries in order to limit the scope for diverting inflows through alternative channels.[26] Nevertheless, in periods of significant market turmoil, they may provide policymakers with some additional time to react and implement more fundamental policy adjustments.

6.5.5 Changes in Statutory Reserve Requirements

Increases in unremunerated reserve requirements on (resident and nonresident) deposits in domestic banks have been used as a complement to market-based instruments in various countries—including Chile, Korea (1988-90), Malaysia (1989-94), and the Philippines (1990)—particularly in cases where capital inflows were intermediated directly or indirectly by the banking system. The main effect of higher, across-the-board statutory reserve requirement rates is to lower the **money multiplier**, reduce domestic credit and money supply expansion, and dampen inflationary pressures associated with large inflows of capital.[27]

However, increases in unremunerated reserve requirements are not necessarily without costs.

---

[26] Garber (1996) discussed ways by which reserve requirements aimed at penalizing short-term inflows in favor of longer-term investments can be evaded through the use of derivative instruments in the absence of tight controls on capital outflows.

[27] Higher reserve requirements on *foreign currency* deposits only (as imposed by Chile, Peru, and Sri Lanka, in particular) are more appropriately viewed as a form of capital controls, which aim at discouraging the accumulation of a particular type of financial liabilities in the banking system, as opposed to restraining overall lending.

- They can undermine the *profitability* and *soundness* of the banking system. In cases where banks are faced with solvency problems, unremunerated reserve requirements may worsen banks' financial positions by encouraging excessive risk taking.

- They may reduce the *efficiency* of bank intermediation and promote alternative domestic channels of intermediation (such as nonbank financial intermediaries), thereby complicating the process of banking supervision and the conduct of monetary policy.

- They may increase the fragility of banks that are under financial stress, without fully absorbing the excess liquidity held by healthy banks, particularly when liquidity is not evenly distributed across banks (as a result of an uneven distribution of the increase in the deposit base associated with the inflow of capital) and the interbank market foir short-term funds does not operate efficiently.

6.5.6   Other Policy Responses

Various other policy responses have been implemented by countries attempting to cope with large inflows, in addition to those reviewed earlier. Some countries have required commercial banks to hold *liquid deposits* abroad. Foreign liquidity requirements may be preferable to reserve requirements because they force commercial banks to be more cautious and address the **currency mismatch** that may characterize their balance sheets. However, they may not be sufficient to satisfy the demand for foreign exchange resulting from an abrupt outflow of capital taking the form of a reduction in foreign-currency deposits from a segment of the banking system. In such conditions, a perceived shortage of official reserves may well be sufficient to transform a bank run into a full-blown financial crisis. Moreover, unless they are only applied to foreign exchange deposits, foreign liquidity requirements expose commercial banks to **currency risk**. If the exchange rate is not credibly fixed, this risk (and the cost of hedging against it) can be substantial.

In some, mostly Asian countries, the transfer of **public sector deposits** from commercial banks to the central bank (or an increase in reserve requirement rates on deposits of the public sector held in commercial banks) has also been used to offset the liquidity effects of capital inflows. Malaysia and the Philippines, for instance, adopted this policy during 1992-94 (World Bank (1997)). This measure can be more flexible and easier to implement than an increase in reserve requirements and less costly to the central bank than a sterilization operation. However, it may also penalize excessively those banks whose deposit base consists mostly of public sector deposits. Moreover, if used aggressively, it can hamper the development of an active interbank market.

6.6   Summary

- The *surge in capital flows* to developing countries in the early 1990s contrasts sharply with the experience of the mid-1980s, when most of these countries attracted very little foreign capital or recorded large net outflows. It also contrasts with the experience of the 1970s and the 1980s in that a substantial part of these flows consists now of *private, non-debt-creating flows*—such as **foreign direct investment** and acquisitions of **equity** in local stock markets. They have also been highly concentrated, with about 10 countries receiving almost 80 percent of total net private capital flows.

- **Foreign direct investment** is in general less prone to abrupt reversals than **portfolio investment**; the determinants of its growth, location, and sectoral composition are longer term and more dependent on structural factors than the short-term risk-return factors that influence portfolio flows.

- Foreign direct investment also has more direct effects on economic growth than other cross-border flows, because it facilitates **technology transfers** and generates spillovers into other sectors.

- Empirical studies have found that capital inflows respond to both external and internal factors, the relative importance of which varies across countries. **External** or **push factors** include changes in international interest rates and rates of return on foreign assets, the business cycle in industrial countries, and institutional changes affecting the propensity of investors in major industrial countries to diversify their portfolios internationally.

- **Internal** or **pull factors** are related to the domestic macroeconomic policy stance and the process of liberalization of foreign trade and opening of financial markets. The evidence suggests that capital inflows have occurred not only where fiscal adjustment took place in the preceding years (as in *Thailand*) but also in countries where it did not (as in *Turkey*). In the latter case, the combination of a lax fiscal policy and a tight monetary stance led to high interest rates, stimulating short-term speculative capital inflows.

- A *liberalization* of capital *outflows* may also cause an increase in capital *inflows*, because granting to foreign investors more freedom to repatriate their capital reduces the **implicit cost** of foreign investment in the country.

- The recent evidence suggests that *short-term* investment flows are more *volatile* (and thus more susceptible to large and abrupt reversals) than other types of capital flows, including direct investment.

- The *level* and *composition* of capital inflows have important macroeconomic effects. Large surges in inflows in the early stages of financial integration may lead to an unsustainable **credit boom** (which may increase the vulnerability of the domestic financial system), a *real appreciation*, and higher *macroeconomic volatility*.

- The fact that capital flows to Latin America were associated mostly with an increase in *consumption* (with a large component consisting of expenditure on nontradable goods), rather than *investment*, and the fact that countries like Argentina, Brazil, and Peru were pursuing exchange-rate-based stabilization programs during the first part of the 1990s, explains the large real appreciations observed in that region.

Policy responses to capital inflows have included a combination of market-based and non-market-based instruments.

- **Sterilization**, narrowly defined, is the offsetting of reserve inflows so as to leave the *monetary base* unaffected, through sales of government interest-bearing debt or central bank paper. Broadly defined, sterilization is the offsetting of inflows so as to leave the *broad money supply* unaffected, for instance, through increases in reserve requirements placed on commercial banks.

- Sterilization can be effective in the short term to dampen the effects of surges in inflows, but its effectiveness is more limited in the medium term, notably because of its impact on **quasi-fiscal deficits**. Sterilization conducted through open market operations may lead to central bank losses because the government bonds or central bank liabilities used for sterilization operations may carry higher interest rates than those earned by the central bank on its holdings of foreign-currency assets. Moreover, because sterilization through open-market operations tends to raise domestic interest rates, capital inflows may be exacerbated.

- A *more flexible* exchange rate policy (in the context, for instance, of an exchange rate band with an adjustable central rate) may be an effective way to insulate domestic liquidity from highly volatile capital flows. By increasing uncertainty in the behavior of the exchange rate, it may reduce speculative movements of capital. However, to the extent that nominal appreciations translate into real appreciations, it may have and adverse effect on the current account.

- *Cuts in government spending* can alleviate upward pressures on domestic prices and dampen the real appreciation that may be associated with capital inflows. However, fiscal policy is generally geared to long-term objectives and may not be flexible enough (as a result of various institutional constraints) to deal with surges in capital flows.

- *Restrictions* over international capital flows take a variety of forms, including multiple exchange rate arrangements, taxes or quantitative limits on capital movements, minimum reserve requirements on foreign loans or credits, ceilings on foreign borrowing, interest rate equalization taxes, limits on the share of foreign currency liabilities of domestic commercial bank in their total liabilities, and prohibitions on residents from selling short-term monetary instruments to nonresidents.

- Experience in several countries has shown that capital controls (on both *inflows* and *outflows*) tend to lose effectiveness over time as financial markets find ways to bypass existing regulations. However, the evidence also suggests that controls in some countries appeared to have been effective in limiting short-term capital inflows and that they may have induced a change in the composition of aggregate flows, increasing long-term flows relative to short-term flows. While controls on short-term capital inflows impose costs (in terms of foregone access to capital and efficiency losses), they also provide important benefits to the extent that they allow countries to insulate themselves from potentially unstable capital movements and to put in place more fundamental policy measures. These benefits can be significant in periods of market turbulences.

- Increases in **statutory reserve requirements**, by limiting banks' capacity to lend, may dampen the liquidity effects and inflationary pressures associated with surges in capital inflows. However, changes in requirement rates lack flexibility and may promote financial disintermediation.

- Two common methods of estimating the *degree of capital mobility* are **tests of monetary autonomy**, which examine the extent to which the effect of changes in the central bank's net domestic assets on the monetary base is offset by changes in official net foreign assets, and tests of **uncovered interest parity**, which examine whether the nominal rates of return (adjusted for the *expected* rate of change in the exchange rate) on comparable domestic and external financial instruments are equalized. Some recent studies allow the degree of capital mobility to vary over time; they suggest that, although capital mobility has increased significantly in some countries in recent years, it remains imperfect in most cases.

Appendix
Measuring the Degree of Capital Mobility

Among the methods that have been used in the literature to measure the degree of capital mobility (or more generally the degree of integration of domestic and foreign financial markets) in developing countries, tests of **monetary autonomy** and tests based on the **uncovered interest parity (UIP) condition** have played an important role.[28]

Tests of **monetary autonomy** examine the extent to which the effect of changes in the central bank's net domestic assets on the monetary base are offset by changes in official net foreign assets through the balance of payments. Under perfect capital mobility, the **offset coefficient** should be equal to *minus unity*. Most of the early work in this area (see, for instance, Cumby and Obstfeld, 1983, and Kamas, 1985) concluded that developing countries retained significant amounts of monetary autonomy in the sense that the effect of changes in net domestic credit on the monetary base were offset only slowly by changes in official reserves. More recent work (see Fry, 1995), however, suggested higher coefficients in absolute value and thus an increase in the degree of capital mobility.

The **uncovered interest parity (UIP) condition** implies that the nominal rates of return (adjusted for the *expected* rate of change in the exchange rate) on comparable domestic and external financial instruments should be equalized if the degree of capital mobility is high.[29] Early studies massively rejected the UIP condition for developing countries, often arguing that this was a consequence of the existence of various barriers that made domestic and foreign assets imperfect substitutes. These barriers to capital mobility included existing capital controls, high transactions costs, high information costs, discriminatory tax laws (based on the country of residence), high premia related to default risk, and the risk of *future* capital controls.

More recent analyses have used a more direct approach to estimate the degree of capital mobility, and allowed this measure to *vary over time*. This is particularly important because, as noted in the introduction to this chapter (and as also discussed in Chapter 14), many developing countries in recent years relaxed the controls imposed during the 1970s and early 1980s on capital movements. Moreover, even in countries where the *legislation* on capital controls has not been changed, it is possible that the *cost* of evading them may have changed significantly over time; as a result the degree of capital mobility may also have changed significantly. Faruqee (1992), in particular, found evidence that the

---

[28] Other methods that have been used in the literature are reviewed by Agénor and Montiel (1999, Chapter 5); see also Maloney (1997) for a recent application. The evidence on capital mobility for industrial countries is reviewed by Obstfeld (1995).

[29] Note that for *real* interest parity to hold, one must have not only uncovered interest parity, as defined in the text, but also *ex ante* relative *purchasing power parity*, that is, the expected rate of depreciation must be equal to the difference between expected domestic and foreign inflation rates. However, in practice, goods markets are *not* perfectly integrated; purchasing power parity is thus unlikely to hold. The possibility of an expected real depreciation implies that real interest parity may fail even if the nominal interest parity condition holds.

degree of integration between interest rates in the money markets in Korea, Malaysia, Singapore, and Thailand and the offshore three-month Japanese yen LIBOR rate increased during the 1980s.

In general, the existing evidence for developing countries suggests that the degree of capital mobility, although it increased in recent years (in some cases quite dramatically), remains *imperfect*. This has important analytical implications, as formally discussed in Chapter 8: domestic interest rates become determined through general equilibrium interactions rather than solely by foreign interest rates and exchange rate expectations.

Chapter 7

Currency Crises and Financial Volatility

> All economic events, by their very nature, are motivated by crowd psychology...Men think in herds;...they go mad in herds, while they only recover their senses slowly, and one by one.
>
> Preface to the second edition of Charles Mackay's *Memoirs of Extraordinary Popular Delusions and the Madness of Crowds*, 1852.

Asset price volatility and speculative currency attacks have been a recurrent feature of the international financial scene for quite some time. However, the increased degree of capital mobility and the sheer amount of capital flowing across borders (as documented in the previous chapter) has led to a greater incidence of exchange rate crises in recent years. This chapter analyzes the sources of these crises, reviews the recent experience of developing countries caught up in such crises, examines the sources and effects of financial volatility, and considers what appropriate policy responses policymakers can implement to mitigate excessive volatility.

The first part of the chapter presents the two main classes of analytical models of currency crises. The second part reviews two recent cases of exchange rate collapse: the Mexican peso crisis of December 1994, and the Thai baht crisis of July 1997. The links between banking and currency crises are examined in the third and fourth parts, from an analytical as well as empirical perspective. The last two parts focus on the determinants and effects of financial volatility on world capital markets (particularly the role of contagious shocks and herding behavior) and on ways to limit the adverse effects of such volatility. Among the measures that can be implemented are the introduction of taxes on capital flows transactions, and the use of appropriate guidelines for foreign debt management. The appendix discusses some practical aspects of speculative attacks involving bank lending, and the use of interest rates to fend off speculative pressures.

7.1 Sources of Exchange Rate Crises

The analytical literature on exchange rate crises is dominated by two types of models. Conventional or first-generation models tend to emphasize *inconsistencies* between fiscal, monetary, and exchange rate policies and the role of speculative attacks in "forcing" the abandonment of a currency peg. More recent models, by contrast, emphasize the vulnerability of exchange rate systems even in the presence of consistent macroeconomic policies and sound market fundamentals. They explicitly account for **policymakers' preferences** and the **trade-offs** that they face in their policy objectives. In this setting, an exchange rate "crisis" (a devaluation or a switch to a floating rate regime) is viewed as an *ex ante* optimal decision for the policymaker. These models also highlight the role of **self-fulfilling mechanisms, multiple equilibria,** and **credibility factors**.

7.1.1 Inconsistent Fundamentals

The conventional or first-generation model of currency crises was formulated by Krugman (1979) and Flood and Garber (1984). The main features of their analysis can be presented in the context of a single (tradable) good, full-employment, small open-economy model with exogenous output. The basic assumptions of the model can be summarized as follows.

- The foreign-currency price of the good is fixed (at, say, unity). The domestic price level is equal, as a result of **purchasing power parity**, to the nominal exchange rate.

- Agents are endowed with **perfect foresight** and hold three categories of assets: domestic money (which is not held abroad), and domestic and foreign bonds, which are **perfect substitutes**.

- The *demand for money* depends positively on output and negatively on the domestic interest rate.

- **Uncovered interest parity** equates the domestic interest rate to the foreign rate plus the expected (and actual, under perfect foresight) rate of depreciation of the nominal exchange rate.

- There are no private banks, so that the money stock (the *monetary base*) is equal to the sum of domestic credit issued by the central bank and the domestic-currency value of foreign reserves held by the central bank. The central bank pegs the exchange rate through **unsterilized intervention**.

- *Domestic credit* expands at a constant growth rate to finance the government budget deficit.

Formally, the conventional model can be defined by the following set of equations:

$$m^d = p + y - \alpha i, \quad \alpha > 0, \tag{7.1}$$

$$h^s = \gamma d + (1 - \gamma)R, \quad 0 < \gamma < 1, \tag{7.2}$$

$$\dot{d} = \mu > 0, \tag{7.3}$$

$$p = e, \tag{7.4}$$

$$i = i^* + \dot{e}, \tag{7.5}$$

where m^d denotes nominal money demand, p the price level, y real output (assumed exogenous), h^s the nominal supply of base money, d domestic credit, R the domestic-currency value of the foreign reserves held by the central bank, e the spot exchange rate, i^* the constant foreign interest rate, and i the domestic interest rate. All variables except i and i^* are measured in logarithms.

Equation (7.1) shows that money demand is homogeneous in prices, positively related to income and negatively to the domestic interest rate. Equation (7.2) is a log-linear approximation to the identity defining the *monetary base* as a weighted average of the sum of *domestic credit* and the stock of *foreign reserves* held by the central bank; the coefficient γ reflects the proportion of domestic credit in the money stock at the point of linearization. Equation (7.3) indicates that domestic credit grows at the rate μ. Equations (7.4) and (7.5) define, respectively, purchasing power parity and uncovered interest parity.

To simplify notations, suppose that $\gamma = 0.5$, and let $m^s = 2h^s$; Equation (7.2) therefore becomes

$$m^s = d + R. \tag{7.6}$$

In what follows, m^s will be referred to as the money supply. Similarly, interpreting m^d as twice the demand for base money implies that the money market equilibrium condition is

$$m^s = m^d = m.$$

Setting for simplicity $i^* = 0$ and using Equations (7.1), (7.4), and (7.5), money market equilibrium implies that

$$m - e = y - \alpha \dot{e}. \tag{7.7}$$

As long as the exchange rate is credibly fixed at $e = \bar{e}$, devaluation expectations will be zero and $\dot{e} = 0$; the above equation therefore becomes

$$m = \bar{e} + y, \tag{7.8}$$

which indicates that, with nominal money demand fixed at $\bar{e} + y$, the *nominal supply* of money by the central bank must also remain *fixed over time*. Put differently, under a fixed-exchange-rate regime, the rate of depreciation is zero and (because output is constant) real money balances are also constant. Thus, the central bank must accommodate any change in domestic money demand through the purchase or sale of foreign reserves to the public.

To see what the above condition implies for the behavior of official reserves in a setting in which credit is growing over time, note that by substituting Equation (7.6) in (7.8) yields

$$R = y + \bar{e} - d. \tag{7.9}$$

Differentiating this equation with respect to time, noting that output is constant and using Equation (7.3) implies

$$\dot{R} = -\mu. \tag{7.10}$$

Equation (7.10) shows that, in order for the nominal money supply to remain constant and ensure equilibrium of the money market, *official reserves must fall at the same rate as the rate of credit expansion.*

This result has an important implication: in a setting in which the nominal credit stock is growing exogenously, any *finite stock of official reserves will be exhausted in a finite period of time.* Once foreign reserves reach a *lower bound* (say, R_{min}) the central bank will be *unable* to defend the prevailing parity and will be forced (unless credit policy can be altered to ensure that $\mu = 0$) to abandon the pegged-rate regime. This is, in a sense, a **natural collapse**. By contrast, when domestic credit is not growing ($\mu = 0$), there is no policy inconsistency and the fixed exchange rate regime can in principle survive indefinitely.

Suppose, however, that the central bank cannot credibly commit to setting $\mu = 0$ when the lower bound R_{min} is reached. Instead, it announces that it will abandon the prevailing fixed exchange rate once $R = R_{min}$ and adopt a *permanently floating exchange rate regime* thereafter.

With a positive rate of domestic credit growth, rational agents will anticipate that, without speculation, reserves will eventually fall to the lower bound, and will therefore foresee the ultimate collapse of the system. At that point, the rate of depreciation of the nominal exchange will jump from zero to a positive value; from Equation (7.5) the domestic interest rate will also jump upward, and from Equation (7.1) the demand for money will fall. To maintain money market equilibrium, the *real* money supply must also fall; and because the *nominal* money stock cannot change in a discrete manner (reserves are constant after the collapse and credit continues to grow smoothly), the nominal exchange rate must undergo a *step depreciation*. The rise in prices imposes therefore a **capital loss** on agents holding domestic-currency assets.

However, speculators endowed with perfect foresight will not wait passively to absorb the capital loss arising from an abrupt depreciation of the exchange rate at the time of collapse; they will attempt to reduce their holdings of domestic assets and in the process will force a crisis *before* the lower bound on reserves is reached—that is, before the regime collapses naturally. The issue is thus to determine the exact moment at which the fixed-exchange-rate regime is abandoned or, equivalently, the **transition time** to a floating-rate regime.

As first shown by Flood and Garber (1984), this transition time can be calculated through a **backward-induction process**, which can be characterized as follows.

- In equilibrium, under perfect foresight, agents can never expect a *discrete jump* in the level of the exchange rate, because a jump would provide them with profitable arbitrage opportunities.

- As a consequence, **arbitrage** in the foreign exchange market requires the exchange rate that prevails immediately after the attack to be *equal* to the fixed rate prevailing at the time of the attack.

Formally, the time of collapse is found at the point where the **shadow floating rate**, the exchange rate that would prevail if reserves had fallen to the minimum level and the exchange rate were allowed to float freely, is *equal* to the prevailing fixed rate. The reason is that if the shadow floating rate falls below the prevailing fixed rate, speculators would not profit from driving the government's stock of reserves to its lower bound and precipitating the adoption of a floating-rate regime, because they would experience an instantaneous capital loss on their purchases of foreign exchange. On the contrary, if the shadow floating rate is above the fixed rate, speculators would experience an instantaneous capital gain. Neither anticipated capital gains nor losses at an infinite rate are compatible with a perfect-foresight equilibrium. Speculators will compete with each other to eliminate such opportunities.

A first step in calculating the time of the speculative attack is thus to solve for the shadow floating exchange rate. A simple method to do so is to use the **method of undetermined coefficients**, which consists here of postulating that the (floating) exchange rate is a linear function of the money supply:

$$e = \kappa_0 + \kappa_1 m, \tag{7.11}$$

where κ_0 and κ_1 are coefficients that must be solved for given structural parameters of the model. In the above equation, m is the postattack value of the money supply, given by [using Equation (7.2)]

$$m = d + R_{min}. \tag{7.12}$$

Taking the rate of change of Equation (7.11), noting that κ_0 is constant and that from Equation (7.12) $\dot{m} = \dot{d}$ under a floating-rate regime implies

$$\dot{e} = \kappa_1 \mu. \tag{7.13}$$

In the **postcollapse regime**, therefore, the exchange rate depreciates steadily and *proportionally* to the rate of growth of domestic credit. Substituting Equation (7.13) in (7.7) yields, with $y = 0$ for simplicity,

$$e = m + \alpha \kappa_1 \mu. \tag{7.14}$$

Comparing Equations (7.14) and (7.11) yields

$$\kappa_0 = \alpha \mu, \quad \kappa_1 = 1,$$

which implies that the shadow exchange rate will depreciate at the rate

$$\dot{e} = \mu.$$

From Equation (7.3), $d = d_0 + \mu t$. Using the definition of m given in Equation (7.12) and substituting in Equation (7.14) yields

$$e = d_0 + \alpha\mu + R_{min} + \mu t. \tag{7.15}$$

The fixed-exchange-rate regime collapses when the prevailing parity, $\bar{e}$, equals the shadow floating rate, e. From Equation (7.15) the exact time of collapse, t_c, is obtained by setting $\bar{e} = e$, so that

$$t_c = (\bar{e} - d_0 - R_{min})/\mu - \alpha,$$

or, because from Equations (7.2) and (7.8) $\bar{e} = d_0 + R_0$,

$$t_c = (R_0 - R_{min})/\mu - \alpha, \tag{7.16}$$

where R_0 denotes the initial stock of reserves.

Equation (7.16) has the following implications.

- The higher the initial stock of reserves, the lower the critical level, or the lower the rate of credit expansion, the longer it will take before the collapse occurs.

- With no speculative demand for money, that is, with $\alpha = 0$, the **natural collapse** occurs when reserves are run down to the minimum level; the time of collapse, t_n, is thus

$$t_n = (R_0 - R_{min})/\mu.$$

- The interest rate (semi-) elasticity of money demand determines the size of the downward shift in money balances and reserves that takes place when the fixed-exchange-rate regime collapses and the nominal interest rate jumps to reflect a positive (expected) rate of depreciation of the domestic currency. The larger α is, the earlier the crisis.

The analysis implies, therefore, that the speculative attack *always* occurs before the central bank would have reached the minimum level of reserves in the absence of speculation. Using Equation (7.9) with $y = 0$ yields the stock of reserves just before the attack (that is, at t_c^-):

$$R_{t_c^-} \equiv \lim_{t \to t^-} R_{t_c} = \bar{e} - d_{t_c^-},$$

where $d_{t_c^-} = d_0 + \mu t_c^-$, so that

$$R_{t_c^-} = \bar{e} - d_0 + \mu t_c^-. \tag{7.17}$$

Using Equation (7.16) yields

$$\bar{e} - d_0 = \mu(t_c^- + \alpha) + R_{min}. \tag{7.18}$$

Finally, combining Equations (7.17) and (7.18) yields

$$R_{t_c^-} = R_{min} + \alpha\mu. \tag{7.19}$$

The two panels of Figure 7.1 illustrate the behavior of all variables before and after the crisis. The path continuing through point A in the upper panel corresponds to the **natural collapse** scenario ($\alpha = 0$), which occurs at t_n. As shown in the lower panel, at that point the rate of depreciation of the exchange rate jumps from zero to μ and the domestic interest jumps from i^* to $i^* + \mu$ (that is, from G to G'), requiring a discrete depreciation of the nominal exchange rate from B' to C. The expected capital loss leads to a speculative attack that brings the regime down at $t_c < t_n$. The exchange rate remains constant at $\bar{e}$ until the collapse occurs and begins depreciating smoothly at point B in the lower panel. The domestic interest rate, as a result of the interest parity condition (7.5), jumps by μ at the moment the attack takes place (from point F to F'), as implied by Equation (7.13) with $\kappa_1 = 1$. Prior to the collapse at t_c, the money stock is constant, but its composition varies because domestic credit rises at the rate μ and reserves decline at the rate μ. In the postcollapse regime, the money stock is equal to R_{min} plus domestic credit, and grows also at the rate μ. An instant before the regime shift, a speculative attack occurs, and both reserves and the supply of money fall by $\alpha\mu$. The size of the attack, $\alpha\mu$, corresponds exactly to the reduction in money demand induced by the upward jump in the domestic interest rate.

This basic theory has been extended in a variety of directions (see Agénor and Flood, 1994). Important extensions include

- the nature of the *fiscal constraint* that underlies the assumption of an exogenous rate of credit growth and the factors that may prevent policy-makers from adjusting their fiscal and credit policies to prevent a crisis;[1]

- the nature of the **postcollapse exchange-rate regime**;

- the *output, real exchange rate,* and *current account* implications of an anticipated exchange-rate crisis;

- the role of *external borrowing* and **capital controls**;

- and *uncertainty* over the critical threshold of reserves and the credit policy rule.

Ozkan and Sutherland (1995), for instance, suggested that a fixed exchange rate system can survive longer with capital controls. However, it has also been

---

[1] In this model the central bank could choose, before reserves are exhausted, to change its credit policy rule to make it consistent with a fixed exchange rate—that is, set $\mu = 0$.

shown that the *anticipation* of controls may have exactly the opposite effects. In general, the anticipation of capital controls has the same effect as the anticipation of a devaluation, because both reduce the future value of domestic assets for foreign investors. It follows that, paradoxically, the threat of capital controls may generate the very problem that they are supposed to remedy. Dellas and Stockman (1993) modeled the vicious circle that may result in this setting. They showed that the mere possibility of introducing capital controls may generate **self-fulfilling crises**, as discussed below.

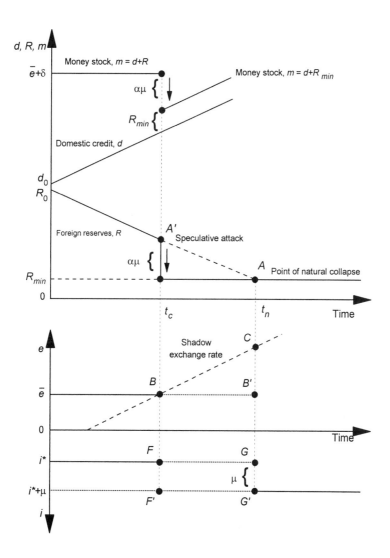

Figure 7.1. The "Conventional" Model of an Exchange Rate Crisis.

Source: Adapted from Agénor and Flood (1994, p. 230).

The introduction of *uncertainty* on domestic credit growth provides a channel through which the sharp increases in domestic nominal interest rates that often precede an exchange-rate crisis can be explained. In addition, the introduction of uncertainty in collapse models has the following implications.

- The transition to a floating-rate regime becomes **stochastic**. As a result, the collapse time becomes a random variable that cannot be determined explicitly, as before.

- There will, in general, always be a *nonzero probability* of a speculative attack in the next period, a possibility that in turn produces a **forward discount** on the domestic currency—the so-called **peso problem**.

- The degree of uncertainty about the central bank's credit policy plays an important role in the speed at which reserves are depleted. In a stochastic setting, reserve losses tend to exceed increases in domestic credit because of a rising probability of regime collapse. Reserve depletion tends therefore to *accelerate* prior to the regime change. Such a pattern has often been observed in actual crises.

A key assumption of the conventional model is that the money supply falls, in line with money demand, at the moment the currency attack takes place. However, if reserve losses are completely *sterilized* (as discussed in the previous chapter), there will be no discrete jump in the money supply.[2] Flood, Garber, and Kramer (1996) argued that in such conditions a fixed exchange rate regime *cannot be viable*; as long as agents understand that the central bank plans to sterilize an eventual speculative attack, they will attack *immediately*. To see this, consider again the money market equilibrium condition, Equation (7.7), with $y = i^* = 0$. If the money stock is constant as a result of sterilized intervention (at, say, $m = m^s$) and the exchange rate is fixed, this condition is

$$m^s - \bar{e} = 0,$$

whereas in the postattack floating-rate regime, with $\dot{e} = \mu$:

$$m^s - e = -\alpha\mu.$$

Subtracting the second expression from the first yields

$$e - \bar{e} = \alpha\mu > 0.$$

Thus, if the money supply is not allowed to change when the attack takes place, the shadow exchange rate (consistent with money market equilibrium) will always exceed the prevailing fixed exchange rate—thereby provoking an immediate attack. By adding a **risk premium** to the above model, Flood,

---

[2] The evidence pertaining to some recent episodes of speculative attacks, including the crisis of the Mexican peso of December 1994 reviewed here, suggests indeed that policymakers may engage in sterilized intervention prior to a currency crisis.

Garber, and Kramer (1996) showed that a fixed exchange rate *can* remain viable under sterilized intervention. Essentially, the risk premium adjusts to keep the demand for money *constant* when the attack occurs, just as sterilization maintains money supply constant. A problematic feature of their analysis, however, is that because the money supply does not change and the exchange rate cannot jump (although its rate of change, $\dot{e}$, does), the *domestic interest rate cannot jump* either—in contrast to what the empirical evidence suggests.

There is considerable evidence suggesting that currency crises (or financial crises in general, as discussed later) tend to be preceded by a real exchange rate appreciation and growing current account deficits. A simple extension of the standard model to account for these facts consists of assuming that the economy produces two goods, one tradable the other nontradable. Suppose also that in the nontradable sector prices are set as a markup over wage costs; and suppose that nominal wages are *forward looking*, that is, set on the basis of the expected *future* evolution of the cost of living (Willman, 1988). If the cost of living is a weighted average of prices of tradables and nontradables (as discussed in Chapter 5), an anticipated future depreciation of the nominal exchange rate (due, as in the standard model, to an expansionary fiscal policy accompanied by reserve losses) will translate into higher nominal wages today and higher prices of nontradables today. Because prices of tradables remain fixed until the actual regime change, the real exchange rate appreciates. In turn, the real appreciation reduces the relative price of importables and thus leads to increased imports and a growing current account deficit prior to the collapse.

7.1.2 Rational Policymakers and Self-Fulfilling Factors

A problem with the conventional model is that the exact timing of an exchange rate crisis may be difficult to pin down if, as first emphasized by Obstfeld (1986), the inconsistency between fiscal and exchange rate policies is *conditional* or *contingent* on the occurrence of a speculative attack. Suppose that the foreign exchange market is atomistic, so that no single speculator can, individually, launch an attack that drives international reserves to their minimum level and force the central bank to abandon the peg. Then, no agent will attack the currency unless he or she expects that a sufficient number of other agents will do so at the same time. In this case, the timing of a speculative attack becomes *indeterminate*, as it depends on *strategic uncertainty* regarding the coordination of private agents on one particular regime of expectations. In every period during which the official parity is enforced, *two equilibria* are possible: one characterized by a run on international reserves and the abandonment of the peg, and another in which no attack occurs and the official parity is maintained. **Self-fulfilling speculative attacks** are thus possible if private agents expect an easing of monetary policy after the abandonment of the fixed rate regime. Put differently, the mere expectation that monetary policy will become more accommodative following an attack may be sufficient to generate the anticipation of capital losses on domestic-currency assets, associated with a more depreciated exchange rate—thereby validating the attack in the first place. The attack itself brings about the crisis, which may or may not be preceded by a drop in reserves, or a real exchange rate appreciation and growing current account deficits as emphasized in the conventional model and its various extensions.

A key feature of the second-generation literature on currency crises has also been an explicit modeling of *policymakers' preferences* and policy rules. In this setting, and as discussed in Chapter 4, policymakers are viewed as deriving benefits from pegging the currency—by, say, importing the **anti-inflation bias** of a foreign central bank—but as also facing other policy targets, such as the accumulation of foreign reserves, a high level of output, low unemployment, and low domestic interest rates. Thus, depending on the circumstances that they face, policymakers may find it optimal to abandon the official parity. According to this approach, the occurrence of an exchange rate "crisis" (or, to use a more neutral term, an exchange rate change) is not necessarily related to central bank reserves reaching a lower limit. Rather, the abandonment of the peg is the result of the implementation of a **contingent rule** for setting the exchange rate. Each period, the policymaker considers the *costs* and *benefits* associated with maintaining the peg for another period, and must decide—given the relative weights attached to each objective in its policy loss function—whether or not to abandon it. This decision typically is viewed as depending on the realization of a particular set of domestic or external shock(s). For a given cost associated with abandoning the currency peg, there exists a *range of values* for the shock(s) that makes maintaining the peg optimal. However, for sufficiently large realizations of the shock(s), the *loss in flexibility* associated with the discretionary use of the exchange rate may exceed the loss incurred by abandoning the peg; in such circumstances, it is optimal for the policymaker to operate a regime change.

Another implication of such models—as emphasized early on by Obstfeld (1986)—is the existence of **multiple equilibria** and the possibility that shifts across these equilibria may be **self-fulfilling**: the economy may switch from an equilibrium in which devaluation expectations are low and the peg is sustainable, to an equilibrium in which devaluation expectations are high and the peg becomes impossible to defend.

Obstfeld (1995) provides a simple model that illustrates self-fulfilling crises and multiple equilibria. The model extends the Barro-Gordon framework discussed in Chapter 5 to account for labor market rigidities and aggregate demand shocks. The existence of such shocks creates a role for stabilization policy. For instance, an adverse shock to aggregate demand at the initial real wage will lead to a fall in output; in order to offset this effect, the policymaker can devalue the nominal exchange rate and thus lower real wages—but at the cost of higher inflation. The extent to which adverse shocks are accommodated by exchange rate adjustment will depend, in particular, on the form of the policy loss function.

Specifically, Obstfeld's model assumes purchasing power parity, so that (with the foreign-currency price level constant and normalized to zero) the logarithm of the domestic price level, p, is equal to the logarithm of the nominal exchange rate, e. The logarithm of output, y, depends negatively on the logarithm of the real wage, $w - e$ (with w denoting the logarithm nominal wage) and a serially independent shock, u, which captures shifts in aggregate demand:

$$y = -\alpha(w - e) - u, \quad \alpha > 0. \tag{7.20}$$

In this equation α measures the responsiveness of output to changes in the real wage, $w - e$. In what follows it will be assumed that u can take only nonnegative values in the interval $(0, u_m)$, where $u_m > 0$.

Nominal wages are set on the labor market *before* the demand shock is observed, so as to maintain a constant *expected* real wage:

$$w = E_{-1}e, \tag{7.21}$$

where E_{-1} is the expectations operator conditional on information available at period $t - 1$.

The policymaker's loss function is quadratic in inflation and output deviations and is given by

$$L = \frac{1}{2}(y - \tilde{y})^2 + \theta\frac{\pi^2}{2}, \quad \theta > 0, \tag{7.22}$$

where $\tilde{y}$ is the desired level of output, π is inflation, and θ the weight attached to inflation in the loss function. The first term on the right-hand side reflects the cost of deviations from the desired level of output, whereas the second captures the cost of deviating from zero inflation. Using Equation (7.20) and noting that inflation is simply $\pi = \Delta e$, Equation (7.22) can be rewritten as

$$L = \frac{1}{2}[-\alpha(w - e) - u - \tilde{y}]^2 + \theta\frac{(\Delta e)^2}{2}. \tag{7.23}$$

Suppose that the policymaker cannot precommit to a fixed exchange rate, and that it chooses discretionarily the nominal exchange rate e to minimize L given the nominal wage set at period $t - 1$. Minimizing Equation (7.23) over e yields the first-order condition

$$\frac{\partial L}{\partial e} = \alpha[-\alpha(w - e) - u - \tilde{y}] + \theta\Delta e = 0,$$

which yields the following reaction function:

$$e = e_{-1} + \lambda(w - e_{-1}) + \frac{\lambda}{\alpha}(u + \tilde{y}), \tag{7.24}$$

where

$$\lambda = \frac{\alpha^2}{\theta + \alpha^2}.$$

Equation (7.24) indicates that high nominal wages (relative to prices in the previous period) and a negative shock to aggregate demand (an increase in u) bring a partially offsetting devaluation of the nominal exchange rate. The coefficient λ can be viewed as measuring the extent to which the policymaker accommodates wage movements and demand shocks; λ is higher the greater the adverse impact of changes in the real wage on output are (as measured by α), and is smaller the greater the weight attached to inflation (measured by θ) in the policymaker's loss function is. Thus $\lambda \to 0$ in two particular cases:

- $\alpha \to 0$, so that output is independent of movements in real wages;

- $\theta \to \infty$, in which case the policymaker is only concerned about maintaining a zero rate of inflation.

In either case, Equation (7.24) implies that $e = e_{-1}$; when the penalty for inflation, in particular, is infinitely large, a fixed exchange rate is optimal.

Firms and wage setters know the policymaker's reaction function and set wages (as indicated earlier) so as to take the policymaker's expected exchange rate adjustment into account. Equations (7.21) and (7.24) therefore imply that, in equilibrium:

$$w = e_{-1} + \lambda(w - e_{-1}) + \frac{\lambda}{\alpha}(E_{-1}u + \tilde{y}),$$

or, setting $E_{-1}u = \bar{u}$,

$$w = e_{-1} + \frac{\lambda(\bar{u} + \tilde{y})}{\alpha(1 - \lambda)}. \tag{7.25}$$

Combining Equations (7.24) and (7.25), the equilibrium level of the exchange rate is given by

$$e = e_{-1} + \lambda u + \frac{\lambda(\bar{u} + \tilde{y})}{\alpha(1 - \lambda)}. \tag{7.26}$$

Equation (7.26) indicates that, under a discretionary policy regime, a fixed exchange rate ($e = e_{-1}$) prevails in equilibrium only if inflation is infinitely costly ($\lambda \to 0$). It also shows that the economy is characterized by a systematic **devaluation bias** (proportional to the level of desired output and the mean value of the aggregate shock), which reflects the policymaker's attempt to exploit the potential short-run trade-off between output and inflation created by predetermined nominal wages. But although a precommitment to a fixed exchange rate would eliminate the devaluation bias, it would also prevent the policymaker from responding to unpredictable shocks to aggregate demand. Put differently, there is a trade-off, as discussed in Chapter 5, between *credibility* and *flexibility*. In choosing whether or not to maintain a fixed exchange rate or to devalue, the policymaker will select the alternative that minimizes its loss.

Describing the nature of the choice facing the policymaker proceeds as follows. Because the policymaker faces a predetermined nominal wage when deciding the value of the nominal exchange rate at period t, the (predetermined) expected rate of inflation, π^e, is given by the expected change in the exchange rate. Specifically, Equation (7.21) implies that nominal wage growth, $w - e_{-1}$, is equal to the expected inflation rate, so that

$$\pi^e = w - e_{-1} = E_{-1}e - e_{-1}. \tag{7.27}$$

Under a fixed exchange rate, $e = e_{-1}$. Inflation is thus constant and the second term on the right-hand side of Equation (7.23) vanishes. Noting that $w - e = (w - e_{-1}) - (e - e_{-1})$ and using Equation (7.27), the policy loss derived from (7.23) is

$$L^F = \frac{1}{2}(\alpha\pi^e + u + \tilde{y})^2. \tag{7.28}$$

If the policymaker decides, instead, to devalue according to the reaction function described in Equation (7.24), it incurs a **fixed cost** c (measured in terms of, say, units of domestic output), in addition to the policy loss given by, after substituting Equation (7.24) in (7.23):

$$L^D = (\frac{1-\lambda}{2})(\alpha\pi^e + u + \tilde{y})^2. \tag{7.29}$$

The decision to devalue will thus take place whenever the policy loss associated with maintaining the exchange rate fixed exceeds the total loss associated with a discretionary adjustment:

$$L^F > L^D + c,$$

that is, using Equations (7.28) and (7.29), when

$$\frac{\lambda}{2}(\alpha\pi^e + u + \tilde{y})^2 > c.$$

This expression must be turned into an equality in order to determine the threshold value(s) of u. Rearranging terms yields

$$u^2 + 2(\alpha\pi^e + \tilde{y})u - \{2c/\lambda - (\alpha\pi^e + \tilde{y})^2\} = 0.$$

Assuming that the last term in brackets is positive, **Descartes' rule of signs** (see Gandolfo, 1996, p. 54) implies that this quadratic equation has two solutions, one negative and one positive. By assumption, u cannot take negative values; the (unique) threshold value of u, denoted U, is thus equal to the positive root

$$U = \sqrt{2c/\lambda} - \alpha\pi^e - \tilde{y} > 0. \tag{7.30}$$

Thus the policymaker devalues whenever $u > U$. The ex post optimal level of the exchange rate is given by Equation (7.24). Intuitively, when the adverse demand shock is large, the cost associated with low output (or high unemployment) is so high that the benefits of a stimulus (a fall in real wages) outweighs the inflationary cost induced by a devaluation.

From the definition of U, it is clear that a shift in market expectations, π^e, or in the cost of realignment, c, can lead to a change in the position of the threshold point and to a currency crisis—although none might have occurred in the absence of this shift. More precisely, the potential for a self-fulfilling exchange rate crisis arises in the above setting from a **circularity problem**.

- The threshold point U, which determines whether the policymaker devalues or not, depends on prior expectations of depreciation, π^e, as shown by Equation (7.30).

- In turn, these expectations depend on market perceptions of where the point U (that is, the value of u beyond which the policymaker finds it suboptimal to defend the prevailing exchange rate) lies.

To see how inflation expectations depend on the position of U, suppose for instance that the shock u follows a **uniform distribution**, $g(u)$, in the interval $(0, u_m)$. Agents, again, anticipate a devaluation whenever $u > U$. To solve for π^e requires

- calculating the expected rate of depreciation given an anticipated trigger point U;

- calculating the actual threshold given the expected rate.

The expected depreciation rate can be written as the weighted average of two possible outcomes: either $u \leq U$ and the fixed exchange rate is maintained, or $u > U$, and it is devalued by a given amount Δe. Thus, In probabilistic terms,

$$\pi^e = \Pr(u \leq U) \cdot 0 + \Pr(u > U) \cdot E(\Delta e \mid u > U), \qquad (7.31)$$

where $E(\Delta e \mid u > U)$ measures the expected size of the devaluation, given that $u > U$. With a uniform distribution, using Equation (7.24), and noting that $\pi^e = w - e_{-1}$:

$$\Pr(u > U) = \frac{u_m - U}{u_m} > 0, \qquad (7.32)$$

$$E(\Delta e \mid u > U) = \frac{\lambda}{\alpha} E(u \mid u > U) + \frac{\lambda}{\alpha}(\alpha \pi^e + \tilde{y}),$$

where $E(u \mid u > U)$, the conditional expectation of u given that $u > U$, is equal to the mean of the conditional distribution of u, given that $u > U$:

$$E(u \mid u > U) = \int_U^{u_m} u g(u \mid u > U) du.$$

Again, from the properties of the uniform distribution,

$$E(u \mid u > U) = \int_U^{u_m} \frac{u}{u_m - U} du = \frac{u_m^2 - U^2}{2(u_m - U)} = \frac{u_m + U}{2},$$

which implies that

$$E(\Delta e \mid u > U) = \frac{\lambda}{\alpha}\left(\frac{u_m + U}{2}\right) + \frac{\lambda}{\alpha}(\alpha \pi^e + \tilde{y}). \qquad (7.33)$$

Substituting Equations (7.32) and (7.33) in (7.31) yields therefore

$$\pi^e = \left(\frac{u_m - U}{u_m}\right)\left[\frac{\lambda}{\alpha}\left(\frac{u_m + U}{2}\right) + \frac{\lambda}{\alpha}(\alpha \pi^e + \tilde{y})\right],$$

which can be rewritten as

$$\pi^e = F(U) = \lambda(\frac{u_m - U}{u_m}) \left[(\frac{u_m + U}{2}) + \frac{\tilde{y}}{\alpha} \right] \div \left[1 - \lambda(\frac{u_m - U}{u_m}) \right]. \quad (7.34)$$

Substituting this solution in Equation (7.30) implies that the largest value of the aggregate demand shock consistent with maintaining the prevailing exchange rate fixed is a positive value u^* that solves the quadratic equation

$$\frac{\lambda}{2} [\alpha F(U) + u^* + \tilde{y}]^2 - c = 0,$$

or, because equilibrium requires setting $U = u^*$:

$$\alpha F(u^*) + u^* + \tilde{y} = \sqrt{2c/\lambda}.$$

Figure 7.2 illustrates the possibility of multiple devaluation trigger points in the above setting. The curve $\alpha F(u^*) + u^* + \tilde{y}$ is convex with respect to the origin and may intersect the horizontal line corresponding to the quantity $\sqrt{2c/\lambda}$ (which depends on the devaluation cost, c) only once, as is the case at point A. In general, however, the two curves will intersect twice at, say, points B and B'. As can be inferred from Equation (7.34), at the high value u_H^*, the expected rate of depreciation is relatively low, and at the low value u_L^* (corresponding to point A), devaluation expectations are relatively high. At this level of the expected depreciation rate, wages are so high and output so low that even a small adverse shock to output will lead to a devaluation. Again, a shift in market expectations, or in the (perceived) cost of realignment can lead to a change in the position of the threshold point u^* and to a currency crisis—although none might have occurred in the absence of this shift. If the private sector adopts the high value u_H^* as the value that will trigger the abandonment of the fixed-exchange rate rule, then u_H^* will also solve the policymaker's optimization problem. Consequently, this value of the disturbance will indeed be the one that leads the policymaker to abandon the peg and devalue the currency. Similarly, if the private sector adopts the low value u_L^* as the value that it believes will induce an exchange rate regime switch, then it will also be optimal for the policymaker to adopt it as well. Thus, the economy can jump from one equilibrium to another; the shift in perceptions that triggers the jump can be completely unrelated to the behavior of macroeconomic fundamentals.

Figure 7.2 also shows that, as pointed out by Flood and Marion (1999), an increase in the cost of abandoning the peg may increase the likelihood of a crisis. Suppose for instance that the initial position of the economy is at point B, corresponding to the lower threshold u_L^*. An increase in c translates into an upward shift of the horizontal curve $\sqrt{2c/\lambda}$, thereby reducing the lower threshold value (from B to C) of the disturbance that makes a devaluation more likely.

The importance of market perceptions in determining the timing of a currency crisis suggests that a reputation for "toughness" may help policymakers to fend off speculative attacks and preserve a peg (see Chapter 5). However, as pointed out by Drazen and Masson (1994), toughness can be counterproductive. Speculators may infer that a policymaker resisting a speculative attack is indeed "tough," thus deterring them from future attacks, or they may instead infer that the defense against the first speculative attack was so costly that the policymaker could not possibly resist a future attack.[3]

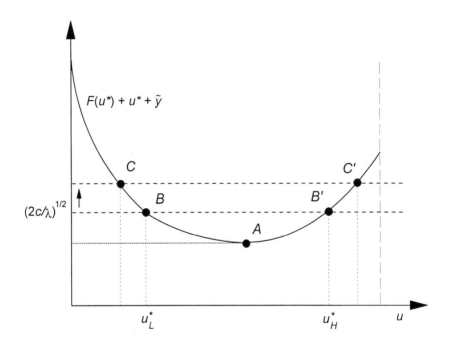

Figure 7.2. Multiple Solutions in the Obstfeld Model.
Source: Adapted from Obstfeld (1995).

As discussed by Obstfeld (1996), various other sources of policy trade-offs, and thus trigger mechanisms, have been suggested in the recent literature on self-fulfilling crises. A particular channel, as discussed by Agénor and Masson (1999), focuses on the adverse effects of *high interest rates*, as discussed in the appendix to this chapter. For instance, banks may come under pressure if market interest rates rise unexpectedly. To avoid a costly bailout, policymakers may want to implement a quick devaluation—although the incentive to devalue may be curtailed if banks face a high burden of unhedged, foreign-currency debt (see below). Or, with sticky domestic prices, an increase in *nominal* interest rates may translate into a rise in *real* interest rates, which may generate self-fulfilling devaluation pressures. In models such as those of Calvo (1998) and

---

[3] A good example is the case of Sweden, as noted by Obstfeld (1995) and Obstfeld and Rogoff (1995). In September 1992, Sweden's central bank successfully resisted an attack on the krona by raising the domestic interbank rate up to an annualized value of 500 percent. However, it responded to a second attack in November 1992 by floating the krona. The cost of defending the peg, given high unemployment, was just too high.

Sachs, Tornell, and Velasco (1996a), it is a large volume of **short-term debt**, denominated either in domestic or foreign currency, that puts a country's exchange rate peg in a vulnerable position, where a self-fulfilling panic can lead to a sudden and massive speculative attack.

- A large stock of *domestic-currency* short-term debt may generate doubts about public-sector solvency, raise fears that the authorities may inflate to reduce the real value of public debt, and may impose constraints on the ability of policymakers to use high interest rates to fend off speculative attacks (see the appendix to this chapter). These factors may lead creditors to refuse to rollover the existing stock of debt and may increase the currency's vulnerability.

- A large stock of *foreign-currency* short-term debt (which cannot be reduced by domestic inflation) may also raise concerns about *external* solvency. These concerns may be heightened if, again, currency depreciation has an immediate impact on the local-currency value of foreign debt obligations, as discussed below in the context of the Asia crisis. In general, when the ratio of short-term foreign debt relative to official reserves is high, the risk of short-term liquidity problems may increase the vulnerability of the exchange rate to a sudden shift in expectations or perceptions.

An important implication of this analysis is that *flow measures* of the adequacy of reserves (such as the ratio of imports to official reserves) and vulnerability (such as the ratio of the current account deficit to output), as well as long-term solvency indicators (such as the ratio of total foreign debt to output) have limited usefulness as indicators of exchange rate vulnerability relative to *stock measures* such as the ratio of short-term external debt to official reserves, or the ratio of total (domestic and foreign) short-term debt to reserves. An alternative indicator of short-term vulnerability, as proposed by Calvo (1998), is the ratio of *broad money* to official reserves—on the ground that these components of money holdings represent contingent liabilities for the authorities in case of a currency crisis. However, even an indicator based on broad money may understate potential exchange market pressures if, for instance, holders of short-term domestic public debt become concerned about the sustainability of the exchange rate or about the government's ability to service its debt (as noted earlier). In such conditions, an aggregate consisting of all short-term government liabilities would be more appropriate. Judging which indicator is best in a particular set of circumstances is an empirical matter; the point is that flow measures can be misleading indicators of exchange rate viability.

A more general message of the new literature on currency crises is that the possibility of self-fulfilling crises makes any pegged rate regime precarious. In most of the models discussed earlier, fundamentals, viewed as reflecting the policymaker's preferences and the economy's structure, affect the multiplicity of equilibria. But the policymaker is incapable of enforcing its preferred equilibrium should market expectations focus on an inferior one. Furthermore, **sunspots**—seemingly minor random events, such as the resignation of some key economic minister—could shift the exchange rate from a position where it is vulnerable to only very bad realizations of domestic and external shocks—a phenomenon with very low *ex ante* probability—to one where output is so low absent a devaluation and a fall in real wages that even relatively small shocks will induce policymakers to devalue.

At least two important issues remain. First, as noted by Obstfeld (1995), if currency crises are viewed as a manifestation of possible multiple equilibria, there are no convincing explanations of the mechanisms through which market expectations coordinate (at a given moment in time) on a particular self-fulfilling set of expectations. Second, the evidence on the role of self-fulfilling factors in exchange rate crises remains limited. The approach followed by Eichengreen, Rose, and Wyplosz (1996) is to compare, using nonparametric statistical tests, the behavior of macroeconomic variables during periods of speculative pressure with their behavior during more "tranquil" periods. Significant differences in the behavior of these variables across periods are deemed to provide support for the view that speculative pressures are triggered by inconsistencies in the macroeconomic policy stance. If no differences are found, episodes of speculative pressures are viewed as the result of arbitrary shifts in expectations. Such tests, however, have limited power, and more robust methods remain to be devised.[4]

7.2 Currency Crises: Recent Experiences

Exchange rate crises have been a recurrent feature of the macroeconomic experience of developing countries, particularly in Latin America. Argentina and Brazil, for instance, experienced several such episodes during the 1980s (see Agénor and Montiel, 1999, Chapter 16). This section focuses on two recent crises that had significant repercussions on world capital markets: the Mexican peso crisis of December 1994, and the Thai baht crisis of July 1997. In part because of their systemic implications, understanding the events in Mexico and Thailand has been a major preoccupation of academics and policymakers alike. A key issue in recent discussions has been the role of economic "fundamentals" and "pure" speculation (as discussed earlier) in causing these crises.

7.2.1 The 1994 Crisis of the Mexican Peso

Between 1988 and 1993, macroeconomic stabilization and economic reform in Mexico led to a sharp reduction in inflation and a significant improvement in the operational balance of the public sector (Figure 7.3).[5] A key factor in bringing down inflation to single-digit levels was the exchange rate policy, which involved the fixing of the Mexican peso-U.S. dollar exchange rate in December 1987 (which lasted until January 1989), followed by a preannounced narrow

---

[4]The fourth part of this chapter discusses other general issues that arise in predicting financial crises.

[5]See Aspe (1993) for a comprehensive overview of Mexico's reform and stabilization during that period.

margin crawling peg and the adoption in November 1991 of a crawling peg with adjustable bands. The floor of the band was kept constant while its ceiling was allowed to depreciate relative to the U.S. dollar at a predetermined rate. As a result, the intervention band widened from 1 percent in November 1991 to 9 percent at the end of 1993. Between January 1990 and December 1993, the peso depreciated in nominal terms by about 17 percent; it continued to depreciate albeit at a slower rate, between January and early December 1994 (Figure 7.4).

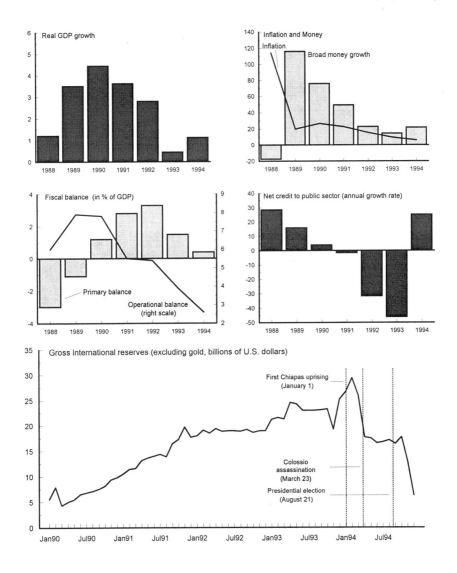

Figure 7.3. Mexico: Macroeconomic Indicators, 1988-94.

Source: International Monetary Fund.

Figure 7.4. Mexico: Nominal Exchange Rate and Intervention Bands, 1994 (Pesos per U.S. dollar).

Source: Bank of Mexico and Bloomberg, Inc.

However, nominal depreciation over the period did not prove sufficiently large to prevent a growing appreciation of the real exchange rate. Between January 1990 and December 1993, the real effective exchange rate based on consumer prices appreciated by almost 35 percent; the index based on unit labor costs appreciated by an even larger amount (Figure 7.5). At the same time, the current account deficit widened from 3.2 percent of GDP in 1990 to 4.8 percent in 1991 and 6.6 percent in 1992-93, averaging $24 billion in these two years (Figure 7.5). Despite the growing external deficit, a surge in capital inflows led to a significant increase in gross international reserves, which stood at $19.4 billion at the end of 1992 and $25.4 billion at the end of 1993, compared with $6.5 billion in 1989 (Figure 7.3). In order to sterilize capital inflows, the authorities issued large amounts of short-term treasury bills (*Certificados de Tesoreria*, or *Cetes* bonds) denominated in pesos.

Large capital inflows continued during the first quarter of 1994, after the approval of the North American Free Trade Agreement (NAFTA) by the U.S. Congress in November 1993. As a result, the interest rate differential between Cetes bonds and interest rates in the United States declined significantly. Figure 7.6 decomposes this differential into two components:

- the interest rate differential between Cetes and *Tesobonos* (short-term dollar liabilities repayable in pesos), which represents an indicator of **currency risk**;

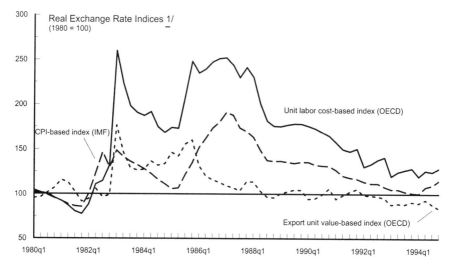

Figure 7.5. Mexico: Current Account and Real Exchange Rate Indices, 1980-94.
Source: International Monetary Fund and OECD.
1/ An increase is a depreciation.

- the Tesobono-U.S. certificate of deposit (CD) rate differential, which represents an indicator of country or **default risk**.[6]

The figures show that both components of the Cetes-U.S. interest rate differential narrowed in early 1994. The Cetes-Tesobono differential fell from a peak of about 10 percent in early November 1993 to about 3 percent in early

---

[6] Using the yield on U.S. treasury bills instead of the interest rate on CDs to calculate the risk of default does not make much difference.

April 1994, whereas the Tesobono–U.S. CD rate differential dropped from about 2 percent in December 1993 to less than half a percentage point in early March 1994.

However, the macroeconomic policy stance weakened considerably in 1994. Fiscal policy became more expansionary, as the government increased expenditure financed through state-controlled development banks.

- Credit to the financial system expanded sharply between March and June 1994, from 15.7 to 33.5 billion pesos. It rose further by about 10 percent (to 36.5 billion pesos) in September 1994.

- Net credit to the public sector also expanded, from -12.5 billion pesos in March to -2.1 billion pesos and -1.6 billion pesos in June and September, respectively (Figure 7.3).

- Credit extended by official development banks (such as *Nacional Financiera*) grew at an annual rate of more than 40 percent in the first three quarters of the year.

The overall expansion in credit largely offset the effect on liquidity of the fall in net foreign assets of the Bank of Mexico. The monetary base fell only slightly, from 47.1 billion pesos in March 1994 to 45.3 billion in June and 45.8 billion in September 1994. Overall, the supply of base money expanded in 1994 at the same rate as in 1993 (about 18 percent), but credit extended by the banking system to the private sector expanded at a rate of 32 percent.

The expansion in domestic credit and relaxation of the fiscal stance (which appear to have been related to electoral considerations) and a series of adverse political events (unrest in Chiapas in January and the assassination of presidential candidate Luis D. Colosio in March), brought the Mexican peso under severe pressure in the second quarter of 1994. The Cetes-Tesobono interest rate differential rose above 10 percentage points in April (Figure 7.6). The stock of international reserves fell from $26.8 billion at the end of March to $16.9 billion by the end of June 1994. To stem capital outflows, the authorities raised domestic interest rates and allowed the peso to move to the upper limit of the exchange rate band. Reserves then remained relatively stable through the period of the presidential election in August, as negotiations continued on the social-economic pact (the *Pacto*) into September. During that period, the exchange rate remained at or near the ceiling of the authorities' intervention bands (Figure 7.4). The authorities also substituted short-term debt denominated in foreign currency for peso-denominated debt. As a result of these swap operations, the outstanding stock of Tesobonos more than doubled between March and April 1994 from 14.0 billion to 36.4 billion pesos, reaching 47.5 billion pesos in June and 64.9 billion pesos in July. The share of Tesobonos in proportion of the total stock of Cetes and Tesobonos held by the private sector rose from less than 10 percent in January-February 1994 to more than 40 percent in April and almost 60 percent in July (Figure 7.7).

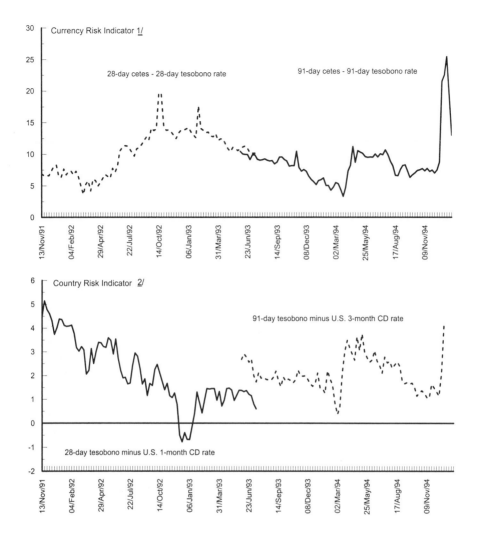

Figure 7.6. Mexico: Currency Risk and Country Risk Indicators, 1991-94 (In percent).

Source: Bank of Mexico and Bloomberg, Inc.

1/ Based on monthly averages of weekly auction rates.

2/ Based on monthly averages of weekly auction rates of tesobonos.

The current account deficit continued to deteriorate in the third quarter of 1994 (reaching 7.6 percent of GDP on average for the year as a whole), heightening concerns about the sustainability of Mexico's external position. Political unrest in Chiapas intensified after the Zedillo administration took office on December 1, 1994. These developments were accompanied by increased exchange rate pressures and large capital outflows. Despite relative stability from end-April until August and a slight improvement between September and October

(Figure 7.3), official reserves fell further to $10 billion in mid-December. The stock of Tesobonos continued to increase, from 78.4 billion pesos in September to 85.2 billion pesos in November. As a proportion of the privately held stock of Cetes and Tesobonos, the share of Tesobonos reached 80 percent in that month (Figure 7.7). The continued accumulation of short-term U.S. dollar liabilities offset to some extent movements in reserves but exposed the authorities' debt servicing operations to greater exchange rate risk. Although currency risk and default risk indicators did not deteriorate significantly during that period (Figure 7.6), the Cetes-Tesobono interest rate differential remained significantly above its first quarter level—indicating that investors' devaluation expectations were somewhat higher toward the end of the year.[7]

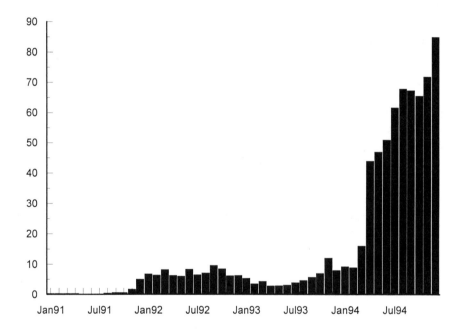

Figure 7.7. Mexico: Share of Tesobonos Held by Commercial Banks and the Nonfinancial Private Sector, 1991-94 1/ (In proportion of total stock of Cetes and Tesobonos).

Source: Bank of Mexico.

1/ Includes residents and nonresidents.

On December 20, the exchange rate band was widened by 15.3 percent and the Mexican authorities announced their intention to support the currency at about 4 pesos to the U.S. dollar. But the Bank of Mexico was unable to hold the exchange rate there. Widespread investor fears put further pressure on foreign exchange and financial markets (leading to a loss of reserves of about $4

---

[7]See Agénor and Masson (1999) for a more detailed discussion of the behavior of exchange rate expectations prior to the Mexican peso crisis.

billion in two days) and forced the adoption of a floating exchange rate regime on December 22. The peso, which had closed at 3.47 to the U.S. dollar on December 19, quickly depreciated in the ensuing days to around 5.5 to the U.S. dollar. It recovered slightly afterwards, but between December 20 and January 3, 1995, the peso depreciated by about 30 percent from its pre-devaluation rate. Domestic interest rates rose sharply, with the 28-day Cetes rate increasing nearly threefold to an annualized level of 45 percent by January 10, 1995. At end-December 1994, the value of the outstanding stock of Tesobonos amounted to about 29 billion U.S. dollars, or approximately 156 billion pesos, at the prevailing exchange rate.

7.2.2 The Thai Baht Crisis

As noted in the previous chapter, Thailand experienced a surge in capital inflows beginning in 1988. To a large extent, these inflows were a response to improved economic prospects; between 1986 and 1988, in particular, Thailand turned an overall fiscal deficit of 4.3 percent of GDP to a surplus of 2.6 percent. Various other economic reforms were also initiated during that period; these reforms included a reduction or elimination of government controls over economic activity, the privatization of state-owned firms, a reduction in tariffs and quantitative import barriers, and a removal of capital controls. Capital inflows were associated with a sharp increase in investment; the ratio of gross capital formation to GDP increased from an average of 21.8 percent a year in 1984-88 to 28.4 percent in 1989-93. During the same period, public consumption spending fell sharply, from 13.6 percent of GDP to 9.9 percent.

Beginning in 1984 and until the 1997 crisis, the Thai baht was pegged to a weighted basket of currencies of Thailand's major trading partners. But in practice, the U.S. dollar remained the most important currency in the basket.[8] Because inflation in Thailand in the early 1990s exceeded the levels recorded by its trading partners (including the United States), the pegged exchange rate regime led to a significant real appreciation. The *de facto* peg to the US dollar implied also that swings in the nominal and real values of the U.S. dollar relative to the Japanese Yen and European currencies had significant effects on Thailand's real exchange rate. In particular, as a result of the nominal depreciation of the U.S. dollar relative to the yen and the deutschemark between 1991 and 1995 (with the U.S. currency reaching a low of 80 yens per U.S. dollar in the spring of 1995), the baht depreciated in real terms. After the spring of 1995, the dollar started to appreciate (from 80 yens per U.S. dollar to over 125 in the summer of 1997, a 56 percent appreciation) taking the baht in its wake. Using 1990 as a base year, Thailand's real exchange rate had appreciated by 12 percent by the spring of 1997. Taking spring 1995 as a base period, the real

---

[8] Glick, Hutchison, and Moreno (1997) estimated that over the period 1979-92, the weight of the U.S. dollar in Thailand's currency basket amounted to about 92 percent, compared with 5 percent for the Yen and 3 percent for the Deutschemark. The exchange rate was also adjusted discretionarily at times between 1984 and mid-1997—with, for instance, a 15 percent devaluation in November 1984.

appreciation of the baht was larger, and amounted to 17-18 percent.

The appreciation of the real exchange rate led, in turn, to a worsening of external accounts. Thailand's current account deficit grew significantly during the 1990s, reaching about 8 percent of GDP in late 1996 (Figure 7.8). For quite some time, Thailand's external deficits were viewed as relatively harmless, because they did not result from large public-sector imbalances and because foreign borrowing was being used mainly to increase domestic investment—rather than domestic consumption as occurred, for instance, in Mexico during the years preceding the peso crisis.[9] The public sector fiscal balance, in fact, remained in surplus throughout the 1990s.[10] But in 1996 and early 1997, markets grew increasingly concerned about Thailand's macroeconomic problems and financial sector vulnerability.

- Several factors led to questions about the vulnerability to sudden reversals in capital inflows and the *sustainability* of Thailand's external deficits.

    – Merchandise exports slowed down sharply in 1996 and early 1997, reflecting in part the real appreciation of the baht and the loss in competitiveness.[11] In volume terms, exports fell by -0.7 percent in 1996, after growing by 14.2 percent in 1995 (Radelet and Sachs, 1998, p. 31).[12]

    – Real output growth dropped to 6.4 percent in 1996, compared with 8.6 percent in 1995.

---

[9] The logic of the argument here relies on the saving-investment identity discussed in Chapter 3 and in the next chapter. If net government saving is close to zero or positive, external deficits merely indicate that, from a macroeconomic accounting point of view, the country is investing more than it is saving. From that perspective, external deficits are not symptomatic of a "problem."

[10] Part of the reason for the fiscal performance is the budgetary legislation in effect in Thailand. As noted by Glick, Hutchison, and Moreno (1997), deficits are limited to a small percentage of the year's total outlays, and there is an upper limit on the proportion of public expenditure that can be allocated to servicing the foreign public debt. The preparation and formulation of the budget is also the primary responsibility of technocrats in the civil service, and the parliament has, by law, limited ability to alter their decisions.

[11] The slowdown in exports in 1996 was also partly related to continued economic weakness in Japan (which accounts for about 14 or 15 percent of Thailand's exports) and the slowdown in the world semiconductor market.

[12] Some analysts have argued that the devaluation in China's official exchange rate in January 1994 also worsened competitiveness in Thailand and other countries of the region. However, the actual nominal exchange rate devaluation in China was much smaller than implied by the official devaluation, because it served essentially to unify the dual exchange rate regime then prevailing. Most external trade transactions were already being conducted at a more depreciated exchange rate (the swap market rate) prior to 1994. The weighted net devaluation for all exporters is estimated by the World Bank as being only in the range of 7-8 percent. In addition, as a result of high domestic inflation, China's *real* exchange rate *appreciated* between 1994 and 1997—by about 31 percent between January 1994 and June 1997, according to IMF estimates.

Figure 7.8. Thailand: Macroeconomic Indicators, 1990-97 (In percent per annum, unless otherwise indicated).

Source: International Monetary Fund and Bank of Thailand.

Note: The vertical line corresponds to the date of flotation of the Baht (July 2, 1997).

- There was also a perceived shift in regional comparative advantage in some industries (such as telecommunications, semi-conductors, and garments) to lower-wage countries such as China, India, and Vietnam.[13]

---

[13] During the 1990s, China, with wage levels much lower than those in other countries of

Figure 7.8. (continued) Thailand: Macroeconomic Indicators, 1990-97 (In percent per annum, unless otherwise indicated).

Source: International Monetary Fund and Bank of Thailand.

Note: The vertical line corresponds to the date of flotation of the Baht (July 2, 1997).

– Net private capital inflows into Thailand averaged more than 10 percent of GDP during the 1990s and reached 13 percent of GDP in 1995

the region, started to produce and compete in many manufacturing sectors that had been the source of export growth for East Asia. As noted earlier, however, the 1994 devaluation of the Chinese currency did not have a significant *de facto* effect on competitiveness throughout the region.

alone (see Chapter 6). However, 46 percent of the flows recorded during 1990-96 were in the form of short-term borrowing (excluding portfolio equity and international bonds).[14]

- The early favorable perception of the high levels of investment (relative to domestic savings) as a sign of economic strength gave place to questions and concerns about the allocation of capital outlays and their sources of financing. It became apparent that much of the investment was risky and of low quality, going to low-productivity and speculative activities—overambitious infrastructure projects, inefficient government monopolies, and real estate development.[15]

- Weaknesses in the banking system (in a context of inadequate prudential regulation and supervision) began to emerge. In particular, banks were saddled with a large proportion of nonperforming loans, particularly in the real estate and property sectors. Between 1993 and 1996, domestic credit to the private sector grew at annual rates exceeding 20 percent, and the ratio of total credit to output almost doubled.[16]

- There were also growing concerns that financial institutions had exposed themselves to significant risk by relying heavily on *short-term borrowing in foreign currency*, combined with *long-term loans in bahts*. This created a *mismatch* in terms of both *maturity* and *currency* on commercial banks' balance sheets.

Speculative pressures on the Thai baht started to build up around December 1996. During that month alone, the Central Bank lost about 2.3 percent of its foreign exchange reserves in defense of the currency.[17] On February 14, 1997, a massive attack led to a drop in the value of the baht by almost 1 percent against the U.S. dollar. The authorities responded to these pressures through **sterilized intervention** (a strategy that proved largely ineffective), increases in interest rates,[18] and restrictions on foreign exchange movements. On May 14-15, 1997,

---

[14]The existence of an offshore banking center provided an important channel for raising short-term capital by domestic financial firms.

[15]A crude macroeconomic indicator of the quality of investment is ICOR, the incremental capital output ratio (as measured by the ratio of the investment rate to the growth rate of output; see Chapter 9). In Thailand, ICOR increased from 2.9 in 1987-89 to 4.6 in 1990-92 and 5.2 in 1993-95, suggesting indeed a reduction in the productivity of investment; see Radelet and Sachs (1998, p. 40).

[16]Foreign capital inflows also contributed to the credit boom of the early 1990s and thus to the consequent overvaluation of asset prices.

[17]Growing signs of tensions were evident before that date. In September 1996, Thailand's short-term debt rating was downgraded by Moody's, which cited the country's overreliance on short-term debt to finance the growing current account deficit. Between February 1996 and May 1997, the stock market index fell by about 60 percent (Figure 7.8).

[18]The interbank overnight interest rate rose from 10 percent to 12 percent in the first two months of 1997. The authorities, nevertheless, resisted further increases in interest rates as a response to speculative pressures, in order to avoid a negative effect on economic activity and a further weakening of banks' balance sheets. This perceived trade-off is consistent with the model of Agénor and Masson (1999); see the previous section.

renewed speculative pressures on the baht led to heavy intervention by the Thai Central Bank, with assistance from the monetary authorities of Singapore. The Bank of Thailand also attempted to strengthen controls on capital transactions by imposing restrictions on the ability of domestic banks to extend credit in baht to offshore banks and sell baht for U.S. dollars in the spot market to nonresidents (speculators) in the offshore market, as well as restrictions on the ability of domestic banks to engage in foreign exchange swaps involving baht for U.S. dollars.[19] However, sustained speculative pressures continued in June, forcing the central bank to intervene to defend the exchange rate. In June alone, the Bank of Thailand lost about $4 billion defending the baht and incurred a $23 billion forward position. But the accelerated rate at which reserves were being lost forced them, on July 2, to announce a *managed float regime* and to seek assistance from the International Monetary Fund. The baht was effectively devalued by about 15 percent (relative to its level of the previous two months), ending the day at 28.8 to the U.S. dollar. The ratio of the country's gross short-term liabilities to reserves (taking into account forward contracts) was in the range of 6 to 8 prior to the July 2 devaluation—clearly a potential source of vulnerability, as emphasized in recent models of self-fulfilling currency crises.[20]

During the months that followed the flotation of the baht, it was discovered that the financial difficulties faced by financial and nonfinancial firms were far worse than originally thought. This generated uncertainty about the possibility of a full-blown financial crisis developing. In turn, this uncertainty led to a further weakening of the baht—which worsened further the situation of highly indebted domestic firms and validated initial expectations. Between the end of 1996 and September 1997, the baht depreciated relative to the U.S. dollar by 42 percent. The currency depreciation worsened the real burden of external debt faced by public sector entities, private financial institutions, and nonfinancial firms that had borrowed heavily in foreign currency.

The Bank of Thailand tightened significantly its monetary policy stance and increased interest rates only after the currency had collapsed and after a continuing period of depreciation. Unfortunately, the timing of the policy change did nothing but aggravate the financial situation of domestic firms, because the depreciation had already increased sharply the domestic-currency value of their foreign-currency liabilities. A sharp fall in domestic credit was accompanied with a fall in output, as well as an increase in the bankruptcy rate and the proportion of nonperforming loans (from about 15 percent to 25 percent) —which further weakened an already fragile banking system.

In conclusion, Thailand's growing external deficits and a weak and poorly supervised financial system were the two main factors triggering the baht crisis. Because the corporate sector in Thailand—and in other fast-growing Asian countries as well, as noted below—had accumulated large stocks of U.S. dollar

---

[19]The appendix to this chapter discusses the various ways by which restrictions on foreign exchange transactions can be implemented, in order to limit access to local funds by speculators trying to establish a net short domestic currency position.

[20]As shown in Figure 7.8, Thailand's total external debt was about US$90 billion in mid-1997. See also Figure 7.13 and the discussion of the sources of the Asia crisis.

liabilities in place of local currency debt in an attempt to reduce borrowing costs, the devaluation of the baht led to a full-blown financial and economic crisis. The stability of (and the high degree of confidence in) the fixed exchange rate had a perverse effect: most borrowers did not hedge their foreign-currency liabilities; as a result, they felt the brunt of the devaluation. The inability of domestic firms to service their foreign-currency debt was compounded by the continuing depreciation of the baht and the deepening economic recession, which led to a sharp increase in nonperforming loans and a rise in the bankruptcy rate. But the delayed policy response to the mounting problems faced in 1996 (with warning signs such as slowing export growth, real appreciation, a growing current account deficit increasingly financed by short-term private capital inflows, rapid domestic credit growth, and a dramatic fall in stock prices), and the authorities' resistance to an early adjustment of the exchange rate, also exacerbated the crisis.

7.3 Currency and Banking Crises

As argued earlier, one of the key aspects of the Mexican peso crisis of December 1994 was the reluctance of the authorities to raise domestic interest rates in order to avoid further weakening the position of bank debtors and thus the overall situation of the banking system. Similar considerations appear to have played a role in Thailand in early 1997. More generally, the recent evidence on financial crises reveals the existence of close links between currency crises and banking crises. This section and the next review some of the recent analytical and empirical literature on these issues.

A first step in this analysis is to define what constitutes a **banking crisis**. Unlike currency crises, definitions vary among economists because banking crises have several dimensions. Following Caprio and Klingebiel (1996), a banking crisis can be defined as a situation in which either

- the capital of the banking system is practically exhausted;

- nonperforming loans amount to or exceed 15 to 20 percent of total bank loans;

- the cost of resolving these problems (through bank recapitalization, for instance) amounts to at least 3 to 5 percent of GDP.

Kaminsky and Reinhart (1999), by contrast, identified banking crises by an *event*, indicating either

- a **bank run**, associated with the closure, merging, or takeover by the public sector of at least one large financial institution; or,

- in the absence of a bank run, the closure, merging, or takeover of, or large-scale government assistance to, at least one important financial institution.

These definitions raise, of course, a number of problems. The last two characteristics of the Caprio-Klingebiel definition, in particular, relate to the *consequences* of banking crises and may be subject to wide margins of uncertainty. Differences in estimates can have a significant impact in comparing alternative methods for predicting crises (see below).

Leaving these definitional issues aside, the recent literature has emphasized a variety of causes of banking crises. One branch of the literature, dwelling on the seminal work of Diamond and Dybvig (1983), argues that banking crises may be purely **self-fulfilling**, because depositors think that other depositors think that there will be a significant amount of withdrawals in the very near future. With **fractional reserves** and a **first-come first-served rule**, depositors at the end of the sequential service line may suffer losses. To avoid these losses, all depositors try to place themselves at the head of the line, causing a panic in the process.

A brief description of the Diamond-Dybvig model is as follows.[21] There are two categories of agents in the economy: households (whose preferences are identical *ex ante*) and a financial intermediary (a bank). The number of households is large and there is no aggregate uncertainty. There are three periods, $h = 0, 1$, and 2, and a single consumption good available to agents in each period. Each household has an initial endowment of one unit of the consumption good at period 0 and none in subsequent periods. They all deposit their endowment, C_0, with the bank at period 0 in return for consumption in periods 1 or 2. They observe in period 1 an idiosyncratic preference shock that is not observed by the bank; depending on the value of the shock, they decide to either withdraw their deposit and consume now (in period 1) or keep their deposit at the bank and consume later (in period 2). Households are also able to store consumption between periods 1 and 2, if they so choose.

Let u be a differentiable, strictly increasing and strictly concave utility function, and C_h is consumption at period h. Households who realize the utility function $u(C_1)$ [respectively, $u(C_2)$] at period 1 (respectively, period 2) are called type-E (respectively, type-L) agents; E standing for *early* and L for *late* consumers. Let θ be the probability that a household will indeed choose to withdraw its endowment from the bank and consume now. Given the assumptions described above, the cross-sectional distribution of preference shocks realized at period 1 is the same as the probability distribution of these shocks for an individual household at period 0. Thus, θ is also the proportion of type-E households realized at period 1, and $1 - \theta$ the proportion of type-L households.

Formally, the representative household's preferences are given by

$$u(C_0, C_1, C_2) = \begin{cases} u(C_1) & \text{with probability } \theta, \\ u(C_2) & \text{with probability } 1 - \theta. \end{cases}$$

The bank accepts a deposit of one unit from each depositor and knows that a fraction θ of them will be type-E agents. In exchange for the deposit, the

---

[21] See Chang and Velasco (1998) for an extension of the Diamond-Dybvig model that emphasizes the type of financial sector weaknesses discussed in Chapter 15.

bank offers each household a contract that allows it to withdraw either C_1 units of consumption at period 1 or C_2 units at period 2. The bank has access to two investment technologies: the first, corresponding to investment in a short-term asset, yields one unit of consumption at period 1 for every unit of investment made at the beginning of that period. The second, corresponding to investment in the long-term asset, yields $R > 1$ units of consumption at period 2 for every unit of investment made in period 1. In case of withdrawals in period 1, the bank must finance them by liquidating L units (per capita) invested in the long-term asset in period 1, receiving only $R(1 - L)$ in period 2.

The bank therefore chooses (C_1, C_2, L) to maximize the *ex ante* expected utility of individual agents. It thus solves the problem

$$\max_{C_1, C_2, L} \left[\theta u(C_1) + (1 - \theta)u(C_2) \right],$$

subject to

$$\theta C_1 = L,$$

$$(1 - \theta)C_2 = R(1 - L).$$

Given the restrictions imposed on u, any interior optimum must satisfy

$$u'(\tilde{C}_1) = Ru'(\tilde{C}_2),$$

$$\tilde{C}_1 = \frac{L}{\theta}, \quad \tilde{C}_2 = \frac{R(1 - L)}{1 - \theta}. \tag{7.35}$$

These equations, together with $R > 1$, imply that

$$\tilde{C}_2 > \tilde{C}_1.$$

A sufficient condition for $\tilde{C}_2/\tilde{C}_1$ to be less than R is to have $Cu'(C)$ decreasing in C. Thus, if u has a coefficient of **relative risk aversion** greater than unity (as assumed in what follows), type-E households will share in the higher returns of illiquid assets.

Is the first-best allocation $(\tilde{C}_1, \tilde{C}_2, \tilde{L})$ defined by Equation (7.35) achievable? A key insight of the Diamond-Dybvig analysis is that in attempting to implement Equation (7.35) the bank faces a **coordination problem**. In defining the first-best allocation problem above, it was assumed that only type-E households consumed C_1 and only type-L households consumed C_2. However, because preference shocks are privately observed, the bank is not able to guarantee this. In fact, the type-L household's decision whether to withdraw C_1 at period 1 and store it for later consumption or to withdraw C_2 at period 2 is a *strategic* one, which depends on what other households do. Diamond and Dybvig found, with fractional reserves and a first-come first-serve rule, that there are two equilibrium outcomes in this setting:

- In the first, only those households with a true preference for early consumption choose to make an early withdrawal.

- In the second equilibrium, agents who actually prefer late consumption, fearing withdrawals by others of the same type, also choose to withdraw early—there is therefore a *bank run*. This run is costly and inefficient because the bank is forced to liquidate prematurely some of its higher-yielding investments.

In practice, however, bank runs seldom have a purely self-fulfilling character. In developing countries, in particular, runs are often triggered by a noisy signal that nonetheless contains some information about the bank's ultimate solvency. More generally, according to Goldstein and Turner (1996), the primary causes of banking crises in these countries are related to the following factors:

- *external* and *domestic macroeconomic volatility*, the main elements of which are often sudden adverse movements in the country's *terms of trade* and sharp fluctuations in *world interest rates*, real exchange rates, and inflation rates;

- *lending booms*, characterized by rapid increases in bank credit growth to the private sector and unsound financing during economic expansions;

- rapidly increasing *bank liabilities*, with large mismatches with respect to *liquidity*, *maturity*, and *currency denomination* (as noted earlier, for instance, in the context of the Thai baht crisis);

- insufficient strengthening of *bank supervision* and *regulation* prior to financial liberalization, which leaves bank supervisors ill prepared to prevent banks from engaging in *overly risky* lending activities;

- heavy *government involvement* in the banking system and loose controls on *connected lending*, that is, loans extended to banks' owners or managers and to their related businesses;

- weaknesses in the *accounting, disclosure,* and *legal infrastructure*, which hinder the operation of market discipline and effective banking supervision;

- *distorted incentives*, such as pressures for *regulatory forbearance* created by insufficient political protection of bank supervisors and the absence of suitable financial incentives for bank owners, managers, and depositors to avoid excessive risk and monitor lending activities;

- a *rigid exchange rate regime*, such as a **currency board**, which severely constrains the lender-of-last-resort function of the central bank and thus prevents it from reacting quickly to stop, for instance, a bank run by injecting liquidity.

Links between currency and banking crises operate in both directions. There are two major channels through which a currency crisis can lead to a banking crisis.

- In the absence of **sterilization**, the large loss in international reserves that results from the speculative attack that precedes the abandonment of a fixed-exchange-rate regime may translate into a sharp decline in the base money stock and the supply of credit. In turn, the fall in credit may have an adverse effect on output and lead to a rise in nonperforming loans, and consequently to a banking crisis.[22]

- The exchange rate depreciation that often accompanies a currency crisis can create **solvency problems** among banks that are subject to large, unhedged foreign exchange exposures.[23] Even if the foreign exchange position of the banks themselves is small, borrowers in the nontradables sector (such as the real estate sector) may be highly indebted in foreign currency. To the extent that such borrowers face solvency problems and that a large proportion of bank loans are made to that sector, the depreciation of the exchange rate could also lead to a weakening of the banking system's position as well.

There are also two major channels through which a banking crisis can lead to a currency crisis; both relate to a situation in which the central bank must inject liquidity to bail out ailing banks or depositors, because of an explicit or implicit **deposit insurance** scheme. The difference between the two channels stems from the two options that the central bank has to finance the bailout.

- The central bank may allow an excessive expansion of domestic credit to provide liquidity. As emphasized in the conventional model of currency crises, the expansionary credit stance will eventually lead to an equilibrium speculative attack that forces the central bank to abandon the exchange rate peg.

- The central bank may finance the bailout by issuing large amounts of *domestic debt* as the counterpart to assuming a large portfolio of nonperforming loans. As a result, market participants may perceive that the authorities have an incentive to reduce the burden of the debt through inflation or currency devaluation (as noted in Chapter 5) and this may lead to a **self-fulfilling crisis**, as discussed earlier.

It is also possible, of course, that *both* currency and banking crises may result from *common macroeconomic shocks*. In particular, an unexpected sharp increase in world interest rates may be accompanied by abrupt capital outflows. To the extent that the capital inflows, to begin with, were intermediated by the

---

[22] Moreover, to the extent that depositors attempt to switch away from domestic-currency assets and acquire foreign exchange instead they may force the commercial banks to reduce lending abruptly and liquidate existing loans to raise cash. Alternatively, the government may impose an outright suspension of the convertibility of deposits into cash.

[23] As argued by Garber and Lall (1998) in the context of the Mexican peso crisis, the degree of sophistication of financial instruments available on world capital markets nowadays is such that prudential bank regulations—in particular with respect to foreign exchange exposures— can easily be avoided.

banking system (as noted in Chapter 6), the outcome may well be a weakening of the banking system (as a result of a sharp reduction in banks' domestic deposits) and severe pressures on official reserves, which would eventually prevent the central bank from defending the official exchange rate. This outcome is particularly likely in countries where the monetary and exchange rate regime is such that the authorities have limited capacity to act promptly and inject liquidity into the banking system.

7.4 Predicting Financial Crises

A flurry of recent studies have attempted to devise indicator systems, or **early warning indicators**, aimed at predicting currency and banking crises. Among those that have attempted to study *jointly* the empirical determinants of these crises, the study of Kaminsky and Reinhart (1999) is the most representative. Their analysis covered the period 1970-95 and was based on a group of 20 countries, 14 of which are developing countries: Argentina, Bolivia, Brazil, Chile, Colombia, Indonesia, Israel, Malaysia, Peru, the Philippines, Thailand, Turkey, Uruguay, and Venezuela. They examined a total of 76 episodes of currency crises and 26 episodes of banking crises. The data indicated that the *incidence* of both types of crises increased sharply between the early 1980s and the end of their sample period: the average number per year of currency crises in the sample rose from 2.6 during the period 1970-79 to 3.1 in 1980-95; for banking crises, the numbers are 0.3 and 1.4 for the same period. These data are corroborated by those shown in Figure 7.9; in addition, however, the figure suggests that the incidence of currency crises during the 1990s was not higher than in the early 1980s.

Kaminsky and Reinhart identified currency crises by calculating an index of *currency market turbulence*, defined as a weighted average of exchange rate changes and reserve changes.[24] Values of the index that were at least *three standard deviations* above the mean were identified as crises. In practice, this definition appeared to coincide with some major events, such as devaluations, a change in the exchange rate regime, and the suspension of external convertibility of the domestic currency. As noted earlier, Kaminsky and Reinhart identified a banking crisis by either a bank run or (in the absence of a run), the closure, merging, takeover, or large-scale government assistance to at least one important financial institution.

Kaminsky and Reinhart used a large series of indicators to assess the extent to which they help predict banking and balance-of-payments crises. These variables included output and stock prices, financial sector variables (in particular the broad money multiplier, the domestic credit-to-GDP ratio, real deposit interest rates, the lending-deposit interest rate spread, and the broad money-official reserves ratio), and external sector variables (including exports, imports,

---

[24]Interest rates were excluded from the index, because the authors were unable to obtain reliable data on market-oriented rates for several of the developing countries included in their sample.

the terms of trade, the real exchange rate, changes in net foreign assets, and interest rate differentials). As noted earlier, the use of the ratio of broad money to official reserves as an indicator of currency crises was first suggested by Calvo (1998). It captures the extent to which a central bank has sufficient foreign exchange reserves readily available to absorb a run by holders of domestic currency assets. If the ratio is relatively high, the currency can be viewed as vulnerable to speculative attacks.

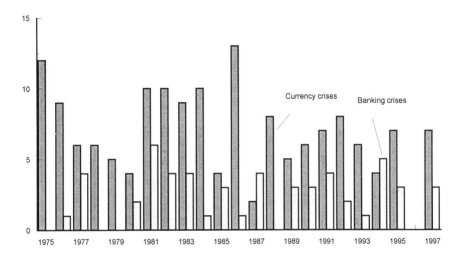

Figure 7.9. Incidence of Currency and Banking Crises, 1975-97 (Number of crises).

Source: International Monetary Fund.

The main conclusions of the study were the following:

- **Banking crises** are often *preceded* by *financial liberalization*, that is, periods during which interest rates were deregulated and other restrictions on the financial system removed.

- Banking and currency crises appear to share *common causes*. Long before a crisis episode, several of the indicators begin to send *stress signals*.

- The best predictors of currency crises are the degree of *overvaluation* of the real exchange rate, adverse movements in exports, an increasing ratio of broad money over official reserves, falling stock prices, and output.[25]

- The best predictors of banking crises are (in that order) the *real exchange rate*, the *broad money multiplier*, the stock market, output, and real interest rates. A real exchange rate appreciation lowers the profitability of

---

[25] By contrast, interest rate differentials, imports, bank deposits, and bank lending-deposit spreads were found to have no predictive power.

exports, and often precedes losses on unmatched currency positions (as discussed earlier). Reductions in equity prices have a negative effect on firms' net worth and the collateral on which bank loans are based. Increases in the broad money multiplier are associated with reductions in required reserve ratios, which often result from financial liberalization. Rises in domestic real interest rates, and adverse movements in output, often lead to an increase in the rate of default on bank loans.

- On average, the earliest signals provided by the best predictors are between 17 months and a year before a currency crisis occurs, and between 18 months and as late as 6 months prior to the occurrence of a banking crisis.

- Both currency and banking crises appear to be more severe in *Latin America* than in other regions. Devaluations are in general larger, and the cost of bailing out troubled banks is greater.

- The pre- and postcrisis behavior of most of the indicators show very similar patterns across regions, for both currency and banking crises. In Latin America, however, nearly all of the indicators show larger deviations from their behavior during precrisis periods; these deviations (such as the degree of real exchange rate overvaluation) also tend to be more persistent. Another important peculiarity in the case of Latin America is the *collapse of bank deposits* following a banking crisis.

Some other recent studies have either corroborated or questioned the findings of Kaminsky and Reinhart (1999). Demirgüç-Kunt and Detragiache (1998a), for instance, found that banking crises during the period 1980-94 tended to erupt when growth is low, and inflation and real interest rates are high. Vulnerability to currency crises (as measured by a high ratio of the broad money stock to official reserves) and the existence of an explicit deposit insurance scheme also played a role. In a subsequent study (Demirgüç-Kunt and Detragiache, 1998b) they also found that banking crises are more likely to occur in liberalized financial systems.[26]

Berg and Pattillo (1998) assessed the ability of several empirical models of currency crises—including those of Kaminsky, Lizondo, and Reinhart (1998) and Sachs, Tornell, and Velasco (1996b)—to predict the Asian exchange rate crises that started with the collapse of the Thai baht reviewed earlier. They concluded that although none of the models reliably predicted the timing of the crises, they did have some value in the sense that variables such as a high credit growth rate, an overvalued exchange rate, and a high ratio of broad money to reserves, did affect positively the probability of a crisis. They concluded that although accurately predicting currency crises remains a difficult (if not impossible) task, there are some indicators that policymakers should monitor

---

[26]This, of course, is not an argument against financial liberalization *per se*, but rather against *premature* liberalization, because it is conducive to financial instability. See Chapter 15.

closely—most notably movements in the real exchange rate. However, given the lack of robustness across existing studies, what should constitute the critical set of indicators remains a matter of debate.

7.5   Sources and Effects of Financial Volatility

As noted in the previous chapter, the growing integration of world capital markets in recent years has increased the opportunities for investors to diversify risks. At the same time, however, the volatility of capital flows in the new global economy has created substantial risks. This section begins by examining the sources of volatility of capital flows and the role of herding behavior and contagion effects. It then discusses specifically the contagion effects of the Mexican peso and the Thai baht crises reviewed earlier.

7.5.1   Volatility of Capital Flows

In general, the degree of volatility of capital flows is related to both actual or perceived movements in economic fundamentals, as well as external factors—which include not only movements in world interest rates (as documented in Chapter 6) but also investor herding and contagious factors (as discussed below). Volatility can also be magnified by actual or expected *policy responses*. As noted in the previous chapter, private capital flows are increasingly channeled to the domestic economy through commercial banks. Credit market inefficiencies can magnify the effect of changes in, for instance, external interest rates, and lead to fluctuations in domestic output that may have feedback effects on capital flows (Agénor and Aizenman, 1998). More generally, the fact that investor sentiment (particularly that of highly leveraged, speculative trading institutions, such as *hedge funds*) is constantly changing in response to new information creates the potential for markets to overshoot on a scale that can generate financial crises with unacceptably large costs.[27]

The evidence suggests that volatility in capital inflows has tended to translate into exchange rate instability (under flexible exchange rates) and large fluctuations in official reserves (under a pegged exchange rate regime) and (in the absence of full sterilization) the money supply. There is also evidence that instability has also increased in domestic equity markets, although the evidence there is less clear-cut. Financial volatility may have adverse effects on the real side as well—nominal exchange rate volatility, in particular, may hamper the expansion of exports (Grobar, 1993).

---

[27] The Bank for International Settlements (BIS) estimated average daily turnover in the global foreign exchange market at about $1,200 billion in April 1995. By comparison, during the same period, average daily turnover in the world's ten largest stock markets was around $40 billion.

7.5.2 Herding Behavior and Contagion

More than long-term capital flows, portfolio flows tend to be particularly sensitive to **herding behavior** and **contagion effects**. Many economists view herding among investors—large movements into certain types of assets, followed by equally large movements out, without no apparent reason—as evidence of *irrational behavior*, as the quotation at the beginning of this chapter would appear to indicate. Some recent literature, however, suggests differently; as noted by Devenow and Welch (1996), herding can also occur in the presence of several effects:

- **payoff externalities**, which are related to the fact that the payoff to an agent (investor) adopting a specific action may be positively related to the number of other agents adopting the same action;

- **principal-agent considerations**, which result from the fact that a manager, in order to maintain or improve his or her reputation when markets are imperfectly informed, may prefer either to *hide in the herd* to avoid evaluation and criticism, or to *ride the herd* to generate reputational gains;

- **information cascades**, which are due to the fact that (small) agents that are only beginning to invest in a country may find it optimal to ignore their own information and follow the behavior of larger and more established investors.

Consider, for instance, the model of Calvo and Mendoza (1997), which assumes a global market with many identical investors forming decisions simultaneously. Investors determine optimally (for given means and variances of asset returns) the optimal trade-off between diversification and costly-information collection. They showed that with *informational frictions*, rational herding behavior may become more prevalent as the world capital market grows. The reason is that globalization reduces the incentives to collect country-specific information to discredit rumors and increases the likelihood that fund managers who worry about their relative performance will each select the same portfolio. Consequently, *small rumors* can induce herding behavior and lead to large capital outflows (seemingly unrelated with a country's economic fundamentals) and a self-fulfilling speculative attack on the domestic currency—of the type discussed earlier.

Volatility of capital flows can also result directly from contagion effects. **Financial contagion** occurs when a country suffers massive *capital outflows* triggered by a perceived increase by international investors in the *vulnerability* of a country's currency, or, more generally, a *loss of confidence* in the country's economic prospects, as a result of developments elsewhere.[28] Examples of financial contagion (or cross-border spillover effects) are the **Tequila effect** and the Asia crisis discussed in the next section.

It should be noted also that contagion can occur through two other channels, with indirect effects on the volatility of capital flows.

---

[28] Such phenomena may be compounded by perceived changes in the country's policy stance.

- Contagious shocks may take the form of *terms-of-trade shocks*. The Asia crisis led to a sharp reduction in demand for imports and a sharp drop in world commodity prices. Between June 1997 and April 1998,

  - *oil* prices dropped by almost 30 percent; this had adverse consequences on oil producers and exporters such as Saudi Arabia, Nigeria, and Mexico;

  - *coffee* prices dropped by 21 percent, hurting Brazil and Colombia;

  - *Copper* prices fell by 27 percent, hurting Chile and Zambia.

  By increasing the degree of uncertainty regarding the short-term economic prospects of a country, terms-of-trade shock may translate into financial contagion—as appeared to have happened in the case of Brazil and Chile in late 1997 and early 1998.

- Contagion can also occur through a *competitiveness effect*. The sharp depreciation of the Thai baht that began in July 1997 put pressure on the currencies of neighboring countries that maintained a fixed exchange rate (as discussed later), in part because it implied a loss of competitiveness.

7.5.3 The Tequila Effect and the Asia Crisis

An example of contagion is the so-called **Tequila effect**, which followed the collapse of the Mexican peso on December 20, 1994 (see Section 2). The Mexican crisis triggered exchange market pressures and increased financial market volatility in a number of developing countries. In Latin America, two economies were hit particularly severely: *Argentina* and *Brazil*. External interest rate spreads rose sharply in Argentina (see Figure 7.10), reflecting an adverse shift in sentiment on world capital markets. In both countries, gyrations in market sentiment led in early 1995 to a sharp reduction in net capital inflows, a fall in official reserves, and intense pressure on asset prices. Between December 1994 and February 1995, the cumulative decline in stock market prices (measured in terms of U.S. dollars) reached 24.8 percent in Argentina and 22.6 percent in Brazil.

Whereas in subsequent months most countries that initially suffered from market turbulences regained financial and exchange market stability, a *full-fledged economic crisis* developed in *Argentina*—which had been operating a fixed exchange rate regime (a currency board, as noted in Chapter 4) since the **Convertibility Plan** was introduced in April 1991. As illustrated in Figure 7.11, output contracted significantly in 1995, whereas bank deposits and domestic credit (as measured by bank claims on the private sector) fell dramatically. For 1995 as a whole, industrial output fell by 6.7 percent, real GDP by 4.6 percent, real private consumption by 6.1 percent, real domestic investment by 16 percent, and bank credit to the private sector by 5.5 percent in real terms.[29] The

---

[29] The decline in bank credit to the private sector in 1995 may have been exacerbated by the

unemployment rate increased sharply, peaking at 18.5 percent in May 1995.[30] The liquidity crunch led to a sharp rise in bank lending rates, on both peso- and US dollar-denominated loans. The spread between the lending rates on these two categories of loans widened significantly between February and May 1995 (as shown in Figure 7.11), reflecting an increase in the perceived risk of a collapse of the currency board regime and a subsequent large exchange rate depreciation. Although the contraction in output and the expansion of merchandise exports (by 27 percent in volume terms for 1995 as a whole) led to an improvement in the trade balance, the massive shift away from peso deposits, capital flight and the reduction in new borrowing led to a collapse of foreign reserves, and a dramatic fall in the monetary base.

Of course, whether a crisis would have occurred anyway in 1995, given the large *appreciation* of the real exchange rate and the consumption-induced deterioration in the external accounts recorded after the adoption of the Convertibility Plan in April 1991, is difficult to say. The logic of the **boom-recession cycle** (as discussed in Chapter 5) that often characterizes exchange-rate-based stabilization programs would have indeed predicted an eventual recession. In part due to high residual inflation (an average of 24.9 percent in 1992 and 10.6 percent in 1993 compared with 171.7 percent in 1991), Argentina's real effective exchange rate based on consumer prices appreciated by nearly 27 percent between April 1991 and December 1994.[31] At the same time, the current account deficit increased from 0.1 percent of GDP in 1991 to 2.8 percent in 1992, 3.1 percent in 1993, and 3.7 percent in 1994—reflecting a sharp increase in consumption and gross domestic investment, the latter rising by more than 5 percentage points of GDP between 1991 and 1994. Nevertheless, the timing and severity of the economic downturn in Argentina suggests a contagious effect—massive capital outflows triggered by a loss of confidence of international investors in the country's economic prospects, and the perception that the exchange rate regime was about to suffer the same fate as Mexico's.

---

process of concentration in the banking industry, which is widely perceived to have entailed a loss of information about borrowers' net worth, thereby making banks more cautious in their lending decisions. It should also be noted that *total* credit (including credit to the public sector) actually *increased* between end-1994 and end-1995.

[30] The recession compounded the already unfavorable trends in the labor market. Unemployment rose steadily from around 6 percent in the immediate aftermath of the introduction of the Convertibility Plan to 12.5 percent in October 1994, despite an average rate of real output growth of more than 7 percent during the same period. The low output-employment elasticity has been attributed by some observers to a rise in the *participation rate* and increased substitution of capital for labor.

[31] This estimate is based on calculations made by the International Monetary Fund. It should be noted, however, that (as could be expected from the discussion in Chapter 4) estimates of the real effective exchange rate based on *wholesale prices* and *unit labor costs* show a significantly lower cumulative appreciation during the same period.

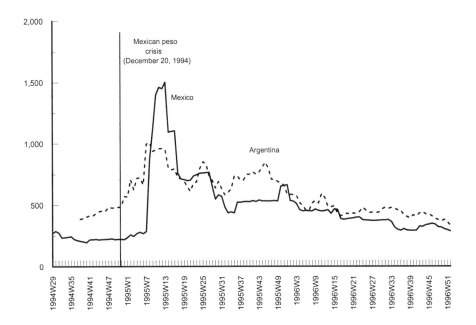

Figure 7.10. Argentina and Mexico: Secondary Market Yield Spreads on U.S. Dollar-Denominated Eurobonds, 1994-96 1/ (In basis points).

Source: Bloomberg and Reuters.

1/ Republic of Argentina fixed-coupon bond issued on December 8, 1993 and due December 20, 2003. United Mexican Statesfixed-coupon bondissued September 17, 1992 and due September 15, 2002. The spread is calculated with respect to a U.S. Treasury fixed-coupon bond issued on August 16, 1993, with maturity date of August 15, 2003.

Following the Thai baht crisis described earlier, currencies of several other Asian countries (most notably Hong Kong, Korea, Malaysia, the Philippines, Singapore, and Taiwan) came under severe speculative pressures. Several of these countries were eventually forced to abandoned their exchange rate regime: the Philippines floated its currency on July 12, Indonesia widened its currency band from 8 percent to 12 percent and then floated the exchange rate on August 14, and Malaysia stopped defending its exchange rate peg in mid-July. Despite some positive developments on the macroeconomic side (including low inflation, relatively high output growth rates, and the absence of significant fiscal imbalances), all of these countries were suddenly viewed by investors as suffering from similar weaknesses in economic fundamentals: overvalued exchange rates pegged to the U.S. dollar, growing current account deficits (particularly Korea and Malaysia), declining equity prices, and weak banking systems.[32] As

---

[32] It should be noted that the evidence regarding the degree of *overvaluation* (as opposed to the degree of *real appreciation*) of Asian currencies prior to the crisis is somewhat ambiguous. Chinn (1998), for instance, estimated a model that determines the degree of overvaluation

shown in Figure 7.12, nominal exchange rates depreciated significantly and equity prices fell dramatically after the collapse of the Thai baht in all of these countries.[33]

Two factors interacted to transform the initial market turbulences into a vicious circle of currency depreciation and deteriorating confidence in the region's economic prospects:

- *Overborrowing* on world capital markets at short maturities and excessive exposure to *foreign exchange risk* in the financial and corporate sectors, both encouraged by the implicit guarantee provided by pegged exchange rate regimes and the **moral hazard** created by expectations of a government bail-out in case of inadequate returns on (overly risky) investment projects. Figure 7.13 shows the sharp increase in foreign borrowing by bank and nonbank private sector entities in East Asia during 1995-97. Most of this borrowing was short term in nature. As shown in Figure 7.14, in the periods preceding the crisis, short-term external debt exceeded by a large amount the level of official reserves. In particular, the ratio of short-term foreign liabilities to official reserves exceeded 170 percent in Indonesia and 210 percent in Korea in June 1997.

- *Weak asset portfolios* of domestic banks (as measured by high ratios of nonperforming loans), in part by inadequate prudential regulations and lax supervision, and in part by distorted incentives for project selection and monitoring—which resulted from the moral hazard created by the belief that the government would intervene to bail out lenders or borrowers and thus prevent bankruptcy.

The perception of these financial fragilities may have led speculators to believe that pegged exchange rate regimes in several countries of the region could not be defended very long with high interest rates—because of their adverse effect on bankruptcy rates and nonperforming loans, as noted earlier—and thus led to persistent pressures on foreign exchange markets.[34] The currency depreciations, in turn, led to a deterioration of the financial positions of banks and nonfinancial corporations (many of them, as in Thailand, carrying large unhedged positions in foreign currency) and an increase in the proportion of nonperforming loans. This, in turn, heightened concerns about the viability of

---

as the difference between actual and equilibrium values of the real exchange rate. Using consumer price indices to measure real exchange rate, Chinn found that in May 1997, the degree of overvaluation was 30 percent for Indonesia, 17 percent for Malaysia, 24 percent for the Philippines, and 13 percent for Thailand. However, using producer price indices, the results were -5 percent, 8 percent, 19 percent, and 7 percent, respectively—relatively small numbers, compared with the subsequent nominal depreciations that these countries experienced.

[33] The impact of the Asian crisis was not confined to Asia. Currencies in Latin America and South Africa, in particular, also came under severe pressure.

[34] During the first stages of the crisis, political uncertainties and doubts about the resolve of policymakers to implement appropriate adjustment measures exacerbated pressures on currencies throughout the region.

domestic banking systems and created doubts about the extent to which corporate and financial sector foreign liabilities were effectively "insured" by implicit government guarantees. Both factors further undermined confidence—leading to renewed pressure on foreign exchange markets.[35]

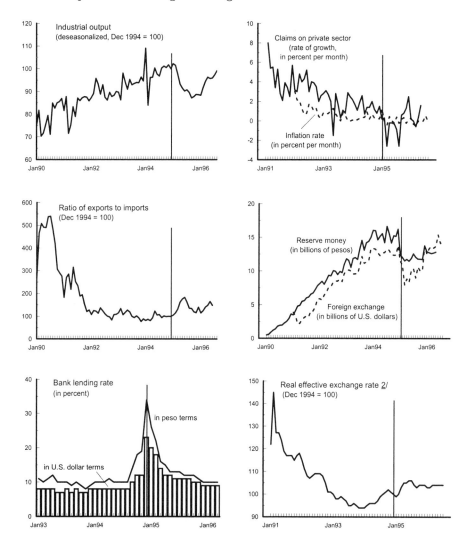

Figure 7.11. Argentina: Macroeconomic Indicators, 1990-96 1/.

Source: FIEL; International Monetary Fund.

1/ The vertical line corresponds to the Mexican peso crisis (December 1994).

2/ An increase is a depreciation.

---

[35] For a detailed analysis of the causes, propagation, and policy responses to the Asian crisis, see Alba et al. (1999), and Radelet and Sachs (1998).

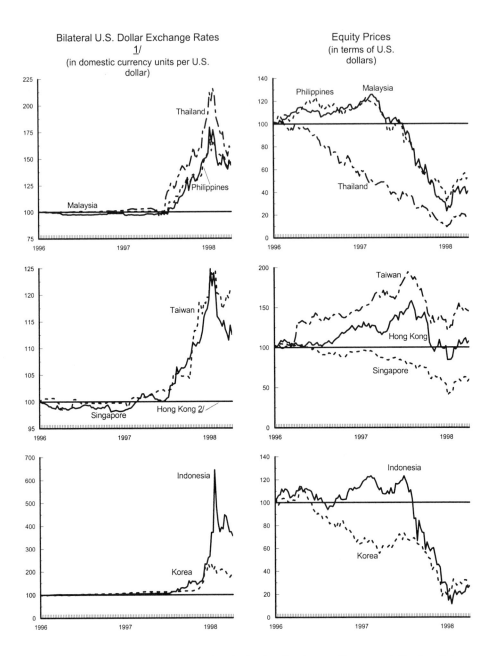

Figure 7.12. Asia: Bilateral U.S. Dollar Exchange Rates and Equity Prices, 1996-98 (January 5, 1996 = 100).

Source: International Monetary Fund.

1/ An increase is a depreciation.

2/ Pegged to the U.S. dollar.

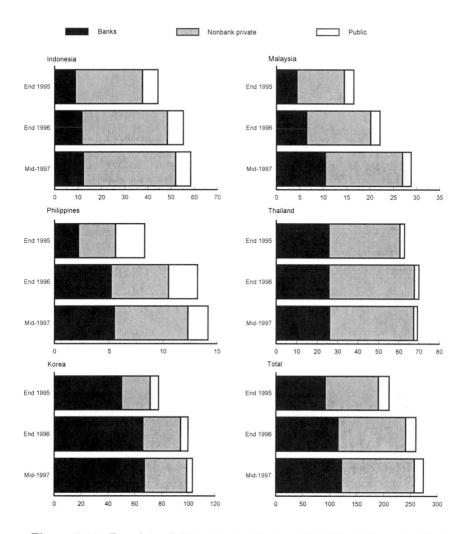

Figure 7.13. East Asia: Debt to Foreign Banks, 1995-97 (In billions of dollars). Source: Radelet and Sachs (1998, p. 26).

7.6   Coping with Financial Volatility

As noted in the previous chapter, an important benefit of financial integration is that it allows countries to use international capital markets to diversify and hedge against both idiosyncratic and global risks. But if these same markets are prone to *overexuberance* in good times and *excess pessimism* (leading to sudden withdrawals of capital) in bad times, then the benefits of portfolio diversification and risk insurance can easily be overwhelmed. Financial integration in this case *increases risks* instead of *reducing* them. The benefits of capital inflows can be completely offset by large and sudden outflows. The foregoing discussion suggested indeed that international capital markets can be prone to sharp shifts in sentiment regarding a country's short- and longer-term economic prospects. The discipline that they exercise over government policies, although beneficial in some respects, can be abrupt, excessive, and indiscriminate.

Figure 7.14. East Asia: Short-term Debt and Foreign Exchange Reserves, 1995–97 (In billions of dollars).

Source: Radelet and Sachs (1998, p. 26).

Note: Ratio is short-term debt over reserves. For Mexico it reached $33.2/6.4 = 5.2$ at the end of 1994.

What type of preventive measures policymakers can put in place before markets force a more costly resolution of (actual or perceived) policy inconsistencies has been an issue to which much thinking has been devoted in recent years. Among the suggestions that have emerged are a renewed emphasis on macroeconomic discipline, information disclosure, and the possibility of throwing *sand in the wheels* of capital markets by imposing a tax on foreign exchange transactions.

7.6.1   Macroeconomic Discipline

Various economists have argued that the constraints imposed by financial globalization are best addressed not by imposing restrictions on capital movements (as documented in the previous chapter), but by following transparent, disciplined, and sustainable macroeconomic policies. Monitoring exchange rate levels to ensure consistency with underlying fundamentals, implementing appropriate policy adjustments to correct fiscal imbalances and prevent an excessive buildup of domestic debt, maintaining a monetary policy consistent with low inflation, and ensuring that the ratio of unhedged foreign debt over official reserves remains sufficiently low are all preventive measures that are likely to reduce the risk of sudden changes in market sentiment. The better the economic fundamentals, the longer the track record of macroeconomic discipline, and the less susceptible the country is likely to be to potentially volatile flows or contagion effects—and thus the lower the probability of a financial crisis.

The adequate management of the public foreign-currency debt, in particular, has been viewed as an important component of a strategy aimed at reducing the volatility of capital flows and ensuring the viability of a fixed exchange rate.[36] As indicated earlier, some recent theories of currency crises have emphasized the fact that a large ratio of short-term (public and private) foreign-currency debt relative to official reserves may put a country in a vulnerable position where a self-fulfilling speculative attack may occur. In addition, a large stock of foreign-currency debt may magnify the impact of adverse external shocks on the economy (particularly when these shocks translate into a depreciation of the nominal exchange rate), and may constrain the policy options available to policymakers during a financial crisis.

More generally, a large, unhedged foreign-currency debt carries risks resulting not only from its *maturity profile* but also from its *currency composition*. In 1995, the ratio of foreign-currency debt held (or guaranteed) by governments in developing countries to total international reserves (excluding gold) reached 270 percent (International Monetary Fund, 1997*b*, p. 215). Governments are thus exposed to a large degree of *currency risk*.[37] In addition, a short-term foreign-

---

[36]It should also be noted that financial markets in many developing countries are using more and more sophisticated hedging techniques and financial instruments that allow both domestic and foreign investors to manage their exposure to foreign exchange and interest rate risk and dampen the impact on domestic markets of volatility on world financial markets.

[37]During the period 1980-94, in an attempt to take advantage of relatively low interest rates in Japan relative to the United States, several of the larger East Asian countries increased significantly their borrowing in Japanese yen. Most of these countries did not hedge their yen exposure either in domestic currency or in U.S. dollars, which account for a large part of their foreign-currency earnings. As a result, the appreciation of the yen vis-à-vis the U.S. dollar

currency debt at floating rates—often indexed on the London Interbank Offer Rate, LIBOR—exposes countries to *interest rate risk* resulting from abrupt changes in world interest rates.

However, macroeconomic discipline and improved management of foreign debt are by no means *sufficient* to prevent speculative attacks and highly volatile capital flows.

- Unwarranted changes in expectations can and do occur, even when underlying economic fundamentals appear strong. A case in point is *Chile* in the aftermath of the Asia crisis; severe exchange market pressures developed, despite apparently solid fundamentals—high growth rates, high saving rates, small fiscal deficits, and low inflation.

- The strengthening of the financial system (including improved supervision and accounting standards) *takes time*. During the transition to a more efficient financial system, distortions in domestic capital markets may continue to exacerbate the adverse effects of external volatility.

For both reasons, policymakers may need during a transitory period to resort to additional instruments to prevent excessive volatility from adversely affecting domestic stability. Short-term controls on capital flows, as discussed in the previous chapter, may be part of the arsenal that they need to consider, despite limitations.

7.6.2   Information Disclosure

As noted earlier, when international investors can allocate their wealth over many risky foreign investments and face a fixed cost of information about each country, it may pay for individuals to diversify widely without waiting to become informed. In such conditions, capital flows can be volatile and subject to herding effects (Calvo and Mendoza, 1997). A mechanism aimed at providing appropriate and timely information to markets (such as data on official foreign reserves, the maturity of public and private foreign borrowing, and the quality and composition of bank loans) may thus be beneficial in reducing volatility. However, the argument faces two problems: countries have limited incentives to provide *bad news* quickly to markets, and markets have limited ability to *verify* (at least in the very short run) the information that is provided. Knowing this, countries may be tempted to exploit this advantage by *falsifying* the information—particularly in bad times. There is therefore a need for a principal to, in a sense, *certify* in some way the information provided by countries. In that regard, current efforts by multilateral institutions such as the International Monetary Fund and the World Bank to encourage countries to provide more timely data on their economies and at the same time impose *quality standards* are important. At the same time, however, it is not obvious that any of these

---

and the Asian currencies in the first half of the 1990s led to a significant rise in the dollar value of their external liabilities.

institutions possesses clear incentives to play an explicit monitoring role in that area; the reason is that such a role (in addition to being unpopular) may create the very problem that it is aimed at avoiding—overreaction by markets to what may be perceived, incorrectly, as a potential deterioration of economic fundamentals.

7.6.3 The Tobin Tax

Some economists recently revived the idea, first advanced by James Tobin in the late 1960s, to uniformly tax spot transactions in foreign exchange (that is, all transactions involving the conversion of one currency into another in foreign exchange markets) as a way to reduce volatility on world financial markets. A key feature of the tax, according to its proponents, is that it would reduce *noise* from market trading while allowing traders to react to changes in economic fundamentals. It would therefore be superior to various forms of capital controls (see Chapter 6). By making currency trading more costly, it would *discourage speculation*—thereby reducing the volume of destabilizing short-term capital flows and leading to greater stability in exchange rate and reserve movements.

An extension of the Tobin tax to a **two-tier tax** was also recently proposed by Spahn (1995) for countries operating flexible exchange rate or band regimes. The proposal consists in imposing a **minimal-rate transaction tax** (of, say, 0.02 percent) that would not impair market efficiency under normal market conditions, and an **exchange surcharge** that would be activated only in periods of *heavy speculative trading*—which are defined by Spahn as periods during which the trading price for a currency crosses an **admissible band**, consisting of a $+/- x$ percent margin around a target, the moving average exchange rate. The idea is that in periods during which the surcharge is triggered, transactions costs would rise sufficiently to cause some traders to delay transactions, thus smoothing out fluctuations in exchange rates. The surcharge is thus a **variable tax** on (cash) transactions in foreign exchange. The exchange rate would thus be kept within a target range through taxation rather than central bank intervention.

There are, however, several potential difficulties that may considerably limit the effectiveness of the Tobin tax and most of its variants, such as Spahn's proposal. These difficulties lie in four areas (see Garber, 1996): establishing the tax base, identifying taxable transactions, setting the tax rate, and implementing the tax across borders.

To limit financial market distortions, the *base* for any tax on international financial transactions would have to be relatively broad. However, there are strong economic arguments for exempting certain types of trades from the tax— for instance, transactions made by *market makers* and those that increase *market liquidity*. In particular, trading by *financial intermediaries* plays generally a stabilizing role. The difficulty is that in practice it is hard to distinguish, on an institutional basis, between normal trading that assures the efficiency and stability of financial markets and destabilizing noise trading, which should be the only target of the tax. By reducing trading, it may paradoxically lead to less liquid markets and entail *greater volatility*.

Applying the Tobin tax only to *spot transactions* involving foreign currencies is likely to be ineffective, because market operators would eventually avoid the tax by trading in more sophisticated financial instruments such as over-the-counter **derivatives**.[38] The high degree of substitutability between financial instruments may thus hamper the application of the Tobin tax. Moreover, financial derivatives such as forward transactions, futures, and financial swaps allow market participants to transform *long trading* into *short trading* activities, with important repercussions on spot markets (see Garber and Lall, 1998). The volume of such transactions has grown at a very high pace over the past few years and now accounts for a significant share of all foreign exchange transactions.

Tobin's initial proposal called for a *low*, uniform tax rate. Given the small margins that traders realize on foreign exchange market transactions, even a 0.02 percent tax (as proposed by Spahn) may represent a significant tax on trading activities in normal times. In addition, because some financial transactions are undertaken by several intermediaries, taxes on these transactions may have a **cascading effect**—implying that the *effective tax rate* may be significantly higher than the nominal rate applied to a single transaction. However, during periods of heavy speculation, even a tax of, say, 3 percent on round-trip transactions (sale and repurchase of foreign currencies) is unlikely to deter speculators who expect a *significant short-term change* in the exchange rate (a devaluation of, say, 15 percent). On the other hand, a tax rate that is high enough to deter speculation even in such periods would hamper the functioning of financial markets. The possible (or uncertain) benefits in terms of reducing short-term speculative trading would thus be outweighed by the possible costs associated with impairing the efficiency of financial intermediation.

Finally, the *mobility* of financial transactions would make the tax easy to avoid—unless it is implemented and enforced around the world (Shome and Stotsky, 1996). However, the likelihood of a universal tax can only be viewed as a remote possibility, in part because of the difficult political and economic issues that the distribution of proceeds raises. For this reason, Eichengreen, Tobin, and Wyplosz (1995) favored a more indirect means to tax foreign exchange transactions, which is a *tax on lending to nonresidents*. This tax can be applied in one country because it applies to resident lenders. Although it would not be universal, it would reduce loans of domestic banks to foreign speculators, which constitutes an important channel of speculation (see the appendix to this chapter).

---

[38] Derivatives are synthetic financial instruments derived from underlying assets. *Futures* and *options* are commonly traded derivative contracts. A futures contract is an agreement between two parties to buy or sell a specific quantity of a financial instrument at a specific price. The buyer and seller agree on a price (exchange rate) for the product to be delivered, or paid for at a specified time in the future known as the *settlement date*. An option on a financial instrument futures contract is a binding agreement between two parties that confers on the buyer or seller the right (but not the obligation) to buy or sell the underlying asset at or up to a specified point in the future. The buyer and seller agree on a price known as a *premium*. *Calls* confer the right to buy, while *puts* confer the right to sell at a predetermined price. The option (call or put) terms determine the time period within which the buyer can exercise the option.

7.7 Summary

- **Conventional** or first-generation models of **currency crises** predict that a fixed-exchange-rate regime is not viable without long-run *consistency* between monetary, fiscal, and exchange-rate policies. Excessive domestic credit growth leads to a gradual loss of foreign reserves and ultimately to a **natural collapse** of the regime, once the *minimum level of reserves* is reached and the central bank can no longer defend the pegged rate.

- Speculators, knowing that the system is doomed to a natural collapse, and willing to avoid *capital losses* that would result from a discrete change in the exchange rate, will attack the currency and force the central bank to abandon the pegged rate *before* the minimum level of reserves is reached.

- The speculative attack takes place at the point in time when the **shadow floating exchange rate** equals the prevailing fixed rate. This also corresponds to the moment in time when remaining international reserves at the central bank, which are gradually being depleted, *precisely match* the portfolio reallocation indicated by the postattack interest rate shift.

- **Second-generation** models of currency crises explicitly account for **policymakers' preferences** and the **trade-offs** that they face in their policy objectives. In this setting, an exchange rate "crisis" (a devaluation or a switch to a floating rate regime) is viewed as an *ex ante* optimal decision for the policymaker. These models also highlight the role of **self-fulfilling mechanisms, multiple equilibria,** and **credibility factors**.

- For instance, an arbitrary increase in inflation expectations (induced by a perceived incentive to relax monetary and fiscal policies in the face of persistent unemployment) may raise *interest rates* to such an extent that the cost of preserving the peg (that is, foregoing the possibility to stimulate output by raising prices and lowering real wages) becomes so large that the authorities may find it optimal to devalue or to abandon altogether the pegged rate.

- Market expectations may thus take on the characteristics of **self-fulfilling prophecies**—crises arising without obvious policy inconsistencies. A speculative attack undermining the viability of a peg can be viewed as a *sudden switch* from one regime of expectations to the other. Thus, the exact timing of an exchange rate crisis becomes *indeterminate* and difficult to predict.

- The new theories suggest that, in examining the determinants of currency crises, it may be necessary to consider a broader set of fundamentals than simply credit growth or the real exchange rate. In particular, the *ratio of short-term foreign currency liabilities to official reserves* appears to be an important indicator of exchange rate vulnerability. Heavy reliance on short-term foreign borrowing increases the economy's exposure to foreign exchange risk and to a potential reversal of capital flows.

- The fact that macroeconomic policies are not regarded as predetermined but are taken as responding to agents' expectations creates the possibility of self-fulfilling crises. However, models of self-fulfilling crises based on an arbitrary selection among multiple equilibria by financial market operators can only *rationalize* speculative attacks; they cannot truly *explain* them, despite being consistent with some of the events that may surround these attacks. They do not explain why the shift between equilibria occurs.

- Some of the new models do not assert that exchange rates can be attacked irrespective of economic fundamentals. Rather, they suggest that the ability of a sudden change in expectations to trigger an attack is *bounded* by the *position of fundamentals*, such as the amount of short-term debt that the government has to roll over.

- A combination of adverse political shocks, a large and growing current account deficit, and policy shortcomings led to increasing reserve losses and growing dependence on short-term external borrowing in 1994 in Mexico. A devaluation on December 20, 1994, triggered a loss of confidence that led to a full-blown financial and economic crisis. Events in Mexico led to serious pressures and increased volatility in financial and exchange markets in a number of Asian and Latin American countries, particularly in Argentina (the **Tequila effect**).

- Thailand's *growing external deficits* and a *weak and poorly supervised financial system* were the two main factors triggering the crisis of the Thai baht in July 1997. Large, unhedged stocks of *U.S. dollar liabilities* held by the banks and the corporate sector compounded the effects of the initial devaluation of the baht and led to a full-blown financial and economic crisis. *Delayed policy response* (despite various warning signs in the previous months) and the authorities' resistance to an early adjustment of the exchange rate also exacerbated the crisis.

- Banking crises result from various factors, including *external* and *domestic macroeconomic volatility* (including *terms-of-trade* shocks and sharp fluctuations in *world interest rates*), excessive **lending booms**, *large mismatches* with respect to *liquidity*, *maturity*, and *currency denomination* of assets and liabilities), *inadequate preparation* for financial liberalization, heavy *government involvement* in the banking system, and loose controls on *insider lending*.

- Exchange rate crises and banking crises are related in various ways. A currency crisis can lead to a banking crisis because an unsterilized, large *loss in international reserves* that results from the speculative attack that precedes the abandonment of a fixed exchange rate regime may translate into a sharp decline in the base money stock and credit availability. In turn, the credit crunch may lead to a rise in nonperforming loans and an increased incidence of bankruptcies by nonfinancial firms. Or, the sharp exchange rate depreciation that often accompanies a currency crisis can create **solvency problems** among banks that are (directly or indirectly, through their customers) exposed to large foreign exchange liabilities.

- A banking crisis can lead to a currency crisis if the central bank allows an *excessive expansion* of domestic credit to finance the bailout of ailing banks, depositors, or both under an explicit or implicit **deposit insurance scheme.** *Both* currency and banking crises may also result from *common macroeconomic shocks*—such as an unexpected sharp increase in world interest rates, which may lead to a bank run and large capital outflows.

- Recent empirical studies of the determinants of currency and banking crises suggest that banking crises are often preceded by **financial liberalization.** In the study by Kaminsky and Reinhart (1999), the best predictors of currency crises are the real exchange rate, exports, the ratio of broad money over official reserves, stock prices, and output. The best predictors of banking crises are the real exchange rate, the broad money multiplier, the stock market, output, and real interest rates. However, the possibility of predicting the actual *timing* of currency and banking crises appears very limited—in part because of the existence of self-fulfilling factors.

- Financial markets are prone to herding, panics, contagion, and boom-bust cycles. However, herding behavior is not necessarily a reflection of irrationality. Portfolio allocation to any given country can be subject to abrupt changes in response to very small changes in perceived expected returns. In addition, the benefits of collecting country-specific information to corroborate the investor's prior expectations regarding the rate of return on the country's assets tends to diminish. Thus, diversification reduces incentives to acquire information; uncorroborated rumors may trigger large capital flows.

- Volatility in capital inflows translates into exchange rate instability (under flexible exchange rates) or large fluctuations in official reserves (under a pegged exchange rate regime) and (without sterilization) the money supply.

- Macroeconomic policy discipline, improved prudential rules on banks, information disclosure, and improved management of foreign-currency debt (to avoid, in particular, excessive reliance on short-maturity debt) can reduce the risks associated with a high degree of financial openness but cannot eliminate them.

- The **Tobin tax** is a proposal to tax uniformly spot transactions in foreign exchange in an attempt to reduce exchange rate volatility induced by large capital flows. However, there is no evidence suggesting a close relationship between transactions costs and volatility on asset markets, and thus no evidence that the Tobin tax would, in fact, reduce market volatility. On the contrary, by increasing transactions costs it may hinder (at a sufficiently high level) the operation of financial markets. It may create a disincentive to trade assets, and may raise the cost of capital—thereby exerting an adverse effect on investment and growth. There are also serious practical difficulties in implementing it; it would penalize both stabilizing and destabilizing traders, because these two groups are difficult to identify in practice.

- To fend off speculative attacks, a first line of defense for the central bank is to raise interest rates to impose a squeeze on short sellers of the domestic currency. This interest rate defense is designed to raise the finance cost to speculators, prior to a possible devaluation, above their anticipated capital gains in the event the devaluation indeed takes place—a situation that might force an eventual closing of the short positions.

- However, the interest rate defense may not be effective if sophisticated financial instruments are used by speculators. Moreover, the potential costs of maintaining high interest rates in periods of heavy speculative currency pressures can also be high. In particular, the interest costs of a squeeze are imposed both on speculators and on agents who are short in the currency for commercial reasons; thus high interest rates will over time affect economic activity. If these costs are large, the central bank may not be able to convince agents of its commitment to defend the fixed exchange rate.

Appendix
The Mechanics of Speculative Attacks
and Interest Rate Defense ˙

Whereas the main focus of the first part of this chapter was a discussion of the *economics* of speculative attacks, this appendix describes the practical aspects or *mechanics* of speculative attacks—particularly the role of bank lending. It also discusses the use of high interest rates to fend off speculative pressures.[39]

A speculator whose objective is to initiate an attack on a given currency (say, the peso) must create a **short peso position**. This is often done by short-selling pesos through a **forward contract**, whose maturity is sufficiently long (say, one month) to a financial intermediary (say, a domestic bank). The first panel of Table 7.1 describes how this transaction takes place. Suppose that the *spot exchange rate* of the domestic currency, the peso, is 25 pesos per US dollar and that the speculator short-sells 2,500 pesos. The bank thus commits to providing a payment of US 100 dollars in one month to the speculator, in exchange for 2,500 pesos.

The bank engaged in the operation has now a **long peso position** as a result of this transaction. The **currency mismatch**, in turn, creates a **currency risk**. If, for instance, a depreciation of the currency takes place (from, say, 25 to 50 pesos per US dollar) before the settlement date (that is, within a month), the bank will need 5,000 pesos to make the scheduled payment of US 100 dollars. In order to balance its domestic-currency position, the bank will *immediately* sell pesos on the **spot market** for foreign exchange for the conventional settlement period—say, two days. Thus, the bank will pay 2,500 pesos in two days, and receive in exchange US 100 dollars. The second panel of Table 7.1 summarizes this transaction.

However, although the bank has now eliminated its currency mismatch, it still faces a **maturity mismatch** in both pesos and US dollars:

- it must borrow 2,500 pesos overnight to cover settlement of the spot sale but it will receive pesos only in 30 days, once the US dollars are actually sold to the speculator in exchange for pesos;

- in the opposite direction, it buys 100 US dollars on the spot market today, but will need them only in 30 days from now; so it will lend overnight US dollars and effectively has borrowed 30-day US dollars.

In order to close this maturity mismatch, the bank can engage in a **foreign exchange swap**—that is, an agreement to exchange a specified payment obligation denominated in one currency for a specified payment obligation denominated in a different currency. In this particular case, the swap entails

- a delivery of 100 US dollars for 2,500 pesos in 2 days;

---

[39] The first part of this section draws largely on the International Monetary Fund (1997*a*, pp. 37-38) and Garber (1998).

- a delivery of 2,500 pesos for 100 US dollars 30 days forward.

The third panel in Table 7.1 summarizes the complete set of transactions performed by the speculator and the bank.

What happens if the central bank intervenes in the forward market for foreign exchange? Suppose that it purchases pesos forward by an amount that matches exactly the forward sale of the speculator (that is, 2,500 pesos). The forward intervention in that case will absorb the spot sale of pesos by the lending bank, without any need for the central bank to intervene directly in the spot market. Thus, intervention in the forward market by the central bank is tantamount to supplying implicitly domestic-currency credit directly to short sellers of pesos.

In a period of market turbulence in which the probability of a devaluation is high, net suppliers of domestic credit are likely to be difficult to find. Nevertheless, as can be inferred from the first part of Table 7.1, the banking system as a whole (commercial banks and the central bank) must provide credit to short sellers of pesos to finance a speculative attack. The previous example shows clearly that the bank's domestic currency receipts from the forward contract correspond to a *one-month loan* to the short seller. If the central bank does not supply the credit implicitly through forward intervention (as in the case considered earlier), the credit must come through either its money market operations or its loan facilities. In either case, the pesos provided by the banking system are essentially a **pass-through** of credit from the central bank, which is the ultimate counterparty in both segments of the position-balancing transactions initiated by domestic lenders.

In periods of large capital outflows, exchange market pressures, and losses in official reserves, one line of defense for policymakers is to increase interest rates. In particular, by raising its lending rate (and thus indirectly rates charged by commercial banks), the central bank can impose losses on speculators—that is, short sellers of pesos. As shown in the previous example, short sellers need to borrow in order to deliver pesos for US dollars under the forward contract; raising interest rates increases the cost of domestic funds and thus reduces the expected return from speculation.[40]

---

[40] More generally, to the extent that the increase in lending rates translates into higher interest rates on other domestic-currency assets, the attractiveness of these assets will increase.

Table 7.1

The Mechanics of Forward Contract Operations

Step 1. Forward contract: creates a currency mismatch			
Receipts		Payment	
Pesos in 1 month	2,500	Dollars in 1 month	100

Step 2. Forward contract + spot sale: creates a maturity mismatch			
Pesos in 1 month	2,500	Pesos in two days (spot)	2,500
Dollars in two days (spot)	100	Dollars in 1 month (forward)	100

Step 3. Forward + spot + swap = balanced position			
Pesos in 1 month (forward)	2,500	Pesos in 1 month (swap)	2,500
Pesos in two days (swap)	2,500	Pesos in two days (spot)	2,500
Dollars in 1 month (swap)	100	Dollars in 1 month (forward)	100
Dollars in two days (spot)	100	Dollars in two days (swap)	100

Source: International Monetary Fund (1997a, p. 38) and Garber (1998, p. 23).

Note: The assumed spot exchange rate is 25 pesos per US dollar.

However, hikes in interest rates may not always have their intended effect on speculators or on the exchange rate. If short sellers of the domestic currency have secured sufficient financing *before* the increase in interest rates is implemented, they will not suffer from it—unless the central bank maintains rates high for a sufficiently long period. The increased degree of sophistication of **derivative markets** may also have weakened the ability of a policy of high interest rates to fend off speculative attacks (Garber, 1998). Specifically, Garber and Spencer (1996) showed that the interest rate defense, which aims to squeeze speculators of liquidity, may not work because of **dynamic hedging strategies** that may trigger off *massive sales* of the domestic currency. A dynamic hedging strategy requires asset holders to adjust continuously the structure of their portfolios according to a certain rule, so as to achieve a *risk-exposure target*; in some of these strategies, a rise in the spread between foreign and domestic interest rates automatically triggers a forward or spot sale of the domestic currency. How widespread such dynamic trading securities are is not entirely clear; nevertheless, their existence suggests that an interest rate hike by the central bank could have the perverse effect of *inducing sales of the domestic currency*—and thus exacerbate exchange market pressures.

In addition to these limitations, increases in interest rates aimed at defending an exchange rate target may entail *various costs*.

- The increase in lending rates raises the cost of borrowing not only for speculators but also for other financial intermediaries (particularly those involved in securities markets), which often finance their positions through short-term lines of credit. This creates a potential constraint on how high the central bank can let interest rates rise without creating financial stress.[41] Such considerations would be particularly important if commercial banks are already suffering from heavy losses on their loan portfolio; the rise in interest rates may exacerbate these problems. It could also increase the expected size of the *fiscal deficit* if these banks are insolvent and explicit or implicit government insurance of commercial bank liabilities is present (see Chapter 14). This, in turn, may reinforce exchange market pressures.

- If total debt and debt service ratios of the nonfinancial private sector are already high, a rise in interest rates may bring these ratios to unsustainably high levels and lead to *insolvencies* and *outright default*—thereby weakening an already fragile banking system. The reduction in aggregate demand and output that high interest rates may entail could also exacerbate the position of firms and other debtors.

- In countries where fiscal imbalances are large and public debt is to a large extent short-term and contracted at floating rates, a large increase in interest rates can feed back quickly into higher interest payments and an increase in the government's fiscal deficit. Increases in interest rates may have a perverse effect and actually weaken the attractiveness of the domestic currency if markets believe that the increase in debt service may be monetized, or if interest rate volatility rises sufficiently beyond what is considered to be an acceptable level of risk.

- A high interest rate defense against speculative attacks may be viewed as having a high *opportunity cost* in terms of domestic economic activity, particularly where the economy has already been slowing down, where the unemployment rate is high or increasing, and inflation is low or falling. In such a situation, even a highly independent central bank (as discussed in Chapter 5) may be reluctant to maintain this policy for a long period of time.

---

[41] To mitigate this cost, a central bank can in principle charge higher interest rates only to those identified as speculators and maintain low (or normal) rates to financial intermediaries through *credit controls*. In practice, countries have tended to identify as speculators foreign residents who engage in foreign exchange swaps with domestic banks and either ban such swaps or ensure that heavy forward discounts be imposed on the forward segments of these operations. Similarly, domestic banks may be forbidden to provide on-balance-sheet overnight or longer maturity credit to foreign residents. However, experience suggests that such controls generate a spread between onshore and offshore interest rates on domestic-currency loans (as was the case in Thailand) and generate strong incentives to evade them.

Chapter 8

Aggregate Accounts, Budget Constraints, and Model Consistency

An integrated and consistent set of economic accounts is a prerequisite for any modeling exercise in macroeconomic analysis. This chapter discusses the relationships between national accounting, stock and flow budget constraints, and the consistency requirements that macroeconomic models must satisfy. The first part of this chapter discusses the basic accounting concepts upon which macroeconomic analysis dwells (production, income, and expenditure) and the national income accounting concepts derived from them. The second part presents a **consistency accounting matrix**, the purpose of which is to summarize in a convenient format all current and financial transactions in an economy during a given period of time. The third part derives various aggregate identities and some key macroeconomic relationships and shows how they relate to the sectoral budget constraints.

The fourth and fifth parts present two types of macroeconomic models in which flow and stock budget constraints are used. The first is a *static*, three-good framework with *imperfect capital mobility*—an adequate characterization for many developing countries, as noted in Chapter 6. Another important feature of the model (which is also consistent with the evidence for developing countries) is the assumption that banks play a key role in the transmission process of macroeconomic shocks, because firms' working capital needs are financed by domestic credit. A graphical solution is provided and the effects of an external shock (a rise in the world interest rate) are examined. The second type of model is a one-good, two-period *intertemporal* model of the current account. Although simpler in its structure than the static, three-good model, it imposes explicitly *stock* budget constraints (as opposed to only flow constraints) in a *dynamic* setting. The model is used to analyze the effects of financial openness on external accounts.

8.1 Production, Income, and Expenditure

Macroeconomic analysis is organized around three basic accounting concepts: production, income, and expenditure.

- **Production** of goods and services is carried out by domestic agents, including firms, self-employed workers (in the formal or informal sector), financial institutions (banks, insurance companies, mutual funds), and the government.

- **Income** consists of wages and salaries, firms' operating surpluses, property income (including interest and dividends), and imputed compensation (for self-employed workers or property owners).

- **Expenditure** consists of outlays on durable and nondurable final consumption goods and investment. In general, production and spending units are different—except for subsistence production by households and the production of government services.

The three concepts of production, income, and expenditure are linked by three basic macroeconomic relationships, which result from the *budget constraints* faced by each category of agents:

- **Production and income.** The value of production, for the economy as a whole, must equal the value of income (excluding transfers) generated domestically. Such income, however, may accrue to either *resident* economic agents or to *nonresident* agents. Similarly, resident agents may receive factor payments from abroad. Income accruing to residents, or **national income**, is thus defined as gross domestic product (GDP) plus net factor payments from abroad.

- **Income, expenditure**, and **savings.** For any economic agent, income earned (regardless of whether the source is domestic or foreign) plus transfers must be equal to expenditure plus savings (which may be positive or negative).

- **Savings** and **asset accumulation.** Savings plus borrowing must equal asset acquisition for any economic agent. These assets may be **physical assets** (capital goods, for instance, but not consumer durables) or **financial assets** (such as government bonds). Borrowing, just like savings, may be either positive or negative.

8.2 A Consistency Accounting Matrix

This section sets out an integrated macroeconomic accounting framework that stresses two types of transactions between agents: transactions in goods and services, and financial transactions. Such a framework (which thus combines income and flow-of-funds accounts) is an important step in the design of a consistent macroeconomic model, such as the **RMSM-X model** of the World Bank described in the next chapter.

This integrated accounting framework records all incoming and outgoing transactions for each category of agent. Thus, the balance of all transactions (real and financial) for each and every one of them is necessarily equal to zero, and the balance of income-expenditure transactions is equal and of opposite sign to the balance of financial transactions. As a result, several equivalence relationships, or *identities*, emerge among the various magnitudes recorded in the accounts.

Consider an economy in which the following four categories of agents operate:

- The *private nonfinancial sector*, which includes the household sector as well as the private corporate sector.

- The *financial sector*, which includes both the central bank and commercial banks, as well as other financial intermediaries (private savings banks, finance companies, and public savings institutions).[1]

- The *government*, defined as general government, thereby comprising all levels of government (central, state, and local) as well as public sector corporations funded through the government budget.[2]

- The *external (nonresident) sector*, which includes all transactions of non-residents with residents.

Following Easterly (1989), Table 8.1 presents the transactions between these agents in the form of a **consistency matrix**, which essentially describes the sources and uses of funds in the economy. Five sets of accounts are incorporated in the consistency framework:

- the national accounts;

- the accounts of the nonfinancial private sector;

- the government accounts;

- the balance sheets of the financial sector;

- the balance of payments, which captures the consolidated accounts of the external sector—that is, transactions between residents and nonresidents.

---

[1] The analysis here focuses only on the role of the financial system as an intermediary for channeling savings across sectors. A high degree of aggregation is thus reasonable. A disaggregated financial structure would, of course, be more appropriate to analyze, for instance, how regulations imposed by the central bank on commercial banks—such as cash reserve ratios or statutory liquidity ratios—affect the money supply.

[2] In general, whether public-owned enterprises are included in the government sector or in the private nonfinancial sector varies across countries; it depends on whether public enterprises are viewed as primarily *profit-seeking* entities (like private enterprises) or as primarily *government-controlled* entities.

Table 8.1 CONSISTENCY ACCOUNTING MATRIX

Uses (columns) and Sources (rows)	Current Account Of					Capital Account Of					Total
	A National Accounts	**B** Government	**C** Financial System	**D** Nonfinancial Private Sector	**E** External Sector	**F** Government	**G** Financial System	**H** Nonfinancial Private Sector	**I** External Sector	**J** Total Investment	Total
1 National Accounts		C^g		C^p	X	I^g		I^p		$I = I^p + I^g$	$Y = C^g + C^p + X - J + I$
2 Government	$T_I - SUB + OS^g$			T_D	NT^{gf}						$T^g = T_I - SUB + OS^g + T_D + NT^{gf}$
3 Financial System											
4 Nonfinancial Private Sector	$W + II + II_s$	$NT^{pg} + INT^{pg}$			$NT^{pf} + NFP^{pf}$						$Y^P = W + II + II_s + NT^{pg} + INT^{pg} + INT^{pg} + NT^{pf} + NFP^{pf}$
5 External Sector	J	INT^{fg}		INT^{-fp}							$J + INT^{gf} + INT^{pf}$
Savings and Borrowings Of:											
6 Government		S^g					ΔL^{gb}	ΔB^p	ΔFB^g		$S^g + \Delta L^{gb} + \Delta B^p + \Delta FB^g$
7 Financial System								ΔM			ΔM
8 Nonfinancial Private Sector				S^p			ΔL^{pb}		ΔFB^p		
9 External Sector				S^p	CA		ΔR^*				$CA + \Delta R^*$
10 Total Savings (Sum of previous 4 rows)		S^g		S^p	CA	I^g	$\Delta L + \Delta R^*$	$I^p + \Delta B^p + \Delta M$		$I = I^p + I^g$	$S^p + S^g + CA$
Total	$Y + J = TI - SUB + OS^g + (W + II) + J$	$G + S^g$		$CC^p + S^p$	CA	I^g	$\Delta L + \Delta R^*$	$I^p + \Delta B^p + \Delta M$		$I = I^p + I^g$	

Source: Adapted from Easterly (1989).

Notes: G in column B is defined as $G = C^g + NT^{pg} + (INT^{pg} + INT^{-fp})$.
CC^p in column D is defined as $CC^p = C^p + T_D + INT^{-fp}$.
ΔL in column G is defined as $\Delta L = \Delta L^{gb} + \Delta L^{pb}$.

ERRATUM

In Chapter 8, "Aggregate Accounts, Budget Constraints, and Model Consistency," Table 8.1 on the Consistency Accounting Matrix was not included in the text. It is reproduced on the following page for the readers' convenience.

Agénor: *Adjustment and Growth*
ISBN: 0-12-044555-7

Reading across rows (labeled 1, 2, etc.) in Table 8.1 provides the *sources* of finance for each sector, whereas reading down columns (labeled A, B, etc.) indicates the *uses* of finance. *Ex post*, each sector's deficit must be financed and, as such, the sum of the rows is always equal to the sum of the columns. *Ex ante*, these sectoral balances become *constraints* for modeling the behavior of each group of agents.

8.2.1 Current Account Transactions

Row 1 and column A, the **national accounts**, consolidate the current-period activities of *all production units* together, regardless of the type of good or service produced: incorporated enterprises (financial and nonfinancial), informal sector firms, producers of government services, and production by households for own consumption. Across row 1, the table describes how goods and services that are produced domestically, Y, or imported, J, are allocated between

- government consumption, C^g;

- private consumption, C^p;

- exports, X;

- the acquisition of *physical assets* by the government and the private sector, or investment, I^g and I^p, with $I = I^p + I^g$.

Column A decomposes the value of current domestic production, Y, defined as *GDP at current market prices*, into the various types of income that are generated through the sale (plus own consumption) of domestic output. Income consists of

- net indirect taxes, that is, indirect taxes, T_I, less subsidies, SUB;

- the operating surplus of government enterprises, OS^g;

- wages and salaries, W, and profits, Π;

- incomes of the self-employed and own-account producers, Y_s.

The sum of wages, salaries, and the incomes of own-account producers—referred to, in the United Nations System of National Accounts (SNA) as *employee compensation*—along with the operating surpluses of all enterprises (including funds set aside for depreciation by producing units), is value added at producers' prices and is referred to as *GDP at factor cost*, Y_{fc}. By convention, *value added at factor cost*, V_{fc}, accrues to households (and to the government, in the case of the operating surplus of state-owned enterprises) even though a fraction of these earnings might be retained by enterprises or the government to finance capital formation. Adding *net indirect taxes* to V_{fc} yields *value added at market prices*, that is, what purchasers actually pay for goods and services. The sum of value added at market prices and imports is equal to the *total amount of goods and services* available for final use.

Row 2 and column B account for the current transactions of the **government**. The sources of current government *revenue*, T^g, are identified across row 2 and consist of

- net indirect taxes, $T_I - SUB$;

- the operating surpluses of government-owned enterprises, OS^g;

- direct taxes levied on the nonfinancial private sector, T_D;

- net transfers to the government from the rest of the world, NT^{gf}.

Column B provides a decomposition of total current government *expenditures*, G, into

- government consumption of goods and services, C^g, which essentially represents the cost of producing government services;

- net transfers to the nonfinancial private sector, NT^{pg};

- interest paid to the private sector on domestic public debt, INT^{pg};

- interest payments on public foreign debt, INT^{fg}.

Government savings, S^g, shown at the bottom of column B, is thus the difference between current government revenue and expenditure, that is

$$S^g = T^g - G,$$

with

$$T^g = T_I - SUB + OS^g + T_D + NT^{gf},$$
$$G = C^g + (NT^{pg} + INT^{pg}) + INT^{fg}.$$

Row 3 and column C describe the balance sheet of the consolidated **financial sector**. In the case considered here, again, the financial system operates as a *pure intermediary*; it has therefore no independent revenue and expenditure accounts. The revenues of financial institutions minus their costs represent the value added of these institutions to the economy. Because this value added is included in the production accounts of the domestic economy as income to the nonfinancial private sector or to the government, row 3 and column C are empty.

Row 4 and column D describe the accounts of the **nonfinancial private sector**. Row 4 identifies the *sources* of income of the private sector, Y^p, which consist of

- factor income, including wages and salaries, W, profits, Π, and incomes of the self-employed, Π_s;

- net transfers received from the government, NT^p;

- interest payments from the government on its domestic debt, INT^{pg};

- net transfers, NT^{pf}, plus net factor payments from abroad, NFP^{pf}.

Column D describes the *allocation* of private sector income into

- private consumption, C^p;

- payment of direct taxes, T_D;

- interest payments on private external debt, INT^{fp}.

Private saving, S^p, shown at the bottom of column D, is the balancing item and is the difference between total private sector income, Y^p, and total current expenditures of the private sector, CC^p:

$$S^p = Y^p - CC^p,$$

where[3]

$$CC^p = C^p + T_D + INT^{fp} + S^p.$$

Row 5 and column E depict the **current account** of the **balance of payments.** Row 5 provides the sources of income accruing *to* foreign residents, which consist of

- the value of imports of goods and services, J;[4]

- public and private sector interest payments on their respective external debts, INT^{fg} and INT^{fp}.

Column E describes the sources of income accruing *from* foreign residents. These sources of income are

- exports of goods and services, X;

- net current (as opposed to capital) transfers to the government and private sectors, NT^{gf} and NT^{pf};

- net factor payments to the private sector, NFP^{pf}.

Savings by foreign residents, shown at the bottom of column E, is the balancing item between external receipts and payments, that is, the *current account balance*, CA:

$$CA = X + (NT^{gf} + NT^{pf}) + NFP^{pf} - J - INT^{fg} - INT^{fp}.$$

---

[3]Note that *property income* paid and received by resident households does not appear as separate entries in Table 8.1. Such incomes are accounted for in the operating surpluses of producing units and cancel each other out.

[4]Note that, following conventional practice, payments of *principal* on the external debt are recorded in net terms in the capital account (see rows 6 to 9 and columns F through I), not in the current account of the balance of payments.

8.2.2   Capital Account Transactions

While rows 1 to 5 and columns A through E describe the current accounts of the economy, rows 6 to 9 and columns F through J describe the corresponding capital account transactions, that is, the financing of *asset acquisition* by the government, the private nonfinancial sector, and the external sector.[5]

Row 6 describes the sources of financing of asset accumulation by the **government**, which consist of

- government savings, S^g;

- net borrowing from the financial system, ΔL^{gb};

- net borrowing from the private sector, ΔB^p;

- net foreign borrowing, ΔFB^g.

Column F contains only one item, gross fixed capital investment by the government, I^g.[6]

Row 7 and column G depict the accounts of the **financial sector**. Row 7 indicates that, as an intermediary, the financial system acquires liabilities principally in the form of new domestic currency issues, demand deposits and time deposits, ΔM.[7] Column G indicates that assets of the financial system consist of loans to the government, ΔL^{gb}, loans to the private sector, ΔL^{pb}, and net foreign assets, ΔR^*.

Row 8 and column H describe the capital account transactions of the nonfinancial private sector. Row 8 indicates that asset acquisition by the private sector is financed by private sector savings, S^p, net borrowing from the financial system, ΔL^{pb}, and net borrowing from abroad, ΔFB^p. Asset acquisition is detailed in column H and consists of

- private investment, I^p, which includes physical assets, inventories and working capital, as well as intangible nonfinancial assets;

- net lending to the government (that is, acquisition of government securities), ΔB^p;

- increases in holdings of monetary assets, ΔM, that is, liabilities issued by the financial sector.

---

[5] The block consisting of rows 1 to 5 and columns A through E represent the *flows-of-funds matrix*, which can be used separately if the focus of analysis is on the determination of the economy's investment-savings balance.

[6] Asset acquisition by the government may also take the form of acquisition of financial assets in the form of loans to the private sector and acquisition of foreign assets. However, the last two items have been *netted out* from government borrowing from the private sector, ΔB^p, and foreign borrowing of the government, ΔFB^g, and therefore do not appear explicitly as separate entities in Table 8.1.

[7] For simplicity, it is assumed that the financial sector does not hold net government liabilities, such as treasury bills.

Row 9 and column I depict the capital account transactions of the external sector. Row 9 indicates that savings by foreign residents (that is, the current account deficit), CA, plus acquisition of net foreign exchange reserves by the financial system, ΔR^*, are the counterpart to net foreign borrowing of the government, ΔFB^g, and the private sector, ΔFB^p, as shown in column I.

Finally, row 10 and column J describe the overall **savings-investment balance** of the economy. Row 10 indicates that total domestic savings (the sum of government saving, S^g, private saving, S^p, and foreign saving, that is, the current account deficit, CA) must finance total investment (given by I in column J), that is, the sum of government investment, I^g, and private investment, I^p.

8.3 National Income Identities and Budget Constraints

The current and capital account transactions of the four categories of agents that are summarized in the consistency accounting matrix of Table 8.1 can be used to show that standard national income identities are essentially *flow budget constraints*, that is, basic relationships that relate income and expenditure of each category of agents.

8.3.1 Gross Domestic Product and Absorption

Gross domestic product (GDP), or the value of goods and services that are produced by the domestic economy, can be derived from the basic macroeconomic relationship that relates the value of domestic production to the value of incomes that are domestically generated. From Table 8.1, two different approaches can be adopted for estimating GDP: the **expenditure approach** or the **value-added approach**.

- From row 1 and column A, we have

$$C^g + C^p + X + I^g + I^p = W + \Pi + \Pi_s + OS^g + (T_I - SUB) + J. \quad (8.1)$$

  GDP at market prices is given by the sum of private consumption, C^p, public consumption, C^g, private investment, I^p, public investment, I^g, and net exports of goods and services, $X - J$. Thus

$$Y = C + I + X - J, \quad (8.2)$$

  where $C = C^p + C^g$ is total consumption, and $I = I^p + I^g$ is total investment.

- GDP at factor cost, Y_{fc}, is given by the sum of factor incomes, that is, wages, W, profits, Π, own-income of the self-employed, Π_s, augmented by the operating surplus of government enterprises, OS^g:

$$Y_{fc} = W + \Pi + \Pi_s + OS^g. \quad (8.3)$$

Substituting Equations (8.2) and (8.3) into Equation (8.1) yields

$$Y = Y_{fc} + (T_I - SUB),$$

which indicates that GDP at market prices is equal to GDP at factor cost plus indirect taxes net of subsidies.

Equation (8.2) can be rewritten as

$$Y + J - X = C + I = A, \tag{8.4}$$

which equates total supply of goods and services (that is, the sum of domestic output plus net imports) to **domestic absorption**, which consists of the sum of domestic consumption and investment. Equation (8.4) can be rewritten as

$$J - X = A - Y = I - (Y - C) = I - S, \tag{8.5}$$

which relates net imports, $J - X$, to an excess of domestic absorption over output $(A - Y)$, or equivalently an excess of investment over savings, $I - S$. Thus, a reduction in the trade deficit requires either a reduction in absorption or, equivalently, an increase in domestic savings.

8.3.2 The Government Budget Constraint

Equating the sum of the entries in row 2 and column B leads to

$$T_I - SUB + OS^g + T_D + NT^{gf} = C^g + NT^{pg} + (INT^{pg} + INT^{fg}) + S^g. \tag{8.6}$$

Given the definitions of T^g and G provided earlier, this equation can be rewritten as

$$T^g - G = S^g. \tag{8.7}$$

Equation (8.7) indicates that total current revenue of the government, T^g, must be equal to total current public expenditure, G, plus government savings, S^g.

Equating the sum of the entries in row 6 and column F yields

$$S^g + \Delta L^{gb} + \Delta B^p + \Delta FB^g = I^g, \tag{8.8}$$

which indicates that government savings plus net domestic and foreign borrowing must be equal to the (physical) assets acquired by the government.[8] This constraint thus essentially relates government savings, borrowing, and asset acquisition.

Substituting Equation (8.7) into Equation (8.8) and rearranging the resulting expression reveals the sources of financing of the government budget deficit, as discussed in Chapter 3:

$$G + I^g - T^g = \Delta L^{gb} + \Delta B^p + \Delta FB^g. \tag{8.9}$$

[8] Recall that the government acquisition of domestic financial assets (such as loans to the private sector) as well as foreign assets are netted out from foreign borrowing and from domestic borrowing, respectively.

The expression on the left-hand side of Equation (8.9) represents the overall fiscal deficit of the government (with G now defined to include interest payments on the public debt), whereas the expression on the right-hand side indicates the sources of deficit financing—direct borrowing from the banking system and the private sector, and borrowing from abroad.

8.3.3   The Private Sector Budget Constraint

The private sector budget constraint can be derived in a similar fashion. Equating the sum of the entries in row 4 and column D shows that

$$W + \Pi + \Pi_s + NT^{pg} + INT^{pg} + NT^{pf} + NFP^{pf} = C^p + T_D + INT^{fp} + S^p.$$

Defining total private sector income as

$$Y^p = W + \Pi + \Pi_s + NT^{pg} + INT^{pg} + NT^{pf} + NFP^{pf},$$

and private expenditure as

$$CC^p = C^p + T_D + INT^{fp},$$

the above expression can be rewritten as

$$Y^p = CC^p + S^p, \tag{8.10}$$

as shown earlier. Equating the sum of the entries in row 8 and column H implies

$$S^p + \Delta L^{pb} + \Delta FB^p = I^p + \Delta B^p + \Delta M. \tag{8.11}$$

Substituting out for S^p in Equation (8.11) by using Equation (8.10) yields the private sector budget constraint:

$$Y^p - CC^p + \Delta L^{pb} + \Delta FB^p = I^p + \Delta B^p + \Delta M. \tag{8.12}$$

Equation (8.12) equates private sector income plus (domestic and foreign) borrowing less total current expenditure to private sector asset acquisition in the form of money (currency plus demand and time deposits), physical investment, and lending to the government.

8.3.4   The External Sector Budget Constraint

Equating the sum of the entries in row 5 and column E yields

$$J + INT^{fg} + INT^{fp} = X + NT^{gf} + NT^{pf} + NFP^{pf} + CA, \tag{8.13}$$

whereas equating the sum of all entries in row 9 and column I implies

$$CA = \Delta FB^g + \Delta FB^p - \Delta R^*. \tag{8.14}$$

Equation (8.14) indicates that a current account deficit (or positive savings by the external sector) must be financed either by an increase in net foreign borrowing and a capital inflow (implying an increase in the country's external debt) or by drawing down the stock of reserves held by the financial sector.

Let **J** denote *gross payments* by the domestic economy, that is, the sum of imports and all interest payments on external debt, and let **X** be *gross receipts* to the domestic economy, obtained by adding to exports net transfers and net factor payments from abroad:

$$\mathbf{J} = J + INT^{fg} + INT^{fp},$$

$$\mathbf{X} = X + NT^{gf} + NT^{pf} + NFP^{pf}.$$

Using these definitions, and substituting Equation (8.13) into (8.14) yields the *external sector budget constraint*:

$$\mathbf{J} - \mathbf{X} = \Delta F - \Delta R^*, \tag{8.15}$$

where $\Delta F = \Delta FB^g + \Delta FB^p$ denotes total capital inflows. The expression on the left-hand side of Equation (8.15) represents the *net resource inflow* in terms of goods and services, whereas the expression on the right-hand side is **net foreign asset acquisition**, or **net foreign borrowing** by domestic residents.

8.3.5   The Balance Sheet of the Financial System

As indicated earlier, the financial system in the present accounting framework is a pure intermediary. It does not, therefore, face a budget constraint *per se* but rather a balance sheet accounting identity. Equating the sum of the entries in row 7 and column G yields

$$\Delta L + \Delta R^* = \Delta M, \tag{8.16}$$

where $\Delta L = \Delta L^{gb} + \Delta L^{pb}$. Equation (8.16) states that assets of the financial system, which consist of credit to the government and private sectors and net foreign assets, must be equal to its liabilities, which consist of broad money.

Equation (8.16) can be rewritten as

$$\Delta R^* = \Delta M - \Delta L,$$

which indicates that the change in foreign exchange reserves is equal to the demand for money (assuming that the money market is in equilibrium) less the change in total domestic credit. This equation suggests that if the demand for money is held constant, then increases in domestic credit are offset by decreases in reserves on a one-to-one basis. Alternatively, it implies that given a desired level of reserves, and with the demand for money exogenously determined, the required change in domestic credit can be estimated. As discussed in the next chapter, this basic relationship is at the heart of the International Monetary Fund's model of **financial programming**.

8.3.6   The Savings-Investment Balance

Adding the budget constraints of the government and private sectors, that is, Equations (8.9) and (8.12), and using Equation (8.7) and (8.10), yields

$$S + \Delta L + \Delta F = I + \Delta M, \tag{8.17}$$

that is, using Equation (8.15) to eliminate ΔF:

$$S + \Delta L + (\mathbf{J} - \mathbf{X}) + \Delta R^* = I + \Delta M.$$

Using Equation (8.16), the above equation yields the **savings-investment balance**:

$$I = S + (\mathbf{J} - \mathbf{X}), \tag{8.18}$$

which states that aggregate domestic investment, I, is financed by domestic savings, S, and foreign saving, $\mathbf{J} - \mathbf{X}$, the latter being synonymous to the current account deficit, CA. Equation (8.18) is identical to the result obtained by equating the sum of the entries in row 10 and column J, thereby indicating that the overall savings-investment balance is a *macroeconomic budget constraint* obtained by summing up the *sectoral budget constraints*.

Equation (8.18) can also be rewritten as

$$(S^g - I^g) + (S^p - I^p) = \mathbf{X} - \mathbf{J},$$

which implies, as discussed in Chapter 3, that an improvement in the current account balance can occur only to the extent that government or private savings rise relative to government or private investment.

Similarly, Equation (8.17) can be rewritten as

$$S - I + \Delta F = \Delta M - \Delta L.$$

From Equation (8.5), $S - I = Y - A$. Substituting this result in the above equation yields

$$Y + \Delta F - A = \Delta M - \Delta L, \tag{8.19}$$

which links money, domestic credit, and absorption. The term $Y + \Delta F$ in the above expression can be viewed as representing *total resources available* for domestic consumption and investment. Equation (8.19) thus indicates that domestic absorption, A, will exceed total available resources by the amount by which domestic credit expansion, ΔL, exceeds the flow demand for (or the flow supply of) money, ΔM. The identity also shows that with available resources fixed and ΔM fixed, a reduction in domestic credit ΔL will improve the balance of payments, that is, increase reserves, ΔR^*, by reducing absorption.

8.4   A Three-Good Model with Banks

This section presents a simple open-economy macroeconomic model that is quite useful to illustrate how the various accounting relationships derived earlier can be integrated with behavioral equations for analyzing the transmission process of macroeconomic policy and exogenous shocks. The economy considered has now five types of agents: households, producers, commercial banks, the government, and the central bank. All households are identical in their endowments and behavior; in particular, they possess identical ownership shares of firms' profits. Similarly, all firms and banks are identical. The choices made by a representative firm in each sector, a representative household, and a representative bank are therefore the focus of the analysis.

The nominal exchange rate E is fixed. The economy produces two goods: a home good that is used only for final domestic consumption, and an exportable good, the price of which is fixed on world markets. In addition, domestic agents consume an importable good which is not produced domestically. The capital stock in each sector is fixed within the time frame of the analysis, and workers are perfectly mobile across sectors. By the assumption of a small open economy, the demand for domestically produced exportables is perfectly elastic at the exogenous world currency price, so that output of these goods is supply determined. For simplicity, it will be assumed that output of exportable goods is entirely sold abroad.

8.4.1 Households

Households supply labor inelastically, consume both home and importable goods, and hold four categories of financial assets in their portfolios: domestic money (which bears no interest), deposits with the banking system, domestic bonds, and foreign bonds. In line with the discussion in Chapter 6, all assets are taken to be **imperfect substitutes**. Foreigners do not hold domestic assets. Total domestic financial wealth is constant during the time frame of the analysis.

Consumption decisions follow a *two-stage process*. The representative household first determines *total* consumption, and then allocates that amount between consumption of the two goods. Total consumption expenditure C is assumed to depend positively on disposable income:[9]

$$C = (1 - s)(Y - T), \quad 0 < s < 1, \tag{8.20}$$

where Y denotes net factor income (defined below), T lump-sum taxes imposed by the government, and s the marginal propensity to save.[10] C, Y, and T are all measured in terms of the price of exportables.

In the second stage of the consumption process, the representative household determines consumption of imported goods (in quantity C_I) and home goods (in quantity C_N). Suppose, for simplicity, that the world price of imported goods, P_I^*, is constant and normalized to unity. The domestic-currency price of these

---

[9] As noted in Chapter 1, the life-cycle model would predict a relationship between wealth and consumption, rather than income. However, as also noted in that chapter, in the presence of liquidity constraints current income may have large effect on consumption expenditure.

[10] For simplicity, the value of output and income are assumed equal. As noted in the previous chapter, the value of output generally exceeds that of income as a result of indirect taxes, net factor payments to nonresidents, and net unrequited transfers from the rest of the world.

goods is thus also equal to the nominal exchange rate, E. The allocation of total consumption expenditure is given by[11]

$$C_I = (1 - \delta)C, \quad 0 < \delta < 1 \tag{8.21}$$

$$P_N C_N = \delta EC, \tag{8.22}$$

where δ measures the share of home goods in total private expenditure.

Let $z \equiv E/P_N$ be the relative price of imported goods in terms of home goods; z will be referred to in what follows as the *real exchange rate*.[12] Equation (8.22) can thus be rewritten as, using Equation (8.20):

$$C_N = \delta z C = \delta z (1 - s)(Y - T). \tag{8.23}$$

Asset demand equations are given as follows. First, the demand for money is assumed to be related negatively to the opportunity cost of holding cash (measured by the interest rate on domestic bonds, i_b) and positively to factor income:[13]

$$M^d = M^d(\overset{-}{i_b}, \overset{+}{Y}). \tag{8.24}$$

Second, the demand for bank deposits is taken to depend positively on factor income and the bank deposit rate, i_d, and to depend negatively on the rate of interest on domestic bonds:

$$D^p = D^p(\overset{+}{i_d}, \overset{-}{i_b}, \overset{+}{Y}). \tag{8.25}$$

Third, the (flow) demand for foreign bonds, B^*, is assumed to be increasing in the spread between the interest rate on domestic bonds and the rate of interest on foreign bonds, i^*, augmented by the expected rate of devaluation of the nominal exchange rate, ε^a:

$$\Delta B^* = \gamma(i^* + \varepsilon^a - i_b), \quad \gamma > 0, \tag{8.26}$$

where γ can be viewed as a measure of the **degree of substitutability** between domestic and foreign bonds, or what amounts to the same thing here, the degree of capital mobility. In the particular case in which $\gamma \to \infty$, domestic and foreign bonds are perfect substitutes, capital is perfectly mobile, and the **uncovered interest parity condition** will hold:

$$i_b = i^* + \varepsilon^a.$$

Finally, because total financial wealth, W, is given, the demand function for domestic bonds, B, can be readily derived from Equations (8.24), (8.25), and (8.26) as

$$B = W - M^d - D^p - B^*.$$

---

[11] It can be shown that the allocation rule given here is optimal if the utility derived from consuming home and importable goods is approximated by a *Cobb-Douglas* function.

[12] For the economy as a whole, a more conventional definition of the real exchange rate would imply defining z in terms of a weighted average of both categories of goods produced and traded in the economy—exportables and imported goods. This would be a particularly important consideration if changes in the terms of trade are considered.

[13] Assuming that the opportunity cost of holding cash also depends on the interest rates on bank deposits and foreign bonds would not qualitatively affect the implications of the analysis.

8.4.2 Firms and the Labor Market

Firms in each sector must finance their **working capital needs** prior to the sale of output, and therefore borrow from commercial banks. For simplicity, it is assumed that there is no substitute for bank loans, so that firms cannot issue and trade equities or bonds (claims on their capital stock) to finance their borrowing needs. Firms producing exportables and nontradables are modeled symmetrically, although in practice their behavior can differ substantially given differences in factor intensities.

Working capital needs are assumed to consist solely of **labor costs**. Total production costs faced by the representative firm in each sector are thus equal to the wage bill plus **interest payments** made on bank loans needed to pay labor in advance.

The maximization problem faced by the representative firm in each production sector can be written as

$$\max_{Y_h} Y_h - \omega_h N_h - i_L L_h, \tag{8.27}$$

where the subscript h is used to denote the exportable ($h = X$) and nontradable goods ($h = N$) sector. Y_h denotes output of good h, N_h the quantity of labor employed in sector h, ω_h the **product wage** in sector h, L_h the amount of bank loans obtained by the firm operating in sector h, and i_L the nominal bank lending rate.

The output-employment relationship in each sector takes the form

$$N_h = Y_h^\alpha, \qquad \alpha > 1, \tag{8.28}$$

which shows that, because $\alpha > 1$, technology for the production of both categories of goods is characterized by **decreasing returns to labor**.

The typical firm's financial constraint is given by

$$L_h \geq \omega_h N_h, \tag{8.29}$$

which requires the amount of bank loans to be at least as large as nominal wage costs. Constraint (8.29) is assumed to be continuously binding, because the only reason for firms to demand loans is to finance labor costs.

Maximizing Equation (8.27) subject to (8.28) and (8.29) yields the output supply equation in sector h:

$$Y_h^s = \left\{ \frac{1}{\alpha \omega_h (1 + i_L)} \right\}^{1/(\alpha - 1)}, \tag{8.30}$$

which shows that output supply in h is inversely related to the **effective product wage** in that sector, $\omega_h(1 + i_L)$. Substituting Equation (8.30) in (8.28) yields labor demand in sector h as

$$N_h^d = N_h^d[\omega_h(1 + i_L)]. \quad N_h^{d'} < 0 \tag{8.31}$$

Using Equations (8.29)—holding with equality—and (8.31), the representative firm's demand for credit can be written as

$$L_h^d = \omega_h N_h^d \equiv L_h^d[\overset{?}{\omega_h}, \overset{-}{i_L})],$$ (8.32)

which shows that, in general, an increase in the product wage has an ambiguous effect on the demand for credit. On the one hand, it directly raises labor costs; on the other, it lowers the demand for labor. If the elasticity of the demand for labor is sufficiently large, the net effect will be negative.[14] This is the case assumed in what follows.

The next step is to examine the process of wage determination. As a first approximation, the model assumes that nominal wages are *perfectly flexible*; given *perfect labor mobility across sectors*, unemployment therefore cannot emerge. Moreover, by definition, the product wage in the nontradable sector is equal to the real exchange rate times the product wage in the exportable sector:

$$\omega_N = z\omega_X.$$ (8.33)

Thus, wage flexibility implies that (for a given level of z) the product wage in the exportable sector, ω_X, equilibrates the supply and demand for labor. This equilibrium condition is given by, using Equations (8.32) and (8.33):

$$N_X^d[\omega_X(1 + i_L)] + N_N^d[z\omega_X(1 + i_L)] = N^s,$$

where N^s denotes the constant supply of labor. Solving this equation for ω_X shows that the equilibrium real wage (measured in terms of the price of exportables) is negatively related to the real exchange rate and the bank lending rate:

$$\omega_X = W_X(\overset{-}{z}, \overset{-}{i_L}),$$ (8.34)

where

$$\frac{\partial W_X}{\partial z} \equiv -\frac{N_N^{d\prime}(1 + i_L)}{N_X^{d\prime}(1 + i_L) + N_N^{d\prime}(1 + i_L)} = -\frac{N_N^{d\prime}}{N_X^{d\prime} + N_N^{d\prime}},$$

which implies that $|\partial W_X/\partial z| < 1$.

Substituting Equations (8.33) and (8.34) in Equation (8.30) yields the sectoral supply equations:

$$Y_X^s = Y_X^s(\overset{+}{z}, \overset{-}{i_L}), \quad Y_N^s = Y_N^s(\overset{-}{z}, \overset{-}{i_L}).$$ (8.35)

These equations show that output of exportables (home goods) is positively (negatively) related to the real exchange rate, and that an increase in the bank lending rate has a negative effect on activity in both sectors.

Net factor income is given by

$$Y = Y_X^s + z^{-1}Y_N^s.$$

---

[14]By definition $dL_h^d/d\omega_h = \tilde{N}_h^d + \tilde{\omega}_h(\partial N_h^d/\partial\omega_h)$. Multiplying both sides by $\tilde{\omega}_h/\tilde{L}_h^d$ yields $\eta_{L_h^d/\omega_h} = 1 + \eta_{N_h^d/\omega_h}$, which therefore requires $\left|\eta_{N_h^d/\omega_h}\right| > 1$ for $dL_h^d/d\omega_h$ to be negative.

To determine the sign of Y_z note that

$$Y_z = \frac{\partial Y_X^s}{\partial z} + \tilde{z}^{-1}\frac{\partial Y_N^s}{\partial z} - \tilde{z}^{-2}\tilde{Y}_N^s,$$

where a '~' is used to denoted an initial equilibrium value. The **envelope condition** for production (resulting from profit maximization) implies that

$$\frac{\partial Y_X^s}{\partial z} + \tilde{z}^{-1}\frac{\partial Y_N^s}{\partial z} = 0,$$

so that $Y_z < 0$. A depreciation of the real exchange rate lowers aggregate output because it reduces the value of output of nontradables measured in terms of the price of exportables. Thus, using Equations (8.35):

$$Y = Y(\overset{-}{z}, \overset{-}{i_L}). \tag{8.36}$$

Total demand for credit, L^d, measured in terms of the price of exportables, is given by

$$L^d = L_X^d + z^{-1}L_N^d = L^d(\overset{-}{z}, \overset{-}{i_L}), \tag{8.37}$$

which shows again that a real exchange rate depreciation (an increase in z) lowers the demand for credit.

8.4.3 Commercial Bank

Assets of the representative commercial bank consist of credit extended to firms, L^s, and reserves held at the central bank, RR; for simplicity, banks hold no excess reserves. *Bank liabilities* consist of deposits held by households. The balance sheet of the representative commercial bank can therefore be written as

$$D^p = L^s + RR, \tag{8.38}$$

where all variables are measured in terms of the price of exportables.

Reserves held at the central bank do not pay interest and are determined by

$$RR = \mu D^p, \quad 0 < \mu < 1, \tag{8.39}$$

where μ is the *coefficient of reserve requirements*.

The actual level of deposits held by the private sector is demand determined and, from Equations (8.38) and (8.39), the *supply of credit* is

$$L^s = (1 - \mu)D^p. \tag{8.40}$$

Banks have *no operating costs*. Under a **zero-profit condition**, the relationship between the lending rate and the deposit rate is given by

$$i_L = \frac{i_d}{1 - \mu}. \tag{8.41}$$

This condition requires the marginal revenue per unit of currency lent to equal the bank's net interest payment per unit of currency deposited, which is equal to the deposit rate adjusted for the reserve requirement tax.

Using Equations (8.25), (8.40), and (8.41), the supply of credit is thus given by

$$L^s = (1 - \mu)D^p[(1 - \mu)i_L, i_b, Y], \tag{8.42}$$

which shows, in particular, that L^s is increasing in the lending rate, i_L.

8.4.4 Government and the Central Bank

The government, as noted earlier, levies lump-sum taxes on households. It also consumes home goods, in quantity G_N.

The key function of the central bank is to ensure the *costless conversion* of domestic currency holdings into foreign currency at the prevailing fixed exchange rate, E. The central bank lends only to the government. The real money supply, M^s, measured in terms of the price of exportables, is thus given by

$$M^s = L^g + R^*, \tag{8.43}$$

where R^* is the central bank's stock of net foreign assets (measured in foreign-currency terms) and L^g real credit to the government, which is assumed exogenous.

Changes in official reserves are determined by the behavior of the balance of payments, that is, the sum of the current account and the capital account. Ignoring interest payments on net foreign assets for simplicity, the balance of payments is

$$\Delta R^* = Y_X^s - C_I - \Delta B^*,$$

that is, using Equations (8.21), (8.26) and (8.35):

$$\Delta R^* = Y_X^s - (1 - \delta)C + \gamma(i_b - i^* - \varepsilon^a). \tag{8.44}$$

Thus, changes in official foreign reserves translate into one-to-one changes in the domestic money supply. Put differently, the central bank does not engage in **sterilized intervention** (see the discussion in Chapter 6).

8.4.5 Equilibrium Conditions

To close the model requires specifying the equilibrium conditions of the markets for domestic bonds, domestic money, credit, and nontradable goods. By **Walras' law**, the first three conditions are not independent; one of them can be eliminated. The analysis here will focus on the equilibrium conditions of the money and credit markets.

The money market

Using Equation (8.24), the equilibrium condition of the money market is given by

$$M^s = M^d(i_b, Y). \tag{8.45}$$

For a given level of the money supply, M^s (that is, for a given level of official reserves, R^*), and using Equation (8.36) to eliminate Y, Equation (8.45) defines the combinations of the real exchange rate and the interest rate on domestic bonds for which the money market is in equilibrium. Solving this equation for i_b yields

$$i_b = i_b(\overline{z}, \overset{-}{i_L}; \overset{-}{M^s}). \tag{8.46}$$

For instance, a real depreciation lowers aggregate output (measured in terms of the price of exportables) and the transactions demand for money, requiring a fall in interest rates to maintain equilibrium of the money market.

The credit market

The equilibrium condition of the credit market is given by

$$L^s = L^d,$$

so that, using Equations (8.37) and (8.42):

$$D^p[(1-\mu)i_L, i_b, Y] = \frac{L^d(z, i_L)}{1-\mu}, \tag{8.47}$$

Using Equation (8.36) again to eliminate Y, the above equation can be solved for the equilibrium bank lending rate:

$$i_L = i_L(\overset{?}{z}, \overset{+}{i_b}). \tag{8.48}$$

Equation (8.48) shows that an increase in the interest rate on domestic bonds, by lowering the demand for bank deposits by households, creates an excess demand for loans—requiring therefore an increase in the bank lending rate. A real depreciation, by contrast, has an ambiguous effect on the lending rate.

- On the one hand, it lowers output, the demand for bank deposits by households, and thus the supply of bank credit. This tends to increase the equilibrium lending rate;

- on the other, it also lowers the demand for loans, which then requires a fall in the bank lending rate to maintain credit market equilibrium.

The net effect is assumed in what follows to be negative ($\partial i_L/\partial z < 0$). This assumption requires that the sensitivity of the demand for bank deposits with respect to income be sufficiently small.

The market for home goods

The equilibrium condition of the market for home goods is given by

$$C_N + G_N - Y_N^s = 0, \qquad (8.49)$$

which can be solved for the equilibrium real exchange rate, using Equations (8.23) and (8.35):

$$z = \Omega(\overset{-}{i_L}; \overset{+}{T}, \overset{-}{G_N}). \qquad (8.50)$$

Equation (8.50) shows that an increase in the bank lending rate (which reduces the supply of nontraded goods) or an increase in government spending on home goods requires an *appreciation* of the real exchange rate (a fall in z) to eliminate excess demand and maintain equilibrium of the market for nontraded goods. An increase in taxes, by lowering private expenditure, creates an incipient excess supply of nontraded goods and therefore requires a *depreciation* of the real exchange rate to maintain market equilibrium.

8.4.6 Graphical Solution

The *logical structure* of the model is illustrated in Figure 8.1. A compact formulation of the equilibrium solution can be derived and illustrated in a simple diagram, in the bank lending rate-real exchange rate space. To do so, the first step is to combine the money market and credit market equilibrium conditions by substituting out i_b, using Equation (8.46), in (8.48). The resulting equation is

$$i_L = \phi(\overset{-}{z}; \overset{-}{M^s}), \qquad (8.51)$$

which will be referred to as the MM curve. It is downward sloping, because, for given M^s,

$$\left. \frac{di_L}{dz} \right|_{MM} = \phi_z < 0.$$

The equilibrium condition of the market for nontraded goods, Equation (8.50), gives a relationship between z and i_L that will be referred to as the NN curve. This curve is also downward sloping, because

$$\left. \frac{di_L}{dz} \right|_{NN} = \Omega_{i_L}^{-1} < 0.$$

Finally, using Equation (8.51) to substitute out for i_L in Equation (8.46) yields the following alternative expression for the market-clearing interest rate on domestic bonds:

$$i_b = i_b[z, \phi(z; M^s), M^s] = \eta(\overset{-}{z}; \overset{-}{M^s}). \qquad (8.52)$$

Using this result to substitute out for i_b, and using the supply equation of traded goods, Equation (8.35), changes in official reserves [Equation (8.44)] are given by

$$\Delta R^* = Y_X^s(z, i_L) - (1 - \delta)(1 - s)[Y(z, i_L) - T] + \gamma[\eta(z; M^s) - i^* - \varepsilon^a].$$

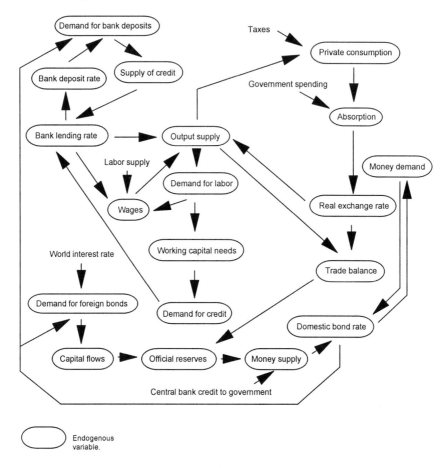

Figure 8.1. Logical Structure of the Three-Good Model.

Setting $\Delta R^* = 0$ in the above equation yields the combinations of z and i_L that ensure equilibrium of the balance of payments, that is, equality between the sum of the current and capital accounts. In the present setting, because credit to the government by the central bank is constant, external equilibrium implies a constant money supply, because from Equation (8.43) $\Delta M^s = \Delta R^*$. The balance-of-payments equilibrium condition can be written as[15]

$$z = \kappa(\overset{+}{i_L}; \overset{+}{i^*}, \overset{-}{T}, \overset{+}{M^s}). \tag{8.53}$$

[15] The signs of the partial derivatives in (8.53) are derived from
$$\partial Y_X^s / \partial z - (1 - \delta)(1 - s)Y_z + \gamma \eta_z > 0,$$
$$\partial Y_X^s / \partial i_L < (1 - \delta)(1 - s)Y_{i_L}.$$

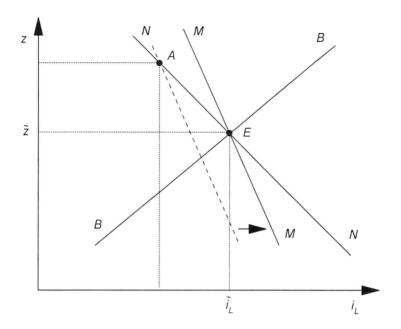

Figure 8.2. Equilibrium in the Three-Good Model.

Equation (8.53) defines a curve in the z-i_L space, the BB curve, which is upward sloping because

$$\left.\frac{di_L}{dz}\right|_{BB} = \kappa_{i_L}^{-1} > 0.$$

Curves MM, NN, and BB are illustrated in Figure 8.2.[16] Points located to the right (left) of MM represent combinations of the lending rate and the real exchange rate for which both the money and credit markets are characterized by excess supply (demand). Points located to the left (right) of NN represent combinations of z and i_L for which the market for nontraded goods is characterized by excess supply (demand). Finally, points located to the left (right) of BB represent situations in which the balance of payments is in deficit (surplus).

Suppose, for instance, that the initial position of the economy is at point A, characterized by equilibrium of the market for nontraded goods, and the credit and money markets. The short-run equilibrium, being to the left of the BB locus, corresponds to a balance-of-payments deficit; domestic interest rates are too low to generate an inflow of capital that is large enough to finance net imports. The deficit leads over time to a fall in official reserves and a reduction in the domestic money supply, until the balance of payments is in equilibrium ($\Delta R^* = 0$). The curve MM therefore continuously shifts to the right, until point E is reached. The external deficit at that point is eliminated, the money

---

[16]Although the figure assumes that MM is steeper than NN, in general it cannot be determined a priori whether ϕ_z is larger than $\Omega_{i_L}^{-1}$ in absolute terms.

supply is constant, and all three curves intersect. Equilibrium values of the lending rate and the real exchange rate are given by $\tilde{z}$ and $\tilde{i}_L$.

The monetary contraction involved during the adjustment process has the following effects. The fall in the money supply leads [as implied by (8.52)] to a rise in the domestic bond rate, which induces an inflow of capital and lowers the demand for bank deposits [see Equation (8.25)]. In turn, the fall in bank deposits lowers the supply of credit and puts upward pressure on the bank lending rate [see Equation (8.48)]. At the same time, the increase in i_L tends to lower output of nontraded goods, and the incipient excess demand leads to an appreciation of the real exchange rate [see Equation (8.50)]. The real appreciation, by reducing aggregate income and the demand for credit (and given the assumption that $\partial i_L/\partial z < 0$), leads to further upward pressure on the equilibrium lending rate. Over time, although the continuing real appreciation tends to lower exports and to enlarge the trade deficit, the increase in capital inflows induced by higher domestic interest rates is large enough to entail a gradual reduction in the external deficit. The adjustment process continues until the economy reaches its equilibrium position at point E.

8.4.7   Rise in the World Interest Rate

Consider now a rise in the rate of return on foreign bonds, i^*. The immediate impact of a rise in i^*, as can be inferred from Equation (8.26), is to raise the demand for foreign bonds and reduce net capital inflows. At the initial levels of the bank lending rate and the real exchange rate, official reserves fall, reducing therefore the domestic money supply [see Equation (8.43)]. From Equation (8.46), maintaining equilibrium of the domestic money market requires an increase in the rate of return on domestic bonds, i_b. The increase in i_b, in turn, tends to reduce the demand for bank deposits by households and thus the supply of credit—requiring therefore an increase in the bank lending rate to maintain equilibrium of the credit market. At the same time, however, the incipient increase in i_L puts downward pressure on supply of (traded and) nontraded goods. To eliminate excess demand for nontraded goods and restore market equilibrium requires an appreciation of the real exchange rate. Although the real appreciation tends to lower the supply of exportables and to increase imports, the deficit in the balance of payments gradually falls as a result of the increase in domestic interest rates.

Graphically, as shown in Figure 8.3, the rise in i^* entails a rightward shift of the BB curve to $B'B'$. Thus, the initial situation is characterized by a balance-of-payments deficit, induced by a reduction in capital inflows. The adjustment process is similar to the one described earlier; the monetary contraction is associated with a gradual rightward shift of the MM curve, until the general equilibrium point E' is reached. Throughout the adjustment process, domestic bank rates increase and the real exchange rate appreciates.

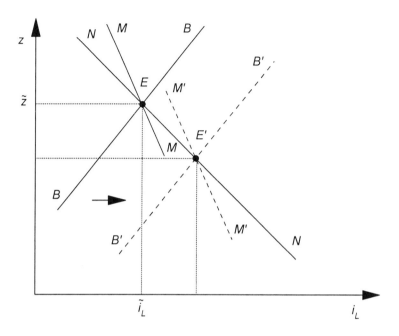

Figure 8.3. Increase in the World Interest Rate.

8.4.8 Extensions

The three-good structure described earlier provides a useful framework for addressing a variety of other macroeconomic issues of importance to developing countries.

- The model can be used to study the effects of changes in *government spending* on the real exchange rate, domestic interest rates, and capital flows.

- The production structure adopted here allows a distinction, in principle, between the *terms of trade* and the real exchange rate—unlike a *dependent-economy framework*, which distinguishes only between tradable and nontradable goods. An important application of the model, therefore, is an analysis of the macroeconomic effects of *terms-of-trade shocks*.[17] As

---

[17]The exports earnings of virtually all sub-Saharan African countries, for instance, are heavily concentratred on one or two commodities. This feature of their economic structure makes them highly vulnerable to adverse movements in the terms of trade. As documented for instance by Deaton and Miller (1995), in sub-Saharan Africa the contemporaneous effects of export price shocks on output were substantial during the 1980s.

illustrated in Figure 8.4, *prices of non-oil commodities* tend to fluctuate quite dramatically, both in *nominal* and *real* terms.[18]

- *Credit market imperfections*, along the lines discussed in Chapter 2, can also be introduced through **markup pricing** by banks (see Agénor and Aizenman, 1999).

- *Production of importables* and *imported intermediate inputs* can also be integrated in the analysis. As discussed in Chapter 4, imported intermediate goods play an important role in the production process in many developing countries.

Nevertheless, although these extensions would provide valuable insight, the model remains subject to two limitations:

- *Behavioral functions* for consumption and asset demand functions are *postulated* rather than derived from microeconomic considerations. Relating consumption to current income only may be a good approximation if the majority of households face liquidity constraints, but it may be misleading in a more general setting.

- The static nature of the model implies that the *stock budget constraints* that the various agents faced are not explicitly accounted for. Consequently the links between flows and changes in stocks over time are also ignored.

An extensive literature in international economics and development macroeconomics has demonstrated that the impact of policy shocks may depend crucially on some arbitrary assumption about, say, the nature of the consumption function. In addition, the static nature of the model means that it cannot, in particular, account for the effects of current account imbalances on net external debt and the impact of investment on the economy's stock of capital. Thus it can only describe the short-term effects of macroeconomic policies on external balance and not the longer-run effects that result from the interaction of stocks and flows. For instance, a policy (such as a fiscal expansion) that leads to a current account deficit—by appreciating the real exchange rate—will lead over time to an increase in the country's foreign debt and debt service payments—thereby increasing the deficit of the services account. For the current account to remain at a given level requires an increase in the trade surplus. This, in turn, requires a real exchange rate depreciation. Thus, the initial exchange rate appreciation will gradually be reversed over time as external debt and debt service grow. Accounting for these longer-run effects is important to assess the sustainability of a given current account position.

---

[18] A commodity boom can give rise to the *Dutch disease* phenomenon, which, as noted in Chapter 3, occurs when a rise in earnings on commodity exports leads to an expansion in domestic spending, a real exchange rate appreciation, a shrinkage of the tradable sector, and a deterioration in export performance.

Figure 8.4. Developing Countries: Non-oil Commodity Prices, 1980-94 (1990 = 100).

Source: International Monetary Fund and The Economist.

1/ Deflated by the price of exports of manufactured goods by industrial countries.

8.5   An Intertemporal Framework

This section presents an **intertemporal** model, which addresses the two main limitations of the three-good model presented earlier:

- it explicitly derives behavioral rules from an optimization framework (as in the life-cycle model presented in Chapter 1);

- it accounts for agents' *flow* and *stock* budget constraints in a dynamic setting, ensuring, in particular, that such constraints are respected across periods.

The intertemporal approach has proved to be particularly useful to understand the nature of *current account deficits*. As shown in the first part of this chapter, such deficits fundamentally reflect the excess of domestic expenditure (or absorption) over output, or equivalently a shortfall of domestic saving relative to domestic investment. Because they represent international borrowing and lending decisions that are a reflection of intertemporal consumption and investment decisions by households, firms, and the government, movements in the current account are best analyzed in a multiperiod macroeconomic framework.

8.5.1 Basic Structure

The intertemporal model presented here, for pedagogical purposes, is a *two-period model* with no financial assets and only one good. This framework is sufficient to analyze the role of intertemporal decisions of *households* in determining current account behavior.[19] The model assumes perfect foresight, optimal behavior of individual agents, and perfect capital mobility. Output is supply determined as full employment is assumed. These assumptions make the model more appropriate for a longer-run analysis in which aggregate demand effects on output may be ignored.

As shown in the first part of this chapter, the gross national product (GNP) of a country, Y, is equal to the gross domestic product (GDP), Q, plus net factor payments from abroad (such as remittances or interest on foreign assets), Z:

$$Y = Q + Z. \tag{8.54a}$$

GNP plus net unilateral transfers from abroad, R, can be used for consumption, C, gross private saving, S^p, and taxes, T:

$$Y + R = C + S^p + T. \tag{8.55}$$

Government saving, S^g, is given by $T - G$, where G is government consumption of goods and services. Equilibrium of the goods market requires

$$Y = C + I + G + X - J. \tag{8.56}$$

As also shown earlier, the current account surplus, CA, can be defined in three equivalent ways:

---

[19]Various extensions of the intertemporal approach to consider capital accumulation, a more diversified production structure, and a government sector (with both taxes and expenditure) are discussed by Frenkel and Razin (1995).

- as exports minus imports of goods and services plus unilateral transfers and net factor payments from abroad (income transfers, for short),

$$CA = X - J + Z + R, \qquad (8.57)$$

- as national income minus domestic absorption,

$$CA = Y - (C + I + G) + R, \qquad (8.58)$$

- as national saving minus domestic investment,

$$CA = S - I, \qquad (8.59)$$

where $S = S^p + S^g$.

Although these three definitions are equivalent, the analysis that follows focuses on the third one because it permits a clear emphasis on the role of intertemporal choices in determining saving, investment, and the current account.[20]

To begin with, consider a world in which there are only two periods, the present (indexed $t = 1$) and the future ($t = 2$). The country considered is represented by a single household whose utility function is $U(C_1, C_2)$, where C_h denotes consumption at period h. The first step in the analysis is to specify the *supply side* of the model.

Suppose that agents in the economy are initially endowed with quantities Y_1^0 and Y_2^0 of output (or income). The endowment Y_1^0 in period 1 may be consumed, or it may alternatively be invested to increase output in the next period. Investment decisions, therefore, possess an intertemporal dimension which alters available output flows. During the second (and last) period, total income is fully spent. Formally, output in the second period, Y_2, is linked to the endowment Y_2^0 through the following relationship:

$$Y_2 = Y_2^0 + I_1^\alpha, \quad 0 < \alpha < 1, \qquad (8.60)$$

where I_1 represents investment, which is equal to the level of output not consumed in period 1, that is,

$$I_1 = Y_1^0 - C_1.$$

For simplicity, the production function that transforms investment in output is assumed to be Cobb-Douglas.

Investment opportunities in the economy consist of a *set of projects*, each of which involves a trade-off between lower consumption today, C_1, and higher consumption tomorrow, C_2. Thus, the gross rate of return, $1 + r$, on a project is given by the ratio of its return, ΔC_2, to its cost, $-\Delta C_1$:

$$-\frac{\Delta C_2}{\Delta C_1} = 1 + r. \qquad (8.61)$$

---

[20] The analysis that follows is based largely on Frenkel and Razin (1995, Chapter 1) and Lee and Szenberg (1994).

Adding projects according to their rates of return traces out a *concave* **production possibility frontier** (PPF) reaching Northwest from point E in Figure 8.5; the slope of the PPF at any point is $-(1+r)$, where r is now the rate of return on the *marginal* project.

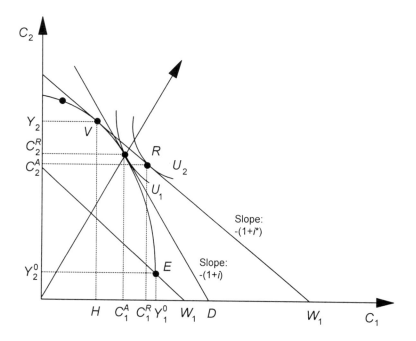

Figure 8.5. The Two-Period Intertemporal Model.
Source: Lee and Szenberg (1994, p. 994).

In *autarchy*, the household's PPF is also its **consumption possibility frontier**. Its problem is thus

$$\max_{C_1, C_2} U(C_1, C_2),$$

subject to the **production constraint**

$$F(C_1 - Y_1^0, C_2 - Y_2^0) = 0.$$

The equilibrium solution is obtained at the point of tangency between the PPF and the indifference curve U^A, that is, the point at which the slopes of these curves are equal:

$$F_1/F_2 = U_{C_1}/U_{C_2}.$$

The absolute slope of the indifference curve is

$$-\frac{dC_2}{dC_1} = \frac{U_{C_1}}{U_{C_2}} = 1 + \frac{U_{C_1} - U_{C_2}}{U_{C_2}} = 1 + \rho,$$

where ρ denotes the **rate of time preference**, which can be viewed as measuring the proportion by which the value of consumption today exceeds that of consumption tomorrow. The absolute slope of the PPF is

$$-\frac{dC_2}{dC_1} = \frac{F_1}{F_2} = 1 + \frac{F_1 - F_2}{F_1} = 1 + r,$$

so that, in equilibrium, $\rho = r$.

At the optimal production and consumption point, A, the household has determined not only its rate of saving and investment (both of which equal $Y_1^0 - C_1^A$), but also its equilibrium rate of time preference, $\tilde{\rho}$, which serves as the *ex post* discount rate as well as the *autarchy interest rate*, i. Therefore in autarchy, saving (that is, postponing consumption today to finance investment) must necessarily equal investment.[21] However, as shown below, once the possibility of borrowing and lending on world capital markets is accounted for, the saving-investment equality need no longer hold.

8.5.2   Financial Openness

Suppose now that the country considered is opened up to world capital markets, where it can borrow at the going world interest rate, i^*, which is lower than the autarchy interest rate i. It can be shown that it is now optimal—because it is consistent with profit maximization by the firm and utility maximization by the household—for the country to *borrow* on world capital markets, thereby incurring a current account deficit (and a capital account surplus).

Suppose, indeed, that the firm acts to maximize the present value of profits, PV, given by

$$PV = \frac{I_1^\alpha}{1 + i^*} - I_1.$$

Financial openness results in a fall in interest rates from i to i^*. The firm will therefore increase the level of investment, I_1, until the rate of return on the marginal project, r, equals the world interest rate. The present value-maximizing level of investment, $\tilde{I}_1$, now occurs at point V in terms of Figure 8.5, where the (absolute value of the) slope of the transformation function equals that of the isovalue locus VW_1. $\tilde{I}_1$ is measured in a leftward direction from Y_1^0 to H and the *maximized present value of profits*, PV_m, can be measured by the distance DW_1, for the line ED is a zero-value locus. The **isovalue line**, VW_1, then, is associated with the maximum attainable level of wealth W_1, which is defined as the present value of the flow of income (net of investment outlays) discounted at the world interest rate:

$$H + \frac{Y_2}{1 + i^*} = Y_1^0 + \frac{Y_2^0}{1 + i^*} + PV_m \equiv W_1.$$

[21] At the *ex post* discount rate i, the household (or the firm that it owns) undertakes all investment projects for which $r > \rho$, or, equivalently, all projects for which future flows have *positive present value* when discounted at rate i.

Given this definition, the household's **intertemporal budget constraint** is

$$C_1 + \frac{C_2}{1+i^*} = Y_1^0 + \frac{Y_2^0}{1+i^*} + PV_m. \tag{8.62}$$

This present-value budget constraint highlights the fact that the key decisions that the household makes are with respect to C_1 and C_2 as well as the *magnitude of external borrowing*, which appears *explicitly* in the two temporal budget constraints below.

The first-period budget constraint is

$$C_1 = Y_1^0 + L_1 - \tilde{I}_1, \tag{8.63}$$

and the second-period budget constraint is

$$C_2 = Y_2^0 + \tilde{I}_1^\alpha - (1+i^*)L_1, \tag{8.64}$$

where L_1 denotes first-period borrowing and $-(1+i^*)L_1$ gross repayment in the second period. These two temporal budget constraints imply that

- the first-period current account surplus, CA_1, is equal to domestic savings, $Y_1^0 - C_1$, minus investment:

$$CA_1 = Y_1^0 - C_1 - \tilde{I}_1.$$

It is also equal to the trade balance, TB_1, and the inflow of capital that represents the counterpart to foreign borrowing, L_1.

- The second-period current account surplus, CA_2, is again equal to domestic savings, $Y_2 - C_2 - i^*L_1$, which excludes repayment on the principal of the first-period loan, L_1:

$$CA_2 = Y_2 - C_2 - i^*L_1,$$

it differs now from the trade balance, $TB_2 = Y_2 - C_2$, which must be in surplus, but remains equal to the outflow of capital that represents repayment of the principal on foreign borrowing.

Intertemporal solvency implies that the discounted sum of the first-period trade account deficit and second-period surplus be equal to zero:

$$TB_1 + \frac{TB_2}{1+i^*} = 0.$$

The appropriate condition for the current account is given by

$$CA_1 + \frac{CA_2 - L_1}{1+i^*} = 0.$$

As under autarchy, suppose that the household's maximization problem is

$$\max_{C_1, C_2} U(C_1, C_2),$$

subject to Equation (8.62). The optimal solution to this problem is obtained at a point where the indifference curve U^B is tangent to the budget line associated with point W_1, that is, at point R in Figure 8.5. The optimal intertemporal allocation of consumption (C_1^R, C_2^R) is such that the marginal rate of time preference is equal to the world rate of interest.

Suppose, for simplicity, that the utility function is **homothetic**—an assumption that implies that, for a given rate of interest, the *ratio* of consumption in the two periods is *independent* of the level of wealth (see, for instance, Varian, 1992, pp. 146-147). The **wealth-consumption path** in this case is simply the ray from the origin going through the initial equilibrium point A. Figure 8.5 shows that the household borrows $C_1^R - H$ in period 1—an amount that represents the excess of investment $Y_1^0 - H$ over saving, $Y_1^0 - C_1^R$—and repays $Y_2 - C_2^R = (1 + i^*)(C_1^R - H)$ in period 2. The economy's current account deficit (which is also its trade deficit) is equal to the amount of borrowing, $C_1^R - H$. In a sense, the country borrows because its available investment opportunities (relative to its capacity to save) are highly productive.

Because of the homotheticity assumption, it can be shown that the first-period level of consumption C_1^R is greater than C_1^A, the first-period level of consumption under autarchy, because the wealth and substitution effects operate in the same direction. The second-period level of consumption is also shown to be higher than the autarchy level C_2^A if it is assumed that the positive wealth effect more than offsets the negative substitution effect that is due to the increase in the relative price of future consumption, namely, $1/(1 + i^*)$.

To see how the above framework can be used to analyze the behavior of the current account in response to exogenous shocks, suppose that initially the domestic interest rate is equal to the world interest rate, and that the current account is initially balanced. In terms of Figure 8.5, the initial equilibrium position (representing both a production and a consumption optimum) would be at point V, where the highest indifference curve attainable (which is not drawn to avoid cluttering the figure) is tangent to the PPF. Suppose now that there is a shift in domestic agents' demand from future consumption to present consumption, that is, *an increase in the domestic rate of time preference*. The equilibrium position would move from point V to a point such as A, in the absence of international capital movements, as the domestic indifference curves shift so as to increase relative preferences for present versus future consumption. The drop in domestic saving would then have to be accompanied by a corresponding *drop in domestic investment* and a *rise in the domestic interest rate*. By contrast, in a financially open economy, the current account would move into deficit, as new general equilibrium levels of investment, consumption, savings, and the various accounts of the balance of payments emerge at point R. Thus, the fall in domestic saving would translate into lower net exports (a higher trade deficit) with no effect on domestic investment. Thus, what this analysis suggests is that steps aimed at reducing the current account deficit can only be effective if they also reduce the gap between national saving and investment.

8.6 Summary

- Macroeconomic analysis is organized around three basic accounting concepts: production, income, and expenditure. These three concepts are linked by three *basic macroeconomic relationships*, which result from the *budget constraints* faced by each category of agents.

- A **consistency accounting matrix** integrates transactions in goods and services as well as financial transactions among agents. By imposing various *identities* among these magnitudes, it provides a useful accounting framework for designing consistent macroeconomic models.

- Standard *national income identities*, such as the ones relating the gross domestic product and absorption, and savings and investment, are essentially *flow budget constraints*, that is, basic relationships that relate income and expenditure of each category of agents.

- The combination of basic identities and behavioral equations in a macroeconomic model is well illustrated in a static, three-good model with a credit-supply side link and imperfect capital mobility—both of which are key macroeconomic features of developing countries. The model, however, imposes only *flow* budget constraints, and is therefore better suited to analyze the short-term effects of policy and exogenous shocks.

- An **intertemporal framework** allows the explicit derivation of behavioral functions from microeconomic considerations and to account explicitly for the *stock* budget constraints that the various agents faced—thereby allowing the modeler to impose a natural link between flows and changes in stocks over time.

- The intertemporal approach is particularly useful to interpret *current account imbalances* as the outcome of saving, lending, and borrowing choices across periods by households, firms, and governments. A simple two-period framework illustrated how adverse movements in domestic saving (as a result, for instance, of an increase in the *rate of time preference*) translate into an increase in the current account deficit.

Chapter 9

Policy Tools for Macroeconomic Analysis

Since the early 1950s, a variety of empirical techniques and quantifiable models have been developed and used in formulating macroeconomic and adjustment programs in the developing world. One of the main features of this chapter is its focus on the analytical foundations of some of these operational models and the assessment of their usefulness from a variety of perspectives—most notably, their ability to capture some of the key macroeconomic features identified in the previous chapters, their data requirements, and the ease with which they can be implemented.

The first part describes a simple empirical method for assessing business cycle regularities, based on cross correlation among macroeconomic variables. The second outlines a simple technique for evaluating the macroeconomic effects of external shocks, which tend to have a disproportionately large effect on macroeconomic fluctuations in developing countries. Part 3 presents the analytical framework (in both its basic and extended forms) that has been at the heart of stabilization programs designed by (or prepared with the assistance of) the International Monetary Fund (IMF), the financial programming approach. Part 4 presents the World Bank's basic model, which focuses on medium-term growth. In contrast to financial programming models, productive capacity and the rate of capital accumulation are endogenously determined; however, the demand and financial sides of the economy are completely ignored. Part 5 hows how the two models can be integrated to analyze jointly stabilization and medium-term growth issues. Part 6 discusses the three-gap model developed by Bacha (1990). Part 7 presents a static, computable general equilibrium model that has proved useful in assessing the medium- and longer-term effects of fiscal adjustment and tariff reform in developing countries. The last part discusses the role of various types of lags in the transmission process of policy shocks and their impact on short-term macroeconomic projections.

9.1 Assessing Business Cycle Regularities

Understanding and distinguishing among the various factors affecting the short- and long-run behavior of macroeconomic time series has been one of the main areas of research in quantitative macroeconomic analysis in recent years. However, much of the research on these issues has focused on industrial countries, with relatively limited attention paid to developing economies. At least two factors may help account for this.

- Limitations on *data quality* and *frequency* continue to be constraining factors in some cases. For instance, quarterly data on national accounts are available for only a handful of developing countries; even when they are available, they are considered to be of significantly lower quality than annual estimates.

- Developing countries tend to be prone to *sudden crises* and marked gyrations in macroeconomic variables, often making it difficult to discern any type of *cycle* or economic regularities.

At the same time, there are at least three reasons why more attention to the analysis of the stylized facts of macroeconomic fluctuations in developing countries could be useful.

- Determining the regular features of economic cycles in an economy helps to specify *applied macroeconomic models* that may capture some of the most important correlations.

- The sign and magnitude of *unconditional correlations* can provide some indication of the *type of shocks* that have dominated fluctuations in some macroeconomic aggregates over a particular period of time.

- Assessing the pattern of *leads* and *lags* between aggregate time series and economic activity can be important for the design of stabilization programs. For instance, as discussed later, the cross correlation between changes in private credit and domestic output may play an important role in the decision to allocate a given level of credit between the government and the private sector.

To characterize short-run fluctuations (measured as deviations of a variable from its long-run trend) in macroeconomic time series and analyze unconditional correlations between them and detrended output, the *first step* involves choosing a measure of real activity. Real GDP is often chosen in annual studies, whereas an index of industrial output is often selected in quarterly studies— usually because few developing countries produce consistent national accounts data at that frequency. However, it is important to note that using total GDP as a measure of output may not always be appropriate. The reason is that agricultural output, which depends on factors that may be unrelated to other macroeconomic variables (such as weather conditions) may represent a large fraction of GDP. As shown in Figure 9.1, for instance, although agriculture represents a smaller share of output in most developing countries in 1995 compared with 1980, it remains quite important in many of them. In such conditions, using *nonagricultural GDP* may be preferable.

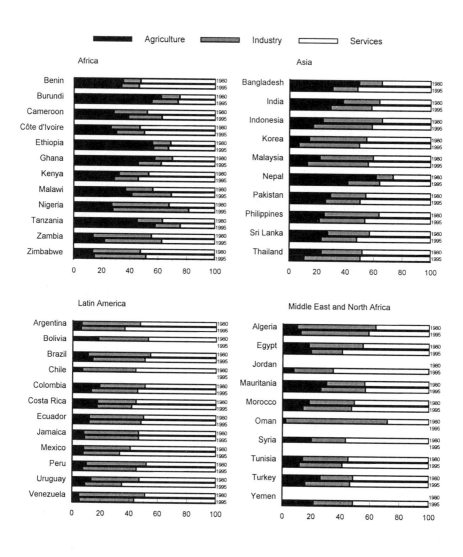

Figure 9.1. Structure of Output (Value added, in percent of GDP).
Source: World Bank.

The *second step* in the analysis consists in decomposing all macroeconomic series into nonstationary (trend) and stationary (cyclical) components, because most of the techniques that are commonly used to characterize the data empirically (including cross correlations) are valid only if the data are stationary. As noted in the appendix to Chapter 2, the most common procedure to test for **unit roots** is to use the **Augmented Dickey-Fuller (ADF) test**, by running the following regression:

$$\Delta x_t = \alpha + \beta t + (\rho - 1)x_{t-1} + \sum_{h=1}^{k} \Phi_h \Delta x_{t-h} + u_t,$$

where u_t is an error term and $k \geq 0$. The null hypothesis of nonstationarity (that is, that the series contains a **unit root**) is H_0: $\rho = 1$. For x_t to be stationary, $\rho - 1$ should be negative and significantly different from zero.

Suppose that the observed variable x_t has no seasonal component and can be expressed as the sum of a trend x_t^* component and a cyclical component, x_t^c:

$$x_t = x_t^* + x_t^c. \tag{9.1}$$

At period t, the econometrician can observe x_t but cannot measure either x_t^* or x_t^c. The second step is thus to estimate the trend component of x_t. A possible option is to use the **Hodrick-Prescott (HP) filter**. It consists essentially in specifying an adjustment rule whereby the trend component of the series x_t moves continuously and adjusts gradually. Formally, the unobserved component x_t^* is extracted by solving the following minimization problem:

$$\min_{x_t^*} \left[\sum_{t=1}^{T}(x_t - x_t^*)^2 + \lambda \sum_{t=2}^{T}[(x_{t+1}^* - x_t^*) - (x_t^* - x_{t-1}^*)]^2 \right]. \tag{9.2}$$

Thus, the objective is to select the trend component that minimizes the sum of the squared deviations from the observed series, subject to the constraint that changes in x_t^* vary gradually over time. The coefficient λ is a positive number that penalizes changes in the trend component. The larger the value of λ, the smoother is the resulting trend series.[1] It can be shown that the trend component x_t^* can be represented by a **two-sided symmetric moving average** expression of the observed series:

$$x_t^* = \sum_{h=-n}^{n} \alpha_{|h|} x_{t+h}, \tag{9.3}$$

where the parameters $\alpha_{|h|}$ depend on the value of λ.

The *third step* is to assess the degree of co-movement of each series, y_t, with output, x_t. This is done by measuring the magnitude of the **contemporaneous correlation coefficient**, $\rho(0)$, between the filtered components of y_t and x_t. A series y_t is said to be

---

[1] In general, the choice of the value of λ depends on the degree of of the assumed stickiness in the series under consideration. The usual practice is to set, for instance, λ to 100 with annual time series, and 1600 with quarterly time series. However, it should be noted that this choice is somewhat arbitrary; a more appropriate procedure would be to choose a value of λ using a data-dependent method. See Agénor, McDermott, and Prasad (1998).

- *procyclical* if $\rho(0)$ is positive;

- *countercyclical* if $\rho(0)$ is negative;

- *acyclical* if $\rho(0)$ is zero.

To establish which correlations are significantly different from zero, it can be noted that the statistic

$$\ln[\frac{1 + \rho(0)}{1 - \rho(0)}]/2,$$

has an asymptotically normal distribution with a variance equal to $T - 3$, where T is the number of observations. With about 30 observations, this implies that positive correlations of 0.3 or larger are significantly different from zero at the 10 percent level, and of 0.5 or greater are significant at the 1 percent level. Using a 10-percent significance threshold, for instance, the series y_t can be said to be

- *strongly contemporaneously correlated* with output if $0.3 \leq |\rho(0)| < 1$;

- *weakly contemporaneously correlated* with output if $0.1 \leq |\rho(0)| < 0.3$;

- *contemporaneously uncorrelated* with output if $0 \leq |\rho(0)| < 0.1$.

The last step is to determine the **phase shift** of y_t relative to output, by studying the **cross-correlation coefficients** $\rho(j)$, $j \in \{\pm 1, \pm 2, ...\}$. Specifically, y_t is said to

- *lead the cycle* by j period(s) if $|\rho(j)|$ is maximum for a negative j;

- *lag the cycle* if $|\rho(j)|$ is maximum for a positive j;

- be *synchronous* if $|\rho(j)|$ is maximum for $j = 0$.

The pattern of lead-lag correlations (in particular, the lag at which the peak positive correlation occurs) can be interpreted as indicating the speed at which innovations in variable y_t are transmitted to real activity x_t.

A comprehensive analysis of macroeconomic fluctuations in 12 developing countries based on the above approach and using quarterly data is provided by Agénor, McDermott, and Prasad (1998). Table 9.1 illustrates a more narrow application to two countries, Kenya and Venezuela, using annual data. The table suggests the following results.

- Private consumption, investment, and credit to the private sector are *procyclical* in both cases; they are also *less volatile* than output and tend to move synchronously with it—except for investment in Kenya. The relatively low volatility of consumption can be viewed as evidence in favor of **consumption-smoothing** behavior, as discussed in Chapter 1.

- The fiscal stance (measured by the ratio of government spending to tax revenue) is *countercyclical* in Kenya and *procyclical* in Venezuela—suggesting in the latter case that fiscal policy may magnify output fluctuations.

- The trade ratio (the ratio of merchandise exports over imports) has no strong association with movements in detrended output in Kenya; whereas in Venezuela, the association is *countercyclical*—possibly as a result of a close correlation between imports and activity.

- Broad money has no significant correlation with output, and seems to be *lagging* movements in activity.

Table 9.1
Cross Correlations with real GDP
(Sample period: 1970-1995)

	Kenya	Venezuela
Private consumption	Procyclical	Procyclical
Contemporaneous correlation	0.82	0.61
Relative volatility[1]	1.93	1.33
Phase shift	Synchronous	Synchronous
Gross domestic investment	No pattern	Procyclical
Contemporaneous correlation	0.34	0.83
Relative volatility[1]	3.27	5.56
Phase shift	Lagging	Synchronous
Fiscal stance[2]	Countercyclical	Procyclical
Contemporaneous correlation	-0.57	0.43
Phase shift	No pattern	No pattern
Trade ratio[3]	Countercyclical	Countercyclical
Contemporaneous correlation	-0.26	-0.58
Phase shift	No pattern	Synchronous
Broad money	Countercyclical	Procyclical
Contemporaneous correlation	-0.26	0.17
Phase shift	No pattern	Lagging
Credit to private sector	Procyclical	Procyclical
Contemporaneous correlation	0.73	0.64
Relative volatility[1]	2.01	3.15
Phase shift	Synchronous	Synchronous
GDP deflator, level	Countercyclical	Acyclical
Contemporaneous correlation	-0.84	-0.08
Phase shift	Synchronous	Leading
Inflation, GDP deflator	Countercyclical	Countercyclical
Contemporaneous correlation	-0.38	-0.32
Phase shift	No pattern	No pattern
Terms of trade	Countercyclical	Countercyclical
Contemporaneous correlation	-0.18	-0.54
Phase shift	Leading	Synchronous

[1]Ratio of the standard deviation of the detrended component of the variable to the standard deviation of detrended real output.

[2]Ratio of government spending to tax revenue.

[3]Ratio of merchandise exports over merchandise imports at current prices.

- The terms of trade (the ratio of export prices to import prices) are significantly *countercyclical* in Venezuela only. This result is not general: for most of the countries in their sample, for instance, Agénor, McDermott, and Prasad (1998) find a *procyclical* effect.

- Both prices and their rate of change (inflation) are *countercyclical* in Kenya; in Venezuela, this is the case only for inflation. A negative cross correlation between (detrended) prices and (detrended) output is generally viewed as indicating the predominance of *demand shocks*, whereas a positive cross correlation is indicative of *supply shocks*.[2]

One limitation of the procedure outlined above relates to the use of the HP filter, which remains the subject of much criticism. In particular, it has been argued that it removes potentially valuable information from time series and that it may impart *spurious cyclical patterns* to the data. It also assumes, as indicated in Equation (9.1), that the trend and cyclical components are *independent*. In reality, the choice of the relationship between the trend and cyclical components is arbitrary. Nevertheless, the HP filter remains widely used. One reason might be that *any* detrending filter is, to some extent at least, arbitrary and is bound to introduce distortions that may affect the robustness of reported business cycle regularities.[3] Used concurrently with other detrending techniques for robustness checking, the HP filter—or improvements over the standard specification, such as the variant based on the optimal choice of the smoothing parameter (see Agénor, McDermott, and Prasad, 1998)—remains a useful tool for applied macroeconomic analysis.

9.2   Assessing the Effects of External Shocks

Because they are so vulnerable to external shocks, developing countries often face the issue of quantifying the effects of these shocks, during a given period, on the economy's performance. In the absence of a fully specified and estimated macroeconomic model, a useful method to do so is the three-step methodology developed by McCarthy, Neary, and Zanalda (1994).

The *first step* involves estimating the effects on the balance of payments of three components of external shocks—changes in the trade-weighted terms of trade, changes in global demand, and changes in international interest rates—all measured in percentage of output.[4]

- The *terms-of-trade shock* is measured as the *net import effect*, that is, the change in export prices multiplied by the volume of exports minus the change in import prices multiplied by the volume of imports.

---

[2] Supply shocks are usually defined as those shocks that have *permanent* effects on output (and possibly other real variables); whereas demand shocks are those that have only *temporary*, but often persistent, effects on output. This teminolgy is somewhat misleading because most shocks perturb both demand and supply. More sophisticated methods, based on *structural vector autoregression techniques*, have been used to identify demand and supply shocks; see, for instance, Hoffmaister and Roldós (1997), and Hoffmaister, Roldós, and Wickham (1998).

[3] In fact, a large literature has highligthed that so-called *stylized facts* of business cycles in industrial countries may have been distorted by prefiltering procedures.

[4] The three measures are based on a strong *ceteris paribus* assumption, and should be viewed as yielding broad orders of magnitude.

- The *interest rate effect* is calculated as the change in world interest rates (approximated by changes in the London interbank offered rate, LIBOR) multiplied by the estimated stock of interest-sensitive external debt in the previous year.

- The impact of *changes in global demand* is calculated as the deviation of the growth of world export volumes from its estimated trend multiplied by the initial volume of the country's exports.

In the *second step*, the economy's response to these shocks is disaggregated into various measures of adjustment:

- Reductions in the *level of demand* affecting economic activity. The adjustment in imports induced by the reduction in aggregate demand is calculated as the difference between import volumes expected on the assumption of the historical import elasticity of GDP using the trend growth rate versus the actual GDP growth rate.

- *Expenditure-switching* measures. These are captured by changes in export performance (measured as the initial export volume multiplied by the excess of actual export volume growth over world export volume growth) and the degree of import intensity (calculated as the difference between import volumes expected on the assumption of historical import elasticity of GDP and actual import volumes).

The *third step* involves calculating the additional net external financing as the difference between the effect of all shocks and the economy's responses.

McCarthy, Neary, and Zanalda (1994) used the above procedure to explore the response of the Philippines to external shocks during the period 1972-91. The average value of these shocks over the period amounted to 2.6 percent of GDP during the 1970s and 1.8 percent during the 1980s. The terms-of-trade effect was the dominant source of external shocks in the first period, whereas the interest rate effect predominated in the second. In terms of the economy's response, net external financing was the dominating factor during the 1970s, whereas reductions in aggregate demand represented the main adjustment mechanism during the 1980s.

The procedure outlined above suffers from several limitations. In particular, the decomposition of the effects of external shocks on the balance of payments takes everything else equal (*ceteris paribus* assumption), and may provide incorrect orders of magnitude. In addition, the fact that the domestic economy's responses are evaluated in terms of deviations from historical trends implies that they cannot be attributed solely to changes in policies; other factors may have played a significant role, including indirect effects of the shocks themselves on the balance of payments through their impact on income and wealth. Nevertheless, without a complete macroeconomic model at hand, the McCarthy-Neary-Zanalda procedure provides broad orders of magnitude of the economy's response to external shocks that may be useful to policymakers.

9.3   Financial Programming

Financial programming is at the core of macroeconomic policy exercises conducted by the International Monetary Fund. The first model of financial programming was developed by Polak (1957); essentially, the model can be viewed as a systematic attempt to integrate *monetary* and *credit* factors in discussions of balance-of-payments issues. The first part of this section presents the Polak model, and the second considers a more elaborate financial programming framework.

9.3.1   The Polak Model

The Polak model considers a small open economy operating a fixed exchange rate regime. It is specified in *nominal terms* and consists of two identities, one behavioral equation, and an equilibrium condition.

- The first equation defines changes in the *nominal money supply*, M^s. Suppose, for simplicity, that all foreign assets are held by the central bank.[5] M^s is thus the sum of *domestic credit*, L, and *official foreign exchange reserves, R*:[6]

$$\Delta M^s = \Delta L + \Delta R. \tag{9.4}$$

- The second equation relates changes in official reserves to the *current account* (which is identical to the trade balance, assuming for now that there are no interest payments on foreign debt), and *capital inflows*, ΔF, which are treated as exogenous:

$$\Delta R = X - \alpha Y + \Delta F, \quad 0 < \alpha < 1, \tag{9.5}$$

where *exports*, X, are taken as exogenous, and *imports* are a constant fraction, α, of nominal income, Y. Given the earlier assumption that all net foreign assets are held by the central bank, the change in net official reserves is identical to the balance of payments.

- The third equation specifies changes in the nominal demand for money, ΔM^d, as a function of changes in nominal income, ΔY:

$$\Delta M^d = \nu^{-1} \Delta Y, \quad \nu > 0, \tag{9.6}$$

where ν, the *income velocity of money*, is assumed to be constant over time.

---

[5] This assumption can be rationalized by either assuming that there are no commercial banks operating in the economy, or commercial banks are required to surrender all their foreign exchange receipts to the central bank. Accounting explicitly for net foreign assets held by commercial banks can be done by straightforward modifications to Eqs. (9.4) and (9.5).

[6] More precisely, R is the book value, in domestic currency terms, of official reserves. Of course, with a fixed exchange rate normalized to unity, the foreign- and domestic-currency values of oficial reserves are the same.

- The fourth and last equation assumes that the money market is in *flow equilibrium*:

$$\Delta M^s = \Delta M^d. \tag{9.7}$$

The structure of the Polak model is summarized in Table 9.2. The change in net official reserves, ΔR, is the *target* variable. The change in the nominal money stock and nominal output, ΔM and ΔY, and imports, $J = \alpha Y$, are *endogenous* variables. Exports and capital inflows, X and ΔF, are *exogenous* variables. ΔL is the *policy instrument*. It is important to note that in the model there is no explicit decomposition of changes in nominal output into changes in prices and changes in real activity.

Table 9.2
Structure of the Polak Model

Variables	Definition
Target	
ΔR	Change in official foreign reserves
Endogenous	
$J = \alpha Y$	Imports
ΔM	Change in nominal money balances
ΔY	Change in nominal output
Exogenous	
X	Exports
ΔF	Change in net capital flows
Policy instrument	
ΔL	Change in domestic credit
Parameters	
ν	Income velocity of money
α	Marginal propensity to import

Source: Adapted from Polak (1957).

The main use of the Polak model is to assess the effects of *changes in domestic credit* on the balance of payments—or, more precisely here, official reserves in foreign exchange. Using Equations (9.4), (9.6), and (9.7) yields

$$\Delta R = \nu^{-1}\Delta Y - \Delta L, \tag{9.8}$$

which indicates that the change in net official reserves will be positive only to the extent that the desired increase in nominal money balances exceeds the change in domestic credit. The *structure* of the balance of payments (that is, the relative importance of trade flows and capital movements) plays no direct role in this relationship; it matters only for the *adjustment process* to credit shocks.

To illustrate this result and analyze how credit shocks are transmitted in this setting, consider a once-and-for-all increase in L at period $t = 0$ by ΔL_0. The adjustment process operates as follows.

- The increase in ΔL_0 expands on impact the nominal supply of money by the same amount [Equation (9.4)]. This brings about an identical increase in the demand for money, as implied by Equation (9.7). Because velocity is constant, this increase in money demand requires a rise in nominal income by $\nu\Delta L_0$ [Equation (9.6)], which in turn raises imports by $\alpha\Delta Y_0 = \alpha\nu\Delta L_0$. Official reserves therefore fall by $-\alpha\nu\Delta L_0$ on impact.

- Because the initial increase in domestic credit remains fixed at ΔL_0, the money supply, at the beginning of period $t = 1$, increases by only $(1 - \alpha\nu)\Delta L_0$. Nominal income therefore increases by $\nu(1 - \alpha\nu)\Delta L_0$ and the first-period increase in imports is $\alpha\nu(1 - \alpha\nu)\Delta L_0$. The *cumulated fall* in reserves at the end of the first period is consequently

$$\Delta R|_{t=1} = -\alpha\nu\Delta L_0 - \alpha\nu(1 - \alpha\nu)\Delta L_0,$$

and the *cumulated change* in the money supply at the end of the first period is

$$\Delta M^s|_{t=1} = \Delta L_0 - \alpha\nu\left[1 + (1 - \alpha\nu)\right]\Delta L_0 = (1 - \alpha\nu)^2\Delta L_0,$$

which is also equal to the increase in the money supply at the beginning of period $t = 2$.

With the same reasoning, the cumulated fall of reserves over an infinite horizon $(t \to \infty)$ is given by

$$\Delta R|_{t\to\infty} = -\left[\alpha\nu + \alpha\nu(1 - \alpha\nu) + \alpha\nu(1 - \alpha\nu)^2 + ...\right]\Delta L_0.$$

The term in brackets in the above expression can be written as

$$\alpha\nu\left[1 + (1 - \alpha\nu) + (1 - \alpha\nu)^2 + ...\right].$$

For the geometric series in brackets to converge, the term $1 - \alpha\nu$ must be less than unity; because $\alpha\nu > 0$, this condition is always satisfied. Thus, the above expression can be written as

$$\alpha\nu\frac{1}{1 - (1 - \alpha\nu)} = 1,$$

so that

$$\Delta R|_{t\to\infty} = -\Delta L_0.$$

The *cumulative fall in official reserves*, over an infinite horizon, is thus equal to the initial *increase in domestic credit*. Equation (9.4) therefore implies that

$$\Delta M^s|_{t\to\infty} = 0.$$

In the long run, the initial expansion in money supply through an increase in domestic credit is *completely offset* by the reduction in official reserves. Thus, nominal income and imports also return to their original levels after increasing initially.

Because the only long-run effect of a change in domestic credit is on foreign reserves, establishing a given target level of ΔR (given a projected path for money demand) allows the policymaker to estimate the *maximum allowable increase* in domestic credit, that is, a **credit ceiling**. Specifically, if $\Delta\tilde{R}$ denotes the reserve target, and ΔY^p the projected level of nominal income, the required change in credit is given by, using Equation (9.8):

$$\Delta L = \nu^{-1}\Delta Y^p - \Delta\tilde{R}.$$

Thus, controlling *domestic credit expansion* (in a setting in which exports, the income velocity of money, and capital flows can be treated as exogenous) is crucial in attaining a balance-of-payments objective. This implication of the model has been at the heart of the stabilization programs advocated by (or put in place with the support of) the IMF. The demand function, as shown in the foregoing example, plays a critical role in the analysis. The particular form used here is actually not essential for the main implication of the model; a more general function (involving, for instance, interest rates or inflation, as discussed in Chapter 2) can readily be specified—as long as it is assumed stable and independent of changes in domestic credit (International Monetary Fund, 1987, p. 14).

The importance of controlling domestic credit expansion for balance-of-payments performance is also the key message of the **Monetary Approach to the Balance of Payments** (MABP), which in its most popular form relies on the assumptions of a stable demand for money, purchasing power parity, and continuous *stock equilibrium* of the money market (Kreinin and Officer, 1978). There is, however, a key difference between the Polak model and the MABP: in the latter, any increase in domestic credit expansion (everything else equal) instantly crowds out official reserves by an equivalent amount.[7] In the Polak model, complete crowding out also occurs but only *in the long run*, and takes place through a series of adjustments in nominal income, imports, and the money supply. This adjustment process may be viewed as more realistic than the assumption underlying the MABP.

A key limitation of the Polak model is the assumption that changes in domestic credit have no effect (even in the short run) on the determinants of money demand, such as real income or domestic interest rates. As noted in the previous chapter, in many developing countries the bank credit-supply side link is often a critical feature of the economy. Another problem with the model (as well as many of its extensions) is that it assumes a stable money demand function. In practice, especially over short horizons, the demand for money balances tends to be unstable—often as a result of volatile inflation expectations. In such conditions, it may provide an unreliable tool for macroeconomic projections.

9.3.2 An Extended Framework

The Polak model continues to be at the core of the financial programming framework that underlies IMF stabilization programs designed for economies operating under a fixed exchange rate. In practice, the model has been modified and expanded in several directions. This subsection examines one version of the model, adapted from Khan, Haque, and Montiel (1990), that distinguishes explicitly between changes in real and nominal output and the sources of credit

---

[7]Specifically, an excess supply of real money balances brought about by an increase in domestic credit gives rise to an excess demand for other financial assets as well as goods and services. In an open economy, this excess demand translates immediately into changes in net foreign reserves.

growth.[8]

Consider an economy producing one good, which is an imperfect substitute for imported goods. Let nominal income, Y, be defined as

$$Y = Py, \tag{9.9}$$

where P denotes the *overall price index* and y *real output*, which is assumed exogenous. The change in nominal income is given by

$$\Delta Y = Py - P_{-1}y_{-1} = Py + P_{-1}(\Delta y - y) = Py + P_{-1}\Delta y - P_{-1}y,$$

that is,

$$\Delta Y = \Delta Py + P_{-1}\Delta y = \Delta P(\Delta y + y_{-1}) + P_{-1}\Delta y = \Delta Py_{-1} + P_{-1}\Delta y + \Delta y \Delta P.$$

Assuming that both ΔP and Δy are small, the last term on the right-hand side in the above expression can be ignored and so

$$\Delta Y = \Delta Py_{-1} + P_{-1}\Delta y. \tag{9.10}$$

Changes in the overall price index are a function of changes in domestic prices, ΔP_D, and changes in foreign prices measured in domestic-currency terms, $\Delta E + \Delta P^*$:

$$\Delta P = \delta \Delta P_D + (1 - \delta)(\Delta E + \Delta P^*), \quad 0 < \delta < 1 \tag{9.11}$$

where E is the nominal exchange rate, P^* the price index of foreign goods measured in foreign-currency terms, and δ (respectively $1 - \delta$) a parameter that measures the relative weight of domestic goods (respectively imported goods) in the overall price index.

Domestic credit, L, consists now of *credit to the private sector*, L^p, and *credit to the government*, L^g:[9]

$$\Delta L = \Delta L^p + \Delta L^g. \tag{9.12}$$

Changes in credit to the private sector reflect demand for working capital (as discussed in the previous chapter) and, as such, are assumed proportional to changes in nominal output:

$$\Delta L^p = \theta \Delta Y, \quad 0 < \theta < 1. \tag{9.13}$$

The *money supply identity* is given as in the Polak model by[10]

$$\Delta M = \Delta L + \Delta R, \tag{9.14}$$

---

[8] A limitation of the model presented here is that it assumes that the economy produces only one domestic good, which is used for both domestic consumption and exports. A more appropriate framework for developing economies would distinguish between exportables, non-tradables, and importables, as done in Chapter 8.

[9] L^g is defined net of government deposits. In practice, the definition of government used for programming exercises varies across countries. In what follows *government* and *public sector* are used as synonymous.

[10] Equation (9.14) assumes that capital gains and losses on foreign exchange reserves associated with changes in the nominal exchange rate are not monetized, but rather are treated as an off-balance sheet. Khan, Haque, and Montiel (1990) provide an alternative treatment.

where ΔR is equal to $E\Delta R^*$, that is, the change in the foreign-currency value of official reserves ΔR^*, valued at the current exchange rate.

Changes in official reserves are again related to the trade balance and capital inflows, ΔF, assumed exogenous:

$$\Delta R = X - J + \Delta F. \qquad (9.15)$$

X, J, and ΔF are all measured in domestic-currency terms. ΔF consists now of both private and public flows, ΔF^p and ΔF^g, which are both assumed to be given in foreign-currency terms, so that $\Delta F = (1 + \Delta E)\Delta F^*$.

Exports are again exogenous. Imports in *nominal* terms are given by $J = EQ_J$, where Q_J is the volume of imports. Consequently, assuming that $\Delta E\Delta Q_J$ is small,

$$J = J_{-1} + \Delta EQ_{J-1} + E_{-1}\Delta Q_J.$$

Changes in the volume of imports are assumed to depend on changes in real output and changes in the price of domestic goods relative to the price of foreign goods:

$$\Delta Q_J = \alpha\Delta y + \eta[\Delta P_D - (\Delta E + \Delta P^*)],$$

where $\eta > 0$ measures the sensitivity of (the change in) imports to (changes in) relative prices. Substituting this result in the previous equation yields:

$$J = J_{-1} + (Q_{J-1} - \eta E_{-1})\Delta E + E_{-1}[\alpha\Delta y + \eta(\Delta P_D - \Delta P^*)], \qquad (9.16)$$

which shows that, as long as Q_{J-1} is not too large, a devaluation of the nominal exchange rate $(\Delta E > 0)$ will lower imports, improve the trade balance, and increase official reserves.[11]

As in the Polak model, the income velocity of money is taken to be constant, implying that

$$\Delta M^d = \nu^{-1}\Delta Y, \quad \nu > 0. \qquad (9.17)$$

The money market is again assumed to be in *flow equilibrium*:

$$\Delta M^s = \Delta M^d. \qquad (9.18)$$

The *government budget constraint* relates the budget deficit $G - T$, where G is total expenditure and T is total tax revenue, to changes in *foreign borrowing*, ΔF^g (which is exogenous), and changes in central bank credit:[12]

$$G - T = \Delta L^g + \Delta F^g. \qquad (9.19)$$

Table 9.3 summarizes the structure of the extended Polak (or financial programming) model. The change in domestic prices, ΔP_D, and the change in net

---

[11] The model can easily be modified to endogenize exports as a function also of relative prices. See Khan, Haque, and Montiel (1990).

[12] It is assumed that the government cannot borrow directly from the domestic private sector by issuing bonds. This assumption has become particularly restrictive and untenable for a number of middle-income developing countries.

official reserves, ΔR, are *target* variables. Changes in the nominal money stock, ΔM, nominal output, ΔY, credit to the private sector, ΔL^p, the overall price index, ΔP, and imports, J, and the budget deficit, $G - T$, are *endogenous* variables. Changes in real output, Δy, foreign prices, ΔP^*, and exports and capital inflows, X and ΔF, are *exogenous* variables. Changes in domestic credit to the government ΔL^g and the nominal exchange rate ΔE are the *policy instruments*. It is worth emphasizing that in this setting it is the government budget deficit *as a whole* that is considered endogenous. As discussed below, whether the adjustment occurs through movements in government spending (changes in G) or in taxes (changes in T) is left unspecified at this stage.

To relate targets, exogenous variables, and policy instruments in this setup, substitute first Equations (9.12), (9.13), (9.14), and (9.17) in (9.18) to give

$$\Delta R = (\nu^{-1} - \theta)\Delta Y - \Delta L^g,$$

where it is assumed that $\nu\theta < 1$.

Using Equation (9.10) to eliminate ΔY, and (9.11) to eliminate ΔP, yields

$$\Delta R - (\nu^{-1} - \theta)y_{-1}\delta\Delta P_D = \Lambda, \tag{9.20}$$

where

$$\Lambda = (\nu^{-1} - \theta)[y_{-1}(1 - \delta)(\Delta E + \Delta P^*) + P_{-1}\Delta y] - \Delta L^g.$$

Similarly, substituting Equation (9.16) in (9.15) yields

$$\Delta R + \eta\Delta P_D = X + \Delta F - J_{-1} + (Q_{J-1} - \eta E_{-1})\Delta E + \eta\Delta P^* - \alpha E_{-1}\Delta y. \tag{9.21}$$

These two equations can be solved in two different modes.

- In the **positive mode**, Equations (9.20) and (9.21) are used to determine *simultaneously* ΔR and ΔP_D, for given values of X, ΔF, ΔP^*, Δy, and the policy instruments, ΔE and ΔL^g. This solution is obtained *independently* of Equations (9.11), (9.10), (9.13), (9.12), and (9.19), which determine, respectively, ΔP, ΔY, ΔL^p, ΔL, and $G - T$.

Table 9.3
Structure of the Extended Financial Programming Model

Variables	Definition
Targets	
ΔR	Change in official foreign reserves
ΔP_D	Change in domestic prices
Endogenous	
ΔY	Change in nominal output
ΔL^p	Change in private sector credit
ΔM	Change in nominal money balances
ΔP	Change in the overall price index
ΔJ	Change in imports
$G - T$	Fiscal deficit
Exogenous	
Δy	Change in real output
ΔP^*	Change in foreign prices
X	Exports
$\Delta F = \Delta F^p + \Delta F^g$	Change in net capital flows
Policy instruments	
ΔL^g	Change in domestic credit to government
ΔE	Change in the nominal exchange rate
Predetermined	
y_{-1}	Real output in previous period
P_{-1}	Price level in previous period
Q_{J-1}	Volume of imports in previous period
Parameters	
ν	Income velocity of money
δ	Share of domestic goods in the consumer price index
α	Marginal propensity to import
θ	Response of private sector credit to output
η	Response of imports to relative prices

Source: Adapted from Khan et al. (1990, p. 163).

- In the **programming mode**, ΔR and ΔP_D are policy targets, denoted $\Delta \tilde{R}$ and $\Delta \tilde{P}_D$, in Equations (9.20) and (9.21). These two equations are now solved for the two policy instruments, ΔE and ΔL^g. Again, this solution is obtained *independently* of Equations (9.12), (9.13), and (9.19). Given the value of the instrument ΔL^g, and values for the exogenous variable ΔF^g, Equation (9.19) determines residually (from *below the line*) the government fiscal deficit, $G - T$. This *programmed deficit* is achieved by adjusting either tax revenue, T, or public expenditure, G. The target for domestic prices (given the assumption that real output is exogenous) generates endogenously a programmed value for the change in the overall price index, ΔP, the change in nominal output, ΔY, and thus private sector credit, ΔL^p through Equations (9.10), (9.11), and (9.13).

The solution of the extended model is illustrated in Figure 9.2, in the ΔR-ΔP_D space. Curve MM is given by Equation (9.20) and has a positive slope. Curve BB is derived from Equation (9.21) and has a negative slope. The intersection of the two curves (at point E) defines the solution values for ΔR and ΔP_D in the **positive mode** (that is, for given values of the exogenous variables and the policy instruments). To see how the model operates in **programming mode**, suppose, for instance, that the policymaker's objectives are to lower inflation and increase official reserves, by moving from the initial position at E to a point such as E'. This outcome can be achieved through a combination of two policy actions:

- by reducing domestic credit to the government, ΔL^g, which implies a leftward shift in MM, with no change in BB;

- by depreciating the nominal exchange rate, ΔE, which implies a leftward shift in MM and a rightward shift in BB.

The actual solution values for ΔE and ΔL^g can be calculated *recursively*: Equation (9.21) can be used to obtain the appropriate level of ΔE, for given values of $\Delta \tilde{R}$ and $\Delta \tilde{P}_D$; substituting the solution for ΔE in Equation (9.20) yields the required value of ΔL^g. Graphically, the new equilibrium is obtained at point E' in Figure 9.2, where MM and BB intersect. What this experiment suggests, therefore, is that it is necessary to use *two policy instruments* to achieve *two policy targets*, as suggested by the **Meade-Tinbergen principle**.

9.4   The World Bank RMSM Model

The World Bank currently uses for the macroeconomic projections that underlie some of its loan operations the RMSM-X model, which is discussed in the next section. The present section focuses on the precursor to that model, the **Revised Minimum Standard Model** (RMSM), which was developed in the early 1970s.

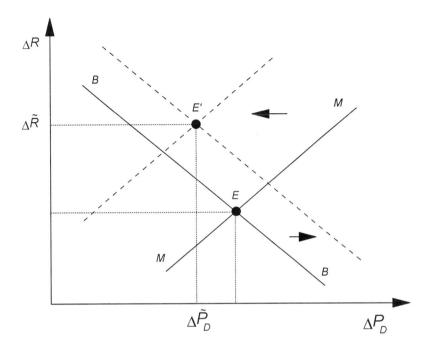

Figure 9.2. The Extended Financial Programming Model.
Source: Adapted from Khan, Montiel, and Haque (1990, p. 161).

The main objective of the model is to make explicit the link between *medium-term growth* and its *financing*. The basic model takes prices as given. It consists of five relationships.

- The first basic relationship relates the *desired level* of investment, I, to the *change* in real output, Δy:

$$I = \Delta y / \sigma, \quad \sigma > 0, \tag{9.22}$$

where σ is the inverse of the **incremental capital-output ratio** (ICOR).

- The second relationship relates *imports*, J, and real output:

$$J = \alpha y, \quad 0 < \alpha < 1. \tag{9.23}$$

- The third relationship defines (as in the three-good model of Chapter 8) *private consumption*, C^p, as a fraction of *disposable income*, defined as income, y, minus taxes, T:

$$C^p = (1 - s)(y - T), \tag{9.24}$$

where $0 < s < 1$ is the marginal propensity to save.

- The balance-of-payments identity is defined, as above, by

$$\Delta R = X - J + \Delta F, \tag{9.25}$$

where X again denotes exports (assumed exogenous) and ΔF net capital inflows or net foreign borrowing.

- The last relationship is the *national income identity*, which is given by

$$y_{-1} + \Delta y = C^p + G + I + (X - J), \tag{9.26}$$

where G is government expenditure.

The structure of the RMSM model is summarized in Table 9.4. Changes in real output, Δy, and the change in net official reserves, ΔR, are *target* variables. Government spending, G, tax revenue, T, and the change in foreign borrowing, ΔF, are the *policy instruments*. Exports, X, are *exogenous*.

To see how targets, exogenous variables, and policy instruments are related in this setup, substitute Equations (9.22), (9.23), (9.24) in (9.26) to give

$$\Delta y = \frac{(s + \alpha)y_{-1} + (1 - s)T - (X + G)}{\sigma^{-1} - (s + \alpha)}. \tag{9.27}$$

Substituting (9.23) in (9.25) yields

$$\Delta R = X - \alpha(y_{-1} + \Delta y) + \Delta F. \tag{9.28}$$

The system consisting of Equations (9.27) and (9.28) can be solved in two different modes.

- In the **positive** or **policy mode**, Equations (9.27) and (9.28) are used to solve for Δy and ΔR. The system is in fact **recursive**: Equation (9.27) can first be used to determine Δy, for given values of X and the policy instruments, T and G. Given this solution, Equation (9.28) is then used to determine ΔR, for given values of X and ΔF.

- In the **programming mode**, the solution can again be obtained *recursively*: Equation (9.27) can be used to determine either the value of G or T for a given target value of Δy; and for given target values of Δy and ΔR, Equation (9.28) can be used to determine the value of net capital inflows, ΔF. With $\Delta \tilde{y}$ and $\Delta \tilde{R}$ denoting the target levels of output and reserves, this solution is

$$\Delta F = \alpha(y_{-1} + \Delta \tilde{y}) - X + \Delta \tilde{R}. \tag{9.29}$$

The solution of the RMSM model in the positive mode is illustrated in Figure 9.3, in the Δy-ΔR space. The horizontal curve YY is given by Equation (9.27). Curve BB is derived from Equation (9.28) and has a negative slope. The intersection of the two curves (at point E) defines the equilibrium values of Δy and ΔR, for given values of the exogenous variables and the policy instruments.

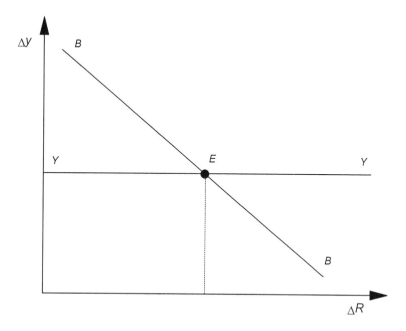

Figure 9.3. The RMSM Model in the Positive Model.

Because setting a target level of output is tantamount to fixing imports and thus the trade balance (recall that exports are exogenous), the programming mode of the RMSM model described above is often described as the **trade-gap mode**: for $X - J$ given, the model calculates the appropriate level of external financing, ΔF, that satisfies the balance-of-payments identity, Equation (9.25).

Ignoring the trade gap, and assuming that policymakers exert sufficient control over capital inflows to determine ΔF as in Equation (9.29) may not, of course, be warranted in all circumstances. In practice, countries do face *limits on foreign borrowing*. By treating external financing ΔF as given, the RMSM model—just as the RMSM-X model described later—can alternatively be closed by fixing, instead, the level of saving that is consistent with the programmed level of investment that is consistent with the targeted level of output, $\Delta \tilde{y}$; specifically, using Equation (9.22), the required level of saving is $\Delta \tilde{y}/\sigma$. This is what is referred to as the **saving-gap mode**. In this case, it is often assumed that total consumption ($C = G + C^p$) is determined *residually* from the national income identity, Equation (9.26). Assuming further that public consumption expenditure of the government is policy determined yields private consumption as the residual variable, that is, using Equations (9.22) and (9.23):

$$C^p = y_{-1} + \Delta \tilde{y} - \Delta \tilde{y}/\sigma - X - m(y_{-1} + \Delta \tilde{y}) - G.$$

The trouble with this functioning mode, of course, is that there is no reason a priori to expect the level of private consumption derived from the above equation to be equal to the desired level of private spending (derived from consumption-smoothing considerations, for instance), or with the level consistent with the national accounts identity (9.26).

In general, of course, both the trade gap and the saving gap may represent binding constraints on the determination of output and changes in official reserves, implying that either one or both of these targets may need to be adjusted to accommodate a shortage in foreign exchange restrictions. The version of the RMSM model in which a (possibly binding) foreign exchange constraint is added is the **two-gap mode**.[13] Neither constraint is suppressed a priori so that either one of the two gaps might be binding. In such a two-gap situation, depending on which constraint is binding, observed domestic saving (imports) may be different from desired or required saving (imports).

The main use of the two-gap version of the RMSM model in the programming mode is to determine the *financing requirements* for alternative target rates of *output growth* (given also a target for official reserves) or, equivalently, to determine the feasibility of a particular rate of output growth given alternative foreign financing scenarios. To illustrate, rewrite the national income accounting identity (9.26) as

$$I = (y - T - C^p) + (T - G) + (J - X). \tag{9.30}$$

This formulation now equates domestic investment, I, to the sum of private sector savings, $y - T - C^p$, public sector savings, $T - G$, and foreign savings (or the trade surplus), $J - X$. Using Equation (9.24) to substitute out for C^p and (9.25) to substitute out for $J - X$ in (9.30), and with target levels of output and reserves given by $\Delta \tilde{y}$ and $\Delta \tilde{R}$, Equation (9.30) implies that investment is constrained by total saving, that is,

$$I \leq \kappa_S + \Delta F, \tag{9.31}$$

where

$$\kappa_S = s(y_{-1} + \Delta \tilde{y}) + [(1 - s)T - G] - \Delta \tilde{R}.$$

Equation (9.31) is the **saving constraint**. It is depicted (in equality form) in Figure 9.4 as curve SS in the I-ΔF space. The figure assumes that κ_S, which is in general ambiguous, is positive. Below curve SS the inequality (9.31) is satisfied, whereas above SS it is not. The constraint $I = \kappa_S + \Delta F$ is thus binding above SS. Changes in the policy instruments, T and G, and changes in the policy targets, $\Delta \tilde{y}$ and $\Delta \tilde{R}$, imply horizontal shifts in SS because they affect κ_S.

To derive the second constraint that operates in the two-gap version of the RMSM model requires rewriting the balance-of-payments constraint (9.25) in

---

[13] The two-gap model, with its focus on foreign exchange and domestic saving as alternative constraints on growth, was developed by Chenery and Strout (1966). See Taylor (1994) for a more recent treatment.

the form

$$J - X = \Delta F - \Delta \tilde{R}, \tag{9.32}$$

which gives the level of the trade account (or, again, imports) consistent with a given value of ΔF and a target level for reserves.

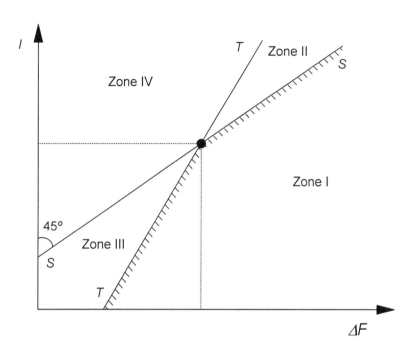

Figure 9.4. The RMSM Model in Two-Gap Mode.

Substituting the import demand function, Equation (9.23), in the above equation and rearranging yields

$$\Delta y = (X - \Delta R + \Delta F)/\alpha - y_{-1}. \tag{9.33}$$

From Equation (9.22), $\Delta y = \sigma I$. Substituting Equation (9.33) for Δy in this expression implies that investment is also constrained by

$$I \leq \kappa_T + \Delta F/\alpha\sigma, \tag{9.34}$$

where

$$\kappa_T = (X - \Delta \tilde{R})/\alpha\sigma - y_{-1}/\sigma.$$

Table 9.4
Structure of the World Bank's RMSM Framework

Variables	Definition
Targets	
Δy	Change in output
ΔR	Change in official foreign reserves
Endogenous	
I	Investment
C^p	Private consumption
J	Imports
Exogenous	ΔF
X	Exports
Policy instruments	
G	Government expenditure
T	Tax revenues
ΔF	Change in net foreign borrowing
Predetermined	
y_{-1}	Real output in previous period
Parameters	
σ	Inverse of the incremental capital-output ratio
s	Saving rate
α	Marginal propensity to import

Source: Adapted from Khan et al. (1990, p. 169).

Equation (9.34) is the **trade constraint**. It is represented in (equality form) in Figure 9.4 as curve TT, which is drawn under the assumption that $\kappa_T < 0$. In practice, the ICOR, $1/\sigma$, varies usually between 2 and 5; in general, therefore, $\alpha\sigma < 1$. Curve TT (whose slope is $1/\alpha\sigma$) is thus typically steeper than SS. As before, the position of TT depends also on $\Delta\tilde{R}$. In addition, here, it also depends on the (exogenous) value of exports, X. But with X given, the only way to generate a shift in TT is through a revised target level for official reserves.

Both constraints, (9.31) and (9.34), provide an estimate of the level of investment. The constraint that yields the lowest level of the two is called the **binding constraint**. Curves SS and TT separate Figure 9.4 into four zones:

- Zone I, in which *no constraint is binding*;

- Zone II, in which only the *saving constraint is binding*;

- Zone III, in which only the *trade constraint is binding*;

- Zone IV, in which *both constraints are binding*.

Clearly, because TT is steeper than SS, the impact of foreign borrowing on investment, and thus output and growth, will be larger if the trade constraint is binding, as opposed to the saving constraint.

To see how the two-gap version of the RMSM model operates in the programming mode (that is, with target levels for both official reserves and output), suppose that foreign financing is the constraining factor. The values of investment, changes in output, imports and official reserves that are mutually consistent with each other (as well as with the policy instruments and the exogenous variables) are then determined through an *iterative process* which involves the following steps.

- *Step 1.* Specify values for a) the parameters σ, s, and α; b) the predetermined variable, y_{-1}; c) the exogenous variables, X and ΔF; d) the policy instruments, T and G; e) and the policy targets, $\Delta \tilde{y}$ and $\Delta \tilde{R}$.

- *Step 2.* Given the policy target $\Delta \tilde{y}$, determine the **required level of investment** as $I_R = \Delta \tilde{y}/\sigma$.

- *Step 3.* Determine the levels of investment, I_S and I_T, implied by the saving constraint [Equation (9.31)] and the trade constraint [Equation (9.34)]. Determine the **binding level of investment** given by the hatched area in Figure 9.4, as
$$I_{min} = \min(I_S, I_T). \tag{9.35}$$

- *Step 4.* If the required level of investment does not exceed the minimum level, that is, if $I_{min} \geq I_R$, no constraint is binding, and the intersection of ΔF and I_R occurs in Zone I in Figure 9.4. Then proceed to step 6. If not, proceed to either step 4a, 4b, or 4c:

  - *Step 4a.* If $I_{min} \leq I_R$, and if the savings constraint is binding, the intersection of ΔF and I_R will occur in Zone II in Figure 9.4. Either increase taxes, T, and/or reduce public expenditure, G, and/or reduce the desired change in official reserves, $\Delta \tilde{R}$, until the constraint is relaxed or until further changes in the policy or target variables are ruled out as unfeasible.[14] If the constraint is relaxed so that the required investment level can be achieved, proceed to step 6. If not, proceed to step 5.

  - *Step 4b.* If $I_{min} \leq I_R$, and if the trade constraint is binding, the intersection of ΔF and I_R will occur in Zone III in Figure 9.4. Reduce the desired change in official reserves, $\Delta \tilde{R}$, until the constraint is relaxed or until further changes in the policy or target variables are ruled out as unfeasible.[15] If the constraint is relaxed so that the

---

[14]From Eqs. (9.31) and (9.34), it can be seen that an increase in T or a reduction in G (by raising κ_S) shifts only SS to the left, increasing the feasibility region (zone I). A reduction in $\Delta \tilde{R}$, by contrast, shifts *both* SS and TT to the left. The shift in TT, however, is inconsequential, because the trade constraint was satisfied in the first place.

[15]From Eqs. (9.31) and (9.34), it can be seen that an increase in T or a reduction in G (by raising κ_S) would shift SS to the left. This, however, would be inconsequential, because the saving constraint was satisfied in the first place. There must therefore be a leftward shift in TT in order to increase the feasibility region. In turn, this can occur only through a reduction in $\Delta \tilde{R}$ (because X is given), which shifts *both* SS and TT to the left.

required investment level can be achieved, proceed to step 6. If not, proceed to step 5.

- *Step 4c.* If $I_{min} \leq I_R$, and if both constraints are binding, the intersection of ΔF and I_R occurs in Zone IV in Figure 9.4. Reduce the desired change in official reserves, $\Delta \tilde{R}$ and/or adjust policy instruments T and G, until both constraints are relaxed or until further changes in the policy or target variables are ruled out as unfeasible.[16] If both constraints are relaxed so that the required investment level can be achieved, proceed to step 6. If not, proceed to step 5.

- *Step 5.* If step 4 does not yield the required level of investment needed to achieve the desired level of increase in output, then the targeted change in output must be changed and a new (lower) value must be set according to

$$\Delta \tilde{y} = \sigma I_{min},$$

which by definition is consistent with the binding(s) constraint(s).

- *Step 6.* Determine the required level of imports, J_R, as

$$J_R = \alpha(y_{-1} + \Delta \tilde{y}).$$

- *Step 7.* Given the required level of imports and the exogenous levels of X and ΔF, reestimate the targeted change in official reserves as follows:

$$\Delta \tilde{R}[1] = X - J_R + \Delta F.$$

For consistency reasons, this revised targeted change in reserves must be compared to the original target value used in the saving and trade constraints. If both estimates $\Delta \tilde{R}[1]$ and $\Delta \tilde{R}$ are identical (a very unlikely outcome after only one iteration), go to step 8. If not, go back to step 3 and re-solve the model again with the revised target $\Delta \tilde{R}[1]$. Continue iterations until the estimate of $\Delta \tilde{R}$ used in step 3 is almost identical to the one provided by step 7, that is, until the values obtained between iterations h and $h-1$, $\Delta \tilde{R}[h]$ and $\Delta \tilde{R}[h-1]$, are very close.

- *Step 8.* Once convergence has been achieved, the model yields inter-related consistent values of the levels of investment, the change in output, imports, and the change in official reserves.

- *Step 9.* Use Equation (9.24), along with the new value of output, (given by $y = y_{-1} + \Delta \tilde{y}$) and the (possibly modified) value of taxes to estimate private consumption, C^p.

---

[16] As indicated earlier, a change in $\Delta \tilde{R}$ is necessary to shift the TT curve. Because as a result of a reduction in $\Delta \tilde{R}$ both SS and TT shift to the left, there may be no need to adjust T or G to expand sufficiently the feasibility region.

Various criticisms have been offered of the two-gap version of the RMSM model. Two of the most important ones are the following.

- It is often difficult, in practice, to decide a priori which constraint is binding. The RMSM framework assumes that *imports are essential for investment* and that the availability of foreign exchange, by allowing such imports, raises the growth rate of output. However, it has been argued that the saving gap can be closed by *reducing imports* or *increasing exports* (or both), thereby freeing foreign exchange necessary for investment.

- The model is largely incomplete because it is essentially a growth-oriented model with emphasis on a small number of real variables and no financial side. For instance, relative prices and induced *substitution effects* among production factors (and their possible impact on exports, for instance) are neglected.

9.5   The Merged Model and RMSM-X

The RMSM model has been extended in recent years and has been superseded by the **RMSM-X** framework. Essentially, RMSM-X integrates into the RMSM framework the financial programming approach of the IMF, described earlier. The analytical structure of the merged IMF-World Bank model, which is at the core of RMSM-X, is described in the first subsection; The RMSM-X framework itself is presented in the second subsection.

9.5.1   The Merged IMF-World Bank Model

The merged IMF-World Bank model combines the extended financial programming model described earlier and the World Bank's RMSM model. As in the extended IMF model, which assumes imperfect substitutability between domestic and imported goods, relative prices (and thus the nominal exchange rate) affect the demand for imports and domestic absorption.

The merged model consists of the following equations:

- The change in *real output* is given by an equation similar to (9.22):

$$\Delta y = \sigma I/(1 + \Delta P), \tag{9.36}$$

where investment expenditure is now measured in real terms, deflated by the price level.

- The change in *nominal output* is given, as in Equation (9.10), by

$$\Delta Y = \Delta P y_{-1} + P_{-1}\Delta y, \tag{9.37}$$

- and changes in the *overall price index* are given by an equation similar to (9.11):

$$\Delta P = \delta \Delta P_D + (1 - \delta)\Delta E, \tag{9.38}$$

where, for simplicity, foreign prices are taken as constant $(\Delta P^* = 0)$.

- *Domestic credit* consists again of credit to the private sector and credit to the government, as in Equation (9.12):

$$\Delta L = \Delta L^p + \Delta L^g, \tag{9.39}$$

with changes in private sector credit given by a relation similar to Equation (9.13):

$$\Delta L^p = \theta \Delta Y. \tag{9.40}$$

- Ignoring again capital gains on official reserves due to exchange rate fluctuations, the *money supply identity* is given by an equation similar to (9.14):

$$\Delta M = \Delta L + \Delta R, \tag{9.41}$$

where ΔR is equal to $E\Delta R^*$.

- Changes in *official reserves* are given by an equation similar to (9.15):

$$\Delta R = X - J + \Delta F, \tag{9.42}$$

where X, J, and ΔF are all measured in domestic-currency terms, with ΔF consisting of private and public flows, ΔF^p and ΔF^g. Again, ΔF is assumed given in foreign currency terms, so that $\Delta F = (1 + \Delta E)\Delta F^*$.

- *Exports* are exogenous and changes in *nominal imports* are again determined by a relation similar to Equation (9.16), with $\Delta P^* = 0$:

$$J = J_{-1} + (Q_{J-1} - \eta E_{-1})\Delta E + E_{-1}(\alpha \Delta y + \eta \Delta P_D). \tag{9.43}$$

- With constant income velocity, money demand is given by a relation identical to Equation (9.17):

$$\Delta M^d = \nu^{-1}\Delta Y. \tag{9.44}$$

- The *money market* is assumed as before to be in *flow equilibrium*, as in Equation (9.18):

$$\Delta M^s = \Delta M^d. \tag{9.45}$$

- The *government budget constraint* is given again by Equation (9.19):

$$G - T = \Delta L^g + \Delta F^g. \tag{9.46}$$

To close the model requires an equation for investment. The *private sector budget constraint* is given by

$$(Y - C^p - T) - I = \Delta M^d - \Delta L^p - \Delta F^p,$$

which relates saving minus investment to changes in money balances, net of liabilities (change in bank liabilities and foreign borrowing). Assuming, as in (9.24), that $C^p = (1 - s)(y - T)$, this constraint implies that

$$I = s(Y_{-1} + \Delta Y - T) + \Delta L^p + \Delta F^p - \Delta M^d. \tag{9.47}$$

Table 9.5 summarizes the structure of the merged model. The change in real output, Δy, domestic prices, ΔP_D, and the change in net official reserves, ΔR, are *target* variables. Changes in the nominal money stock, ΔM, nominal output, ΔY, credit to the private sector, ΔL^p, the overall price index, ΔP, and imports, J, the budget deficit, $G - T$, and investment are *endogenous* variables. Exports, X, and changes in foreign borrowing, ΔF, are *exogenous* variables. Changes in domestic credit to the government, ΔL^g, taxes or government spending (T or G), and the nominal exchange rate, ΔE, are the *policy instruments*.

As before, a condensed form of the system can be derived in three steps. First, substitute Equation (9.44) in (9.47), and then both (9.46) and (9.47) in (9.36), together with (9.39), to give

$$\Delta y = \sigma(1 + \Delta P)^{-1}[s(Y_{-1} + \Delta Y) + (1 - s)T - G + \Delta L + \Delta F - \nu^{-1}\Delta Y],$$

so that, using Equation (9.40):

$$\Delta y = \sigma(1 + \Delta P)^{-1}[sY_{-1} + \tau\Delta Y + (1 - s)T - G + \Delta L^g + \Delta F],$$

where $\tau = s + \theta - \nu^{-1}$ is assumed positive, that is,

$$\nu(s + \theta) > 1.$$

Using Equation (9.37) to substitute for ΔY in the above expression, and multiplying both sides by $1 + \Delta P$ yields, noting that $\Delta P \Delta y \simeq 0$ and setting $P_{-1} = 1$,

$$\Delta y = \frac{\kappa + \tau y_{-1}\Delta P}{\sigma^{-1} - \tau}, \tag{9.48}$$

where

$$\kappa = sY_{-1} + (1 - s)T - G + \Delta F + +\Delta L^g, \tag{9.49}$$

and it is assumed that

$$\sigma\tau < 1.$$

Substituting Equation (9.38) for ΔP yields

$$\Delta y = \frac{\kappa + \tau y_{-1}[\delta\Delta P_D + (1 - \delta)\Delta E]}{\sigma^{-1} - \tau},$$

which can be rewritten as

$$\Delta P_D = \frac{-\kappa + (\sigma^{-1} - \tau)\Delta y}{\delta\tau y_{-1}} - (1 - \delta)\delta^{-1}\Delta E. \tag{9.50}$$

Table 9.5
Structure of the Merged IMF-World Bank Model

Variables	Definition
Targets	
ΔR	Change in official foreign reserves
ΔP_D	Change in domestic prices
Δy	Change in real output
Endogenous	
ΔY	Change in nominal output
ΔL^p	Change in private sector credit
ΔM	Change in nominal money balances
ΔP	Change in the overall price index
ΔJ	Change in imports
$G - T$	Fiscal deficit
Exogenous	
X	Exports
$\Delta F = \Delta F^p + \Delta F^g$	Change in net capital flows
Policy instruments	
ΔD^g	Change in domestic credit to government
ΔE	Change in the nominal exchange rate
G or T	Government spending or taxes
Predetermined	
y_{-1}	Real output in previous period
P_{-1}	Price level in previous period
Parameters	
ν	Income velocity of money
δ	Share of domestic goods in consumer prices
α	Marginal propensity to import
θ	Response of private sector credit to output
η	Response of imports to relative prices

Source: Adapted from Khan et al. (1990, p. 172).

Second, as in the extended financial programming model, substituting Equations (9.39), (9.40), (9.41) and (9.44) in (9.45) yields

$$\Delta R + \tau \Delta Y = -\Delta L^g.$$

Using Equation (9.37) to eliminate ΔY, and (9.38) to eliminate ΔP yields, with $P_{-1} = 1$,

$$\Delta R + \tau(y_{-1}\delta\Delta P_D + \Delta y) = \Phi, \qquad (9.51)$$

where

$$\Phi = \tau y_{-1}(1 - \delta)\Delta E - \Delta L^g.$$

Third, substituting Equation (9.43) in the balance-of-payments Equation (9.42) implies

$$\Delta R = X - J_{-1} - (Q_{J-1} - \eta E_{-1})\Delta E - E_{-1}(\alpha \Delta y + \eta \Delta P_D) + \Delta F. \quad (9.52)$$

Equations (9.50), (9.51), and (9.52) represent the condensed form of the model. Equation (9.50) can be rewritten as

$$\Delta P_D = \chi_{10} + \chi_{11}\Delta y, \quad (9.53)$$

with

$$\chi_{10} = \frac{-\kappa}{\delta \tau y_{-1}} - (1 - \delta)\delta^{-1}\Delta E, \quad \chi_{11} = \frac{\sigma^{-1} - \tau}{\delta \tau y_{-1}},$$

which can be substituted in (9.51) to give

$$\Delta R = (\Phi + \tau y_{-1}\delta \chi_{10}) - \chi_{21}\Delta y, \quad (9.54)$$

and in (9.52) to give

$$\Delta R = \chi_{30} - \chi_{31}\Delta y, \quad (9.55)$$

where

$$\chi_{21} = \tau(y_{-1}\delta \chi_{11} + 1),$$

$$\chi_{30} = X - J_{-1} - (Q_{J-1} - \eta E_{-1})\Delta E - E_{-1}\eta \chi_{10} + \Delta F,$$

$$\chi_{31} = E_{-1}(\alpha + \eta \chi_{11}).$$

Equations (9.53), (9.54), and (9.55) can be solved, as before, in two different modes.

- In the **positive mode**, the system is *recursive*: Equations (9.54) and (9.55) jointly determine Δy and ΔR, for given values of the policy instruments and the exogenous variables. Given the solution value for Δy, Equation (9.53) determines ΔP_D, again for given values of the policy instruments and the exogenous variables.

- In the **programming mode**, Δy, ΔR, and ΔP_D are policy targets (denoted $\Delta \tilde{y}$, $\Delta \tilde{R}$, and $\Delta \tilde{P}_D$) and the instruments are T or G, ΔE, and ΔL^g. All four possible instruments appear directly in all three equations—T and G, for instance, through κ, as shown in Equation (9.49), and thus χ_{10}. The system is thus *fully simultaneous*: values of three policy instruments (ΔE, ΔL^g and, say, G) must be solved at the same time from Equations (9.53)-(9.55) for given targets $\Delta \tilde{y}$, $\Delta \tilde{R}$, and $\Delta \tilde{P}_D$ and given values of X, ΔF, T and the predetermined variables.

Given the solution values for the instruments G and ΔL^g and for given values of T and ΔF^g, Equation (9.46) is always satisfied. The target values for changes in real output and the domestic price level—and thus, from Equation (9.38), the target value for the *overall* price level—generate from Equation (9.37) a programmed value for nominal output and thus private sector credit, ΔL^p, through Equation (9.40).

The solution of the merged model is illustrated in Figure 9.5. In the panel on the right-hand side, two curves are shown in the Δy-ΔR space. Curve MM is derived from Equation (9.54) and its slope is given by

$$\left.\frac{\Delta y}{\Delta R}\right|_{MM} = -\chi_{21}^{-1} < 0.$$

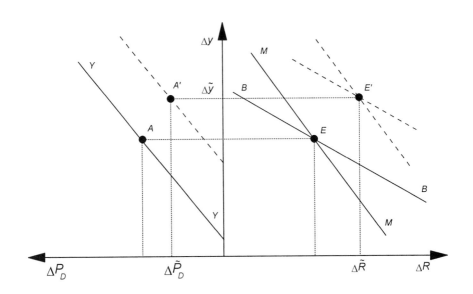

Figure 9.5. The Merged IMF-World Bank Model.

The second curve is denoted BB and depicts the combinations of Δy and ΔR that satisfy Equation (9.55); its slope is assumed to be less than that of MM and is given by

$$\left.\frac{\Delta y}{\Delta R}\right|_{BB} = -\chi_{31}^{-1} < 0, \quad |\chi_{31}| > |\chi_{21}|.$$

In the panel on the left-hand side, the curve YY depicts the combinations of Δy and ΔP_D that satisfy Equation (9.53). Its slope is given by

$$\left.\frac{\Delta y}{\Delta P_D}\right|_{YY} = \chi_{11}^{-1} > 0.$$

In the **positive mode** (that is, for given values of the exogenous variables and the policy instruments), the intersection of MM and BB (at point E)

yields the solution values for Δy and ΔR; the corresponding equilibrium value for ΔP_D is found at the intersection of the horizontal line originating from E and curve YY.

Suppose, for instance, that the policymaker has three objectives, to increase output, lower inflation, and increase official reserves by moving from the initial position at E to a point such as E' in the panel on the right-hand side of Figure 9.5 and point A' in the panel on the left-hand side. This outcome can be achieved through a combination of three policy actions: a *reduction* in domestic credit to the government, ΔL^g; a *depreciation* of the nominal exchange rate, ΔE; and a *reduction* in government spending, G. In general, as can be inferred from Equations (9.53)-(9.55), a change in any of these instruments shifts all three curves, MM, BB, and YY; but as shown in Figure 9.5, all three curves must eventually shift to the right for all three objectives to be satisfied and this can only be achieved by using *simultaneously* all three policy instruments. This result illustrates once again the **Meade-Tinbergen principle**.

9.5.2   The RMSM-X Framework

The RMSM-X model is the expanded version of the RMSM model previously used by the World Bank for its macroeconomic projections (see World Bank (1997b)). Its conceptual basis is the merged IMF-World Bank model described earlier, which again essentially adds to the RMSM model a price sector, a monetary sector, and government accounts, along the lines of the financial programming approach.

In practice, RMSM-X models are fairly detailed; they often consist of four economic sectors: the public sector, the private sector, the consolidated banking system, and the external sector, although some models disaggregate further the public sector (into government and public enterprises) and the banking system (into commercial banks and the central bank). A budget constraint is associated with each sector. These constraints are represented within the framework of a **consistency accounting matrix,** similar to the one developed in Chapter 8. National accounts are derived via aggregation of the sectoral budget constraints and serve to close the RMSM-X model. On the financial side, standard versions of the model include as before two types of assets, money and foreign assets, but some versions (particularly for middle-income countries) also include domestic bonds—requiring therefore explicit assumptions regarding interest rate formation.

The specification of the money demand function follows in most cases the Polak model, in which (nominal) money demand is linked to (nominal) income via the assumption of a constant income velocity of money. In models where the structure of the banking system is disaggregated, the money supply (which represents the liabilities of the entire banking system) is not simply the sum of central bank credit and official reserves but rather is obtained as the product of the *monetary base* (which represents the total liabilities of the central bank) and a (constant) *money multiplier.*

The RMSM-X framework, just like the RMSM model, also includes a central relationship between ICOR (which may or may not vary over time), investment, and the growth rate of output. Relative prices are introduced by assuming that domestic and foreign goods are imperfect substitutes, so that substitution effects can be analyzed on the demand side. Imports are often divided into several categories (for instance, food, other final consumption goods, intermediate goods, and capital goods) and the demand for each category of imports is specified as a function of the real exchange rate and either real GDP or, in the case of imports of capital goods, gross domestic investment. Imports of food are also sometimes made a direct function of private consumption. As was also the case in the RMSM approach, consumption is generally assumed to depend only on disposable income—thereby excluding consumption-smoothing effects.

Within the RMSM-X framework, several **model closures** can be specified, with each yielding an alternative solution.

- In the **public sector closure**, values for all variables except public sector expenditure and domestic borrowing are specified; the latter two variables are then determined by the model.

- In the **private sector closure**, values for government expenditure and revenue are specified, and the model estimates private sector variables.

In both of these approaches, likely disbursements from external donors provide an estimate of external financing. The *needed* amount of external borrowing is determined separately, through the balance-of-payments identity. If there is a gap between what is expected to be available and what is required to equilibrate external accounts, a marginal economic agent is assumed to provide it. Under a public sector closure for instance, the marginal borrower is the central government. The marginal foreign creditor in both the private and public sector closures can also be chosen, although in general it is assumed to be foreign commercial banks.

- In the **policy closure**, the values of macroeconomic policy variables as well as the expected behavior of private sector agents are specified so that the model can generate time paths of nominal and real GDP and some key variables, such as inflation. All external financing is identified in advance and imports are adjusted (positively or negatively) in order to equilibrate the balance of payments. Hence, this type of closure is also called the *availability mode*.

The RMSM-X model is most often operated in the **programming mode**; given a set of macroeconomic objectives, it can be solved for a mix of fiscal, monetary and exchange rate policies that are consistent with the targeted values. The solution sequence is as follows:

- *Step 1.* Set targets for the inflation rate, potential GDP growth rate (evaluated at full employment), real exchange rate, real interest rate, and international reserves (specified in months of imports).

- *Step 2*. Calculate investment requirements, given estimates of ICOR and the actual growth rate of output, the latter being determined by adjusting the potential growth rate on the basis of the projected rate of capacity utilization;

- *Step 3*. Calculate the demand-side relationships based on the projections of the exogenous variables.

- *Step 4*. Estimate the initial supply of foreign borrowing on the basis of likely disbursements of external agencies. Calculate the foreign reserve requirements of the central bank for an exogenously given target of imports. Given the demand for foreign borrowing as well as the initial supply, determine the amount of additional foreign borrowing needed.

- *Step 5*. Determine the growth rates of the monetary base and the broad money supply, given the policy targets for inflation and the output growth rate and estimates of velocity and the money multiplier. Estimate residually the amount of domestic credit to be supplied by the central bank or the banking system, given the reserve accumulation target.

- *Step 6*. Close the model by determining the following residuals in the relevant markets: consumption of goods and services, that is, public (private) consumption in the public (private) sector closure; borrowing from the foreign external sector; and credit allocated by the banking system (or, in more specific cases, central bank credit to the nonfinancial public enterprises).

Although the RMSM-X framework is a significant step toward an integrated framework for analyzing the feasibility and sustainability of stabilization and growth-oriented policies, it retains the limitations of the two models that underlie it. The financial programming framework of the IMF remains rudimentary; its static nature makes it particularly problematic for short-term projections, given the importance of lags (see the discussion below).[17] It does not incorporate many important features of modern-day developing countries, particularly on the financial side: bond financing of fiscal deficits and its effects on domestic interest rates is often ignored, and so is the endogeneity of private capital flows. The short-run link between production and bank credit (a key feature of many developing countries, as emphasized in Chapter 8) is often not taken into account—thereby obviating a critical channel through which monetary policy can affect the real economy. The supply-side of the RMSM-X also reflects the limitations of the basic RMSM model. It does not account for the complementarity between public investment (in infrastructure, most notably) and private investment, as discussed in Chapter 1. Most importantly, the fixed-coefficient production function (the ICOR relationship) remains subject to a

---

[17] There is an extensive literature analyzing the outcomes (as opposed to the analytical foundations) of IMF stabilization programs. See Conway (1994), Doroodian (1993), and especially Killick (1995).

number of analytical and practical difficulties. In a study on 146 countries over the period 1950-92, Easterly (1999) found that the assumed *linear* relationship between growth and investment is significantly rejected by the data. In addition, the ICOR specification rules out *substitutability* between capital and labor and therefore is unable to account for observed fluctuations in real wages. Relative prices (and the real exchange rate) influence the allocation of resources only through the demand side, not the supply side. Finally, the model provides no role to expectations (and thus the degree of policy credibility, as discussed in Chapter 5) and no explicit role for the labor market. It is thus incapable of explaining fluctuations in unemployment.

9.6   Three-Gap Models

The two-gap approach discussed earlier in the context of the RMSM model was extended to a three-gap framework by Bacha (1990) to account for the possibility of a third constraint, the **fiscal gap**.[18] In contrast to the *financing needs approach* described earlier, Bacha's model links foreign exchange availability directly to the rate of growth of productive capacity and only indirectly to the actual level of real output.

The first equation of the model is an **ICOR relationship** similar to Equation (9.22), which is repeated here for convenience:

$$I = \Delta y/\sigma, \quad \sigma > 0. \tag{9.56}$$

In addition, total investment is now assumed to require *imported capital goods*, in quantity J_K:

$$J_K = \delta I, \quad 0 < \delta < 1. \tag{9.57}$$

Let X be total exports of goods and nonfactor services, J total imports of goods and nonfactor services, and let X_N be the level of exports net of other (noncapital) imports, that is,

$$X_N = X - (J - J_K).$$

Define ΔF_N as net capital inflows, ΔF, minus changes in foreign exchange reserves (previously denoted ΔR), and let O_S be net factor services to the rest of the world (namely, external debt service and other transfers). The standard balance-of-payments identity, given by

$$\Delta R = (X - J) - O_S + \Delta F, \tag{9.58}$$

can thus be written as

$$\Delta F_N - O_S + (X_N - J_K) = 0.$$

This equation yields, together with Equation (9.57):

$$I = (X_N + H)/\delta. \tag{9.59}$$

---

[18] A useful survey of gap models is provided by Taylor (1994).

where $H = \Delta F_N - O_S$.

Suppose that other (noncapital) imports are invariant to the level of domestic income, and that X_N is subject to an upper bound $\tilde{X}_N$, determined by external demand. Equation (9.59) implies therefore a *foreign exchange constraint* on investment, given by

$$I \leq (\tilde{X}_N + H)/\delta. \tag{9.60}$$

Equations (9.56) and (9.60) imply therefore a constraint on capacity growth as well.

To derive the second gap, consider now the basic national income accounting identity, as derived in Chapter 8:

$$I = (y - C^p - G) + (J - X),$$

where C^p denotes private expenditure and G current spending of the government. Using Equation (9.58), this equation can be rewritten as

$$I = (y - C^p - G) + H. \tag{9.61}$$

Defining private saving as $S^p = y - T - C$, where T denotes government net tax revenue, Equation (9.61) becomes

$$I = S^p + (T - G) + H,$$

which simply decomposes the financing of investment into domestic private and public sector saving, and foreign saving (see Chapter 8).

Suppose, for simplicity, that private consumption is exogenous.[19] Because, as noted earlier, y is bounded from above by full-capacity output, S^p (being an increasing function of output) is also bounded from above by private saving at full capacity output, $\tilde{S}^p = \tilde{y} - C^p$. Thus, investment is subject to a **saving constraint**, given by

$$I \leq \tilde{S}^p + (T - G) + H. \tag{9.62}$$

Suppose now that money is the only asset available as a store of value to private agents; all foreign capital inflows serve to finance the government's budget deficit. The private sector's budget constraint can thus be written as

$$S^p - I^p = \Delta M/P, \tag{9.63}$$

where I^p denotes private investment, M the nominal stock of base money, and P the price level. Assuming constant real money balances, $\Delta M/P$ measures both seigniorage and the inflation tax (see Chapter 3). Revenue from this tax is written as a function of the inflation rate, $\pi \equiv \Delta P/P$, and the **propensity to hoard**, θ, which can be defined as the proportion of any increase in income allocated to the accumulation of cash balances:

$$\Delta M/P = h(\pi, \theta), \quad \theta > 0, \ h_\theta > 0. \tag{9.64}$$

---

[19] It is straightforward to extend the analysis to consider the case where consumption is a linear function of disposable income.

Because, as indicated earlier, all foreign capital flows accrue to the government, the budget constraint of the consolidated public sector can be written as

$$I^g = h(\pi, \theta) + (T - G) + H, \tag{9.65}$$

where I^g is public investment. Total investment is thus

$$I = I^p + I^g. \tag{9.66}$$

Suppose that private and public investment are *complements*, so that private investment is bounded from above by the level of public investment:

$$I^p \leq \phi I^g, \tag{9.67}$$

where ϕ is the ratio of private to public capital in the composite capital stock. As discussed in Chapter 1, this assumption is particularly relevant empirically in cases where public sector investment is mostly on infrastructure.

From Equations (9.65) to (9.67), the **fiscal constraint** on total investment is thus given by

$$I \leq (1 + \phi)[h(\pi, \theta) + (T - G) + H]. \tag{9.68}$$

Equations (9.56), (9.60), (9.62), and (9.68) determine simultaneously the level of output, the inflation rate, the current account, and the rate of growth of productive capacity. To illustrate the mechanisms at play, a useful first step is to analyze the effects of a change in the level of foreign financing, H, in the presence of the foreign exchange and saving constraints.

Figure 9.6 plots aggregate investment, I, against H. The foreign exchange and saving constraints, Equations (9.60) and (9.62), are plotted as curves FF and SS, respectively. The slope of SS is unity, whereas the slope of FF is $1/\delta$. The latter is greater than unity, because δ is a fraction.[20] The hatched areas beneath the curves represent the feasible regions for I, that is, the values of I that satisfy the inequalities in (9.60) and (9.62). Three cases can be considered.

- If net foreign inflows H are equal to H^*, both constraints are binding and investment is equal to I^*.

- If H is less than H^*, only the foreign exchange constraint binds. Investment (and therefore capacity growth) is determined by foreign exchange availability. Because investment will therefore be less than the level that would satisfy Equation (9.62) as an equality, and because the other components of aggregate demand are fixed, the economy will suffer from *excess capacity* and actual output will be given by

$$y = C^p + G + (1 - \delta)I^c + \tilde{X}_N, \tag{9.69}$$

where I^c is the actual, constrained level of investment.

<hr>

[20] The relative positions of the two curves in the figure assumes that $\tilde{X}_N/\delta < \tilde{S}^p + (T - G)$.

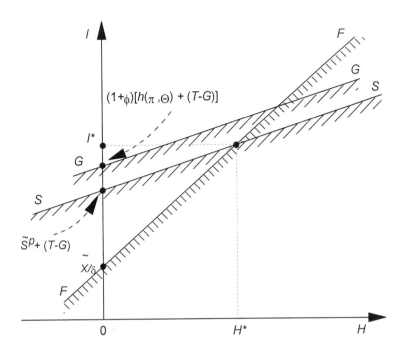

Figure 9.6. The Three-Gap Model.
Source: Adapted from Bacha (1990, p. 291).

- If H *exceeds* H^*, the economy will be constrained by domestic saving. Investment will now be determined along SS, and output will be at full capacity, $\tilde{y}$. The actual value of adjusted exports, X_N, will thus be less than their maximum value $\tilde{X}_N$, given by foreign demand; domestic demand, in a sense, "squeezes" exports to

$$X_N = \tilde{y} - C^p - G + (1 - \delta)I^c, \tag{9.70}$$

where I^c denotes the saving-constrained level of investment.

The foregoing discussion is essentially similar to the previous discussion of the two-gap mode of the RMSM model. Graphically, adding the fiscal gap leads to the following modifications to Figure 9.6.

- Inequality (9.68) is represented by an area bounded from above by a curve called GG, with slope $1+\phi$ and vertical intercept $(1+\phi)[h(\pi, \theta)+(T-G)]$. The quantity $1+\phi$ may be greater or less than $1/\delta$, so GG may be steeper or flatter than FF; the case illustrated in the figure assumes that $1/\delta > 1+\phi$ and GG is steeper than FF.

- Curves GG and SS have the same slope. However, their relative heights depend on the values of π and ϕ. As long as I^p is positive, the private sector budget constraint, Equation (9.63), implies that

$$\tilde{S}^p > h(\pi, \theta).$$

- However, the difference between $\tilde{S}^p$ and $h(\pi, \theta)$ decreases with π. Thus, a larger value of π raises the height of GG relative to SS. A larger value of ϕ has a similar effect.

The fiscal constraint can be incorporated in the foregoing analysis in a variety of ways. Two possibilities are the following:

- Treat inflation as an *endogenous* variable, whose role is to ensure that Equation (9.68) holds as an equality. In this simple case, the fiscal constraint serves only to determine the rate of inflation. Given the value of I, Equations (9.66) and (9.67)—the latter holding as an equality—would determine the levels of I^p and I^g, and, given the latter, Equation (9.68) holding as an equality would determine π.[21]

- Treat inflation as an *exogenous* policy variable, so that GG serves as an independent constraint.

In this mode, two cases must be considered. If the fiscal constraint *does not bind*, then ϕ becomes the slack variable. Given I and I^g, private investment I^p is then determined residually, and the constrained value of ϕ implied by I^p and I^g, ϕ_c, may be smaller than the initial value of ϕ. If the fiscal constraint *does bind*, then a rise in H will increase capacity growth, because increased foreign financing will result in higher public investment, which, in turn, will induce more private investment outlays. The actual level of output will rise, through a positive demand effect stemming from higher levels of both private and public investment—bringing the economy closer to full capacity utilization, at a lower level of net exports.

An important lesson of the three-gap model is that a country may face a fiscal constraint independently of its overall saving constraint. However, the model remains subject to a number of limitations. Some of the main variables are only partially endogenized; inflation, for instance, depends on a host of factors in addition to public finance considerations (see Chapter 5). The government budget constraint does not account for the possibility of bond financing—an option, again, that has become available to a number of governments in middle-income developing countries. It also does not account for movements in relative prices.

---

[21] Graphically, the introduction of the fiscal constraint would entail a shift in the GG curve (brought about by changes in π) to intersect whichever of the two other curves happens to be binding at a point directly above the actual value of $(\Delta F - H)$. An increase in $(\Delta F - H)$ would in this case not only serve to increase the rate of capacity growth by raising I (as in the two-gap approach), but would also reduce inflation by allowing external financing of the fiscal deficit and reducing reliance on seigniorage.

9.7   The 1-2-3 Model

The 1-2-3 model, developed at the World Bank by Devarajan et al. (1997), captures well the main features of more complex, highly-disaggregated **computable general equilibrium (CGE) models**. CGE models are highly disaggregated models (on both the demand and the supply side) designed to study issues such as the allocational and distributional effects of domestic and external shocks (see Bandara, 1991). On the demand side, for instance, they typically consider several types of households, depending on their ownership of production factors. Relative price movements play a central role in CGE models, although price adjustment is not always Walrasian in nature; that is, prices do not always adjust to clear markets instantaneously. Price rigidities are, in fact, common in many CGE models.

Although mostly microeconomic in nature, CGE models also have a macroeconomic dimension due to the identity that relates aggregate saving and investment. The mechanism that ensures that this identity holds *ex post* is defined as a **closure rule**. As discussed by Dewatripont and Michel (1987), three types of closure rules are commonly used in the CGE literature:[22]

- *classical rule*, whereby investment is endogenous and determined by aggregate saving.

- *Keynesian rule*, whereby investment is exogenous and real wages are taken to adjust to changes in aggregate income—thereby permitting saving to equal investment. The labor market, however, may not clear and unemployment can emerge.

- *Johansen rule*, whereby endogenous public or private consumption equates total saving to exogenous investment.

The specification of the saving-investment balance is also an important issue in the 1-2-3 model. The first part of this section presents the simplest version of the model (with no saving and no investment), and the second uses it to analyze the effects of a terms-of-trade shock. The last part extends the model to account for government activities and investment.

9.7.1   The Minimal Setup

Consider a small open economy in which two representative agents operate: a producer (or firm) and a household. The economy produces two goods: a **home good** which is used only for final domestic consumption, and an **exportable good**, the price of which is fixed on world markets. In addition, the household consumes an **imported good** which is not produced domestically.[23] The capi-

---

[22]In practice, the sensitivity of numerical results to the particular closure rule chosen is not always clear and may vary depending on the issue under consideration.

[23]As noted in the previous chapter, a three-good structure (rather than a dependent-economy framework) is necessary to analyze the effects of changes in the terms of trade (as discussed later) and changes in tariffs on imports. Adding domestic production of importables is straightforward.

tal stock is fixed within the time frame of the analysis. Given that the economy is assumed small, the demand for domestically produced exportables is perfectly elastic at an exogenous foreign currency price, so that output of these goods is supply determined. For simplicity, it will be assumed that output of exportable goods is entirely sold abroad. For the moment, it is also assumed that the economy has no access to capital markets; external equilibrium requires therefore equality between exports and imports or a zero trade balance.

The domestic **production possibility frontier** (PPF), which defines the maximum achievable combinations of exportables and nontradables that the economy can supply, is given by

$$Y = F(Y_X, Y_N^s; \theta), \qquad (9.71)$$

where Y denotes aggregate production, Y_X output of exportables, Y_N output of home goods, and θ a technological parameter. The quantity Y (which is the economy's net output, because no intermediate inputs are used in the production process) will be assumed to be fixed—an assumption that is tantamount to assuming full employment of all production factors. In the standard, practical implementation of the 1-2-3 model—as in many CGE models—the functional form $F(\cdot)$ is taken to be of the **constant elasticity of transformation** (CET) type:

$$Y = [\delta Y_X^\mu + (1 - \delta) Y_N^\mu]^{1/\mu}, \quad 0 < \delta < 1, \ 1 < \mu < +\infty,$$

with the parameter θ measuring the **elasticity of transformation**, given by

$$\theta = \frac{1}{\mu - 1}.$$

The *efficient ratio* of output of exportables to nontradables can then be written as a function of their relative prices:

$$Y_X / Y_N^s = h^1(P_X, P_N), \qquad (9.72)$$

where P_N is the (domestic) price of the home good and P_X the domestic price of exportables, given by the product of the nominal exchange rate, E, and the world (foreign-currency) price of the exportable good, P_X^*:

$$P_X = E P_X^*. \qquad (9.73)$$

The *price of aggregate output, P_Y*, is defined as a function of both P_X and P_N as[24]

$$P_Y = g^1(P_X, P_N). \qquad (9.74)$$

The identity relating aggregate domestic output in nominal terms to output of exportables and nontradables is thus

$$P_Y Y \equiv P_X Y_X^s + P_N Y_N^s. \qquad (9.75)$$

---

[24]Technically, the price function g^1 in Eq. (9.74) is the *cost function* dual to the firm's first-order condition for profit maximization, from which Eq. (9.72) is derived. See, for instance, Varian (1992, Chapters 5 and 6).

The household consumes both domestic and imported goods. These goods are imperfect substitutes; their combination describes a **composite good**, Q, defined by

$$Q^s = q(Y_N^d, J; \sigma), \tag{9.76}$$

where σ is a technological parameter. In numerical applications of the 1-2-3 model—again, as in many CGE models—the functional form $q(\cdot)$ is taken to be of the **constant elasticity of substitution** (CES) variety:

$$Q^s = [\phi Y_N^\rho + (1 - \phi)J^\rho]^{1/\rho}, \quad 0 < \phi < 1, \ -\infty < \rho < 1,$$

with the parameter σ measuring the **elasticity of substitution**, given by

$$\sigma = \frac{1}{1 - \rho}.$$

Assuming that utility is linear in Q, and that the household maximizes its utility yields the *desired ratio* of home goods and imported goods as a function of relative prices:

$$J/Y_N^d = h^2(P_J, P_N), \tag{9.77}$$

where P_J is the domestic price of imported goods, given by the product of the nominal exchange rate, E, and the world (foreign-currency) price of these goods, P_J^*:

$$P_J = E P_J^*. \tag{9.78}$$

The price of the composite good is given by[25]

$$P_Q = g^2(P_J, P_N). \tag{9.79}$$

The identity relating aggregate supply of the composite good to imports and demand for nontradables is thus

$$P_Q Q^s \equiv P_J J + P_N Y_N^d. \tag{9.80}$$

The household's *total income* in nominal terms, V, is given by

$$V = P_Y Y. \tag{9.81}$$

Assuming that all income is spent on the composite good yields the household's demand for this good as

$$Q^d = V/P_Q. \tag{9.82}$$

This equation can be written in the form of an identity:

$$V \equiv P_Q Q^d, \tag{9.83}$$

---

[25] Again, the price index defined by Eq. (9.79) can be interpreted as the *cost function* dual to the first-order condition for utility maximization, from which Eq. (9.78) is derived.

which simply indicates that total purchases of composite goods by the household must be equal (in fact, identical) to the value of expenditure on these goods.

In the above system, Equations (9.71) and (9.76) are **linearly homogeneous** (that is, homogeneous of degree one): doubling, for instance, the quantities of exportables and nontradables produced would double aggregate output. The price equations (9.74) and (9.79) are also linearly homogeneous. By contrast, Equations (9.72), (9.77), and (9.82) are **homogeneous of degree zero** in all prices (including the exchange rate). Thus only *relative prices* affect the demand for composite goods, the exportables-to-nontradables output ratio, and the home goods-and-imports expenditure ratio.

To close the model requires specifying the *equilibrium conditions* between supply and demand.

- The first condition is the equality between *demand and supply of nontradables*:

$$Y_N^s = Y_N^d. \tag{9.84}$$

- The second condition requires equality between *demand and supply of composite goods*:

$$Q^s = Q^d. \tag{9.85}$$

- Finally, because the economy cannot borrow on world capital markets, the third condition requires that *trade be balanced*, that is,

$$P_J^* J - P_X^* Y_X = 0. \tag{9.86}$$

These three constraints, however, are *not independent*, as implied by **Walras' Law**. The reason is that the model must satisfy three identities: Equations (9.75), (9.80), and (9.83). Multiplying both sides of Equation (9.84) by P_N, both sides of (9.85) by P_Q, and both sides of (9.86) by E yields, adding all three equilibrium conditions,

$$P_N(Y_N^s - Y_N^d) + P_Q(Q^s - Q^d) + P_J J - P_X Y_X = 0,$$

which shows that, as long as, say, the equilibrium conditions (9.84) and (9.85) are satisfied, condition (9.86) will also be satisfied.

The model is summarized in Table 9.6. As indicated earlier, only relative prices affect demand for composite goods and the ratios Y_X/Y_N^s and J/Y_N^d. A **numéraire price** (that is, a *unit of account*) must thus be defined. A conventional choice is to assume that it is the price of foreign exchange, $E = 1$. It is also convenient to normalize world prices to unity, so that $P_X^* = P_J^* = 1$.

The equilibrium of the model is illustrated in Figure 9.7. The PPF, as given by Equation (9.71), is shown in the Southeast quadrant. For any given price ratio P_N/P_X, the point of tangency with the transformation frontier determines the allocation of total resources between production of exportables and production of nontradables (point A). The balance of trade constraint, which requires equality between exports and imports $(J - Y_X = 0)$ is shown as the 45-degree line in the Northeast quadrant. Given the level of output of exportables determined at point A, the level of imports is determined at point B. The **consumption possibility frontier** (CPF), which shows the combinations of the domestic and imported goods that the household can purchase (given the production technology as reflected in the PPF and the foreign exchange constraint), is depicted in the Northwest quadrant. Because foreign trade is balanced, the CPF is simply the mirror image of the PPF. The composite quantity Q defined by Equation (9.76) can be called **absorption**; it is also shown in the Northwest quadrant. Maximizing the level of absorption requires tangency between an **isoabsorption curve** and the CPF; the tangency point, C, determines the optimal allocation of imports and nontradables demanded by the household, given the price ratio P_N/P_J.

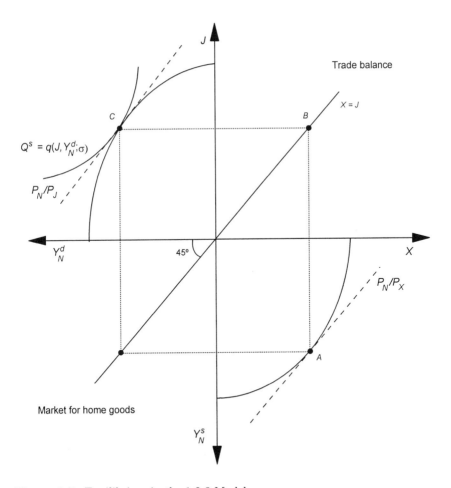

Figure 9.7. Equilibrium in the 1-2-3 Model.
Source: Adapted from Devarajan et al. (1997, p. 164).

The case illustrated in Figure 9.7 corresponds to the case in which the **elasticity of substitution** between imports and home goods in the composite good aggregation function, σ, is positive and less than infinite ($0 < \sigma < \infty$). With $\sigma \to 0$, the indifference curves in the Northwest quadrant would be L-shaped; whereas with $\sigma \to \infty$, the indifference curves would be *almost flat*. Distinguishing the three cases is important in assessing the general equilibrium effects of policy and exogenous shocks.

Table 9.6
The "Minimal" 1-2-3 Model

Equation	Definition
	Flows
$Y = F(Y_X, Y_N^s; \theta)$	Production possibility frontier
$Y_X/Y_N^s = h^1(P_X, P_N)$,	Allocation of production resources
$Q^s = q(Y_N^d, J; \sigma)$	Composite good
$J/Y_N^d = h^2(P_J, P_N)$	Allocation of demand
	between home and imported goods
	Prices
$P_X = EP_X^*$	Domestic price of exports
$P_Y = g^1(P_X, P_N)$	Output deflator
$P_J = EP_J^*$	Domestic price of imports
$P_Q = g^2(P_J, P_N)$	Cost-of-living index
	Equilibrium conditions
$Y_N^s = Y_N^d$	Market for home goods
$Q^s = Q^d$	Supply and demand of composite good
$P_J^* J - P_X^* X = 0$	Balanced trade
	Identities
$P_Y Y \equiv P_X X + P_N Y_N^s$	Value of output of domestic goods
$P_Q Q^s \equiv P_Z Z + P_N Y_N^d$	Value of composite goods
$V \equiv P_Q Q^d$	Sales and purchases of composite goods

Source: Adapted from Devarajan et al. (1997, p. 159).

9.7.2   An Adverse Terms-of-Trade Shock

To illustrate the functioning of the simple version of the 1-2-3 model, suppose that there is an adverse terms-of-trade shock, captured by an increase in the world price of the imported good, P_J^*. The results are illustrated in Figure 9.8, in the general case in which $0 < \sigma < \infty$. At the initial level of P_N/P_X, output of exportables does not change; however, the increase in P_J^* implies that the country must *reduce* the quantity of goods imported. Graphically, the line capturing the balanced trade constraint in the Northeast panel rotates *clockwise*, that is, its slope becomes less steep. At the same time, the fall in the relative price of home goods, P_N/P_J, leads to an inward rotation of the CPF, as shown in the Northwest quadrant. The new equilibrium consumption point, B', is obtained at a lower level of utility. Consumption of both home and imported goods falls. The equality between demand and supply of home goods (as shown in the Southwest quadrant) implies that the equilibrium allocation of resources on the supply side is now at A'. Because the value of imports rises (the increase in import prices is proportionally higher than the fall in the volume of imports), exports must increase to maintain trade balance equilibrium. The increase in output of exportables is brought about through an increase in the relative price of these goods, which shifts incentives away from the production of nontradables. Thus, the *real exchange rate* (defined either as P_X/P_N or as a weighted average of P_X and P_J over P_N) must *depreciate* in the case illustrated in Figure 9.8.

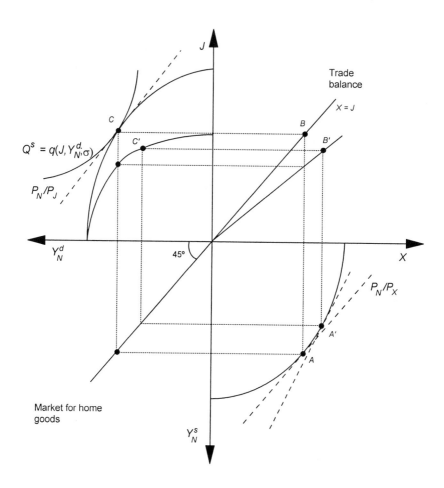

Figure 9.8. An Adverse Terms-of-Trade Shock in the 1-2-3 Model.
Source: Adapted from Devarajan et al. (1997, p. 167).

In general, however, whether the real exchange rate depreciates or not in response to an adverse shock in the terms of trade depends crucially on the value of the elasticity of substitution between imports and home goods, σ.[26]

- If $\sigma \to 0$, so that (as indicated earlier) the isoabsorption curves are L-shaped, both production and consumption of home goods will fall, and

---

[26] A formal algebraic analysis of the relationship between the response of the economy to a terms-of-trade shock and the elasticity of substitution in the 1-2-3 model is provided by Devarajan, Lewis, and Robinson (1993).

the real exchange rate will *depreciate*, as in Figure 9.8.

- If $\sigma \to \infty$, the isoabsorption curves are flat; the tangency point between one of these curves and the new CPF will necessarily occur **to the left** of the initial equilibrium consumption point, C. This is because, as shown in Figure 9.8, the rotation flattens the CPF curve. The demand for home goods therefore increases; output of home goods rises and the real exchange rate *appreciates*.

The effect of the shock on the real exchange rate depends also on whether σ is less than, greater than, or equal to 1. The reason is that the increase in the price of imports generates two types of effects: an **income effect**, which captures the reduction in the household's real income, and a **substitution effect**, which results from the fact that home domestic goods have now become relatively cheaper. The resulting equilibrium will depend on which effect dominates.

- If $\sigma < 1$ (that is, there is relatively low substitutability between imports and home goods) the income effect dominates. The equilibrium response is a reduction in output of nontradables and an increase in output of exportables, which is brought about through a real depreciation.

- If $\sigma > 1$, substitutability between imports and home goods is relatively high; the substitution effect dominates. The equilibrium response is to reduce output of exportables (and therefore also imports) and increase output of nontradables. In that case, the real exchange rate appreciates.

- If $\sigma = 1$, there is no change in either the real exchange rate or the allocation of productive resources in the economy.

9.7.3   Investment, Saving, and the Government

The minimal version of the 1-2-3 model described earlier can be extended in various directions. Two of these extensions are now considered: the introduction of a government sector (with both taxes and expenditure) and investment.[27] The first extension is important to analyze the effect of fiscal policy measures on relative prices and resource allocation, whereas the second is important to integrate the saving-investment balance.

The PPF remains as defined earlier in Equation (9.71), with the allocation of resources given as in (9.72). The domestic price of exports and the output deflator are also given by Equations (9.73) and (9.74), respectively. The identity relating aggregate domestic output in nominal terms to output of exportables and nontradables is again given by Equation (9.75).

The composite good is defined as before by Equation (9.76), with the desired ratio of home goods and imports given as a function of relative prices [Equation

---

[27] Other extensions to the static 1-2-3 framework are discussed by Devarajan, Lewis, and Robinson (1990). A dynamic formulation of the model is presented by Devarajan and Go (1998).

(9.77)]. However, because the government is now assumed to impose a tariff on imported goods at the rate $0 < \iota_J < 1$, the domestic price of imported goods, P_J, is now determined by

$$P_J = (1 + \iota_J)EP_J^*. \tag{9.87}$$

Although the price of the composite good remains given by Equation (9.79), the *sales price* of the good (or the *cost-of-living index*) is now different from P_Q because the government levies a *sales tax*, at the rate $0 < \iota_S < 1$, on domestic sales. Thus

$$P_S = (1 + \iota_S)P_Q. \tag{9.88}$$

The accounting identity relating domestic sales and purchases of goods is now determined by, instead of Equation (9.80),

$$P_Q Q^s \equiv P_J J + P_S Y_N^d. \tag{9.89}$$

The household's *total income* in nominal terms, V, is now written as

$$V = P_Y Y + P_Q NT_g^h + E \cdot NT_f^h, \tag{9.90}$$

where NT_g^h are net transfers from the government, and NT_f^h net transfers from abroad, measured in foreign-currency terms. It is now assumed that only a fraction of the household's income is spent on the composite good, specifically,

$$P_S Q_h^d = (1 - s_h - \iota_V)V, \tag{9.91}$$

where s_h is the household's saving rate, and $0 < \iota_V < 1$ the (direct) tax rate on income. Note also that expenditure is now valued at the sales price, P_S. Assuming that the government consumes a quantity G of composite goods, and that investment requires a quantity I of composite goods, total demand for the composite good is now written as

$$Q^d = Q_h^d + I + G. \tag{9.92}$$

Consider now the government sector. Total government revenue, T, consists of both direct and indirect tax revenue and is given by

$$T = \iota_J EP_J^* J + \iota_S P_Q Q^d + \iota_V V. \tag{9.93}$$

Government spending consists of purchases of composite goods, $P_Q G$, and transfers to households, $P_Q NT_g^h$. Government saving, S^g, is thus given by the difference between revenue and expenditure:

$$S^g = T - P_Q G - P_Q NT_g^h. \tag{9.94}$$

Aggregate saving, S, is therefore given by

$$S = s_V V + S^g. \tag{9.95}$$

To close the model requires again specifying the market-clearing conditions. Equations (9.84) and (9.85)—with Q^d defined as in Equation (9.76) remain identical. Because of the existence of private transfers from abroad, the external balance condition, Equation (9.86), now takes the form

$$P_Z^* Z - P_X^* X - NT_f^h = 0. \tag{9.96}$$

There is an additional condition now, which is the *equality between investment and saving*:

$$P_S I = S. \tag{9.97}$$

It can be verified that the four equilibrium conditions, (9.84), (9.85), (9.96), and (9.97), are not independent, given the identities that the model satisfies—Equations (9.75), (9.89), and (9.92).

The extended model, assuming again that the nominal exchange rate is used as numéraire, is summarized in Table 9.7. The government, in this setup, possesses three tax instruments: the import tariff rate, ι_J, the (indirect) tax rate on domestic sales, ι_S, and the (direct) tax rate on income, ι_V. In the present setting aggregate output is fixed, and foreign saving is fixed. Thus, aggregate saving is given, and *investment adjusts to savings*. The closure rule is thus *classical* in nature, as noted earlier. The model possesses 19 endogenous variables. By **Walras' law**, as discussed earlier, one of the equations [for instance the savings-investment identity, Equation (9.97)] can be dropped from the system, as it is implied by the others.

Various experiments can be performed with the extended model: a terms-of-trade shock similar to the one considered earlier, or fiscal policy shocks, such as a reduction in tariffs compensated by an increase in the sales tax to maintain government budget balance. In the latter exercise, the implications of the analysis for the structure of the budget can be drawn—after properly taking into account general equilibrium effects.

Despite its simplicity, the 1-2-3 model (in both its minimal and extended forms) is an informative setup for analyzing a variety of policy issues of crucial importance to policymakers in developing countries. In particular, it is a useful device to understand and quantify the effects of changes in fiscal policy instruments (such as a domestic indirect taxes), trade policy instruments (such as a reduction in tariffs), as well as external shocks (as illustrated earlier), on relative prices and resource allocation in the medium term. However, because changes in *productive capacity* are not accounted for, the model cannot adequately address longer-term issues related, for instance, to the linkages between stabilization and growth.

Table 9.7

The 1-2-3 Model with a Government Sector

Equation	Definition
	Flows
$Y = F(Y_X, Y_N^s; \theta)$	Production possibility frontier
$Y_X/Y_N^s = h^1(P_X, P_N),$	Allocation of production resources
$Q^s = q(Y_N^d, J; \sigma)$	Composite good
$J/Y_N^d = h^2(P_J, P_N)$	Allocation of demand
	between home and imported goods
	Prices
$P_X = EP_X^*$	Domestic price of exports
$P_Y = g^1(P_X, P_N)$	Output deflator
$P_J = (1 + \iota_J)EP_J^*$	Domestic price of imports
$P_Q = g^2(P_Z, P_N)$	Price of the composite good
$P_S = (1 + \iota_S)P_Q$	Sales price of the composite good
	Equilibrium conditions
$Y_N^s = Y_N^d$	Market for home goods
$Q^s = Q^d$	Supply and demand of composite goods
$P_J^* J - P_X^* X - NT_f^h = 0$	Balanced trade
$P_S I = S$	Savings-investment balance
	Identities
$P_Y Y \equiv P_X X + P_N Y_N^s$	Value of output of domestic goods
$P_Q Q^s \equiv P_J J + P_S Y_N^d$	Value of composite goods

Source: Adapted from Devarajan et al. (1997, p. 172).

Another limitation of the 1-2-3 model is that it is built only around the real side. In recent years, much effort has gone into strengthening the macroeconomic dimension of CGE models. A good example is the **Maquette**, developed by Bourguignon, De Melo, and Suwa (1991), and described as a *micro-macro framework* that attempts to combine the long-run features of CGE models, which are essential for the analysis of the allocational and distributional effects of adjustment policies (such as trade and tax policies), and the short-run features of macroeconomic models—namely a detailed *financial side*. Specifically, the Maquette attempts to capture the short-run effects through which stabilization policies affect the distribution of income and wealth, and to link them with the effect of structural adjustment measures that alter relative prices. There are a number of methodological issues associated with the introduction of financial variables in CGE models, and some of these are not yet fully resolved.[28]

9.8 Lags and Behavioral Functions

As noted earlier, accounting for lags can be critical for establishing short-term projections. From a policy perspective, it is convenient to distinguish between

---

[28] See Robinson (1991) and Adam and Bevan (1998) for a discussion of some of these issues.

two types of lags:

- **Inside lags**, which refer to the legal and institutional delays involved in implementing a change in policy;

- **Outside lags**, which relate to the delay involved between implementation of a policy and its effects on the target variables.

Empirical studies suggest that structural policies often involve relatively long lags of both types relative to short-term macroeconomic policies, with outside lags being typically much longer. Among the latter group of policies, there are also significant differences; monetary policy is usually considered to encompass relatively short inside lags and relatively long outside lags. A change in *domestic credit*, for instance, may take a substantial amount of time to affect the ultimate target variables—aggregate demand, inflation, and the current account. Changes in the *nominal exchange rate* often have a rather rapid impact on prices (because, for instance, domestic prices are set as a markup over the cost of domestic and imported inputs) but they usually take time (up to 18 months) to affect trade flows and the trade balance. By contrast, *fiscal policies* are often characterized by relatively long inside lags and relatively short outside lags.

Accounting for lags in the adjustment process to policy and exogenous shocks is important in practice, particularly when projections are required at a relatively short horizon—say, on a quarterly basis.[29] Lags can generate complex dynamics; the way they are introduced in the model may thus have a significant effect on the formulation and validity of macroeconomic projections.

Unfortunately, such lags are often difficult to estimate with any degree of precision—thereby complicating policy responses and the timing of policy measures. Moreover, lags may be to some extent *endogenous*; they are often affected by private agents' expectations about the sustainability of the various policies. A policy that is perceived to be *highly credible* (that is, with a low probability of reversal) may exert its effect on the target variable relatively fast, compared with the average historical lag.

Another source of endogeneity in lags is the fact that the behavioral functions themselves may change over time. In particular, behavioral functions are often difficult to estimate in the context of a country undergoing a comprehensive reform program or large shifts in policy. Money demand functions, for instance, are notoriously difficult to estimate in an environment of financial liberalization. In such a context, the use of relatively sophisticated econometric techniques (such as the **error correction framework** described in the appendix to Chapter 2) may not be enough to detect stable relationships. This instability in behavioral parameters will make the timing of policy effects even more difficult to establish and may make the lag between changes in policy instruments and the economy's response more uncertain.

---

[29]Medium-term policy analysis using tools such as the 1-2-3 model is less sensitive to this issue.

9.9   Summary

- Analyzing macroeconomic fluctuations is useful to *specify applied macro-economic models*, to assess the *type of shocks* that have dominated fluctuations over a particular period of time, and to assess the likely effect (given the pattern of *leads* and *lags*) between changes in policy instruments and domestic output.

- A simple procedure is first to use the **Hodrick-Prescott (HP) filter** to extract the trend component of each series. The two main hypotheses underlying the HP decomposition are that the trend is *stochastic* but moves slowly over time, and that the *secular* and *cyclical components* are *independent*. Other filtering techniques can also be used for checking robustness.

- In the absence of a fully specified and estimated macroeconomic model, the McCarthy-Neary-Zanalda method provides a useful framework for assessing the effects of external shocks and policy responses.

- **Financial programming**, based on the **Polak model** and its extensions, remains at the core of macroeconomic policy exercises conducted by the International Monetary Fund. The extended model endogenizes prices but continues to take real output as given.

- The World Bank's RMSM model makes explicit the link between medium-term growth and its financing. It is a real sector model that takes prices as given and highlights the interplay between the domestic **saving constraint** and the **foreign exchange constraint**.

- The **merged IMF-World Bank** model endogenizes both real output and prices. It forms the analytical basis of the RMSM-X model, currently used by the World Bank for its macroeconomic projections. The model remains, however, subject to a number of limitations, related in particular to a rudimentary supply side, an inadequate financial structure, and mechanical behavioral rules.

- **Three-gap models** extend the two-gap approach of the RMSM model to include a third one, the **fiscal constraint**. However, they are also subject to limitations due, in particular, to the complete absence of relative price effects.

- The **1-2-3 model**, also developed at the World Bank, is a simple, static, computable general equilibrium model with two production sectors and three goods. It provides a useful and tractable framework for the analysis of the medium-term effects of external shocks and policies such as tariff and tax reforms on relative prices and the allocation of resources.

- Macroeconomic policies operate with lags that can be fairly long, although short-run policies are deemed to have a more rapid impact than, say, supply-side measures. Long policy lags may be partly related to private agents' expectations about the perceived sustainability of the policy measures—the higher the probability of policy reversal, the more delayed the response. Accounting for these lags in operational exercises is important but not always done.

Chapter 10

Growth, Poverty, and Income Distribution: Some Basic Facts

After a long period of relative neglect in mainstream economics, the study of economic growth has gone through a revival since the early 1980s. A key motivation for this renewed interest is the observation that average annual growth rates (calculated over several decades) vary substantially across countries. The conventional neoclassical theory, which attributes growth to (mostly exogenous) technological progress, has proved incapable of explaining in a satisfactory manner the wide disparities in the rates of per capita output growth across countries.

This chapter and the next three provide a thorough discussion of recent theories and evidence on the determinants of economic growth. The present chapter reviews some basic empirical facts and is organized as follows. Part 1 reviews the evidence on economic growth for both industrial and developing countries from 1820 to the early 1990s. Part 2 uses simple arithmetic to illustrate the dramatic effects that small differences in growth rates can have on standards of living. Part 3 summarizes some of the basic facts that appear to characterize the process of economic growth in developing countries. It discusses, in particular, the links between growth, poverty, and inequality, as well as the interactions between inflation, financial development, and economic growth.

10.1 A Long-Run Perspective

Tables 10.1 and 10.2 summarize the evidence on long-run growth compiled by Maddison (1995). Table 10.1 shows that per capita growth since 1820 has been the fastest in countries that were already the most prosperous in the early nineteenth century. Gross domestic product (GDP) per capita recorded a 13-fold increase in European countries such as France and Germany, and a 17-fold increase in North America. By contrast, in Latin America, real per capita income increased by only seven times between 1820 and 1992. Africa (which was the region with the lowest per capita income in 1820) had an average income in 1992 that was about the same as some European countries achieved in... 1820. Some of the Asian countries had an income per capita that was actually below the average observed in Africa in 1950, but they are now well ahead. Within Asia, per capita income in Japan rose by nearly 28-fold between 1820 and 1992 (by far the largest increase ever recorded) and in 1992 was the third highest in the world.

Table 10.2 shows the average rate of growth per capita for the same group of countries shown in Table 10.1 and for the five **phases of growth** identified by Maddison (1995): 1820-70, 1870-1913, 1913-50, 1950-73, and 1973-92.[1]

- The data suggest that during the first period (1820-70) growth occurred mostly in the now-industrial countries, at relatively low rates.

- By contrast, in the second phase (1870-1913) growth accelerated in all industrial countries (as well as in some developing regions), in part as a result of a sharp increase in *international trade, factor mobility* (both capital and labor), and improved *communication technologies.*

- The period 1913-50 was characterized by a sharp slowdown in rates of economic growth, again in almost all countries and regions—reflecting partly the disruptions of the two World Wars, the *collapse of world trade,* and the *economic crisis* of the 1930s.

- The years from 1950 to 1973, the so-called **golden age of prosperity**, were characterized by unprecedented increases in incomes and growth rates. During that period, world real income per capita grew by about 2.9 percent per annum, more than three times as fast as during the period 1913-50 (Maddison, 1995, p. 73). Although the acceleration in growth rates was recorded in all regions, it was particularly impressive in Asia.[2]

- The last period, 1973-92, was characterized by *severe disruptions* to world economic activity (such as the two oil shocks of 1973 and 1979, and the developing-country debt crisis of the early 1980s) and a sharp reduction in growth rates—except in Asia.[3] In Africa, in particular, with high growth rates of population, average real per capita income fell by about 8 percent between 1973 and 1992 (Maddison, 1995, p. 78). The growth performance of most Latin American countries—several of which were characterized

---

[1] These phases do not correspond to *stages of development*, as identified for instance by Rostow (1960). They are not derived either from a Kondratieff-type view of long-run fluctuations. See Maddison (1995, pp. 59-86) for a full discussion.

[2] Various factors were at play—including a large increase in physical capital, improved skill levels of the labor force, and a significant expansion of trade among the most advanced economies (which provided a strong impetus to world economic activity). Many of these factors are discussed in the next chapters.

[3] See Cline (1995) for a recent retrospective on the debt crisis of the early 1980s.

throughout the period by major macroeconomic imbalances, such as high inflation and large fiscal deficits—was also poor. By contrast, in Asia, per capita growth accelerated further relative to the period 1950-73, in part as a result of a reduction in the rate of population growth and large imports of capital goods (see Chapters 12 and 13).

The overall pattern suggested by Tables 10.1 and 10.2 is one of *convergence* in income per capita levels over the very long run among the group of the currently most advanced industrial countries, but also *significant divergence between rich and poor countries* over time. According to calculations made by Pritchett (1997) and based in part on Maddison's data, from 1870 to 1990, the ratio of per capita incomes between the richest and the poorest countries increased by a factor of five. The standard deviation of per capita income of rich and poor countries increased from 0.51 in 1870 to 0.88 in 1960 and 1.06 in 1990.

The data also suggest that the *pace* of economic growth as well as patterns of convergence and divergence have changed considerably across periods. Most importantly, there appears to have been a *substantial catch-up* among some groups of countries since 1950. In that year, in particular, the United States had a per capita income that was about 1.7 times the per capita income in France and Germany. By 1992, the gap was substantially narrowed. In Asia, after a long period of almost 130 years during which growth in per capita income was limited and gaps with respect to the now-industrialized countries rose substantially, a significant narrowing of income differentials occurred between 1950 and 1992. For instance, the difference in levels of income per capita between the United States and South Korea dropped from 11:1 in 1950 to about 2:1 in 1992. For Thailand, the difference (which was roughly the same as the one recorded by South Korea in 1950) dropped to about 5:1 in 1992. Thus, there is evidence within Asia of a significant catch-up—even though large differences remain across countries of the region. The adverse impact of the recent economic and financial crisis in the region (as discussed in the previous chapters) on standards of living has also been large and will take time to reverse.

Table 10.1
GDP per Capita, in 1990 U.S. Dollars

	1820	1870	1900	1913	1950	1973	1992
Industrial countries							
Canada	893	1,620	2,758	4,213	7,047	13,644	18,159
France	1,218	1,858	2,849	3,452	5,221	12,940	17,959
Germany	1,112	1,913	3,134	3,833	4,281	13,152	19,351
Italy	1,092	1,467	1,746	2,507	3,425	10,409	16,229
Japan	704	741	1,135	1,334	1,873	11,017	19,425
United Kingdom	1,756	3,263	4,593	5,032	6,847	11,992	15,738
United States	1,287	2,457	4,096	5,307	9,573	16,607	21,558
Developing countries							
Argentina	—	1,311	2,756	3,797	4,987	7,970	7,616
Brazil	670	740	704	839	1,673	3,913	4,637
Chile	—	—	1,949	2,653	3,827	5,028	7,238
Colombia	—	—	973	1,236	2,089	3,539	5,025
Mexico	760	710	1,157	1,467	2,085	4,189	5,112
Peru	—	—	817	1,037	2,263	3,953	2,854
Venezuela	—	—	821	1,104	7,424	10,717	9,163
Bangladesh	531	—	581	617	551	478	720
India	531	558	625	663	597	853	1,348
Indonesia	614	657	745	917	874	1,538	2,749
Pakistan	531	—	687	729	650	981	1,642
Philippines	—	—	1,033	1,418	1,293	1,956	2,213
South Korea	—	—	850	948	876	2,840	10,010
Thailand	—	717	812	846	848	1,750	4,694
Egypt	—	—	509	508	517	947	1,927
Ethiopia	—	—	—	—	277	412	300
Ghana	—	—	462	648	1,193	1,260	1,007
Kenya	—	—	—	—	609	947	1,055
Morocco	—	—	—	—	1,611	1,651	2,327
Nigeria	—	—	—	—	547	1,120	1,152
Tanzania	—	—	—	—	427	655	601

Source: Maddison (1995, pp. 23-24).

Table 10.2
Average Annual per Capita Real GDP Growth Rates

	1820-1870	1870-1913	1913-1950	1950-1973	1973-1992
Industrial countries					
Canada	1.2	2.2	1.4	2.9	1.5
France	0.8	1.5	1.1	4.0	1.7
Germany	1.1	1.6	0.3	5.0	2.1
Italy	0.6	1.3	0.8	5.0	2.4
Japan	0.1	1.4	0.9	8.0	3.0
United Kingdom	1.2	1.0	0.8	2.5	1.4
United States	1.3	1.8	1.6	2.4	1.4
Developing countries					
Argentina	—	2.5	0.7	2.1	-0.2
Brazil	0.2	0.3	1.9	3.8	0.9
Chile	—	—	1.0	1.2	1.9
Colombia	—	—	1.4	2.3	1.9
Mexico	-0.1	1.7	1.0	3.1	1.1
Peru	—	—	2.1	2.5	-1.7
Venezuela	—	—	5.3	1.6	-0.8
Bangladesh	—	—	-0.3	-0.6	2.2
India	0.1	0.4	-0.3	1.6	2.4
Indonesia	0.1	0.8	-0.1	2.5	3.1
Pakistan	—	—	-0.3	1.8	2.7
Philippines	—	—	-0.2	1.8	0.7
South Korea	—	—	-0.2	5.2	6.9
Thailand	—	0.4	0.0	3.2	5.3
Egypt	—	—	0.0	2.7	3.8
Ethiopia	—	—	—	1.7	-1.7
Ghana	—	—	1.7	0.2	-1.2
Kenya	—	—	—	1.9	0.6
Morocco	—	—	—	0.1	1.8
Nigeria	—	—	—	3.2	0.1
Tanzania	—	—	—	1.9	-0.5

Source: Maddison (1995, pp. 62-63).

In contrast to the experience of Asian countries such as South Korea and Thailand, the postwar evidence for African and Latin American countries shows *no sign of convergence*. Between 1950 and 1992, the per capita income gap vis-à-vis the United States rose for almost all of the African countries and for four out of the seven Latin American countries shown in Table 10.1. In the three cases in which the income gap narrowed, the improvement was relatively small. Thus, there are *large disparities* in patterns of growth in the developing world, both across countries and over time. For instance, during the period 1973-92, average growth rates per annum ranged from -1.7 percent in Ethiopia and Peru to 6.9 percent in South Korea.

10.2 Some Simple Arithmetic

10.2.1 Growth and Standards of Living

The data displayed in Tables 10.1 and 10.2 are useful to understand the importance of even small differences in output growth for standards of living over a relatively long period. Consider, for instance, the United States and India. In 1992, measured in 1990 U.S. dollars, income per capita was U.S. $21,558 in the United States, and U.S. $1,348 in India; per capita income in India represented thus only 6.3 percent of income in the United States. Suppose that both countries experience, for the next two centuries, the same annual growth rate that they recorded on average during the period, say, 1913-92—1.8 percent for the United States, and 1.2 percent for India. Under these conditions, in the United States, per capita income will reach U.S. $21,558 \cdot (1.018)^8 =$ U.S. $24,865 in the year 2000, U.S. $60,671 in the year 2050, and U.S. $148,036 in the year 2100. The same numbers for India will be, respectively, U.S. $1,348 \cdot (1.012)^8 =$ U.S. $1,483, U.S. $2,693, and U.S. $4,889. Thus, in proportion of U.S. per capita income, India's income per person will fall to 6.0 percent in the year 2000, 4.4 percent in the year 2050, and 3.3 percent in the year 2100.

10.2.2 How Fast Do Economies Catch Up?

Now suppose that, given the average growth rates achieved during the period 1913-92, one wants to calculate the amount of time (in years) that it would take for both countries to double their real per capita income, from the levels observed in 1992. For India, doubling of income in N years requires that $y_N = 2 \cdot 1,348 = 1,348 \cdot (1.012)^N$, so that

$$2 = (1.012)^N \Rightarrow N = \ln 2 / \ln(1.012) \simeq 58.11$$

For the United States, the same calculations yield $N = \ln 2 / \ln(1.018) \simeq 38.85$. Thus, it would take India about 58 years and the United States about 39 years to achieve these results.

By way of comparison, suppose that both South Korea and the United States continue to grow at the average rate observed during the period 1950-92 (6.1

percent and 1.9 percent, respectively). How long would it take South Korea to reach the same level of per capita income as the United States, using 1992 as a base period? This value is obtained by solving for N from the equation

$$21,558 \cdot (1 + 0.019)^N = 10,010 \cdot (1 + 0.061)^N,$$

so that

$$N = \ln(21,558/10,010)/\ln(1.061/1.019) \simeq 18.993,$$

which indicates that it would take Korea only 19 years.

Another interesting question is the following: suppose that India's objective is to attain a per capita income that is equal to 30 percent of the level of the United States by the year 2100. By how much should India grow per year? Let y_0^{US} (y_0^{IN}) denote per capita income in the United States (India) in the year 1992, and $g_{US} = 0.018$ and g_{IN} the average growth rate over the period 1913-92 for each country. Because it takes 108 years to reach 2100 beginning in 1992, the value of g_{IN} that is to be calculated is the solution of

$$0.3 \cdot y_0^{US}(1.018)^{108} = y_0^{IN}(1 + g_{IN})^{108},$$

so that

$$(1 + g_{IN})^{108} = C, \quad C \equiv 0.3 \cdot y_0^{US}(1.018)^{108}/y_0^{IN},$$

or

$$\ln(1 + g_{IN}) = \ln C/108 \Rightarrow 1 + g_{IN} = e^{\ln C/108},$$

and finally $g_{IN} = e^{\ln C/108} - 1 \simeq 0.0329$.

Put differently, the target growth rate of output must be about 3.3 percent per annum—almost three times the level observed during the period 1913-92. If, instead of 3.3 percent, India grows by a slightly lower number of 3.0 percent per annum, in the year 2100 its per capita income will be only about 22 percent of the U.S. level. Thus, when compounded over fairly long periods of time, even small differences in growth rates can have dramatic effects on standards of living.

10.3 Some Basic Facts

Studies of the growth patterns of industrial and developing economies suggest a set of propositions (or *basic facts*) that can be viewed as broadly consistent with long-run trends. This section summarizes some of these facts as they relate to the growth experience of developing countries.

10.3.1 Output Growth, Factor Inputs, and Population

The evidence on the growth rates of output, production inputs, and population across countries suggests the following basic facts.

> **Fact 1. Output per worker** (or average labor productivity) tends to grow over time, albeit at **widely different rates** across countries.

Fact 2. The rate of growth of **factor inputs** (capital and labor) does not fully account for the rate of growth of output.

Fact 3. The mean growth rate of output is **unrelated** to the **initial level** of per capita income across countries.

Fact 4. Population growth rates are **negatively related** with both the **level** of income per capita and the **rate of growth** of income per capita across countries.

The first fact is directly corroborated by the evidence reviewed in the first part of this chapter. The second empirical observation, which will be discussed at length in Chapter 13, has important analytical implications. It suggests that even after appropriate adjustments are made to measure factor inputs (such as the *degree of utilization* of the capital stock, or *quality adjustments* for labor categories), other factors need to be introduced to fully explain the growth rate of output.

Fact 3 is illustrated in Figure 10.1. The horizontal axis in the figure measures the ratio of per capita income in a given country relative to that in the United States in 1980, with incomes in both countries measured in 1980 U.S. dollars. The vertical axis measures the growth rate of per capita income during the period 1980-95. The data cover 99 industrial and developing countries. The figure suggests, indeed, that the growth rate of output bears *no systematic correlation* with the initial level of income. Similar results are obtained when the sample period is extended to cover the 1960s and 1970s (Barro and Sala-i-Martin, 1995). This is in contrast to the main prediction of the standard neoclassical model, which (as discussed in the next chapter) suggests that low-income countries should *grow faster* (at least during a transitory period of time) than rich countries.

Fact 4 is illustrated in Figure 10.2 for a group of about 30 developing countries, again for the period 1980-95. It also holds for a broader sample that includes industrial countries. As discussed in the next chapter, the standard orthodox model does predict a relationship between the population growth rate and the *level* of income per capita, but no relationship between the former variable and the *growth rate* of income per capita.

10.3.2   Saving, Investment, and Growth

The evidence on saving, investment and output growth rates across countries suggests the following basic facts.

Fact 5. Saving rates are **positively related** to the **level** and the **growth rate** of income per capita.

Fact 6. Both the **rate of growth of investment** and the **share of investment in output** are **positively related** to the rate of growth of income per capita.

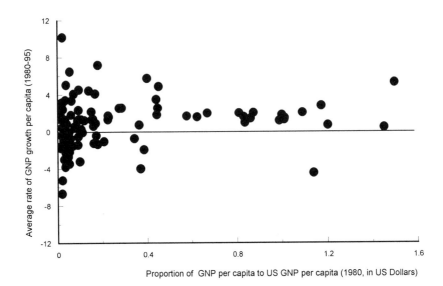

Figure 10.1. Average Rate of Growth Per Capita and Proportion of GNP Per Capita to US GNP Per Capita (1980-95).
Source: World Bank.

Fact 5 captures the widely held view that saving is crucial to economic growth. Countries that have achieved high saving rates have also tended to enjoy high levels and growth rates of per capita income—although the direction of *causality* between savings and growth remains a matter of controversy (see Chapter 13). Figure 10.3 shows cross-sectional scatter plots of domestic saving rates in developing countries—measured as gross domestic savings as a fraction of GDP—against both the *level* and the *rate of growth* of per capita real income over the period 1980-95. The data suggest a positive association between these variables. This evidence is corroborated by a large number of studies, as discussed for instance by Schmidt-Hebbel, Servén, and Solimano (1996).

Figure 10.4 displays the positive relation between the rate of growth of investment, the share of investment in output, and the rate of growth of income per capita for a group of developing countries, as summarized by Fact 6. It is important to note that the data shown in the figure refer to the accumulation of *physical* capital; as discussed in Chapters 12 and 13, new theories of growth have suggested that the accumulation of *human* capital plays a critical role in the growth process. Figure 10.5 shows scatter diagrams relating the rate of growth of real income per capita and two proxies for human capital accumulation: the **gross enrollment ratio** and the **adult literacy rate**. The data do not suggest a close correlation. However, in part because of the limitations of the measures used, firm conclusions cannot be established on the basis of these figures alone.

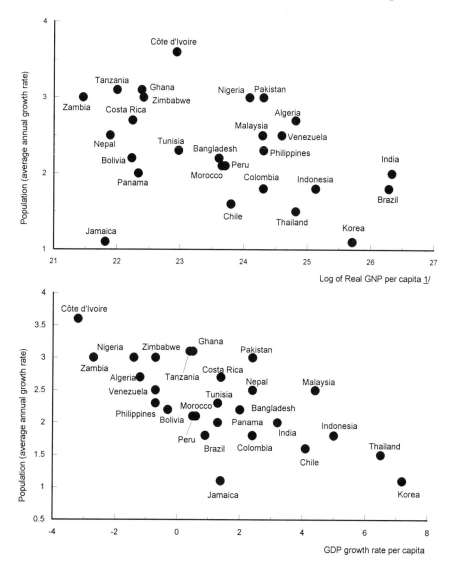

Figure 10.2. Population Growth and Real Income Per Capita (Averages over 1980-95).

Source: World Bank.

1/ In terms of US dollars at 1987 prices.

10.3.3   Poverty and Growth

Economists typically use two indicators to measure poverty:[4]

---

[4]See Ravallion (1994) and Lipton and Ravallion (1995) for a discussion of the limitations of these indicators.

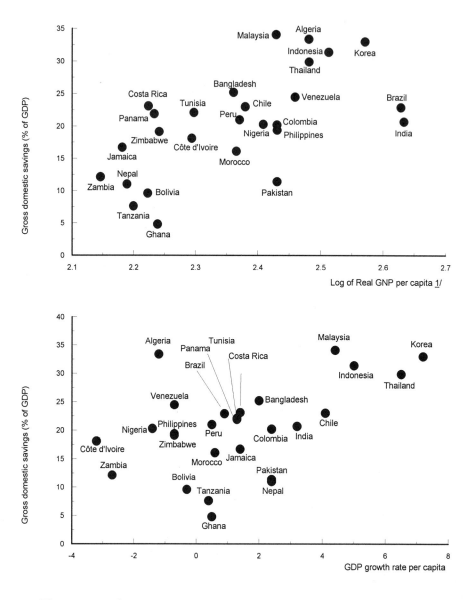

Figure 10.3. Saving Rate and Per Capita Income (Averages over 1980-95).
Source: World Bank.
1/ In terms of US dollars at 1987 prices.

- the **poverty headcount index**, which measures the proportion of individuals or households earning less than a given absolute level of income;

- the **poverty gap**, which is the average shortfall of the income of the poor
  with respect to the poverty line, multiplied by the headcount ratio.

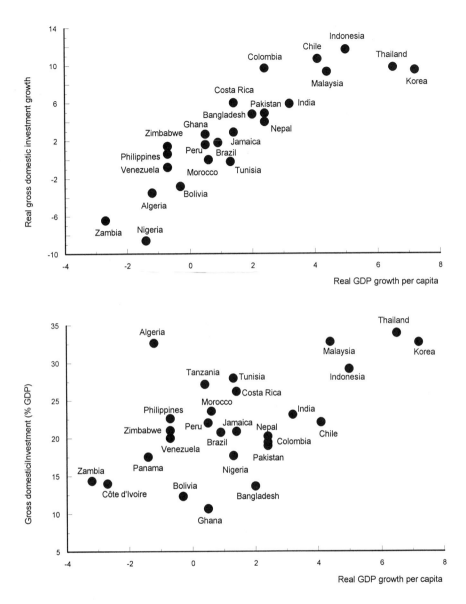

Figure 10.4. Investment Growth, Investment Share, and Growth (Averages over 1980-95).

Source: World Bank.

Ravallion and Chen (1997) used both types of indicators in their recent study on poverty. They used a uniform, 1985 PPP-adjusted, U.S. dollar-a-day line to measure poverty across countries.[5] The results (which are summarized in Figure

---

[5] Some researchers have argued that a *country-specific* poverty line should be used for cross-country comparisons, because there are significant differences in consumption pattters

10.6) suggest that the *incidence* of poverty in developing countries, as measured by the headcount index, fell somewhat between 1987 and 1993, from 31 percent to 29 percent. The *depth* of poverty, however, as measured by the average distance below the poverty line, did not change much in the aggregate over the same period. In most countries, although poverty is becoming an increasingly urban problem, the rural poor are still poorer than the urban poor. There were also sharp differences across regions; poverty incidence fell in East Asia, South Asia, and the Middle East and North Africa, and rose in Eastern and Central Europe, Latin America, and sub-Saharan Africa.

The evidence linking poverty and growth leads to the following observation.

Fact 7. Durable reductions in **poverty rates** require maintaining **sustained rates** of **economic growth** over time.

Figure 10.7 displays average growth rates of GNP per capita over the period 1981-93 and the proportion of poor—those earning less than US$ 60 a year in both the rural and urban sectors—in a group of 22 developing countries. The data suggest indeed a negative correlation between poverty and economic growth. More generally, the empirical evidence suggests also that the depth of poverty, as reflected in the poverty gap index, is more responsive to growth than is the incidence of poverty (Lipton and Ravallion, 1995).

It is also worth emphasizing that growth seems to have an *asymmetric effect* on poverty: in Latin America, for instance, poverty deteriorated significantly during the 1980s, but improved only little in the 1990s, despite the economic recovery and an increase in GDP per capita in the region of almost 6 percent in real terms between 1990 and 1995 (Londoño and Székely, 1997).

What this outcome suggests is that, as shown in various empirical studies, several other factors affect poverty in addition to the rate of growth. The cross-country econometric results presented by Agénor (1999) suggested that *inflation* has a significant effect on the poor. The top panel of Figure 10.8, which displays the evolution of poverty and inflation in Latin America during the period 1970-96, suggests also a positive (albeit weak) correlation between price increases and the incidence of poverty during the 1980s.[6] Londoño and Székely (1997) have suggested that, at least in Latin America, poverty is strongly associated with a *skewed distribution* of income (see below). Other important variables are access to *education, health services*, and employment opportunities, and the *degree of urbanization* (Lipton and Ravallion, 1995).

---

across countries and over time—differences that make it difficult to establish a common criterion. However, it has been shown that the elasticity of the poverty line with respect to average income appears to be very low in practice, implying that it is unlikely that changes in consumption patterns over time will significantly alter the value of country-specific poverty lines.

[6]In the figure, one 1985 PPP-adjusted U.S. dollar-a-day line is used to measure *extreme* poverty, and two 1985 PPP-adjusted U.S. dollars per day to measure *moderate* poverty.

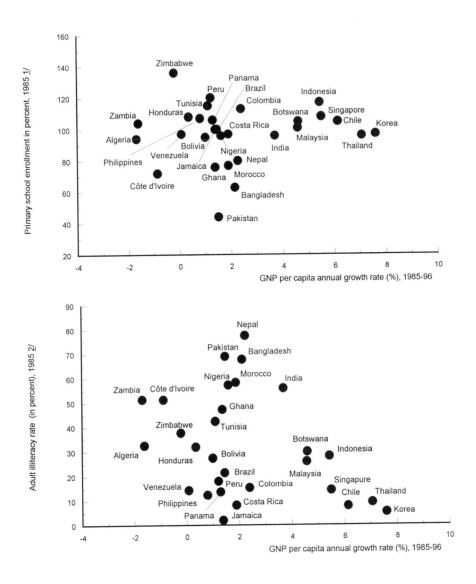

Figure 10.5. Enrollment Ratio, Literacy Rate, and Growth.

Source: World Bank.

1/ The gross enrollment ratio is the ratio of total enrollment, regardless of age, to the population of the age group that officially corresponds to the level of education shown.

2/ The adult illiteracy rate is the proportion of adults aged 15 and above who cannot, with understanding, read and write a short, simple statement on their everyday life.

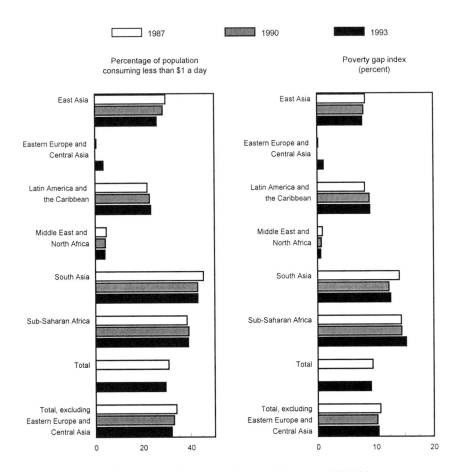

Figure 10.6. Developing Countries: Poverty Measures, 1987-93.
Source: Ravallion and Chen (1997, p. 374).

1/ Using an international poverty line of $1 a day per person at 1985 purchasing power parity exchange rates.

10.3.4 Inequality, Growth, and Development

To measure income inequality and capture some of the most important characteristics of income distribution in a given country, economists often use three types of indicators:

- The share of the top to the bottom income deciles or quintiles, which only attaches weight to the two tails of the income distribution.

- The **Gini coefficient**.

- The **Theil inequality index**, which can be decomposed into two terms: one that captures inequality due to differences *between groups*, and another that captures inequality *within groups*.

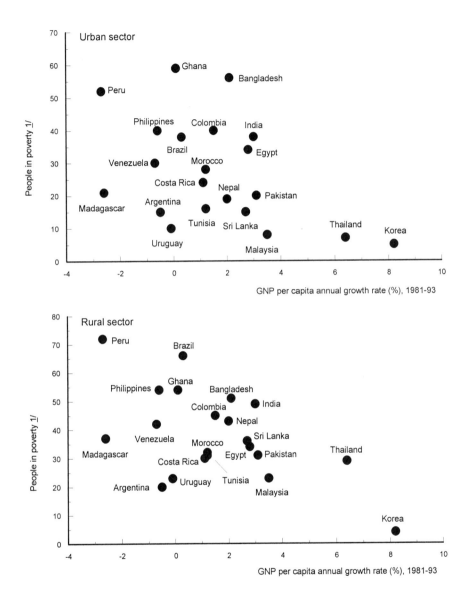

Figure 10.7. Growth and People in Poverty (Period average, in percent).
Source: World Bank.

1/ Proportion of the population earning one U.S. dollar or less, in 1985 ppp-adjusted U.S. dollars, various survey years.

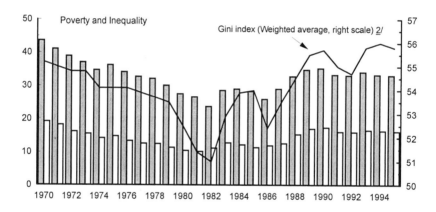

Figure 10.8. Latin America: Poverty, inflation, and Income Inequality, 1970-96, 1/.

Source: Londoño and Székely (1997).

1/ Extreme poverty is one U.S. dollar a day, in 1985 PPP-adjusted U.S. dollars. Moderate poverty is two U.S. dollars a day, in 1985 PPP-adjusted U.S. dollars.

2/ For 13 countries.

In practice, the **Gini coefficient** remains the most widely used indicator. Like the first indicator, it is derived from the **Lorenz curve**, which shows the cumulative share of total income received by cumulative shares of the population, starting from the poorest income-receiving groups. The graph of the Lorenz curve contains a reference line representing *perfect equality*, which indicates what the distribution would be if every individual received an identical

income. The Gini coefficient measures the area between the actual curve for a
population and the line of perfect equality; it varies between 0 (maximum equality) and unity (maximum inequality).[7] Figure 10.9 shows the Lorenz curve and
the Gini coefficient for a hypothetical country. The horizontal axis shows the
cumulative proportion of the population (in terms of quintiles and deciles), and
the vertical axis represents the proportion of total income accruing to the corresponding proportion of the population. The distance AA' in the figure measures
the income share of the poorest 40 percent of the population, whereas the distance BB' measures the income share of the richest 20 percent. The more
unequal the distribution of income, the greater the distance of the Lorenz curve
from the diagonal, and the greater the Gini coefficient.[8]

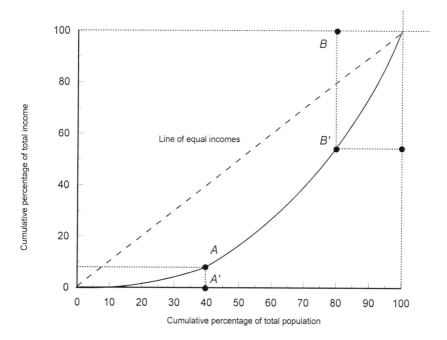

Figure 10.9. The Lorenz Curve and the Gini Coefficient.

The evidence on income shares for *industrial countries* suggests that the
share of income accruing to capital (and thus labor) is approximately constant,
although in some cases there appears to be a slight reduction (increase) over long
periods of time (Romer, 1989). The evidence for developing economies, however,
does not point in the same direction. Figure 10.10 shows the correlation for a

---

[7] In practice, many researchers (see, for instance, Londoño and Székely, 1997) use the
Villaseñor-Arnold procedure to obtain the arc of the Lorenz curve even when information is
only available by quintiles (see Lipton and Ravallion, 1995). The method uses a quadratic
equation to estimate, using available data, the parameters of the Lorenz curve.

[8] The Gini index may not always fully capture changes in inequality. A complementary
measure, discussed in the appendix to this chapter, is the *polarization index*.

group of about 30 countries between the rate of growth of income per capita and two measures of income inequality, both derived (as indicated earlier) from the Lorenz curve: the ratio of the share of the richest 20 percent to the share of the poorest 20 percent, and the Gini coefficient. The data do not suggest any clear pattern. However, it should be recognized that Figure 10.10 focuses on a relatively short period (about 15-16 years); there are good theoretical reasons, related in particular to political economy considerations, to argue that the link between growth and inequality may be ambiguous at relatively short horizons (Bénabou, 1997).

A related but different issue (because of its longer-run perspective) is the link between inequality, the *pattern of growth*, and development. In fact, a long-held view in development economics is that income distribution changes in a predictable manner during the process of economic development. According to the **Kuznets hypothesis**, income inequality increases in the early stages of development and then decreases. This **inverted-U shape** reflects the view that the process of economic development involves a transition from a *low-productivity, agrarian economy* to a *high-productivity, industrial economy*. More specifically, during the process of industrialization, income inequality tends to rise not only on account of earnings differentials between agriculture and industry, but also because of the increased importance of industrial incomes, which are distributed less equally than agricultural incomes. However, as industry takes over and average incomes rise, earnings differentials associated with productivity differences tend to fall. Consequently, a *turning point* is eventually reached; beyond that point, income distribution begins to improve as the level of income rises. On this view, therefore, *growth is first unequalizing, then equalizing*. A trade-off exists between equity and prosperity in the short run (Galor and Tsiddon, 1997).

Early evidence based on cross-country analysis of the relationship between per capita income and inequality broadly confirmed the existence of the inverted-U pattern in which inequality is lowest in low-income and high-income countries and highest in middle-income countries. A number of more recent studies, however, have failed to corroborate this result, as indicated in two comprehensive surveys, by Bruno, Ravallion, and Squire (1998) and Fishlow (1995). This can be summarized in the following fact.

Fact 8. The link between **income inequality** and **growth** appears to be nonlinear, but there remains some controversy about the nature and robustness of this relationship.

In addition to growth, there appears to be significant evidence of an adverse effect of **education inequality** on the distribution of income, as is the case for poverty. Psacharopoulos et al. (1995), for instance, suggested that educational attainment has the greatest correlation with both income inequality and the probability of being poor. Londoño and Székely (1997) suggested also that changes in income inequality in Latin America during the past two decades have largely reflected growing inequalities in educational opportunities. Moreover, the evidence reviewed by Lipton and Ravallion (1995) suggests that the relationship between education levels and inequality is typically *nonlinear*. The first phases of growth in education are associated with *increased inequality*; for example, an increase from 1 to 2 years of education in the labor force is typically associated with a 3-point increase in the Gini coefficient. An increase from 4 to 5 years is associated with a 1 point increase. The turning point arises when the work force attains between 5 and 6 years of education. From that point on, the inequality decreases; on going from 6 to 7 years, inequality *falls* by half a point. On passing from 9 to 10 years, it falls by 2 points. The link between education and income distribution has, of course, important implications for *public policy*. Improving access to education and the quality of education may lead over time to a reduction in income differentials associated with disparities in average levels of schooling, and should contribute significantly to reductions in income inequality and foster growth (see Chapter 12).

In addition to growth and education, studies have shown that various other factors may affect the pattern of income distribution. Cardoso et al. (1995), for instance, have identified *inflation* and *unemployment* as determinants of income inequality in Brazil during the 1980s. In a more recent cross-section study of 75 countries, Bulir (1998) showed that inflation and income inequality (as measured by the Gini coefficient) are positively related. This relationship appears to be *nonlinear*: a reduction in inflation from very high levels significantly lowers inequality, whereas further reduction toward very low levels (below, say, 5 percent a year) bring about negligible improvements in income equality. The bottom panel of Figure 10.8, which shows the evolution of poverty and income distribution in Latin America during the period 1970-96, suggests indeed a positive relation between these variables.[9] Finally, several studies suggested that inequality in developing countries is often closely associated with considerable concentration of *material wealth*. Inequality in the ownership and distribution of assets (including land) tend to interact with the other variables listed above, such as education, and often compound their effects.

10.3.5 Trade, Inflation, and Financial Deepening

Fact 9. Growth in the **volume of exports** and **imports** are both **positively related** to the rate of growth of output. Evidence on the correlation between the **degree of openness** and growth, however, is less robust.

Figure 10.11 shows indeed that growth in both export volumes and import volumes are closely related to real output growth in developing countries. The first fact is at the heart of the debate between advocates and opponents of *export-led growth* strategies. The second fact may be related to the importance of imports of capital goods and intermediate products in total imports of most developing countries (see the discussion in Chapters 1 and 5). Figure 10.12, which displays the correlation between the rate of growth of income per capita and the **degree of openness**, measured as the sum of exports plus imports

---

[9]Sarel (1997), however, found no significant effect of inflation (in either level or in terms of variability) on income distribution.

of goods and services divided by GDP, does not strongly suggest that outward orientation is associated with high standards of living, although other measures of openness, such as the index devised by Sachs and Warner (1997*a*), indicate a stronger correlation.[10]

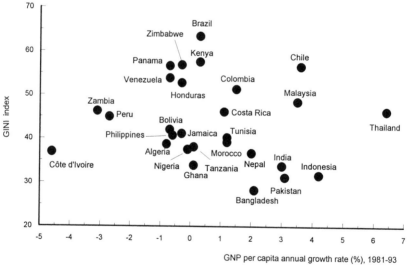

Figure 10.10. Growth and Income Distribution (Average over 1981-93). Source: World Bank.

---

[10] See Edwards (1998*b*), Harrison (1996), and Harrison and Hanson (1999) for further discussion of measures of openness and their relation with the rate of economic growth. Harrison and Hanson, in particular, argue that the Sachs-Warner index is not a robust measure of trade openness.

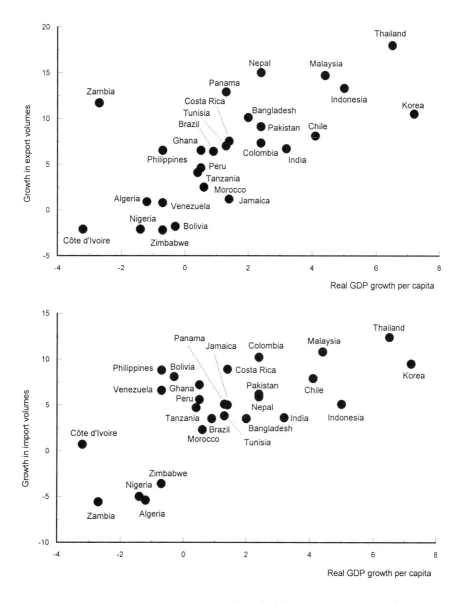

Figure 10.11. Exports, Imports, and Growth (Averages over 1980-95).
Source: World Bank.

Fact 10. The association between **inflation** and growth is **negative** and **nonlinear**.

The negative correlation between inflation and growth (possibly resulting from the effect of the former variable on the incentive to invest) is shown in Figure 10.13. This link is often viewed as a key argument for advocating **macroeconomic stability**. Much of the recent literature, however, suggests that the inflation-growth link is nonlinear: at low levels of inflation, changes in inflation have only a negligible impact on growth rates; at higher levels (above, say, 30-40 percent per annum), inflation stabilization is conducive to higher growth rates. These issues are discussed further in Chapters 12 and 13.

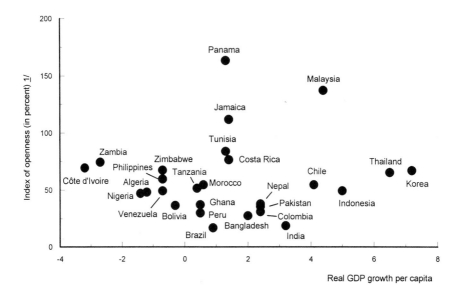

Figure 10.12. Openness and Growth (Averages over 1980-95).

Source: World Bank.

1/ Openness is measured by the ratio of the sum of exports of goods and services and imports of goods and services (both at current prices), relative to GDP at current prices.

Fact 11. The degree of development of the **financial system** is **positively** related to the rate of growth of output.

The link between financial deepening and economic growth is documented by Levine (1997). Various indicators have been used to measure the degree of financial development in empirical work. Figure 10.14 relates one of those indicators, the ratio of private sector credit to GDP, to real growth in per capita terms over the period 1980-95. The figure suggests indeed a positive correlation between these two variables. Other indicators, such as the proportion of quasi-money in the broad money stock, yield similar results. However, although the link between finance and growth is a well-documented fact, the direction of *causality* remains a matter of controversy, as discussed in subsequent chapters.

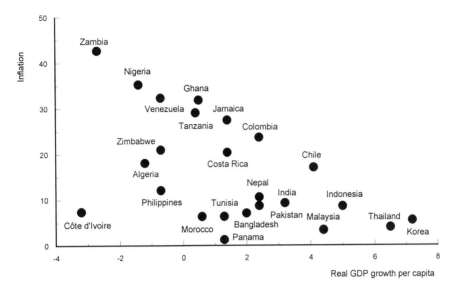

Figure 10.13. Inflation and Growth (Average annual % change, 1980-95).
Source: World Bank.

10.4   Summary

- The evidence on growth since the end of the nineteenth century suggests a pattern of *convergence* in income per capita levels among the group of the currently most advanced *industrial countries*, but also significant *divergence* between *rich* and *poor countries.*

- Simple arithmetic reveals that even *small* differences in growth rates, once compounded, can add up over time to *very large* differences in levels of income and standards of living.

Empirical evidence on the patterns of growth in industrial and developing countries suggest the following basic facts, which theories of growth must explain:

- Output per worker grows at widely different rates across countries.

- Growth of capital and labor does not fully account for the rate of growth of output.

- Output growth rates across countries appear to be unrelated to *initial* levels of per capita income.

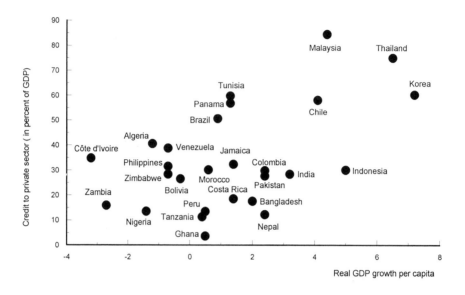

Figure 10.14. Private Sector Credit and Growth (Average annual % change, 1980-95).
Source: World Bank.

- *Population growth* rates are negatively related with both the level of income per capita and the rate of growth of income per capita across countries.

- Countries with low (high) *saving rates* and *investment rates* tend to have low (high) income levels and growth rates per capita.

- Whereas **poverty** rates appear to be negatively related with growth, the link between **income inequality** and growth is less robust. The importance of *education* (or the lack thereof) as a source of poverty and income inequality has critical implications for public policy.

- Income inequality in developing countries is often closely associated with considerable concentration of *material wealth*, including land and other real assets.

- Growth in the volume of *exports* and *imports*, and the **degree of openness**, are positively correlated with growth.

- The association between **inflation** and growth is negative and **nonlinear**.

- The degree of development of the *financial system* is positively related to the rate of growth of output.

A reduction in poverty is not necessarily accompanied by reduced inequality as conventionally measured. A policy, for instance, that leads to income being redistributed toward the *extreme groups* of the distribution, accompanied at the same by a fall in the percentage received by the middle groups, may lead to an increase in **polarization** even though it reduces inequality at the same time.

Appendix
Income Distribution and Polarization

Conventional measures of income distribution, such as the Gini index defined in the text, may not fully capture changes in inequality. An alternative (or, rather, complementary) measure that economists often use is the **polarization index**. Generally speaking, income distribution in country 1 for instance is said to be more polarized than in country 2 if incomes in country 1 tend to be *more bimodal*, in that there are more poor and rich, but fewer people in the middle (Wolfson, 1994). In concrete terms, following Ravallion and Chen (1997), consider an economy composed of 4 individuals (A, B, C, and D), with incomes of $100, $200, $300, and $400 respectively. Suppose that $50 are taken by a benevolent government from individual B, with income of $200, and given to individual A, with income of $100. Suppose also that the same amount is taken from individual D, with income of $400, and given to individual C, with income of $300. The new distribution is thus $150, $150, $350, and $350. Inequality, as measured by the **Gini index**, *has fallen* because the gainers (individuals A and C) were poorer than the losers (individuals B and D); but *polarization has increased* because the new distribution is more sharply divided between "poor" individuals (A and B) and "rich" individuals (C and D).

A commonly-used index of polarization is the **Wolfson index**, W, which is defined as

$$W = 2(\mu^* - \mu_L)/m,$$

where μ^* is the distribution-corrected mean income (given by the actual mean times 1 minus the Gini index), μ_L is the mean income of the poorest half of the population, and m is the median income.

Although in practice common measures of inequality and polarization are often closely associated (see, for instance, Ravallion and Chen, 1997), there may be situations in which measuring inequality through conventional indicators may miss relevant aspects of how distribution has changed. This may be particularly important from a political economy point of view; a more polarized distribution may exacerbate social tensions and lead (as discussed in Chapter 17) to the collapse of a reform program.

Chapter 11

Growth and Technological Progress: The Solow-Swan Model

The starting point of many of the attempts aimed at explaining analytically the facts described in the previous chapter is the so-called neoclassical growth model, developed in the 1950s by Solow (1956) and Swan (1956). For or against it, the Solow-Swan model continues to be at the center of the debate between "old" and "new" theories of economic growth. It is therefore important to understand its properties and predictions, regarding notably the effects of the allocation of output between consumption and investment on capital accumulation, and the critical role played by technological progress.

The first part of this chapter presents the basic structure and the main assumptions of the Solow-Swan model. The second part derives the dynamic path of output and the capital stock, under the assumptions that labor and knowledge grow exogenously. The third part considers briefly the case in which the rate of growth of the population is nonlinearly related to the capital-effective labor ratio. The fourth part analyzes the effects of changes in the rate of growth of the labor force and the saving rate on the rate of growth of output per capita in the short and in the long run. Factors affecting the speed at which adjustment to the long-run equilibrium proceeds are analyzed in the fifth part. The last part assesses the model's ability to explain some of the basic facts discussed in the previous chapter.

11.1 Basic Structure and Assumptions

The basic version of the Solow-Swan model considers a closed economy producing one single (composite) good using both *labor* and *capital*. It takes **tech-**

nological progress as given and the *saving rate* as exogenous.[1] There is no government; there is a fixed number of firms in the economy, each with the same production technology. Normalizing the number of firms to unity for simplicity, aggregate output can thus be characterized by an *aggregate production function*. The price of output is constant and factor prices (including wages) adjust to ensure full utilization of all available inputs.

Formally, the model focuses on four variables:

- the flow of output, Y;

- the stock of capital, K;

- the number of workers, L;

- *knowledge* or the **effectiveness of labor**, A.

The economy combines capital, labor and knowledge to produce output. The aggregate production function is[2]

$$Y = F(K, AL), \tag{11.1}$$

where capital and effective labor are assumed to be **gross (Edgeworth) complements** ($F_{KL} > 0$).

Three features of the production function (11.1) must be noted at the outset.

- Because K and L are *stock* variables, strictly speaking it is the *flow rates of services* of these factors—for instance, the stock of capital times the rate of utilization of capital services—that should enter the production function. For simplicity, the utilization rates of both factors are set to unity.

- *Time* does not enter directly, but only through K, L, and A. That is, output changes over time only if the production inputs change.

- A and L enter multiplicatively. AL is referred to as **effective labor**, and technological progress that enters in this fashion is known as **labor augmenting** or **Harrod neutral**.

If knowledge enters in the form $Y = F(AK, L)$, technological progress is deemed **capital augmenting** or **Solow neutral**. If it enters in the form $Y = AF(K, L)$, technological progress is **Hicks neutral**. The assumption that technological progress is Harrod-neutral implies, as shown below (and given the other assumptions on which the model relies), that the relative shares of capital and labor in output remain *constant* along paths for which the capital-output

---

[1] More precisely, the model takes the saving *function* as given.

[2] In practice, there are serious aggregation problems involved in the measurement of aggregate stocks of inputs—particularly stock of physical capital—as specified in Equation (11.1). However, such issues do not arise here, because of the assumption that the economy produces only one good.

ratio itself remains constant. Although there exists limited evidence on the relevance of these facts for developing countries, they appear to hold over the long run for industrial countries (see Romer, 1989).

Several additional assumptions characterize the model:

- The **marginal product** of each factor is positive ($F_h > 0$, where $h = K$, AL) and there are **diminishing returns** to each input ($F_{hh} < 0$).

- The production function exhibits **constant returns to scale** (CRS) in capital and effective labor; that is, doubling the quantities of K and AL doubles the amount of output produced. More formally, the CRS assumption implies that, multiplying K and AL by any nonnegative constant m changes output by the same factor:[3]

$$F(mK, mAL) = mF(K, AL), \quad m \geq 0.$$

- Inputs other than capital, labor and knowledge are relatively unimportant. In particular, the model neglects *land* and other *natural resources*. If natural resources are important—as one would expect to be the case in, say, island economies—doubling capital and effective labor could less than double output. The assumption of constant returns to capital and effective labor alone may therefore be inappropriate. Nevertheless, it will be assumed to hold.[4]

Under the CRS assumption, the production function can be written in terms of the *ratio* of production factors. Setting $m = 1/AL$ in Equation (11.1) results in

$$F(\frac{K}{AL}, 1) = \frac{1}{AL} F(K, AL), \tag{11.2}$$

where K/AL is the amount of physical capital per unit of effective labor, and $F(K, AL)/AL$ is Y/AL, output per unit of effective labor.

Let $k = K/AL$, $y = Y/AL$, and $f(k) = F(k, 1)$. Equation (11.2) can be rewritten as

$$y = f(k), \quad f(0) = 0. \tag{11.3}$$

Equation (11.3) relates output per unit of effective labor to capital per unit of effective labor. The term $f(k)$ is defined as the *intensive-form* production function. Positive output is assumed to require a positive level of capital; put differently, capital is an indispensable factor of production.

Given the earlier assumptions regarding the signs of F_K and F_{KK}, the intensive-form production function must satisfy the following conditions:

$$f'(k) > 0; \quad f''(k) < 0.$$

---

[3]The CRS condition is an important assumption of the Solow-Swan model and will be further discussed later.

[4]Romer (1995) discusses an extension of the Solow-Swan model in which the presence of natural resources implies the existence of diminishing returns to capital and labor. The next chapter will examine the implications of increasing returns.

The quantity $f'(k)$ is the marginal product of capital, F_K, because

$$Y = F(K, AL) = ALf\left(\frac{K}{AL}\right) \Rightarrow F_K = \frac{\partial F(K, AL)}{\partial K} = ALf'\left(\frac{K}{AL}\right) \cdot \frac{1}{AL} = f'(k),$$

and is thus positive. Similarly, $f''(k) < 0$ because

$$F_{KK} = \frac{\partial^2 F(K, AL)}{\partial K^2} = \frac{\partial}{\partial K}\left\{ALf'\left(\frac{K}{AL}\right) \cdot \frac{1}{AL}\right\} = \frac{\partial}{\partial K}\left\{f'\left(\frac{K}{AL}\right)\right\} = \frac{f''(k)}{AL}.$$

Thus, the above assumptions imply that

- the marginal product of capital is *positive*;

- the marginal product of capital *decreases* as capital (per unit of effective labor) rises.

In addition, the intensive-form production function is assumed to satisfy the **Inada conditions**:

$$\lim_{k \to 0} f'(k) = \infty, \qquad \lim_{k \to \infty} f'(k) = 0.$$

These conditions state that the marginal product of capital is very large when the capital stock is sufficiently small, and that it becomes very small as the capital stock becomes very large; their role is to ensure that the path of the economy does not diverge, as discussed below.[5]

A specific production function satisfying all the above conditions is the **Cobb-Douglas function**:

$$Y = F(K, AL) = K^\alpha (AL)^{1-\alpha}, \quad 0 < \alpha < 1. \tag{11.4}$$

This production function is easy to use, and it appears to be a reasonable first approximation to actual production technologies. To show that the Cobb-Douglas function has constant returns to scale, multiply both inputs by m to obtain

$$(mK)^\alpha (mAL)^{1-\alpha} = m^\alpha m^{1-\alpha} K^\alpha (AL)^{1-\alpha} = mY.$$

The intensive-form Cobb-Douglas function is obtained by dividing both inputs in Equation (11.4) by AL, so that

$$y = f(k) = \left(\frac{K}{AL}\right)^\alpha = k^\alpha. \tag{11.5}$$

Equation (11.5) implies that

$$f'(k) = \alpha k^{\alpha-1} > 0, \quad f''(k) = -(1-\alpha)\alpha k^{\alpha-2} < 0.$$

---

[5] These conditions are, in fact, stronger than is needed for the model's central results. See Burmeister and Dobell (1970, pp. 25-26).

It can also be verified that the Inada conditions are satisfied:

$$\lim_{k \to 0} \alpha k^{\alpha-1} = \infty, \qquad \lim_{k \to \infty} \alpha k^{\alpha-1} = 0. \tag{11.6}$$

The function k^α is illustrated in Figure 11.1. The *slope* of the function is the marginal product of capital, $\alpha k^{\alpha-1}$. It becomes flatter as k increases, as implied by the assumption of diminishing marginal product of capital.

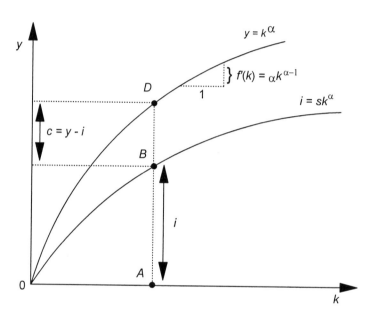

Figure 11.1. The Production Function in the Solow-Swan Model.

It can also be verified that, with the Cobb-Douglas production function, labor-augmenting, capital-augmenting, and Hicks-neutral technological progress (as discussed earlier) are all basically the same. This is because all factors of production enter multiplicatively. Because of its tractability, the Cobb-Douglas specification will be used systematically in what follows.

To complete the description of the model requires specifying the allocation of resources between consumption, saving, and investment, and the evolution over time of the stocks of capital, labor, and knowledge. Both labor and knowledge are assumed to grow at exogenous, constant rates:

$$\dot{L}/L = n, \quad \dot{A}/A = \gamma, \tag{11.7}$$

where γ can be interpreted as the rate at which knowledge, other than technological know-how embodied in equipment, improves—for instance, efficiency gains in organizational structures and management procedures.

The expressions in (11.7) imply that, denoting by L_0 and A_0 the initial values of L and A:[6]

$$L = L_0 e^{nt}, \quad A = A_0 e^{\gamma t}. \tag{11.8}$$

Output is divided between consumption, C, and investment, I:

$$Y = C + I. \tag{11.9}$$

Savings, S, defined as $Y - C$, is assumed to be a constant fraction, s, of output:

$$S \equiv Y - C = sY, \quad 0 < s < 1. \tag{11.10}$$

All savings are assumed absorbed by firms for capital accumulation. Combining Equations (11.9) and (11.10) the savings-investment equality can therefore be written as:

$$S = I = sY, \tag{11.11}$$

which shows that the saving rate is also the fraction of output allocated to investment.[7]

Finally, assuming that one unit of output allocated to investment yields one unit of new capital, that the existing capital stock depreciates at the constant rate $\delta > 0$, and using Equation (11.11), changes in the capital stock (or net investment) can be written as

$$\dot{K} = sY - \delta K. \tag{11.12}$$

Let $c = C/AL$ and $i = I/AL$ denote consumption and investment per effective units of labor, respectively. Using Equation (11.4) yields:

$$c = (1 - s)k^{\alpha}, \quad i = sk^{\alpha}. \tag{11.13}$$

Figure 11.1 shows graphically how output (per effective units of labor) is allocated between consumption, saving, and investment.

11.2   The Dynamics of Capital and Output

To determine the behavior of the economy over time under the preceding set of assumptions requires only examining the behavior of the capital stock, because labor and knowledge grow exogenously. To do so, it is convenient to focus on the *capital stock per units of effective labor*, k, rather than the capital stock itself. Differentiating the expression $k = K/AL$ with respect to time implies that

$$\dot{k} = (\frac{1}{AL})\dot{K} - (\frac{K}{A})\frac{\dot{L}}{L^2} - (\frac{K}{L})\frac{\dot{A}}{A^2},$$

---

[6] To verify this, note, for instance, that $L = L_0 e^{nt}$ implies that $\dot{L} = nL_0 e^{nt} = nL$ and that the initial value of L is $L_0 e^0 = L_0$.

[7] For simplicity, the assumption that savings are a constant fraction of income will be maintained in this chapter and the next two. Models with a variable saving rate can be derived from full-blown optimization problems by households but are mathematically more demanding. For a discussion, see Barro and Sala-i-Martin (1995).

or equivalently

$$\dot{k} = \frac{\dot{K}}{AL} - (\frac{K}{AL})\frac{\dot{L}}{L} - (\frac{K}{AL})\frac{\dot{A}}{A} = \frac{\dot{K}}{AL} - (\frac{\dot{L}}{L} + \frac{\dot{A}}{A})k. \qquad (11.14)$$

From Equation (11.8), $\dot{L}/L = n$ and $\dot{A}/A = \gamma$; and $\dot{K}$ is given by Equation (11.12). Substituting these expressions into the right-hand side of Equation (11.14) results in

$$\dot{k} = \frac{sY - \delta K}{AL} - (n + \gamma)k,$$

or

$$\dot{k} = \frac{sY}{AL} - \delta k - (n + \gamma)k,$$

and finally, using the fact that, from Equation (11.4), $Y/AL = k^{\alpha}$:

$$\dot{k} = sk^{\alpha} - (n + \gamma + \delta)k, \quad n + \gamma + \delta > 0, \qquad (11.15)$$

with initial condition $k_0 = K_0/A_0L_0$.

Equation (11.15) is a *nonlinear, first-order differential equation*; it represents the key equation of the Solow-Swan model. It states that the rate of change of the capital stock per units of effective labor is the difference between two terms:

- sk^{α}, which measures *actual investment* per unit of effective labor. Output per units of effective labor is k^{α}, and the fraction of that output that is invested is s.

- $(n + \gamma + \delta)k$, which measures *required investment*, that is, the amount of investment that must be undertaken in order to keep k at its existing level.

There are two reasons why some investment is needed to prevent k from falling.

- The existing capital stock is depreciating; this capital must be replaced to prevent the capital stock from falling. This is measured by the term δk in Equation (11.15).

- The quantity of effective labor is growing. Thus, investing just enough to keep the capital stock, K, constant is not sufficient to maintain capital per unit of effective labor, k, constant. Instead, because the quantity of effective labor is growing at the rate $n + \gamma$, the capital stock must grow at the rate $n + \gamma$ to keep k constant. This is the $(n + \gamma)k$ term in Equation (11.15).

Equation (11.15) indicates, therefore, that the capital-effective labor ratio rises at a rate proportional to the difference between actual and required investment:

- When actual investment exceeds required investment, so that $sk^{\alpha} > (n + \gamma + \delta)k$, k is rising.

- When actual investment falls short of required investment, k is falling.

- When the two terms are equal, k is constant.

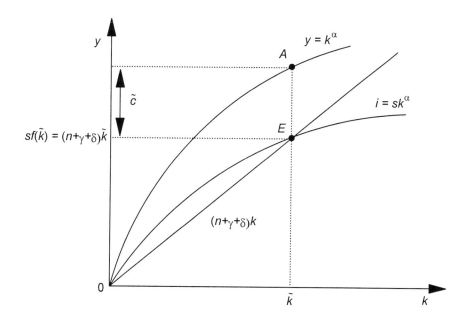

Figure 11.2. The Equilibrium Capital-Labor Ratio.

Figure 11.2 extends Figure 11.1 to represent both terms of the expression for $\dot{k}$ as functions of k. Required investment, $(n + \gamma + \delta)k$, is proportional to k and is represented as a *straight line* with a positive slope. Actual investment is a *concave curve*, because it is a fraction of output per units of effective labor and, as shown earlier, $\alpha k^{\alpha-1} > 0$, $-(1 - \alpha)\alpha k^{\alpha-2} < 0$.

At $k = 0$, $y = 0$ and actual investment and required investment are equal. To show that this equality does occur only once for $k > 0$ proceeds in three steps.

- The first Inada condition in (11.6) implies that for k slightly greater than 0, the marginal productivity of capital $\alpha k^{\alpha-1}$ is large, and thus that the sk^{α} curve is steeper than the $(n + \gamma + \delta)k$ line. Thus, for positive but small values of k, actual investment is larger than required investment.

- The second Inada condition in (11.6) implies that $\alpha k^{\alpha-1}$ falls toward zero as k becomes large. At some point, the slope of the actual investment line falls below the slope of the required investment line. With the sk^α curve flatter than the $(n + \gamma + \delta)k$ line, the two must eventually cross.[8]

- The fact that $-(1 - \alpha)\alpha k^{\alpha - 2} < 0$ implies that the two curves will intersect *only once* for $k > 0$—at the unique value of k for which actual investment equals required investment.

Let $\tilde{k}$ denote this unique value, which is the *equilibrium point* of the system; it is determined by setting $\dot{k} = 0$ in Equation (11.15) and is implicitly defined by

$$s\tilde{k}^\alpha - (n + \gamma + \delta)\tilde{k} = 0, \tag{11.16}$$

the solution of which is

$$\tilde{k} = \left\{\frac{s}{n + \gamma + \delta}\right\}^{1/(1-\alpha)} \tag{11.17}$$

This equation implies that, in particular, $\partial\tilde{k}/\partial s > 0$. An increase in the saving rate raises the equilibrium capital-effective labor ratio.

Figure 11.3 shows the **phase diagram** relating $\dot{k}$ to k.

- If initially $k < \tilde{k}$, actual investment exceeds required investment and so $\dot{k}$ is positive, that is, k is rising.

- If initially $k > \tilde{k}$, $\dot{k}$ is negative and k is falling.

- If initially $k = \tilde{k}$, $\dot{k}$ is zero.

Thus, regardless of where the economy's initial stock of capital is (as long as it is positive), it converges to $\tilde{k}$—the point at which the phase line crosses the horizontal axis.[9] The dynamic process described by Equation (11.15) is thus **globally stable**. The explicit dynamic path of k is derived in the appendix to this chapter.

In the steady-state equilibrium, with k constant at $\tilde{k}$, the capital stock, which by definition is equal to ALk, is growing at the rate

$$\tilde{g}_K = \left.\frac{\dot{K}}{K}\right|_{k=\tilde{k}} = \frac{\dot{A}}{A} + \frac{\dot{L}}{L} = n + \gamma, \tag{11.18}$$

which is also the growth rate of the effective labor force, AL.

Output is given by ALy. Its steady-state growth rate, $\tilde{g}_Y$, is thus

$$\tilde{g}_Y = \frac{\dot{A}}{A} + \frac{\dot{L}}{L} = n + \gamma, \tag{11.19}$$

---

[8] Clearly, if there is no range of values of k for which the sk^α curve is above the $(n+\gamma+\delta)k$ line, the two curves cannot intersect and there is no equilibrium.

[9] If k is initially zero, it remains there. This possibility is ignored in what follows.

because y is constant at $\tilde{k}^\alpha$, so that $\dot{y}/y|_{k=\tilde{k}} = 0$. Thus, output is also growing at the same rate as capital and effective labor.

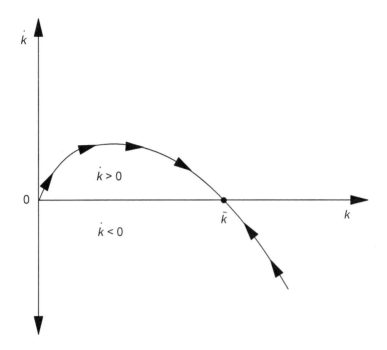

Figure 11.3. Adjustment Process of the Capital-Labor Ratio.

From the above results, the rates of growth of capital per worker, and output per worker (that is, labor productivity), are given by

$$\tilde{g}_{K/L} = \tilde{g}_K - \frac{\dot{L}}{L} = \gamma, \quad \tilde{g}_{Y/L} = \tilde{g}_Y - \frac{\dot{L}}{L} = \gamma. \tag{11.20}$$

Thus, the Solow-Swan model implies that, regardless of its starting point, the economy converges to a **balanced growth path**—a situation where each variable of the model is growing at a constant rate. On the balanced growth path, the growth rate of output per worker is determined solely by the rate of growth of technological progress. It depends, in particular, neither on the saving rate nor on the specific form of the production function.

By definition, if markets are competitive, the **rate of return on capital**, r, must equal its marginal product, $\alpha k^{\alpha-1}$, minus depreciation, δ:

$$r = \alpha k^{\alpha-1} - \delta,$$

whereas the *wage rate*, w, is given by

$$w = \frac{\partial}{\partial L}(ALk^\alpha) = (1-\alpha)Ak^\alpha.$$

On the balanced growth path, therefore, the rate of return on capital (or the net real interest rate) is constant, and the real wage is rising at the rate γ. Using the above results, the *relative shares of capital and labor*, as given by

$$\frac{(r+\delta)K}{Y} = \frac{(r+\delta)k}{y} = \frac{\alpha k^{\alpha-1}k}{k^\alpha} = \alpha,$$

$$\frac{wL}{Y} = \frac{w}{Y/L} = \frac{w}{Ay} = \frac{(1-\alpha)Ak^\alpha}{Ak^\alpha} = 1-\alpha,$$

are also constant along the balanced growth path.

11.3 A Digression on Low-Income Traps

The foregoing discussion assumed that the population growth rate, n, was exogenous [Equation (11.7)]. Suppose for a moment that the rate of population growth is *endogenous* and *nonlinearly* related to the capital-effective labor ratio. As shown in early contributions by Buttrick (1958) and Nelson (1956), in such conditions the Solow-Swan model can lead to a **dynamically stable, low-steady-state** level of per capita income.[10]

Formally, suppose that $n = n(k)$; the basic dynamic equation of the Solow-Swan model, Equation (11.15), becomes

$$\dot{k} = sk^\alpha - [n(k) + \gamma + \delta]k.$$

Suppose, specifically, that the function $n(k)$ is such that the population growth rate is

- *negative* at low levels of the capital-effective labor ratios, because the population is unable to satisfy its basic needs;

- *positive* at intermediate values of k (and thus the real wage);

- again *negative* at higher values of k.

Such a scenario may be a very plausible one for developing countries. A function $n(k)$ that satisfies these conditions is illustrated in the upper panel of Figure 11.4, which is taken from Burmeister and Dobell (1970). As shown in the lower panel of the figure, the nonlinearity of $n(k)$ implies that **multiple equilibria** (some of them unstable) may emerge.[11] In particular, the figure illustrates the possibility of a **low-level trap** (point E) at which, for small changes in k, population effects prevent any increase in the capital-effective labor

---

[10] Becker, Murphy, and Tamura (1990) provide a more modern treatment of this idea by endogenizing *fertility rates.*

[11] Burmeister and Dobell (1970, pp. 36-38) discuss endogenous labor growth in the basic Solow-Swan model by relating participation rates to the going wage. As discussed later, this extension does not affect the qualitative properties of the model, only the *speed of convergence* to the balanced growth path.

ratio and force a return to the stable equilibrium, $\tilde{k}_S$. A **big push**, however, taking the form of an exogenous increase in the saving rate for instance, would increase the capital-effective labor ratio beyond the high, unstable equilibrium point $\tilde{k}_U$, and would set the economy on a path of rising capital and income per capita. This possibility was pointed out by Rosenstein-Rodan (1961); a modern restatement of this view is offered by Murphy, Shleifer, and Vishny (1989).

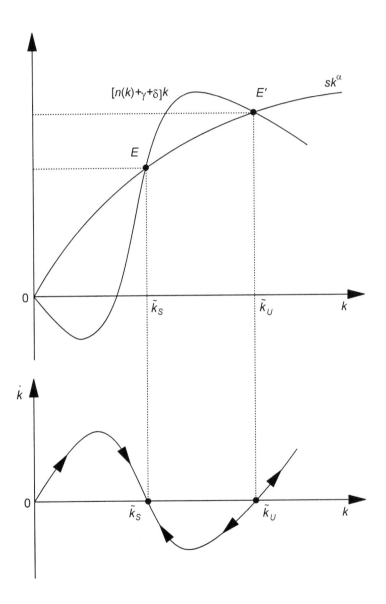

Figure 11.4. Endogenous Labor Force in the Solow-Swan Model.
Source: Adapted from Burmeister and Dobell (1970, p. 37).

11.4   Population, Savings, and Steady-State Output

Return now to the case in which the rate of growth of the labor force is indeed exogenous, and consider the effects of a change in n and a change in the saving rate, s.

Suppose that the economy's initial position is on the balanced growth path and assume first that the rate of population growth falls, at $t = 0$, from n_H to n_L. Figure 11.5 illustrates the effects of this change. The break-even investment line shifts downward; on impact, with k given at $k_0 = \tilde{k}_H$, the fall in required investment relative to actual investment (by the quantity EA) implies that $\dot{k}_0 > 0$. Thus k begins to rise and continues to do so until reaching the new steady state, which is characterized by a higher capital stock per worker ($\tilde{k}_L > \tilde{k}_H$). Output per worker, which is equal to $A\tilde{k}^\alpha$, is thus also higher in the new steady state. This positive long-run effect can be directly verified from Equation (11.17). However, the rate of growth of all variables measured in per capita terms is not affected in the long run; although the reduction in n is *permanent*, the increase in the growth rate of output per worker is only *transitory*. In the long run, Y/L grows at the same rate γ.

Suppose now that the saving rate, s, increases—as a result, say, of a sudden appetite for thrift. The increase in s (from s_L to s_H) shifts the actual investment curve, sk^α as illustrated in Figure 11.6. The steady-state capital stock therefore increases from $\tilde{k}_L$ to $\tilde{k}_H$. At the initial level of k, actual investment exceeds required investment (by the quantity EA) and so $\dot{k}_0 > 0$; k begins to rise and continues to do so until the new steady-state level $\tilde{k}_H$ is reached. Thus, an increase in the saving rate raises the capital-effective labor ratio in the long run as can be seen, again, directly from Equation (11.17).

Output per worker, Y/L, is equal to Ak^α. When k is constant, Y/L grows at rate γ, as shown earlier. During the transition from $\tilde{k}_L$ to $\tilde{k}_H$, with k increasing, the rate of growth of Y/L will exceed γ. Thus, a *permanent* increase in the saving rate leads only to a *transitory* increase in the growth rate of output per worker. Moreover, the increase in the saving rate has *no long-run effect* on the rate of growth of output and the capital stock.

As shown earlier [Equation (11.13)], consumption per unit of effective labor, c, is initially given by

$$c = (1 - s_L)k^\alpha. \tag{11.21}$$

By definition, k cannot change in discrete fashion. Thus, the step increase in s from s_L to s_H implies that consumption jumps downward. After falling initially, consumption rises gradually as k rises and s remains at s_H.

To establish whether consumption per unit of effective labor rises or falls in the long run relative to its initial level, note that on the balanced growth path, $\tilde{c}$ is given by the difference between output and actual investment:

$$\tilde{c} = \tilde{k}^\alpha - s\tilde{k}^\alpha, \tag{11.22}$$

which is given in Figure 11.2 by the distance EA. As shown by Equation (11.16), on the balanced growth path, actual investment, $s\tilde{k}^{\alpha}$, is also equal to required investment. Substituting Equation (11.16) in (11.22) results in

$$\tilde{c} = \tilde{k}^{\alpha} - (n + \delta + \gamma)\tilde{k},$$

which implies that

$$\frac{\partial \tilde{c}}{\partial s} = [\alpha \tilde{k}^{\alpha-1} - (n + \gamma + \delta)]\frac{\partial \tilde{k}}{\partial s} \gtrless 0.$$

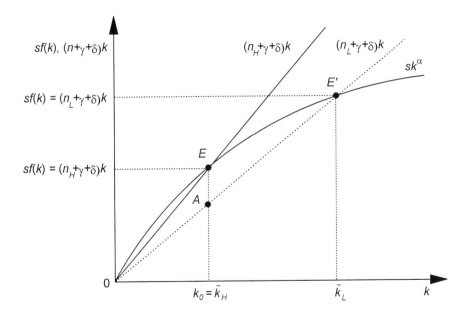

Figure 11.5. Reduction in the Population Growth Rate in the Solow-Swan Model.

Because $\partial \tilde{k}/\partial s > 0$, the sign of $\partial \tilde{c}/\partial s$ depends on whether the marginal product of capital, $\alpha \tilde{k}^{\alpha-1}$, is greater or lower than $n + \gamma + \delta$.

- If $\alpha \tilde{k}^{\alpha-1}$ is *less* than $n + \gamma + \delta$, then the additional output from the increased capital is not enough to maintain the capital stock at its higher level. In this case, consumption must fall to maintain the higher capital stock.

- If $\alpha \tilde{k}^{\alpha-1}$ is *greater* than $n + \gamma + \delta$, there is more than enough additional output to maintain k at its higher level, and so consumption rises.[12]

---

[12] The value of $\tilde{k}$ for which an increase in the saving rate has no effect on consumption

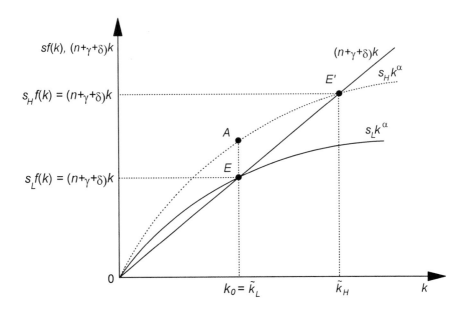

Figure 11.6. Increase in the Saving Rate in the Solow-Swan Model.

Establishing the effect of the increase in the saving rate on the long-run value of output per unit of effective labor is a bit more involved. As derived in the appendix, the long-run elasticity of y with respect to s, η, is given by

$$\eta = \frac{\alpha}{1 - \alpha}. \tag{11.23}$$

Suppose that α, the share of income paid to capital, is about 0.3—a value that appears to be largely consistent with the evidence for developing countries. Substituting this value in the above expression yields

$$\eta = \frac{0.3}{1 - 0.3} \simeq 0.43.$$

This result implies that, for instance, a 10 percent increase in the saving rate (from, say, 10 percent of output to 11 percent) raises output per unit of effective labor by only 4.3 percent in the long run relative to its initial path. Even a 50 percent increase in s (from, say, 10 percent to 15 percent) would raise $\tilde{y}$ by only about 21 percent. Thus, large changes in saving rates have only *moderate effects* on the level of output on the balanced growth path.

$(\partial \tilde{c}/\partial s = 0)$ is known as the *golden-rule* level of the capital stock. Consumption is at its maximum possible level among balanced growth paths. The golden-rule growth path is defined as the point where the marginal product of capital equals the rate of economic growth. See Barro and Sala-i-Martin (1995).

Intuitively, a small value of α makes the impact of saving on output low for two reasons (Romer, 1995, p. 21):

- a low value of α means that the impact of a change in $\tilde{k}$ on $\tilde{y}$ is small;

- it implies that the actual investment curve, sk^{α}, bends fairly sharply; as a result, an upward shift of the curve moves its intersection with the required investment line relatively little. Thus the impact of a change in s on $\tilde{k}$ is small.

11.5   The Speed of Adjustment

The foregoing discussion has focused on the *long-run* effects of changes in the population growth rate and the saving rate; in practice, it is also important to assess the *speed* at which adjustment to the new equilibrium proceeds, that is, how fast is k approaching $\tilde{k}$.

Consider first the behavior of the capital stock per unit of effective labor. As shown in the Appendix to this chapter, changes in k in the vicinity of the balanced growth path can be approximated by

$$\dot{k} \simeq \Lambda(k - \tilde{k}), \tag{11.24}$$

where

$$\Lambda = -(1 - \alpha)(n + \gamma + \delta) < 0.$$

Equation (11.24) indicates that (in the neighborhood of the balanced growth path), capital per unit of effective labor evolves toward its steady-state level at a speed *proportional to its distance* from $\tilde{k}$, with a coefficient of proportionality Λ.

Equation (11.24) is a *first-order, nonhomogeneous differential equation*, whose solution, as derived for instance in Chiang (1984, pp. 472-474), is given by

$$k - \tilde{k} \simeq e^{\Lambda t}(k_0 - \tilde{k}),$$

where k_0 denotes the initial value of k. As shown in the appendix, y approaches $\tilde{y}$ at the same rate that k approaches $\tilde{k}$:

$$y - \tilde{y} \simeq e^{\Lambda t}(y_0 - \tilde{y}). \tag{11.25}$$

Equation (11.25) can be used to assess the speed at which a Solow-Swan economy approaches its balanced growth path. Specifically, $|\Lambda|$ in the above equation measures the **speed of adjustment** of output per worker, that is, the rate at which the economy catches up to its steady-state level of y, given some initial position y_0. Put differently, Equation (11.25) indicates that $|\Lambda| \cdot 100$ percent of the initial gap between the actual level of output per worker and its steady-state level is closed every year. In particular, the speed of adjustment is a decreasing function of the capital share, α.

Suppose, for instance, that the annual rate of growth of the labor force, n, is 2 percent, technological progress γ grows at the yearly rate of 2 percent, and that the annual rate of depreciation of the capital stock, δ, is 4 percent (which implies that capital lasts an average of 25 years). Suppose, again, that capital's share in output is about 0.3. Thus,

$$\Lambda = -(1 - 0.3)(0.02 + 0.02 + 0.04) \simeq -0.056,$$

that is, output per worker (as well as the capital-effective labor ratio) moves about 6 percent of the remaining distance toward its long-run equilibrium value $\tilde{y}$ each year. Let the **adjustment ratio**, μ, be defined as the fraction of the change from y_0 to $\tilde{y}$ completed after t years:

$$\mu = \frac{y - y_0}{\tilde{y} - y_0}.$$

Using (11.25), this equation can be rewritten as

$$\mu = \frac{(y - \tilde{y}) + (\tilde{y} - y_0)}{\tilde{y} - y_0} = 1 - e^{\Lambda t},$$

or equivalently

$$e^{\Lambda t} = 1 - \mu. \tag{11.26}$$

The time taken to achieve a given fraction μ of the adjustment from y_0 to $\tilde{y}$ is thus given by[13]

$$t^* = \ln(1 - \mu)/\Lambda \simeq -\mu/\Lambda, \tag{11.27}$$

where the last result is obtained by using the approximation $\ln(1 + x) \simeq x$, for x small enough. For instance, calculating the **half-life** of the process—the time needed to eliminate one half of the initial deviation of y from its steady-state value—requires setting $\mu = 0.5$. Given the value of Λ calculated earlier, Equation (11.27) yields

$$t^* = -0.69/(-0.056) \simeq 12.4,$$

that is, it takes approximately 12 years to get half-way to the steady state $\tilde{y}$. Table 11.1 provides a more complete set of numerical results for $\delta = 0.04$. In particular, for $\alpha = 0.3$, $n = 0.01$ and $\gamma = 0.02$, the speed of adjustment is 4.9% and it takes 32.8 years to achieve 80 percent of the adjustment from y_0 to $\tilde{y}$. Thus, as emphasized very early on by Sato (1963), reaching the steady-state equilibrium in the Solow-Swan model can be a fairly long process.

---

[13] Equation (11.26) can also be used to calculate the percentage μ^* of the steady-state value achieved for a given convergence rate after t years as $1 - e^{-\Lambda t} \simeq -\Lambda t$.

Table 11.1
Solow-Swan Model: Years to Adjustment

γ	μ	$\alpha = 0.3$		$\alpha = 0.4$	
		$n = 1\%$	$n = 2\%$	$n = 1\%$	$n = 2\%$
		$|\Lambda| = 4.2\%$	$|\Lambda| = 4.9\%$	$|\Lambda| = 3.6\%$	$|\Lambda| = 4.2\%$
	0.2	5.3	4.6	6.2	5.3
0.01	0.5	16.5	14.1	19.3	16.5
	0.8	38.3	32.8	44.7	38.3
		$|\Lambda| = 4.9\%$	$|\Lambda| = 5.6\%$	$|\Lambda| = 4.2\%$	$|\Lambda| = 4.8\%$
	0.2	4.6	4.0	5.3	4.6
0.02	0.5	14.1	12.4	16.5	14.4
	0.8	32.8	28.7	38.3	33.5
		$|\Lambda| = 5.6\%$	$|\Lambda| = 6.3\%$	$|\Lambda| = 4.8\%$	$|\Lambda| = 5.4\%$
	0.2	4.0	3.5	4.6	4.1
0.03	0.5	12.4	11.0	14.4	12.8
	0.8	28.7	25.5	33.5	29.8

Note: These results assume that the rate of depreciation of the capital stock is 4 percent.

Source: Author's calculations.

The implication of these results is also that policy changes in the model may be associated with very long periods of adjustment. Suppose indeed that $|\Lambda| = 0.056$. In the previous example of a 10 percent increase in the saving rate, output per worker is $0.056(5\%) = 0.28\%$ above its previous path after 1 year; $0.5(5\%) = 2.5\%$ above after about 12 years; and asymptotically approaches 5% above the initial path. Thus not only is the overall impact of a substantial change in the saving rate modest, it does not occur very quickly.

A procedure similar to the one outlined above can be used to study the speed of adjustment of the *growth rate* of output, as opposed to its *level*, to its steady-state value. To do so, note first that the solution to Equation (11.24) can be written as

$$k = \tilde{k} + \eta e^{\Lambda t},$$

where η is a **constant of integration**. Substituting this result back in Equation (11.24) then yields

$$\dot{k}/k = \Lambda \left\{ 1 - \frac{\tilde{k}}{\tilde{k} + \eta e^{\Lambda t}} \right\}. \tag{11.28}$$

Because output is equal to $Y = ALk^{\alpha}$, the actual growth rate of output is equal to

$$g_Y \equiv \dot{Y}/Y = \alpha \dot{k}/k + n + \gamma = \alpha \dot{k}/k + \tilde{g}_Y, \tag{11.29}$$

where, as shown earlier [Equation (11.19)], $\tilde{g}_Y = n + \gamma$.

Substituting Equation (11.28) in (11.29) yields

$$g_Y = \alpha \Lambda \left\{ 1 - \frac{\tilde{k}}{\tilde{k} + \eta e^{\Lambda t}} \right\} + \tilde{g}_Y. \tag{11.30}$$

Setting $t = 0$ in this equation implies that

$$\alpha\Lambda\left\{1 - \frac{\tilde{k}}{\tilde{k} + \eta}\right\} = g_Y^0 - \tilde{g}_Y,$$

where g_Y^0 is given by the initial condition. Solving this equation for the constant term η yields

$$\eta = \frac{(g_Y^0 - \tilde{g}_Y)\tilde{k}}{\tilde{g}_Y - g_Y^0 + \alpha\Lambda},$$

which can be substituted back into Equation (11.30) to give

$$g_Y = \alpha\Lambda\left\{1 - \tilde{k}\left[\tilde{k} + \frac{(g_Y^0 - \tilde{g}_Y)\tilde{k}e^{\Lambda t}}{\tilde{g}_Y - g_Y^0 + \alpha\Lambda}\right]^{-1}\right\} + \tilde{g}_Y. \qquad (11.31)$$

The **adjustment ratio** can now be defined as

$$\mu = \frac{g_Y - g_Y^0}{\tilde{g}_Y - g_Y^0}. \qquad (11.32)$$

Substituting Equation (11.31) in (11.32) and solving for the time t^* (in years) required to get a fraction λ of the way from g_Y^0 to $\tilde{g}_Y$ yields

$$t^* = \Lambda^{-1}\ln\left\{\frac{(1-\mu)(\tilde{g}_Y - g_Y^0 + \alpha\Lambda)}{(1-\mu)(\tilde{g}_Y - g_Y^0) + \alpha\Lambda}\right\}.$$

11.6   Model Predictions and Empirical Facts

The following are the predictions of the Solow-Swan model regarding the long-run behavior of output, consumption, and investment and the response of these variables to changes in the population growth rate and the saving rate.

- The capital-effective labor ratio, the marginal product of capital, and output per units of effective labor, are constant on the balanced growth path.

- The steady-state growth rate of capital per worker K/L and output per worker Y/L are determined solely by the rate of technological progress. In particular, neither variable depends on the saving rate or on the specific form of the production function.

- Output, the capital stock, and effective labor all grow at the same rate, given by the sum of the growth rate of the labor force and the growth rate of technological progress.

- A reduction in the population growth rate raises the steady-state levels of the capital-effective labor ratio and output in efficiency units and lowers the rate of growth of output, the capital stock, and effective labor.

- A rise in the saving rate also increases the capital-effective labor ratio and output in efficiency units in the long run, but has no effect on the steady-state growth rates of output, the capital stock, and effective labor.

How do these predictions compare with the empirical evidence on growth and the basic facts described in the previous chapter? First, the evidence for *industrial countries* suggests that it is a reasonable first approximation to argue that the growth rates of labor, capital, and output are each about roughly constant (Romer, 1989). The growth rates of output and capital are about equal (so that the capital-output ratio is approximately constant) and are larger than the growth rate of labor; as a result, output per worker and capital per worker are rising over time. The limited evidence available for developing countries, however, does not allow any generalization.

Second, the model's predictions regarding the effects of changes in the population growth rate and the saving rate on the *level* of income (or standards of living) are also consistent with the evidence. The upper panel of Figure 10.2 showed that, indeed, as predicted by the model, lower population growth rates tend to be associated with higher levels of income per capita.[14] Similarly, the upper panel in Figure 10.3 showed that the saving rate is positively associated with the level of income per capita.

However, there are several stylized facts that the model is unable to explain. First, as discussed in the previous chapter, and as shown in the lower panels in Figures 10.3 and 10.4, both the *saving rate* and the *share of investment in output* are positively correlated (over a sufficiently long period of time) with the growth rate of income per capita (or approximately output per worker). Variations in the accumulation of physical capital do appear to account for a significant part of cross-country income differences in economic growth (see Chapter 13). By contrast, the Solow-Swan model predicts *no association* between these variables in the steady state.

Second, differences in *physical capital per worker* cannot account for the observed differences in output per worker (or income per capita)—at least if capital's contribution to output is roughly reflected by its private returns. Specifically, two difficulties arise:

- The required differences in capital are *far too large*. For instance, output per worker in the United States today is on the order of *ten times* larger than it is in, say, India today. With the Cobb-Douglas production technology used earlier, the share of capital in output, α, is also the elasticity of output with respect to the capital stock. Accounting for a tenfold difference in output per worker on the basis of differences in capital requires a difference of a factor of $10^{1/\alpha}$ in capital per worker. For $\alpha = 0.3$, this is a factor of one thousand. Even if $\alpha = 0.5$, a value that exceeds most estimates available, one still needs a difference of a factor of one hundred.

---

[14]It should be noted that a more appropriate test of the effect of per capita income on individual decisions is to look at *fertility rates*, which correct for the age structure of the population, and subtract out the effects of mortality and migration.

However, capital per worker in the United States is no more than twenty to thirty times larger than in India.[15]

- Attributing differences in output to differences in capital without differences in the effectiveness of labor implies large variations in the rate of return on capital (Lucas (1990)).

As noted earlier, the rate of return on capital, r, equals its marginal product, $\alpha k^{\alpha-1}$, minus depreciation, δ. Because the production function can be written as $k = y^{1/\alpha}$, the marginal product of capital is $\alpha y^{-(1-\alpha)/\alpha}$; this implies that the elasticity of the marginal product of capital with respect to output is $-(1-\alpha)/\alpha$. If $\alpha = 0.3$, a *tenfold difference* in output per worker arising from differences in capital per worker thus implies a *hundredfold difference* in the marginal product of (and the rate of return on) capital. Again, there is no evidence of such differences in rates of return across countries; they would lead to massive and sustained flows of capital from rich to poor countries—none of it is observed in practice, despite the evidence of the early 1990s (see Chapter 6).

Third, and most importantly, the only source of variation in the growth rate of output per worker (or income per capita) in the Solow-Swan model in the long run is the rate of growth of labor effectiveness, γ. But the model is *incomplete* because the driving force of long-run growth, the rate of increase in the effectiveness of labor, is *exogenous*.[16] The effectiveness of labor is no more than just a catchall for factors other than labor and capital that affect output. Much of the recent research in this area has focused on defining what the effectiveness of labor is, and what causes it to vary over time, in order to understand cross-country differences in the growth rates of real income. The next chapter will consider in detail several alternative interpretations.

11.7   Summary

The Solow-Swan growth model makes the following predictions.

- The capital-effective labor ratio, the marginal product of capital, and output per units of effective labor, are *constant* on the **balanced growth path**.

- The steady-state growth rates of capital per worker are determined only by the rate of technological progress.

---

[15] The same argument can be presented in terms of the rates of saving, population growth, and so on, that determine capital per worker. For instance, the elasticity of $\tilde{y}$ with respect to s is $\alpha/(1 - \alpha)$; see Eq. (11.23). Thus, accounting for a difference of a factor of ten in output per worker on the basis of differences in s would require a difference of a factor of one hundred in s if $\alpha = 0.3$ and a difference of a factor of ten if $\alpha = 0.5$. Variations in actual saving rates are much smaller than this.

[16] It should be noted that, away from the steady state, fluctuations (over time as well as across countries) in the rate of growth of output per worker can result not only from differences in the rate of growth of the effectiveness of labor, A, but also from differences in the growth rate of capital per worker, K/L. As discussed earlier, however, in most reasonable cases the impact of changes in capital per worker on output growth rates is likely to be modest.

- Output, the capital stock, and effective labor grow at the *same rate*, given by the sum of the growth rate of the labor force and the growth rate of technological progress.

- Changes in the *population growth rate* and the *saving rate* affect the steady-state *levels* of the capital-effective labor ratio and output per worker but have *no effect* on the *steady-state growth rate* of income per capita.

- If the rate of growth of the population is *nonlinearly* related to the capital-effective labor ratio (or income), the Solow-Swan model may lead to a *dynamically stable, low-steady-state level of per capita income.*

Several of these predictions are consistent with the empirical evidence on long-run growth in industrial and developing countries. The basic model remains, however, subject to a number of limitations.

- It does not account for the positive correlation between *saving* and *investment rates* and *growth* in income per capita across countries, as documented in the previous chapter.

- Differences in long-run per capita income levels across countries can result in the model only from differences in capital-effective labor ratios—which in turn may differ across countries only as a result of differences in population growth rates, rates of technological progress, and saving rates. However, observed differences in capital per worker are *far smaller* than those needed to account for the differences in output per worker (or income per capita) shown in the data.

- It provides an *incomplete* description of the growth process, because the driving force of long-run growth, the rate of increase in the effectiveness of labor, is *exogenous.*

Appendix
Dynamics of k, the Output Effect of s,
and the Speed of Adjustment

To find the explicit dynamic path of k, note that Equation (11.15) can be written as

$$\dot{k} + (n + \gamma + \delta)k = sk^{\alpha},$$

whose particular form is known as a **Bernoulli equation** (see Chiang, 1984, p. 500). Let $z = k^{1-\alpha}$, so that $\dot{z} = (1 - \alpha)k^{-\alpha}\dot{k}$; from these two results,

$$k = zk^{\alpha}, \quad \dot{k} = \frac{\dot{z}k^{\alpha}}{1 - \alpha},$$

so that the above equation can be written as

$$\dot{z} + (1 - \alpha)(n + \gamma + \delta)z = (1 - \alpha)s,$$

which is a standard linear nonhomogeneous differential equation in z, whose solution is therefore

$$z = \left\{ z_0 - \frac{s}{n + \gamma + \delta} \right\} e^{-(1-\alpha)(n+\gamma+\delta)t} + \frac{s}{n + \gamma + \delta}.$$

Substituting for z yields

$$k^{1-\alpha} = \left\{ k_0^{1-\alpha} - \frac{s}{n + \gamma + \delta} \right\} e^{-(1-\alpha)(n+\gamma+\delta)t} + \frac{s}{n + \gamma + \delta},$$

which shows that, because $(1-\alpha)(n+\gamma+\delta) > 0$, $k^{1-\alpha}$ tends to $s/(n+\gamma+\delta)$—or the solution $\tilde{k}$ given in Equation (11.17).

To establish the effect of the increase in the saving rate on output per unit of effective labor on the balanced growth path, note that because $\tilde{y} = \tilde{k}^{\alpha}$ it must be that

$$\frac{\partial \tilde{y}}{\partial s} = \alpha \tilde{k}^{\alpha-1} \left(\frac{\partial \tilde{k}}{\partial s} \right). \tag{A1}$$

As shown above, $\tilde{k}$ is determined by the equality between actual and required investment [Equation (11.16)], that is,

$$s\tilde{k}^{\alpha} - (n + \gamma + \delta)\tilde{k} = 0. \tag{A2}$$

Implicit differentiation of this expression with respect to s yields

$$s\alpha \tilde{k}^{\alpha-1}\left(\frac{\partial \tilde{k}}{\partial s} \right) + \tilde{k}^{\alpha} - (n + \gamma + \delta)\frac{\partial \tilde{k}}{\partial s} = 0,$$

which can be rearranged as

$$\frac{\partial \tilde{k}}{\partial s} = \frac{\tilde{k}^{\alpha}}{(n + \gamma + \delta) - s\alpha \tilde{k}^{\alpha-1}}.$$

Substituting this expression for $\partial \tilde{k}/\partial s$ in (A1) results in

$$\frac{\partial \tilde{y}}{\partial s} = \frac{\alpha \tilde{k}^{\alpha-1} \tilde{k}^{\alpha}}{(n + \gamma + \delta) - s\alpha \tilde{k}^{\alpha-1}}.$$

To interpret this expression, it is convenient to use Equation (11.16) to substitute for s and convert it into an elasticity by multiplying both sides by $s/\tilde{y}$.

The result is

$$\eta \equiv \frac{\partial \tilde{y}/\tilde{y}}{\partial s/s} = \left(\frac{s}{\tilde{k}^{\alpha}}\right)\frac{\alpha \tilde{k}^{\alpha-1} \tilde{k}^{\alpha}}{(n + \gamma + \delta) - s\alpha \tilde{k}^{\alpha-1}},$$

or, noting from (A2) that $s\tilde{k}^{\alpha-1} = (n + \gamma + \delta)$:

$$\eta = \frac{\alpha(n + \gamma + \delta)\tilde{k}^{\alpha}}{[(n + \gamma + \delta) - \alpha(n + \gamma + \delta)]\tilde{k}^{\alpha}},$$

which can be simplified to give Equation (11.23) in the text.

To derive Equation (11.24), note first that from Equation (11.15), $\dot{k}$ is a function of k; this relationship can be written as

$$\dot{k} = \Phi(k). \tag{A3}$$

When $k = \tilde{k}$, $\dot{k}$ is zero. Around the long-run equilibrium $(k = \tilde{k})$, therefore, a **first-order Taylor-series approximation** of $\Phi(k)$ yields (see Chiang, 1984, pp. 256-258):[17]

$$\dot{k} \simeq \Phi(\tilde{k}) + \Phi'|_{k=\tilde{k}} (k - \tilde{k}),$$

or, because $\Phi(\tilde{k}) = 0$ when $\dot{k}$ is zero (in the neighborhood of the long-run equilibrium):

$$\dot{k} \simeq \Phi'|_{k=\tilde{k}} (k - \tilde{k}), \tag{A4}$$

where $\Phi'|_{k=\tilde{k}}$ is the first-order derivative of $\dot{k}$ evaluated at $k = \tilde{k}$.

Differentiating Equation (11.15) with respect to k and evaluating the resulting expression at $k = \tilde{k}$ yields

$$\Phi'|_{k=\tilde{k}} = s\alpha \tilde{k}^{\alpha-1} - (\gamma + n + \delta),$$

or, using Equation (11.16) to substitute for s:

$$\Phi'|_{k=\tilde{k}} = \Lambda = -(1 - \alpha)(n + \gamma + \delta) < 0,$$

---

[17] The speed of adjustment derived from this procedure provides, strictly speaking, a reliable estimate only in an arbitrarily small neighborhood around the balanced growth path. For the Solow-Swan model with conventional production functions, and for moderate changes in parameter values (such as the change in s considered earlier), the Taylor-series approximations are deemed reliable. In general, however, Taylor-series approximations do not provide reliable estimates for *finite changes*. See Mulligan and Sala-i-Martin (1993) for a discussion.

which can be substituted in (A4) to yield Equation (11.24).

To show that y approaches $\tilde{y}$ at the same rate that k approaches $\tilde{k}$, note first that, from Equation (11.5), $\dot{y} = \alpha k^{\alpha-1}\dot{k}$; using (A3) and the fact that $k = y^{1/\alpha}$ yields

$$\dot{y} = \alpha k^{\alpha-1}\Phi(k) = \alpha y^{(\alpha-1)/\alpha}\Phi(y^{1/\alpha}) = \Gamma(y).$$

A *linear approximation* in the vicinity of $y = \tilde{y}$ now yields, because $\Gamma(\tilde{y}) = 0$,

$$\dot{y} = \Gamma'|_{y=\tilde{y}}\,(y - \tilde{y}),$$

where, because $\Phi(\tilde{y}^{1/\alpha}) = 0$,

$$\Gamma'|_{y=\tilde{y}} = \alpha y^{(\alpha-1)/\alpha}\,\Phi'|_{y=\tilde{y}} = \alpha\tilde{y}^{(\alpha-1)/\alpha}[sy - (\gamma + n + \delta)y^{1/\alpha}]'_{y=\tilde{y}},$$

that is,

$$\Gamma'|_{y=\tilde{y}} = \alpha s\tilde{y}^{(\alpha-1)/\alpha} - (\gamma + n + \delta).$$

Using Equation (11.16) yields $s = (\gamma+n+\delta)\tilde{y}^{1/\alpha}/\tilde{y}$, which can be substituted in the above expression to give $\Gamma'|_{y=\tilde{y}} = \Lambda$.

Chapter 12

Knowledge, Human Capital, and Endogenous Growth

The Solow-Swan model studied in the previous chapter does not fully explain some of the basic facts about economic growth in developing countries identified in Chapter 10. Apart from capital, the only determinant of per capita income in the model is the effectiveness of labor, A, whose exact meaning is not specified and whose behavior is taken as exogenous. Moreover, assuming that the rate of return on capital reflects its contribution to output and that its share in total income is set at plausible levels, differences in capital intensity cannot account for cross-country income differences.

Understanding the sources of growth and the divergent patterns of income observed across countries has been the subject of much thinking in the past few years. This research has highlighted the existence of a variety of *endogenous mechanisms* that foster economic growth, and has suggested new roles for public policy. This revival of interest has largely been the result of the influential contributions of Lucas (1988), Grossman and Helpman (1991), and Romer (1986). This chapter considers several of these new perspectives on growth.[1]

The first part of this chapter focuses on the view that the driving force of growth is the *accumulation of knowledge*. It examines various mechanisms through which knowledge is produced and resources allocated to knowledge production. The second perspective, examined in the second part, takes a broader view of capital to include *human* capital. These models (which in some regards can be seen as extensions of the Solow-Swan model) imply that the income share of *physical* capital alone may not be an accurate measure of the overall importance of capital. A broad measure of capital raises the possibility that dif-

---

[1] For comprehensive overviews, see Aghion and Howitt (1998), and Barro and Sala-i-Martin (1995). Jones and Manuelli (1997) provide a more technical survey of some important classes of endogenous growth models.

ferences in capital intensity may be able to account, after all, for cross-country differences in incomes per capita. The third part discusses the links between human capital accumulation, public policy toward education, and growth. The last part considers various other determinants of growth emphasized in the recent growth literature—including fiscal policy (changes in government spending, taxation, and fiscal deficits), inflation and macroeconomic stability, trade liberalization, the degree of financial development, political factors and income inequality, and the role of institutions.

12.1   The Accumulation of Knowledge

There are two main mechanisms through which the creation of knowledge is captured in endogenous growth models: as a by-product of economic activity, or as a production activity in its own right. Of course, these approaches are rather mechanical; in reference to the latter, Solow (1994, pp. 51-52), for instance, wrote

> There is probably an irreducibly exogenous element in the research and development process, at least exogenous to the economy. Fields of research open up and close down unpredictably, in economics as well as in science and technology. This is reflected, for instance, in the frequency with which research projects end up by finding something that was not even contemplated when the initial decisions were made. There is an internal logic—or sometimes non-logic—to the advance of knowledge that may be orthogonal to the economic logic. This is not at all to deny the partially endogenous character of innovation but only to suggest that the "production" of new technology may not be a simple matter of inputs and outputs.

Nevertheless, it is worth presenting illustrative models of both mechanisms because they have very different implications regarding the determinants of an economy's steady-state growth rate.

12.1.1   Knowledge As a By-Product: Learning by Doing

A key source of technological progress, as emphasized by Arrow (1962), results from **learning by doing**. In such a framework, experience, measured in various ways (in terms, for instance, of cumulative past investment or output) plays a critical role in raising labor productivity over time.

A simple way to illustrate Arrow's learning-by-doing approach is to assume that the level of productivity, A, is related to the absolute size of the capital stock and to an autonomous factor, Z, so that

$$A = ZK^\theta,$$

where θ is a positive coefficient. Differentiating this expression with respect to time yields

$$\frac{\dot{A}}{A} = \theta(\frac{\dot{K}}{K}) + \gamma, \quad 0 < \theta < 1, \tag{12.1}$$

where $\gamma \ (\equiv \dot{Z}/Z)$ can be viewed, as before, as the exogenous rate of labor-augmenting technical change. The parameter θ is often described as the *learning coefficient*, which may depend, in particular, on government spending on education (see below). Thus, technological change is partly *exogenous*, and partly *endogenous*. The Solow-Swan model corresponds to the case in which $\theta = 0$.[2]

To examine the implications of this specification, consider again the case in which the production technology is Cobb-Douglas, which in intensive form is given by

$$y = k^{\alpha}, \tag{12.2}$$

where $k = K/AL$. Capital accumulation and the labor force growth rate are again given by

$$\dot{K} = sY - \delta K, \quad \dot{L}/L = n. \tag{12.3}$$

From Equations (12.2) and (12.3), the growth rate of the capital stock is given by

$$\frac{\dot{K}}{K} = s\left(\frac{Y}{AL}\right)\left(\frac{AL}{K}\right) - \delta = \frac{sk^{\alpha}}{k} - \delta, \tag{12.4}$$

whereas the growth rate of labor in efficiency units is given by, using Equation (12.1):

$$\frac{\dot{A}}{A} + \frac{\dot{L}}{L} = \theta\left(\frac{\dot{K}}{K}\right) + \gamma + n. \tag{12.5}$$

Differentiating the expression $k = K/AL$ with respect to time yields

$$\frac{\dot{k}}{k} = \frac{\dot{K}}{K} - \left(\frac{\dot{A}}{A} + \frac{\dot{L}}{L}\right), \tag{12.6}$$

so that, using Equations (12.4) and (12.5):

$$\dot{k} = s(1 - \theta)k^{\alpha} - [\gamma + n + \delta(1 - \theta)]k, \tag{12.7}$$

which is a nonlinear, first-order differential equation in k similar to the one derived in the previous chapter for the Solow-Swan model. The equilibrium capital-effective labor ratio is thus given by

$$\tilde{k} = \left\{\frac{s(1 - \theta)}{n + \gamma + \delta(1 - \theta)}\right\}^{1/(1-\alpha)},$$

from which it can readily be established that an increase in the learning coefficient θ, by raising the level of effective labor, reduces the steady-state value of the capital-effective labor ratio.

Setting $\dot{k} = 0$ in Equation (12.6), the steady-state growth rate of the capital stock is thus given by, using Equation (12.5),

$$\tilde{g}_K \equiv \left.\frac{\dot{K}}{K}\right|_{k=\tilde{k}} = \theta\tilde{g}_K + \gamma + n,$$

---

[2] Assuming that knowledge accumulation occurs as a *side effect of goods production* rather than capital accumulation leads to qualitatively similar conclusions to those derived here.

so that

$$\tilde{g}_K = \frac{\gamma + n}{1 - \theta}.$$

The steady-state growth rate of output, ALk^α, is thus equal to

$$\tilde{g}_Y = \theta\tilde{g}_K + \gamma + n = \frac{\gamma + n}{1 - \theta},$$

so that income per worker, Y/L, grows on the balanced growth path at the rate

$$\tilde{g}_{Y/L} = \tilde{g}_Y - n = \frac{\gamma + \theta n}{1 - \theta}. \tag{12.8}$$

Thus, in Arrow's model, although the learning coefficient has a *positive* effect on the steady-state growth rate of output, the latter remains *independent of the saving rate*. In addition, this model predicts that an increase in the population growth rate, n, *raises* the steady-state growth rate of output per worker—in contrast to the Solow-Swan model, where an increase in n has no effect on Y/L. The evidence reviewed in Chapter 10, however, suggests that the population growth rate and the growth rate of income per capita (or output per worker) are *negatively* related.

The upshot of the above analysis is thus that although Arrow's formulation of learning by doing is capable of explaining differences in growth rates in per capita incomes by differences in the ability to learn from experience (going in this sense beyond the Solow-Swan model, which relies only on differences in the rate of technological progress), it still gives *no role to saving* and *investment rates*.

An extension of Arrow's learning-by-doing model presented by Villanueva (1994) addresses this issue. Specifically, the introduction of learning through experience in Villanueva's model has three attractive consequences.

- The equilibrium growth rate becomes *endogenous* and may be influenced by government policies.

- The *speed of adjustment* to the equilibrium growth path is faster than in the Solow-Swan model, and enhanced learning reduces adjustment time.

- The equilibrium rate of output growth exceeds the sum of the exogenous rates of technical change and population growth.

The key relationship of Villanueva's modified Arrow model is the equation driving the efficiency of labor, which is given by, instead of Equation (12.1),

$$\dot{A} = \theta(\frac{K}{L}) + \gamma A, \quad \theta > 0, \tag{12.9}$$

Equation (12.9) indicates that technical change is positively related to the capital stock per worker, K/L.[3] Put differently, the productivity of workers

---

[3] This specification is reminiscent of an early contribution by Conlisk (1967), who related the rate of growth of the labor force not only to an exogenous component, n, but also to output per worker, Q/L.

increases when the relative availability of capital goods (for instance, the stock of high-performance computers) rises.

Suppose again that the production technology is Cobb-Douglas [as shown in Equation (12.2)] and that capital accumulation and the labor force growth rate are given by Equation (12.3). The growth rate of the capital stock is thus again given by Equation (12.4). Using Equation (12.9), the growth rate of labor in efficiency units is now given by

$$\frac{\dot{A}}{A} + \frac{\dot{L}}{L} = \theta k + \gamma + n. \tag{12.10}$$

Differentiating the expression $k = K/AL$ with respect to time and substituting Equation (12.10) now yields

$$\dot{k}/k = sk^{\alpha-1} - \theta k - (\gamma + n + \delta), \tag{12.11}$$

an equation for which no explicit solution can be derived—in contrast to the case studied in the appendix to Chapter 11, which corresponds to $\theta = 0$. The equilibrium capital-effective labor ratio can nevertheless by obtained from Equation (12.11) by setting $\dot{k} = 0$, so that

$$s\tilde{k}^{\alpha-1} - \theta\tilde{k} - (\gamma + n + \delta) = 0.$$

Using the **implicit function theorem**, it can be established from the above expression that $\partial\tilde{k}/\partial\theta < 0$.[4] Thus, as in Arrow's model, an increase in the speed of learning lowers the equilibrium capital-effective labor ratio.

The steady-state growth rates of the capital stock and output are now equal to

$$\tilde{g}_Y = \tilde{g}_K = \theta\tilde{k} + \gamma + n,$$

whereas income per worker, $Y/L = Ak^{\alpha}$, which grows away from the steady state at the rate

$$\frac{\dot{Y}}{Y} - n = \alpha(\frac{\dot{k}}{k}) + \theta k + \gamma, \tag{12.12}$$

has an equilibrium growth rate given by

$$\tilde{g}_{Y/L} = \theta\tilde{k} + \gamma.$$

In contrast to Arrow's model [Equation (12.8)], $\tilde{g}_{Y/L}$ now depends on the steady-state value of the capital-effective labor ratio—as long as θ is different from zero.

The determination of the equilibrium growth in the modified Arrow model is depicted in Figure 12.1.

---

[4]The implicit function theorem states that for a given equation in the form $H(y, x_1, ...x_n) = 0$ to define an implicit function $y = h(x_1, ...x_n)$ it is sufficient that a) the function H has continuous partial derivatives; and b) at a point $(y^0, x_1^0, ...x_n^0)$ satisfying the equation $H(\cdot) = 0$, H_y is not zero. In this case, $H(\cdot)$ is defined as $H(\tilde{k}, s, n, \theta)$, with $y = \tilde{k}$. See Chiang (1984, pp. 206-208) for more details.

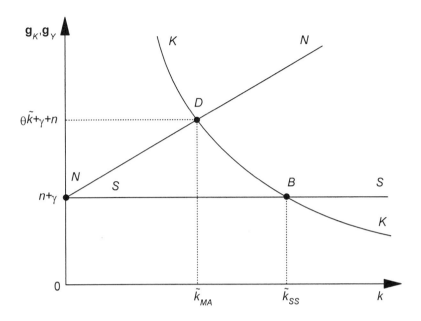

Figure 12.1. The Steady-State Growth Rate in the Solow-Swan and Modified Arrow Models.

Source: Adapted from Villanueva (1994, p. 8).

- Curve KK corresponds to Equation (12.4), and shows the growth rate of the capital stock, $\dot{K}/K$, as a function of the capital-effective labor ratio, k. It is *downward sloping* as a result of diminishing marginal returns to capital ($\alpha < 1$).

- The line NN corresponds to the growth rate of effective labor in the modified Arrow model, as given by Equation (12.10); it is *upward sloping* because $\theta > 0$.

- The curve SS corresponds to the growth rate of effective labor in the Solow-Swan model, which is equal to $n + \gamma$ [that is, Equation (12.10) with $\theta = 0$].

The balanced growth path of the Solow-Swan model is obtained at point B, which corresponds to the intersection of KK and SS. The balanced growth path of the modified Arrow model, by contrast, is obtained at the intersection of KK and NN (point D). The growth rate of output, g_Y, is thus *higher* in the modified Arrow model by the magnitude $\theta \tilde{k}$, which reflects induced learning by doing. The capital-effective labor ratio, however, is lower in the modified Arrow model ($\tilde{k}_{MA} < \tilde{k}_{SS}$), because of a higher level of effective labor.

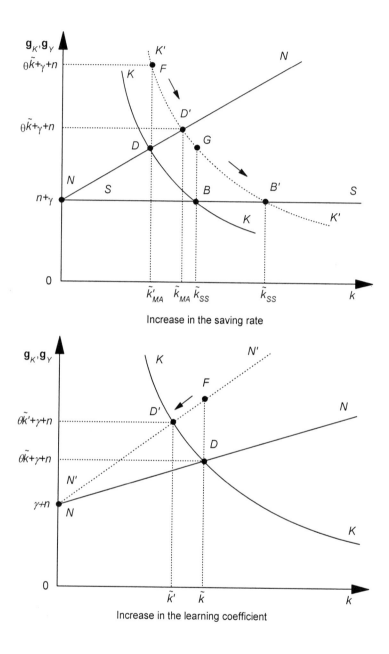

Figure 12.2. Properties of the Modified Arrow Model.

Source: Adapted from Villanueva (1994, pp. 11 and 13).

To illustrate the properties of this model, it is worth examining the effects of an *increase in the saving rate*, s, as was done in the previous chapter in the context of the Solow-Swan model. Such effects are illustrated in Figure 12.2, in which the initial positions of the Solow-Swan and modified Arrow models are indicated by Points B and D, respectively. An increase in the saving rate shifts the KK curve to the right in both models. The new equilibrium positions are given respectively by point B' in the Solow-Swan model and point D' in the modified Arrow model. In both models, the capital-effective labor ratio rises, although the new ratio remains lower in the modified Arrow model (as a result of learning by doing) compared with the Solow-Swan model. But the new steady-state growth rate *rises* in the modified Arrow model, whereas it does not change in the Solow-Swan model.

During the transition between equilibrium points B and B', the rate of output growth in the Solow-Swan model is temporarily higher—as measured by the distance BD—than the natural rate $n + \gamma$ because the growth of capital increases as a result of the rise in the saving rate. Formally, from Equation (12.12) with $\theta = 0$, because $\dot{k}/k$ is positive anywhere between $\tilde{k}_{SS}$ and $\tilde{k}'_{SS}$, $\dot{Y}/Y$ must be greater than $n + \gamma$ throughout the transition from B to B'. Nevertheless, the growth rate of output falls over time (the vertical distance between the horizontal curve SS and $K'K'$ diminishes continuously between $\tilde{k}_{SS}$ and $\tilde{k}'_{SS}$) as a result of diminishing marginal returns. In the new steady state (point B'), because $\dot{k} = 0$, $\dot{Y}/Y$ is again equal to $n + \gamma$. Thus, as shown in the previous chapter, the long-run effect of a rise in the saving rate is an increase in the capital-effective labor ratio, with no change in the economy's steady-state rate of output growth.

In the modified Arrow model, by contrast, the increase in the saving rate shifts the long-run equilibrium position (the point of intersection of $K'K'$ and NN) to D'. At the initial level of the capital-effective labor ratio $\tilde{k}_{MA}$, the growth rate of the capital stock jumps from point D to point F (implying that the growth rate of output jumps also), and the capital-effective labor ratio begins to increase along $K'K'$. This increase tends to reduce over time the marginal (and average) product of capital, thereby lowering the level of saving per unit of capital and reducing the growth rate of the capital stock—from point F to point D'. At the same time, because the increase in the capital-effective labor ratio tends to raise the rate of labor-augmenting technical change, the rate of growth of effective labor begins to increase also—rising from point D to point D' along NN. This process continues until a new long-run equilibrium is achieved, in which the growth rates of the capital stock and effective labor are equal (point D').

Another important feature of the modified Arrow model is the dynamic adjustment process associated with an *increase in the learning coefficient*, θ. As illustrated in the lower panel of Figure 12.2, an increase in θ shifts the NN curve to the left, and its slope becomes steeper. The adjustment dynamics are as follows. Following the increase in θ, and at the initial equilibrium point $\tilde{k}_{MA}$, the rate of change of effective labor rises above $\gamma + n$ [as implied by Equation (12.10)], jumping from point D to point F, whereas the rate of change of the capital-effective labor ratio, $\dot{k}/k$, turns negative [as implied by Equation (12.11)]. From Equation (12.6), this last result implies that the rate of growth of effective labor is higher than the growth rate of the capital stock, and the capital-effective labor ratio begins to fall toward $\tilde{k}'_{MA}$. As k falls, income per unit of capital [Y/K, which is equal to $1/k^{1-\alpha}$ from Equation (12.4)] increases, stimulating saving and investment, and the growth rate of the capital stock begins rising. At the same time, the fall in the capital-effective labor ratio reduces over time the rate at which technological progress is occurring [$\dot{A}/A = \theta k + \gamma$, from Equation (12.9)]. The growth rate of effective labor, $\dot{A}/A + n$, therefore falls also over time [Equation (12.10)]. This process continues until the growth rates of the capital stock and effective labor are equal (point D'). The new long-run equilibrium is characterized by a lower level of the capital-effective labor ratio and a higher growth rate of per capita output and income.

The model also has interesting implications—as does the original Arrow model of learning by doing presented earlier—for the *speed of adjustment* to the steady state. From Equation (12.11), it can be shown that[5]

$$\dot{k} = \Lambda(k - \tilde{k}), \quad \Lambda < 0. \tag{12.13}$$

As in the previous chapter, the speed of adjustment of the actual growth rate of output to its steady-state value, $\tilde{g}_Y = \theta\tilde{k} + \gamma + n$, can be easily calculated. The **adjustment ratio** can again be defined as

$$\mu = \frac{g_Y - g_Y^0}{\tilde{g}_Y - g_Y^0}.$$

Solving for g_Y and substituting the result in this equation implies that the time t^* (in years) required to get a fraction μ of the way from g_Y^0 to $\tilde{g}_Y$ is given by

$$t^* = \Lambda^{-1} \ln\left\{\frac{(1-\mu)(\tilde{g}_Y - g_Y^0 + \alpha\Lambda)}{(1-\mu)(\tilde{g}_Y - g_Y^0) + \alpha\Lambda}\right\}.$$

Simulation results performed by Villanueva (1994) showed that the adjustment time in this model is about a quarter to a third of what is derived from the Solow-Swan model, depending on the value of the learning coefficient θ (which affects Λ). Thus, the presence of learning by doing implies that convergence to the balanced growth path occurs *more quickly*. Of course, the generality or empirical relevance of Villanueva's specification remain open to question. At the conceptual level, nevertheless, it provides a useful illustration (consistent with various other models) of the importance of learning for the growth

---

[5]Following the procedure outlined in the appendix to Chapter 11, Eq. (12.11) can be written as

$$\dot{k} = sk^\alpha - \theta k^2 - (\gamma + n + \delta)k = \Phi(k).$$

Taking a linear approximation in the neighborhood of $\tilde{k}$ yields

$$\dot{k} \simeq \Phi(\tilde{k}) + \Phi'\big|_{k=\tilde{k}}(k - \tilde{k}),$$

which, because $\Phi(\tilde{k}) = 0$, corresponds to Eq. (12.13) with

$$\Phi'\big|_{k=\tilde{k}} = \Lambda \equiv s\alpha\tilde{k}^{\alpha-1} - 2\theta\tilde{k} - (\gamma + n + \delta).$$

Note that Λ is, in general, ambiguous; ensuring stability requires assuming that $\Lambda < 0$.

process. More generally, Villanueva's variant of Arrow's specification of endogenous technical change is potentially capable of explaining the diversity in per capita growth rates across countries indicated by the data. Such diversity can be explained not only in terms of differences in population growth rates, but also in terms of differences in saving rates and parameters that influence the learning process—such as government spending on education (see below).

12.1.2   The Production of Knowledge

The foregoing discussion assumed that the accumulation of knowledge occurs as a natural *by-product* of economic activity. This section discusses the case where, on the contrary, knowledge must be produced, like any other good.

Following Romer (1990), consider an economy with two production sectors:

- a *goods-producing sector*, which uses physical capital, knowledge, and labor in the production process; and

- a *knowledge-producing sector*, where additions to the stock of knowledge are made using the same inputs.

A fraction ϕ_L of the labor force is used in the knowledge-producing sector, and a fraction $1 - \phi_L$ in the goods-producing sector. Similarly, a fraction ϕ_K of the capital stock is used in the knowledge-producing sector, and a fraction $1 - \phi_K$ in the goods-producing sector. Both sectors use the *full stock of knowledge*, A. The rationale here is **nonrivalry**: the use of an element or component of knowledge in one sector does not preclude its use in the other sector.

Output in the goods-producing sector is given by a conventional Cobb-Douglas function

$$Y = [(1 - \phi_K)K]^\alpha [A(1 - \phi_L)L]^{1-\alpha}, \quad 0 < \alpha < 1, \tag{12.14}$$

which implies constant returns to *both* capital and (effective) labor. By contrast, the production of knowledge is determined by the **generalized Cobb-Douglas** form

$$\dot{A} = \gamma(\phi_K K)^\beta (\phi_L L)^\eta A^\kappa, \quad \beta \geq 0, \ \eta \geq 0, \tag{12.15}$$

with no restriction placed on θ in Equation (12.15). If $\kappa = 1$, $\dot{A}$ is proportional to A; the effect is stronger if $\kappa > 1$, and weaker if $\kappa < 1$. The production function for knowledge is not assumed to have constant returns to scale to capital and labor.[6] Setting $\beta = \eta = \phi_K = \phi_L = 0$, and $\kappa = 1$, the production function for knowledge accumulation becomes $\dot{A}/A = \gamma$, which implies that A grows at a constant rate—as in the Solow-Swan model.

Unlike the previous models of learning by doing, the dynamics of the above model cannot be characterized by a single differential equation in the capital-effective labor ratio. The dynamics involve the two endogenous stock variables,

---

[6] The fact that the function does not necessarily have constant returns to scale is the reason for referring to it as a generalized Cobb-Douglas function.

K and A, making the model more complicated to analyze. As shown by Romer (1990), under the same assumptions as above regarding capital accumulation and the labor force growth [Equation (12.3)], the steady-state growth rates of knowledge and capital are given by

$$\tilde{g}_A = \frac{\beta + \eta}{1 - (\kappa + \beta)} n, \quad \tilde{g}_K = \tilde{g}_Y = n + \tilde{g}_A,$$

and the growth rate of output per worker by

$$\tilde{g}_{Y/L} = \tilde{g}_K - n = \tilde{g}_A.$$

Thus, the economy's growth rate is an increasing function of population growth and is zero if population growth is zero—because in that case $\tilde{g}_A = 0$. The fractions of the labor force and the capital stock used in the knowledge-producing sector, ϕ_L and ϕ_K, have no effect on the growth rate, nor does the saving rate, s. Thus the specific mechanism by which a knowledge-producing sector was introduced does not alter significantly the predictions of the Solow-Swan model. Consequently, the model suffers from the same limitations regarding its ability to explain some of the basic empirical facts that appear to characterize the growth process in developing countries.

12.2 Human Capital and Returns to Scale

Another strand of the recent literature on growth focuses on the accumulation of human capital—as distinct from the accumulation of knowledge. Human capital is viewed as consisting of the abilities, skills, and knowledge of individual workers. In that perspective, it has been emphasized that human capital, very much like conventional economic goods, is *rival* (use of a particular good by one individual precludes its use by another individual at the same time) and *excludable* (an individual can prevent others from using the good that he or she is using). By contrast, as indicated earlier, aggregate knowledge is typically nonrival. This section presents two models of growth with both physical and human capital accumulation: the model of Mankiw, Romer, and Weil (1992), and the so-called AK model of Rebelo (1991).[7]

12.2.1 The Mankiw-Romer-Weil Model

Aside from the inclusion of human capital, the model developed by Mankiw, Romer, and Weil (1992) resembles the Solow-Swan model in the sense that it assumes constant returns to scale. However, as shown below, it differs in an important way from that model because relatively small changes in the resources devoted to physical and human capital accumulation may lead to large changes

---

[7]For other models of human capital accumulation and growth, see Lucas (1988) and Azariadis and Drazen (1990).

in output per worker. As a result, it is more able to account for large differences in real incomes across countries.

There is only one production sector, with output given by

$$Y = K^{\alpha} H^{\beta} (AL)^{1-\alpha-\beta}, \quad \alpha, \beta > 0, \ \alpha + \beta < 1, \tag{12.16}$$

where H is the stock of human capital, and L the number of workers, as before. Thus, there are *constant returns* to K, L and H. As before, it is assumed that

$$\dot{K} = s_K Y - \delta K, \quad \dot{L}/L = n, \tag{12.17}$$

where now s_K denotes the fraction of output devoted to investment.

As in the Solow-Swan model, technological progress is taken to be exogenous:

$$\dot{A}/A = \gamma. \tag{12.18}$$

Investment in human capital is also assumed to represent a fixed fraction of output:[8]

$$\dot{H} = s_H Y. \tag{12.19}$$

Let $h = H/AL$ be the **human capital-effective labor ratio**. The production function (12.16) can be written in intensive form as

$$y = k^{\alpha} h^{\beta}, \tag{12.20}$$

where, as before, $k = K/AL$ and $y = Y/AL$.

To determine the dynamics of k, note that from the definition of k, as shown in the previous chapter,

$$\dot{k} = \frac{\dot{K}}{AL} - \left(\frac{K}{AL}\right)\frac{\dot{L}}{L} - \left(\frac{K}{AL}\right)\frac{\dot{A}}{A},$$

which can be written as, using Equations (12.17) and (12.18):

$$\dot{k} = s_K y - \varphi k,$$

where $\varphi = n + \gamma + \delta$. Equivalently, using Equation (12.20), this equation can be rewritten as:

$$\dot{k} = s_K k^{\alpha} h^{\beta} - \varphi k. \tag{12.21}$$

Similarly, from the definition of h,

$$\dot{h} = \frac{\dot{H}}{AL} - \left(\frac{H}{AL}\right)\left\{\frac{\dot{L}}{L} + \frac{\dot{A}}{A}\right\},$$

---

[8] See Cohen (1996*b*) for a more general specification of the law of motion of human capital. Cohen's specification assumes that knowledge and output are not proportional, and that human capital plays a larger role in the production of knowledge than in the production of goods.

which can be written as, using Equations (12.18), (12.19) and (12.20):

$$\dot{h} = s_H k^\alpha h^\beta - \varphi h. \tag{12.22}$$

Equations (12.21) and (12.22) form a first-order differential equation system in k and h, which can be linearized around the steady state to give

$$\begin{bmatrix} \dot{k} \\ \dot{h} \end{bmatrix} = \begin{bmatrix} a_{11} & a_{12} \\ a_{21} & a_{22} \end{bmatrix} \begin{bmatrix} k - \tilde{k} \\ h - \tilde{h} \end{bmatrix}, \tag{12.23}$$

where

$$a_{11} = \alpha s_K \tilde{k}^{\alpha-1} \tilde{h}^\beta - \varphi, \quad a_{12} = \beta s_K \tilde{k}^\alpha \tilde{h}^{\beta-1} > 0,$$

$$a_{21} = \alpha s_H \tilde{k}^{\alpha-1} \tilde{h}^\beta > 0, \quad a_{22} = \beta s_H \tilde{k}^\alpha \tilde{h}^{\beta-1} - \varphi,$$

and $\tilde{k}$ and $\tilde{h}$ are the steady-state values obtained by setting $\dot{k} = 0$ and $\dot{h} = 0$ in Equations (12.21) and (12.22):

$$s_K \tilde{k}^\alpha \tilde{h}^\beta = \varphi \tilde{k}, \quad s_H \tilde{k}^\alpha \tilde{h}^\beta = \varphi \tilde{h}.$$

Because $0 < \alpha < 1$ and $0 < \beta < 1$, these two equations imply that $a_{11} < 0$ and $a_{22} < 0$. They also yield two relationships between k and h,

$$\tilde{k} = \left\{ \left(\frac{s_K}{\varphi} \right) \tilde{h}^\beta \right\}^{1/(1-\alpha)}, \quad \tilde{k} = \left\{ \left(\frac{\varphi}{s_H} \right) \tilde{h}^{1-\beta} \right\}^{1/\alpha}, \tag{12.24}$$

which can be solved for $\tilde{k}$ and $\tilde{h}$.

The first equation of (12.24) is shown in Figure 12.3 as curve KK in the k-h space.[9] The slope of this curve is positive and given by

$$\left. \frac{dh}{dk} \right|_{KK} = -\frac{a_{21}}{a_{22}} > 0. \tag{12.25}$$

In addition, Equation (12.21) implies that $\dot{k}$ is increasing in h. Thus, $\dot{k}$ is positive (negative) to the right (left) of the KK curve, as illustrated by the horizontal arrows. Similarly, the second Equation in (12.24) is illustrated in Figure 12.3 as curve HH. The slope of HH is positive and given by

$$\left. \frac{dh}{dk} \right|_{HH} = -\frac{a_{11}}{a_{12}} > 0. \tag{12.26}$$

Again, Equation (12.22) implies that $\dot{h}$ is positive (negative) above (below) HH as shown by the vertical arrows.

For the linearized system (12.24) to be **locally stable** requires that

- The determinant of the matrix of coefficients, **A**, must be positive, to guarantee that the two roots of the system have the same sign:

$$\det \mathbf{A} = a_{11}a_{22} - a_{12}a_{21} > 0;$$

---

[9] See Chiang (1984, pp. 628-634) for a discussion of two-variable phase diagrams.

- The trace of matrix $\mathbf{A}$ must be negative, to ensure at least one negative root:

$$\det \mathbf{A} = a_{11} + a_{22} < 0.$$

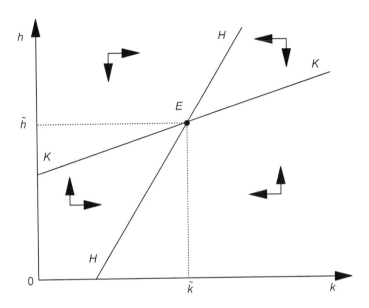

Figure 12.3. Dynamics of Human and Physical Capital per Unit of Effective Labor in the Mankiw-Romer-Weil Model.

The second condition is always satisfied, whereas the first requires HH to cut KK from below. This case is illustrated in Figure 12.3, with a long-run equilibrium position given at point E.[10] The long-run equilibrium values of physical and human capital are given by $\tilde{k}$ and $\tilde{h}$, which can be solved from Equations (12.23) and (12.25):

$$\tilde{k} = \left\{ \frac{s_K^{1-\beta} s_H^\beta}{\varphi} \right\}^{1/(1-\alpha-\beta)} \quad , \quad \tilde{h} = \left\{ \frac{s_K^\alpha s_H^{1-\alpha}}{\varphi} \right\}^{1/(1-\alpha-\beta)} .$$

Total physical capital, human capital, and output (K, H, and Y) are growing at rate $n + \gamma$; and physical capital per worker, human capital per worker, and output per worker (K/L, H/L, and Y/L) are growing at rate γ. Thus, as in the Solow-Swan model, the long-run growth rate of output per worker is determined by the exogenous rate of technological progress.

---

[10] In fact, it can be shown that the Mankiw-Romer-Weil model is *globally stable*: whatever the initial values of k and h, the economy *always converges* to the balanced growth path. See Romer (1996, pp. 128-131).

Consider again an increase in the *saving rate* s_K, under the assumption that the economy is initially on a balanced growth path. The economy's path is illustrated in Figure 12.4. Because, as shown in Equation (12.24), the dynamics of h do not depend on s_K, the curve HH is not affected; its slope, as given by Equation (12.26), remains the same. The slope of the KK curve, on the contrary, becomes steeper, as can be inferred from Equation (12.25). The new balanced growth path is now at E', located on the North-East of E. Initially (at $t = 0$) k increases ($\dot{k}_0 > 0$). The economy's position therefore moves above HH, implying that the stock of human capital-effective labor ratio begins to rise also. During the transition, both k and h increase until the new balanced growth path is reached at point E'.

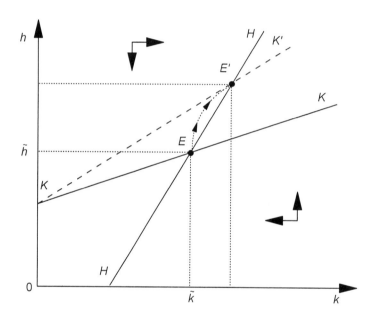

Figure 12.4. An Increase in the Saving Rate in the Mankiw-Romer-Weil Model.

From Equation (12.20), output per worker is equal to

$$Y/L = Ak^\alpha h^\beta.$$

During the transition between the two balanced growth paths, output per worker is rising both because A is rising and because k and h are rising. Thus, output per worker is growing at a rate greater than γ. When the economy reaches the new balanced growth path, k and h are again constant, and the rate of growth of output per worker returns to γ. Thus, as in the Solow-Swan model, a permanent increase in the saving rate leads to only a *temporary increase* in the economy's growth rate.

However, the implication of the model regarding the *magnitude* of the effects of changes in the saving rate and the population growth rate differ considerably from the Solow-Swan model. To see this, calculate first the level of y on the balanced growth path, $\tilde{y}$. From Equations (12.21) and (12.24), with $\dot{k} = \dot{h} = 0$ on the balanced growth path,

$$s_K \tilde{k}^\alpha \tilde{h}^\beta = \varphi \tilde{k}, \quad s_H \tilde{k}^\alpha \tilde{h}^\beta = \varphi \tilde{h},$$

which can be rewritten, in log-form, as

$$\alpha \ln \tilde{k} + \beta \ln \tilde{h} = \ln \varphi + \ln \tilde{k} - \ln s_K,$$

$$\alpha \ln \tilde{k} + \beta \ln \tilde{h} = \ln \varphi + \ln \tilde{h} - \ln s_H.$$

These two equations are linear in $\ln \tilde{k}$ and $\ln \tilde{h}$. The solution is

$$\ln \tilde{k} = \frac{1}{1 - \alpha - \beta} \left\{ (1 - \beta) \ln s_K + \beta \ln s_H - \ln \varphi \right\},$$

$$\ln \tilde{h} = \frac{1}{1 - \alpha - \beta} \left\{ \alpha \ln s_K + (1 - \alpha) \ln s_H - \ln \varphi \right\}.$$

From the production function (12.20),

$$\ln \tilde{y} = \alpha \ln \tilde{k} + \beta \ln \tilde{h}.$$

Substituting in this expression the solutions for $\ln \tilde{k}$ and $\ln \tilde{h}$ derived above yields

$$\ln \tilde{y} = \frac{\alpha}{1 - \alpha - \beta} \ln s_K + \frac{\beta}{1 - \alpha - \beta} \ln s_H - \frac{\alpha + \beta}{1 - \alpha - \beta} \ln \varphi. \tag{12.27}$$

The analogous expression for the Solow-Swan model is identical to Equation (12.27) with $\beta = 0$, and is thus given by

$$\ln \tilde{y} = \frac{\alpha}{1 - \alpha} \ln s_K - \frac{\alpha}{1 - \alpha} \ln \varphi. \tag{12.28}$$

Suppose, for instance, that β, human capital's share in output, is equal to 0.4, and that $\alpha = 0.35$. Equation (12.27) implies that with these parameter values output has elasticities of 1.4 with respect to s_K, 1.6 with respect to s_H, and -3 with respect to φ. In the model without human capital, by contrast, a value for α of 0.35 implies that the elasticity of output with respect to s_K is 0.54 and its elasticity with respect to φ is -0.54. Thus, unlike the Solow-Swan model, the Mankiw-Romer-Weil model can, because of the large elasticities of output with respect to its underlying determinants, potentially account for the observed large income differences across countries. Empirical tests of the Mankiw-Romer-Weil model are discussed in the next chapter.

Finally, because the model assumes diminishing marginal products of physical and human capital, it also implies that rates of return are lower in rich than in poor countries. Thus the model does not answer the question of why capital does not flow to poor countries—at least not in the massive and sustained amounts that the theory predicts.[11]

12.2.2 The AK Model

The foregoing analysis focused on the case of diminishing returns to physical and human capital taken together. But it is possible that there are **constant** or **increasing returns** to capital. There are at least three reasons for this to happen.

- Production methods can lead to **internal economies of scale**, once output reaches a sufficiently high level.

- Knowledge can occur as a by-product of capital accumulation (as in the learning-by-doing models discussed earlier), which then creates **positive externalities**.

- The production technology may generate **external economies of scale**. For instance, a doubling of inputs by a single firm may only doubles its own output, but a doubling of inputs by all firms *together* may more than double their total output.[12]

A simple growth model that views production as exhibiting constant returns to scale to physical and human capital together is the so-called AK model proposed by Rebelo (1991). All production inputs in the model are viewed as *reproducible capital*, including not only physical capital (as emphasized in the basic neoclassical framework), but also human capital. Specifically, denoting by K this composite measure of capital, the production function is assumed given by the linear form

$$Y = AK, \qquad (12.29)$$

where A is again a parameter that captures factors affecting the level of technology.[13]

---

[11]Tax policies, the possibility of expropriation, capital-market imperfections, and so on, could cause capital not to flow to poorer countries in the face of rate-of-return differentials—even if these differentials are large.

[12]For instance, the presence of a large number of firms producing similar products can foster the development of specialized support firms, thereby making the production process at any given firm more efficient.

[13]Another route to obtaining an equation like Eq. (12.29) is to postulate that an increasing variety or quality of machinery or intermediate inputs offsets the propensity to diminishing returns. In this interpretation, K now represents the variety or quality inputs. Research and development are necessary to obtain this variety and firms devote skilled labor to this activity. To ensure that outlays for research and development that generate these inputs are recuperated (in the form of rents) by firms that engage in such activities, markets are assumed to be monopolistically competitive. See Grossman and Helpman (1991) and Romer (1990).

Using (12.3), the steady-state growth rate of the capital stock per worker can be shown to be equal to

$$g_{K/L} = sA - (n + \delta),$$

with the steady-state growth rate of output per worker given by

$$g_{Y/L} = sA - (n + \delta), \tag{12.30}$$

which implies that the growth rate is, for $sA > n + \delta$, positive and constant over time. An important implication of the AK model is thus that, in contrast to the Solow-Swan and Mankiw-Romer-Weil models discussed earlier, an increase in the saving rate raises *permanently* the growth rate of output per capita. In addition, and again in contrast with the neoclassical growth model, which predicts that poor countries should grow faster than rich countries during the transition to the steady state, the AK model implies that poor countries whose production process is characterized by the same degree of technological sophistication as richer countries should always grow at the same rate as these countries, *regardless* of the initial level of income. Thus, the AK model does not predict convergence in per capita income even if countries share the same technology and are characterized by the same pattern of saving—a prediction that seems to accord well with some of the empirical evidence. However, recent time-series tests do not appear to support the basic assumptions of the AK model (Jones, 1995).

12.3 Human Capital, Public Policy, and Growth

Educational attainment is a crucial determinant of an individual's earnings capacity and of a country's stock of human capital. Poor families are often caught in a **low-education, low-skill**, and **low-income trap**: they cannot afford to forego current income and invest in education.[14] The higher the initial degree of inequality in income and asset distribution, the more likely it is that the trap will operate and poverty will be self-perpetuating. The evidence discussed in Chapter 10 seems to corroborate these assertions.

Endogenous growth theories have emphasized that in the absence of adequate collateral and other forms of credit market imperfections, (poor) individuals may find it impossible to borrow on capital markets and finance human capital accumulation (De Gregorio, 1996). Thus, restrictions on the ability to borrow may act as a constraint on the rate of economic growth in the long run. Some economists have argued that, in such conditions, the provision of *free basic education* (at the primary and secondary levels) or the creation of *public credit schemes* to cover the costs of skill acquisition may be welfare enhancing (Stern, 1989). The social value of this investment is clear: it creates **positive**

---

[14]Skill acquisition through on-the-job training and apprenticeship provides in some cases the possibility to escape from the poverty trap, but may typically be the case only for jobs requiring *moderate levels* of education.

externalities (because they benefit society as a whole), raises the steady-state rate of economic growth, and reduces income disparities.

However, while intuitively appealing, these conclusions must be treated with caution, as suggested in two studies.

- Zhang (1996) argued that although government *subsidies* to private education unambiguously stimulate growth, the *direct provision of education* by the public sector may actually *reduce* growth—despite reducing income inequality. This may occur if public education is financed through a **distortionary tax**. Even in this case, however, the positive externalities generated by higher education levels may be sufficient for government intervention to be welfare improving.

- Upadhyay (1994) showed that government *subsidies* can produce *too much education.* This is because a subsidy may increase the demand for higher education at the cost of investment in physical capital and could lead to *inefficient substitution* between skilled and unskilled labor in the long run. Paradoxically, in the long run, output can be constrained by a lack of unskilled labor, while at the same time skilled workers may be unemployed.[15]

12.4   Other Determinants of Growth

In addition to the endogenous channels of growth highlighted in the foregoing discussion, the recent literature has identified a number of other mechanisms through which government intervention can affect, directly or indirectly, the rate of growth in the long run. This section offers a review of some of these mechanisms. It focuses, in particular, on the role of fiscal policy, inflation and macroeconomic stability, openness to trade, financial development, and the role of institutional factors.

12.4.1   Fiscal Policy

Recent models of endogenous growth have shown that there are a variety of channels through which fiscal policy can have long-run effects on growth. In particular, different types of government expenditure and different types of taxes may have very different effects on growth.

Government Spending

As suggested by Tanzi and Zee (1997), government expenditure may affect the rate of economic growth in at least two ways:

- directly by increasing the economy's capital stock through, for instance, public investment in *infrastructure* (which, as noted in Chapter 1, can be *complementary* to private investment) or investment by public enterprises;

---

[15]This is akin to a situation of *luxury unemployment* discussed in Annex A in a static framework.

- indirectly by raising the marginal productivity of privately supplied factors of production—through spending on education, health, and other services that contribute to the accumulation of human capital.

Regarding the first channel, however, it should be noted that public capital, like any other production factor, is subject to diminishing marginal returns. This raises the possibility that excessive government spending on infrastructure (relative to private investment) may be *inefficient*. A key policy issue is thus to determine the optimal ratio of government to private capital formation. Another issue, of course, is that the effect of public investment also depends on the way these outlays are financed. Cashin (1995), in particular, analyzed how the effect of public investment on private investment and growth may depend on the form of taxation used to finance it. For instance, if public capital expenditure is financed by an increase in *direct taxes* and a reduction in private saving, the net effect on growth may be *negative* despite a positive effect on the marginal productivity of capital. As discussed next, there may be a trade-off involved if the only financing instrument available is **distortionary taxation**.

The Dual Effects of Taxation

In assessing the effects of taxes on economic growth, the distinction made in Chapter 3 between **lump-sum taxes** and **distortionary taxes** is essential. In practice, most taxes are distortionary; they tend therefore, everything else equal, to distort the allocation of resources through their impact on saving and investment.[16] However, whether or not they have a detrimental effect on growth *in net terms* depends on the growth benefits of the expenditures that they serve to finance. More generally, not all distortionary taxes have adverse effects on long-run economic growth; the net effect depends on whether the tax considered is used as an instrument to correct for **negative externalities** or other related distortions.

Barro (1990) developed a model that illustrates well the *dual effects* of taxation. The key idea of Barro's model is that government activities, such as the provision of public infrastructure and the protection of property rights, complement private capital. Specifically, Barro considered the following production function for firm h, with $h = 1, ...n$:

$$Y_h = AG^{1-\alpha}L_h^{1-\alpha}K_h^{\alpha}, \quad 0 < \alpha < 1, \tag{12.31}$$

where K_h is the capital stock held by h, L_h the amount of labor used by h, and G denotes the *flow* of government spending.[17] This specification implies that for each firm h, the production function exhibits constant returns to G and K_h.

---

[16] The impact of taxation on the level of investment operates through the cost of capital. As discussed in Chapter 1, the evidence on this effect is limited for developing countries. Taxation may, nevertheless, affect the *composition* of investment through a differentiated structure of tax rates on profits.

[17] The derivations that follow are actually based on Barro and Sala-i-Martin (1992, pp. 153-155). Cashin (1995) extends Barro's analysis to include the *stock of public capital*, rather than the flow of government spending in the production function.

Suppose that the government runs a *balanced budget* financed by a proportional tax on output, τ, so that

$$G = \tau Y, \quad 0 < \tau < 1, \tag{12.32}$$

where Y is aggregate output. Given that G rises along with the aggregate private capital stock and that the individual firm's production function exhibits constant returns to G and K_h, the model produces endogenous steady-state growth. Barro shows that in fact the economy's growth rate of output per capita is given by

$$\tilde{g}_{Y/L} = \alpha A^{1/\alpha} \tau^{(1-\alpha)/\alpha}(1 - \tau) - (\rho + \delta), \tag{12.33}$$

where ρ is the subjective **rate of time preference** (as discussed in Chapter 1) and δ the rate of depreciation of capital.[18]

Equation (12.33) shows that the effect of government spending on growth operates through two channels:[19]

- the term $1 - \tau$, which represents the *negative* effect of taxation on the after-tax marginal product of capital; and

- the term $\tau^{(1-\alpha)/\alpha}$, which represents the *positive* effect of the provision of public services on the after-tax marginal product of capital.

Expression (12.33) implies therefore that the growth rate rises at first with increases in the tax rate (with the positive effect dominating the negative effect), reaches a maximum at τ^*, and then begins to *decrease* with further rises in the tax rate, as illustrated in Figure 12.5. Thus for $\tau > \tau^*$, taxation and government expenditure are *inefficient* as argued earlier.

The optimal tax rate is such that it maximizes the growth rate given in Equation (12.33), that is, $d\tilde{g}_{Y/L}/d\tau = 0$. The condition that determined τ^* is thus

$$\frac{d\tilde{g}_{Y/L}}{d\tau} = \alpha A^{1/\alpha} \tau^{(1-\alpha)/\alpha} \left[\frac{(1-\tau)(1-\alpha)}{\alpha \tau} - 1 \right] = 0,$$

which yields

$$\tau^* = 1 - \alpha.$$

In a related contribution that bears particular relevance for developing countries, Loayza (1996) proposed a model that captures the idea that the imposition of high tax rates in the **formal sector** by governments that lack the capability to enforce compliance leads to a growing **informal sector**, where taxes are evaded. High tax rates therefore lower the capacity of the government to generate revenue and exert an adverse effect on growth.

---

[18] The derivation of the growth rate is relatively involved and is thus omitted here. The expression given in Eq. (12.33) assumes that the *degree of intertemporal substitution* (as defined in Chapter 1) is unity.

[19] Empirical evidence on these two effects is provided by Cashin (1995).

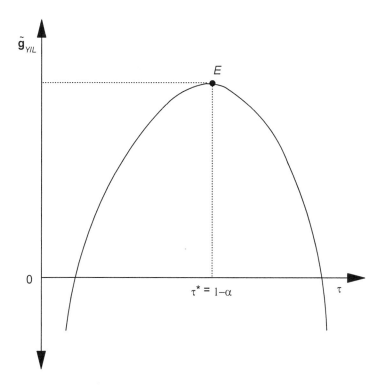

Figure 12.5. Growth and the Tax Rate in Barro's Model.
Source: Barro and Sala-i-Martin (1995, p. 155).

Loayza's model rests on Barro's (1990) analysis which, as indicated earlier, accounts explicitly for the provision of public goods. Specifically, Loayza considered an economy producing one good, which can be either consumed or invested. Agents are endowed with a broad measure of **human** and **physical capital**, and production takes place using a technology that exhibits constant returns to capital, as in the AK model of Rebelo (1991) discussed earlier.[20] As in Barro, production depends also on the *flow* of public services, G, so that

$$Y_h = A(\frac{G}{Y})^\alpha K_h, \quad 0 < \alpha < 1, \tag{12.34}$$

where Y_h is production of firm h, K_h the stock of capital owned by h, A an exogenous productivity parameter, and Y the economy's aggregate output. The coefficient α measures the elasticity of output with respect to G/Y.

At any point in time, each firm can choose to belong either to the formal economy or to the informal sector.

---

[20] Thus, *raw labor* does not have a direct role in the production process.

- Firms operating in the formal economy are subject to a proportional tax on income, τ, the proceeds of which are used to finance government expenditure, which consists not only of the flow of services that are used in the production process, but also of the spending required to *enforce the rule of law.*

- Firms operating in the informal sector are able to evade the tax on profits paid by firms in the formal sector, but they lose a fraction of their income, $\phi < \tau$, to maintain their informal sector status (say, *bribes* to government officials). At the same time, because of their illegal status, informal firms have access only to a fraction of public services that are available to society at large.

Thus, if firm h belongs to the formal sector, its net-of-tax income is given by

$$Y_h^F = (1 - \tau)A(\frac{G}{Y})^\alpha K_h, \quad 0 < \tau < 1, \tag{12.35}$$

whereas if it belongs to the informal sector, its income is

$$Y_h^I = (1 - \phi)A(\frac{\theta G}{Y})^\alpha K_h, \quad 0 < \phi, \theta < 1, \tag{12.36}$$

where θ is the fraction of public services to which firms operating in the informal sector have access to.

The flow of public services that are used in the production process are financed by a fraction η of the taxes levied on formal-sector output, such that

$$G = \eta(\overset{+}{q}, \overset{-}{\lambda})\tau Y^F, \quad 0 < \eta \leq 1. \tag{12.37}$$

The coefficient $1 - \eta$ represents the fraction of government revenue that is either used unproductively (to finance enforcement costs) or misused, and thus wasted. η is assumed to be related positively to the *quality* (or *efficiency*) of government institutions, measured by the parameter q, and negatively to the government's capacity to enforce the rule of law, measured by the parameter λ. In addition, it is assumed that $\eta_{q\lambda} > 0$; this captures the idea that the amounts of resources it takes to raise enforcement strength decreases with the quality of government institutions.

Let Ω denote the relative size of the informal sector, defined as

$$\Omega = Y_I/Y, \tag{12.38}$$

where Y is total output. Using Equations (12.37) and (12.38), the ratio of public services to output can be written as

$$\frac{G}{Y} = \eta(q, \lambda)\tau(1 - \Omega). \tag{12.39}$$

Finally, the fraction of income spent by informal-sector firms to maintain their illegal status, ϕ, is assumed to depend positively on the size of the informal sector. Specifically, ϕ is assumed given by

$$\phi = \kappa\Omega, \quad \kappa > 0. \tag{12.40}$$

In equilibrium (given *unrestricted mobility* between the formal and informal sectors), rates of return in both sectors must be equalized. This equality determines the relative size of the informal sector. To see this, note that from Equations (12.35), (12.36), and (12.40):

$$(1 - \kappa\Omega)\theta^\alpha = 1 - \tau,$$

so that[21]

$$\Omega = \frac{\theta^\alpha - (1 - \tau)}{\kappa\theta^\alpha} = \Omega(\overset{-}{\kappa}, \overset{+}{\tau}, \overset{+}{\theta}, \overset{-}{\alpha}). \tag{12.41}$$

Equation (12.41) shows, in particular, that the relative size of the informal sector *increases* with the tax rate in the formal economy and the fraction of public services to which firms operating in the informal sector have access.

The equilibrium **after-tax rate of return on capital**, r, is given by

$$r = A(1 - \tau)\tau^\alpha[\eta(q, \lambda)(1 - \Omega)]^\alpha. \tag{12.42}$$

The term $A(1-\tau)\tau^\alpha$ represents the economy's after-tax rate of return in the absence of waste ($\eta = 1$) and with no informal economy ($\Omega = 0$). In the presence of an informal sector, this term is multiplied by the quantity $[\eta(1 - \Omega)]^\alpha$—which is less than unity, because both η and Ω are less than unity. Thus, the economy's after-tax rate of return is *lower* than it would be otherwise.

Equation (12.42) shows that, as in Barro's model, with no informal activities ($\Omega = 0$), an increase in the tax rate has at first a *positive* and then a *negative* effect on the after-tax rate of return. In the presence of an informal sector ($\Omega > 0$), there is an *additional, negative* effect of the tax rate on capital's rate of return resulting from the positive effect of τ on the size of the informal sector.

As shown by Loayza, the model has *no transitional dynamics*: capital and formal and informal sector output (and thus aggregate output) all grow at the constant rate of growth of per capital income, $\tilde{g}_{Y/L}$, given by[22]

$$\tilde{g}_{Y/L} = A(1 - \tau)\tau^\alpha[\eta(1 - \Omega)]^\alpha - (\rho + \delta). \tag{12.43}$$

It can be seen from Equation (12.43) that an increase in the tax rate can have either a positive or negative effect on the steady-state growth rate—as

---

[21] For Eq. (12.41) to provide an *interior solution* for s_I (that is, $0 < s_I < 1$) requires imposing the following parameter restrictions:

$$\delta^\alpha - (1 - \tau) > 0, \quad (1 - \kappa)\delta^\alpha - (1 - \tau) < 0.$$

[22] The derivation of the growth rate is relatively involved and is omitted here. Again, the expression given in Eq. (12.43) assumes that the *degree of intertemporal substitution* is unity.

shown earlier in the analysis of Equation (12.42)—depending on the initial level of taxation. At low levels of taxes, an increase in the tax rate leads to an increase in the amount of public services that is large enough to offset the adverse effect of public-service congestion due to increased informality, and its negative impact on the private net rate of return.

The optimal tax rate is determined, as in Barro's model, as the rate τ^* that maximizes the growth rate, Equation (12.43). In Loayza's model, however, in the general case, there is no explicit solution for τ^*.[23] Nevertheless, by applying the **implicit function theorem** (as defined in the previous chapter) it can be shown that[24]

$$\tau^* = \tau(\overset{+}{\alpha}, \overset{+}{\kappa}, \overset{-}{\delta}). \tag{12.44}$$

Equation (12.44) indicates, in particular, that an increase in the cost of remaining informal, which makes informality less attractive, implies that a sufficiently small increase in the tax rate does not lead to more public-service congestion due to informality.

There are a number of important aspects of the links between informal sector activities and growth that Loayza's model does not account for, such as labor market regulations and segmentation, the size of production units, and differences in factor intensity, which may be important for understanding the size of the informal sector.[25] Nevertheless, a key implication of the model is that in countries where taxation is larger than optimal and the enforcement system is weak, the relative size of the informal sector will be *negatively* correlated with the rate of economic growth. Thus, measures aimed at reducing the tax burden and improving the quality of government institutions, for instance, will not only help reduce the relative size of the informal economy but will also promote economic growth.

Other models have identified various additional channels through which the level and nature of government taxes affect economic growth, particularly through their impact on the supply and demand for capital and labor. For instance, Milesi-Ferretti and Roubini (1998) recently examined the effects of *consumption* and *income taxes* on growth. Their analysis emphasized, in particular, the adverse role that taxation of human capital accumulation may have on the expansion of the *education sector*. Labor income taxation reduces individuals' incentive for human capital accumulation and may thus affect the rate

---

[23] In the particular case where $\kappa = 1$ (the cost of bribery is so high that no firm would choose to operate in the informal sector), it can be shown that the optimal tax rate is

$$\tau^* = \alpha/(1 + 2\alpha).$$

[24] If $1 - \theta^\alpha < \alpha\lambda/(\alpha + \kappa + \alpha\kappa)$, the growth-maximizing tax rate would imply some informality. If this inequality is reversed, the optimal tax rate would bring about a fully formal economy. The first inequality is assumed to hold.

[25] Another limitation of the model is that it does not capture the effect of taxes on *labor supply*, that is, the effect on agents' *labor-leisure trade-off*. A reduction in taxes, for instance, by increasing income, may lead agents to opt for more leisure, which would lower the steady-state rate of economic growth.

of economic growth when tax revenues are spent unproductively by the government. As discussed below, *trade taxes* may also affect steady-state effects on growth: *tariffs*, for instance, can raise the relative price of *intermediate goods*, and thus reduce the steady-state marginal rate of return of these inputs. Finally, it should be noted that the effect of taxes on growth can operate through their effect on macroeconomic stability (as discussed below) and may, as a result, be *nonlinear*. For small tax rates, the effect might be positive because of the contribution of taxes to macroeconomic stability (the **automatic stabilizer** effect); for higher tax rates, however, the relationship could become *negative*, as the distortionary effects (on, say, production incentives and the supply of labor) start to dominate.

Budget Deficits and Growth

In addition to spending and taxes, the government's *overall* budgetary position may also affect growth, through three channels:

- By lowering *aggregate saving*, in the realistic case in which Ricardian equivalence does not strictly hold (see Chapter 1).

- By contributing to higher *inflation* (as discussed below), when deficits are monetized. Inflation may in turn distort *relative price signals* and increase **macroeconomic instability** (as discussed below), thereby contributing to inefficiencies in the allocation of resources.

- By leading to a buildup of *domestic debt* when deficits are financed by issuance of liabilities; this type of financing may **crowd out** private investment through pressures on interest rates or the availability of domestic credit.[26] It may also raise the risk of *future taxation* and thus adversely affect private saving and investment decisions.

Weak fiscal discipline may also have an indirect, adverse effect on long-run growth if it leads to a weak external position and stop-go implementation of corrective policies. Both factors may increase macroeconomic uncertainty (the former by raising the prospects of a nominal devaluation, the second by affecting the *credibility* of the policy process) and thus reduce investment.

12.4.2   Inflation and Macroeconomic Stability

Endogenous growth models identify various channels, direct and indirect, through which inflation can affect steady-state growth. De Gregorio (1993), for instance, suggested that inflation may have a negative effect on steady-state growth because it reduces the *rate* of investment and lowers the *efficiency* of investment. At the heart of De Gregorio's model is the assumption that firms (as well as

---

[26] The latter possibility is particularly relevant in the case of *financial repression* (as discussed in Chapter 2), in which the structure and regulation of the financial system are deeply dependent on the financing needs of the government.

households) use money because it reduces **transactions costs**. Inflation lowers the optimal level of real money balances and raises the cost of investing; it thus lowers the rate of capital accumulation and the productivity of capital, thereby adversely affecting the rate of growth in the long run. In a related analysis, Palokangas (1997) argued that inflation affects negatively the steady-state growth rate because higher inflation raises *nominal interest rates*, and reduces real money balances—thereby subjecting private agents to larger transactions costs. This, in turn, lowers the rate of return on physical and human capital and reduces investment and long-run growth rates.[27]

What *causes* inflation is important, not only to assess its ultimate effects on growth, but also to understand the type of policies that may be needed to limit these effects. As indicated in Chapter 5, inflation in developing countries is often caused by large fiscal deficits and a high degree of monetization. In such conditions, reductions in government spending may be necessary. Roubini and Sala-i-Martin (1995), for instance, argued that, to the extent that inflation can be viewed as a proxy for financial repression, the negative effect of inflation on growth may reflect government-imposed *restrictions* on financial markets—which may exert also other distortionary effects of inflation on investment. An alternative, and probably more general, interpretation is to view inflation directly as a *tax*, which is determined (as discussed in Chapter 3) by the government to maximize seigniorage revenue (given an expenditure or deficit target) subject to the constraint that *conventional* taxes are subject to **rising marginal collection costs**. In that perspective, then, what causes inflation (and thus low growth) is an *inefficient tax system*, as emphasized most notably by De Gregorio (1993).

The data reviewed in Chapter 10 suggested a negative correlation between inflation and growth. As discussed in the next chapter, this result is largely corroborated by formal econometric studies. In addition, several of these studies have shown that the effect of inflation on growth is *nonlinear*, being small at low levels of inflation but significantly negative at high levels. Achieving and maintaining inflation in the single-digit range may thus be beneficial for increasing output growth.

High inflation, large fiscal deficits, and real exchange rate overvaluation are often viewed as key symptoms of **macroeconomic instability**. Such instability is, in general, more pronounced in developing countries relative to industrial countries because the former tend to be *less diversified* and less able to absorb external shocks. In addition, however, macroeconomic instability often reflects weaknesses in macroeconomic management. By increasing *overall uncertainty* and *distorting information* on underlying economic fundamentals, macroeconomic instability hampers private investment and saving decisions, thereby leading to an inefficient allocation of resources. Macroeconomic instability also has an adverse effect on *confidence*, which can discourage domestic investment and

---

[27]It is is worth noting that this result appears to be in contrast with the prediction of early monetary growth models, which argued that higher inflation would lead to increased output through a shift away from money balances (as real interest rates fall) toward real capital accumulation; see Burmeister and Dobell (1970).

lead to capital flight—with potentially adverse effects on long-run growth.

The effect of macroeconomic policy uncertainty on growth is well illustrated in the model developed by Aizenman and Marion (1993).[28] Endogenous growth emerges in their model because knowledge is one input in the production process and investment in human capital and physical capital are linked. Policy uncertainty arises because the *future tax rate on capital* is unknown at the moment investment decisions are made.

The key result of the model stems from the interaction between **irreversibility** effects in investment decisions and **policy persistence**. As noted in Chapter 1, when investment is subject to sunk costs, uncertainty generates an **option value of waiting**. Put differently, irreversibilities in the investment process generate *delays*, as entrepreneurs may opt to wait for the resolution of uncertainty. Firms are cautious in their decisions to expand capacity under uncertainty because investment today can lead to excessive capacity tomorrow if circumstances change. Aizenman and Marion showed, however, that macroeconomic policy uncertainty generates an option value of waiting only if policy is characterized by persistence. With persistence, higher macroeconomic uncertainty alters the expected net present value of the marginal product of capital and hence the pattern of investment. Moreover, with investment in physical capital linked to investment in human capital, the interaction of macroeconomic uncertainty and persistence influences the steady-state growth rate of output.[29]

12.4.3   Trade and Openness

Conventional trade theory, as discussed in Chapter 14, suggests that openness generates **static economic gains**—under free trade, productive resources tend to be reallocated toward activities where they are used with comparatively greater efficiency and away from less efficient activities. However, these gains (which tend to be relatively small in practice) generally take the form of a *level* effect on output, not a *growth* effect.[30] Recent research in growth theory provides various mechanisms through which trade and openness may generate **dynamic gains** and thereby affect the economy's rate of growth in the long run. In particular, it has been shown that trade openness may have the following effects.

- It may lead to improved allocation of resources among sectors by eliminating distortions—including lower incentives to engage in **rent-seeking activities**.[31]

---

[28] Another study that suggests that policy variability lowers the economy's steady-state growth rate is by Hopenhayn and Muniagurria (1996).

[29] In the Aizenman-Marion model, policy uncertainty affects growth only through the *supply side*. This is because the household utility function that they specify prevents any effect of uncertainty on consumption and saving decisions. In general, of course, the effects of policy uncertainty on growth may also result from the demand side.

[30] In practice, of course, a level effect can appear as a growth effect for a *given period of time*, because the adjustment process to any given shock in real economies can be very slow.

[31] The concept of rent seeking is attributed to Krueger (1974). The argument, essentially, is that public policy—especially in the domain of import duties, tariffs, quotas, and licensing

- It may facilitate the acquisition of new inputs, intermediate goods, and improved technologies, which enhance the *overall productivity* of the economy.

- It may reduce the **risk premium** on world capital markets (see Chapter 16), thereby improving the terms under which a country can borrow to finance domestic capital formation. If the marginal productivity of domestic investment is *higher* than the world interest rate, trade openness will also increase the supply of foreign capital and may improve domestic welfare.

The second channel, the international diffusion and adoption of new technologies or new goods, has been a major focus of attention in the recent literature. Grossman and Helpman (1991) and Rivera-Batiz and Romer (1991), for instance, developed models in which technology is produced by profit-maximizing firms. They showed that openness to international markets can increase the growth rate of technology by increasing the *size of the market* available to technology producers and allowing those countries with a comparative advantage in technology production to specialize in that activity. International trade may also improve domestic productivity and economic growth by increasing **knowledge spillovers** from more advanced trading partners. The empirical evidence provided by Coe, Helpman, and Hoffmaister (1997) suggest indeed that trade flows provide a conduit through which advanced production techniques and technological knowledge are transmitted across countries.[32] The empirical evidence also suggests that the learning-by-doing and growth effects of these spillovers are largest in countries with *higher levels of education.* As discussed in the next chapter, this appears to have played an important role in the rapid growth of some Asian countries since the end of World War II.

Another important idea that has been explored in some recent models of growth is that trade liberalization increases the *variety of goods* available to domestic agents and raises productivity by providing *less expensive* or *higher-quality intermediate goods.* Romer (1994), for instance, emphasized both the productivity of specialized resources and the limitations given by the size of the market. In an economy subject to trade restrictions, only a narrow range of specialized intermediate goods or capital goods can be profitably produced and therefore the full range of technological possibilities, which rely on a potentially broader range of inputs, cannot be exploited effectively. In this model a *greater variety of inputs* does more for production than a *greater quantity of a narrow range of inputs.* Thus, access to a variety of foreign inputs at a lower cost

---

systems—has the potential of increasing the incomes of certain individuals and groups. These incomes accrue in the form of *rents.* Pressure groups, acting rationally, seek rents by spending money and lobbying in order to get governmnent authorities to allocate to them import licences, foreign exchange allocations, and the like.

[32] As discussed in Chapter 6, *foreign direct investment* provides another, perhaps more direct, route through which technology and advanced managerial and production techniques can flow from industrial to developing countries.

shifts the economy-wide *production possibility frontier* outward, thereby raising productivity.

In contrast to the early literature on trade and growth, which emphasized solely the role of *exports* as an engine to growth, the new literature provides important new insights. A number of caveats, however, are worth highlighting.

- The effects of scale economies and learning-by-doing emphasized in the new theories of trade and growth take place mostly in the production of advanced manufactured products, such as *high-technology goods*. Exports of many developing countries continue, however, to consist of *raw materials* (including energy and agricultural products) and relatively *low-technology* manufactured goods (such as *textiles*). It may be argued, nevertheless, that openness to trade (and capital flows) may help these countries *over time* to assimilate technologies and production techniques, thereby enabling them to shift eventually toward the production of goods and services that are characterized by dynamic gains.

- Some models suggest that, under some conditions, opening an economy to trade may discourage *domestic* research and development activities, for instance by inducing the poorer countries to allocate too much of their limited supply of skilled labor to the production of manufactured goods. In such conditions, paradoxically, restrictions on trade may *accelerate* growth.

- In several models, the mechanism through which increased productivity and growth rates occur as economies become open to international trade focuses on the adoption of more specialized intermediate inputs and machinery available from trading partners. However, there are many types of useful knowledge that are not embodied in material inputs, such as *production engineering* and information about changing product patterns, which can also be transferred as a result of trade with more advanced countries. As argued by Romer (1992), in practice, the *transmission of ideas* may be as important, if not more important, than the *transmission of new inputs*.

12.4.4   Financial Development

As noted in Chapter 2, *government restrictions* imposed on financial institutions (such as interest rate ceilings, high reserve requirements, and directed credit programs) restrain the process of financial intermediation and, consequently, impede economic growth. Recent developments in growth economics have highlighted the fact that financial institutions play a key role in evaluating prospective entrepreneurs and financing those that carry the best promise of future innovation—with the resulting increase in *productivity* leading to higher growth. As noted in Chapter 1, financial development also leads to higher saving rates, and thus higher rates of economic growth.

Several contributions in the recent literature on endogenous growth have examined the potential linkages between economic growth and financial markets. A key feature of these contributions is the idea that financial institutions emerge to mitigate problems such as economies of scale in information gathering and the allocation of risk under **asymmetric information** (see Chapter 2). Greenwood and Jovanovich (1990), for instance, stressed the role of financial intermediaries in *pooling funds* and *acquiring information* that enables them to allocate capital to its highest valued use, thereby raising the *average return* to capital. Specifically, Greenwood and Jovanovich considered a situation in which capital can be invested in *safe, low-yielding* investments or *risky, high-yielding* investments. Risk results from both *aggregate* and *project-specific* shocks. Potential entrepreneurs cannot differentiate between the two types of shocks. With large portfolio holdings, however, financial intermediaries can experiment with a small sample of high-yielding projects to determine the *state of the world*. By spending on the collection and analysis of information, financial intermediaries determine their investment strategies knowing the realization of the current-period aggregate shock. Provided the cost of information collection and analysis is sufficiently small, the ability to choose the appropriate set of projects knowing the realization of the aggregate shock raises the expected return on the intermediaries' portfolios above that of individuals who must choose one or the other technology without any information about the aggregate shock. Thus, financial intermediation improves the allocation of resources and raises the long-run rate of economic growth.

Another approach is followed by Bencivenga and Smith (1991, 1992) and Greenwood and Smith (1997).[33] Their analysis emphasized the fact that, with the introduction of banks, individuals can hold deposits that financial intermediaries (essentially banks) then invest in currency and capital. At the same time, banks can exploit the **law of large numbers** to estimate *deposit withdrawals* (which are unpredictable individually but predictable for the economy as a whole) and thus ensure that they never have to liquidate capital prematurely.[34] Hence, banks avoid the uncertainty that leads individuals to misallocate resources. By engaging in **maturity intermediation** (one of the key functions of banks, as noted in Chapter 2) financial institutions offer liquidity to savers and, at the same time, long-term funding to entrepreneurs. In so doing, they stimulate productive investment by inducing savers to switch from unproductive investment in tangible assets to productive investment in firms. By ensuring that capital is not wasted, financial intermediation leads to higher

---

[33] Yet another approach is developed by Boyd and Smith (1996), who emphasize the role of *monitoring costs* (in a context where the returns associated with the various technologies available are not costlessly observable *ex post*) in the interactions between growth and the evolution of debt and equity markets. As noted in Chapter 2, monitoring costs may also lead to credit rationing.

[34] Consider a set of n independent random variables that follow the same distribution function with mean μ. Then the mean of these variables, $\bar{x}_n$, also has mean μ, whatever the value of n. The (weak) law of large numbers states that, in effect, $\bar{x}_n$ becomes more and more *narrowly dispersed* about μ as n increases. This theorem remains valid even if the *variance* of the underlying random variables does not exist.

capital-labor ratios and higher steady-state rates of economic growth.

12.4.5   Political Factors and Income Inequality

Although there exists a large literature, by both economists and political scientists, focusing on the linkages between economic performance in general and political factors (see Chapter 17), the recent analytical literature on endogenous growth focusing on the interactions between these factors and growth is somewhat more limited. Moreover, much of this literature, as reviewed by Alesina and Perotti (1994), remains largely inconclusive. In particular, most *developed* countries today are *democracies* but democratic regimes in many developing countries have failed in the past to support economic growth; much of the evidence (as discussed in the next chapter) is ambiguous on whether democracy is good or bad for growth.

There is more robust evidence suggesting, for instance, that fertility is lower in countries where citizens enjoy more civil and political liberties (Dasgupta, 1995). There is also some empirical support, as discussed in the next chapter, for the view that political instability may have an adverse effect on long-run growth. One possible explanation for this negative effect is that the political environment has an influence on the *choice of public policy*, which in turn affects growth. Different political environments may set different constraints on the available public policy instruments. For instance, the quantity and quality of public investment, the role of the government in production activities, the extent of regulation, and many other factors, may be determined by the characteristics of the political system.

Another possibility is that political instability affects long-run growth through its effect on investment. Alesina and Tabellini (1989), for instance, examined the implications of political uncertainty in a model in which two governments with *conflicting distributional objectives* randomly alternate in office. Each government represents a different interest group; as a result, the incumbent government makes transfers only to its constituent interest group. These transfers are financed by taxing the other group and by borrowing. However, the incumbent government recognizes the possibility of a different type of government coming to power in the future and having to service the debt. To the extent that the future cost of debt servicing is not fully internalized in the borrowing decision, the result will be an above-optimal level of borrowing.[35] Private agents realize that the future costs of debt servicing will fall disproportionately on one group depending on which government is in power. They accumulate foreign assets as insurance against the risk of taxation. Political uncertainty thus generates overborrowing, capital flight, and low domestic investment—with potentially adverse effects on the rate of economic growth.[36]

---

[35] That is, the level of debt will be higher than that consistent with economic efficiency; it will, of course, still be constrained by the lending limit imposed by lenders.

[36] Overborrowing may also occur when, in addition to political uncertainty, *polarization*—defined as the extent of disagreement over the composition of public goods—prevails, leading to a stronger preference for present government consumption (Ozler and Tabellini, 1991).

The link between income inequality and growth has also been the subject of much investigation in recent years. The recent literature goes beyond the **Kuznets curve**, which (as noted in the previous chapter) relates income distribution and the *level* of income. It has also emphasized the role of the political system in affecting this link, because of the key role played by the political process in aggregating conflicting interests into public policy decisions (Persson and Tabellini, 1994).

A common argument is that income inequality is necessary for rapid capital accumulation because the rich have a higher propensity to save and invest than the poor. Recent research has shown, however, that there are at least two channels through which inequality in income distribution can lower the rates of capital accumulation and economic growth.[37]

- Inequality can trigger *political and social pressures* that contribute to social and political instability, which may eventually undermine incentives to save and invest. The adverse effect on growth may further increase inequality, leading to a **vicious cycle** of increasing inequality and low growth.

- Inequality can reduce the average *skill level* of the labor force by making it more difficult for the poor to finance their education and that of their children. This effect may be particularly large if, as discussed earlier, low-income families have only limited access to capital markets.

Galor and Zeira (1993), in particular, showed that in the presence of credit market imperfections and indivisibilities in investment in human capital, the initial distribution of wealth affects aggregate output and investment both in the short run and in the long run. Alesina and Rodrik (1994) presented a theoretical model that suggested that income inequality affects growth negatively:

- income (and wealth) inequality causes the tax rate to rise above its optimal level, because the median voter gains from the redistributive effects of a higher tax rate if the degree of inequality is large;

- a higher than optimal tax rate reduces the propensity to invest.

12.4.6 Institutions and the Allocation of Talent

Various economists have argued in recent years that one reason why growth rates differ across countries is that the *economic environment* in which individuals operate also differs. This environment comprises the country's laws, institutions, and government rules, policies and regulations. An environment that provides adequate protection for *property rights* and gives agents the incentive to produce, invest, and accumulate skills is a *pro-growth* environment.

---

[37] See Alesina and Rodrik (1994), Alesina and Perotti (1996), Bruno, Ravallion, and Squire (1998), and Persson and Tabellini (1994). Alesina and Perotti (1994) and Bénabou (1997) provide recent surveys of this literature.

An *anti-growth* environment, by contrast, discourages production and effort and has an adverse effect on economic performance. A highly corrupt bureaucracy, for instance, operates as a *tax* on production activities.[38] Entrepreneurs must allocate some of their time and resources to bribing government officials, to obtain the necessary authorizations (such as permits and licenses) for operating. As Shleifer and Vishny (1993) argued, if the structure of government is such that different groups of bureaucrats have *hold-up power* over an investment project, the result may be a level of capital formation that is dramatically lower than would be achievable in different circumstances: because the bureaucrats may be unable to collude or coordinate, the total sum of bribes required to have the project approved may exceed the private gains from investing in the first place.

The opportunity to divert resources in this way through government can have important dynamic consequences for the **allocation of talent**, as emphasized by Baumol (1990) and Murphy, Shleifer, and Vishny (1991). Individuals who might have chosen to become entrepreneurs may instead devote their energies to **rent seeking** or other forms of diversion in the public sector. Individuals may be tempted to accumulate not the type of skills that would increase the productive capacity of the economy but rather those that maximize their own chance of securing a *strategic position* in the government bureaucracy. Douglass North's description of pirates investing in technologies and skills to make piracy more effective is a classic example of this diversion of talent (see North, 1990, pp. 77-78):

> To be a successful pirate one needs to know a great deal about naval warfare; the trade routes of commercial shipping; the armament, rigging, and crew size of potential victims; and the market for booty. Successful pirates will acquire the requisite knowledge and skills. Such activities may well give rise to a thriving demand for improved naval warfare technology by both the pirates and the victims... If the basic institutional framework makes income redistribution (piracy) the preferred (and most profitable) economic opportunity, we can expect a very different development of knowledge and skills than a productivity-increasing ... economic opportunity would entail... The incentives that are built into the institutional framework play the decisive role in shaping the kinds of skills and knowledge that pay off.

A key implication of this analysis is that effective government institutions are essential to avoid biasing individual choices in favor of rent seeking instead of production. Such institutions include a *strong judiciary* and *secure property rights*.[39]

Related arguments were made by Hall and Jones (1999) and Olson (1996). Hall and Jones argued that differences in *social infrastructure* (which they define as institutions and government policies that determine the environment within

---

[38] See the appendix to Chapter 17 for a discussion of corruption and its economic costs.

[39] In an environment characterized by a strong judicial system, limited resources may actually be needed to enforce the laws, because of the *deterrent effect* of a credible threat of enforcement.

which economic agents operate) are key factors in explaining cross-country differences in capital accumulation, educational attainment, productivity, and thus income per capita. Olson argued that a key factor that explains the low-growth performance of poor countries is that they tend to *waste more resources* (both capital and knowledge) than richer countries. The problem, then, may not be to accumulate more resources (by investing in physical and human capital, for instance) but to waste less of the resources that *already exist*. This, in turn, calls for the adoption of policies and institutions that can raise the ability to use existing resources more efficiently.

12.5 Summary

- Recent developments in the theory of economic growth have emphasized the potential growth-enhancing roles of knowledge, **human capital**, and **research and development**, as well as the possibility of **increasing returns** to scale at the aggregate level.

- This literature contrasts with the traditional, neoclassical model, in which capital accumulation raises the *level* of output but not its *long-term growth rate*. In the Solow-Swan model, because of the assumption of *constant returns to scale* in all inputs (and hence diminishing returns to capital), policies that stimulate saving and investment raise output growth only *temporarily* because each addition to the capital stock is assumed to generate diminishing amounts of additional output.

- By contrast, the new endogenous growth theories assume either that investment does not have such diminishing returns, or that some of the additional output is used in activities that directly increase the rate of technological change and economic growth.

- The production of knowledge may occur either as a *by-product* of economic activity (as in **learning-by-doing** models) or through a production activity. In such models, an increase in the *saving rate* may raise the steady-state growth rate of income per capita.

- The Mankiw-Romer-Weil model extends the Solow-Swan model to include human capital. Although it retains the assumption of constant returns to scale in all inputs (and thus diminishing returns to physical and human capital taken together), it differs in an important way from the Solow-Swan model because relatively small changes in the resources devoted to physical and human capital accumulation may lead to large changes in output per worker. As a result, it is better equipped to account for large differences in *levels* of real income across countries.

- The AK model assumes that there are *constant returns* to capital, defined broadly to include both physical and human capital. In the AK model, an increase in the saving rate raises *permanently* the growth rate of output per capita. Whereas the Solow-Swan model predicts that poor countries should grow faster than rich countries, the AK model implies that poor countries with the *same level of technology* and the same structural parameters as richer countries should grow at the same rate as these countries, *regardless* of the initial level of income. Thus, the AK model *does not predict* (absolute) *convergence*.

New growth theories have identified various other factors, both structural and policy related, that may alter the long-run growth process.

- *Fiscal policy* affects steady-state growth through *direct effects* stemming from expenditures and taxes and *indirect effects* through macroeconomic stability.

- Public investment in infrastructure (which is generally *complementary* to private investment) has a direct effect on growth by increasing the economy's capital stock. Government spending may also alter growth indirectly by raising the *marginal productivity* of privately supplied factors of production—through spending on *education, health,* and other services that contribute to the accumulation of human capital.

- An increase in the tax rate lowers the after-tax marginal product of capital (and thus investment and growth) because of its direct impact on rates of return; it also raises it, however, because of its impact on the provision of *public services*. Taxes and growth are thus *nonlinearly* related. High rates of taxation, in addition, may contribute to the growth of the **informal economy**.

- *Inflation* has a negative effect on steady-state growth through various channels. In particular, it may reduce both the *rate* and the *efficiency* of investment. If firms use money because it reduces *transactions costs*, inflation will lower the optimal level of real money balances and raise the cost of investing. By lowering the rate of capital accumulation and the productivity of capital, inflation adversely affects the rate of growth in the long run.

- High inflation, large fiscal deficits, and real exchange rate overvaluation are key symptoms of *macroeconomic instability*. Such instability is pervasive in countries that are *poorly diversified* (and thus less able to absorb domestic and external shocks) and where macroeconomic management is weak. By increasing *overall uncertainty* and *distorting information* on underlying economic fundamentals, macroeconomic instability hampers private investment and saving decisions, and thus long-run growth.

- There are various mechanisms through which **trade** and **openness** may generate **dynamic gains** and thereby affect the economy's rate of growth in the long run. The specialization in production that results from free improving technology. All these effects have the potential to raise growth rates.

- *Financial development* affects long-run growth through a variety of channels. Financial institutions play a key role in screening among potential entrepreneurs and financing the best prospects. The resulting increase in productivity may lead to higher growth.

- Financial development also leads to higher saving rates, and thus higher rates of economic growth. Financial institutions possess *economies of scale* in gathering and processing information, monitoring performance, and enforcing contracts, and therefore help reduce the cost of transforming savings into productive investment.

- By pooling together the assets of a multitude of individual savers, such institutions can also finance projects that would not be undertaken otherwise because of their *size*, their *riskiness*, or their long *gestation period*. Moreover, combining assets allows financial institutions to reduce any single individual's exposure to the risks of liquidity and failure inherent in any project compared with a situation in which financing is provided directly.

- *Political instability* may have an adverse effect on long-run growth. A possible reason is that the political environment has an influence on the *choice of public policy*, which in turn affects growth.

- The *economic environment* in which individuals operate (a country's laws, institutions, and policies) may have a strong impact on its growth performance. An environment that provides agents with the incentive to produce, invest, and accumulate skills fosters economic growth. By contrast, an environment that discourages production and effort will have an adverse effect on economic performance. A highly corrupt bureaucracy, for instance, operates as a *tax* on production activities. The opportunity to divert resources through government can have important dynamic consequences for the **allocation of talent**. Individuals who might have chosen to become entrepreneurs may instead devote their energies to **rent-seeking** activities in the public sector.

Appendix
The Savings Trap and Coordination Failures

Studies of the pattern of growth in developing countries suggest that the saving rate tends to evolve from

- an initial period of **low savings** (5 percent of GDP or less) and slow economic growth;

- the **takeoff** period, during which the saving rate increases dramatically to more than, say, 10 percent of GDP, and perhaps to as much as 20 or 30 percent;

- the **mature** phase, marked by declining saving and growth rates.

Breaking out of the initial phase may be the most important step toward economic development (Rostow, 1960). However, reaching the take-off point can be difficult, as a result of a **savings trap**, which was described by Ragnar Nurkse (1953, p. 5) in the early 1950s:

> On the supply side, there is a small capacity to save, resulting from the low
> level of income. The low real income is a reflection of low productivity, which in
> its turn is due largely to the lack of capital. A lack of capital is the result of the
> small capacity to save, and so the circle is complete.

Various models of the savings trap have been developed in recent years. Some models emphasize the role that *cultural* and *institutional factors* may have on saving rates. Several other models have emphasized the idea that a low savings equilibrium may result from a *lack of coordination* among agents and that, in the absence of policy interventions or other exogenous shocks, such an outcome may persist over time. In an important contribution, Azariadis and Drazen (1990), for instance, developed a model in which sufficient *human capital* must be acquired before the economy can take off. Specifically, they showed that in an extended Solow-Swan setting in which the *private* rate of return on human capital depends positively on the existing *average* quality of the stock of human capital (that is, when the technology that drives human capital accumulation is characterized by *positive externalities*), small differences in initial conditions may lead to very different equilibrium growth paths. In particular, if the private return to training is too low to induce agents to acquire training and accumulate skills—a possibility that arises when the average initial stock of human capital is relatively low—the economy will converge to a no-training, low-income equilibrium path. This occurs even if the *social return* to higher average human capital is high.

Chapter 13

The Determinants of Economic Growth: An Empirical Overview

The past few years have witnessed a flurry of empirical studies on the determinants of economic growth, in parallel with the development of the various endogenous approaches to growth reviewed in the previous chapter. Two main techniques have been used: *growth accounting*, which evolved mostly from the Solow-Swan growth model that was discussed in Chapter 11, and *cross-country regressions*, which rely on econometric techniques and large data sets. This chapter reviews the recent evidence on the determinants of growth suggested by both approaches and highlights some of the methodological issues confronting many of the existing studies. Part 1 presents the growth accounting methodology and part 2 illustrates its usefulness (and limitations) by analyzing the controversy over the sources of growth in East Asia since the early 1950s. Part 3 discusses the econometric issues that arise in using cross-country growth regressions. The fourth part provides a partial summary of the recent literature in this area, highlighting, in turn, the role played by saving and physical and human capital accumulation, fiscal policy, inflation and macroeconomic stability, the degree of trade openness, and political variables and income inequality. The last part concludes by assessing the evidence on the speed of convergence in income per capita across countries.

13.1 Growth Accounting

A widely used methodology to explain differences in growth rates across countries is **growth accounting**, which consists essentially in adding the different contributions of the growth of basic factor inputs (labor and capital) and an *unexplained element* or residual that captures *improvements in technology*.

To derive the basic growth accounting equation, suppose that aggregate output in the economy can be described by the production function

$$Y = AF(K, L), \tag{13.1}$$

where K is the stock of capital, L the number of workers, and A measures the efficiency of the production process or the level of *technological progress*. This specification implies that technological progress raises the level of output that can be produced with a given combination of inputs, without affecting their marginal products. In standard terminology (see Chapter 11), technological progress is assumed to be **Hicks neutral.**

Differentiating Equation (13.1) with respect to time yields

$$\dot{Y} = \dot{A}F + AF_K\dot{K} + AF_L\dot{L},$$

which can be rewritten as

$$\frac{\dot{Y}}{Y} = \frac{\dot{A}}{A} + F_K(\frac{AK}{Y})\frac{\dot{K}}{K} + F_L(\frac{AL}{Y})\frac{\dot{L}}{L} = \frac{\dot{A}}{A} + (\frac{KF_K}{F})\frac{\dot{K}}{K} + (\frac{LF_L}{F})\frac{\dot{L}}{L}.$$

Equivalently, letting $\mathbf{g}_x = \dot{x}/x$ and denoting by $\eta_K = F_K K/F$ and $\eta_L = F_L L/F$ the elasticity of output with respect to capital and labor, the above expression yields

$$\mathbf{g}_Y = \mathbf{g}_A + \eta_K\mathbf{g}_K + \eta_L\mathbf{g}_L.$$

Let w and r denote, respectively, the wage rate and the rental rate of capital. Under conditions of perfectly competitive factor pricing, factors are paid their marginal product, so that $w = F_L$ and $r = F_K - \delta$, where δ is the rate of depreciation of capital. Thus, with $\delta = 0$ for simplicity, $\eta_L = wL/Y$ and $\eta_K = rK/Y$; η_L and η_K are equal, respectively, to the share of labor and capital income in total output. **Euler's theorem** on homogeneous functions—see for instance Chiang (1984, pp. 411-414)—guarantees that for a CRS function $F(K, L)$,

$$\frac{KF_K}{F} + \frac{LF_L}{F} = 1,$$

or equivalently that the sum of the share coefficients η_K and η_L is equal to unity ($\eta_K + \eta_L = 1$). The equation for $\mathbf{g}_Y$ can thus be rewritten as

$$\mathbf{g}_Y - \mathbf{g}_L = \mathbf{g}_A + \eta_K(\mathbf{g}_K - \mathbf{g}_L),$$

or equivalently

$$\mathbf{g}_{Y/L} = \mathbf{g}_A + \eta_K\mathbf{g}_{K/L}, \tag{13.2}$$

which relates the growth of output per worker to the rate of technological progress (often referred to as the **Solow residual** or as the rate of growth of **total factor productivity**, TFP) and the rate of growth of capital per worker.

In practice, researchers often use a **Cobb-Douglas** specification, that is,

$$Y = AK^\alpha L^{1-\alpha}.$$

This function, as discussed in Chapter 11, is characterized by *constant returns to scale* and *constant factor income shares*, with a capital share of α $(= \eta_K)$ and a labor share of $1 - \alpha$.

Once estimates of the growth rates of output, capital, and the labor force are obtained, and an estimate of η_K (or α) is derived, Equation (13.2) can be solved for the rate of technological progress:

$$g_A = g_{Y/L} - \eta_K g_{K/L} = \eta_K g_{K/Y} + (1 - \eta_K) g_{Y/L}, \tag{13.3}$$

where the last expression defines **TFP growth** as the weighted average of the growth rates of output per unit of labor and the capital-output ratio.

In practical applications, income is generally measured in per capita terms rather than per worker; Equation (13.2) in this case is written as

$$g_{Y/N} = g_Y - g_N = g_A + \eta_K g_{K/N} + (1 - \eta_K) g_{L/N},$$

where g_N is the rate of growth of the population as a whole. The Solow residual is thus given by

$$g_A = g_{Y/N} - \eta_K g_{K/N} + (1 - \eta_K) g_{L/N}. \tag{13.4}$$

The basic growth accounting framework has been extended in various ways to include not only investment in physical and human capital, but also a large number of additional variables, such as, as noted by Maddison (1995, pp. 40-49), changes in the *composition* and *quality* of factor inputs, changes in levels of research and development, foreign trade, economies of scale in domestic markets, government regulations, labor hoarding, and changes in rates of capacity use.[1]

Nevertheless, growth accounting exercises remain fraught with difficulties. The role of *land* as a separate factor of production is generally ignored—partly because of inadequate data. The share of capital in the production function is, as a result, overstated, and the rate of TFP growth underestimated. No standard measurement method exists for estimating the growth rates of capital and labor. Capital stock series are typically constructed by using the **perpetual inventory method**, which essentially consists in cumulating data on investment flows at constant prices, obtained either from national sources or international databases, such as the *Penn World Tables*, assuming a constant depreciation rate (generally in the 4-6 percent range). The choice of the starting year for the sample, however, is often arbitrary and may lead to large estimation errors—particularly in the early periods. Several authors have attempted to use a *quality-adjusted measure of capital*. Roldós (1997b), for instance, estimated an index of the quality of capital in Chile as a weighted average of investment in machinery and equipment, on the one hand, and investment in buildings and structures, on the other, with weights given by relative rental rates. However, quality adjustments (which may have drastic implications for measured TFP growth rates) are often viewed as having an *ad hoc* nature.

---

[1] However, the inclusion of these variables often proceeds in an *ad hoc* manner, and is not always based on well-accepted theoretical considerations. It should be noted also that some researchers have questioned the very use of a Cobb-Douglas production function.

Labor is often measured from data on participation rates and working hours. Differences among types of workers and data reliability across countries create serious problems for comparative analysis. To answer the first problem, several researchers (for example, see Young, 1995) have used measures of *quality-adjusted labor* as a production input. In several studies, an index of quality-adjusted labor is constructed as a weighted average of labor with different levels of education, with weights given by relative wages. It has been argued, however, that such adjustments may lead researchers to *underestimate* the true rate of TFP growth by attributing a larger part of the increase in output to a better or more educated labor force (Sarel, 1997).[2]

Estimation of factor shares—the parameter η_K or α given above, which may affect significantly estimates of TFP growth—can also be problematic. The most commonly used method to estimate these shares is to use *national accounts* data to calculate (generally period by period) the share of income that is distributed to each factor of production.[3] As noted earlier, this approach requires that markets of capital and labor be perfectly competitive and that the income of each factor be equal to the value of its marginal product. In practice, of course, market imperfections abound. Noncompetitive wage determination and monopolistic product markets may significantly distort the relationship between income shares and marginal products. The absence of perfect competition, in the context of a constant returns to scale production function, can lead to large errors in estimating the elasticity of output with respect to each input, because factor shares need no longer reflect output elasticities. In particular, to the extent that monopoly profits are reflected in capital income, capital's share of income will tend to overstate the elasticity of output with respect to capital. Researchers often attempt to adjust for such biases, but the practice has an *ad hoc* nature with potentially large effects on estimated TFP growth rates.

The method also ignores government policies and regulations, most notably tax policy, which may have a significant impact on the rate of return to capital. Subsidies to capital-intensive industries, for instance, may raise the rate of return to capital above its technological marginal product; estimating factor shares by using income shares would thus lead to an overestimation of the share of capital in the production process. There are also additional problems involved in using national accounts data, related notably to the classification of workers (see Sarel, 1997, pp. 386-387). Finally, the presence of **positive externalities** implies that standard growth accounting techniques can provide *misleading estimates* of total factor productivity growth. In particular, if the aggregate production function is indeed characterized by **increasing returns to scale**—as a result, for instance, of externalities generated by the economy-wide capital stock, as discussed by Romer (1986)—then the standard approach

---

[2] This argument loses some strength if TFP growth is viewed merely as a measure of ignorance, a true residual.

[3] The second approach used to estimate factor shares is the *regression approach*, which suffers in particular from the assumption that the estimated weights are constant over the estimation period. In practice, the relative importance of production inputs is likely to change over time, especially when an economy undergoes rapid transformation and structural change.

based on the assumption of constant returns to scale will *underestimate* the contribution of capital and the residual obtained will *overestimate* TFP growth. A simple illustration of this result, due to Barro (1998), is presented in the appendix to this chapter.

13.2 The East Asian "Miracle"

A particularly interesting application of the growth accounting framework has been to the issue of growth in East Asian countries since the early 1950s. Growth in some of these countries averaged 6 percent between 1950 and 1992. Output per worker increased by more than 5 percent during the period 1960-94 in Korea, Singapore, Thailand, and Taiwan (Table 13.1). Just during the period 1980-95, Indonesia, Malaysia, Singapore, and Thailand more than doubled their real income per capita, compared with an increase of only 20 percent in the United States (Sarel, 1997, p. 369). In all of these countries, investment in *physical capital* appears to have played an important role. In Singapore for instance, the rate of growth during the period 1960-91 averaged 6.3 percent a year in per capita terms. The scale of investment (mostly by the private sector) since the early 1960s has been impressive: the ratio of gross fixed investment to GDP has exceeded, on average, 35 percent since the early 1970s and remains one of the highest in the world—far exceeding that of the other fast-growing Asian economies. On the basis of cumulative net investment data, Singapore's capital stock has increased 33-fold between 1960 and 1992, doubling on average once every 6 years. This rapid pace of physical investment resulted in a *tenfold increase* in the capital-labor ratio between 1960 and 1992. However, whether investment in physical capital alone accounts for the high growth rates observed in East Asia remains a hotly debated issue among economists.

In a well-publicized study, Young (1995) argued, using the framework described above, that the very high growth rates experienced by Hong Kong, Singapore, South Korea, and Taiwan over the past three decades are almost entirely due to rising investment, increasing labor-force participation, and improving labor quality (as reflected in an increase in the proportion of skilled workers), and not to rapid technological progress and other forces affecting the Solow residual. More specifically, Young estimated the growth rate of TFP in these countries to be very low in comparison with industrial countries. Thus, in Young's view, there is *nothing miraculous*—in the sense of something that can be explained only by referring to divine intervention—about growth in East Asian countries. These conclusions found some support in a subsequent study by Collins and Bosworth (1996), as illustrated in Table 13.1. For the period 1960-94, they estimated that of an average growth of output per worker equal to 4.2 percent for East Asia, 1.1 percentage points can be attributed to TFP growth; most of the increase (2.5 percentage points) resulted from the high rate of accumulation of physical capital per worker. Results for individual countries (most notably Korea and Singapore) suggested a similar pattern.

Several authors, including Pack and Page (1994) and Sarel (1997) questioned the validity of Young's calculations and argued that TFP growth in East Asia was *much higher* than Young's results suggested. Sarel's analysis focused on five East Asian countries: Indonesia, Malaysia, the Philippines, Singapore, and Thailand (with the United States as a comparator country) for the period 1978-96. Sarel's approach differed from the standard growth accounting framework used by Young in that he estimated technological factor shares not by using *income shares* (as described earlier) but by a method that attempted to capture differences in the structure of production across countries and differences in the level of development.[4] The estimated capital share, α, varied from 0.28 for Thailand to 0.34 for Singapore. Young (1995), in contrast, obtained a capital share of 0.5 for Singapore. Sarel's growth accounting exercises are summarized in Table 13.2. The results indicate that the rates of TFP growth were very strong in Singapore (2.2 percent), Malaysia and Thailand (2 percent), and much less so in Indonesia (1.2 percent). These rates are well above the rate observed in the United States for the sample period (0.3 percent) and those obtained by Collins and Bosworth (1996). In all four Asian countries, TFP growth rates accounted for a significant proportion of the growth rate of output per capita during the period.

Thus, Sarel's results differ significantly from Young's calculations. Several methodological factors may account for these differences. In the case of Singapore, in particular, the difference between the two studies appears to result essentially from the use of different estimates of the capital share. But for the other countries, various other factors may also be important. The studies cover different periods; and the methods used for the measurement of the capital stock and the stock of labor differed substantially. In particular, Sarel did not adjust his measure of labor input for education levels, in contrast to Young and many other authors.

The conclusion of this brief overview of growth accounting studies is that no consensus has yet emerged regarding the relative importance of productivity growth versus growth in factor inputs in accounting for the high growth rates observed in East Asia during the early 1960s to the mid 1990s. Various aspects of the methodology, as indicated earlier, remain sources of controversy; it is thus legitimate to ask whether a consensus will ever emerge. The experience of industrial countries does suggest that the accumulation of physical capital is an important source of growth in the early stages of development; once a relatively high level of capital intensity (as measured by the capital-to-labor ratio) is reached, technological progress tends to become the principal driving force. At the same time, it is worth emphasizing that it is not only the *quantity* of investment that matters, but also its *quality*. As noted in Chapter 7, this

---

[4] Specifically, Sarel calculated the aggregate capital share in each country, for every year during the sample period, as the weighted average of the capital shares in each major economic activity (as defined in the United Nations' *National Accounts Statistics*), using as weights the relative shares of these activities in output at factor cost. Implicit in this approach, however, is the assumption that no systematic differences in factor shares would exist once cross-country differences are controlled for in the structure of production and the level of development. As can be inferred from the previous section, this is far from being an innocuous hypothesis.

may have been one of the key lessons of the recent crisis in East Asia.

Table 13.1

Growth Accounting, 1960-94

(Percentage points per annum)

	Output per worker	Contribution by Component		
		Physical capital per worker[a]	Education per worker[b]	TFP[c]
Indonesia	3.4	2.1	0.5	0.8
Korea	5.7	3.3	0.8	1.5
Malaysia	3.8	2.3	0.5	0.9
Philippines	1.3	1.2	0.5	-0.4
Singapore	5.4	3.4	0.4	1.5
Thailand	5.0	2.7	0.4	1.8
Taiwan	5.8	3.1	0.6	2.0
East Asia	4.2	2.5	0.6	1.1
South Asia	2.3	1.1	0.3	0.8
Africa	0.3	0.8	0.2	-0.7
Middle East	1.6	1.5	0.5	-0.3
Latin America	1.5	0.9	0.4	0.2
United States	1.1	0.4	0.4	0.3

[a]The contribution of physical capital per worker is given by its growth rate times capital's share in output ($\alpha = 0.35$).

[b]The contribution of education per worker is given by the growth rate of the labor quality index, H, times labor's share in output ($1-\alpha = 0.65$).

[c]Total factor productivity, given by the difference between the first column and the sum of the second and third columns.

Source: Adapted from Collins and Bosworth (1996, pp. 157-159).

Table 13.2

East Asia: Growth Accounting, 1978-96

(Growth in percent per annum and relative contributions in percent)

	Output[a]	Capital Share	Capital[a]		Labor[a]			Residual
Indonesia	4.7	0.326	9.0	62%	0.9	13%	1.2	25%
Malaysia	4.5	0.315	6.9	47%	0.6	9%	2.0	44%
Philippines	0.2	0.297	1.8		0.6		-0.8	
Singapore	5.1	0.337	6.5	42%	1.1	14%	2.2	44%
Thailand	5.2	0.289	7.3	41%	1.5	21%	2.0	39%
Average[b]	4.9	0.313	7.4	48%	1.0	14%	1.9	38%
U.S.	1.1	0.292	1.6	44%	0.4	28%	0.3	27%

[a]Per person.

[b]Excluding the Philippines.

Note: The growth residual in the last column is derived using Equation (??).

Source: Adapted from Sarel (1997, p. 378).

13.3   Growth Regressions and Convergence

13.3.1   Diminishing Returns and Convergence

An issue that has attracted considerable attention in the recent empirical litera-ture on growth is whether poor countries tend to grow faster than rich countries; that is, whether a process of *convergence* in growth rates occurs over time. As discussed in Chapter 11, the Solow-Swan model predicts that countries with different production technologies, saving rates, and population growth rates but with the same rate of technological progress, γ, will all converge to a balanced growth path in which the rate of growth of income per capita is equal to γ. Moreover, if production technologies, saving rates, and population growth rates are the same across countries, they will all converge to the same level of income per capita as well.

But to the extent that countries are at different points in their *transition* to the balanced growth path, differences in output per worker will arise; one would then expect the poorer countries to grow faster than the richer countries— even with identical technology, saving rates, and population growth rates. The reason is that *diminishing returns to capital* imply that each addition to the capital stock generates large additions to output when the capital stock is small to begin with (see Chapter 11). The opposite is true when the capital stock is large initially. This observation has important implications for econometric testing.

13.3.2   Convergence and Cross-Section Regressions

From an empirical point of view, various concepts of convergence have been used in the literature. The two concepts emphasized by Barro and Sala-i-Martin (1995) and Mankiw, Romer, and Weil (1992) are β-convergence (absolute and conditional) and σ-convergence, which are commonly analyzed through cross-country regression techniques.

- **Absolute β-convergence**, or **mean reversion**, occurs in a cross section of countries if a negative relationship can be found between the growth rate of real income per capita and the *initial level* of real income per capita. Put differently, absolute β-convergence occurs if poor economies tend to grow *faster* than richer ones, as indicated earlier.[5]

- **σ-convergence** occurs across a group of countries when the *dispersion* of real per capita income tends to fall over time. In other words, σ-convergence requires that the distribution of world income become *more equitable* over time.

To see how these two concepts of convergence are related, consider a group of N countries, with real per capita income for country h given by y_h, $h = 1, ...N$. Consider also the following regression model, in discrete time, of y_h over a constant term, a_0, and its lagged value:

$$\ln y_{ht} = a_0 + (1 - \beta) \ln y_{ht-1} + u_{ht}, \quad h = 1, ...N, \qquad (13.5)$$

where β is a parameter to be estimated. u_{ht} is a disturbance term with mean zero and constant variance σ_u^2, which captures temporary shocks to the production technology, the propensity to save, and so on. This term is also assumed to be *independent* over time and across countries. Equation (13.5) can also be written as

$$\ln(y_{ht}/y_{ht-1}) = a_0 - \beta \ln y_{ht-1} + u_{ht}, \quad h = 1, ...N. \qquad (13.6)$$

Equation (13.6) shows that for β-convergence to hold, the condition $\beta > 0$ must be satisfied; indeed, $\beta > 0$ implies *mean reversion* because the annual growth rate of per capita income, $\ln(y_{ht}/y_{ht-1})$, is inversely related to $\ln y_{ht-1}$.[6] The higher β is, the greater the tendency to converge.[7]

In the long run, with $y_{ht-1} = y_{ht}$, *expected real income per capita* is

$$\mathrm{E} \ln y_h = a_0/\beta,$$

---

[5] An alternative statistical technique to test for β-convergence, based on changes in the ranking of income levels over time, is proposed by Boyle and McCarthy (1997).

[6] The condition $\beta < 1$ is also generally required to exclude the possibility that real income per capita in poor countries exceed income per capita in richer ones at some point in the future.

[7] As shown by Bernard and Durlauf (1996), with *ordinary least squares* estimation, β can be written as a weighted average of the ratio of differences of growth rates from the sample mean to differences of initial incomes from the sample mean. The requirement that $\beta > 0$ in a cross-section regression may therefore be expressed as requiring that a weighted average of countries with above-average initial incomes grows at a slower rate than the mean growth for the cross section.

where **E** is the mathematical expectations operator.

To define σ-convergence, consider as a measure of the dispersion of income across countries the **sample variance** of $\ln y_{ht}$:

$$\sigma_t^2 = \frac{1}{N-1} \sum_{h=1}^{N} (\ln y_{ht} - \mu_t)^2, \qquad (13.7)$$

where μ_t is the sample mean of $\ln y_{ht}$. If N is sufficiently large, then the sample variance can be viewed as a relatively accurate measure of the **population variance**. Equation (13.5) can then be used to calculate the process driving σ_t^2 over time:

$$\sigma_t^2 \simeq (1-\beta)^2 \sigma_{t-1}^2 + \sigma_u^2. \qquad (13.8)$$

Equation (13.8) is a **first-order difference equation** in σ_t^2, which, as long as $0 < \beta < 1$, provides a stable steady-state solution, $\tilde{\sigma}^2$, given by (see Chiang, 1984, pp. 554-556):

$$\tilde{\sigma}^2 = \frac{\sigma_u^2}{1 - (1-\beta)^2}. \qquad (13.9)$$

Equation (13.9) shows that the long-run value of the variance of per capita income across countries is increasing in the variance of the disturbance term σ_u^2, and decreasing in β.

Equation (13.8) also reveals that if absolute β-convergence does not hold in the sample, that is if $\beta < 0$, $(1-\beta)^2$ will be greater than unity and the process driving σ_t^2 will be **unstable**: the cross-sectional variance of income will tend to increase over time without bound. Thus, absolute β-convergence is *necessary* for σ-convergence to occur.

The solution of Equation (13.8) can be written as

$$\sigma_t^2 - \tilde{\sigma}^2 = (1-\beta)^2 (\sigma_{t-1}^2 - \tilde{\sigma}^2), \qquad (13.10)$$

which shows that if absolute β-convergence holds $(\beta > 0)$, then σ_t^2 will approach its long-run value $\tilde{\sigma}^2$ monotonically. Equation (13.10) also shows that whether σ_t^2 is rising or falling toward $\tilde{\sigma}^2$ depends on whether its initial value is greater, or lower, than the long-run value. In particular, σ_t^2 may be increasing during the transition even if $\beta > 0$. Thus, although absolute β-convergence is *necessary* for σ-convergence (as shown earlier), it is *not sufficient*.[8] Figure 13.1 provides some evidence on σ-convergence for a group of 82 developing countries covering the period 1960-90, and a group of industrial countries. The figure suggests that whereas there has been increased σ-convergence between industrial countries since the early 1960s, a pattern of divergence has occurred in developing countries—particularly among countries in Africa and Asia.

The third concept of convergence emphasized in the literature is the concept of **conditional β-convergence**, which is taken to occur in a group of countries

---

[8] Quah (1996a,1996b) explains the difference between β- and σ-convergence by means of *Galton's fallacy*: the convergence to the intergenerational mean in the height of the members of a family (β-convergence) does not imply that the dispersion of heights within the population diminishes throughout time (σ-convergence).

if the *partial correlation* between the rate of growth of, and the initial level of, per capita real income is *negative*. To illustrate this concept, consider a cross-section regression of per capita income growth rates on initial per capita income and various other *control variables* summarized in the vector Z_t, which captures other determinants of income—such as inflation, the degree of openness, or the degree of political polarization (as discussed below):

$$\ln y_{ht} = a_0 + a_1 Z_t + (1 - \beta) \ln y_{ht-1} + u_{ht}. \qquad (13.11)$$

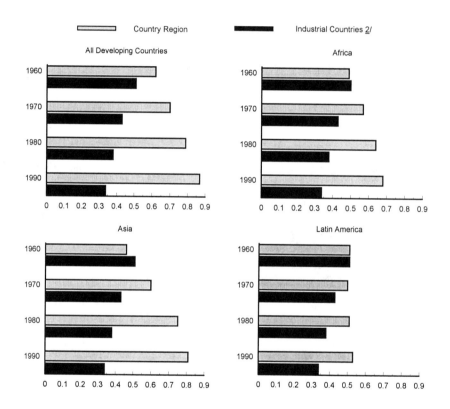

Figure 13.1. Sigma Convergence Across Countries 1/ (Coefficient of variation of per capita income).

Source: United Nations.

1/ Based on data for 82 developing countries covering the period 1960-90.

2/ Excluding the former socialist countries of Eastern Europe.

It can be shown that, as long as the process driving the variables contained in Z is stable, conditional β-convergence once again requires $\beta > 0$. Similarly, σ-convergence can also be defined in the context of Equation (13.11); and once again, conditional β-convergence is *necessary* for σ-convergence to occur. There are, however, two differences:

- Even if $0 < \beta < 1$, σ_t^2 does not approach its steady-state value *monotonically*: there may be, during the transition process, periods during which σ_t^2 increases and then falls, depending on the process driving the variables contained in Z_t, as well as their initial and long-run values.

- The dispersion of income per capita in the long run depends not only [as in Equation (13.9)] on the variance of the shocks, σ_u^2, but also on the dispersion of *country-specific characteristics*, as summarized by σ_Z^2.

13.3.3 Testing the Mankiw-Romer-Weil Model

A key implication of the growth model with physical and human capital accumulation developed by Mankiw, Romer, and Weil (1992), as indicated in the previous chapter, is that differences in population growth and capital accumulation can potentially account for the observed large variations in incomes across countries. The income per capita equation of their model, as derived earlier, is

$$\ln \tilde{y} = \frac{\alpha}{\Omega} \ln s_K + \frac{\beta}{\Omega} \ln s_H - \frac{\alpha + \beta}{\Omega} \ln(n + \gamma + \delta),$$

where $\Omega = 1/(1 - \alpha - \beta)$. To test this equation, Mankiw, Romer, and Weil use the following measures:

- y: the logarithm of output per person in the population of working age (15 to 64);

- n: average population growth rate;

- s_K: the ratio of gross savings to GDP;

- s_H: the average fraction of the population of working age that is enrolled in secondary school over the period 1960-85;[9]

- $\gamma + \delta$: set to 0.05 for all countries.

Mankiw, Romer, and Weil estimate their income equation in the form

$$\ln y_i = a_0 + a_1 [\ln s_{Ki} - \ln(n_i + 0.05)] + a_2 [\ln s_{Hi} - \ln(n_i + 0.05)] + u_i,$$

where i is a country index and u_i is an error term. The results obtained for a group of 98 industrial and developing countries are the following:

$$a_1 = \underset{(0.12)}{0.73}, \quad a_2 = \underset{(0.07)}{0.67}, \quad \bar{R}^2 = 0.78, \quad \hat{\sigma}_u = 0.51,$$

---

[9]This variable may be subject to large *measurement errors*. In general, proxies for human capital, such as the average number of years of schooling of the labor force, the proportion of the labor force with higher education, and so on, are not only largely arbitrary measures but they also fail to reflect fully the large differences across countries in the quality of education.

where numbers in parentheses are standard errors. The values of α and β implied by the estimates of a_1 and a_2 are

$$\alpha = \underset{(0.04)}{0.31}, \quad \beta = \underset{(0.03)}{0.28}.$$

Thus, the model fits the data fairly well: the estimates of α and β are reasonable, and the regression accounts for almost 80 percent of cross-country variation in output per worker. However, the estimation method used by Mankiw, Romer, and Weil (*ordinary least squares*) exposes them to both **omitted variable** and **endogeneity bias**, as discussed below.

To examine the issue of *convergence*, Mankiw, Romer, and Weil begin by noting that the model implies that countries with different levels of s_K, s_H, and n have different levels of output per worker on their balanced growth paths; thus there is a component of cross-country income differences that persists over time. But differences that arise because countries are initially at different points on their balanced growth paths gradually disappear as convergence to those paths occurs. The model therefore predicts convergence once the determinants of income on the balanced growth path are properly controlled for, that is, **conditional convergence**, as defined earlier.

Specifically, the model implies that, in the vicinity of the balanced growth path, y converges to $\tilde{y}$ at the rate

$$|\Lambda| = (1 - \alpha - \beta)(n + \gamma + \delta),$$

which differs from the speed of adjustment derived for the Solow-Swan model (see Chapter 11) by the term in β. By definition, therefore, changes in real income over time can be approximated by

$$\frac{d \ln y}{dt} \simeq -|\Lambda|(\ln y - \ln \tilde{y}).$$

This equation implies that $\ln y$ approaches $\ln \tilde{y}$ exponentially:

$$\ln y - \ln \tilde{y} \simeq e^{-|\Lambda|t}(\ln y_0 - \ln \tilde{y}), \tag{13.12}$$

where y_0 is some initial value. If α and β are each 0.3 and $n + \gamma + \delta$ is 6 percent, $|\Lambda|$ is 2.4 percent; this implies that a country moves half way to its balanced growth path in $\ln(0.5)/\Lambda \simeq 29$ years.

Adding $\ln \tilde{y} - \ln y_0$ to both sides of Equation (13.12) yields an expression for the growth of income:

$$\ln y - \ln y_0 \simeq -(1 - e^{-|\Lambda|t})(\ln y_0 - \ln \tilde{y}). \tag{13.13}$$

Equation (13.13) implies **conditional convergence**: countries with initial incomes that are low relative to their balanced growth paths have higher growth. Finally, using the solution for $\ln \tilde{y}$ derived in the previous chapter [Equation (27)] yields

$$\frac{\ln y - \ln y_0}{1 - e^{-|\Lambda|t}} \simeq \frac{\alpha}{\Omega}[\ln s_K - \ln(n + \gamma)] + \frac{\beta}{\Omega}[\ln s_H - \Delta \ln(n + \gamma)] - \ln y_0,$$

which can be estimated in the form

$$\ln y_i = a_0 + a_1[\ln s_{Ki} - \ln(n_i + 0.05)] + a_2[\ln s_{Hi} - \ln(n_i + 0.05)] + a_3 \ln y_0 + u_i.$$

The parameter estimates obtained by Mankiw, Romer, and Weil are

$$a_1 = \underset{(0.08)}{0.50}, \quad a_2 = \underset{(0.06)}{0.24}, \quad a_3 = \underset{(0.06)}{0.30}, \quad \bar{R}^2 = 0.46, \quad \hat{\sigma}_u = 0.33,$$

which imply the following values for α, β, and $|\Lambda|$:

$$\alpha = \underset{(0.07)}{0.48}, \quad \beta = \underset{(0.05)}{0.23}, \quad |\Lambda| = \underset{(0.002)}{0.014}.$$

These estimates are broadly in line with the predictions of the model: countries converge toward their balanced growth paths at about the rate that the model predicts, and the estimated capital shares appear to be broadly similar to the available evidence. Overall, the results obtained by Mankiw, Romer, and Weil suggest that a model that maintains the assumption of diminishing returns to capital but that adopts a *broader definition of capital* than traditional physical capital, and therefore implies a total capital share closer to 0.7, appears to provide a good approximation to the cross-country data.

Results qualitatively similar to those obtained by Mankiw, Romer, and Weil were obtained by Gundlach (1995). De la Fuente (1997), however, reestimated the Mankiw-Romer-Weil model over two subperiods (1960-75 and 1975-85) and found that it does not explain well the growth slowdown that characterized the 1975-85 period—suggesting some important *omitted variables* in the model. Grossman and Helpman (1994) criticized the assumption of an identical rate of technological progress for all the countries in the sample considered by Mankiw, Romer, and Weil. Specifically, Grossman and Helpman (1991, p. 29) argued that

> If technological progress varies by country, and [these variations are] treated as part of the unobserved error term, then ordinary least squares estimates of the... equation will be biased when investment-GDP ratios are correlated with country-specific productivity growth. In particular, if investment rates are high when productivity grows fast, the coefficient on the investment [or saving] variable will pick up...part of the variation due to their different experiences with technological progress...[In addition, one] would certainly expect investment to be highest where capital productivity is growing the fastest.

Thus, the estimate of the effect of the saving-investment variable derived by Mankiw, Romer, and Weil is overstated and the slope-coefficient test is consequently biased. How large this bias is has not been precisely evaluated. But in any case it relates only to the ability of the model to explain cross-section differences in income levels, not in growth rates.[10]

---

[10] Islam (1995) provided a panel-date approach to conditional convergence regressions that allows some production function parameters to differ across countries. His approach, however, retains the assumption that the rate of technological progress is the same for all countries.

At a more conceptual level, another criticism of the Mankiw-Romer-Weil approach is offered by Barro, Mankiw, and Sala-i-Martin (1995), who introduced not only human capital but also **partial capital mobility** in a Solow-Swan framework by assuming that only a fraction of the capital stock can be used as *collateral* against borrowing on world capital markets. Specifically, in the model physical capital is assumed to be mobile across countries, but human capital is not. Moreover, physical capital can be used (at least in part) as collateral for international borrowing, but human capital cannot.

In this setting, adjustment to the steady-state level of physical capital is fast due to the possibility of international borrowing, but adjustment to the steady-state level of human capital is relatively slow. The relative size of the accumulated stocks of physical and human capital determines the fraction of the capital stock that can be used as collateral. These assumptions have no effect on the predicted steady state itself, but affect the rate of convergence. Specifically, the convergence rate derived by Barro, Mankiw, and Sala-i-Martin (1995), based on a production function similar to the one used by Mankiw, Romer, and Weil, is

$$|\Lambda| = (1 - \frac{\beta}{1 - \alpha})(n + \gamma + \delta).$$

For instance, assuming again that α and β are each 0.3 and that $n + \gamma + \delta$ is 6 percent, $|\Lambda|$ is 3.4 percent; a country would move half way to its balanced growth path now in only $\ln(0.5)/\Lambda \simeq 20$ years.

The main implication of the analysis is that the speed of convergence predicted for a *closed economy* (with no capital mobility) is very similar to the speed predicted by an *open-economy* model where the share of mobile capital that can be used as collateral—physical capital only—does not exceed one half. For all practical purposes, therefore, the assumption of a closed economy is not completely misleading, as long as *capital mobility is imperfect*—a view that is supported by much of the evidence (see Chapter 6). Thus, the neoclassical model with partial capital mobility appears to be consistent with the empirical evidence on convergence in levels of per capita income.

13.4   The Empirics of Growth: Econometric Issues

Much of the empirical literature on growth, following an early study by Barro (1991), has focused on estimating **cross-country regressions** in search of a set of stable relations among the various variables suggested by the old and new theories. This literature has been plagued, however, by severe methodological problems.[11] From an econometric standpoint, many studies suffer from an in-

---

[11] A comprehensive methodological and conceptual review of the early cross-country empirical studies of economic growth was prepared by Levine and Renelt (1992). They made general recommendations aimed at improving the econometric techniques used to estimate cross-country growth equations and improve the database. They also provided a more detailed discussion of the general statistical problems (sampling, aggregation, causality, data

appropriate treatment of **measurement** and **specification errors**, and lack of appreciation of the potential for **simultaneity bias**.

A first difficulty is that the data necessary to adequately test the predictions of the new models of growth do not exist or are difficult to construct. In many cases, the quality of the data is also inadequate. As a result, the explanatory variables typically introduced in cross-sectional growth regressions suffer from **measurement errors**. Arcand and Dagenais (1995), in particular, argued that results derived from Barro-type regressions, as well as those of Mankiw, Romer, and Weil (1992) reviewed earlier, are fragile when such errors are properly accounted for in the econometric procedure. A few authors—such as Persson and Tabellini (1994)—have attempted to gauge the sensitivity to measurement errors of the parameter estimates obtained in their cross-section studies by using more appropriate econometric techniques (such as *instrumental variables*), but the practice is far from being systematic.

Even with adequately measured variables, the basic approach that characterizes many cross-country empirical studies of growth (consisting of regressing the *time-averaged* growth rate for a group of countries on a set of ad hoc explanatory variables) faces a number of other difficulties.

- Heterogeneity between developing countries regarding growth patterns may be such that it is simply inappropriate to perform cross-country regressions. The practice of using **regional or continent dummies** in pooled cross-section, time-series analyses is based on the presumption that geographical factors may yield a homogeneous sample.[12] In practice, however, appropriate **statistical tests for pooling** are seldom applied.

- There are considerable variations in *data definitions* across countries; classifications of government expenditures, for instance, vary depending on the institutional coverage (for example, central government or general government), and on arbitrary conceptual definitions. Such differences are seldom taken into account.

- The behavior of the actual growth rate of output reflects both a *trend* (or *long-term*) component and a *cyclical* component—that is, **transitional movements** around the steady state (see Chapter 9). Attempts to measure the trend component often take the form of *averaging* both output growth rates and explanatory variables over a relatively long period (sometimes up to 30 years). However, the *length of the period* used to average the data is in practice *largely arbitrary*, because the frequency of cycles is not generally known (making it difficult to separate the trend component from the cyclical component), and because cycles have different frequencies across countries and across variables. Using a *uniform* averaging period is thus likely to distort the long-run relationships between variables.

---

selection, measurement errors, etc.) that cross-country econometric analysis faces. The more recent survey by Temple (1999) provides an updated presentation (and criticism) of the new econometric procedures used in the current literature.

[12] Alternatives followed by some authors are to focus only on one specific region (for instance, Rodrik, 1998a) or to exclude a subset of countries—such as major oil-exporting countries.

- In addition, as emphasized by Pesaran and Smith (1995), whereas the dependent variable is a time average of growth rates, explanatory variables are often a combination of time averages of *flows* (such as fixed investment) and beginning-of-period *stock* variables (such as an index of schooling). Such variables, however, have different time-series properties; mixing **stationary** and **nonstationary** variables in estimation can lead to spurious results—a point well emphasized in modern time-series econometrics (see Greene, 1997).

- Finally, averaging implies that cross-country regressions do not represent *typical behavioral equations*. Parameter estimates represent cross-country averages which may not be representative of any individual country.

Other criticisms focus on the econometric techniques used by some researchers in estimating cross-country regressions. Particularly in the early literature, *linear* models and *ordinary least squares* (OLS) were used most of the time. Caselli, Esquivel, and Lefort (1996) and Pesaran and Smith (1995), for instance, argued that such techniques give *unreliable results* because they are subject to the following problems:

- An **omitted variable** (or **specification**) **bias**, resulting from the incorrect treatment of country-specific effects—associated notably with differences in technology and tastes. OLS estimates in a cross-section regression are consistent only to the extent that the individual effects are *uncorrelated* with other explanatory variables. This condition is unlikely to hold in practice.[13]

- An **endogeneity** (or **simultaneity**) **bias**, resulting from the failure to account for the endogenous nature of some of the explanatory variables.

The specification bias may also result from the fact that the growth regression takes the relationship between the explanatory variables and growth to be *linear*, whereas in fact it is *nonlinear*—as discussed for instance in the last chapter in the case of taxation; this makes it difficult to detect empirically a significant correlation.

Some more recent studies have attempted to correct for these problems; but almost none of them has tried to do so simultaneously. The estimation method used by Knight, Loayza, and Villanueva (1993), for instance, provided a proper treatment of country-specific effects but failed to address the endogeneity issue. In contrast, Aizenman and Marion (1993) used instrumental variables estimation to account for simultaneity bias but did not correct for specification bias. Only Caselli, Esquivel, and Lefort (1996) and Easterly, Loayza, and Montiel (1997) attempted to address simultaneously both issues in their estimation procedure.

---

[13]Pesaran and Smith (1995) also argued that the assumption that the error term is uncorrelated with the explanatory variables is likely to be violated due to the inherently *dynamic nature* of growth regressions.

Finally, the early literature was characterized by considerable diversity in the country coverage, the periods examined, and the set of explanatory variables; this made it difficult to generalize or to consider any particular study as reliable. Moreover, the *lack of clear theoretical underpinnings* for many empirical studies made it difficult to attach any analytical interpretation to some of these results. As noted earlier, a comprehensive review of the early literature on cross-country empirical studies of economic growth was provided by Levine and Renelt (1992); their conclusion was that almost all of the cross-country regression results that they reviewed were fragile: minor alterations in the list of explanatory variables often destroyed the properties of the growth equation. This *lack of robustness* appeared to be related to the omitted-variable bias discussed earlier.

Several alternative approaches to the standard cross-country regression framework discussed above have been developed in recent years. Quah (1996*a*, 1996*b*, 1997) argued that focusing on cross-section averages over long periods of time may be misleading, and proposed to analyze the evolution of the entire distribution.[14] Other researchers, such as Bernard and Durlauf (1996) and Arestis and Demetriades (1997), suggested that **time-series regression** for *individual* countries may be more appropriate to assess the effects of various variables on growth. As indicated earlier, cross-country regressions typically involve averaging out variables over relatively long periods of time—a procedure that makes cross-country variations in results difficult to interpret. In addition, the question of *causality* is difficult to address in a cross-section framework. The time-series approach allows the investigator not only to analyze the possibility of **bidirectional causality** but also to account for differences in the *institutional framework* and the *policy regimes*, which may affect (as noted in the previous chapter) in a crucial manner the effect of various variables on growth.

Arestis and Demetriades (1997), in particular, use a **cointegration approach** (as briefly discussed in the appendix to Chapter 2) to analyze the determinants of growth in an individual-country context. This alternative approach, of course, also has its limitations. One is the *limited number of observations* available in a time-series context for many developing countries. Another is the fact that cointegration analysis does not allow the investigator to capture changes in the *steady state itself*, which may result from structural change. Recent developments in *panel data econometrics* and their application to growth issues (as discussed by Temple, 1999) provide a promising framework for integrating the cross-country and time-series approaches.

13.5   The Econometric Evidence: An Overview

This part provides a *selective overview* of the recent literature on cross-country growth regressions, broadly along the lines of the discussion on the determinants of growth provided in Chapters 11 and 12. The focus on recent studies is motivated by the results of the extensive review of Levine and Renelt (1992),

---

[14]Specifically, Quah suggested jointly analyzing β- and σ-convergence using *stochastic kernels* for the dynamics of the distribution of income per capita.

which, as indicated earlier, emphasized the fragility of many of the cross-country regression results they reviewed. Although some of the recent studies continue to suffer from some of the problems identified by Levine and Renelt, many of them have used improved econometric methods and can therefore be viewed, at least to some extent, as more reliable.

13.5.1 Saving and Physical and Human Capital

Levine and Renelt (1992), in their careful review of the early evidence on the determinants of growth, suggested that both *saving* and *physical investment* rates were positively and significantly correlated with average growth rates across a wide variety of samples and specifications. These results have been corroborated in a variety of more recent studies, including Easterly, Loayza, and Montiel (1997). However, very few researchers have attempted to account for the *quality* of investment in their growth regressions; as the Asia crisis discussed earlier amply demonstrated, high rates of investment are not necessarily conducive to sustained growth.

As indicated in the previous chapters, investment in education and *human capital* leads to the acquisition of skills that increase efficiency, raises the intensity with which existing technologies are used, and promotes technological advances. Econometric evidence provided by Barro (1991, 1997), Benhabib and Spiegel (1994), and various other researchers suggested that, indeed, the *initial level of education* (a proxy for human capital), especially at the primary level, was an important determinant of subsequent growth. Higher education and public spending on education as a share of GDP have been found to have a relatively strong positive impact on growth. The more recent literature also suggests that the *quality* of education is important. This is in contrast to the early review by Levine and Renelt (1992), which suggested that the significance of human capital indicators in growth regressions was not always robust to the inclusion of other variables.

Some of the recent evidence, however, is not entirely conclusive for at least two reasons.

- As noted by Pack and Page (1994), most cross-section regressions do not take into account changes in the *sectoral composition* of output, although such shifts in the production structure may explain part of aggregate growth. They argued that some of the growth effects attributed to investment and education may reflect the fact that they facilitate a change in the *sectoral structure* of production.

- Bils and Klenow (1998) emphasized that the positive correlation between initial schooling enrollment and subsequent movements in growth rates found in several empirical studies may be consistent with *causality* running from *expected* growth to schooling (through its effect on expected earnings, for instance), rather than the other way around. They noted, in particular, that for the group of 93 countries in their sample, schooling attainment implied by enrollment rates increased by one third between 1960 and 1975; yet the average growth rate of per capita income in the same group fell from 2.9 percent per year during 1960-75 to 11.1 percent during 1975-90.[15]

13.5.2   Fiscal Policy

A large part of the recent empirical growth literature has examined the impact on growth of the levels of government current and investment expenditure, and the composition of such expenditure. Overall, the evidence on the nature of this relationship is mixed. Devarajan, Swaroop, and Zou (1996), for instance, found no significant relationship between growth and the *level* of expenditures (as measured by their share in GDP). The empirical literature on the effects of the *composition* of expenditures has also produced mixed results. Barro (1997) found that government consumption expenditures—calculated by deducting defense and education expenditures from general consumption spending—measured in proportion of GDP was negatively correlated with growth. Devarajan, Swaroop, and Zou (1996), in contrast, found a positive relationship between public consumption expenditures (as measured by current outlays as a share of total expenditures) and economic growth. Caselli, Esquivel, and Lefort (1996) also found a positive effect on growth of government expenditure (net of military and educational spending) as a share of output. Easterly, Loayza, and Montiel (1997) found no significant effect of the share of government consumption in GDP on growth in Latin America.

Recent analytical studies have emphasized the differential role of public and private investment in the growth process. As discussed in Chapters 1 and 12, public investment in infrastructure, to the extent that it proves *complementary* to private investment, can increase the marginal product of private capital— thereby raising the economy's growth rate. This is a particularly important link in developing countries. In contrast, if public production activities *compete* with private initiative, there may be **substitution** or **crowding-out effects** that may lead to adverse effects on growth. However, the evidence on the relationship between public investment and growth remains ambiguous. Using a sample of 95 developing countries over the period 1970-90, Khan and Kumar (1997) found that the effects of private and public investment on growth differed significantly, with private investment being consistently more productive than public investment. Knight, Loayza, and Villanueva (1993) and Nelson and Singh (1994) also found that the level of public investment in infrastructure had a significant effect on growth, particularly during the 1980s. Using a cross-section study of 119 countries, Easterly and Rebelo (1993) estimated that public investment in *transportation* and *communications* was positively related to growth. In contrast, public investment in *state-owned enterprises* had no effect on growth, whereas public investment in *agriculture* had a negative effect. Devarajan, Swaroop and Zou (1996) obtained evidence of an inverse relationship

---

[15] The drop in the growth rate of per capita income between the two periods was actually larger in countries where growth in schooling exceeded the average rate.

between public investment and growth, suggesting that, in fact, governments may have been misallocating expenditures in favor of capital expenditures (as opposed to outlays on, say, infrastructure maintenance).

Several empirical studies have found evidence of an inverse relationship between *taxes* and economic growth, but overall the results are not very robust. Finally, Nelson and Singh (1994) found no significant effect of **fiscal deficits** on growth in developing countries during the 1970s and 1980s. Rodrik (1998a), in contrast, provided evidence suggesting that long-term growth in sub-Saharan Africa during 1965-90 was significantly affected by fiscal policy (in addition to human resources, demography, and a catchup variable). Low central-government surpluses tended to slow the rate of growth in income per capita in the region.

The lack of robustness of the evidence on fiscal policy and growth may be related in part to the *nonlinear* nature of the relationship between these variables. As discussed in the previous chapter, in Barro's (1990) model, growth increases with taxation and expenditures at low levels and then decreases as the distortionary effects of taxation exceed the beneficial effects of public goods. Government expenditures and growth are positively correlated when government expenditures are below the optimum amount, negatively related when they are above, and are uncorrelated when governments are providing the optimal amount of services. Cross-country empirical studies have, in general, failed to account for this nonlinearity and may therefore be unable to detect it in the data. Despite the inconclusive nature of the empirical literature, however, the consensus view seems to be that changes in the composition of government spending toward higher outlays on health, education, and basic infrastructure tend to have a positive impact on growth.

13.5.3   Inflation and Macroeconomic Stability

The effect of inflation and macroeconomic stability on long-run growth has been a key area of investigation, at both the analytical and empirical level. In one of the early contributions to this literature, Fischer (1993) found empirical evidence for a large group of countries of a positive link between growth and macroeconomic stability— defined in terms of the level of inflation and its volatility, the parallel market exchange rate premium (the ratio of the parallel exchange rate to the official rate, as defined in Annex C), the ratio of the budget deficit to GDP, and changes in the terms of trade. The negative correlation between the overall budget deficit and growth appeared particularly robust. De Gregorio (1992, 1993) also found evidence of a negative relationship between the level of inflation (an indicator of tax system inefficiency rather than financial repression, as argued earlier), the variability of inflation, and growth in Latin America, using a cross section of 12 Latin American countries over the period 1950-85.

In a more recent contribution, Sarel (1996) found that the effects of inflation on economic growth are *nonlinear*. When inflation is low, it has no significant effect on growth. But when inflation is high (above 8 percent per annum), it has a negative and statistically significant effect on growth. A doubling in the rate of inflation (from, say, 20 to 40 percent) reduces the economy's growth rate by 1.7 percentage points. This is much higher than the estimate derived in several other studies. Barro (1997) also found that inflation has a negative effect on output growth rates per capita (and the share of investment in output) in a cross-country regression over the period 1960-90. This effect, however, is not large; an increase in average inflation by 10 percentage points per year lowers the growth rate of real per capita GDP on impact by 0.2 to 0.3 percentage point per year.[16] In addition, it exists only when the high-inflation observations, that is, countries in which inflation exceeded 40 percent a year (a sample that included a large proportion of Latin American countries), are included in the sample. Along the same lines, Bruno and Easterly (1998) found no robust evidence of a long-run relationship between inflation and growth at annual inflation rates less than 40 percent. They argued that the significant effect reported in some early cross-country studies was an *artifact* that resulted from both the sample period used and the inclusion of some high-inflation outliers.

Various other studies have used a series of indicators, in addition to inflation variability, to assess the degree of uncertainty associated with macroeconomic policies. A simple (albeit crude) *composite* indicator of macroeconomic instability is the unweighted sum of the mean inflation rate, the standard deviation of inflation, mean budget and external current account deficits as a percentage of GDP, and mean terms-of-trade changes. A more precise measure of *policy variability* was proposed by Aizenman and Marion (1993); they used the standard deviation of the real exchange rate, the standard deviation of inflation, and domestic credit growth, as well as composite indicators including all of the foregoing variables. The evidence that they provided generally supported a negative relationship between policy variability and growth, although the relationship was not robust for some indicators. Bleaney (1996), in a cross-section study covering the period 1980-90, found that macroeconomic instability (measured by the fiscal balance and the degree of volatility of the real exchange rate) had a significant negative effect on the rate of economic growth and possibly also a negative effect on investment.

13.5.4 Financial Factors

The recent evidence on the role of financial variables on growth, as reviewed in the extensive survey prepared by Levine (1997), appears to be highly supportive of a positive link between these variables. King and Levine (1993), for instance, found a robust correlation between the degree of financial development and growth, investment, and the efficiency of capital. The financial indicators that they used included the size of the formal financial sector (as measured by the liquid liabilities to the financial system) relative to output, the importance of banks relative to the central bank, the ratio of credit allocated to firms relative to output, and the share of total credit allocated to firms.

---

[16] As noted in Chapter 9, however, even small reductions in the rate of growth of output may translate over a sufficiently long period of time (say, 20 or 30 years) into large effects on standards of living.

The problem with most of the cross-section literature, however, is that (as noted earlier) it does not address the issue of *causality*. Demetriades and Hussein (1996), using time-series data and appropriate econometric techniques for 16 countries, suggested that the causality between financial depth—as measured by the ratios of bank deposits to GDP and bank claims on the private sector to GDP—and growth varies across countries. In only two cases (Honduras and Sri Lanka) did financial development appear to cause economic growth. In about seven of the countries in their sample (Guatemala, Honduras, India, Korea, Mauritius, Thailand, and Venezuela) they detected a **feedback relationship** between finance and growth; and in four of them (El Saldavor, Pakistan, South Africa, and Turkey) the causality relationship was instead *from growth to finance*—which may occur as a result, for instance, of an increased demand (induced by higher income) for financial services.

There is also some evidence showing that **financial repression** has an adverse effect on economic performance. Roubini and Sala-i-Martin (1995), for instance, found a negative effect of the *bank reserve ratio* on growth. However, this evidence is not entirely conclusive because reserve ratios can be a poor proxy for the degree of financial repression. As an alternative approach, Arestis and Demetriades (1997) used as proxy a weighted index of the principal components of five types of controls on the banking sector—the ceiling on deposit rates, the ceiling on lending rates, the proportion of total credit covered by the directed credit program, and the minimum reserve requirement rate on demand and time deposits. Their econometric results suggested a mildly positive effect of financial repression on economic growth in *Korea*.

13.5.5 Openness and External Trade

As noted in the previous chapter, endogenous growth models emphasizing the role of international trade suggest that trade openness allows poorer countries to benefit from **technology spillovers**, such as through the stock of knowledge embedded in *capital goods*. Openness to international trade may also increase the number of *specialized inputs*, thereby increasing growth rates in the long run.[17] Studies that highlighted the importance of the degree of openness and, more generally, an outward orientation for growth are those of Dollar (1992), Edwards (1993), Khan and Kumar (1997), Knight, Loayza, and Villanueva (1993), and Sachs and Warner (1997a, 1997b). Trade distortions, in all of these studies, had a negative effect on growth.[18]

---

[17] Note that if the degree of openness to international trade and the resulting transfer of knowledge and inputs affects the rate of *productivity growth*, then the standard growth accounting framework described earlier (which is based on a pure production function approach) may be inadequate because the level of technology will change with the allocation of output between domestic sales and exports—partly offsetting the effect of diminishing returns to capital.

[18] The parallel market premium was used in a number of studies as an indicator of structural distortions, particularly in the trade and financial areas; see, for instance, Easterly (1992). Results were often highly significant but, as noted by Levine and Renelt (1992), the precise channels through which the premium may affect growth were usually not specified.

Sachs and Warner (1997*a*) in particular focused on a sample of 117 countries classified into two groups: those that protected *property rights* and kept trade open during the 1970-89 period, and those that did not. The *index of openness* that they constructed was based on five criteria—nontariff barriers, average tariff levels, the parallel market exchange rate, whether state monopolies existed for major exports, and whether the economy was socialist or not. They found that, on average, the more open countries grew by 2 to 2.5 percentage points more than others. As noted in Chapter 10, however, the robustness of the Sachs-Warner index of trade openness has been questioned by Harrison and hanson (1999).

A more recent econometric study by Greenaway, Morgan, and Wright (1998) used a cross-country data set covering 73 countries. The regression model that they specified includes not only a measure of openness but also various other control variables—initial income per capita, the ratio of domestic investment to output, and an index of the terms of trade. They also used three indicators of openness, among which was the Sachs-Warner index described earlier, and an index based on **average nominal tariffs**, the extent of **quantitative restrictions** on imports, and average parallel market premia. In contrast to earlier studies, Greenaway, Morgan, and Wright used a *dynamic* regression framework to investigate potential lagged effects. They found that trade openness appeared to have an identifiable impact on growth; this effect was robust relative to the indicator used. At the same time, however, the growth effect had a **J-curve** feature: the initial impact of trade openness on output growth rates was found to be small or negative; only over time did it becomes positive. This result has implications for the *sustainability of trade reforms*, as discussed in the next chapter.

There is also evidence of a direct link between imports of *capital goods* and growth. Lee (1993), for instance, found a close relationship between these two variables in a large group of developing countries. Along the same lines, Roldós (1997) found that in Chile over the period 1971-95 TFP growth appeared to be correlated with the ratio of imported capital to total physical capital—perhaps reflecting the process of technology diffusion and adoption. There is also some suggestive firm-level empirical evidence of the importance of transfers of knowledge, rather than machinery, for several Asian countries (including Korea and Taiwan), as pointed out by Pack and Page (1994).

As noted in the previous chapter, the growth in productivity stemming from increasing international trade may be facilitated by improved domestic absorptive capacity made possible by higher levels of *human capital*; education, in particular, increases the ability of individuals to deal with rapid changes in knowledge. What this suggests is that the effect of the degree of openness on growth may be *nonlinear*: low in countries with low levels of education, and high in countries with a highly skilled workforce. Although there does not appear to be formal econometric evidence supporting this view, a review of the East Asia growth experience by the World Bank (1993) did suggest that Asian countries benefited from the interaction of rapid transfers of technology and a highly skilled labor force to adapt the technology to local needs.

Nevertheless, it should be emphasized that the empirical evidence has not yet clearly established the direction of *causality* between trade openness and growth. There are several mechanisms that could imply a positive effect of growth on openness, or channels through which other factors may affect *both* openness and growth in the same direction. For instance, as income grows, the demand for luxury imported goods may rise fast enough to lead to an increase in the degree of openness, as conventionally measured. In such conditions, the case for advocating outward orientation as a growth-enhancing strategy would be significantly weakened.

13.5.6   Political Variables and Income Inequality

As noted in the previous chapter, it is now well recognized that *political* and *civil liberties* are not only desirable in themselves; by providing a foundation for imposing the rule of law, and thereby ensuring the security of property and the enforcement of contracts, they may play also an important economic role. Indeed, recent evidence suggests that these liberties are positively and significantly correlated with improvements in income per capita, life expectancy at birth, and the infant survival rate (Dasgupta, 1995).

Specifically, the *growth effects* of political factors have been the subject of a variety of cross-country empirical studies. Brunetti (1997) classified the political variables used in these studies in five groups:

- Measures of democracy, which include indicators such as the *Gastil index*—an annual rating of political rights and civil liberties in individual countries based on a seven-point scale.

- Measures of government (or institutional) instability, namely the number of, or the probability of, changes in government. These measures sometime include not only the number of regular executive transfers (through conventional legal procedures) but also the number of irregular transfers of power (or successful coups).

- Indicators of political violence, including measures of political strikes, protest demonstrations, riots, armed attacks, political assassinations, and executions.

- Subjective political indicators, as measured by surveys of the perceptions of local or international experts of the political situation in various countries. The empirical growth literature has often relied on indicators provided by three well-established country-risk evaluation firms: Business International, the International Country Risk Guide (ICRG), and Business Environmental Risk Intelligence (BERI).

The results summarized by Brunetti (1997) suggested that democracy indicators, measures of government stability, and indicators of political violence were not robustly correlated with growth. The same conclusion was reached by

Levine and Renelt (1992) in their sensitivity analysis of the early literature, including studies such as Barro's (1991), which found that social indicators of war, revolution, and civil liberties were negatively related to growth. Survey-based measures of political risk appear, in contrast, to be more closely correlated with growth, as suggested, for instance, by Mauro (1997).

The available evidence also suggests no clear correlation between the degree of income inequality and the rate of economic growth. In most empirical studies, inequality and growth were found either to be unrelated or the relationship lost its significance when other variables were included (see Alesina and Perotti, 1994, and Fishlow, 1995). Even where an inverse relationship was found, the impact of inequality on growth was fairly small (Clarke, 1995).[19]

13.6   Catching Up or Falling Behind?

As discussed earlier, the Solow-Swan model implies convergence across countries in both growth rates and income levels if all structural parameters (notably the production technology and the saving rate), and the rate of technological progress, are the same. Poor countries will initially exhibit lower capital-labor ratios than richer ones, implying a higher marginal product of capital. Given equal rates of technological progress, labor force growth, and domestic saving rates, their capital stock growth will exceed that in richer countries during a transitional period but they should ultimately converge to the capital-labor and capital-output ratios (and income levels) of richer countries. Of course, convergence will not occur if countries differ in their production technology, their saving rates, or their rate of technological progress. For instance, if trade barriers are such that poor countries have limited possibilities to access the more advanced technologies available in the richer countries, the rate of income growth per capita in the poor countries may well be permanently lower than in rich countries, implying sustained and growing differences in standards of living.

Many endogenous growth models (such as the AK model), indeed, imply the possibility of sustained differences in both levels and rates of growth of income. Because of the externalities or the productivity gains obtained from the availability of specialized inputs made possible by research and development activities, diminishing returns to human and physical capital do not occur, and the main force behind convergence disappears. Thus, the fact that the Solow-Swan model (with uniform parameters) predicts convergence and endogenous growth models do not, explains in part why the convergence hypothesis has received so much attention in the empirical literature of the last few years: it has been viewed as one way to discriminate between the two models. However, as pointed out in particular by Romer (1989), the convergence hypothesis is strictly speaking a test of the absence of diminishing returns, not a test of endogenous growth; the two issues should not be confused. For instance, suppose that the production process in the Solow-Swan model is characterized by a *constant elasticity of*

---

[19]Studies have also found no systematic relationship and no clear causal link between income inequality and political instability.

substitution (CES), as defined in Chapter 9. It can then be shown that, for a sufficiently high elasticity of substitution, the model can generate an endogenous steady-state growth and at the same time guarantee convergence (see Jones and Manuelli, 1997). The reason is that the key condition for endogenous growth is the violation of the **Inada conditions** (given in Chapter 11), whereas the key for ensuring convergence is the existence of diminishing returns to capital. The CES production function displays diminishing returns to capital, and therefore predicts convergence, but it violates the Inada conditions—thereby generating making it possible for the model to generate endogenous growth.[20]

The informal evidence discussed in Chapter 10 suggested that poor countries do not grow faster than richer countries; *absolute* β-convergence (in the sense defined above) did not appear to hold. However, several cross-country studies based on the econometric framework described earlier have confirmed the existence of *conditional* convergence: the level of GDP per capita at the start of the period is generally found to have a negative sign, once other factors are controlled for. Put differently, relative income levels eventually stabilize; but the long-run equilibrium position itself varies across countries, reflecting underlying differences in economic fundamentals—the level of education (a proxy for human capital), the rate of investment, the degree of openness, and so on. Thus, divergence in income levels across countries may persist over time. Early empirical estimates based on the econometric approach described earlier suggested that the rate of convergence was between 1 and 2 percent—although estimates tended to be quite sensitive to sample size and the list or control variables. A more recent study by Caselli, Esquivel, and Lefort (1996), however, using an estimator that relies on first differencing and instrumental variable and a general growth regression framework, found that the speed of convergence is very large compared with the early estimates—in the range of 6 to 10 percent per annum. Easterly, Loayza, and Montiel (1997) also found, for Latin America, a rate of 5.4 percent per year (implying a half-life of 12.8 years). The key implication of these results is that observed differences in income per capita may reflect to a significant extent differences in *steady-state levels* of per capita income, rather than differences in countries' *relative positions* along similar transitional paths leading to the same steady state.

The evidence also suggests that since the end of World War II the *dispersion* of levels of income per capita across industrial countries has fallen significantly— an indication of σ-convergence (De la Fuente, 1997). However, the dispersion of income levels between industrial and developing countries has increased substantially at the same time, as illustrated in Figure 13.1. Poor countries, particularly those in sub-Saharan Africa, appear to be more and more concentrated in the tails of the distribution of income. A similar tendency for divergence of cross-country incomes is obtained in a series of studies by Quah (1996*a*, 1996*b*, 1997). His analysis suggested that in the postwar era, rich countries have tended to become richer and poor countries poorer—leading to the emergence of **convergence clubs.**

---

[20] See also the production functions proposed by Jones and Manuelli (1990).

13.7   Summary

- **Growth accounting** aims to quantify the immediate sources of growth by measuring the rates of accumulation of various productive factors and weighting them according to their observed shares in national income.

- The methodology is subject to *important limitations.* The main difficulty with the concept of **total factor productivity** (or **Solow residual**) is that it encompasses the effects of a wide variety of factors, including *technology, efficiency* in resource allocation, *managerial skills* and *administrative efficiency,* and **economies of scale**. It may also reflect changes in the *quality* of factors of production; such changes can be very difficult to measure.

- Growth accounting techniques have been used to assess the sources of economic growth in East Asia between the 1950s and the early 1990s. Some economists have argued that the growth performance in the region was essentially the result of a high rate of *physical capital accumulation;* others have argued that it stemmed mostly from a high rate of growth of *total factor productivity.* The debate is difficult to settle because of a number of methodological and econometric issues.

- The assumption of *diminishing returns to capital* implies that in the Solow-Swan model countries with different production technologies, saving rates, and population growth rates but with the same rate of technological progress, γ, will all converge to a balanced growth path in which the rate of growth of income per capita is equal to γ. If production technologies, saving rates, and population growth rates are the same across countries, they will all converge to the same *level* of income per capita as well.

- This prediction has been tested in both its *absolute form* and *relative form* (given differences among structural parameters and characteristics across countries) using *cross-country regression techniques.* Conditional β-**convergence** of per capita income is defined as the tendency for poor economies to grow faster than rich economies, once the determinants of their steady state are held constant.

- Another concept of convergence is that of σ-**convergence**, which is deemed to occur across a group of countries when the *dispersion* of real per capita income tends to *fall over time.* β-convergence is necessary, but not sufficient, for σ-convergence.

- Cross-country estimates of the model of Mankiw, Romer, and Weil (1992) suggest that maintaining the assumption of diminishing returns to capital but accounting for both physical and human capital yields empirical predictions that appear to be consistent with the observed cross-country differences in *levels* of income. However, further tests for robustness remain appropriate.

- Much of the empirical literature on growth has focused on estimating **cross-country regressions** in search of a set of stable relations among the variables suggested by the old and new theories. This literature has been plagued, however, by severe *methodological problems*. The data necessary to test adequately the predictions of the new models of growth do not exist or are difficult to construct. The *quality* of the data may also be inadequate. From an econometric standpoint, many studies suffer from an inappropriate treatment of **measurement** and **specification errors** (**omitted variable bias** due to incorrect treatment of individual country-specific effects, for instance), **simultaneity bias**, and lack of appreciation of the potential for **bidirectional causality**. As a result, the bulk of the early evidence lacks robustness.

- Some recent cross-country studies have been able to correct some of these problems. An alternative approach that is gaining popularity in the analysis of the determinants of growth is the **time-series approach**, which is more suited to assess, for instance, the issue of *causality* among variables. Detailed case studies may also be able to capture more accurately salient differences in *policy regimes* than may broad cross-country studies.

A selective review of the more recent cross-country evidence suggests the following regularities.

- *Saving* and *physical investment* are positively and significantly correlated with average growth rates across countries in a wide variety of samples and specifications. The evidence on the role of *human capital* is less conclusive.

- Most of the evidence on the effects of taxes and government (current and capital) expenditure on growth is *inconclusive*, although it would appear that public investment in infrastructure, which tends to be *complementary* to private investment, has a positive effect on growth. *Nonlinearities* may explain this apparent lack of robustness. Evidence for sub-Saharan Africa suggests that *fiscal deficits* had an adverse effect on growth.

- The level of *inflation* has an adverse, and possibly *nonlinear*, effect on growth. *Macroeconomic instability* (as measured by the variability of inflation or the standard deviation of the real exchange rate) also tends to be negatively correlated with growth.

- Indicators of *financial depth* (such as the ratio of liquid liabilities to the financial system to GDP, the percentage of credit allocated by commercial banks, the percentage of domestic credit received by the private sector, and the ratio of credit to the private sector in proportion of GDP) have a positive and statistically significant correlation with long-term economic growth, the investment ratio, and total factor productivity. However, time-series evidence suggests that the *causality* may run from growth to finance, or may operate in *both directions*.

- *Trade openness* tends to be positively associated with growth, but again, the direction of causality is not well established. Recent evidence also suggests a *nonlinear* (**J-curve**) pattern: the initial effect on output growth tends to be small or negative; it is only over time that the effect becomes positive.

- *Political variables* (including measures of democracy, measures of government instability, indicators of political violence, and subjective indicators) are not robustly correlated with growth.

- **Absolute** β-convergence does not appear to hold, but **conditional** β-convergence does. Put differently, relative levels of income per capita eventually stabilize; but the long-run equilibrium position *itself* varies across countries, reflecting underlying differences in economic fundamentals, such as the level of education (a proxy for human capital), the rate of investment, and the degree of openness. Thus, divergence in income levels across countries may persist over time. Some early empirical studies suggested that the *rate of convergence* was around 2 percent, but a much higher number was found in some of the more recent studies. These estimates, however, remain quite sensitive to sample size and the list or control variables.

Appendix
Growth Accounting and Increasing Returns

This appendix, which is based on Barro (1998), shows that if the production technology is characterized by **increasing returns to scale**, then standard growth accounting techniques based on the assumption of constant returns to scale will underestimate the contribution of capital and overestimate total productivity growth.

Following Romer (1986), suppose that output Y_h of each firm h in the economy depends not only on the stock of physical capital and the quantity of labor used by the firm, K_h and L_h, but also on the economy-wide capital stock, K. The scale of production at each individual firm is thus a function of the aggregate stock of knowledge, embodied in the capital stock (see Chapter 12). Assuming identical firms and a generalized Cobb-Douglas production function yields

$$Y_h = AK_h^\alpha L_h^{1-\alpha} K^\beta, \quad 0 < \alpha < 1, \ \beta \geq 0, \tag{A1}$$

where A measures the efficiency of the production process or technological progress. Thus production exhibits constant returns to scale only in the firm's specific inputs, K_h and L_h. The coefficient β measures the strength of the spillover effects associated with the diffusion of knowledge across firms.

Let w and r denote again the economy-wide wage rate and the rental rate of capital. Under perfect competition, each firm equates factor prices (taken as given) to the marginal product of each production factor. Assuming, in addition, that the aggregate stock of capital is also taken as given yields, from Equation (A1),

$$r = \frac{\alpha Y_h}{K_h} - \delta, \quad w = \frac{(1-\alpha)Y_h}{K_h},$$

where δ is the rate of depreciation. Factor income shares are thus simply $\eta_K = \alpha$ and $\eta_L = 1 - \alpha$.

Let $k = K/L$, where L is the aggregate supply of labor, denote the economy-wide capital-labor ratio. The production function (A1) can thus be written as

$$Y_h = Ak_h^\alpha L_h L^\beta k^\beta. \tag{A2}$$

In equilibrium, each firm must adopt the same capital-labor ratio. Setting $k_k = k$ in Equation (A2) yields

$$Y_h = Ak^{\alpha+\beta} L_h L^\beta.$$

Linear aggregation across all firms implies

$$Y = Ak^{\alpha+\beta} L^{1+\beta} = AK^{\alpha+\beta} L^{1-\alpha}, \tag{A3}$$

given the definition of k. Equation (A3) shows that, as long as $\beta > 0$, then aggregate production will exhibit increasing returns to scale. A doubling of K

and L, in particular, will raise aggregate output by $1 + \beta$. Taking growth rates, Equation (A3) also implies that

$$g_A = g_Y - (\alpha + \beta)g_K - (1 - \alpha)g_L,$$

which can be rewritten as

$$g_A = g_{Y/L} - \alpha g_{K/L} - \beta g_K. \tag{A4}$$

Comparing Equations (13.3) and (A4) shows that using the conventional growth accounting framework, based on constant returns to scale ($\beta = 0$), will underestimate by β the contribution of the growth rate of capital when in fact production is characterized by increasing returns. It will thus lead to overestimation of the true rate of TFP growth. The larger the difference between the social marginal product of capital, $(\alpha + \beta)Y/K$, and the private marginal product, $r = \alpha Y/K$ (that is, the larger β is), the larger the bias. How to estimate in practice the size of the coefficient β remains, however, a matter of debate.

Chapter 14

Structural Adjustment: Agriculture, Trade, and the Labor Market

Structural reforms are generally defined as policy measures that lead to a rise in the productive capacity, or the degree of flexibility, of the economy. They are also often referred to as *microeconomic policies*, because their ultimate objective is to improve efficiency in resource allocation by reducing the various distortions (government induced or otherwise) that may hinder the functioning of specific markets. In addition to their microeconomic or sectoral effects, however, structural reforms often have a significant impact on the behavior of aggregate variables, such as interest rates, prices, fiscal deficits, and the current account. For instance, as noted in Chapter 2, and as further discussed in the next chapter, ceilings on interest rates that lead to negative real rates of return often have an adverse effect on aggregate savings, investment, and thus on the rate of economic growth. Conversely, structural policies that make markets *more flexible* may enhance the economy's ability to absorb domestic macroeconomic shocks and external disturbances—thereby limiting their effects on inflation and the balance of payments. Recognizing that microeconomic rigidities may have a large impact on macroeconomic imbalances is essential for the overall design of adjustment programs, as further discussed in the last chapter of this book.[1]

This chapter focuses on the conceptual and empirical aspects of structural adjustment policies that directly affect the *real side* of the economy. The first part focuses on price reform in agriculture. The second assesses the benefits, costs, and evidence on trade liberalization, including their effects on wage inequality—an issue that has attracted much attention in recent years. The re-

---

[1] Measuring the effects of structural reforms is in general difficult; there is no straightforward way of assessing, for instance, the increase in the degree of flexibility in response to shocks that structural reforms may bring. The appendix to this chapter discusses an index-based approach that has been used in a recent study on Latin America.

cent trend toward regional trade integration and preferential trade arrangements is discussed next. The last part focuses on the role of the labor market in economic adjustment. It begins with a review of the main features of labor markets in developing countries, including wage formation mechanisms and the sources of labor market segmentation. It then discusses the impact of minimum wages on employment and the role of trade unions in the wage bargaining process. The part concludes with an assessment of measures aimed at increasing labor market flexibility, particularly those aimed at reducing job security provisions.

14.1   Price Reform in Agriculture

A common argument made in much of the development literature is that agriculture has borne a *high implicit tax* burden, through government food price policy, often to the benefit of urban citizens.[2] In several developing countries, food products (often basic staple commodities) continue to be directly subsidized, and government-controlled **marketing boards** continue to pay domestic producers significantly less than the world market prices for their output. Such policies are frequently undertaken as a direct attempt to alter the *distribution of income* in the economy, particularly to increase the per capita consumption of low-income groups. There are at least two problems, however, associated with food subsidies.

- They are not an *efficient means* of redistributing income compared with direct and well-targeted transfers.

- By artificially lowering prices for food products, they tend to *reduce domestic production* (thereby increasing imports) and employment in the rural sector, thereby raising migration flows to urban areas and increasing urban unemployment.

The consequence is that subsidization of food products may not only impose a direct drain on the budget but also exacerbate *balance-of-payments difficulties* and *unemployment*.

Taxation, by lowering the profitability of agricultural activities, may lead to similar effects. Although exports taxes (as documented in Chapter 3) have now lost most of their importance in developing countries, they represented for a long time the main mechanism through which agriculture was taxed.[3] In some countries, agricultural producer prices were kept at artificially low levels; this had an effect on production equivalent to that of a tax on output, and an effect on consumption equivalent to that of a subsidy. Pricing policy can raise significant revenue; for instance, Benjamin and Deaton (1993) concluded that coffee and cocoa pricing policies in *Côte d'Ivoire* had the effect of raising as much as 40 percent of government revenue (broadly defined) in the early 1980s.

---

[2] See Sah and Stiglitz (1992) for an extensive discussion

[3] For a review of explicit and implicit instruments of agricultural taxation in developing countries, see United Nations (1993).

The experience of sub-Saharan Africa illustrates well the dire consequences of excessive agricultural taxation. The tax burden imposed on major export crops through marketing boards has long been considered to be one of the major sources of the region's economic difficulties (notably slow output growth rates and a high incidence of poverty, as discussed in Chapter 10), not only because it has created distortions and disincentives in agriculture, but also because it has shifted income distribution against the rural sector, where most of the poor are located. As argued by Schiff and Valdés (1992), for instance, inadequate agricultural pricing policy, together with currency overvaluations, have led to an **urban bias** in many of these countries.

Partly in response to a better understanding of the cost of these distortions and disincentives, a number of sub-Saharan African countries have in recent years implemented reforms of agricultural pricing and tax policies. These reforms have aimed at increasing the profitability of agricultural production, through either the elimination of export duties or a reduction in the gap between world and domestic producer prices of agricultural commodities. In sub-Saharan Africa, in particular, major areas of reform have been the deregulation of agricultural prices and the dismantling of marketing boards. Price controls have been eliminated, subsidies reduced or eliminated, and prices received by farmers set by the remaining marketing boards are now more closely linked with world prices. Although in some cases it is too early to assess the impact of these reforms on farm income and income distribution, available data on producer prices suggest that the impact has been so far limited in the region. Estimates by the World Bank (1994, Tables A9 and A18) for a group of 27 sub-Saharan African countries indicated that the average *domestic terms of trade* for export crops (as measured by producer prices relative to overall price movements) improved during the periods 1981-83 and 1989-91 in only ten countries. Of course, these results may point toward the possible role of *market imperfections* (such as the fact that markets for export crops are often dominated by a few traders) and shortcomings in the institutional aspects of the implementation of reforms. Nevertheless, a legitimate question is whether policies designed to remove price distortions in agriculture are always sufficient to strengthen incentives for production and promote greater income equality. In many cases, reform of agricultural taxation may need to be complemented with land reform, increased provision of infrastructure, development of rural credit markets, and the encouragement of small-scale production methods in order to achieve these objectives.

Reforms in agricultural tax and pricing policies may also have benefits for other sectors as well. To the extent that they lead to a rise in net agricultural and rural incomes, they may reduce *incentives to migrate* out of agricultural employment.[4] Reduced rural-urban migration has important effects on the determination of urban unemployment and urban informal employment (see below).

---

[4]The World Bank (1993) noted that the gap between urban and rural incomes is generally much smaller in the high-performing Asian developing economies than that in other developing economies; the level of agricultural taxation in the former has typically also been lower than that in the latter.

But such reforms may also have adverse budgetary effects. The elimination of taxes creates a *loss of revenue* that must be addressed. In some cases, therefore, tax reform in agriculture cannot be dissociated from the overall reform of the tax system.

14.2 Trade Liberalization

In recent years, growing recognition of the severe allocative distortions associated with **import substitution strategies** has led an increasing number of countries in the developing world to adopt a more liberal external trade regime.[5] Traditional economic arguments suggest that a reduction in trade barriers (such as *tariffs* and *import quotas*) fosters an adjustment in relative prices that leads to a reallocation of resources toward the exportable sector. In the long run, trade reform leads to an expansion of output of exportables and a contraction of activity in import-competing industries, as well as to an overall transfer of resources from sectors producing nontradables toward those producing tradables. The improvement in the allocation of resources does not only lead to a static output gain; as noted in Chapter 12, there are also *dynamic gains* from free trade. In particular, the removal of barriers to trade may lead to a *permanent increase* in the economy's growth rate as a result of **technological spillovers**.

This part begins by showing, using both partial and general equilibrium settings, the efficiency loss associated with tariffs—and thus the gain from removing them. It then discusses recent experiences with trade reform, and reviews the impact of such reforms on employment and wage inequality. It concludes by examining various obstacles to trade reform, such as political resistance and adverse effects on fiscal deficits.

14.2.1 The Gains from Trade

Understanding the gains from trade reform requires understanding the efficiency loss associated with the imposition of a tariff in the first place. A simple analysis of the impact of tariffs is illustrated in the two panels of Figure 14.1, which are constructed using the assumptions underlying the standard *Hekscher-Ohlin-Samuelson model*—perfectly competitive and efficient markets, incomplete specialization in accordance with relative factor endowments, international immobility of factors, and exogenous terms of trade for the domestic economy (see, for instance, Mikić, 1998). The upper panel in Figure 14.1 describes the case of a small open economy producing one importable good in a *partial equilibrium* setting. D, S, and S^* denote domestic demand, domestic supply, and foreign supply, respectively, of the import substitute. At the world price of P_j^*, OA is consumed, with OB supplied by domestic producers and BA by foreign producers. If an *ad valorem* tariff of ι is levied on imported goods, the domestic price,

---

[5]See Bruton (1989) for a critical discussion of arguments for and against import substitution policies.

P_J, becomes

$$P_J = (1 + \iota)P_J^*.$$

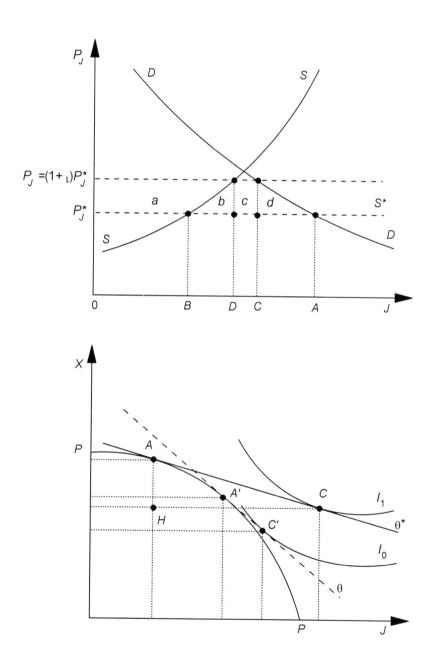

Figure 14.1. Effects of a Tariff in a Small Open Economy.

At this price demand falls by the quantity AC to OC, domestic supply increases by BD to OD, and imports drop to DC. The welfare effects of the imposition of the tariff are

- a reduction in the **consumers' surplus** by the area $a + b + c + d$;

- an increase in the **producers' surplus** by a;

- an increase in **government revenue** by c.

The **deadweight loss** (or net welfare loss) associated with tariff protection is thus equal to $b + d$. The area b represents the excess cost of producing domestically goods that could otherwise be imported; the area d represents the loss resulting from the fact that, at the margin, some consumers are "squeezed out" as a result of the higher cost of importables. The area of triangle b is measured by $\iota(OD - OB)/2$ and the area of d by $\iota(OA - OC)/2$. The welfare loss due to the tariff is thus

$$\Delta W = \iota[(OD - OB) + (OA - OC)]/2 \simeq \iota \Delta J/2,$$

where ΔJ is the change in imports, $(OA - OB) - (OC - OD)$. If the domestic good is measured in units such that its free-trade price, P_J^*, is normalized to unity, the change in imports can be written as $\iota J \eta_J$; in this expression, η_J is the price elasticity of the demand for imports, and ι, the tariff rate, represents the proportionate price change between the two regimes. Using this result, the welfare loss can be approximated by the **Meade formula** given by[6]

$$\Delta W = \iota^2 J \eta_J/2.$$

The lower panel in Figure 14.1 illustrates the same result in a *general equilibrium* setting. Let X denote the exportable good and J the importable good. PP is the **production possibilities frontier** (PPF), which shows the maximum physical production of X and J that can be produced, given the economy's productive resources and the state of technology. It is concave to the origin, as noted in Chapter 9. Its slope, the **marginal rate of transformation** of X into J, reflects the assumption of diminishing marginal productivity of factors of production. The convex curves I_0 and I_1 are **social indifference curves**, which show the various combinations of X and J between which society is indifferent in choosing. The slope of these curves is defined as the **marginal rate of substitution** of X into J. Finally, θ is the relative price of importables in terms of exportables, and is taken as exogenous. The slope of θ measures the rate at which goods can be transformed through trade.

Free trade production is located at point A on the PPF, and consumption at C on the social indifference curve I_1. Trade is shown by triangle AHC; the country exports AH of good X and imports HC of good J.

---

[6] Note that this formula provides a good approximation only in the case of a small market, with (approximately) linear demand and supply schedules.

Suppose now that an *ad valorem* tariff is levied on imports of J. The tariff distorts the domestic relative price ratio from θ^* to

$$\theta = (1 + \iota)P_J/P_X.$$

At this price ratio, production shifts from A to A' as the exportable sector contracts and the importable sector expands. Consumption shifts from point C to C', with the restriction of consumption possibilities taking the economy from I_1 to I_0. The tariff equilibrium is thus *suboptimal*.

- On the producers' side, the shift from A to A' entails a loss in the value of domestic output at world prices.[7]

- On the consumers' side, there is a loss in utility because I_0 is not the highest social indifference curve that can be attained, even at a relative price θ. This is the analogue to the deadweight loss identified in the upper panel of the figure.

The overall conclusion, therefore, is that (in the absence of initial distortions) an import tariff results in net welfare losses in a small open economy.[8] But can an import tariff be nevertheless optimal? It has been argued, for instance, that if collection costs of alternative means of generating revenue—including income and consumption taxes—are relatively high, reliance on tariffs as a revenue-raising device may indeed be optimal. For instance, Aizenman (1987) showed that, in the absence of collection costs associated with tariffs, and with an inelastic supply of labor, the optimal tariff rate is given by

$$\iota = \frac{\phi}{\eta - \phi},$$

where ϕ is the cost of collecting alternative taxes (in percent) and η the price elasticity of the demand for imports. However, the argument that trade taxes are necessary to raise revenue in developing countries (because of their lower administrative costs) was criticized by Dixit (1985), who showed that it is possible to derive a combination of domestic taxes levied neutrally on domestic and foreign goods that yields the same revenue as an import tax, for instance, but with a lower efficiency loss. Moreover, there are many cases where even if *collection* costs associated with tariffs are low (as assumed by Aizenman), *enforcement* costs may be high; thus the net effect may well be a reduction in welfare, as indicated earlier.

The foregoing discussion focused on the *static* gains from trade. As discussed in Chapter 12, the recent growth literature has emphasized that the benefits of trade openness may be largely *dynamic* in nature. As noted by Rivera-Batiz and Romer (1991), lowering barriers to trade could affect economic growth through at least three mechanisms.

---

[7] World prices measure the *true* value of domestic goods, because both goods can be converted at that rate through trade.

[8] This result, however, does not hold for a large open economy; see, for instance, Greenaway and Milner (1994, pp. 14-15).

- Trade integration with the industrial world increases the *transmission of technology* to developing countries (through imports of capital goods), thereby reducing the duplication of research and development activities. Because knowledge is a *public good*, its accumulation increases the rate of technical progress.

- The international integration of sectors characterized by *increasing returns to scale* raises output without requiring more inputs.

- Trade liberalization reduces *price distortions*, reallocating resources across sectors and increasing economic efficiency.

The first two effects unambiguously raise the rate of economic growth; the third raises growth to the extent that greater efficiency leads to more resources being invested in research and development—but it could also lower growth if the change in relative prices causes resources to shift out of research and development activities.[9]

In recent years a new approach to the analysis of the benefits of free trade has led to the development of **strategic trade theory** (Helpman and Krugman, 1985). At the heart of the new approach is the consideration of **scale economies** and **externalities**. Because both factors tend to lower *average costs*, large producers have an advantage over small ones. An important feature of the theory is its emphasis on the role of *alternative market structures* in assessing the impact of trade liberalization. The case considered by Rodrik (1988), for instance, is that of a country where tariffs are high and imperfect competition prevails. In such a setting, trade reform (a reduction in tariffs) affects welfare through a variety of channels, some traditional (such as the *volume of trade* effect, which results from the fact that imports should expand in those sectors where the domestic price rises) and some that depend on assumptions about market structure. Whether the net effect of a reduction in tariffs is beneficial or not is a priori ambiguous, because these effects operate in conflicting directions. Nevertheless, it is possible for trade intervention to be efficient. However, as argued in particular by Baldwin (1992), the results of strategic trade theory are not easily generalizable; the policy recommendations that it leads to are very sensitive to assumptions about market structure, entry and exit restrictions, and intersectoral linkages—information that is in practice very difficult to obtain.

14.2.2   Recent Evidence on Trade Reforms

Trade liberalization (elimination of nontariff barriers and sharp reductions in tariffs) accelerated in many developing countries since the mid-1980s, particularly in *Latin America*. A simple policy indicator of the change in the level of trade intervention is some average measure of nominal tariffs. However, there

---

[9] How to identify and measure the dynamic gains from trade, and thus the net effect of the channels identified here, remains a difficult task, as noted in Chapter 13.

are at least four reasons to be careful in interpreting data on nominal tariff rates (Greenaway and Milner, 1994).

- There may be *instrument substitution* taking place; nominal tariffs may indeed be lowered, but at the same time they may be replaced by other restrictions—such as *antidumping measures.*

- *Nominal* tariffs may decline, but *effective* tariffs may be increasing. This is the case if, at the same time, exemptions are being eliminated.

- There may have been a degree of *tariff redundancy* prior to reform. If so, the overall structure of tariffs may become more, rather than less, protective.

- Trade liberalization, in practice, includes not only tariff cuts but also reductions in *anti-export-biased policies* (such as distorted exchange rate regimes, as discussed in the next chapter), and the substitution of more efficient for less efficient forms of interventions—such as the replacement of tariffs for *quotas.*

The bias of a trade regime is better assessed by looking not at nominal protection rates (that is, the nominal tariffs themselves, if they are ad valorem), but at **effective protection rates,** which are defined as the amount by which the value added in a given sector at domestic prices exceeds the value added in that sector at international prices, expressed as a percentage of the latter (see, for instance, Anderson, 1994). These rates depend therefore not only on the tariff on the (final) good produced in the sector, but also on the *input coefficients* and the *tariffs on inputs.* As a result, calculations of effective rates of protection usually require detailed *input-output tables* and a variety of other microeconomic data for a large number of sectors if they are to be accurate and useful.[10] Thus, despite their limitations, nominal tariff rates are often used as indicators of changes in the trade regime.

Figure 14.2 shows movements in nominal tariffs for a group of developing countries during the period 1980-95. It highlights the fact that average tariff rates fell substantially in several developing countries. In India, for instance, the maximum tariff on imports fell from 400 percent in 1990 to 50 percent in 1995, and average tariff rates dropped from well above 80 percent to under 30 percent over the same period. In Latin America tariffs were cut from 41.6 percent in 1985 to 13.7 percent in 1995 (Lora and Olivera, 1998, p. 13). In South Asia, unweighted tariff averages on *manufactured goods* fell in the early 1990s to 11 percent in Korea, 15 percent in Malaysia, and 11 percent in Taiwan; at the same time, however, they remained at 42 percent in Thailand, 56 percent in India, 64 percent in Pakistan, and 85 percent in Bangladesh (Bandara and McGillivray, 1998). Figure 14.3 suggests that the reduction in mean tariffs was also associated with a reduction in the *dispersion* of tariff rates.

---

[10] Note also that effective rates of protection are relevant only for analyzing the *production* (or supply side) effects of protection, not *consumption* (or demand side) effects, which should still be analyzed in terms of nominal tariff rates on goods.

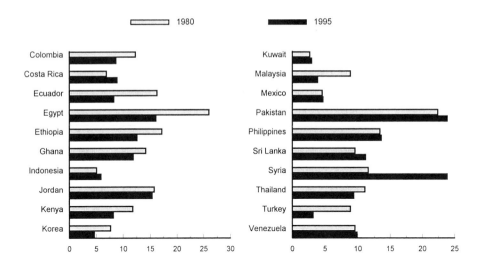

Figure 14.2. Import Duties (In percent of merchandise imports).
Source: World Bank.

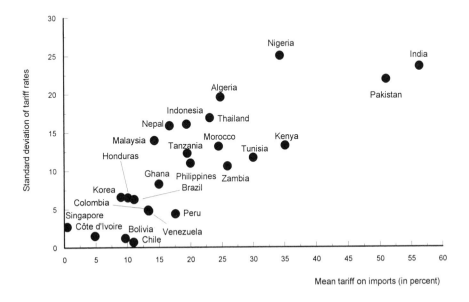

Figure 14.3. Mean Tariffs and Tariff Dispersion (Averages over 1990-93).
Source: World Bank.

Finally, it is worth noting that the region where the least progress has been achieved in trade liberalization is sub-Saharan Africa. In fact, the region's importance in global trade declined significantly over the past 30 to 40 years. Exports from sub-Saharan Africa accounted for about 3 percent of world exports in 1955; by 1990, its share had fallen to barely above 1 percent. Part of this outcome reflects declining global demand for key export products of the region, but part is due to a substantial erosion of its market shares. World Bank estimates suggest that if sub-Saharan Africa had maintained its 1962-64 export shares for major products, the region's exports would now be more than double their current value. In turn, the evidence suggests that the loss of market share and marginalization of the region in world trade appears to be the *antiexport bias* that still characterizes the trade regime in many of the countries of sub-Saharan Africa (Ng and Yeats, 1997). Trade policy reform may thus be an essential component of an adjustment program aimed at reversing the marginalization process that the region has experienced since the early 1960s.

14.2.3 Trade Reform, Employment, and Wage Inequality

While there appears to be broad agreement on the allocative effects of trade liberalization in the long run, the short- and intermediate-run impact of trade reform on wages and employment remains imperfectly understood. The evidence gathered in the comprehensive study of trade reform episodes in developing countries conducted in the early 1980s at the World Bank and summarized by Papageorgiou, Choksi, and Michaely (1990) appeared to be largely inconclusive in that regard. Although most individual-country studies suggested that total employment in the *manufacturing sector* either fell or remained stable in the aftermath of the liberalization program, they often did not distinguish between traded and nontraded manufacturing goods and were therefore unable to characterize changes in the distribution of employment. In addition, almost no evidence was provided on changes in employment in production activities other than manufacturing, or changes in the aggregate unemployment rate. These limitations (which in several cases resulted from the paucity of relevant data) are compounded by the *methodological shortcomings* that affect many of the specific country studies. For instance, although in several cases trade reforms were implemented *simultaneously* with macroeconomic stabilization programs— and in an environment characterized by *severe external shocks*—few authors attempted to disentangle rigorously the employment effects associated with each set of measures (Edwards, 1993). Despite this important caveat, Papageorgiou, Choksi, and Michaely (1990) attributed the fall in manufacturing sector employment observed in a few cases in the aftermath of reform mostly to restrictive macroeconomic policies.

Some more recent studies have attempted to study directly the effects of tariff reform on the labor market.

- Rama (1994) examined the relationship between tariffs, employment, and wages in the manufacturing sector in *Uruguay*. He found no impact of the reform on wages, but a negative effect on employment. Rama's estimates indicated that a reduction in the tariff-inclusive price of imports by 1 percentage point led to an employment drop in manufacturing of between 0.4 and 0.5 percentage points.

- In a study of the trade liberalization program implemented in *Mexico* between 1985 and 1988, Revenga (1997) estimated that the reduction in tariffs during the period (of about 10 percentage points) led to a much smaller reduction in aggregate employment in the manufacturing sector (by 2 to 3 percentage points) and an increase in average wages. However, her study also suggested that, despite relatively limited aggregate effects, significant changes occurred in the *composition* of employment at the industry level.

- Currie and Harrison (1997) found that the comprehensive trade reform that was implemented in *Morocco* between 1984 and 1990—which led to a reduction in the coverage of import licenses from 41 percent of imports in 1984 to 11 percent in 1990, and a reduction in the maximum tariff rate from 165 percent to 45 percent—also had a small, albeit significant, impact on aggregate wages and employment in the formal manufacturing sector. As in the case of Mexico, pronounced *sectoral shifts* in employment appeared to have taken place, particularly in the manufacturing industries that were subject to large tariff reductions.

- Márquez and Carmen Pagés-Serra (1998) estimated the effect of changes in trade openness and real exchange rates on the demand for labor in the manufacturing sector in a group of 18 countries in Latin America and the Caribbean. They found that trade reforms had a negative but small effect on employment growth, and that this effect was reinforced by real exchange rate appreciation. Changes in domestic protection did not have a significant effect on unemployment, suggesting that movements in and out of the labor force dominated over flows into unemployment.

The impact of trade liberalization on *income distribution* has also been the subject of much research in recent years. In a number of countries (particularly in Latin America), openness to trade since the early or mid-1980s has coincided with an increase in the demand of, and the return to, *skilled labor* relative to *unskilled labor*, and a worsening of income distribution.[11] Revenga (1997) noted that the increase in average manufacturing wages in Mexico in the aftermath of trade reform may have reflected a change in the *composition* of the labor force—a shift toward high-skill, high-wage workers. A similar shift in the composition of the workforce was noted by Currie and Harrison (1997) in their analysis of trade reform in Morocco. Increases in relative wages of skilled workers have been noted in several other countries implementing trade reforms; in Chile, wages of university graduates rose by 56 percent relative to those of

---

[11] The link between trade and wage inequality has also been a key policy issue in *industrial countries* in recent years.

high-school graduates between 1980 and 1990. Similar evidence is also available for Argentina, Colombia, Costa Rica, and Uruguay (Robbins, 1996), although more recent studies focusing on the 1990s suggest only that wage differentials may have remained largely unchanged in Argentina, Chile, and Costa Rica (Lora and Olivera, 1998).

The theory often referred to in interpreting these links is the standard *Hecksher-Ohlin-Samuelson* (HOS) *model* of international trade (see, for instance, Bhagwati, Panagariya, and Srinivasan, 1998). The model relies on the **principle of comparative advantage** and predicts the pattern of trade across countries by reference to the relative abundance of factors of production among them. Specifically, the HOS model predicts that between two countries A and B which share the same production technology, country A will export commodities that are produced with relatively more of the factor of production that is relatively abundant in country A and will import commodities produced with relatively more of the factor of production that is relatively abundant in country B.[12]

Two theorems derived from the HOS model deal explicitly with the effect of trade on wages and other factor prices: the **factor price equalization** (FPE) **theorem** and the **Stolper-Samuelson** (S-S) **theorem.**

- The FPE theorem asserts that under the assumptions of the HOS model and a regime of unrestricted free trade, prices of *production factors* will be *equalized* among trading partners.[13] Free trade between the United States and Mexico, for instance, should lead to an equalization of U.S. and Mexican wages for the same category of labor. It will also equalize the price of *land* across these countries—even if land cannot be moved across borders.

- The S-S theorem asserts that an increase in the domestic price of a good, brought about by a higher tariff or increased nontariff protection (such as quotas), will raise the real price of the factor of production that is used *relatively intensively* in producing that good. If computers, for instance, are produced using labor intensively and land sparingly, whereas wheat is produced using land intensively and labor sparingly, then an increase in tariffs on computers will raise the real wage received by workers. By implication, a reduction in tariff protection on manufacturing goods (such as apparel and footwear) that are relatively *intensive in unskilled labor* will tend to reduce the real wage received by that category of workers—relative to wages earned by skilled workers. Thus trade liberalization may lead to an *increase in wage inequality.*

---

[12]The HOS model is subject to a number of limitations. In particular, the validity of the assumption of *constant returns to scale*, which is central for some of the model's predictions, is debatable.

[13]The original proof of the FPE theorem (attributed to Paul Samuelson) was based on a model in which *two inputs* were used to produce *two goods.* It has been shown that the result remains valid under appropriate assumptions for additional goods and factors, as long as the number of goods *exceeds* the number of factors of production.

The S-S theorem is illustrated in Figure 14.4, for the same type of economy described earlier in analyzing the welfare loss from tariffs.[14] w and r are the wage rate and rental rate of capital, respectively. Curves $P_X P_X$ and $P_J P_J$ are the **iso-price curves** for the exportable and importable goods, respectively, produced by the domestic economy.[15] The intersection of the two curves, at point E, determines the economy's equilibrium wage and rental rates consistent with *zero profits* in both industries. At point E, the country produces both goods.

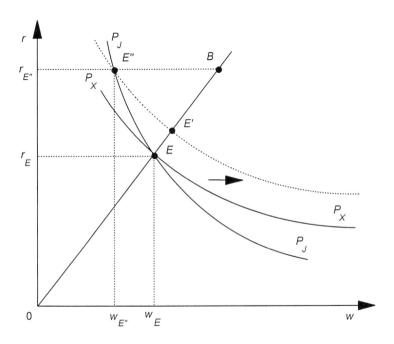

Figure 14.4. The Stolper-Samuelson Theorem.
Source: Adapted from Mikić (1998, p. 91).

Suppose now that the domestic economy begins trading with the rest of the world at prices that reflect the increase in the country's price of exportables. This shifts $P_X P_X$ *outward* by the same proportion as the price increase. Measuring along the ray to the origin and point E, the price increase is given by EE'/OE. But, because it is assumed that the price of importables does not change, curve $P_J P_J$ does not change. As a result, the new intersection of the isoprice curves gives the new competitive equilibrium, point E''. At this

---

[14]For an algebraic proof, see, for instance, Mikić (1998, pp. 91-92).

[15]The isoprice curves are convex to the origin because the capital-labor ratio in each sector is an increasing function of the ratio of the wage rate and the rental rate of capital (for a derivation see, for instance, Mikić, 1998, pp. 131-132). Note also that, as drawn, the curves intersect only once; this is due to the exclusion of *factor intensity reversals*.

new point, factor prices have changed: the price of capital has increased while the price of labor has fallen. Moreover, the increase in the rental rate of capital is relatively *larger* than the increase in the price of exportables because $r_E r_{E''} > EE'/OE$. Put differently, there is a *magnification effect*—the price of a factor changes more than proportionately in response to a change in the price of a good intensive in that factor. Relative to both commodity prices, the rental rate has increased whereas the wage rate has fallen, as predicted by the S-S theorem.

The implication of the theorem is that changes in *factor prices* can be inferred from changes in *relative goods prices*. Assuming continuous full employment of both factors, an increase in the relative price of a good will unambiguously increase the real return to the factor of production used relatively intensively in the production of that good, while the real return to the other factor of production will be reduced in terms of both goods. In the particular case that is being considered here, a reduction in the relative price of unskilled labor-intensive goods (brought about by a reduction in tariffs) will unambiguously reduce the real return to the factor of production used relatively intensively in the production of that good—unskilled labor. Tests of this proposition, however, have been inconclusive, as noted by Robbins (1996) in a study covering seven countries in Latin America and East Asia.

An alternative explanation is that trade liberalization was associated with the introduction of *higher-level technology*, the use of which required highly skilled labor. The reason is that the **cost of capital** depends not only on the relative price of capital goods (as noted in Chapter 1), but also on *financial costs*, *tariffs*, and *taxes* that must be incurred in order to be able to purchase and use an additional unit of capital goods. To the extent that a fall in tariffs translates into a fall in the cost of capital, a high degree of *complementarity* between skilled labor and capital, and a high degree of substitutability between unskilled labor and capital, will entail an increase in the demand for skilled workers—thereby leading to a widening of the wage gap between skilled and unskilled labor. There is indeed evidence, for some countries (including Colombia), that the price of capital fell significantly following the beginning of trade reform. A problem with the argument, however, is that it suggests that one should observe a fairly sizable increase in *imports of capital goods*, and a concomitant expansion in *exports of skill-intensive goods*. Yet the evidence, at least for Latin America, does not suggest anything of the sort. In 1992, for the seven major Latin American countries taken together, investment in machinery and equipment (most of it imported) was *lower* than in the early 1980s. There has been also no dramatic increase in the relative share of skill-intensive goods in the region's total exports.

A recent study by Spilimbergo, Londoño, and Székely (1999) emphasized the role of *relative factor endowments* in analyzing the relationship between trade liberalization, increases in wage differentials, and income inequality. In an analysis covering postwar data and focusing on 88 countries, they found that the relationship between trade liberalization and total income distribution depended essentially on factor endowments (natural resources, skilled and unskilled labor, and capital) relative to world patterns. In turn, world endowment patterns appeared to have changed with trade: growing participation by Asian countries (including China) abundant in unskilled labor altered the traditional comparative advantage patterns of Latin America. They also found that changes in natural resource and capital rates of return that usually accompany trade liberalization tended to have a smaller effect in bridging the income gap in those countries in which assets were more concentrated in a few hands, as was (and continues to be) the case for Latin America.

14.2.4   Obstacles to Trade Reform

Although many developing countries have implemented far-reaching programs of trade liberalization in recent years, progress has remained relatively slow in some countries—particularly in sub-Saharan Africa. In a detailed review of the empirical evidence, Matusz and Tarr (1999) argued recently that adjustment costs associated with trade liberalization (notably in terms of employment losses in manufacturing and increases in fiscal deficits and inflation) are typically very small compared with the benefits of reform. Why, then, is trade reform so unpopular at times? The reason is often that trade policies are heavily influenced by the interests of *powerful groups* and *political considerations* rather than by an assessment of costs and benefits. **Rent-seeking activities** (aimed at maintaining and extending existing tariff protection, or at influencing the allocation of import quotas) for instance, tend to magnify the distortions and inefficiencies in resource allocation. Specifically, two main obstacles to trade reform have been identified in the recent literature (Rodrik, 1995c):

- the **status quo bias**, associated with individual uncertainty regarding the benefits of reform;

- the high *political cost* compared with relatively small efficiency gains associated with trade reform.

Fernández and Rodrik (1991), in particular, argued that **idiosyncratic uncertainty** associated with the effect of reforms (the fact that individual gainers and losers cannot always be clearly identified before implementation) may generate *ex ante* opposition to them, even if, *ex post*, everyone should support them. To illustrate this result in a simple manner, consider the case of an economy populated by 100 workers, employed in two sectors, identified by W and L. Initially, 40 workers operate in sector W and 60 in L:

$$L \qquad\qquad\qquad\qquad W \qquad \|$$

| 60 workers | 20 workers | 40 workers   ‖ |
| -0.2 each | $\Longrightarrow$ | +0.2 each   ‖ |

Consider now a reform whose outcome is such that each worker in sector W gains 0.2, whereas workers in sector L lose each 0.2. The reform is anticipated to induce 20 workers to move from L to W. If there is *full information* regarding the identity of the workers moving from L to W, the majority of voters will approve the reform, because 60 will benefit (the original 40 in W plus the 20 that will be relocated in W).

However, suppose that there is *individual uncertainty* regarding the identity of the workers moving from L to W. Specifically, suppose that the *probability of relocation* is the same for all workers in sector L; this probability can thus be approximated by $20/60$, whereas the probability of remaining in L is simply $40/60$. In the first case, as indicated earlier, each worker gains 0.2, whereas in the second he or she loses 0.2; the *expected gain from the reform* is thus the weighted average given by

$$0.2 * (1/3) - 0.2(2/3) < 0,$$

which implies that each worker expects to *lose* from the reform—implying that the majority of workers in the L sector will rationally *vote against it*. The paradox is that if a benevolent dictator (admitting that such dictators exist) were to implement the reform discretionarily, the majority of workers would *ex post* support it, because *ex post* individual uncertainty disappears.

The preceding example illustrates what Fernandez and Rodrik characterize as a **status quo bias**. As the example illustrates, this bias reduces welfare. Overcoming it requires policies that mitigate personal uncertainty, such as the design of appropriate *transfer schemes* or more generally the operation of an *insurance market*, which would allow individuals to protect themselves from uncertain outcomes. In practice, of course, such markets are difficult to create and may be themselves subject to asymmetric information problems.

Another source of resistance to trade reform stems from the existence of relatively high political costs. Empirical evidence suggests that the welfare cost of trade distortions (such as tariffs and quotas), as measured by **Harberger triangles** (the loss in social welfare resulting from the misallocation of resources due to market imperfections), are frequently relatively small—often of the order of 2 percent of GDP or less.[16] Although trade liberalization will typically improve welfare by eliminating these distortions, they involve at the same time potentially *large reallocations of income*; these movements may be associated with high political costs and may generate resistance to reform (Rodrik, 1992). Consider, for instance, a small open economy facing a given world relative price of importables to exportables, p^*. Initial tariffs are such that the relative price faced by domestic agents is $p_d > p^*$. A reduction in tariffs from p_d to p^*—or, using Figure 14.1 to illustrate, a reduction from P_J to P_J^*—implies that consumers gain areas $a + b + c + d$, the government loses area a (foregone tariff revenue), and producers lose area c. In other words, there is a redistribution of income from producers and the government to consumers (area $a + c$, respectively) and an increase in efficiency given by $b + d$. Rodrik defines the ratio of the income redistributed to the efficiency triangles, that is, $(a + c)/(b + d)$, as

---

[16] See Chapter 15 for a more precise definition of Harberger triangles. Note, however, that the use of these triangles to assess welfare losses has been criticized because they do not take into account the potential benefits of all production activities that are, in a sense, *missing* because of high levels of tariffs. See Romer (1993) for a simple example.

a measure of the political resistance to reform. He points out that this ratio is typically high in practice—possibly reaching values exceeding 10. In another study, Rodrik (1998) argued that the large distributional effects of trade reform (and its potential for increased social conflict) explains the erratic pattern and low credibility of trade reform in many sub-Saharan African countries during the past two decades. What may compound the problem is the fact that opposition to trade reform is often more localized, more organized, and more effective than political opposition to macroeconomic stabilization—which may be more diffuse, less organized, and relatively ineffective (Tommasi and Velasco, 1996).

Another possible obstacle to reform may be the **lack of credibility** of the reform process. As emphasized by Calvo (1989), a low degree of credibility acts fundamentally as a *distortion* or a *production tax* because it impairs the beneficial effects of an otherwise desirable policy. The example considered by Calvo is a situation in which the authorities announce that all tariffs will be permanently abolished, but the private sector expects that such a policy will be modified in the future and that a new set of tariffs will be put in place. If there is no substitution in production and consumption, but consumption goods can be stored at a low cost, the lack of credibility of the tariff reform will trigger speculative accumulations of inventories. Although this activity may be profitable from the point of view of the private sector, it will not necessarily be desirable for the society as a whole because the accumulation of inventories may crowd out the acquisition of other types of assets—such as physical capital—with a higher social rate of return. In this setting, the *social cost* of this misallocation is a function of the structure of capital markets: in a regime of perfect capital mobility, unlimited funds could be obtained from abroad for speculation in inventories; with binding controls on capital flows, a lesser amount of capital could be tied up in this form.[17]

Finally, concerns about possible *adverse revenue effects* may also explain the slow pace of trade liberalization. In countries where the share of trade taxes in total revenues is large, trade barriers have often been dismantled gradually. However, although trade liberalization may lead to a fall in revenue in the *short term* (sometimes forcing governments to implement concomitant cuts in expenditure) some trade liberalization measures (such as the replacement of quotas by tariffs) can be implemented without significant declines in revenue. Lifting *quantitative restrictions* may even lead to an increase in revenue if the newly liberalized categories of imports increase and are subject to tariffs. Moreover, in countries where at the same time the foreign exchange market is being liberalized (see the next chapter) and the official exchange rate depreciates significantly as a result, the increase in the *domestic-currency price* of imports may be large enough to lead to, even with falling tariff rates, a limited fall in revenue.

---

[17]This does not, of course, imply that capital controls should be retained or reintroduced, but rather that reform efforts in other areas should be accelerated.

14.3   Trade and Regional Economic Integration

Since the early 1970s, key changes have taken place in the *composition* of developing-country exports.

- In *Asia*, the share of manufacturing exports relative to that of primary commodities has increased substantially since 1970, from 42 percent of total exports of goods in that year to 48 percent in 1980 and 74 percent in 1990.

- The share of manufactures in total merchandise exports in *Latin America* also increased, from about 12 percent in 1970 to 18 percent in 1980 and 34 percent in 1990.

- By contrast, in *Africa*, the export share of manufactured goods fell from 27 percent in 1980 (after increasing from 15 percent in 1970) to 22 percent in 1990.

These changes in export composition were in part the result of the removal of distortions in domestic markets and reductions in trade barriers. Most importantly, they reflect an underlying shift in the *comparative advantage* of many developing countries toward manufacturing activities. Relatively low wage costs coupled with increased investment have made some developing countries highly competitive in the production of many manufactured goods. This is particularly so in some of the Asian countries where high domestic saving and investment rates have been reflected in increases in the stock of capital. The composition of manufactured exports in a number of Asian countries now includes a significant proportion of advanced, high-technology manufactured goods.[18]

At the same time, there has been an increase in the degree of diversification of export markets of developing countries and a marked rise in *intraregional trade*. Figure 14.5 shows the diversification of export markets for each developing region to other developing regions and to industrial countries between 1984 and 1994. The growth in intraregional trade was particularly marked during the period in Asia, where almost 40 percent of the region's exports are now going to other Asian countries. The expansion of markets in Asia has benefited other regions—all industrial and developing-country regions have increased the share of their exports going to Asia. Intraregional trade has also risen markedly among Latin American countries, although export diversification has been more limited—with almost 50 percent of the region's exports being shipped to North America. Export markets among African countries have also remained relatively undiversified, with almost 50 percent of the region's exports going to Europe, and the level of intraregional trade, although increasing, remains modest. The level of intraregional trade among the countries of the Middle East and Europe is also relatively small, and in contrast to the other developing-country regions,

---

[18]At the same time, the comparative advantage of many industrial countries has shifted toward *services*, many of which are now tradable owing to changes in technology, especially improvements in communications and information technologies.

the importance of intraregional trade actually diminished between 1984 and 1994.

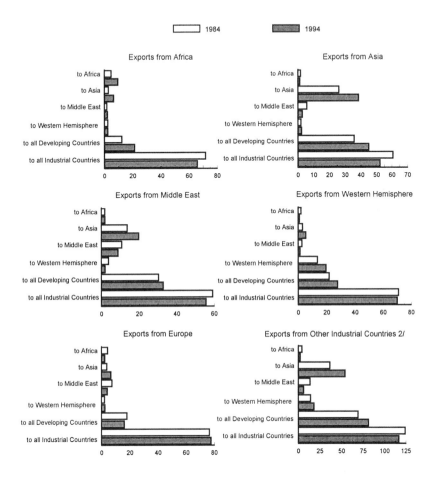

Figure 14.5. Developing Countries: Diversification of Export Markets 1/ (In percent of total exports).

Source: International Monetary Fund.

1/ Export shares of each region to all developing and industrial countries do not add to 100 percent because trade with the countries in transition is excluded and because of some underreporting of trade.

2/ North America, Australia, Japan, and New Zealand. "All industrial countries" includes, in addition, Europe.

The increase in intra-regional trade has coincided with the development of **preferential trade agreements** in almost all regions of the developing world. An example of such arrangements is the *Mercosur agreement* between Brazil, Argentina, Paraguay, and Uruguay that came into force on January 1, 1995. It stipulates a **common external tariff** (CET) structure ranging from 0 to 20 percent on about 85 percent of all traded goods, which can be modified only with the consent of all four partners. The 15 percent of goods currently outside the CET structure are divided into three main categories that are subject to a schedule of adjustments that will bring them into line with the CET rates within the next five to six years.

- **National exceptions**. Each country can identify up to 300 items for temporary exemption from the CET. The tariffs on these goods must be adjusted gradually each year until they converge with the CET by the year 2001.

- **Capital goods**. Capital goods are exempted from the CET structure for all countries but the timetable for convergence for each country will be different. The tariffs on these goods must converge to the CET structure by the year 2001 for Argentina and Brazil, and by 2006 for Paraguay and Uruguay. Brazil's rates under the agreement are to be reduced gradually from an average of 20 percent to 14 percent.

- **Computer goods**. The existing tariffs on these goods are subject to yearly adjustments that are designed to ensure that they will converge to the CET structure by the year 2006. The current average tariff rate in this sector in Brazil, for instance, is 30 percent, and is scheduled to fall to 16 percent by 2006.

Tariffs on trade between Mercosur partners are prohibited, with the exception of the *Adjustment Regime*, which allowed each country to maintain tariffs for items on a preapproved list until January 1, 1997, for Argentina and Brazil, and January 1, 2000 for Paraguay and Uruguay.

Regional trade integration can allow firms to spread the costs of research and development over a larger market, thus reducing unit costs and encouraging greater innovation and technical progress. This can, in turn, generate *positive spillovers* as successful innovations are applied more broadly. Integration can also boost *productivity growth* by allowing increased specialization; there are also *efficiency gains* from increased competition, which can be reinforced by foreign direct investment.[19] Estimating the actual gains from growing regional trade integration is very difficult, because it occurs in different ways and with a variety of different effects.

Preferential trade agreements raise some fundamental policy issues, which have been thoroughly reviewed by Bhagwati and Panagariya (1996). They concluded that some of the common arguments in favor of such agreements are not valid and that they may conflict with *multilateral, nonpreferential trade liberalization*, as pursued through international institutions like the World Trade Organization (WTO).

---

[19] As argued by Eichengreen (1998) in the context of *Mercosur*, realizing the full benefits of trade integration may require, in addition to a customs union, complete monetary integration to prevent potentially disruptive effects of exchange rate changes on trade flows.

- Preferential trade arrangements may lead to **trade creation**, by replacing relatively high-cost domestic production with lower-cost imports from partner countries. However, there is also scope for **trade diversion**, which occurs when imports are switched from efficient nonmember suppliers to less efficient member countries benefiting from tariff preferences.[20]

- Higher trade volumes between member countries that result from the agreement may lead to *greater*, not *smaller*, losses to an individual member Z that joins the agreement from a higher initial set of tariffs, because joining the agreement at a common lower tariff leads to a redistribution of tariff revenues from Z to other member countries with initially lower tariffs.[21]

The concepts of trade diversion and trade creation, attributed to Viner (1950), can be illustrated in a partial equilibrium setting. Consider two countries, A and B, producing the same good and suppose that these countries are considering forming a preferential trade arrangement whose main element is a customs union. Both countries are small relative to the rest of the world; they therefore face a constant world price, P^*, for their imports and exports. Suppose also that country A imports the good before the customs union is created, and that B is a net exporter, but with a volume of exports that does not completely satisfy the demand for imports by A. Country A is thus also importing from the rest of the world. Before the customs union is formed, A imposes a nondiscriminatory tariff of ι on all imports; the same tariff rate is used as the common external tariff by the union (B initially has no tariff). Finally, prior to the creation of the union B exports only to A, and once the union is in place the two countries are self-sufficient at a price P_U which is above the world price P^* but below the tariff-inclusive price $(1 + \iota)P^*$.

As shown in Figure 14.6, before the union is formed the domestic price of the good in country A is $(1+\iota)P^*$, domestic production is Q_E^A, and consumption is $Q_C^A > Q_E^A$. Country A is thus importing $J^A = Q_C^A - Q_E^A$; the quantity $Q_J^A - Q_E^A$ is from country B, whereas the remainder, $Q_C^A - Q_J^A$, is provided by the rest of the world. Country B produces Q_E^B and faces a pre-union domestic price equal to P^*. It consumes Q_C^B and exports a quantity $X^B = Q_E^B - Q_C^B$ (equal to $Q_J^A - Q_E^A$) to country A.

Once the customs union is in place, B channels all its exports to A, and trade with the rest of the world ceases.[22] Demand by member countries for the

---

[20]Yeats (1997) for instance argued that the *Mercosur* agreement has indeed led to the replacement of efficiently produced goods from outside the arrangement by inefficiently produced goods from inside. However, his methodology (based on comparing shifts in intraregional exports with a measure of relative efficiency in production) has been questioned by various researchers.

[21]Bhagwati and Panagariya also stressed that preferential trade arrangements are worth pursuing only for countries whose ultimate goal is complete dismantling of barriers to labor and capital mobility, and complete integration of political structures.

[22]Producers in country B have the incentive to sell to consumers in country A only because P_U, by assumption, is above the world price, P^*.

good is met entirely by union production, at the price $P_U < (1 + \iota)P^*$. Thus, the formation of the customs union has three types of effects in country A:

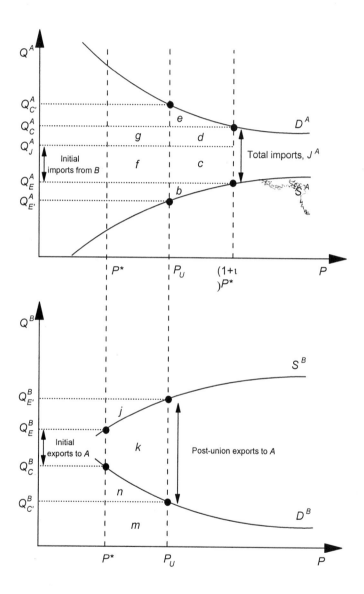

Figure 14.6. Customs Union: Trade Diversion and Trade Creation.

- A *trade creation* effect, which results from the replacement of an amount $Q_E^A - Q_{E'}^A$ of domestic output by cheaper imports from country B. This is measured by area b in Figure 14.6.

- A *trade diversion* effect, as the lower-cost imports from the rest of the world, $Q_C^A - Q_J^A$, are replaced by more expensive imports from the union's other member, B. This is measured by area g in Figure 14.6.

- A *consumption* effect, $Q_{C'}^A - Q_C^A$, which results from the fall in the (tariff-inclusive) domestic price of the good from $(1 + \iota)P^*$ to P_U. This is measured by area e in Figure 14.6.

In country B, production expands by $Q_{E'}^B - Q_E^B$, consumption falls by $Q_C^B - Q_{C'}^B$ and exports increase from $Q_E^B - Q_C^B$ to $Q_{E'}^B - Q_{C'}^B$. The producers' surplus gain in that country is given by the area $k + m + n$, whereas the consumers' loss is given by the area $m + n$. Country B therefore realizes a net welfare gain, equal to k, from the union. Essentially, this gain reflects the increase in exports to country A at a price P_U that exceeds the pre-union price, P^*. For country A, however, the impact of the union on net welfare is in general ambiguous and depends on the relative strength of the three different effects identified earlier. As shown in the figure, the producers' surplus falls by a, the consumers' surplus gain is equal to $a + b + c + d + e$, and tariff revenue falls by the area $c + d + f + g$. The net effect is thus equal to

$$(b + e) - (f + g).$$

Areas b, g and e, as defined earlier, measure the trade creation, trade diversion, and consumption expansion effects; area f measures the *terms-of-trade loss* with country B. Thus country A will incur a net welfare gain only if the gains associated with the trade creation and consumption expansion effects (area $b + e$) exceed the losses resulting from the trade diversion and terms-of-trade loss (area $f + g$).

If country A gains, the union as a whole is also gaining. But in general, whether the union is welfare improving or welfare reducing is ambiguous. In particular, the larger the difference between the union price and the world price, the larger the volume of imports by country A prior to the union; and the lower the price elasticity of domestic supply and demand, the more likely it is that country A will lose. Country A's loss may be large enough to outweigh country B's gain, implying that the union is welfare reducing. As long as the union leads primarily to trade creation (diversion), it will tend to increase (reduce) aggregate welfare.

Analytical research on customs unions have also established a variety of other results.

- The more competitive and the more complementary are the production structures of the union partners, the more likely it is that the customs union will lead to an increase in welfare. The reason is that there is more scope for trade creation among countries whose production structures are similar, because less efficient domestic production tends to be replaced by imports from partner countries.

- The larger the cost differentials7 between the countries of the union in the goods that they both produce, the larger will be the scope for gains from trade creation effects. The reason is that a large cost difference will increase the possibilities for resource reallocation and trade-creation effects.

- The higher the initial tariffs between the union partners, the greater is the scope for trade creation and an increase in welfare. The lower the tariffs imposed on goods imported from the rest of the world, the smaller are the losses resulting from trade diversion.

- The larger the part of trade originally covered by trade between the union partners (that is, the smaller the share of goods imported from nonmember countries in total consumption prior to the union), the greater the likelihood that the union will be beneficial for all members.

In addition, recent research on customs unions and preferential trade arrangements suggests that assessing the net welfare effects of these arrangements requires examining their *dynamic effects*, associated with greater scope for economies of scale, increased competition, and larger investment and technology flows across member countries (see Baldwin and Venables, 1995). However, evaluating the practical importance of these effects may require the use of relatively complex models, whose sensitivity to certain behavioral parameters may be quite high.

14.4   Reforming Labor Markets

A large literature in development economics has emphasized the role of *labor market flexibility* in the process of economic growth. For instance, as argued by a number of observers, one of the alleged key features of the East Asian growth miracle (or whatever is left of it) was the limited impact of trade unions and other distortions on the labor market (Fields and Wan, 1989), and the unusually high levels of employment growth without excessive wage pressures. In turn, this was viewed as the result of large investments in primary and secondary eduction, which have ensured an ample supply of skilled workers and helped to prevent large changes in relative incomes (Fields, 1994).

Advocates of labor market reform have argued that circumventing the scope of hiring and firing regulations, reducing nonwage labor costs, eliminating (or restricting the scope of) minimum wage laws, limiting unemployment benefits, and curtailing the role of trade unions in the wage bargaining process would enhance flexibility and have a positive effect on growth. This section attempts to provide a balanced view of the effects of such reforms. It begins by reviewing some of the known facts about the *structure* of labor markets in developing countries— including the composition of employment, the role of minimum wages, and the role of trade unions in wage negotiations. It then considers various types of labor market reforms aimed at increasing economic flexibility. It concludes by examining the link between *labor market regulations* and *growth*—an issue that has received insufficient attention in the recent literature on structural adjustment.

14.4.1 Labor Markets in Developing Countries

Labor markets play an important role in the transmission process of macroeconomic policy shocks and structural adjustment policies. The degree of **wage inertia**, in particular, plays an important role in determining whether or not a nominal devaluation is *contractionary* (see chapter 4).

Basic Structure

The labor market in developing countries typically consists of three sectors:

- The **rural sector**, which continues to employ a sizable proportion of the labor force in some countries, particularly in sub-Saharan Africa.

- The **informal urban sector**, which is characterized mostly by *self-employment* and a limited proportion of hired labor. Wage flexibility is high and employment security low.[23] *Labor regulations* (including minimum wage laws) do not apply or are not enforced.

- The **formal urban sector**, where workers are hired on the basis of *explicit contracts* and the degree of compliance with labor market legislation is relatively high. Wage determination often departs from *market-clearing mechanisms* as a result of legal restrictions, the existence of labor unions, and considerations internal to firms.

Employment Distribution and Unemployment

Although existing data on employment and unemployment in developing countries are not very reliable, they indicate that the proportion of *wage earners* in total employment is relatively high in Asia and Latin America, and very low in sub-Saharan Africa (about 10 percent). In some countries, the public sector absorbs a large share of formal wage employment. The share of *informal sector employment* in total urban employment is sizable in many developing countries—exceeding, for instance, 60 percent in a countries like India and Kenya. In many countries in Latin America, the informal sector grew in importance during the 1980s and early 1990s, accounting for more than 50 percent of total employment in 1992 (see Agénor, 1996).

Published measures of *unemployment* mostly include unemployed workers looking for jobs in the formal sector, but not *underemployed* workers in the informal and rural sectors—**disguised unemployment**. The available evidence

---

[23] *Nominal* wage flexibility refers to the elasticity of the nominal wage with respect to aggregate prices; *real* wage flexibility refes to the responsiveness of the real wage to unemployment. The degree of real wage flexibility plays an important role in the adjustment process to policy and exogenous shocks.

suggests, nevertheless, that underemployment is *far more pervasive* than open unemployment. Open and disguised unemployment may amount to anywhere between 25 and 60 percent of the labor force in some countries.

Unemployment insurance or **compensation schemes** are not well developed in developing countries. Whether they should be appears to be an open question. It has been argued that such schemes act, to some extent, as a **disincentive to search** for (or to accept) employment, and that they may act as an incentive to enter the labor force in order to collect unemployment benefits. However, unemployment insurance may also have *positive effects* in encouraging labor force participation and favoring regular, as opposed to marginal, employment (Atkinson and Micklewright, 1991). Because of limited data on variables such as the duration of unemployment benefits in the developing countries where they are available, it has proved difficult to test alternative views on these issues. The elasticity of unemployment with respect to replacement rates (benefits before taxes as a percentage of previous earnings) may be relatively low; but whether high unemployment benefits tend to increase unemployment remains an open issue.

Wage Formation and Labor Market Segmentation

A pervasive feature of factor markets in many developing countries is **labor market segmentation**, that is, a situation where *observationally identical* workers (that is, workers with similar qualifications) receive *different wages* depending on their sector of employment. Labor market segmentation may be induced by various factors:

- government intervention in the form of **minimum wages** (discussed below);

- **trade unions**, which may prevent wages from being equalized across sectors by imposing a premium for their members (also discussed below);

- **efficiency wages**, resulting from *nutritional factors* (Bliss and Stern, 1978), *turnover costs* (Stiglitz, 1974) or *productivity considerations* (Stiglitz, 1982).

The basic idea of efficiency wages is that firms set wages so as to minimize labor costs *per efficiency unit*, rather than labor costs *per worker*. For instance, workers' level of effort may depend positively on the wage paid in the current sector of employment (say, the urban formal sector), relative to the wage paid in other production sectors (say the informal economy). The outcome of the firms' wage-setting decisions may be a **markup** of formal-sector wages over informal-sector wages. Because the efficiency wage may exceed the market-clearing wage, such models also help to explain the existence of **involuntary unemployment**.

Annex A presents a model of the urban labor market in developing countries in which efficiency considerations lead to market segmentation and equilibrium unemployment. The model is based in part on the **shirking model** developed by Shapiro and Stiglitz (1984). It also dwells on the rural-urban migration model of Harris and Todaro (1970) and its various extensions (see Bhattacharya, 1993). A key feature of the model is the equality of *expected* (rather than *actual*) wages as the basic equilibrium condition across the rural and urban labor markets— with the *expected urban wage* calculated by multiplying the fixed minimum wage by the urban employment ratio, that is, the probability of being hired. This condition plays a key role in generating unskilled unemployment.

Minimum Wages

Development economists have long debated the role of minimum wage legislation in labor market adjustment. Advocates have often viewed minimum wages as having positive nutritional effects, as being an instrument of income redistribution and social justice, or as a way to raise productivity. By contrast, opponents argue that minimum wage legislation, by preventing wages from adjusting downward to excess supply of labor, imposes an *implicit tax* on employers in the formal economy, leads to *misallocation of labor* (by preventing wages from adjusting downward to excess supply of labor) and creates unemployment (particularly for unskilled workers), induces labor market segmentation, and depresses wages in the informal urban sector—which has an adverse effect on the poor. A high minimum wage increases the relative cost of employing unskilled workers, thereby accelerating the substitution of capital for unskilled labor and reducing profits—and thus firms' capacity to invest. As a result of both factors, high minimum wages restrain the expansion of labor demand over time.

The empirical evidence on the effects of minimum wages on relative earnings and employment in developing countries is mixed and often inconclusive. In part, this is because assessing these effects is inherently difficult in such countries. *Lack of compliance* with the law makes studies based on the formal sector highly imprecise. For instance, a significant share of workers in one formal-sector industry may be paid below minimum wages whereas the other share may earn wages in excess of the minimum wage. Controlling for these differences is not always easy because they are not necessarily related to observable workers' (or firms') characteristics. Nevertheless, some recent studies have suggested that the employment effects of changes in minimum wages are either limited or even positive. Bell (1997) in particular found that although changes in the minimum wage seemed to affect the *distribution* of wages in *Colombia* and *Mexico*, they appeared to have a limited impact on employment. Rama (1995), in a study based on cross-section data for 31 countries in Latin America and the Caribbean covering the period 1980-92, found that minimum wages did not appear to affect significantly the rate of economic growth. Higher minimum wages appeared, in fact, to be *positively correlated* with employment growth. Nevertheless, changes in the minimum wage are likely to have important *distributional effects* among workers, for instance, between those employed in the formal sector and those in the informal sector. Explicit consideration of the informal sector, as is done in Annex A, is thus an essential step in analyzing the aggregate effects of changes in the minimum wage.

Trade Unions and the Bargaining Process

In assessing the role of trade unions in the bargaining process and wage formation in developing countries, two considerations are important (Nelson, 1994).

- Trade union movements in developing countries are typically *not very centralized* (even in Latin America), making it difficult to organize *collective labor action*. In Mexico, for instance, the average union size in the Confederation of Mexican Workers (the country's largest confederation) remains small (about 130 members). Less than half of its members are in *powerful industrial unions* (such as railroads, petroleum, or mining). Nearly half of them are in enterprise-level unions, which are, in turn, loosely related to regional federations.

- The **degree of unionization** is a highly imperfect measure of the influence of trade unions on wage formation and the labor market. Trade unions in certain *strategic* sectors or industries may exert considerable influence on wage formation and working conditions at the national level, even if overall union membership is low in proportion to the work force. Often-cited examples are the trade unions representing tin miners in Bolivia and oil workers in Nigeria. In Singapore, although union density is low, collective bargaining agreements are often extended to the nonunionized workers within individual firms.

Whether a low degree of centralization has beneficial effects on wage formation remains a matter of debate. It has been argued, most notably by Calmfors (1993), that the relationship between the degree of centralization in wage bargaining—defined as the extent to which unions and employers cooperate in wage negotiations—and wage pressures is not monotonic but rather has an **inverted U-shape**. Wage push is *limited* when bargaining is *highly centralized* (that is, conducted at the national level) and when *highly decentralized* (when it takes place at the level of individual firms). The highest degree of influence on wage formation would thus tend to occur in countries where centralization is in the intermediate range, that is, at the industry level.

Various types of **externalities** have been used to explain why centralized bargaining is likely to produce lower aggregate real wages and higher employment (see Calmfors, 1993).

- A high degree of cooperation between unions and employers (as is the case under centralized bargaining) implies that the effects on others of a wage increase in one part of the economy will be *internalized*, thereby lowering the marginal benefit of an increase in wages. In particular, if unions are averse to inflation, they will tend to moderate their wage demands in order to induce the central bank to inflate at a lower rate.

- Decentralized bargaining systems produce real wage moderation because of the restraint imposed by *competitive forces*—although moderation may occur at the cost of increased wage dispersion.

- With intermediate centralization, neither internalization effects nor competitive forces are sufficiently strong to restrain unions' incentives to demand higher wages.

However, some recent research has shown that a higher degree of centralization may not always reduce wage pressures. Cukierman and Lippi (1998), in particular, argued that an increase in the degree of centralization of wage bargaining (as measured by a fall in the number of trade unions in the economy) triggers two opposite effects on real wages.

- The reduction in the number of unions tends to reduce the degree of effective competition among unions; this *competition effect* tends to raise real wages.

- The fall in the number of unions strengthens the moderating influence of inflationary fears on the real-wage demands of each union. This *strategic effect* tends to lower wages.

In addition, it is not always easy in practice to classify wage bargaining systems into completely centralized or decentralized systems. In Argentina in recent years, the government has sought to decentralize collective bargaining agreements from the sectoral to the firm level. In early 1995, Mexico also moved toward terminating centralized wage agreements in favor of decentralized bargaining arrangements. In Brazil, by contrast, the evidence seems to suggest that wage negotiations have become more centralized in a number of industries during the 1980s (Amadeo, 1994). Whether any of these countries can be rigidly categorized under a particular wage bargaining system is unclear.

Evaluating the influence of trade unions in the wage bargaining process can of course be done by assessing their direct impact on wages. Unfortunately, the literature in that area is somewhat limited. Nelson (1994) noted that in Latin America, unions seem to cause wages to rise above the opportunity cost of labor through a combination of union pressure, minimum wage legislation, and wage policies in the public sector. In Taiwan and Korea, the evidence also suggested that unions have limited power in bargaining over wages (Fields, 1994). Other studies have attempted to estimate econometrically the bargaining strength of organized labor, as reflected in the union-nonunion wage differential. Park (1991), for instance, estimated that blue-collar workers in the unionized manufacturing sector in *Korea* are paid on average only 4 percent more than their counterparts in the nonunionized sector. Panagides and Patrinos (1994) estimated that the union-nonunion wage differential in *Mexico* was about 10 percent in the late 1980s, which would appear to indicate the existence of some bargaining strength. Some caution is required, however; if union workers are more productive than their nonunion counterparts (as a result of reduced shirking induced by greater job security, for instance) the productivity differential between the two categories of labor may be large enough to offset the union-nonunion wage differential.

14.4.2   Labor Market Reforms and Flexibility

Various economists have argued that **job security provisions**, despite being commendable in principle (to the extent that their objective is the protection of workers against unsafe work practices and unjustified dismissals), have had in practice a variety of adverse consequences.

- Job security provisions have led in some cases to a general *loss of profitability*, *reduced flexibility* at the firm level to relative price shocks and shifts in aggregate demand, and distortions in favor of more *capital-intensive production techniques*. Tokman (1992), for instance, estimated that during the 1980s labor regulations contributed to an increase in labor costs of about 20 percent on average in a group of Latin American countries; this increase was about equally divided between fringe benefits (such as health insurance and sick leave) and social security contributions.

- Firms tend to become reluctant to take on new employees when faced with high **hiring** and **firing costs**. In addition, employers may become cautious about hiring new workers with contracts of indefinite duration, opting instead to rely on casual labor, subcontracting, or fixed-term contractual relationships. In situations where demand conditions tend to fluctuate, the average level of employment in the affected industries or occupations could thus become lower than optimal.[24]

- High **mandatory severance payments** have effects that are fundamentally similar to a *contingent tax* on labor use; they tend to impede the *speed of adjustment* in employment in response to adverse sectoral and aggregate shocks.

Thus, by inhibiting the reallocation of labor and wage flexibility, labor regulations may lead to higher, and more persistent, unemployment. At the same time, by increasing the incidence of long-term unemployment through reduced labor turnover, regulations may compound the loss of skills among the unemployed and reduce the downward pressure exerted by the unemployed on wages. Moreover, employment security provisions often lead to increased reliance on *temporary labor* and may limit (most notably by raising the cost of dismissing redundant workers) labor mobility across sectors. In effect, as noted by Fallon and Riveros (1989), labor may become a *quasi-fixed factor* of production— thereby raising the short-term costs of adjustment policies. Finally, employment regulations may negatively *reinforce* each other, aggravating their direct effects on the labor market. For instance, it has been argued that high minimum wages and job protection legislation may combine to reduce employment prospects of unskilled workers by pricing them out of jobs and reducing incentives to search and invest in acquisition of new skills. Thus removing (or reducing the scope

---

[24]The use of repeated temporary contracts to circumvent regulations on hiring and firing may also increase with competitive pressures, such as in the aftermath of trade liberalization (Currie and Harrison, 1997).

of) these provisions would reduce nonwage labor costs and eliminate rigidities that impede labor mobility and the efficient allocation of resources.

However, this view has become the subject of renewed controversy in recent years, in both industrial and developing countries. For industrial countries (particularly Europe), there appears to be limited empirical evidence supporting the view that employment protection measures (such as hiring and dismissal procedures) are sources of unemployment persistence. An examination of employment protection measures in Germany, France, and Belgium in the mid-1980s by Abraham and Houseman (1994) found no evidence that changes in such provisions affected the speed of labor market adjustment.[25] In fact, the standardization of contractual rules across firms may reduce **information** and **transactions costs**, thereby making the labor market *more efficient* than it would be otherwise.

In the context of developing countries, high hiring and firing costs may have more limited practical effects than is often thought where (at least segments of) labor markets are highly flexible—precisely in part due to *poor compliance* with existing regulations (Freeman, 1993). Job security provisions may have no direct effects on employment and unemployment, if wages are de facto flexible.[26] More generally, as forcefully argued by Standing (1991), there are several benefits of employment security regulations.

- They can improve workers' commitment to the enterprise and thus raise *work motivation* and *productivity*.

- They may reduce transactions costs associated with employment by reducing *labor turnover*—a consideration that carries particular importance when productivity rises with on-the-job learning.

- They may improve job and work flexibility, that is, improve the willingness of workers to accept (or initiate) occupational and work environment changes.

- They may induce workers to accept lower wage rises.

- They may reduce the probability of **frictional unemployment**, by enabling workers that have been made redundant to get adequate notice and begin searching for alternative opportunities, thereby reducing both individual and social costs of mobility.

In developing countries—where, again, one would expect some types of labor regulations to have limited employment effects, due to extensive noncompliance—it appears that the recent literature has focused almost exclusively on the alleged

---

[25] It should be noted, however, that employment protection measures may only have a *second-order impact* on labor market flexibility in the presence of other (more important) distortions, such as high minimum wages (as in France) or generous long-term unemployment benefits schemes.

[26] However, if employment protection legislation is not applied uniformly to all firms in all production sectors (or if *enforcement* varies according to firm size), it will distort labor allocation and firm size, and foster expansion of the informal economy as producers strive to avoid taxation.

costs of job security provisions. A more balanced evaluation, based on detailed case studies, appears warranted. In the absence of such studies, it appears difficult to conclude (as many observers have done) that easing employment protection regulations (such as minimum wage laws) would, in particular, help increase labor mobility. For instance, high minimum wages may lead formal-sector firms to adopt more efficient managerial practices and to invest in labor-saving technology rather than rely on low wages as the main source of profitability. The overall effect in the longer run may be an increase in productivity and competitiveness, which could outweigh adverse short-term effects on employment. Rama (1995) found that labor market regulations such as social security contributions, minimum wages, and severance pay requirements do not appear to affect significantly the rate of economic growth.[27] Higher minimum wages appear, in fact, to be positively correlated with employment growth. Although these results are preliminary and need to be corroborated by additional evidence, they do cast doubt on the simplistic view that policies aimed at eliminating labor market distortions would necessarily enhance economic performance.[28] Determining the *net cost* of employment security regulations requires taking into account all of their potential benefits.

14.5 Summary

- **Structural policies** operate primarily through the supply side of the economy, by influencing the level of *potential output* and by affecting the *flexibility* with which the economy responds to economic shocks.

- The agricultural sector in many developing countries plays an important role in providing employment opportunities and a source of revenue for government operations. *Tax and pricing policies* with regard to agriculture can, therefore, have a profound effect on the labor market and government revenue.

- *Food subsidies* to households are not an efficient means of redistributing income, compared with direct and well-targeted transfers. By artificially lowering prices for food products, subsidies tend to reduce domestic production.

- Taxation of agricultural exports (often through *marketing boards*), by lowering the profitability of agricultural activities, has also contributed to the creation of distortions and disincentives to produce. In countries where

---

[27] Rama's results also suggest a negative relationship between the relative size of government employment, the unionization rate, and the rate of growth.

[28] In addition, the distortionary effects of employment protection regulations are often judged by comparison to a situation of perfect competition—a probably inappropriate benchmark. As argued by Blank and Freeman (1994), in a setting where government-induced restrictions tend to overlap, some employment security regulations may offset the inefficiencies and distortions caused by other regulations.

much of the labor force is concentrated in rural areas, the *distribution of income* is greatly influenced by agricultural policies.

- Reforms of agricultural pricing and tax policies have aimed at increasing the profitability of agricultural production, through either the elimination of export duties or a reduction in the gap between world and domestic producer prices of agricultural commodities. However, evidence on the impact of these reforms on rural incomes and income distribution remains mixed.

- The trend toward **trade liberalization** in developing countries (except for sub-Saharan Africa) was fostered by the large body of evidence on the high costs of import-substitution policies (including high rates of **effective protection**) and resource losses associated with **rent-seeking activities**. In addition to the traditional *static* gains from trade, it has been increasingly recognized that there are also *dynamic* gains from free trade (resulting, in particular, from **technological spillovers**), which may lead to a *permanent* increase in the economy's growth rate.

- Although the recent literature on **strategic trade theory** does consider cases in which trade intervention can be an efficient form of intervention, its results are not easily generalizable.

- Recent evidence on the effects of trade reform on *employment* suggests that the *level* effect has been limited but that changes in the *composition* of employment (namely, a relative increase in the demand for skilled labor) have been quite pronounced in some cases. Shifts in the structure of employment have been associated with a *worsening of income differentials* between skilled and unskilled workers in many countries.

- One explanation of the movements in relative wages is based on the **Stolper-Samuelson theorem**, which asserts that under the assumptions of the Hecksher-Ohlin-Samuelson model of international trade and a regime of unrestricted free trade, a reduction in the domestic price of a good, brought about by a lower tariff or reduced nontariff protection (such as quotas), will lower the real price of the factor of production that is used *relatively intensively* in producing that good. Thus, a reduction in tariff protection on manufacturing goods that are relatively *intensive in unskilled labor* will tend to reduce the real wage received by that category of workers and *increase wage inequality*. The evidence, however, remains mixed. *Complementarity* between (imported) capital goods and skilled labor provides an alternative explanation of the increase in wage differentials.

- Obstacles to trade liberalization may result from **status quo bias** associated with *individual uncertainty* regarding the benefits of reform, the high political cost compared with the relatively small efficiency gains associated with trade reform, and the lack of credibility of the reform process, which may create expectations of a future *policy reversal.*

- Another obstacle to trade reform is the fact that it may have an adverse effect on the *fiscal deficit,* as a result of the negative impact of a reduction in import duties on revenue. However, if **exchange market unification** occurs at the same time that tariff rates are reduced, the higher domestic-currency price of imports at the liberalized market exchange rate may have an offsetting effect.

- **Intraregional trade** in developing countries (particularly in Asia and Latin America) has increased significantly during the past two decades. **Preferential trade agreements** (such as the *Mercosur agreement*) have also become more common. Such arrangements can be beneficial, because they may generate *positive spillovers* through a broader application of successful innovations. They can also lead to higher *productivity growth* rates by allowing increased specialization.

- At the same time, however, they may conflict with the process of *multilateral, nonpreferential trade liberalization* (as pursued, for instance, through the World Trade Organization) and can lead to **trade diversion** (a shift from low-cost nonmember countries to higher-cost members) instead of **trade creation** (a shift from high-cost domestic producers to lower-cost producers from partner countries).

- The *labor market* plays an important role in the transmission process of macroeconomic policy shocks and structural adjustment policies. It typically consists of three sectors: the **rural sector**, the **informal urban sector** (characterized by **self-employment** and flexible wages), and the **formal urban sector**. **Disguised unemployment** and **labor market segmentation** (induced either by government-imposed minimum wages, trade unions, or efficiency considerations by wage-setting firms) prevail in most countries.

- Labor market regulations have a variety of adverse consequences, including *loss of profitability, reduced flexibility* at the firm level to relative price shocks and *shifts in aggregate demand,* and distortions in favor of more *capital-intensive production techniques.* Firms may rely more on *temporary employment* when faced with high **hiring** and **firing costs**. Such costs also limit labor mobility across sectors.

- At the same time, there are several benefits of employment regulations, including an increase in workers' commitment to the firm that employs them (raising *work motivation* and *productivity*), reduced *labor turnover costs,* improved job flexibility, mitigation of wage pressures, and reduced **frictional unemployment**.

- Assessing the desirability of labor market reforms aimed at enhancing economic flexibility requires a *broad measure* of the benefits and costs of labor market regulations. Available have so far failed to provide such a measure. The limited cross-country evidence that exists does not suggest any adverse effect of labor market regulations on growth.

Appendix
Measuring Reforms: Structural Policy Indices

To assess the effect of structural policy reforms on economic variables such as growth, employment, investment, and financial depth, a number of recent studies have attempted to build a *structural policy index*. A good example is the index devised by Lora (1997) for various countries in Latin America. The index attempts to measure the extent to which structural reforms lead to greater efficiency in resource allocation, essentially by reducing distortions caused by policies that prevent the smooth functioning of markets or that impose large costs on transactions and the production process.[29] It focuses on five areas, each with a set of indicators taking generally a value between 0 and 1, based on the worst and best observations in the sample:

- *Trade policy*, with indicators consisting of average tariffs (including surcharges) and tariff spreads. For lack of information, trade restrictions associated with quotas are not accounted for.

- *Tax policy*, with indicators consisting of the maximum marginal income tax rates on corporations and individuals,[30] the basic value-added tax rate, and the productivity of the value-added tax (defined as the ratio of the basic rate times actual revenue collected over GDP).

- *Financial policy*, with indicators consisting of whether interest rates on deposits and loans are free to vary, the real level of reserves on bank deposits, and the quality of banking and financial supervision. The latter indicator is based on a discrete and subjective scale, with three possible levels.

- *Privatization*, measured as the cumulative sums resulting from sales and other property transfers since a benchmark period (1988 in Lora's study), as a proportion of average public investment over a previous period (1985-87 in Lora's analysis).[31]

- *Labor legislation*, with indicators of flexibility consisting of criteria assessed on a discrete scale of 0 to 2: hiring costs, costs of dismissal after one year of work and ten years of work, overtime pay, and social security contributions.

---

[29] Thus, the index does not attempt to measure in a comprehensive manner the *qualitative* aspects of economic reforms. For instance, it does not capture the fact that changes in labor legislation may increase the *flexibility* of firms to hire and fire workers in response to changes in demand, but at the same time (as discussed earlier) may reduce protection and stability.

[30] An alternative would be to use *average* marginal tax rates, although Lora's measure is more appropriate to assess the effect of taxation on investment and labor supply decisions.

[31] An alternative and perhaps more appropriate measure would be to calculate the percentage of a country's total stock of physical assets held and operated by the private sector. There are, however, considerable practical difficulties in constructing such a measure.

Indices in these five areas are first calculated as simple averages of the indices for the policy variables considered in each case. The *total structural policy index* is then derived as the simple average of the five indices.

Using this index, Lora (1997) showed that structural reforms have made significant progress in Latin America between the mid-1980s and the mid-1990s—although the timing and pace of reform has varied considerably across countries. Without reforms, Lora estimates that on average the rate of economic growth would have been 1.9 percent lower, and income per capita 12 percent lower, than it is at the moment in Latin America. At the same time, however, there appears to remain considerable scope for improvement (particularly in the areas of *labor legislation, tax reform*, and the *regulation and supervision* of *financial systems*), with potentially large effects on investment, growth, and standards of living in the region.

Chapter 15

Fiscal and Financial Sector Reforms

As noted in Chapter 3, many developing countries continue to have tax structures that are overly complex (in some cases several hundred taxes yielding little revenue) and difficult to administer. High rates of taxation levied on a narrow base have contributed (as noted in Chapter 12) to the expansion of the **informal economy**, exacerbating fiscal constraints. Unproductive expenditure, often resulting from rent-seeking activities, and an excessive wage bill, resulting from overstaffed public administrations, are widespread. Large **quasi-fiscal operations**, as also discussed in Chapter 3, have contributed in many countries to distortions in fiscal accounts. At the same time, **financial repression**, often resulting from the inability to extract sufficient resources through conventional taxation, continues to generate serious distortions in the allocation of resources—with adverse effects on rates of economic growth and standards of living.

Growing recognition of the heavy cost associated with these distortions has led many developing countries to implement adjustment programs in which fiscal and financial sector reforms have figured prominently. Issues associated with the design and effects of such reforms are examined in this chapter.[1] Part 1 focuses on fiscal adjustment. It begins by reviewing the efficiency loss of taxation and practical guidelines for tax reform. It then considers issues associated with public expenditure control and management, and civil service reform. The role of fiscal decentralization is also assessed. Part 2 discusses pension reform, which also affects the public sector. The third and fourth parts focus on two aspects of financial reform: interest rate liberalization and its effects on saving and investment, and exchange market unification. The last part considers the benefits and

---

[1] For lack of space, privatization of state-owned enterprises is not addressed here. For a discussion of the analytical issues involved, see International Finance Corporation (1995) and Gylfason (1998a). Campbell, White, and Bhatia (1998) review the experience of sub-Saharan Africa with privatization during the early to mid-1990s.

pitfalls of financial sector reform, particularly its effects on financial volatility.

15.1 Fiscal Adjustment

Fiscal adjustment consists of a variety of policies aimed at improving the efficiency and transparency of public finances. This section focuses on the following aspects of fiscal adjustment: tax reform, expenditure control and management, public sector retrenchment, and fiscal decentralization.

15.1.1 Reforming Tax Systems

Tax reform has been at the heart of adjustment programs in many developing countries. As noted in Chapter 3, the inability to levy sufficient revenue through conventional instruments of taxation has often led to excessive reliance on seigniorage and the inflation tax—a highly distortionary source of revenue. However, conventional taxation may also entail some efficiency and welfare costs.

The Excess Burden of Taxation

There are essentially two types of taxes: lump-sum taxes and ad valorem taxes. A lump-sum tax, by definition, does not alter relative prices; it therefore generates no efficiency losses. By contrast, an ad valorem tax on any given good does distort the relative price of the good and reduces the welfare of consumers through two channels:

- a *direct transfer of income* to the government;

- an indirect effect resulting from the rise in the (tax-inclusive) price of the good relative to other goods that are not subject to taxation. This effect can be decomposed into an (indirect) **income effect** and a **substitution effect**—as in the standard microeconomic analysis of a change in a relative price (see, for instance, Varian, 1992).

The *efficiency loss* of a (distortionary) tax, also called the **deadweight loss** or **excess burden** of the tax, can thus be defined as the excess of the reduction in the consumers' welfare above and beyond that which can be accounted for by the loss in income resulting from the payment of the tax (see Zee, 1995).[2]

In practice, as is the case with tariffs discussed in the previous chapter, the efficiency loss is measured by the loss in the **consumers' surplus** associated with the tax. To illustrate, consider the case of an economy producing a single good. In Figure 15.1, the market demand curve is shown as DD, with Q_A the quantity demanded at the initial, pre-tax price P_A. The consumers' surplus is then the area below DD and above the price line, that is, the triangle BP_AA.

---

[2] More generally, a (distortionary) tax causes an excess burden vis-à-vis a lump-sum tax if it reduces utility in excess of what would have occurred had the tax been collected as a lump-sum payment.

Suppose now that the government imposes an *ad valorem* tax at the rate ι, which brings the market price to $P_T = (1 + \iota)P_A$. The quantity demanded for the good drops from Q_A to Q_T, and the consumers' surplus falls to BP_TA', or equivalently a reduction of $P_TA'AP_A$ relative to the initial situation. The rectangular area $P_TA'CP_A$, however, measures the total amount of taxes paid, $(P_T - P_A)Q_T$, which is $\iota P_A Q_A$. Hence, the **excess burden** of the tax is the triangle $A'AC$, which (as defined earlier) measures the excess of the reduction in the consumers' surplus above and beyond that associated with the payment of the tax. The area $A'AC$ is also known as the **Harberger triangle**.

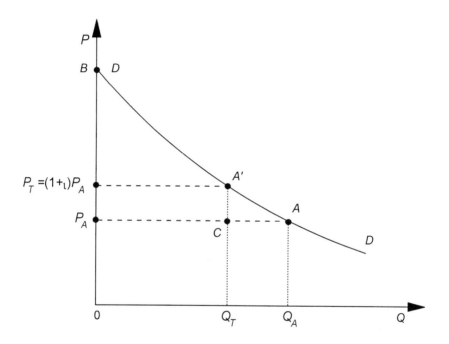

Figure 15.1. The Efficiency Cost of Taxation.

To calculate the area $A'AC$, note that $AC = -(Q_T - Q_A) = -\Delta Q$, and that $A'C = P_T - P_A = \Delta P$. Thus

$$\text{area } A'AC = -\Delta Q \Delta P / 2.$$

By definition, the absolute value of the price elasticity of the demand for the good before the imposition of the tax is $\eta = -(\Delta Q/Q_A)/(\Delta P/P_A)$. As a result,

$$-\Delta Q = \eta \Delta P (Q_A/P_A).$$

Combining the last two equations, and noting that $\Delta P = \iota P_A$, yields

$$\text{area } A'AC = \eta \iota^2 (P_A Q_A)/2, \tag{15.1}$$

which indicates that the excess burden of the tax varies, in particular, with the squared value of the tax rate.[3]

How, then, should taxes be set if the objective is to minimize efficiency losses? The *theory of optimal taxation* suggests that for efficiency reasons tax rates on consumption goods should be inversely related to the elasticity of demand for each commodity (the so-called **Ramsey rule**) and taxation of production should fall on final goods rather than intermediate goods (see, for instance, Stern, 1984). As discussed below, value-added taxes attempt precisely to avoid taxing intermediate inputs and instead focus on final consumption.

In practice, however, taxation of goods and services in many developing countries is far from efficient:

- Tax collection is difficult to administer, leading to revenue losses.

- Tax systems continue to be characterized by the imposition of multiple tax rates on both consumption and production activities.

- Inefficiencies often arise because of a *cascading effect*, resulting from the fact that taxes fall not only on production at a given stage but also on taxes paid in earlier stages.

- Taxes often have an adverse effect on international competitiveness because they are levied at the *manufacturing* stage rather than the *retail* stage in some countries, implying that exporters are also subject to them.

In the area of *income taxation* also, tax systems in developing countries suffer from severe inefficiencies. Legislation often incorporates multiple exemptions and high rates, and it often does not integrate taxation of personal and corporate incomes. Income brackets are usually not indexed on inflation. The implications have been low revenue productivity (As **tax evasion** became pervasive), inequities reflecting narrow tax bases, and inefficiencies in resource allocation.[4]

Guidelines for Reform

During the 1980s several developing countries implemented far-reaching reforms of their tax systems. Simplifying the tax structure and improving the efficiency, equity, and neutrality of the tax system have been key objectives of tax reform in these countries.

Thirsk (1997) summarized the experience of a group of eight countries (Bolivia, Colombia, Indonesia, Jamaica, South Korea, Mexico, Morocco, and Turkey) with tax reform during the 1980s and early 1990s. Although these countries faced very different initial conditions (in terms of both macroeconomic and structural indicators) prior to reform, they all aimed at the same broad objectives: reduce the allocative distortions of their tax systems (notably by reducing

---

[3]Formula (15.1) is not without problems; in particular, as discussed by Zee (1995), it provides a correct approximation only in the case where the market demand curve is approximately linear, as drawn in Figure 8.1. It remains, however, widely used in practice.

[4]The appendix to this chapter reviews standard models of tax evasion.

incentives for rent seeking and tax evasion), broaden their application, improve compliance, and simplify the tax structure in order to reduce administrative requirements and enforcement costs. In all countries, tax rates on both corporate and personal incomes were reduced significantly. Income tax bases were broadened in a variety of ways—including reduced reliance on tax incentives, elimination of exemptions, and greater use of presumptive methods of taxation. A broad-based sales tax (typically a value-added tax, with exemptions for either basic necessities or sectors that are hard to tax) has become a key source of revenue. A good example is Colombia, whose tax reform program during the period 1980-92 led to an increase of 4 percentage points of GDP in the revenue collected by the central administration.[5] The first major step in the reform program occurred in 1983, and was aimed at reducing double taxation (of both enterprises and individuals) and increasing tax incentives for saving and investment.

An important lesson of these experiences, as emphasized by Thirsk (1997, p. 30), is that in developing countries *broad-based indirect taxes* may often be easier to design and implement than broad-based income taxes as a result of a variety of constraints—including a large informal sector (which makes it difficult to production and income comprehensively) and powerful interests that tend to reduce the base of the personal income tax. A somewhat similar conclusion was reached by Burgess and Stern (1993) in their review of the experience of some of the same countries and a few others (Colombia, Indonesia, Jamaica, Korea, Mexico, Sri Lanka, and Turkey) with tax reform during the 1980s: the reform of indirect taxation was in general more successful than that of direct taxation, in part because indirect taxes, being less visible, tend to encounter less political resistance than direct taxes.

There is considerable scope in many developing countries to enhance revenues without worsening distortions and reducing efficiency by *broadening the tax base* and *improving tax collection* and *tax administration.* Another aspect of reform of the tax structure involves a significant reduction in personal and corporate income tax rates and the imposition of strict limitations on ad hoc exemptions that tend to narrow the tax base and reduce efficiency. Lower personal income tax rates, in particular, help to

- promote a more equitable tax system in countries where, because of inadequate tax administration, high marginal tax rates are applied in an ad hoc and discriminatory fashion; and

- reduce the size of the informal economy (by reducing incentives to evade taxes) and improve allocative efficiency.

Reducing *tax evasion* is indeed a key objective of tax reform in many developing countries at the present time. Improving tax enforcement and compliance may allow these countries not only to lower tax rates but also at the same time

---

[5]Other countries also recorded significant increases in their tax revenue-GDP ratios in the aftermath of reform.

to increase tax revenue over the longer term. An important issue that arises in this context is how to design *sanctions* and *penalty systems* that encourage taxpayers to voluntarily comply with their tax obligations. There is general consensus that penalties are more effective than a high probability of detection to deter tax evasion. Theory and empirical evidence also support the intuitive view that lower penalties applied consistently are more effective in deterring tax evasion than high penalties applied fairly infrequently (see Pyle, 1991).

The "ideal" tax system for a developing country would have the following characteristics (Burgess and Stern (1993), and Stotsky (1995)):

- Heavy reliance on a broadly based sales tax, such as the **value added tax**, with one or two rates and minimal exemptions, and excise taxes on petroleum products, alcohol, tobacco, and perhaps a few luxury items. Small production units should be excluded from coverage to lower collection costs and a system of *presumptive assessment* should be used instead (Cnossen, 1991).

- No reliance on export duties, except as a transitory alternative to income taxation.

- Reliance on import taxation for protective purposes only—because the domestic sales tax is assigned the revenue-raising function—with a low average rate and a limited dispersion of rates to minimize effective rates of protection.

- An administratively simple form of the personal income tax, with exemptions limited to allowances for dependents, a moderate top marginal rate, an exemption limit large enough to exclude persons with modest incomes, and a substantial reliance on withholding.

- A corporate income tax levied at only one moderate-to-low rate, with depreciation and other noncash expenditure provisions uniform across sectors and minimal recourse to incentive schemes for new ventures.

It is important to realize that the type of reforms that would bring about this tax system may have significant *distributional implications*. Some of these changes may be *progressive*.

- A simplified tax system reduces opportunities for *tax evasion*. Together with the elimination of special treatments, they tend to reduce the benefits enjoyed by the more influential and higher-income groups.

- Broadening the base of consumption or income taxes may lead to lower tax pressure on middle-income groups that are taxed more heavily to begin with because they are easy to monitor, for example wage earners in the formal sector. This should improve income distribution.

- A more neutral tax system, to the extent that it encourages investment, may lead to the creation of new job opportunities that may benefit the poor.

At the same time, it must be recognized that there can also be *regressive* effects.

- Reducing marginal income tax rates benefits higher-income individuals and corporations.

- Value-added taxes are taxes on consumption; they tax less those who save more, that is, higher-income individuals.

- The elimination of tax exemptions for basic goods and reductions in tax rates on luxury consumption goods hurt the poor and benefit richer households.

- The elimination of special tax exemptions for labor-intensive firms in particular production sectors may have an adverse effect on job creation and raise poverty.

Finally, it should be noted that tax reform may affect *short-* and *longer-term* economic prospects in *opposite directions*. The elimination of an export tax on a commodity such as *cocoa*, for instance, would in the short run tend to reduce public sector revenue and to raise the fiscal deficit—with possibly inflationary consequences. At the same time, however, the removal of the tax tends to increase the domestic price of cocoa, which would not only reduce domestic consumption but also encourage cocoa producers to expand output. This, in turn, may raise exports and lead to an improvement in the trade balance. Thus the microeconomic aspects of fiscal policy (and the possible *trade-offs* that are involved) must be taken into account in the design of stabilization programs.

15.1.2   Expenditure Control and Management

A major source of inefficiencies in the management of public sector resources is the lack of control over expenditure in all four major categories—government consumption (including wages and salaries, and expenditure on materials) public investment, transfers and subsidies, and interest payments on the domestic and external public debt. As noted in Chapter 12, at high levels of taxation, bigger government is not necessarily conducive to higher growth rates.

At the same time, fiscal adjustment is often characterized by excessive and disproportionate cuts in public investment and expenditure on materials, supplies, and maintenance relative to other types of expenditure—most notably wages and salaries. How government spending is cut is, of course, important for growth. But the issue is not only to maintain outlays on key infrastructure projects and high-priority spending on health and education (given their impact on human capital), ensuring the *quality* of spending may be as important as its quantity. In turn, improving *expenditure control systems* (and more transparent budgeting) may play an important role in this process.

Public finance experts regard an efficient public expenditure management system as containing the following elements (see Premchand, 1993):

- A *transparent budget* that integrates current and capital expenditure plans and relies on efficient appraisal techniques to decide among alternative expenditure options;

- Aggregate *expenditure ceilings*, with effective control over expenditure during the year, coordination of domestic- and foreign-financed expenditure, and effective management of cash and public debt;

- A *reporting system* that compiles clear, reliable, comprehensive, and timely data on budget execution.

The public expenditure management system also needs to embed the budgetary process in an appropriate *medium-term macroeconomic framework*, comprising a medium-term, fiscal-policy forecasting component capable of addressing issues such as the sustainability of public debt (see Chapter 3). In practice, however, very few developing countries have so far been able to achieve an efficient system because of administrative and human capital constraints.

15.1.3   Civil Service Reform

In many developing countries government wage and employment decisions are determined more by political considerations than conventional economic considerations. When faced with budgetary pressures, it is easier politically for governments to cut investment outlays or maintenance expenditures (as noted earlier) than fire public sector workers. An unstable political climate may lead to increases in employment or higher wages to attract followers (prior to elections, in participatory democracies) or to retain them (by rewarding key followers). Public sector employment has also been used to offset the effect of adverse shocks on the labor market in part to avoid growing political dissent.

In part because of large and unsustainable fiscal deficits, the downsizing of the public sector labor force has become in recent years a key policy issue in the developing world. Lienert and Modi (1997) for instance examined the process of civil service restructuring in sub-Saharan Africa between the mid-1980s and the mid-1990s. Their analysis suggested that during that period nominal wage bills declined on average (particularly so in CFA franc countries since 1994). To a large extent, however, this decline resulted from a substantial and almost continuous fall in real wages (since 1991 in non-CFA franc countries and since 1994 for CFA franc countries). The number of civil servants did not change much on average, although some progress was made in CFA franc countries after 1994. In many cases, **v**oluntary retirement was encouraged and attractive *severance packages* (based on length of service and, in some cases, the retiree's age) were offered. One problem confronted by many countries is that eligibility for severance packages was not conditional on performance, and many *highly skilled* workers ended up leaving the civil service.

How to alter or design severance packages in a way that induces only poor performers to leave remains a challenge in many countries. A recent analytical overview of some of the issues involved was provided by Rama (1997*b*). The point of departure of his analysis is the observation that *individual productivity* is often difficult to observe in government administration. Thus, identifying the truly redundant workers is also difficult. In such conditions, severance pay may be a potentially *perverse selection mechanism*—in the sense that it may lead to a "wrong" composition between those who stay and those who leave.

To show this, consider the following example, from Rama (1997*b*). Suppose that there are two sectors in the economy, the public and the private sectors. The number of workers is also given; they are all identical, except in their degree of *aversion to effort*. Suppose also, for simplicity, that there are only two levels of effort aversion, so that workers are either *productive* or *unproductive*.[6] Suppose that any worker who leaves (voluntarily or involuntarily) his or her job in one sector is immediately rehired in the other sector. Thus, there is no unemployment. Assume also that private sector firms are effective at monitoring effort; all workers employed there are therefore productive. In contrast, the public sector cannot effectively monitor the level of effort; workers can, if they so choose, be unproductive. The problem is how to identify these unproductive workers.

The first step in the analysis consists in comparing the welfare loss of both types of workers in case of separation. In the above example, both types of workers would earn the same income in the public sector. Because the level of effort is difficult to measure, public sector pay tends to be based on *observable characteristics*, such as education and years on the job, and both types of workers are identical in that respect. Moreover, both types of workers would earn the same income out of the public sector as well, because private sector pay depends on productivity, and monitoring ensures a uniform level of productivity across workers. The change in *income* is therefore the same for both types of employees. But the change in *effort* is not. The effort level remains unchanged for the productive workers, whereas it increases for unproductive ones. The total welfare loss is therefore larger for the latter. In such conditions, if severance pay is used to induce voluntary separations, productive workers would be the first ones to leave, whereas unproductive workers would be the last ones. There is therefore a **perverse selection** effect.

The extent and composition of downsizing depends on the amount of severance offered to induce voluntary departures. In the example considered, there are three possible outcomes.

- The package offered can be less than the loss in income of the productive workers. None of these workers would then leave. However, none of the unproductive workers would leave either, because their welfare loss is even larger.

- The package could be generous enough to offset the welfare loss to unproductive workers. Because the loss to the productive workers is smaller, all workers would then accept the offer and leave.

---

[6] The argument could be easily generalized to the case in which there is a *continuum* of effort levels.

- In between these two possibilities, the package could be higher than the welfare loss to productive workers, but lower than that of unproductive workers. In this case, only the latter would stay.

The *net social benefit* from public sector downsizing differs in each of these three alternatives, but no ranking is valid under all circumstances. In the second and third possibilities, private sector output increases whereas public sector output decreases. Both the increase in private sector output and the decline in public sector output are larger in the second case, because more people are reallocated across sectors. The decline in public sector output could be similar in the second and third cases if the level of effort of unproductive workers was very low to begin with. In turn, this implies that the net social benefit in the second case could be higher than in the third case. It could also be negative in both cases, which implies that offering severance across the board may reduce efficiency.

Various mechanisms have been proposed to mitigate the adverse selection problem that arises when individual productivity is unobservable. In principle, many of these mechanisms try to find ways, through **self-selection**, to separate productive workers from unproductive ones. In practice, however, they remain difficult to implement, as noted by Rama (1997*b*).

15.1.4   Fiscal Decentralization

In recent years, a number of developing countries have begun to decentralize spending and revenue-raising responsibilities from national or central levels of government to subnational levels.[7] This shift can be viewed as reflecting two main factors (Ter-Miniassan, 1997):

- the general tendency of political processes to move toward more *democratic* and *participatory forms* of government, which attempt to make political leaders more accountable for their actions and decisions to their constituencies;

- the attempt to ensure a *closer correspondence* between the level, composition, and quality of goods and services provided by governments and the preferences of beneficiaries or constituents.

From the point of view of macroeconomic management, the process of decentralization may provide some potential benefits. Decentralizing spending responsibilities to the level of government that is most closely associated with potential beneficiaries, for instance, will typically increase the efficiency with which public sector resources are allocated and used—assuming, of course, that these sublevel government institutions are themselves sufficiently competent.

Decentralization may also, however, complicate significantly the conduct of macroeconomic policy (Ter-Miniassan, 1997).

---

[7]In most cases, the central government has retained direct administrative control over foreign borrowing by subnational governments.

- Giving subnational governments too much latitude to tax may excessively reduce the number of tax instruments available for macroeconomic management by the central government.

- Even if subnational governments are limited in their ability to tax and borrow, changes in the *composition* of their expenditures—toward, for instance, higher transfers to consumers or unemployment benefits—can affect aggregate demand and the balance of payments in ways that may conflict with the macroeconomic policy targets set by the central government.

The solution to the latter problem is that expenditures that have a large impact on demand should remain under the control of central governments. The solution to the first is more complicated. Clearly, arrangements that assign all taxing powers to the central government are undesirable, because they imply no connection between the ability to spend and revenue-raising responsibilities. The solution, in practice, is a *revenue-sharing arrangement*, which assigns to each level of government its own source(s) of revenue and provides for various types of intergovernmental transfers to bridge any deficit between revenue and expenditure assignments.

The viability of such arrangements require, however, a high degree of *policy coordination* among the various levels of government. In addition, because most major taxes are typically assigned to the central government, whereas substantial and growing expenditure responsibilities are devolved to regional and local governments, sizable **vertical imbalances** (pretransfer fiscal deficits) frequently emerge at the level of subnational governments. There are also **horizontal imbalances**, which result notably from the fact that the revenue-raising capacity of subnational governments varies across regions. Designing a robust system of *intergovernmental transfers* is crucial not only to redistribute resources within a country but also to ensure that limits on borrowing by subnational governments can be set and properly enforced.

It is worth noting that some recent research suggests that decentralization can lead to *bigger* (and thus *less efficient*) governments. Stein (1997), in particular, found in a study focusing on Latin America that the political distortions associated with decentralization may lead to soft budget constraints. Imposing hard budget constraints on subnational governments requires ensuring that proper limits are in place on vertical fiscal imbalance—as measured by the ratio of intergovernmental transfers from the central government, including tax sharing, over total revenues (own plus transferred) of the subnational level—by proper assignment of revenue bases (on the basis of the degree of efficiency in collection) and by limiting the degree of autonomy in borrowing by lower-level jurisdictions.

15.2   Pension Reform

Pension systems differ in the way they finance and provide pensions, whether they fix *benefits* or *contributions*, and in whether they are run by the state or by the private sector. Until recently, pension systems were mostly state run in developing countries and offered benefits that were determined by law rather than lifetime contributions. These unfunded, defined benefit systems operate on a **pay-as-you-go basis** and transfer resources (collected in part through *payroll taxes* on employers) from the contributors to the beneficiaries. Public pension systems in many countries continue to offer generous coverage—as measured by high **replacement ratios**, that is, the ratio of pension benefits to pensionable income—and extensive protection to retirees.

However, there has been growing recognition that such systems suffer from serious deficiencies. In particular, the lack of a direct relationship between benefits and contributions imposed serious strains on government budgets in some countries—in part exacerbated by the relative increase in the number of retirees due to population aging. In others, the use of payroll taxes to generate revenue distorted labor markets and encouraged tax evasion.

Partly as a result, several developing countries (particularly in Latin America) have moved toward **fully funded pension schemes**, both public and private. The country where the most far-reaching reforms were adopted was Chile. Because of the funding problems developed by the traditional pay-as-you-go system in the late 1970s, pension reform began in 1981 when the fiscal surplus was sufficiently large to finance the transition to a fully funded system, and after the retirement age was increased to 65. A privatized savings plan requiring workers to place 10 percent of their earnings in one of a number of highly regulated intermediaries was also introduced. The legislation allowed workers, at retirement, to choose between a sequence of phased withdrawals or an annuity.[8]

Following Chile, six countries in Latin America reformed their pension systems in the 1990s. But reforms in some of these countries have moved away from exclusive reliance on an individual capitalization system. Peru (1993) and Colombia (1994) opted for a dual pay-as-you-go, fully funded scheme in which the government system and the new private pension funds have to compete with each other. Argentina (1994) and Uruguay (1996) adopted a system in which the two are complementary; and Mexico (1997) is maintaining the public system solely as a guarantor of benefits for those currently enrolled. In all cases, reforms have entailed major corrections of the financial weaknesses and imbalances between contributions and benefits provided by the government pension system.

Countries in East Asia have used fully funded schemes for a number of years. Some have used variants of the defined contribution system, in part as a tool of development policy. The pension systems in Malaysia and Singapore, for

---

[8]However, in contrast to a defined benefit system, uncertainties regarding the length of the working life, the duration of retirement, and the return on invested contributions made pension benefits somewhat unpredictable.

instance, rely primarily on provident-fund, fully funded, defined contribution schemes, where compulsory contributions are maintained in a central fund with separate accounts for individual contributors. Upon retirement, benefits consist of accumulated contributions plus interest and take the form of a lump-sum payment. Compulsory coverage is generally restricted to wage earners in the formal sector, and those with low wages or with short employment records receive limited coverage.

The experience of developing countries that have reformed their pension system suggests that the combination of a *mandatory, fully funded scheme* with a *supplementary, defined-benefit arrangement* may provide the best strategy to reduce pressures on the government budget while at the same time providing adequate protection for retirees. The mandatory, fully funded component of the system may lead to *higher saving* by making households more aware of the need to save for the future, and through *forced saving* (see Chapter 1) the investment needs of pension funds are also likely to foster the development of domestic capital markets. To the extent that pension reform leads to higher saving, it is likely to have a direct, positive effect on growth. The development of domestic capital markets that results from the reform may also lead to higher investment and thus indirectly to higher output growth—which in turn may lead to higher saving.

What is the evidence on these effects? At an informal level, although it is possible that voluntary private saving may be reduced as compulsory saving increases, the experience of Malaysia and Singapore suggests that provident-fund systems may have contributed to high national saving rates (in excess of 30 percent). The more formal evidence reviewed by McKenzie, Gerson, and Cuevas (1997) and Schmidt-Hebbel (1999) suggests also that pension reform may raise saving and spur growth. Preliminary results for Chile, for instance, by Holzmann (1997), suggested that although pension reform may have fostered the development of domestic financial markets (and thus indirectly investment and growth), the direct effect on the private saving rate was negative. In a more recent study, however, Schmidt-Hebbel (1999) provided updated econometric results suggesting that Chile's pension reform led to improved labor market performance and raised saving, investment, total factor productivity, and growth. The overall message, therefore, appears to be largely corroborated by the facts: the shift from an unfunded to a funded pension scheme, supported by an adequate fiscal policy, is likely to lead to higher saving rates and positive externalities (on labor and financial markets) that will accelerate improvements in standards of living.

15.3 Interest Rate Liberalization

Broadly defined, financial liberalization entails, on the one hand, the abolition of explicit controls on domestic interest rates and restrictions on the allocation of credit by commercial banks, and, on the other, the elimination of restrictions on capital movements and access to foreign exchange through official channels. The next section will discuss issues associated with exchange market reform;

the present one focuses on issues associated with interest rate liberalization and the elimination of credit restrictions.

The liberalization of domestic interest rates has been at the core of programs of financial reform in many developing countries—in large part as a result of the growing evidence on the adverse effects associated with **financial repression** (see Chapter 2). Demetriades and Luintel (1997), for instance, found that financial repression—as measured by a composite index based on various types of interest rate controls, reserve and liquidity requirements, and directed credit— had a direct, adverse effect on financial development (as measured by the ratio of bank deposits over GDP) in India during the period 1960-91.

Positive real interest rates have two types of effects:

- They attract savings that were previously held outside the formal financial sector (gold held under the mattress, for instance), which increases the resources available to the financial system, raising the level of investment and stimulating growth.

- They tend to deter entrepreneurs from investing in low-yielding projects that are no longer profitable at the higher cost of loanable funds; hence, the average return to, or *efficiency* of, aggregate investment tends to increase (Fry, 1997, p. 755).

The increase in both the quantity and the quality of investment have positive effects on the growth rate of output. Interest rate liberalization is also an important step toward the development of an *interbank market* and a secondary market for government securities which are necessary, as noted in Chapter 2, for controlling the supply of money through open-market operations.[9]

There are, however, a number of potential dangers associated with financial liberalization.

- To the extent that financial liberalization leads to an easing of *liquidity constraints* (by providing easier access to consumer credit, for instance), it can lead to a temporary expansion of consumption and a *reduction*, rather than an increase, in saving.

- As indicated in Chapter 1, some of the recent empirical studies (notably by Ogaki, Ostry, and Reinhart, 1996) have concluded that the real interest elasticity of total savings is not significantly different from zero for *low-income* countries. Moreover, even in *higher-income* countries, these studies found that the effect of interest rate changes on saving, although significant, remains small. Interest rate liberalization may thus have only a limited impact on aggregate savings. In a review of financial liberalization episodes in the mid-1970s in Chile and Malaysia, and early 1980s

---

[9]Although seldom discussed, the *order* in which interest rates must be freed—taking into account the overall fragility of the financial system—may also be an important consideration. In practice, countries have often started by liberalizing interbank market rates first, then lending rates, and last deposit rates.

in Indonesia, Korea, Malaysia, and Turkey, Atiyas, Caprio, and Hanson (1994) found indeed that higher real interest rates had a small effect on savings rates, except in cases where the change in interest rates was from a severely negative level to a positive one.[10]

- Interest rate liberalization may have an adverse effect on the *fiscal deficit*; a rise in interest rates may increase the cost of borrowing and the interest payments on the domestic public debt. In the presence of fiscal rigidities (namely, the inability to reduce current expenditure and increase conventional tax revenue), the government may be induced to rely more heavily on **the inflation tax.**

- After interest rates are liberalized, endogenous constraints in the credit market, such as those resulting from **imperfect information**, can continue to be significant barriers to efficient credit allocation. Specifically, the Stiglitz-Weiss model discussed in Chapter 2 suggests that even under a regime of free interest rates, banks may not provide loans to potential borrowers that are perceived to be *too risky*.

- The high real interest rates that are often associated with financial liberalization may make the financial system more vulnerable to crises by worsening the problems of **adverse selection** and **moral hazard**, and by raising the **incidence of default** on loan commitments.

15.4   Unification of Foreign Exchange Markets

It is now well recognized that attempts at imposing restrictions on foreign exchange transactions conducted through official markets in developing countries have almost invariably led to the emergence of parallel markets. The evidence gathered in numerous studies suggests that the existence of such markets may entail a variety of economic costs (Montiel, Agénor, and Haque, 1993):

- an increase in **exchange rate** and **price volatility**;

- a **narrowing** of the **tax base**, associated with the development of illegal and informal activities;

- reduced flows of foreign exchange through official channels, as a result of the **diversion** of export remittances and private transfers from the official to the parallel market;

- **efficiency losses**, resulting from the incentives to engage in **rent-seeking activities**—such as corruption and bribery of government officials.

---

[10] However, they also noted that other aspects of financial reform (such as an increase in bank branches, or a greater menu of financial products) may indeed have a positive effect on savings rates.

Recognition of the importance of these adverse and distortionary effects has led policymakers in many developing countries in recent years to seek ways to unify official and parallel markets for foreign exchange. This section examines the effects of exchange market reform on inflation and **quasi-fiscal deficits** in developing countries.[11] It begins by reviewing Pinto's (1991) analysis of the budgetary and inflationary effects of exchange market unification, which emphasizes the role of implicit taxation of exports. It then reassesses Pinto's view and identifies a variety of implicit taxes and subsidies that are associated with multiple exchange rate regimes. The last part reviews Jamaica's experience with exchange market unification and discusses estimates, derived by Agénor and Ucer (1999), of the net fiscal effect of exchange market reform for a group of developing countries that have recently attempted to unify their foreign exchange markets.

15.4.1   Implicit Export Taxation and Inflation

Pinto's (1991) analysis of the fiscal and inflationary effects of exchange market unification is characterized by four features:

- Exporters face *rising marginal costs* to smuggling. The allocation of output between the official and the parallel markets is thus determined in equilibrium by equating marginal returns. The optimal proportion of smuggled exports is in general positive and is an increasing function of the premium.

- Because exports are partly smuggled out and partly sold through the official market, the **parallel market premium** acts as an *implicit tax* on exports repatriated through official channels.

- The government buys imported goods and uses the foreign exchange surrendered by exporters to pay for them. Excess foreign exchange is resold to the private sector at the official exchange rate. Excess private demand for foreign exchange (imported goods) is satisfied through the parallel market. Thus, official reserves remain constant over time (and changes in the money supply are determined only by domestic credit growth.

- In the steady state, the government finances its budget deficit by the **inflation tax** (whose yield depends on holdings of real money balances) and the *implicit tax on exports*. For a given level of the fiscal deficit, therefore, a *trade-off* typically emerges between the inflation tax rate and the premium (see below).

Formally, the government finances its deficit by credit from the central bank, $\dot{D}$:

$$\dot{D} = E(G - T), \tag{15.2}$$

---

[11] The short-run effects of exchange market unification are discussed in Annex C.

where E denotes the official exchange rate, G government imports, and T conventional taxes. Both G and T are assumed fixed in terms of foreign exchange. Equation (15.2) implies that, in the absence of reserve accumulation:

$$\dot{m} = (G - T) - \varepsilon m, \tag{15.3}$$

where m measures the real money stock in terms of the official exchange rate, and ε the constant rate of depreciation of the official exchange rate. Equation (15.3) indicates that in the steady state ($\dot{m} = 0$) the budget deficit is financed entirely by the inflation tax, $\varepsilon \tilde{m}$.

To identify the steady-state revenue from the implicit tax on exports requires moving from the *recorded* deficit measured in terms of the official exchange rate [as given in Equation (15.3)] to the *true* deficit, measured in terms of the parallel exchange rate. Let θ denote (one plus) the parallel market premium. The *true long-run capital loss* incurred by private asset holders as a result of the inflation tax is not $\varepsilon \tilde{m}$, but $\varepsilon \tilde{m} / \theta$. Similarly, while officially recorded taxes (measured in domestic currency) are equal to ET, the **real tax burden** is equal to $T / \tilde{\theta}$

As long as the long-run value of the premium is *positive* ($\tilde{\theta} > 1$), the true fiscal burden imposed by the inflation tax and conventional taxes will be *lower* than the recorded one. However, because real government spending does not depend on the premium (the government always gets enough foreign exchange to satisfy its needs), the difference between the recorded and the true tax burdens corresponds to the **implicit tax on exports**:

$$G - T / \tilde{\theta} - \varepsilon \tilde{m} / \tilde{\theta}.$$

Because $G - T = \varepsilon \tilde{m}$, this expression is equal to

$$G - \frac{T}{\tilde{\theta}} - \frac{(G - T)}{\tilde{\theta}} = G(1 - \frac{1}{\tilde{\theta}}),$$

that is,

$$G - \frac{T}{\tilde{\theta}} - \frac{\varepsilon \tilde{m}}{\tilde{\theta}} = G(1 - \frac{1}{\tilde{\theta}}).$$

Using this result, the steady-state government budget constraint can be written as

$$G = T + \varepsilon \tilde{m} = G(1 - \frac{1}{\tilde{\theta}}) + \frac{T}{\tilde{\theta}} + \frac{\varepsilon \tilde{m}}{\tilde{\theta}}, \tag{15.4}$$

which explicitly shows how the implicit tax on exports serves to finance government expenditure.[12] For a given level of government spending and conventional tax revenue, and under reasonable assumptions, a trade-off will exist between the inflation tax rate and the premium.[13] Put differently, for G and T given, a

---

[12] Note that because in this setting the central bank resells excess foreign exchange to the private sector at the official exchange rate, it provides an *implicit subsidy* to importers. This subsidy is, like government expenditure on imports, financed by the implicit tax on exporters.

[13] The inflation elasticity of the demand for domestic money must be assumed to be less than unity. For the exact formulation of the trade-off, see Proposition 2 in Pinto (1991, p. 129).

decline in the implicit tax on exports must be compensated by an increase in the inflation (devaluation) rate.

The implication of this trade-off is that by unifying foreign exchange markets, the government loses the tax revenue implicit in the premium, $G(1 - 1/\tilde{\theta})$. With no changes in spending or in conventional taxes, the larger the implicit tax on exports is prior to reform, the larger will be the jump in inflation upon unification. Policymakers must compensate for a fall in revenue by an increase in monetary financing of the fiscal deficit and a higher tax on money holdings.

Pinto's emphasis on the trade-off between the premium and inflation in the unification process remains valid under a variety of *rationing schemes* in the official market for foreign exchange. Lizondo (1991), in particular, extended Pinto's analysis by dropping the assumption that private agents are subject to rationing in the official market and by considering the case where the official market for foreign exchange clears through changes in foreign reserves. Of course, if the government is a *net seller* of foreign exchange, Pinto's conclusions are reversed: unification would lead to a fall in inflation, as discussed next.

15.4.2   An Extended Framework

While the emphasis on the implicit taxation of exports appears warranted in view of the experience of some developing countries (notably in sub-Saharan Africa), Pinto's analysis neglects several other potentially important sources of explicit or implicit taxes and subsidies that are often associated with informal dual exchange rate regimes.[14] The first important issue is the extent to which the characterization of the central bank as a *net seller* or a *net buyer* of foreign exchange affects Pinto's analysis of exchange market unification.

In general, the existence of a large differential between the official and parallel exchange rates carries significant implications for the **quasi-fiscal deficit** of the public sector. In conventional accounting terms, the central bank makes a profit every time it buys foreign exchange (from, say, exporters) at a given rate and sells it to importers at a more depreciated rate. Conversely, it incurs a loss when it sells foreign exchange (to, say, the government) at a given rate and buys it at a more depreciated rate. Put differently, if the central bank buys foreign currency from exporters at an exchange rate that is more depreciated than the rate at which it sells it to domestic agents, it will provide a *net implicit subsidy*. Both types of operations affect central bank profits and the consolidated public sector deficit.

If all sales and purchases occur at the official exchange rate, there will typically be no effect on the central bank's profit and loss account as conventionally calculated. However, in a broader economic sense, the central bank would still collect a net implicit tax or provide an implicit subsidy (depending on whether it is a net buyer or a net seller of foreign exchange) in the presence of a parallel market for foreign exchange—even if all of its foreign exchange operations

---

[14]Some of the fiscal effects discussed here were recognized very early on in the literature on multiple exchange rate regimes. See notably Bernstein (1950) and Sherwood (1956).

occur at the same official exchange rate. The central bank provides an implicit subsidy to private agents if it is a net seller of foreign exchange, and collects an implicit tax if it is a net buyer of foreign exchange.

Thus, in broad economic terms, whether exchange market unification raises or reduces implicit profits accruing to the central bank depends not only on the conventionally measured quasi-fiscal effects of foreign exchange operations but also on whether the central bank is a net buyer or seller of foreign exchange. Put differently, there are two types of quasi-fiscal taxes and subsidies: those generated by different exchange rates being applied to particular categories of foreign exchange transactions; and those that are related to the existence of a parallel exchange market, where the exchange rate reflects better than the (overvalued) official rate the marginal value of foreign exchange. Both sets of taxes and subsidies are in a sense implicit, but the former are reflected in (or can be traced from) the accounts of the central bank more directly than the latter. Net sales to the private sector tend to generate losses whereas net purchases tend to generate profits. This is, in substance, the point emphasized by Pinto (1991). In Pinto's formal framework, all foreign exchange operations of the central bank (sales to the government as well as sales to private agents) take place at the official exchange rate; the central bank is a net buyer of foreign exchange from the private sector. As a result, therefore, prior to reform there exists a *quasi-fiscal surplus* (in a broad sense), which is eliminated by unification. In general, of course, this need not be the case, as discussed above. Morris (1995) showed formally that in Pinto's model, if it is assumed that the government is a net seller of foreign exchange—so that, for instance, a devaluation of the official exchange rate lowers the rate of money creation—exchange market unification will lead to a reduction in inflation in the steady state.

More generally, there are a variety of implicit taxes and subsidies associated with multiple exchange rate regimes that are not directly related to foreign exchange operations between the central bank and domestic agents.

- In countries where inflows of foreign assistance take the form of *direct budgetary support* for the government, a depreciation of the official exchange rate toward its market value may raise revenue and reduce the deficit in domestic-currency terms, whereas an appreciation would worsen the deficit.[15]

- In practice, exchange market unification has often taken place in the context of a reform program calling for substantially higher *aid inflows*. In such conditions, the central bank's position can switch from being a *net buyer* to being a *net seller* of foreign exchange. Unification would thus entail a decrease, rather than an increase, in monetary financing of the fiscal deficit.

---

[15] It should be noted that if foreign assistance is treated as a financing item (as is often the case), valuation changes would have no effect on the deficit. The composition of public expenditure financed by foreign aid may, nevertheless, affect indirectly the level of implicit subsidies.

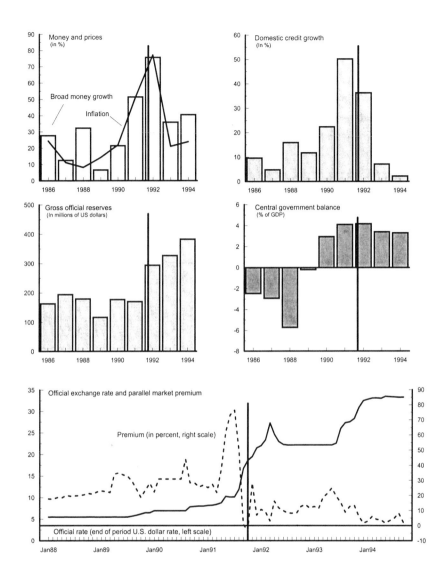

Figure 15.2. Jamaica: Inflation and Financial Indicators.
Source: International Monetary Fund.
Note: A vertical line indicates the date of exchange market reform (October 1991).

- In cases where *guaranteed prices* to local producers of exported goods are fixed in domestic-currency terms, unification will tend to *reduce* expenditure and thereby lower the fiscal deficit.

- As discussed in Chapter 3, *import taxes* remain an important source of fiscal revenue in developing countries, notably in Sub-Saharan Africa. The official rather than the parallel exchange rate is generally used for customs valuation purposes. This practice is tantamount to providing an *implicit subsidy* to importers.[16] The size of this subsidy can be substantial, as was apparently the case during the early 1980s in Nigeria, Tanzania, and Zambia (Nashashibi and Bazzoni, 1994).[17]

To the extent that the net implicit subsidies provided through these other channels are large relative to the revenue generated from the implicit tax on exports, the net effect of exchange market unification may be a *fall* in the steady-state inflation rate—in contrast to Pinto's view. Agénor and Ucer (1999) developed a simple formula for estimating the net effect of exchange market unification on implicit taxes and subsidies (and thus on inflation) that takes into account the foreign exchange operations of the *consolidated public sector* and the various other channels identified above. The application of this formula to several recent experiences is discussed below.

15.4.3   Jamaica's Experience with Unification

Since the early 1980s, a large number of unification attempts have taken place in developing countries in an effort to reduce the role of government in the allocation of foreign exchange and to alleviate some of the costs mentioned above. These countries include Guyana, India, Jamaica, Kenya, Sierra Leone, and Sri Lanka.[18] In many of these countries the postreform regime took the form of the adoption of a flexible exchange rate arrangement operated through an *interbank market* for foreign exchange, rather than a fixed exchange rate or a crawling peg regime.[19]

The experience of *Jamaica* provides a useful example of exchange market unification. The country began to implement stabilization measures and wide-ranging structural reforms in 1989. During the early stages, the record in correcting macroeconomic imbalances appeared mixed. During 1989-92, price increases accelerated, with inflation reaching almost 76 percent in 1992 (Figure 15.2). While the fiscal stance of the central government appeared broadly under control, as reflected in the improvements in the primary and overall fiscal balances through 1994, domestic credit expansion remained strong until 1993. Despite a primary budget surplus throughout, an important financial problem

---

[16]If imported goods sold on the domestic market are valued at market-clearing exchange rate and prices, indirect taxes on domestic sales (such as the value-added tax or excise duties) will not be subject to distortions of this type. However, to the extent that the exchange rate used to value imports is more depreciated than the equilibrium rate, indirect taxes will provide an implicit revenue.

[17]A large premium may also act to reduce *declared imports*, thereby lowering revenue from import taxes by reducing the tax base. There is, however, an offsetting *wealth effect* which may dominate in a general equilibrium context.

[18]Studies on exchange market reform during the past two decades include Ghei, Kiguel, and O'Connell (1997).

[19]McDonald and Lum (1994) examine the operational issues involved in the functioning of interbank markets in sub-Saharan Africa.

during the period was chronic losses by the central bank (that is, a quasi-fiscal deficit), mainly attributable to the interest cost associated with open-market operations.[20] Beginning in 1989, gross reserves started to increase. The buildup accelerated considerably in the aftermath of exchange market reform and continued through 1994.

During most of the 1980s (more precisely, during 1983-89), the value of the Jamaican dollar was determined in a *foreign exchange auction* operated by the central bank.[21] All other foreign exchange receipts were surrendered to the commercial banks at rates quoted by them. Following the suspension of the auctions for about a year, an *interbank exchange rate system* was introduced in September 1990. Initially, certain receipts from exports (mainly of traditional commodities) and tourism, official loan proceeds as well as divestment of government assets, were to be surrendered directly to the central bank. Furthermore, the commercial banks sold a proportion of their purchases from the foreign exchange market to the central bank. After successive modifications to the interbank system, the foreign exchange system was fully liberalized in September 1991; all remaining restrictions on payments and transfers for current and virtually all capital transactions as well as the requirement that foreign exchange earnings be repatriated and surrendered to the banking system, were eliminated. Furthermore, residents and nonresidents were allowed to maintain foreign-currency accounts in Jamaica or abroad without any restrictions. By the end of 1993, proceeds to be sold directly to the central bank included official loans, divestment of government assets, and taxes on the bauxite sector. As the amount of foreign exchange sold directly to the central bank from the above sources fell short of its external debt obligations as well as its international reserve objectives, it began to purchase foreign exchange from the interbank market (including directly from foreign exchange earners) at the prevailing exchange rate.

Since the introduction of the interbank market in September 1990, the value of the Jamaican dollar depreciated gradually, with considerable acceleration in the period surrounding full liberalization in September 1991. After the rate appeared to have stabilized (at about J$22 per U.S. dollar) around mid-June 1992, a further depreciation followed in the latter part of 1993, as the foreign exchange market came under pressure, following mainly a large increase in government wages. The rate stabilized once again in early 1994, albeit at a higher plateau (at around J$33 per U.S. dollar).

Exchange market unification in Jamaica (as in many other countries) took place in the context of a comprehensive reform program which, besides a strong orientation toward more market-oriented economic policies, targeted a relatively restrained fiscal position. In that regard, the country appeared to have achieved some degree of success. Despite sizable exchange rate adjustments, inflation declined substantially in the aftermath of reform. Concurrently, domestic credit

---

[20] It should be noted that such losses complicate the measurement of seigniorage as changes in reserve money in percentage of output.

[21] See Grosse (1994) for a description of the exchange rate system and the characteristics of the parallel market for foreign exchange in Jamaica during the 1980s.

expansion was brought under control (Figure 15.2). Successive devaluations of the official rate were instrumental during the reform process in achieving a unified rate as well as a reduction in the premium; at the end of the reform period, the unified rate was significantly more depreciated than the rate prevailing in the pre-reform period—reflecting in part the extent of the initial disequilibrium in the foreign exchange market. The country also experienced increases in gross reserves in the periods following reform, owing to improved external positions, strong inflows of foreign grants and loans, and rerouting of foreign exchange through official channels. The conclusion, then, is that if one views a successful unification as an exchange market reform that leads to a virtual disappearance of the parallel market premium, without significant increases in domestic inflation or recurrent balance-of-payments problems, Jamaica's experience during the early 1990s appeared fairly successful.

15.4.4   A Simple Formula

Agénor and Ucer (1999) estimated the net effect of exchange market unification using (as mentioned above) a general formula that captures a variety of implicit taxes and subsidies associated with multiple exchange rate regimes. Their results suggested that the subsidy to importers resulting from valuation of imports at the official exchange rate prior to reform (1991) was about 10 percent of GDP for Jamaica. The implicit revenue registered by the central bank (as a result of being a net buyer of foreign exchange prior to reform) amounted to a small positive number. Everything else equal, therefore, the net effect of exchange market reform appeared to have been a reduction in the quasi-fiscal losses of the central bank and the fiscal authorities, thus reducing also reliance on seigniorage revenue. A similar conclusion was reached by Agénor and Ucer (1999) for several of the other countries in their sample (Guyana, India, Sierra Leone, and Sri Lanka).

The Agénor-Ucer findings compared well with those obtained in a study by Ghei, Kiguel, and O'Connell (1997), which summarized the results of a research project on parallel exchange markets involving detailed case studies of exchange market reform in eight developing countries during the 1980s (Argentina, Ghana, Mexico, Sudan, Tanzania, Turkey, and Zambia). These studies covered both cases of *rapid* unification (Argentina at the end of 1989, Mexico in December 1987, and Venezuela in February 1989), and cases of *gradual* unification (Ghana, Sudan, Tanzania, Turkey, Venezuela, and Zambia). The authors found that the existence of a parallel market for foreign exchange was often associated with significant *quasi-fiscal losses*—as appeared to have happened in Jamaica and other countries. To a large extent, these implicit losses (which therefore did not appear directly in budgetary accounts) resulted from *net sales* of foreign exchange to the private sector at below market exchange rates. Ghana, Mexico, Tanzania, Venezuela, and Zambia, in particular, incurred large quasi-fiscal losses as a result of the existence of parallel markets in foreign exchange.[22] In Venezuela for instance, the loss was estimated at between 4.7 and 25.4 percent of GDP, depending on the value used to measure the *true market value* of foreign exchange. In most of these countries (particularly Mexico, Venezuela, and Zambia), the reason why the central bank was a net seller of foreign exchange was related to the position of the consolidated public sector as a *net producer* of foreign exchange, either as a result of large external transfers to this sector, or because public sector enterprises were among the main exporters of the economy—thus representing *captive sources* of foreign currency. In a few other cases, such as Argentina and Tanzania, the central bank was a *net buyer* of foreign exchange from the private sector, thus generating sizable profits. Ghei, Kiguel, and O'Connell (1997) estimated that on net the multiple exchange rate system in Argentina led to profits of the order of 3.5 percent of GDP, whereas in Tanzania it generated a positive effect on the domestic-currency budget equivalent on an annual basis to 2.1 percent of output. As argued earlier, therefore, exchange market reform led to lower reliance on inflationary finance in some cases—Venezuela, for instance—by reducing quasi-fiscal losses.

15.5 Financial Liberalization and Fragility

The previous sections focused on two main aspects of financial liberalization: interest rate liberalization and exchange market unification. There are a number of reasons, as discussed earlier, to suggest that both types of measures can be highly beneficial. But it has also become increasingly clear that interest rate liberalization, in particular, can be risky if undertaken in a *fragile financial environment*. This section begins by reviewing the main sources of financial fragility in developing countries. It then considers various measures aimed at strengthening the financial system and limiting the risks of financial instability associated with liberalization. The analysis, overall, emphasizes two major preconditions for successful financial sector reform: a stable macroeconomic environment and a proper system of bank prudential regulation and supervision.

15.5.1 Sources of Financial Fragility

As noted in Chapter 2, banks remain at the center of the financial system in most developing countries. Any analysis of the sources of financial fragility must therefore pay particular attention to the conditions under which banks operate.

In general, banks are perceived to be more fragile than nonfinancial firms primarily because they tend to have low capital-to-assets ratios (that is, they are *highly leveraged*), a low cash-to-assets ratio (as a result of *fractional reserve banking*), and high ratios of short-term demand deposits to total debt—which create a high potential for a bank run. As discussed later, prudential supervision in many countries has failed to ensure that these **fragility ratios** remain at reasonable levels.

---

[22] In addition, the high premium that prevailed in Ghana in the early 1970s had an adverse effect on declared exports and imports, which limited the revenue generated by trade taxes.

The severity of banking sector problems can be measured in terms of the ratio of *nonperforming loans* to total loans, the volume of *restructured loans*, and the extent of direct and indirect *government support* for the banking system.[23] The evidence reviewed by Lindgren, Garcia, and Saal (1996) for instance suggests that (as also noted in Chapter 7) a significant number of developing countries experienced severe banking sector problems or full-fledged banking crises during the past two decades. The *macroeconomic costs* imposed by these problems have been large in terms of efficiency losses in financial intermediation, adverse effects on output, and pressures on public finances, because the resolution costs have been born mostly by the public sector. As shown in Figure 15.3, the cumulative *fiscal and quasi-fiscal outlays* associated with bank restructuring are on the order of 12 to 15 percent of GDP in Mexico for the period 1994-95, 0 to 17 percent in Venezuela for 1994-96, and 19 to 41 percent in Chile for 1981-85.

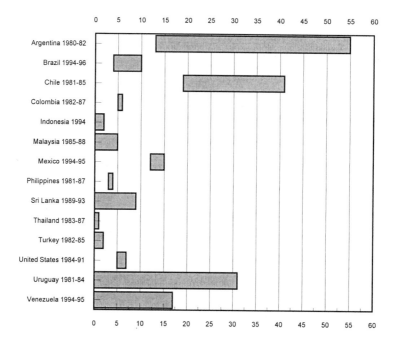

Figure 15.3. Fiscal and Quasi-Fiscal Costs of Banking Crises 1/.

Source: : International Monetary Fund.

1/ Estimated in percent of annual GDP during the restructuring period. Where a range is shown, the lower estimate includes only costs of funds, credit, and bonds injected into the banking system, while the higher estimate includes other fiscal costs, such as exchange rate subsidies.

---

[23] However, the ratio of nonperforming loans is not necessarily a good indicator of bank soundness because banks could be *rolling over* problem loans.

A growing body of evidence suggests that key sources of financial fragility and banking sector weaknesses are *microeconomic* and *institutional failings*. These failings include poor management and weaknesses in the legal framework, inadequate supervision, and perverse incentives and moral hazard created by implicit or explicit government guarantees. In addition, *macroeconomic instability* and *premature liberalization* may have also played an important role.

Microeconomic and Institutional Failings

Poor management within financial institutions is often the first source of fragility. Inadequate internal control procedures, concerted lending, insider dealing, and outright fraud have in many cases led to *excessive risk concentration*—a large proportion of loans allocated to a single borrower (related companies or the banks' own managers), a specific region, or a specific industry. The consequence is often a *poor quality* of loan portfolios and a high ratio of nonperforming loans.[24]

Weaknesses in the *legal framework* have compounded the problems of inadequate management and weak corporate governance, in particular by making it difficult for banks to seize, in case of default, the *collateral* pledged by borrowers on their loans. The absence of effective market discipline (in part resulting from the lack of relevant information about the operations of financial institutions), inadequate prudential regulations, and *supervisory forbearance* have also tended to compound the problem. In many cases supervisors either failed to identify potential weaknesses in banks' balance sheets or did not take appropriate action to force banks to address these weaknesses in a comprehensive and timely fashion. In turn, the *persistence* of these large weaknesses—and inadequate information on the *magnitude* of potential loan losses—affected the effective and uniform enforcement of prudential norms, further delaying the process of strengthening banking supervision and compounding the problems posed by loan losses. As a result, the quality of banks' asset portfolios deteriorated significantly, increasing the vulnerability of the financial system to macroeconomic shocks.

Moral Hazard and Perverse Incentives

The lack of adequate prudential regulation and supervision often leaves too much room for weak financial institutions to take *excessive risks* (as noted above), leading to inefficient intermediation and creating the preconditions for a potential financial crisis. The temptation for banks to *increase the riskiness* of their loan portfolios is in part fostered by the existence of implicit or explicit **government bailout guarantees**, such as **deposit insurance schemes**. Such guarantees create moral hazard problems, that is, weak incentives for banks and borrowers to internalize the consequences of their actions. Such problems tend to be particularly acute when banks and borrowers have low net worth and may

---

[24]Mismatches between assets and liabilities in terms of either currencies or maturities (as discussed later) can also be viewed as a form of mismanagement.

be tempted to "gamble" by engaging in high-return but risky projects.[25]

The adverse incentive effects of implicit government insurance were described for instance by Díaz-Alejandro (1985, p. 18) in a classic review of the financial crises of the early 1980s in Argentina, Chile, and Uruguay that followed financial liberalization:

> "Public opinion," including generals and their aunts, simply [did] not believe that the state would (nor could) allow most depositors to be wiped out by the failure of banks and financial intermediaries. It may be that private financial agents, domestic and foreign lenders, borrowers and intermediaries, whether or not related to generals, (knew) that the domestic political and judicial systems (were) not compatible with [the] laissez-faire commitments [that] a misguided Minister of Finance or Central Bank President may occasionally utter in a moment of dogmatic exaltation. When a crisis hits, agents will reason, bankruptcy courts will break down; when...everyone (who counts) is bankrupt, nobody is!

The increased riskiness of bank portfolios may turn into actual losses when a price bubble bursts or economic activity slows down sharply—as a result either of restrictive macroeconomic policies or adverse external shocks. In such conditions, even loans that are *fully collateralized* can become nonperforming, because the same shock that reduces the borrower's ability to repay may reduce simultaneously the value of the collateral pledged to obtain the loan. For instance, a developer who borrows to invest in real estate and pledges land for collateral would put the lender doubly at risk if property prices experience a sudden collapse. Because banks' own capital generally does not offer sufficient protection against these risks and losses, actual losses often end up being absorbed by the public sector—often at substantial costs, as noted earlier.

The role of **lender of last resort** of the central bank is also a source of moral hazard problems. The rationale for this role is that the central bank should provide liquidity support only to *solvent* but *illiquid banks*, and let *insolvent banks* fail.[26] The reason is that liquidity support to insolvent banks provides perverse incentives and fails to address underlying problems. Abstracting from the issue of whether insolvency problems can be easily distinguished from illiquidity problems in practice, the major problem is that the regulatory authorities cannot credibly commit to such an intervention rule. The reason is the **too-big-to-fail problem**: to avoid a financial crisis, central banks may deviate from their policy and provide liquidity to support large banks, even if they are insolvent. Large banks face therefore perverse incentives.

---

[25]Bhattacharya, Boot, and Thakor (1998) provide a detailed overview of the analytical issues that arise in the context of bank regulation, including measures aimed at reducing moral hazard problems induced by the existence of deposit insurance schemes.

[26]A bank is *solvent* if the value of its assets is greater than the value of its liabilities to depositors and other creditors. A bank is *liquid* as long as it can meet day-to-day operating expenses and withdrawals. A highly leveraged bank can remain liquid even if it is insolvent.

Macroeconomic Instability

As noted on several occasions in previous chapters, macroeconomic instability tends to be high in developing countries. This instability is either induced by inadequate economic management by the government (such as **stop-and-go policies**) or extreme vulnerability to exogenous shocks. Such instability has been associated with serious problems in the financial system, primarily in the banking sector.

The effects of macroeconomic instability on banks operate through both the asset side and the liability side of their balance sheets. Macroeconomic volatility (as measured, for instance, by a highly variable rate of inflation) may considerably distort the accuracy of the rates of return calculated by firms, thereby creating cash-flow problems and repayment difficulties.

More generally, banks' *stock* problems (outstanding amount of nonperforming loans) as well as *flow* problems (operational inefficiencies) tend to be exacerbated by economic downturns. In a highly open economy, as noted in Chapter 7, inconsistent macroeconomic policies tend to exacerbate the volatility of short-term capital flows. To the extent that these flows are intermediated through the banking system, an abrupt reversal can cause a **liquidity crisis** and force banks to default on their obligation to convert deposits into cash at par—a decision that may in turn exacerbate macroeconomic instability. The reasons may be a **maturity mismatch** (the deposit base is *short term*, whereas loans are often for a *longer term*) or a **currency mismatch** (deposits may be in a foreign currency, whereas loans are denominated in the domestic currency). As noted in Chapter 7, greater financial openness and the possibility of abrupt shifts in market sentiment have led to renewed emphasis on maintaining a stable macroeconomic environment. Weak and inefficient banking systems are less able to cope with volatile capital flows and exchange market pressures, and more likely to propagate and magnify the effects of financial crises occurring elsewhere (as a result of **contagion effects**). The implication, again, is to strengthen standards for banking supervision, as discussed next.

Premature Financial Liberalization

There is also evidence that financial liberalization has exacerbated the financial weaknesses present in developing countries. The data compiled by Williamson and Mahar (1998) for more than 30 industrial and developing countries during the 1980s and early 1990s indicated that in more than half of them financial liberalization was followed by a financial crisis. At a more formal level, Demirgüç-Kunt and Detragiache (1998b) constructed an index of financial liberalization (reflecting mostly the deregulation of bank interest rates) for a group of more than 50 developed and developing countries for the period 1980-95 and found that, everything else equal, banking crises were more likely to occur in liberalized financial systems. This relationship was stronger in countries where the institutional environment was weak, particularly in the area of prudential regulation and supervision of financial intermediaries and contract enforcement mechanisms.

Various channels may account for the link between financial liberalization and financial crises. An important element is the fact that prior to financial liberalization, banks and other financial institutions in a number of countries often enjoy substantial *rents*. Financial liberalization leads to *increased competition* for resources and thus a higher marginal cost of funds (as measured by interest rates on bank deposits); in turn, higher funding costs lead to higher lending rates. To compensate for the adverse effect of higher lending rates on the demand for credit, banks often respond by *increasing the riskiness* of their loan portfolios—a strategy that may be exacerbated by the existence of implicit or explicit government bailout guarantees, as noted earlier. The rapid expansion of loans on banks' balance sheets tends also to be associated with a growing concentration of risk exposure to particular sectors (such as the real estate sector) and groups. Again, realized and expected losses impose significant burdens on fiscal and, in some cases, monetary policy as policymakers attempt to preserve financial stability. More generally, if banks are, to begin with, *insolvent*, interest rate liberalization may exacerbate **adverse selection** and **moral hazard effects**, because these banks may be willing to borrow at a very high cost to avoid illiquidity.[27]

The experience of sub-Saharan Africa provides a useful illustration of the potentially adverse effects of premature financial liberalization. As noted by Pill and Pradhan (1995), banks in many sub-Saharan African countries continue to be *publicly owned* and therefore remain susceptible to government interference—even after controls on credit pricing and allocation were formally abolished. Moreover, because of the stock of nonperforming loans inherited from the administratively directed lending programs of the pre-reform period, the *solvency* of many privatized banks has remained dependent on *subsidized credit* from the central bank, even after liberalization. Because banks have remained dependent on the government, and their lending decisions continue to be subject to its discretion, liberalization has done little to improve credit allocation or deepen financial markets in the region.

Another point emphasized by Pill and Pradhan (1995) is that if *competition* among banks in the newly deregulated financial sector is weak, financial liberalization may result in *lower* real deposit rates rather than in higher, positive levels. *Monopolistic banks* can exploit the opportunity offered by the abolition of interest rate controls to widen the margins between their deposit and lending rates to increase profits. Pill and Pradhan argued that the lack of competition explains why in countries like Kenya, Madagascar, and Malawi financial liberalization has in fact led to a *reduction* in the attractiveness of bank deposits to domestic savers, and has so far resulted in little financial deepening in these countries.

These results, of course, do not imply that financial liberalization *per se*

---

[27] In countries where financial liberalization was accompanied by a reduction or removal of restrictions on international capital movements, financial intermediaries took an additional risk (*currency risk*) by increasing their foreign exchange exposure and lending in domestic currency to local borrowers.

should be avoided; rather, what they suggest is that because of its potentially high costs in terms of increased financial fragility, strengthening the financial system is an *important prerequisite* for liberalization to be successful. In cases where administrative constraints are severe (as is the case in many developing countries), a *gradual* process of liberalization may be optimal.

15.5.2 Strengthening Financial Systems

The foregoing discussion suggests that reforming banking systems in developing countries requires a comprehensive approach addressing not only the immediate stock and flow problems of weak and insolvent banks, but also correcting shortcomings in the accounting, legal, regulatory, and supervisory framework.

Bank supervision, in particular, needs to be restructured before financial liberalization in order to cope with the risks that liberalization entails. The globalization of financial markets and the associated increase in the volatility of capital flows has also underscored the importance of strengthening prudential supervision and related information systems in order to deal effectively with interest rate and exchange rate risks, and other banking risks, particularly in the context of capital account liberalization.

Strengthening prudential supervision entails a variety of institutional reforms, including establishing an exposure limit on lending to connected parties (most importantly owners and affiliated companies) and raising *bank capital* to levels commensurate with the volatile macroeconomic environment in many developing countries. **Capital adequacy standards** are particularly needed to compensate for the effect of deposit insurance in weakening market discipline of financial institutions and may be important in mitigating the incentives to take on excessive risk.[28]

In addition to prudential supervision, however, reforming banking systems in developing countries includes a number of other aspects, such as encouraging better public disclosure of banks' financial condition, adopting strict international accounting standards, upgrading banks' internal controls, and legislation to prevent concentration of credit to single borrowers and to ensure arm's length (anonymous) credit allocation decisions. It is also important to bring greater transparency to excessive government involvement or ownership in banking systems (as the example of sub-Saharan Africa illustrates) and redesign official safety nets to include safeguards against strong political pressures for regulatory forbearance.[29] An important question in this context is how to ensure that regulators have the *proper incentives* to intervene. If regulatory action can be interpreted as a signal that the regulatory agency did not perform properly in the past, the agency has an incentive to *cover up* and to be inactive when action

---

[28] However, Rochet (1992) argued that such requirements may distort a bank's investment behavior to such an extent that they may make insolvency more, rather than less, likely.

[29] As discussed in Chapter 6, regulations affecting the assset and liability positions of domestic financial institutions are prudential measures that limit the exchange rate, interest rate, and maturity risk assumed by these institutions, as well as their exposure to sudden changes in capital flows. They can also be viewed as restrictions on capital movements.

is required (Boot and Thakor, 1993).

These reforms, however, take time and require adequate administrative capacity. In many cases, putting in place an adequate system of prudential regulation and effective supervision prior to domestic and external financial liberalization is unlikely to happen. In such conditions, then, there is a strong case for liberalizing the domestic financial system and opening the capital account only gradually. There is thus a *second-best argument* for maintaining some degree of financial repression and limiting capital inflows through various types of controls during a transitional phase.

15.6 Summary

- *Fiscal reform* in many developing countries has led to improvements in the structure of taxation and in tax administration. A number of countries have rationalized and consolidated tax structures to reduce distortionary taxes (particularly taxes on international trade) and have moved toward broad-based consumption taxes. *Public expenditure management* has also been strengthened.

- *Public sector downsizing* has become increasingly important in countries facing budgetary pressures. *Severance pay* is a potentially **perverse selection mechanism**. Because workers differ in unobservable ways, offering severance pay across the board creates an incentive for the most productive workers to leave the public sector and for the less productive ones to stay. Severance pay should be offered only to those workers who are targeted to leave.

- *Fiscal decentralization* can help to improve resource allocation by bringing taxation and spending decisions closer to *voter preferences*. It can also help to make governments more *accountable*. However, it can give rise to *coordination problems*, which may translate into **soft budget constraints**.

- In many developing countries, public pension plans are defined-benefit plans financed on a **pay-as-you go** basis. *Saving* may increase after the establishment of a pay-as-you-go pension system if it induces workers to begin planning for an earlier retirement. In Chile, there are indications that the increase in the retirement age and the fiscal consolidation that accompanied the reforms contributed to the subsequent increase in private saving and the higher output growth rates.

- Advocates of *interest rate liberalization* and abolition of credit ceilings argue that they should lead to an increase in both the quantity of, and the quality of, financial intermediation by the banking system and thereby raise the rate of economic growth. They provide an incentive for borrowers to invest in more productive activities, thereby improving productivity. However, by easing **liquidity constraints**, these measures can lead to a temporary stimulus to consumption and a *reduction*, rather than an increase, in saving. Moreover, the real interest elasticity of total savings is not significantly different from zero for *low-income* countries and remains small in *higher-income* countries; interest rate liberalization may thus have only a limited impact on aggregate savings. Finally, interest rate liberalization may increase the cost of borrowing and interest payments on the domestic public debt and lead to a higher *fiscal deficit*—with consequent inflationary pressures.

- Growing recognition of the substantial economic costs associated with the distortions induced by large differentials between official and parallel exchange rates has led many countries to *unify* their foreign exchange markets. Pinto's (1991) analysis of the unification process emphasizes the view that the loss of the **implicit tax on exports** induced by exchange market unification may lead to a permanently *higher inflation* in the presence of fiscal rigidities.

- There are, however, a variety of implicit taxes and subsidies that must be taken into account in assessing the fiscal effects of exchange market reform. An important issue is to assess the extent to which the use of the official exchange rate for the *valuation of imports* for duty purposes provides an **implicit subsidy** to importers. Pinto's emphasis on the inflationary effect of the loss of the implicit tax on exports is therefore not necessarily warranted. If the reduction in implicit subsidies to importers resulting from levying tariffs at the official exchange rate outweighs the loss in implicit taxes levied on exports repatriated at the official rate, exchange market reform may lead to a *fall* in inflation.

- The perverse nature of the incentive system and regulatory environment is often at the root of banking sector problems in developing countries. The presence of implicit or explicit **government bailout guarantees** (such as **deposit insurance schemes**) creates **moral hazard problems**, that is, weak incentives for banks and borrowers to internalize the consequences of their decisions. Banks, as a result, are often saddled with overly risky loan portfolios.

- The evidence suggests that financial instability in developing countries can be attributed to a wide range of microeconomic and institutional failings, including poor management, an inadequate legal framework, implicit or explicit government guarantees that lead to excessive risk taking (and often translate into large fiscal and quasi-fiscal costs), and macroeconomic instability.

- *Premature financial liberalization* has also played a role in many countries. Perverse incentives and increased risk taking by financial intermediaries in the aftermath of financial liberalization (which translated into a sharp expansion in bank lending and, in some cases, to a growing concentration of loans to particular sectors) have been important sources of financial fragility.

- The speed at which financial liberalization should proceed, the prerequisites for a successful liberalization, and the way financial reforms should be sequenced within an overall reform program are key policy issues. In the absence of improvements in prudential regulation and supervision of the banking system, financial liberalization can be costly and counterproductive. The need for effective prudential supervision may be even greater in a deregulated financial environment than in a regime of financial repression.

- In addition to an adequate regulatory framework, financial liberalization must also be implemented in a stable macroeconomic environment. In particular, to be successful, it may need to be accompanied by *fiscal adjustment* to reduce the need for alternative sources of implicit revenue.

- Other ways to strengthen financial systems include various safeguards that may encourage prudent behavior by banks—including minimum capital standards, criteria for provisioning for nonperforming loans, limits on loan concentration, collateral requirements, and enforcement mechanisms. Financial reporting and disclosure standards are also needed to improve transparency, so that the market and the central bank can play their roles in ensuring financial discipline.

Appendix
Models of Tax Evasion

Limited capabilities to administrate the tax system make tax evasion a wide-spread phenomenon in developing countries. The theoretical literature on tax evasion emphasizes that the level of taxes and the shape of the tax schedule are major factors affecting the decision to evade.[30]

The theoretical literature on tax evasion follows two main approaches: the **expected utility maximization** (EUM) approach, developed by Allingham and Sandmo (1972), and the **expected income maximization** (EIM) approach proposed by Srinivasan (1973).

The EUM approach assumes that the taxpayer has two options:

- to declare his or her *total* actual income, and thus pay the full amount of the taxes due;

- to declare *less* than total actual income—which implies facing a nonzero probability, π, of being detected and penalized.

Given these two options, the taxpayer is assumed to maximize his or her expected utility, $E(U)$. Let Y denote the taxpayer's actual income (assumed exogenous), $0 < \iota < 1$ the statutory tax rate on income (assumed constant), X the income reported to the tax administration, and $0 < \eta \leq 1$ the penalty rate that the taxpayer must face on unreported income, $Y - X$, if detected; expected utility can thus be written as

$$E(U) = (1 - \pi)U(Y - \iota X) + \pi U[Y - \iota X - \eta(Y - X)]. \qquad (A1)$$

The taxpayer chooses reported income, X, to maximize expected utility, Equation (A1). Assuming **decreasing absolute risk aversion** (see the appendix to Chapter 1), Allingham and Sandmo showed that the optimum level of reported income, X^*, responds as follows to changes in ι, η, and π:

$$dX^*/d\iota \gtrless 0, \quad dX^*/d\eta > 0, \quad dX^*/d\pi > 0.$$

The first result implies that a rise in the statutory tax rate on income has an ambiguous effect on the reported value of income. The reason is the interaction between **substitution** and **income effects** associated with a change in the tax rate:

- The substitution effect is *negative* because an increase in ι makes it more profitable (at the margin) to evade taxes.

---

[30]It is common to distinguish tax *avoidance* from tax evasion; the former is legal, whereas the latter is not. From an economic point of view, however, the distinction is less meaningful, because both types of actitivites may have similar fiscal effects.

- The income effect, by contrast, is *positive* because a higher ι lowers (disposable) income; under decreasing absolute risk aversion, this tends to reduce tax evasion.

If the degree of absolute risk aversion is assumed constant, rather than increasing, a rise in the statutory tax rate would unambiguously *reduce* reported income.

The second and third results imply that a rise in the penalty rate, η, or the probability of detection, π, have an unambiguously positive effect on reported income and thus a negative effect on tax evasion, as measured by $Y - X^*$. These effects continue to hold regardless of whether the degree of absolute risk aversion is assumed constant, decreasing, or increasing.

The EIM approach assumes that the objective of the taxpayer is to maximize the expected value of his income, $E(Y)$, after taxes and (possible) penalties. The taxpayer is thus, in contrast to the EUM approach, assumed to be **risk neutral**. Following Srinivasan (1973), let $0 < x < 1$ be the proportion by which income is unreported, $\tau(\cdot)$ the *tax function* based on the reported value of income—Y if total income is reported, or $(1 - x)Y$ if evasion occurs—and $h(x)$ the *penalty function* on tax offenders, which depends on the proportion of income that goes undeclared. Thus, the quantity $h(x)xY$ is the income penalty assessed on the taxpayer if he is caught evading. Formally, the taxpayer chooses the level of reported income so as to maximize

$$E(Y) = (1 - \pi)[Y - \tau[(1 - x)Y]] + \pi[Y - \tau(Y) - h(x)xY].$$

Suppose that the tax function $\tau(\cdot)$ is a positive, increasing, and convex function of declared income–that is, $\tau > 0$, $0 < \tau' < 1$, and $\tau'' \geq 0$. The tax system is therefore **progressive**. Suppose also that the penalty function $h(x)$ is a positive, increasing, and convex function of the proportion by which income is unreported; thus, $h > 0$, $h' > 0$, and $h'' \geq 0$.[31] Under these assumptions, Srinivasan showed that the optimum proportion of unreported income, x^*, responds as follows to changes in π and Y:

$$dx^*/d\pi < 0, \quad \left.\frac{dx^*}{dY}\right|_{\pi \text{ given}} > 0.$$

The first result indicates that an increase in the probability of detection lowers the proportion of undeclared income. The second result indicates that, given a progressive tax function ($\tau'' > 0$), and for π given, the larger the level of income, the larger the optimal proportion of income that is undeclared. This result, however, holds only when the probability of detection is given; Srinivasan showed that if π is an increasing function of income and the tax rate is proportional (so that $\tau'' = 0$), the proportion of understated income will *fall* as total income rises.[32]

---

[31] Imposing $\tau'' \geq 0$ and $h'' \geq 0$ are necessary in Srinivasan's model to ensure the existence of an optimum solution.

[32] Srinivasan's analysis also implies that an increase in the penalty rate lowers tax evasion and increases reported income, as in the EUM approach.

The source of the differences in the qualitative predictions of the two basic EUM and EIM models lies in their treatment of the taxpayer's objective function—not in differences in the treatment of taxation and penalties (proportional in one case, progressive in the other). The Allingham-Sandmo model, which explicitly accounts for attitude toward risk (and therefore excludes a monotonic relation between expected income and utility), can be viewed as a more general approach.

The EUM and EIM approaches have been extended in a number of directions (see Cowell, 1990, and Pyle, 1991). There is general consensus that *penalties*, if properly enforced, can deter tax evasion. There is also agreement that a sufficiently high *probability of detection* tends to reduce the propensity to evade. However, several theoretical contributions have shown that the relationship between an increase in *statutory tax rates* and tax evasion can be either positive or negative; the outcome depends, in particular, on the manner in which penalties are assessed and the shape of the tax schedule. Yitzhaki (1974), for instance, showed that if the penalty imposed on evaders is levied on the evaded tax liabilities (rather than on the amount of unreported income, as assumed by Allingham and Sandmo), an increase in the tax rate will unambiguously reduce evasion. The reason is that in this alternative case the penalty rate will increase *proportionally* with the statutory tax rate, ι. A rise in ι has therefore no substitution effect (as discussed earlier), only a pure income effect. Using also the EUM approach, Koskela (1983) found that a compensated increase in the tax rate *raises* tax evasion if penalties are imposed on the amount of income evaded, whereas it *reduces* tax evasion if penalties are imposed on the amount of income evaded.[33] When penalties are imposed on undeclared income, the negative income effect associated with an increase in the statutory tax rate is offset by a lump-sum transfer from the government, leaving only the positive substitution effect. On the contrary, when penalties are levied on evaded tax liabilities, the amount of penalty will increase proportionally with the tax, as argued by Yitzhaki (1974); an increase in the statutory tax rate has therefore no substitution effect, only a negative income effect.

---

[33] In Koskela's analysis, a compensated increase in the tax rate is a rise in ι that is accompanied by a lump-sum transfer that is such that the expected tax revenue of the authorities remains unchanged.

Chapter 16

Adjustment and External Debt in Low-Income Countries

The debt crisis of the early 1980s had a severe impact on the economic performance of both middle- and low-income developing countries. In many cases, the lack of access to world capital markets led to a surge in inflationary finance of fiscal deficits, a slowdown in investment, and reduced rates of economic growth. But although many of the most severely affected middle-income economies were subsequently able to regain access to world capital markets (in part as a result of international initiatives such as the *Brady Plan*), servicing external debt continues to be a key concern for policymakers in low-income countries. The inability of the poorest of these countries (many of them in sub-Saharan Africa) to meet their debt-service obligations has led in recent years to a variety of new proposals aimed at ensuring that the debt burden does not hamper capital formation and economic growth.

This chapter examines various policy issues associated with the process of growth and adjustment in a highly indebted environment. It begins by presenting a simple endogenous growth model that captures the links between external debt and capital accumulation in a world of imperfect capital markets, and analyzes the short- and long-run response of the economy to fiscal adjustment. Part 2 discusses the notions of debt overhang and debt Laffer curve, which have proved useful to understand the adverse effect of a high burden of debt on investment and production incentives and to justify debt relief. Part 3 reviews various practical measures of a country's debt burden (essentially ratios of debt and debt service to various macroeconomic aggregates) and discusses a more formal approach to assessing the debt burden, namely, external solvency, which dwells on the intertemporal budget constraint of an open economy. The last two parts of the chapter review the mechanics of debt reschedulings as well as recent international initiatives aimed at alleviating the debt burden of the poorest countries in the world.[1]

16.1   Growth, External Debt, and Adjustment

As discussed in Chapter 1, a high level of foreign debt can have adverse effects
of savings and investment. In turn, the strong correlation between savings,
capital accumulation, and growth documented in Chapter 10 suggests that a
high burden of debt can severely constrain growth rates and limit improvements
in standards of living. To illustrate the joint dynamics of foreign debt, capital
accumulation, and growth, this section uses an extension of the learning-by-
doing model of endogenous growth developed by Villanueva (1994) and discussed
in Chapter 11.[2] The relative simplicity of the model makes it a convenient
framework for also analyzing the links between domestic adjustment policies,
foreign borrowing, and growth.

As in Chapter 11, consider the Cobb-Douglas production function

$$Y = K^{\alpha}(AL)^{1-\alpha}, \quad 0 < \alpha < 1, \tag{16.1}$$

where Y is the flow of output, K the stock of capital, L the number of workers,
and A the effectiveness of labor. In intensive form, Equation (16.1) can be
written as

$$y = k^{\alpha}, \tag{16.2}$$

where $y = Y/AL$ and $k = K/AL$ is the capital-effective labor ratio.

Let D^* denote the country's net stock of external debt. National income, Q,
is given by

$$Q = Y - r^* D^*,$$

where r^* is the *cost of borrowing* that the country faces on world capital markets.
National income per unit of effective labor, q, can thus be written as

$$q = k^{\alpha} - r^* d^*, \tag{16.3}$$

where $d^* = D^*/AL$ is foreign debt per unit of effective labor. Changes in net
external debt are equal to foreign saving, S^*:

$$\dot{D}^* = S^*. \tag{16.4}$$

Domestic saving, S, is the sum of private saving, S^p, and government saving,
S^g, which are defined as follows.

---

[1] The debt problems of *middle-income* countries and the various measures aimed at alleviating them (such as the Brady Plan) are not discussed here. For a retrospective on the debt
crisis of the early 1980s and the performance of the Brady Plan since its inception, see Cline
(1995) and Bowe and Dean (1997).

[2] The appendix to this chapter reviews briefly the alternative perspective on debt issues
developed in the literature analyzing *stages in the balance of payments*, which takes foreign
saving as an *outcome* rather than a constraint.

- Private saving is a constant fraction, s, of disposable income, given by $1 - \iota$, where $0 < \iota < 1$ is the tax rate, times national income. Thus

$$S^p = s(1 - \iota)Q. \tag{16.5}$$

- Government saving is the difference between tax revenue (a fraction, ι, of national income) and government spending, G. Thus

$$S^g = \iota Y - G. \tag{16.6}$$

Changes in the capital stock, assuming a depreciation rate of δ, are given by

$$\dot{K} = I - \delta K. \tag{16.7}$$

In equilibrium, domestic investment must be financed by domestic and foreign saving:

$$I = S = (S^p + S^g) + S^*. \tag{16.8}$$

Using Equations (16.4) and (16.7), this condition becomes

$$\dot{K} + \delta K - \dot{D}^* = S. \tag{16.9}$$

Labor is assumed to grow at an exogenous rate:

$$\dot{L}/L = n, \tag{16.10}$$

whereas, following Villanueva's (1994) **learning-by-doing** specification (see Chapter 12), the efficiency of labor changes according to

$$\dot{A} = \theta\left(\frac{K}{L}\right) + \gamma A, \quad \theta > 0.$$

This equation, together with Equation (16.10), implies that the growth rate of labor in efficient units is given by

$$\frac{\dot{A}}{A} + \frac{\dot{L}}{L} = \theta k + n + \gamma. \tag{16.11}$$

The rate of change of foreign debt is assumed to depend on the difference between the marginal productivity of capital, $\alpha k^{\alpha-1}$, net of depreciation, δ, and the marginal cost of funds on world capital markets, r^*:

$$\dot{D}^*/D^* = \beta(\alpha k^{\alpha-1} - \delta - r^*), \quad \beta > 0, \tag{16.12}$$

where β measures the speed of adjustment.

In turn, the marginal cost of funds on world capital markets is assumed to consist of a *risk-free rate*, r_f^*, and a *risk premium*, ρ, which depends on the economy's stock of debt in effective units of labor, d^*:

$$r^* = r_f^* + \rho(d^*, \lambda), \quad \rho_{d^*}, \rho_\lambda > 0, \tag{16.13}$$

where λ represents a shift factor capturing exogenous changes in market perceptions of country risk. This specification captures the idea that the higher the level of foreign debt, the higher the *probability of default*, and thus the higher the cost of borrowing for the domestic country.[3] It is also plausible to assume that the premium rises at an increasing rate (so that $\rho_{d^*d^*} > 0$) and that the domestic economy may lose complete access to world capital markets for a level of debt that is sufficiently high. For the moment, however, it will be assumed that the economy operates in a region in which complete rationing does not occur.

As shown in Chapter 11, changes in the capital-effective labor ratio can be written as

$$\dot{k} = \frac{\dot{K}}{AL} - (\frac{\dot{A}}{A} + \frac{\dot{L}}{L})k,$$

that is, using Equation (16.11):

$$\dot{k} = \frac{\dot{K}}{AL} - [\theta k + (n + \gamma)]k,$$

or, using Equation (16.9):

$$\dot{k} = \frac{(S^P + S^g) - \delta K + \dot{D}^*}{AL} - [\theta k + (n + \gamma)]k.$$

This equation becomes, using Equations (16.5) and (16.6):

$$\dot{k} = [\iota + s(1 - \iota)]q + (\frac{\dot{D}^* - G}{AL}) - [\theta k + (n + \gamma + \delta)]k. \qquad (16.14)$$

Using Equation (16.12), the term $\dot{D}^*/AL$ in the above expression can be written as

$$\frac{\dot{D}^*}{AL} = (\frac{\dot{D}^*}{D^*})(\frac{D^*}{AL}) = \beta(\alpha k^{\alpha-1} - \delta - r^*)d^*.$$

Using this result, setting $\phi = \iota + s(1 - \iota)$ and $g = G/AL$ in Equation (16.14) yields

$$\dot{k} = \phi q + \beta(\alpha k^{\alpha-1} - \delta - r^*)d^* - g - [\theta k + (n + \gamma + \delta)]k.$$

Using Equation (16.3) to substitute out for q in this equation yields

$$\dot{k} = \phi k^\alpha + \{\beta(\alpha k^{\alpha-1} - \delta) - (\phi + \beta)r^*\} d^* - g - [\theta k + (n + \gamma + \delta)]k, \qquad (16.15)$$

with r^* given by Equation (16.13) and g assumed to be constant.

Finally, it can be noted that

$$\frac{\dot{d}^*}{d^*} = \frac{\dot{D}^*}{D^*} - (\frac{\dot{A}}{A} + \frac{\dot{L}}{L}) = \beta(\alpha k^{\alpha-1} - \delta - r^*) - \theta k - (n + \gamma). \qquad (16.16)$$

---

[3] The analysis could be extended to the case in which the risk premium depends on the ratio of the country's debt to its national income, D^*/Q.

Equations (16.15) and (16.16) consist of a system of two differential equations in the capital-effective labor ratio, k, and the external debt-effective labor ratio, d^*, which can be linearized around the steady state to give

$$\begin{bmatrix} \dot{d}^* \\ \dot{k} \end{bmatrix} = \begin{bmatrix} a_{11} & a_{12} \\ a_{21} & a_{22} \end{bmatrix} \begin{bmatrix} d^* - \tilde{d}^* \\ k - \tilde{k} \end{bmatrix}, \qquad (16.17)$$

where

$$a_{11} = -\tilde{d}^* \beta \rho_d < 0,$$

$$a_{12} = \tilde{d}^* [\beta \alpha (\alpha - 1) \tilde{k}^{\alpha-2} - \theta \tilde{k}] < 0,$$

$$a_{21} = -\tilde{d}^* (\phi + \beta) \rho_d - \phi r^* < 0$$

$$a_{22} = \phi \alpha \tilde{k}^{\alpha-1} + \tilde{d}^* \beta \alpha (\alpha - 1) \tilde{k}^{\alpha-2} - 2\theta \tilde{k} - (n + \gamma).$$

The sign of the coefficient a_{22} is in general ambiguous. It will be assumed in what follows that $a_{22} < 0$; a sufficient (although not necessary) condition for this restriction to hold is for the speed of adjustment of external debt, β, to be sufficiently large:

$$\beta > (\frac{\phi}{1 - \alpha}) \frac{\tilde{d}^*}{\tilde{k}},$$

or, equivalently, the initial debt-to-capital ratio must not be too large ($\tilde{d}^*/\tilde{k} < \beta(1 - \alpha)/\phi$).

A graphical illustration of the economy's equilibrium path is provided in Figure 16.1. Curve DD denotes the combinations of d^* and k for which the stock of debt in effective units of labor is constant over time ($\dot{d}^* = 0$), whereas curve KK depicts the combinations of d^* and k for which the capital-effective labor ratio remains constant over time ($\dot{k} = 0$). Stability requires DD to be steeper than KK.[4] The steady-state values of d and k are given at point E.

To illustrate the functioning of the above model, consider an adjustment strategy that calls for a permanent reduction in the ratio of government spending to effective labor, g.[5] As illustrated in Figure 16.2, this shock leads to an upward shift in the KK curve. In the long run, the reduction in government spending increases government saving and reduces the level of foreign borrowing required at the initial levels of domestic saving and investment. The reduction in debt also reduces debt service payments—both directly and indirectly, the latter as a result of the fall in the risk premium—thereby raising national disposable income and thus private saving. The net effect is higher investment and a higher capital stock (measured in effective units of labor) in the long run. During the transition

---

[4]Stability requires that the *trace* of the matrix of coefficients in Eq. (16.17), which is equal to the sum of the roots, be negative ($a_{11} + a_{22} < 0$), and that the *determinant* of that matrix be positive, that is, $a_{11}a_{22} - a_{12}a_{21} > 0$. The first condition is always satisfied, given the assumption that $a_{22} < 0$. The second can be rewritten as $a_{11}/a_{12} > a_{21}/a_{22}$ and is the condition on the slopes of DD and KK given in the text.

[5]Other interesting experiments with the model include an increase in the risk-free interest rate, r_f^*, or in the autonomous component of the risk premium, λ. As discussed by Eaton (1993), the presumption in many endogenous growth models with foreign debt is that an increase in the world interest rate lowers the rate of economic growth.

to the new steady-state equilibrium (located at point E' in Figure 16.2), foreign borrowing falls continuously, whereas the capital-effective labor ratio increases monotonically. The higher capital-effective labor ratio is also associated with a higher growth rate of output per capita in the steady state, which, as shown in Chapter 12, is given by

$$\tilde{g}_{Y/L} = \theta \tilde{k} + \gamma.$$

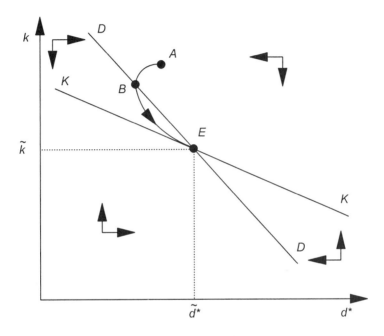

Figure 16.1. Foreign Debt and the Capital-Effective Labor Ratio: Long-Run Equilibrium.

Thus, fiscal adjustment does not only reduce the foreign debt burden; by raising the capital-effective labor ratio, it also has *permanent* (and positive) growth effects.

In practice, as noted earlier, the risk premium that low-income countries may face on world capital markets may be large enough to lead to complete credit rationing. This may explain why, as noted in previous chapters, low-income economies often tend to grow slowly—despite having a high marginal return to capital.[6] It has been argued that, in such conditions, **foreign aid** may lead to higher growth rates through two channels:

---

[6] The Solow-Swan model, for instance, predicts high growth rates during the transition to the steady state if the marginal return to capital is high.

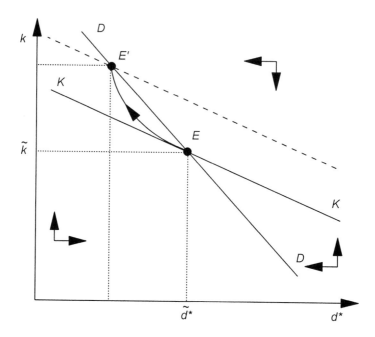

Figure 16.2. Growth, Foreign Debt, and Fiscal Adjustment.

- by leading to a direct increase in public investment and raising the level of the capital stock or the efficiency with which the existing stock is utilized;

- by inducing policy changes that lead to reduced distortions, and thus indirectly stimulate private investment. This latter channel, however, is more debatable, because the donor-recipient relationship may be *noncooperative*.[7]

Two recent studies attempting to measure the impact of foreign aid on growth are those of Boone (1996) and Burnside and Dollar (1997). Boone found that aid has no effect on investment or growth in a sample of developing countries. He argued that in countries in which politicians maximize the welfare of a wealthy elite (unconditional) foreign aid will have a limited effect on standards of living—because it is usually not optimal for politicians to adjust distortionary policies as a result of an increase in aid flows. Burnside and Dollar (1997) considered not only foreign aid but also a variety of indicators of

---

[7]In such conditions, as noted by Svensson (1997), moral hazard problems can lead to aid having little impact on the problems it is intended to alleviate. In particular, aid may simply lead to a relaxation of the budget constraint of the recipient government, without having much impact on the amount of that budget that is used for investment.

economic policies in their growth regressions. They used data for 56 developing countries over six four-year periods over 1970-93, and (in contrast to other studies in the literature) provide a more accurate estimate of foreign aid by adding to outright grants the grant components of concessional loans. Aid was found to have a positive impact on growth only in countries where economic policies were sound—as measured by low inflation, low fiscal deficits, and a high degree of openness. They also found no evidence that aid has had any systematic effect on economic policies, and that aid (particularly on a bilateral basis) had a strong positive impact on government consumption, which in turn has no positive effect on growth. An issue that remains unresolved in the empirical literature, however, is that of *causality* (as discussed in Chapter 13); aid may cause policy changes (owing, say, to conditionality) but policy changes may also result in higher levels of foreign assistance—by increasing donors' confidence in the country's economic prospects.

16.2   The Debt Overhang and the Debt Laffer Curve

A key channel through which a large level of foreign debt affects economic performance in the model of the previous section is the risk premium charged by foreign lenders in their attempt to internalize the risk of default. Several economists have pointed out, however, that the medium-term uncertainty associated with a high burden of debt may have an adverse effect on *investment incentives* domestically—a phenomenon that the model did not capture. Helpman (1989), Krugman (1988), and Sachs (1989) argued that, beyond a certain point, a high level of external debt acts as a marginal tax on investment because a fraction of the gains in output resulting from increased capital formation accrues to creditors in the form of debt repayment. To the extent that individual investors internalize the tax effect of the debt—an assumption that is not as innocuous as it seems—the fear of appropriation will reduce the expected after-tax rate of return on capital. High indebtedness can therefore lead to low investment, low growth, and ultimately to low repayment. Highly indebted countries suffer, in this case, from a **debt overhang**.

More formally, a debt overhang refers to a situation in which the *expected repayment* on foreign debt falls short of its *contractual value*. To illustrate, consider the case of a country whose current level of foreign debt, D^*, must be repaid in full in the next period. Lenders (through *trade sanctions*, for instance) can enforce repayment but only up to a certain extent; the debtor country can always keep a minimum amount, C_{min}, of domestic output, Y, for domestic consumption. Repayment, R, is thus given by

$$R = \min(D^*, Y - C_{min}).$$

Suppose that the production function is given by

$$Y_s = u_s I^\alpha, \quad 0 < \alpha < 1,$$

where s denotes the *state of nature*, I investment output, and u_s a productivity shock that can take two values: a high value $u_s = u_H$ in good states of nature, and a low value $u_s = u_L < u_H$ in bad states of nature. Suppose that there is a physical upper limit on the amount of investment that the country can achieve, I_{max}, and that the two states are so different that there is no overlap of output, that is,

$$Y_L = u_L I_{max}^\alpha < u_H I^\alpha.$$

In this setting, a debt overhang exists if

$$D^* > Y_L - C_{min},$$

because in this case the debt cannot be fully serviced in the bad state of nature. To see how the debt overhang reduces the incentive to invest, suppose that

$$Y_L - C_{min} < D^* < Y_H - C_{min}.$$

In the good state of nature the debt is fully repaid, whereas in the bad state of nature repayment is equal to realized output minus the minimum consumption level. Let π denotes the probability of the good state; for simplicity, this probability is taken to be constant. Because $D^* > Y_L - C_{min}$, the expected marginal return to an additional unit of investment is thus

$$\pi u_H \alpha I^{\alpha-1} + (1 - \pi) \cdot 0,$$

whereas, in the absence of a debt overhang, the expected marginal return to an additional unit of investment is

$$\pi u_H \alpha I^{\alpha-1} + (1 - \pi) u_L \alpha I^{\alpha-1} > \pi u_H \alpha I^{\alpha-1},$$

which implies that investment will never take place. In addition, in the case where $D^* > Y_H - C_{min}$, the expected marginal return to an additional unit of investment is actually zero and the incentive to invest disappears completely.[8]

An alternative way of presenting the concept of a debt overhang is through the derivation of the **debt Laffer curve**, which relates a country's nominal debt obligations to the *market's expectation* of the repayments that these loans will generate.

Let D^* denote once again the contractual value of debt, and V the expected resource transfer that the country is expected to make to service it. The relationship between D^* and V, the debt Laffer curve, is illustrated in Figure

---

[8] However, Aizenman and Borensztein (1993) showed that, in a *strategic investment frame-work*, the effect of the overhang on the incentive to invest can be ambiguous. In particular, there are conditions under which the overhang acts as a *subsidy* to (that is, increases the incentives for) investment. In their model, if a debtor is unable to meet its repayment obligations, then the level of repayment is determined by a *bargaining game*. If domestic capital is a good substitute for imported inputs, the threat of trade sanctions (or autarky) loses its effectiveness. Thus, it is possible that an increase in investment (which increases the stock of domestic capital) strengthens the country's bargaining position and therefore reduces its level of repayment. In such a case high indebtedness may raise the incentive for investment.

16.3. At low levels of D^*, expected repayments increase one for one with the contractual value of debt. The first segment of the debt Laffer curve, OA, is thus along the 45-degree line. As D^* increases, however, the risk of default rises as well, and the probability of repayment, θ, falls below unity. Beyond point E (corresponding to $\tilde{D}^*$) contractual levels of debt and the risk of default are so high that V begins to decline. Additional amounts of debt actually *lower* expected repayments. At that stage, a country is said to be on the *wrong side* of the debt Laffer curve; the disincentive effects on potential investors are so strong that a reduction in the stock of debt would result in an increase in its market value. In such conditions, a reduction in the **debt tax rate**—that is, the proportion of output that is allocated to servicing the debt—would translate into an increase in actual debt payments (Sachs, 1989).

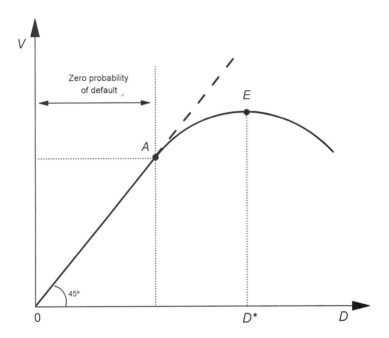

Figure 16.3. The Debt Laffer Curve.
Source: Adapted from Krugman (1989b).

Froot and Krugman (1989) attempted to estimate the position on the debt Laffer curve of various countries in a group of 35 heavily indebted countries (12 of which were low-income countries), by examining the relationship between the *secondary market price* of debt and the face value of debt claims. Multiplying the existing stock of debt by the secondary market price provides an estimate of market expectations of repayments. A debt overhang exists when further increases in obligations are discounted at such a high rate (as implied by a sufficiently large fall in the secondary price) that they are associated with a *decline* in the market value of the debt stock. They found that for 5 of the 12 low-income countries (Bolivia, Madagascar, Nicaragua, Sudan, and Zambia) debt-to-export ratios were sufficiently high to place these countries on the *wrong side* of their debt Laffer curves.[9] However, there are two problems with these results:

- The Froot-Krugman technique cannot be applied to low-income countries for which there is no secondary debt market. This is often because of the relatively small proportion of debt owed to commercial creditors by these countries.

- Claessens (1990), using data for 29 countries for the period 1986-88, found that although the present value of repayment, measured by the secondary market price, is concave with respect to the face value of outstanding debt, there are very few cases (actually, six countries) for which it actually begins to slope downward.

In a more recent study, Deshpande (1997) examined the investment experience of 13 highly indebted countries (including Algeria, Argentina, and Côte d'Ivoire) during the period 1971-92. Deshpande argued that a debt overhang has an adverse effect on investment through two channels:

- a direct disincentive effect, which results from the *fear of appropriation* of funds invested (or the returns from the investment) for the purpose of debt servicing, as described earlier;

- an indirect effect through the *adjustment measures* undertaken to face (or avoid) debt-servicing difficulties—such as cuts in imports (including reductions in imported capital goods) and reductions in public sector investment required to reduce fiscal deficits.[10]

The second argument suggests that to the extent that public and private capital outlays are *complementary* (as discussed in Chapter 1), a fiscal adjustment program that brings about a fall in public capital outlays would also tend to reduce private investment.[11] Deshpande found that there is a significantly negative relationship between the level of external debt and investment. Similar results were obtained by Elbadawi, Ndulu and Ndung'u (1997), in a study focusing on sub-Saharan Africa.

The foregoing discussion therefore suggests that eliminating the debt overhang in a highly indebted country may create renewed incentives for capital

---

[9] The other low-income countries included in the Froot-Krugman sample were Côte d'Ivoire, Honduras, Liberia, Nigeria, Senegal, Togo, and the former Zaire.

[10] As pointed out by Krugman (1988), there is also an *illiquidity effect*, which results from the fact that a debt overhang may shut countries out of world capital markets—preventing them from borrowing to finance high-yielding investments.

[11] At the same time, however, if fiscal consolidation is accompanied by a reduction in (unproductive) government spending, it may lead to an expansion in private investment—by reducing, for instance, the demand for credit by the public sector.

formation, which can benefit *both* the country itself as well as its creditors. In general, for debt relief to benefit creditors, that is, for expected repayment V to increase despite the decline in the contractual value of foreign debt from D^* to $D^* - x$, the increase in the secondary market price of debt (as measured by the ratio of V over the contractual value of debt) must be large enough to outweigh the potential loss to creditors that would occur *ex post* if the state of nature turns out to be so favorable that full repayment would have occurred in the absence of debt relief. Formally, assuming as before that the relation between output and investment is of the form $Y = I^\alpha$, this condition can be written as (Krugman, 1989*b*):

$$\frac{dV}{dx} = -\theta + (1 - \theta)\frac{dI}{dx}\alpha I^{\alpha-1} > 0,$$

where dI/dx measures the increase in investment induced by debt relief, and $\alpha I^{\alpha-1}$ the marginal product of investment in terms of increased debt payment capacity. The first term, θ, represents the loss incurred by creditors in good states of nature, whereas the second measures the expected payoff resulting from debt relief and higher investment. In Figure 16.3, $dV/dD^* < 0$ beyond point A, and $dV/dx > 0$. In the particular case where $dI/dx = 0$,

$$\frac{dV}{dx} = -\theta < 0.$$

Thus, without any induced effect on investment, debt relief would never be optimal from the point of view of creditors.[12]

It is important to stress, however, that the argument for reducing the debt burden of highly indebted countries does not depend only on the existence of a debt overhang. The problem of providing incentives to repay is relevant only insofar as a country has the **ability to repay** (see below). Low growth rates in heavily indebted countries may make full repayment of their outstanding level of debt impossible despite any incentives.[13] To the extent, for instance, that debt relief lowers the *risk premium* charged to borrowers on world capital markets, it may have a direct effect on growth (as indicated in the previous section) and expected repayment.

16.3   Measuring the Debt Burden

A common practice to evaluate the debt burden and the sustainability of the external position of a country is to examine the evolution of the ratios of debt and debt service to various indicators of economic performance. When these

---

[12] As noted by Bowe and Dean (1997, p. 34) these formulas do not account for some of the indirect benefits associated with debt relief, such as the reduction in the costs of default, negotiations with creditors, and enforcement of penalties.

[13] Warner (1993) argued that slow growth in highly indebted middle-income developing countries led to debt difficulties during the 1980s, rather than the reverse.

ratios are so high as to make a country unable to meet its contractual debt-service payments and resort to debt rescheduling, and the ratios are expected to remain at high levels, the external position is deemed unsustainable.

Specifically, conventional measures of the debt burden include

- The ratio of the *stock of debt to output* (or exports of goods and services). This indicator can be misleading to the extent that it fails to capture the effects of new financing and of debt relief on more concessional terms, that is, lower interest rates and longer repayment periods.

- The ratio of *actual debt service to exports*, which captures the impact of debt-service obligations on foreign exchange cash flow. This measure, which is also viewed as a measure of a country's *foreign exchange constraint*, takes into account debt relief provided by debt-service reschedulings (as well as debt cancellations, see below) and arrears on payments. A limitation of this indicator is that, given the uncertain nature of debt relief, a low value may reflect an **unwillingness to pay** (see below).

- The ratio of *scheduled interest payments to exports*, which measures the ongoing cost of the accumulated stock of debt.

The second and third measures tend to diverge as a result of *increased concessionality* in new lending and rescheduling agreements, which often lead to changes in the concessionality of interest rates and changes in grace and repayment periods (see below).

Two conventional measures aim at capturing the *fiscal impact* of the external debt burden:

- The ratio of *scheduled interest payments* to *government revenue*, which measures the country's capacity to repay as scheduled.[14] This ratio is often considered low if it is less than 0.2, moderate if it is between 0.2 and 0.5, and high if it is above 0.5. However, a high value may simply reflect the country's inability to collect revenue.

- The ratio of *scheduled interest payments* to *government expenditure*, which measures the constraint imposed by debt servicing on the country's ability to expand other (current and capital) expenditures.

An alternative to the conventional measures defined above is to compare the discounted present value of *future debt-service obligations* with the discounted present value of *future export receipts*. The discounted present value of debt is obtained by taking all future debt service obligations (including interest payments at the original rate of the loan and amortization payments) until full repayment of the debt, and dividing them by a factor based on a given *discount rate*. If the discount rate is equal to the original interest rate of the loan, the

---

[14]Government revenue in this definition is typically taken to refer only to *permanent* resources, and therefore excludes foreign grants and privatization proceeds.

present value will be equal to the face value of the debt. If the discount rate used is higher than the original interest rate of the loan, future repayments will matter less and the present value will be lower. The present value of future export receipts is obtained in a similar fashion and requires estimates of the growth rate of exports until the horizon of the debt.

A variant of this measure, often used by the World Bank, is the ratio of the present value of *future debt-service payments* to *current exports*. To the extent that the expected future growth rate of exports is higher than the discount rate, this variant would lead to a higher ratio than the present value debt-to-export ratio. Practitioners often consider that a good rule of thumb for this ratio to be consistent with debt sustainability (and thus avoid default or reschedulings, as discussed below) is about 200 percent.

An attractive feature of these alternative indicators is that they take into account the *concessionality* or *grant element* of debt obligations—that is, the fact that loans may be contracted at a rate of interest that is substantially below the prevailing market rate. The present value approach, in particular, can be used to measure the *grant element* of a concessional loan. In that case, the debt service flow is calculated at the concessional rate but is discounted at the higher market rate. The face value of the debt is higher than its present value, and the difference measures the grant element.

However, these indicators are subject to three major weaknesses:

- Data requirements can be quite complex. Estimates of future export receipts needed to construct the ratio of scheduled interest payments to exports, for instance, may be surrounded by considerable *uncertainty* over volume flows and world prices.

- The results can be highly sensitive to the *discount rate* assumed to calculate present values. Applying a discount rate that is *higher* than the original interest rate (concessional or not) on a loan would give a present value that is lower than the face value of the loan, thus understating the actual burden of debt for debtor countries.

- The calculated ratio does no provide information about the *debt-service profile*—which may be of paramount importance for a country contemplating a rescheduling agreement and requiring an assessment of the immediate cash-flow requirements of debt-service obligations associated with alternative options.

Figures 16.4 to 16.8 show both conventional and present-value-based indicators of the debt burden for developing countries. Figures 16.4 and 16.5 show external debt service as a ratio to GDP for a representative group of developing countries. For many countries, not only are these ratios high, they have actually *increased* between 1990 and 1995. For the group of about 40 countries currently classified as **heavily indebted poor countries** (HIPCs) by the International Monetary Fund and the World Bank (see below), the situation is of even greater concern.[15] The external debt of these countries reached $207 billion at the end of 1996, or about 1.5 times their combined GNP. The average growth rate of GDP for the group as a whole was 2.2 percent between 1985 and 1990 and only 1 percent during 1990-95, well below the rate of population growth of 2.7 percent. As indicated in Figure 16.6, the ratio of the present value of foreign debt to exports reached very high levels for most countries in this group, with an average ratio of about 450 percent in 1995. The ratio of actual debt service payments to exports was 17 percent in 1995 for developing countries as a whole, but exceeded 20 percent for the HIPCs. The ratio of actual debt service to government revenue (excluding grants) amounted to more than 70 percent for a country like Uganda during the period 1992-94. Although Figures 16.7 and 16.8 do not suggest a direct and close relationship between either the ratio of debt to GDP and per capita growth rates, or paid debt service in proportion of exports and per capita growth rates, for this group of countries over a relatively recent period, the evidence (as discussed in Chapter 1) does suggest the existence of an *indirect effect* through investment, in line with the debt overhang argument presented earlier.[16]

An alternative approach to assessing the debt burden and its sustaiability is to focus on **external solvency** in a way that is analogous to the assessment of fiscal solvency (see Chapter 3). As derived in Chapter 8, the basic identity defining the *current account deficit* in an open economy is, normalizing the exchange rate to unity,

$$CA \equiv D^* - D^*_{-1} = -(Y - A) - NT + i^* D^*_{-1}, \qquad (16.18)$$

where Y is nominal GDP, D^* net external debt (that is, gross debt minus gross private assets and official reserves), A domestic absorption (the sum of private and public expenditure on goods and services), NT net transfer receipts from the rest of the world, and i^* the interest rate on foreign liabilities. This identity relates the current account deficit (which is algebraically equal to the flow increase in external liabilities) to the difference between total expenditure (absorption and interest payments on foreign debt) to the economy's aggregate income at the end of period t, which consists of domestic income plus net transfers from abroad.

As also shown in Chapter 8, the trade balance surplus, TB (which is equal to the difference between exports and imports of goods and services), is equal to GDP minus domestic absorption:

$$TB = Y - A.$$

---

[15]The definition of a low-income country follows the World Bank and is based on a gross national product per capita being equal to, or less than, a threshold level measured in US dollars. In the early 1990s, for instance, the threshold level was around U.S. $600.

[16]It should be noted that all of the indicators reviewed earlier are typically calculated on the basis of the *consolidated public sector* debt; they generally do not include *private debts* that are *publicly guaranteed*, implicitly or explicitly. In many cases, the fiscal burden of external debt would be substantially larger if these *contingent liabilities* (as discussed in Chapter 3) were taken into account.

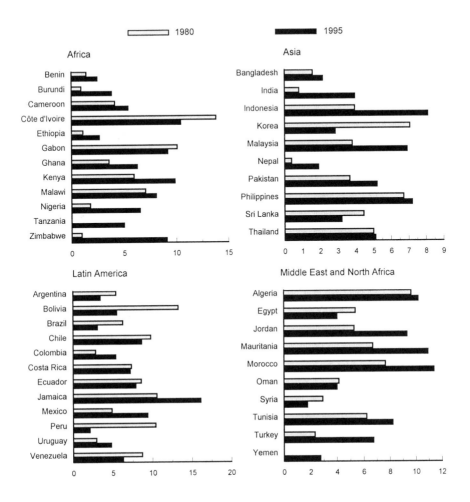

Figure 16.4. Total External Debt Service (In percent of GDP).
Source: World Bank.

Combining this result with Equation (16.18) yields

$$D^* - D^*_{-1} = -(TB + NT) + i^* D^*_{-1},$$

which can be rewritten as

$$D^* = (1 + i^*)D^*_{-1} - Z, \qquad (16.19)$$

where Z_t is the *net external surplus*, defined as

$$Z = TB + NT.$$

Suppose that the world interest rate i^* is constant and that output grows at
the constant rate **g**, so that $Y = (1 + \mathbf{g})Y_{-1}$. Setting $d^* = D^*/Y$ and $z = Z/Y$,

Equation (16.19) becomes

$$d^* = \frac{(1 + i^*)}{(1 + g)} d^*_{-1} - z. \tag{16.20}$$

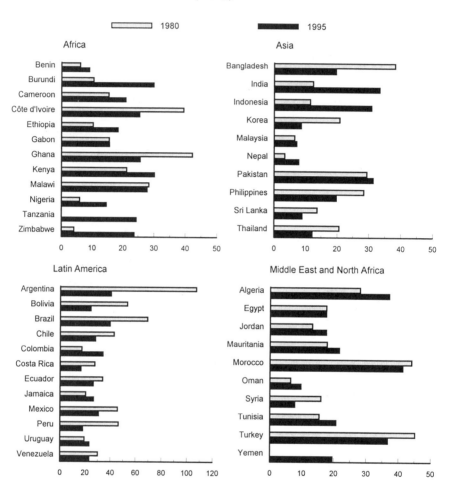

Figure 16.5. Total External Debt Service (% of exports of goods and services). Source: World Bank.

Solving Equation (16.20) recursively forward yields[17]

$$d^*_0 = \sum_{h=1}^{\infty} \left(\frac{1 + g}{1 + i^*}\right)^h z_h + \lim_{N \to \infty} \left(\frac{1 + g}{1 + i^*}\right)^N d^*_N. \tag{16.21}$$

---

[17] The forward solution of Eq. (16.20) with variable output and world interest rates is given by

$$d^*_0 = \sum_{h=1}^{\infty} \Pi_{j=1}^h \left(\frac{1 + g_j}{1 + i^*_j}\right) z_h + \lim_{N \to \infty} \Pi_{j=1}^N \left(\frac{1 + g_j}{1 + i^*_j}\right) d^*_N.$$

Figure 16.6. Heavily Indebted Poor Countries: Debt Indicators, 1992-94 (In percent).

Source: World Bank.

As in Chapter 3, external solvency requires that the **no-Ponzi game condition** hold, so that

$$\lim_{N \to \infty} \left(\frac{1 + g}{1 + i^*}\right)^N d_N^* \leq 0. \qquad (16.22)$$

This condition simply states that a country cannot roll over its external liabilities forever. Thus, from Equation (16.21):[18]

$$d_0^* \leq \sum_{h=1}^{\infty} (\frac{1+\mathbf{g}}{1+i^*})^h z_h. \qquad (16.23)$$

Thus external solvency requires that the current ratio of net foreign liabilities to output be less than or equal to the maximum level of debt that can be sustained by prospective net external surpluses (measured as a fraction of output). The current policy stance is *sustainable* as long as it does not lead to a violation of condition (??).[19] As shown in the context of fiscal solvency, the no-Ponzi game condition matters only if the interest rate on external debt exceeds the growth rate of output; otherwise, the foreign debt-output ratio will *tend to zero* anyway if the horizon N is sufficiently long.

From an analytical standpoint, the concept of external solvency suffers from the same limitations as those faced by the notion of fiscal solvency (see Chapter 3); in particular, the solvency constraint imposes only *weak restrictions* on the size and behavior of the current account deficits that lead to the accumulation of foreign liabilities over time. Practical applications are also hampered by difficulties associated with the projection of trade flows (which depend on the real exchange rate) and the choice of an appropriate interest rate. Nevertheless, a number of recent empirical studies have attempted to estimate operational models of external solvency in developing countries. Sawada (1994), for instance, used various econometric tests to assess external solvency in a group of heavily indebted developing countries in the early 1980s.

16.4 Debt Rescheduling

The theoretical literature on sovereign debt distinguishes two approaches to debt repayment (see Kletzer, 1988):

- the **ability-to-pay** approach, which refers to a situation in which a country is unable to meet its current debt servicing requirements, directly or through further borrowing;

---

[18] With variable output growth and world interest rates, the no-Ponzi game condition for external solvency is

$$\lim_{N \to \infty} \Pi_{j=1}^{N} (\frac{1+\mathbf{g}_j}{1+i_j^*}) d_N^* \leq 0,$$

so that Eq. (??) becomes

$$d_0^* \leq \sum_{h=1}^{\infty} \Pi_{j=1}^{h} (\frac{1+\mathbf{g}_j}{1+i_j^*}) z_h.$$

[19] See Milesi-Ferreti and Razin (1996) for a detailed discussion of the concepts of external solvency and sustainability.

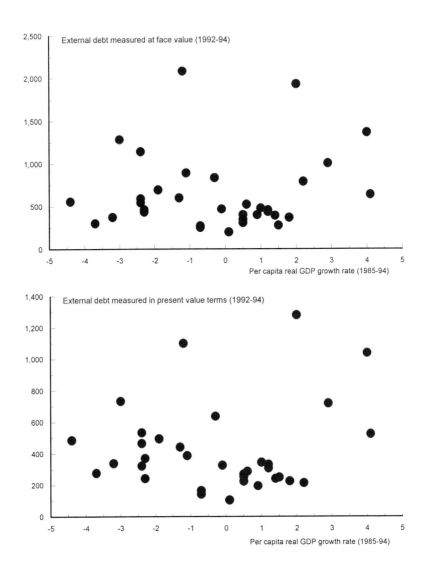

Figure 16.7. Heavily Indebted Poor Countries: Debt to Exports Ratio and Per Capita GDP Growth Rate 1/ (In percent).

Source: United Nations.

1/ Excluding Ethiopia, Cameroon, Congo, Nicaragua, Somalia, and Sudan.

- the **willingness-to-pay** approach, which focuses on the case where the borrower has the resources for repayment but finds it optimal not to repay.

The high levels of foreign debt and debt service faced by the low-income developing countries and the severe difficulties they have encountered in ensuring payments has led to increased recognition that many of these countries face an ability-to-pay problem: required debt service exceeds their debt-servicing capacity. Moreover, this ability-to-pay problem is not in general a reflection of a **liquidity problem** but rather a **solvency problem**—that is, a situation in which the present value of a country's current and future income (taken over the whole future) is less than its debt obligations.[20]

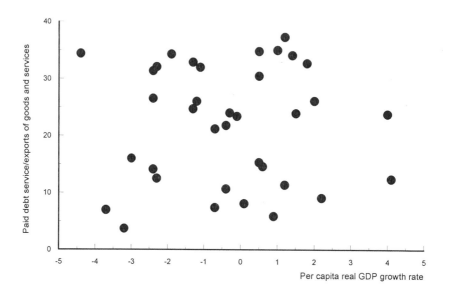

Figure 16.8. Heavily Indebted Poor Countries: Paid Debt Service/Exports and Per Capita GDP Growth Rate, 1985-94 1/ (In percent).

Source: United Nations.

1/ Excluding Ethiopia, Cameroon, Congo, and Uganda.

Debt relief to the poorest countries has often taken the form of debt reschedulings at highly concessional terms by official bilateral creditors. In general, there are two main types of debt rescheduling operations:

- **flow reschedulings**, which provide for the rescheduling of debt service on eligible debt falling due during the so-called *consolidation period*;

- **stock-of-debt operations**, under which the entire stock of eligible debt, before a so-called *pre-cutoff date*, is rescheduled at concessionary terms.[21]

---

[20] A country is illiquid if it is solvent but cannot borrow to meet its current debt servicing requirements. It should be noted that if a country is solvent, lenders should always be willing to lend to it the resources needed to make current repayments—unless they expect the country to *repudiate the debt* at some point in the future.

[21] These operations typically require countries to maintain what is deemed to be a "satisfactory track record" for several years with respect to both payments under rescheduling agreements and performance under a credit arrangement with multilateral institutions.

Debt rescheduling agreements for the poorest most heavily indebted countries have been offered at highly concessional terms by official bilateral creditors (organized through the **Paris Club**) since the mid-1980s. Between October 1988 and June 1991, the conditions describing the terms under which such agreements were made were the **Toronto terms**. Under these terms, creditors were allowed to choose one among (or a combination of) three options:

- *Option A*, or **partial cancellation**. Under this option, one third of consolidated debt-service obligations was canceled and the remaining two thirds rescheduled on the basis of an appropriate market rate over 14 years, including a grace period of 8 years.

- *Option B*, or **extended maturities**. Under this option, consolidated debt-service obligations were rescheduled on the basis of a relevant market interest rate over a period of 25 years, including a grace period of 14 years.

- *Option C*, or **concessional interest rates**. Under this option, consolidated debt-service obligations were rescheduled over a period of 14 years, including an 8-year grace period on the basis of an appropriate market interest rate minus 3.5 percent.

Between December 1991 and December 1994, the **London terms** offered up to 50 percent of debt reduction in net present value (NPV) terms. Since January 1995, new conditions for rescheduling the debt of low-income countries have been put in place by the Paris Club creditors. The following are the key elements of the so-called **Naples terms**.

- **Eligibility** is decided by creditors on a case-by-case basis, taking primarily into account a country's level of income. Countries that have previously received concessional reschedulings (on Toronto or London terms) are eligible for Naples terms.

- **Concessionality**. Most countries receive a reduction in eligible non-ODA (official development assistance) debt of 67 percent in net present value terms. Countries with a per capita income of more than $500 and a debt-to-exports ratio in present value terms of less than 350 percent are given (again, on a case-by-case basis) a 50 percent NPV reduction.

- **Coverage** (inclusion in the rescheduling agreement) of non-ODA pre-cutoff date debt is decided on a case-by-case basis, taking into account balance-of-payments needs.

- **Choice of options**. Creditors have the choice of two concessional options for achieving a 67 percent NPV reduction, namely a *debt reduction* (DR) option (repayment over 23 years with a grace period of 6 years), or a *debt-service reduction* (DSR) option, under which the NPV reduction is achieved by concessional interest rates (with repayment over 33 years).[22]

---

[22] For a 50 percent NPV reduction, the DSR option provides for repayment over 23 years with 6 years of grace and the DR option for repayment over 25 years with 16 years of grace.

- There are, in addition, a *capitalization of moratorium interest* option, which also achieves the NPV reduction by a higher interest rate over the same repayment period as the DSR option, and a *commercial* or *long maturities* option, providing for no NPV reduction (repayment over 40 years with 20 years of grace).[23]

- **ODA credits**. Pre-cutoff date credits are rescheduled on the original concessional interest rates over 40 years with 16 years' grace (30 years' maturity with 12 years' grace for 50 percent NPV reduction).

Uganda was the first low-income rescheduling country to receive an exit rescheduling in the form of a stock-of-debt operation under Naples terms. The February 1995 rescheduling provided for 67 percent NPV reduction of all pre-cutoff date debt, excluding the debt previously rescheduled in 1992 on London terms (which had already received 50 percent NPV reduction). The level of concessionality for debt rescheduled in 1989 on Toronto terms, including arrears and late interest, was increased to 67 percent in NPV terms.

16.5 The HIPC Debt Initiative

As indicated above, official bilateral creditors belonging to the Paris Club improved gradually the terms of rescheduling offered to poor countries over the past few years and increased the percentage of debt reduction. However, it was increasingly recognized that debt reschedulings would not prove to be an effective and durable solution for many low-income countries. Part of the reason is that, for the HIPCs, *multilateral debt* represents a large fraction of total external debt—about 31 percent at the end of 1996, compared with 42 percent for bilateral official creditors and 12 percent for private creditors.

In September 1996, a joint IMF-World Bank proposal, The **HIPC Debt Initiative**, was put forward to tackle the issue of debt owed to multilateral official creditors (see Boote and Thugge, 1999). The HIPC Initiative requires countries to show a track record of *good policy performance* as monitored by the IMF and the Bank. The six-year performance period under the initiative consists of two stages of implementation.

16.5.1 First Stage

During the first three-year period, the debtor country has to establish a track record of good performance, with the Paris Club providing flow rescheduling on Naples terms (67 percent reduction of Paris Club eligible debt on a net present value basis). Other bilateral and commercial creditors must provide at least comparable treatment, whereas bilateral donors and multilateral institutions

---

For flow reschedulings, there is no grace period, and for stock-of-debt operations the grace period is three years.

[23] Creditors choosing this option are required to undertake efforts to change to a concessional option at a later date when feasible.

must continue to provide support in the framework of an adjustment program monitored by the IMF and the World Bank . The end of the first phase is the **decision point**, reached after a three-year track record of good performance. A few months before the decision point, a **debt sustainability analysis** is undertaken to determine whether the debtor country is eligible for further debt relief. The analysis of debt sustainability is often conducted on the basis of a variety of debt indicators (as discussed below) and sometimes also on the basis of a simplified version of the **external solvency approach** described earlier. Once a sustainable path of external debt is estimated, there are three possible scenarios.

- If a Paris Club stock-of-debt operation on Naples terms is sufficient to achieve debt sustainability within three years (that is by the **completion point**, see below), the country is deemed capable of exiting from the debt rescheduling process.

- If such a stock-of-debt operation is not sufficient to achieve debt sustainability, the country becomes eligible for further debt relief.

- In cases where there is doubt about whether sustainability would be achieved by the completion point, the country receives further flow rescheduling under Naples terms from bilateral creditors.

16.5.2   Second Stage

If the country is deemed eligible for support under the HIPC Initiative, it must go through a second stage, of normally three years, during which the Paris Club provides more relief through flow rescheduling (up to 80 percent of the present value of Paris Club debt). Other bilateral and commercial creditors must, again, provide at least comparable treatment, and the country must establish a second track record of good performance under an adjustment program monitored by the IMF and the World Bank. The performance criteria during this second stage include macroeconomic indicators and progress on structural reforms and social reforms. Donors, bilateral creditors and multilateral institutions are also required to provide support in the form of grants and concessional loans. The end of the second stage is the **completion point**.

At the completion point, provided that the country has met the performance criteria under the Initiative, Paris Club creditors provide a stock-of-debt operation of up to *80 percent reduction* in net present value terms—with at least comparable treatment provided by other bilateral and commercial creditors. Multilateral institutions must provide the committed reduction in net present value terms of their claims necessary for the total debt to reach a sustainable level. The World Bank, for instance, must provide assistance for this purpose through the **HIPC Trust Fund**.

16.5.3   Eligibility Criteria and Prospects

To qualify for assistance under the HIPC Initiative, countries must satisfy conditions required by the IMF and the World Bank to be part of the group of poor countries. The **debt sustainability analysis** determines the eligibility of debtor countries, and eventually the amount of debt relief necessary for the country to achieve a sustainable level of debt, on the basis of the following criteria:

- The ratio of the net present value of the *debt-to-export* ratio must fall within a range of 200-250 percent or below, by the completion point.

- The *debt-service-to-exports* ratio (which captures the foreign exchange constraint) must fall within a range of 20-25 percent or below, at the completion point.

- Within the prescribed ranges, debt sustainability must be determined on the basis of various measures of vulnerability, including the burden of external debt on the government budget (as defined earlier), the diversity of the country's export base, its reserve coverage, its resource balance, and other relevant factors.

- The ratio of the net present value of *debt to fiscal revenue* must be below 280 percent, provided that two other criteria are met: an export-to-GDP ratio of at least 40 percent and a minimum threshold ratio of fiscal revenue to GDP of 20 percent.

By December 1998, six countries had benefited from the HIPC Initiative: Bolivia, Burkina Faso, Côte d'Ivoire, Guyana, Mozambique, and Uganda—the first country to reach the second stage in April 1998 (see Boote and Thugge, 1999). Nominal debt relief for this group of countries amounted to U.S. $5.6 billion (that is, a reduction of about U.S. $3 billion in NPV terms), compared with total debt—after other debt-relief mechanisms were accounted for—for all six countries of U.S. $17.4 billion in NPV terms. Critics have argued, however, that the debt relief provided under the initiative has not been sufficient to ensure that beneficiary countries achieve debt sustainability within a reasonable period of time—even with adequate policies in place. In addition, the process is deemed too slow; although the second stage can be shortened for countries that have shown sustained economic performance during the first stage, a six-year performance period appears excessive. The recent meeting of major industrial countries in Cologne (June 18-20, 1999) recognized some of these limitations and the IMF and the World Bank are now considering ways to provide faster and deeper debt relief under the HIPC Initiative. Currently under consideration are reductions in the target levels of the debt-to-exports ratio from 200-250 percent to 150 percent, the debt-to-revenue ratio from 280 to 250 percent, and increases in debt forgiveness provided by the Paris Club for countries that qualify from 80 percent to 90 percent.

16.6   Summary

- In a world of imperfect world capital markets, fiscal adjustment in low-income countries may lead to a lower burden of foreign debt both by reducing the *level* of indebtedness and by lowering the **risk premium** that domestic agents face on foreign borrowing. In an **endogenous growth** setting with learning by doing, the resulting higher capital-effective labor ratio may also lead to a *permanent rise* in the economy's growth rate.

- A **debt overhang** arises in a situation in which a debtor country benefits very little from the return to any additional investment, because of high debt service obligations. It can be measured as the difference between the present value of a country's contractual debt obligations and the expected resource transfers that are needed to service it.

- When foreign obligations cannot be fully met with existing resources and actual debt payments are determined by some negotiation process between the debtor country and its creditors, the amount of payments can become linked to the *economic performance* of the debtor country, with the consequence that at least part of the return to any increase in production would in fact be devoted to debt servicing. This creates a *disincentive to investment*.

- A country is on the *wrong side* of its **debt Laffer curve** when a reduction in the **debt tax rate** (that is, the proportion of output that is allocated to servicing the debt) would translate into an *increase* in actual debt payments. Reducing the debt overhang would benefit both the debtor country and its creditors.

- Conventional measures of the debt burden include the ratio of the stock of debt to output or exports, the ratio of actual debt service to exports (which is also a measure of the foreign exchange constraint), and the ratio of scheduled debt service to exports. Alternative measures include the ratio of the discounted present value of future debt-service obligations relative to either the discounted present value of future export receipts or the current value of exports.

- When loans are contracted (or rescheduled) at concessional interest rates, indicators based on the net present value of foreign liabilities are more meaningful measures of the actual burden of debt than those based on the face value of these liabilities. The lower the concessional rate, the lower the net present value of future debt service obligations discounted at the market rate. The difference between the face value of debt and its present value measures the *grant element*.

- The debt burden can be assessed by evaluating **external solvency**, in a manner analogous to the assessment of *fiscal solvency*. The **no-Ponzi**

game condition prevents a country from rolling over its external obligations indefinitely. Under this condition, external solvency requires the present discounted value of trade surpluses to be sufficiently large to repay the country's existing net stock of foreign liabilities. However, external solvency analysis remains subject to some of the same conceptual and empirical limitations that fiscal solvency analysis faces.

- The debt problem of many low-income countries reflects an **ability-to-pay** problem, rather than a **willingness-to-pay** problem; debt service payments exceed in many cases the country's debt-servicing capacity. Since the mid-1980s many low-income countries have been engaged in rescheduling operations at concessional terms.

- The **HIPC Initiative**, launched in September 1996, is an attempt to recognize the fact that a significant portion of the foreign debt of low-income countries is owed to multilateral institutions. A two-stage process, under a six-year performance period, eventually leads to a *completion point* at which debt relief through *stock-of-debt operations* is implemented. The process, however, has remained slow and the length of the performance period appears excessive.

Appendix
The Theory of Stages in the Balance of Payments

The literature on **stages in the balance of payments** analyzes the pattern of foreign borrowing and lending that an initially capital-poor economy goes through during the process of development. This literature has related the behavior over time of external accounts to *growth paths* in which investment first exceeds saving, then saving overtakes investment. Specifically, five phases are typically distinguished in this literature:

- a *young debtor-borrower stage*, in which both the trade balance and the current account are in deficit and the country is a net debtor;

- a *mature debtor-borrower stage*, in which the trade balance has turned to surplus but the current account is still in deficit due to debt-service obligations;

- a *debtor-repayer stage*, in which the country is still a net debtor but the current account is in surplus;

- a *young creditor-lender stage*, with both the current account and trade balance in surplus, and the country has become a net creditor;

- a *mature creditor-lender stage*, in which the trade balance has turned to deficit but the current account is still in surplus due to interest income from abroad.

In the steady state, a country that has passed through the last two stages will be a net creditor running a trade deficit exactly offsetting its earnings on foreign assets. In summary, therefore, in the early stages of growth when investment opportunities exceed saving, countries tend to borrow abroad. As income and saving rise above investment requirements, and as the marginal productivity of capital falls toward the world rate of interest (thereby reducing the investment motive for borrowing), countries pay back their debt and accumulate foreign assets.

The analytical literature suggests that various conditions must be satisfied for stages in the balance of payments to emerge. In the growth model developed by Fischer and Frenkel (1974), for instance, for a country starting with a low level of capital and low per-capita wealth, a transition from debtor to creditor requires the *assumption* that the steady-state position is one in which the country becomes a net debtor. The model, however, does not necessarily generate non-monotonic dynamics of foreign debt (asset) accumulation; it is also consistent with patterns of foreign borrowing in which debt may increase or decrease continuously over time—raising possibly *solvency* issues (see Chapter 3).

In general, both consumption dynamics and capital accumulation are important in reproducing in analytical models stages in the balance of payments. More importantly perhaps, as pointed out by Manzocchi (1990), is that the whole literature is subject to an important limitation: because of the assumption of perfect international capital markets (which implies a perfectly elastic supply of funds), the balance of payments is viewed as an *outcome* of the process of economic growth, not a *constraint*—a treatment that may appear more realistic for many developing countries. The model discussed in the first part of this chapter illustrates some of the implications of capital market imperfections for the dynamics of growth and external debt.

Chapter 17

Sequencing, Gradualism, and the Political Economy of Adjustment

In designing reform programs in an environment in which various distortions exist, a key issue for policymakers is the choice of an appropriate sequence of policy measures. A related issue is the speed at which economic reforms must be implemented. The answer to both questions depends not only on economic considerations but also on the type of adjustment costs and political constraints that policymakers face.

The political dimension of adjustment has been one of the main areas of interest of the *new political economy*, which studies (using modern analytical tools) the interactions between the political system, institutional structures, and policy formulation. Economic policy decisions are viewed in this perspective as the *endogenous* outcome of these interactions. This approach seeks to provide a better empirical explanation of economic policy formation than conventional models in which policy is chosen either *exogenously* or by a benevolent social planner, often with no interaction between public and private agents. More specifically, the recent literature on the political economy of reform in developing economies has focused on three issues (Williamson and Haggard, 1994):

- The **timing** of reforms, that is, understanding the conditions or circumstances that determine *why* and *when* reforms are implemented.

- The **sequencing** of reforms, that is, the analysis of the reasons why some reforms are implemented *earlier* than others, and why reforms are implemented sometimes in a *piecemeal fashion* and sometimes in the context of a *comprehensive program*.

- The **speed** of reforms, that is, the factors explaining why reform programs, once they are selected, are sometimes implemented *overnight* and sometimes *gradually.*

This chapter reviews various recent contributions to these issues. The first part examines *complementarities* and *trade-offs* that arise in the use of policy instruments for stabilization and adjustment purposes. The second part focuses on the order of liberalization and considers issues associated with both the liberalization of external accounts and the sequencing of domestic and external financial reforms. The links between political constraints and the design of economic reforms is discussed in the third part. It begins by considering alternative approaches to modeling political conflict among agent and then examines the extent to which economic crises may be conducive to reform, including the relation between income distribution, the political acceptability of reform, and the sustainability of the reform process. Part 4 considers how the pace of reform is affected by factors such as preexisting distortions, imperfect credibility of policies, congestion externalities, financial sector weaknesses, and distributional factors.

17.1   Stabilization and Structural Adjustment

Most policy decisions have both short-term and structural effects, which may (or may not) operate in the same direction. A cut in government spending aimed, for instance, at improving macroeconomic performance (by reducing government borrowing needs, money growth, and inflation) may have an effect on the **incentives structure** as well as the efficiency of resource utilization—by leading to a reduction in taxation, and thus reducing the propensity to evade taxes (as noted in Chapter 12). Moreover, although macroeconomic policy measures operate primarily through the *demand side* of an economy, and structural policies primarily through the *supply side*, the ultimate objectives of both sets of policies are often the same: output growth, low unemployment, price stability, and a viable current account. As a result, it has often been argued that stabilization and structural adjustment should proceed in parallel because they may reinforce each other. The existence of **policy complementarities** is one of the main arguments in favor of **shock therapy**, as discussed later.

However, macroeconomic and structural policies may also have *conflicting effects*, particularly in the short run. Eliminating a distortionary *agricultural subsidy*, for instance, may help to improve the government budget in the short run (thereby lowering inflationary pressures) and may raise welfare of consumers of nonagricultural goods in the longer run by improving resource allocation. However, it will also lower farm income and raise food prices in the short run. Agricultural households will suffer, and consumers will pay higher food prices. Similarly, the elimination of a *tax on agricultural exports* may increase exports of these goods and income in the rural sector in the medium and long run, but it may also increase the budget deficit in the short run.

Moreover, structural policies have a *longer time frame* than short-run macroeconomic policies because **potential output** responds more slowly and with highly variable lags to structural policies than does actual output to, say, monetary and fiscal policies. The slow (and uncertain) adjustment of the economy to structural measures and the possible adverse macroeconomic effects of these measures in the short run have led some economists to argue that structural adjustment policies must be introduced gradually, to avoid derailing stabilization objectives and eroding political support to a point where the sustainability of the overall reform process is called into question (see below).

An important economic argument in favor of ensuring that the stabilization objective is achieved first is that in an environment in which inflation is high and relative prices are distorted, the ability of agents to understand and interpret correctly **price signals** (that is, changes in relative prices) may be seriously hampered (Rodrik, 1995a). In such conditions, structural adjustment policies, which operate to a great extent through their effects on the structure of *incentives* faced by agents, may not be successful because markets cannot play their role in allocating resources.

17.2   The Order of Liberalization

Much of the discussion in Chapters 14 and 15 focused on various types of economic reforms aimed at removing or alleviating government-induced distortions. In practice, of course, many of these distortions are present *simultaneously*, and the issue of what to do in such conditions arises. In principle, the **optimal** or **first-best solution** would be to remove all market distortions at once; such a strategy is unambiguously welfare improving. In practice, however, this is almost never a realistic option because of various administrative, political, and other constraints. In such conditions, the issue of sequencing arises. The reason is that, in a **second-best environment**, the impact of a particular measure in a given sector depends on the circumstances in other sectors of the economy. When distortions exist in various sectors of the economy, the removal of a distortion in one sector does not necessarily lead to an improvement in social welfare—despite its direct potential benefits. Consequently, an analysis of the aggregate welfare effects of reform that limits itself to the sector where the policy change is occurring may be misleading. The general implication of the theory of second best is that economic reforms should be broad in scope in order to ensure a first-best solution in the long run. However, as noted earlier, in a world in which policy measures entail short-term **adjustment costs**—resulting from the fact that productive resources cannot move instantaneously among alternative uses, or product and factor prices cannot adjust immediately to clear all markets—economic and political impediments can make an immediate and comprehensive reform of all markets neither feasible nor desirable. In such conditions, the question of what should be the appropriate sequence of economic reforms arises.

More specifically, the sequencing of reforms refers to the order in which individual markets should be liberalized in the transition from a distorted economy toward a market-oriented economy.[1] As noted by Falvey and Kim (1992, p. 909), getting the timing and sequencing of economic reforms right is important because inappropriate timing and sequencing may foster doubts about the *sustainability* of the reform program and deter private agents from undertaking appropriate adjustments in their supply and demand decisions.[2]

The literature on sequencing has focused on two main dimensions of the debate: the order of liberalization of the trade and capital accounts, and whether domestic financial liberalization should precede or follow the opening of the capital account. More recently, there has also been some thinking on the role of labor market reforms in the overall sequence of liberalization measures.

17.2.1 Liberalization of External Accounts

The experience of the Southern Cone countries of Latin America (Argentina, Chile, and Uruguay), Indonesia, and Korea with structural reform in the late 1960s and 1970s was the main source of the initial debate on the order of liberalization. Several economists concluded that the trade account should be opened before the capital account, in order to avoid destabilizing effects associated with capital inflows. Opening the capital account while trade liberalization is still in its initial stages could jeopardize the success of trade reform; this is because the successful liberalization of the trade account requires a *real depreciation* (in order to generate a reallocation of resources from the nontradables sector to the tradables sector, as noted in Chapter 14), whereas opening the capital account may be associated with a *real appreciation* (as documented in Chapter 6).

A more formal analysis of this issue was provided by Edwards and van Wijnbergen (1986). They assessed the desirability of alternative sequences by evaluating their **welfare effects** in the context of a **multi-period model**. The first conclusion of their analysis was that liberalization can have **ambiguous effects** on welfare because of three types of (possibly conflicting) effects:

- **direct effects**, which occur in the market in which the reform has taken place and within the *same time period*;

- **intratemporal indirect effects**, which occur within the period in which the reform occurs because of the interaction between two or more distortions in different markets;

- **intertemporal indirect effects**, which result from the inherently dynamic nature of liberalization policies. They imply that a reform in one period may alter the equilibrium in distorted markets in the *next period*.

---

[1]Note that there are also issues associated with the sequencing of a given set of *policy instruments*. For instance, there is a sequencing issue in the context of *fiscal adjustment*, to the extent that inadequate tax administration may force the government to reduce its fiscal deficit by cutting expenditure (often current outlays on nonwage goods and services and on capital projects,with little reduction in wages and salaries) rather than by increasing revenue. Such cuts may have an adverse effect on growth prospects, as noted in Chapters 12 and 13.

[2]In practice, a politically sustainable reform program requires not only a large degree of social acceptability but also a sufficient degree of parliamentary support for reforms (Tommasi and Velasco, 1996).

The second conclusion reached by Edwards and van Wijnbergen was that the current account should be opened first, because the negative indirect welfare effect of opening the capital account in the presence of trade distortions will be greater than the indirect effects resulting from the opposite ordering. Extension of the Edwards-van Wijnbergen analysis by Kahkonen (1987) to include **financial repression** (as discussed in Chapter 2) broadly supports this policy prescription.

The implication of **uncertainty** in the outcome of reforms (and thus their degree of credibility) for the sequencing of trade and capital account measures was discussed by Conley and Maloney (1995). They considered a two-period model in which the benefits of economic liberalization are uncertain. Specifically, they considered a *two-part liberalization program*:

- A liberalization of the current account—say, a reduction in tariffs—in the first period, which is assumed to translate into an increase in the marginal productivity of capital in the second period. The magnitude of this increase, however, is assumed to fluctuate randomly.

- A complete opening of the capital account, which allows agents to borrow and lend freely on world capital markets—and thus to engage in **intertemporal smoothing** of consumption (see Chapter 2).

Because the benefits of current account liberalization are uncertain, privates agents base their consumption path (for both the first and second periods) on their *expectations* of the value of the marginal productivity of capital in the second period. Conley and Maloney showed that in such conditions, if agents are at the same time free to borrow and lend on world capital markets, economic liberalization will lead to a surge in consumption, a current account deficit, and an increase in foreign borrowing by private agents. However, *ex post*, private sector expectations may turn out to be incorrect; indeed, if private agents borrow in the first period, and the marginal productivity of capital turns out to be significantly *less* than expected, consumption in the second period may have to fall by a large amount to ensure repayment of the first-period debt. Policymakers may be averse to such **boom-bust cycles**; and if the probability of a low realization of the marginal productivity of capital is sufficiently high, they may choose to delay the opening of the capital account. Such outcome depends importantly on the distribution function characterizing the marginal productivity of capital and government preferences.[3] It may occur even if the liberalization program is internally consistent.[4]

---

[3] In the Conley-Maloney model, it is crucial that the government's welfare function depend not only on the expected utility of the representative household but that it also cares about *increases in standards of living*—defined in their model as a situation in which second-period consumption is greater than first-period consumption.

[4] The lack of credibility in this context is thus similar to the one discussed in the context of stabilization in Chapter 4.

17.2.2 Financial Reform and the Capital Account

The experience of developing countries suggests that opening of the capital account has often resulted, at least in the short run, in large destabilizing capital flows. If the capital account is opened at a moment when domestic capital markets are still subject to financial repression, with interest rates in particular fixed at artificially low levels, massive capital outflows are likely to take place—thereby threatening the viability of pegged exchange rate regimes and possibly increasing the fragility of the domestic banking system (see Chapter 15). Such flows may be particularly large in countries where the credibility (and thus sustainability) of the structural reform program within which capital account liberalization is embedded is not fully established. For these reasons, many economists agree that the capital account should only be opened *after* the domestic financial market has been liberalized and interest rates have been raised.

In addition, the experience of the 1980s and 1990s has highlighted the importance of strengthening **prudential supervision** and **regulation** of the banking system at the same time that domestic interest rates are liberalized, before opening the capital account (see Chapter 15). Large capital inflows intermediated by the banking system may, as noted in Chapter 6, lead to excessive risk taking and create or exacerbate financial fragilities if proper regulatory structures are not in place.

17.2.3 Sequencing Labor Market Reforms

As noted in Chapter 14, labor market regulations continue to play a pervasive role in developing countries. Although the extent to which some of these regulations translate into actual distortions is not entirely clear, assessing the role of labor market reform in the overall sequencing of reforms is an important (and as yet unresolved) issue. Edwards (1989) was one of the first to emphasize that labor market reform may need to precede trade reform in order to increase *labor mobility* and facilitate the reallocation of resources across sectors. The issue, however, arises in the context of other policies as well. In particular, reforms aimed at altering the process of wage formation in the formal economy (such as changes aimed at indexing nominal wages on future, rather than past, inflation) may be critical in reducing inflation. It may therefore be argued that labor market reforms should precede (or at least accompany) macroeconomic adjustment measures.

Experience suggests, however, that labor market reforms are often difficult to introduce (Agénor, 1996). They often are relegated, for various political reasons, to the end of the reform sequence—thereby giving the opportunity to some powerful groups to block the overall reform process.. Moreover, the fear of unemployment often retards critical reforms in other areas. Both factors suggest that there may be a strong case for placing labor market reforms early in the overall sequence of economic reform.

17.3   Political Constraints and Economic Reforms

As noted earlier, the new political economy analyzes economic policy formation from both a *normative* and a *positive* perspective.

- The normative perspective focuses, in particular, on issues related to the effect of *institutions* on policy formation.

- The positive perspective focuses on the type of policies that are more likely to emerge from specific political and institutional settings, and thus the specification of politically sustainable policies.

Using both the normative and the positive perspectives, this section examines three issues that have been at the core of the recent research on the new political economy: the modeling of political conflict among interest groups, the role of economic crises in inducing the adoption of reform programs, and the role of distributional factors in affecting the political acceptability and sustainability of reforms.

17.3.1   Modeling Political Conflict

A key step in understanding the *timing* of economic reforms (such as trade liberalization, as discussed in Chapter 14) is to recognize that they typically generate gains for some sectors and losses for others—even if they lead to a net welfare gain for the economy as a whole. If the losing sectors are politically powerful, they may block efforts to adopt adjustment measures that would hurt their interests. Moreover, because *short-run* winners and losers may differ from *long-run* winners and losers, **backtracking** (or policy reversals) may occur in the absence of appropriate compensation schemes, as discussed below.

Analytically, the possibility of conflict (or divergence of interest) between winners and losers suggests that assuming the existence of a welfare-maximizing, **benevolent social planner** that chooses and implements reforms does not describe accurately the way policy decisions are actually made. Instead, as emphasized by Drazen (1996), it must be explicitly recognized that policy choices in reform programs reflect the resolution of *conflicts of interest* between groups with *different goals*. The question then is to identify the reasons why such conflicts, and the mechanisms by which they are resolved, may lead to delays in the adoption of beneficial reforms. Two basic approaches have been proposed in recent years; each is based on heterogeneity of interests and some sort of uncertainty about net benefits of reform, though in quite different ways:[5]

- The **distributional conflict** approach, developed by Alesina and Drazen (1991), and Drazen and Grilli (1993). The basic idea is that there is a conflict over how the *known* cost of policy change will be divided among interest groups, so that what matters is *ex-post heterogeneity*, that is,

---

[5] Drazen (1996) provides an analytical framework that synthesizes the main features of these approaches.

heterogeneity caused by the change in policy. Although each interest group knows the net benefit it would receive from the change under a proposed allocation of costs, each group is *uncertain* about the net benefits other groups will enjoy and hence about their willingness to pay for the reform.

- The **uncertain-benefits** approach. The key idea is that some groups may be uncertain about the net benefits they themselves would receive if a reform is adopted. Thus, reforms that could end up benefitting a majority of the population are not adopted and there is **status quo bias**. An example of this type of model is by Fernández and Rodrik (1991), reviewed in Chapter 14, which focused on the nonadoption of beneficial reforms in a *static* context rather than *delay over time*. But models along the Fernández-Rodrik formulation have also been developed to explain delay in a *dynamic* context.

The distributional conflict approach of Alesina and Drazen (1991) and Drazen and Grilli (1993) are based on models of **war of attrition**. A war of attrition takes place when two (or more) groups disagree over the *burden sharing* that needed policy measures necessarily entail, such as government spending cuts. *Uncertainty* is crucial in this setting—if a group knew it would eventually have to concede, it would be in its interest to do so at the beginning, thus avoiding a costly delay. As time goes by, each group learns about the strength of rival groups (namely, how costly it is for *them* to concede) or the costs of the *status quo*. The war ends when one or both groups find the continuation of the status quo more costly than conceding or compromising. A key factor affecting the length of the period of inaction is an *unequal distribution* of the burden of adjustment—which delays reform because losing is more costly for at least one group. The war of attrition specification may explain why (without resorting to, say, irrationality of economic agents) governments may at first face little difficulty in implementing a reform package, but then become unable to proceed with further reforms. The crucial issue then becomes the identification of a mechanism that can break the deadlock and restart the reform process. Casella and Eichengreen (1996) argued that *foreign assistance* may play such a role.

In the Alesina-Drazen framework, the delay in implementing fiscal stabilization is endogenous, but the initial fiscal deficit is not. Velasco (1997*b*), and Mondino, Sturzenegger, and Tommasi (1996) developed dynamic models that endogenize the deficit (as well as inflation). Velasco (1997*b*) modeled fiscal policy as the outcome of a political process in which spending power is in the hands of several agents (controllers) who represent different interest groups and who behave *noncooperatively*. A key feature of the model is that the benefits of spending are *group specific*, whereas the costs (debt service, in particular) are borne by all groups *jointly*. In this setting, the benefit from public saving, as perceived by each group, is not the rate of interest (that is, the rate of return on saving) but the rate of interest adjusted to account for what other groups spend. As a result, incentives are distorted, each group overspends, and debt accumulates over time. As noted in Chapter 3, this may explain the **deficit bias** that may characterize fiscal policy in some countries.

17.3.2 The Benefits of Crises

A second issue that has been a focus of attention in the new political economy is the role of economic and political crises in generating incentives to reform. The model of Drazen and Grilli (1993), in particular, analyzed the case in which the cost of inflation increases exogenously. They showed that by making delay more costly a sudden upward shock to inflation (a "crisis") can accelerate the implementation of a stabilization program. Crises can even make everyone better off and increase welfare if the indirect, beneficial effect of a "bad" shock (a reduction in delay) outweighs the direct (adverse) effect of the crisis.

The notion that economic crises may facilitate the implementation of economic reforms is appealing and somewhat intuitive. As noted in Chapter 5, the historical record seems to indicate that episodes of **hyperinflation** (which are typically periods of severe economic disruptions) have often been easier to terminate than episodes of chronic inflation. An important reason is that periods of very high price instability may allow governments to gather sufficient political support more rapidly and to implement drastic stabilization measures. However, the argument also faces some difficulties. At the analytical level, as noted by Tommasi and Velasco (1996, pp. 198-199), the definition of crisis used in the Drazen-Grilli framework is somewhat unconventional: a "crisis" in the model consists of an increase in the costs of lax policies that are in place prior to reform, rather than a sharp and unexpected increase in such costs (as would happen, for instance, with a sudden hyperinflation) shortly before a reform program is implemented. In addition, as also noted by Tommasi and Velasco, the Drazen-Grilli analysis relies on dynamic game models which yield equilibria whose features are not robust to relatively minor changes in model specification. The positive link between crisis and reform may thus depend on which specification (or which equilibrium) is being considered by the analyst.

More generally, Rodrik (1996a) argued that the view that crises can be beneficial for reform suffers faces two problems. First, it contains an element of tautology (Rodrik, 1996a, p. 27):

> Reform naturally becomes an issue only when policies are perceived to be not working. A crisis is just an extreme case of policy failure. That reform should follow crisis, then, is no more surprising than smoke following fire.

Second, it is difficult to falsify, because

> If an economy in crisis has not yet reformed, the frequently preferred explanation is that the crisis has not yet become "severe enough."

17.3.3 Political Acceptability and Sustainability

Uncertainty about the distributional consequences of economic reforms also has important implications for the *acceptability* of an adjustment program—particularly, as argued by Wyplosz (1993), in a setting in which reforms raise productivity and lead to full employment in the long run but cause unemployment in the short run. Along lines similar to the Alesina-Drazen approach, Wyplosz also emphasized that in the presence of uncertainty about the distributional consequences of reforms, it is harder politically to *sustain* them over time (that is, to carry out the reform program to its completion) than it is to *start* them.

Formally, Wyplosz's (1993) analysis can be illustrated as follows. Consider an economy in which there are N identical workers. The initial situation, at $t = 0$, is such that each worker's marginal (and average) productivity is θ_L and all workers are employed by the government or public enterprises.[6] National income is thus $Y_0 = N\theta_L$.

In period $t = 1$, an adjustment program, calling for a cut in the public sector labor force, is put in place. Specifically, public enterprises fire a fraction α of their workforce. Employment therefore falls to $(1-\alpha)N < N$ and national income drops to $Y_1 = (1-\alpha)N\theta_L$ (assuming that productivity remains the same as in period 0) and the unemployment rate jumps to α. Because all workers are identical, firing occurs in a *random* fashion. Although the total number of jobs to be cut is known *ex ante*, individual workers do not know for sure who will be affected.

In period $t = 2$, reform leads to an increase in *productivity* from θ_L to $\theta_H > \theta_L$. All workers who lost their job in period 1 regain employment in period 2. National income therefore rises to $Y_2 = N\theta_H$.

Let r denote the constant rate at which agents can borrow and lend—for simplicity, the world interest rate. The reform program is *efficient* if the **present value** of national income rises relative to no reform, that is,

$$Y_1 + \frac{Y_2}{1+r} > Y_0 + \frac{Y_0}{1+r},$$

or equivalently, setting $\beta = 1/(1+r)$:

$$Y_1 + \beta Y_2 > (1+\beta)Y_0. \tag{17.1}$$

Consider a worker who loses his (or her) job when the reform is implemented in period 1 and receives no compensation of any sort. His income is thus 0 in period 1 and θ_H in period 2, because full employment is restored. If the reform is not implemented, his income is θ_L in both periods. In present value terms, the worker would therefore lose from the reform if

$$\theta_L + \frac{\theta_L}{1+r} > 0 + \frac{\theta_H}{1+r},$$

that is,

$$(1+\beta)\theta_L > \beta\theta_H. \tag{17.2}$$

Given the definitions of Y_0, Y_1 and Y_2, Equation (17.1) can be rewritten as

$$(1-\alpha)N\theta_L + \beta N\theta_H > (1+\beta)N\theta_L,$$

---

[6] Wyplosz's argument was developed in the context of transition economies, but it applies with equal force to developing countries engaged in public sector downsizing (see Chapter 15).

that is,

$$(1 - \alpha) + \beta \frac{\theta_H}{\theta_L} > (1 + \beta).$$

This inequality can be rewritten as

$$\frac{\theta_H}{\theta_L} > \frac{1 + \beta}{\beta} - \frac{1 - \alpha}{\beta} = \frac{\alpha + \beta}{\beta}. \tag{17.3}$$

From Equation (17.2), $\theta_H/\theta_L < (1 + \beta)/\beta$. Combining this result with Equation (17.3) implies that the economic reform program must guarantee the **efficiency condition**

$$\frac{\alpha + \beta}{\beta} < \frac{\theta_H}{\theta_L} < \frac{1 + \beta}{\beta}, \tag{17.4}$$

which ensures that from the point of view of society as a whole *and* from the point of view of the individual worker who runs the risk of being fired, the program is worth implementing. Condition (17.4) will be assumed to hold in what follows. However, it does not ensure that the program is *welfare enhancing*. Let $v(c_h)$, where c_h is consumption at period h, denote the utility function of each identical worker; $v(\cdot)$ is taken to satisfy the usual conditions for positive and decreasing marginal utility, $v' > 0$ and $v'' < 0$ (see Chapter 1) . For a reform to be *ex ante* **politically acceptable**, it must be that workers expect their own situation to improve, that is,

$$\mathbf{E}[v(c_1) + \rho v(c_2)] \geq (1 + \rho)v(\tilde{c}), \tag{17.5}$$

where $\mathbf{E}$ is the mathematical expectations operator (conditional on information available at the beginning of period 1), ρ is the **time-preference factor**, which need not be equal to β, and $\tilde{c}$ the (constant) level of consumption if no reform is implemented.

Condition (17.5) is the *ex ante* **political acceptability condition**: when it is not satisfied, all workers will rationally choose to reject an adjustment program that is economically efficient. The reason is that if condition (17.5) is not satisfied, the program will immediately face political opposition upon implementation because, *ex post*, workers are *not* all identical: some become unemployed whereas others end up keeping their jobs. Consequently, the condition for *ex post* political acceptability differs from condition (17.5) and may not be satisfied even when condition (17.5) is, because some workers are worse off.

The question, then, is under what conditions will the government generate sufficient support (or a sufficient degree of consensus) to implement the program anyway? In the present case, suppose that the government cares about income distribution between those workers who retain their jobs and those who become unemployed during the transition period. This concern about income distribution can be captured by the way the government manipulates unemployment benefits in period 1, b.

To begin with, suppose that neither the government nor individuals are able to borrow against future income, either at home or abroad. Workers consume current income ($c_1 = \theta_L$ or 0 in period 1, $c_2 = \theta_H$ in period 2) and the government must finance unemployment benefits out of taxes, τ, levied in period 1 on employed workers who continue to earn pre-reform income θ_L. As a result, *all* citizens are worse off in period 1 compared with their pre-reform situation. The *ex ante* political acceptability condition (17.5) requires that utility increases by a sufficient amount:

$$\mathbf{E}[v(c_1) + \rho v(\theta_H)] \geq (1 + \rho)v(\theta_L),$$

where $\tilde{c} = \theta_L$. In the presence of an unemployment benefit b, given that c_1 depends on the state of nature and that firing occurs randomly (and thus with probability α), this condition can be rewritten as

$$(1 - \alpha)v\left\{\theta_L - \frac{\alpha}{1 - \alpha}b\right\} + \alpha v(b) \geq (1 + \rho)v(\theta_L) - \rho v(\theta_H), \qquad (17.6)$$

where account has been taken of the government budget constraint $\alpha N b = \tau(1 - \alpha)N$, which implies that

$$\tau = \frac{\alpha}{1 - \alpha}b. \qquad (17.7)$$

Ex post, once job losses have actually occurred, workers are not all alike anymore. There are now *two* conditions for *ex post* political acceptability: one for the losers,

$$v(b) \geq (1 + \rho)v(\theta_L) - \rho v(\theta_H), \qquad (17.8)$$

and one for the winners,

$$v\left\{\theta_L - \frac{\alpha}{1 - \alpha}b\right\} \geq (1 + \rho)v(\theta_L) - \rho v(\theta_H). \qquad (17.9)$$

The *ex ante* condition (17.6) is thus a weighted average of the two *ex post* conditions: if (17.8) and (17.9) are both satisfied, (17.6) will also be satisfied, but not the other way around. The range of acceptable income distributions is wider *ex ante* than *ex post*, as seen in Figure 17.1, which displays the left-hand side of the three conditions. This result is important because it may explain why the transition phase of an adjustment program may be difficult. Because the set of politically acceptable distributions tends to narrow, majority support tends to erode during the transition—possibly leading to an abandonment of the adjustment program. For instance, if the initial position is at point A, a shift to a point such as B in the course of the program may lead to a collapse of the adjustment effort.

Maximizing *ex ante* the likelihood that the program will not be abandoned requires the government to choose an income distribution scheme (that is, an unemployment benefit level, b) that maximizes the left-hand side of condition (17.6). The solution is point C in Figure 17.1, where

$$b = \theta_L - \tau,$$

or equivalently, using condition (17.7),

$$b = (1 - \alpha)\theta_L.$$

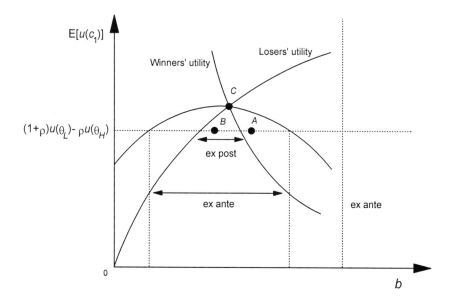

Figure 17.1. Income Distribution and Political Acceptability Regions. Source: Wyplosz (1993, p. 383).

This result implies full *ex post* income equality among *ex ante* identical citizens. If this solution is such that condition (17.6) is satisfied, then both (17.8) and (17.9) will also be satisfied: a reform that is welfare increasing for the country as a whole must also be welfare increasing for each citizen if all receive equal treatment.

To summarize the foregoing discussion, therefore, if all workers face the same probability of becoming unemployed and if economic prospects are expected to improve sufficiently, a redistributional scheme that ensures sufficient support for the implementation of reforms can be readily devised. However, once reforms are implemented and unemployment emerges, even an *ex ante* well-designed redistributional scheme may not prevent individuals that are harmed by the reforms from opposing the continuation of the adjustment program and militate for a policy reversal.

The foregoing discussion assumed that the government was unable to borrow abroad; consequently the compensation scheme had to be financed through taxes on those workers remaining employed in period 1. Suppose now that the government is able to borrow abroad to finance the benefits paid out during the transition. Taxes, τ_1 and τ_2, are levied in both periods to repay the debt. The *ex ante* political acceptability condition (17.6) is now

$$(1 - \alpha)v(\theta_L - \tau_1) + \alpha v(b) \geq (1 + \rho)v(\theta_L) - \rho v(\theta_H - \tau_2), \qquad (17.10)$$

with *ex post* conditions similar to (17.8) and (17.9). The intertemporal government budget constraint is now

$$b = \frac{(1 - \alpha)}{\alpha}\tau_1 + \frac{\beta}{\alpha}\tau_2. \qquad (17.11)$$

Although condition (17.10) is less stringent than (17.6), most of the qualitative results derived earlier continue to apply. In particular, the economic efficiency condition (17.1) still does not necessarily imply *ex ante* support, nor does *ex ante* support provide complete guarantee of *ex post* acceptability. Again, maximizing *ex ante* political support requires the government to maximize Equation (17.10), subject to (17.11), with respect to b; the first-order condition is

$$-\alpha(1 - \alpha)\frac{v'(\theta_L - \tau_1)}{1 - \alpha} + \alpha v'(b) - (\frac{\alpha}{\beta})\rho v'(\theta_H - \tau_2) = 0,$$

which can be rearranged as

$$v'(b) = v'(\theta_L - \tau_1) + (\frac{\rho}{\beta})v'(\theta_H - \tau_2). \qquad (17.12)$$

With a **logarithmic utility function,**[7]

$$v(c) = \ln c, \qquad (17.13)$$

Equation (17.12) becomes

$$\frac{1}{b} = \frac{1}{\theta_L - \tau_1} + \frac{\rho}{\beta(\theta_H - \tau_2)}. \qquad (17.14)$$

Using Equations (17.13) and (17.14), Equation (17.10) can be rewritten as, after some manipulations

$$\frac{\theta_H}{\theta_L} \geq \frac{\alpha + \rho}{\beta}, \qquad (17.15)$$

Given condition (17.4), a *sufficient* condition for political acceptability is thus

$$\beta \geq \rho, \qquad (17.16)$$

that is, the government must be able to borrow at an interest rate that is lower than the rate of time preference. In that case, *ex post* acceptability is guaranteed. On the contrary, a sufficient (although not necessary) condition for (17.15) to be *rejected*, using condition (17.4), is:

$$1 + \beta \leq \alpha + \rho. \qquad (17.17)$$

---

[7]Wyplosz considers a more general utility function, which generalizes conditions (17.16) and (17.17).

Thus, the higher the rate of unemployment in period 1, α, or the lower the discount factor, β (or the higher the interest rate) the more likely condition (17.15) will be rejected. Hence, only in cases where the cost of borrowing is not too high will access to international capital markets and foreign loans (by private agents or the government itself) be able to help alleviate the costs of transition and hence facilitate political sustainability.

The foregoing analysis suggests therefore that assessing the political consequences of its actions is a crucial step for a reform-minded government; these consequences determine, at least in part, the sustainability of the initial decisions and whether or not delays (or partial reversals) occur in the implementation of the reform program. In that perspective, it has been increasingly recognized that adjustment programs must include a **social safety net**, that is, a combination of measures aimed at mitigating the short-term adverse effects of economic reform on *losers*—often the poorest segments of the population. Such measures, advocates claim, may help to enhance the political sustainability of the program. Typical reforms with potentially adverse consequences for the most vulnerable include reduction of generalized price subsidies on basic necessities, restructuring of state enterprises, and civil service downsizing. Safety nets often include the following components:

- *Targeted subsidies* and *cash compensation.* These schemes have sought to protect the consumption of basic food items by the poor in the face of rising prices, while reducing budgetary expenditure.

- *Unemployment benefits, severance pay,* and *public works schemes.* Because reforms usually involve a temporary increase in unemployment, an important aspect of social safety nets has been enhanced unemployment benefit schemes, the provision of severance pay, and low-wage public works schemes.

In practice, however, even a well-designed social safety net may not be politically effective, in the sense of enhancing the political acceptability and sustainability of the reform process. The reason is that losers of economic reform are not necessarily the poor; for instance, a sharp reduction in tariff protection will hurt *producers* (and not only workers) in import-substitution industries. As a group, these producers (who presumably do not benefit from the safety net) may be quite effective in blocking further reform or forcing the government to reverse the process of trade liberalization.

17.4   Shock Treatment or Gradual Approach?

As indicated earlier, various economists have argued that shock therapy is preferable in implementing reform programs, because of complementarities between policy instruments. As also noted earlier, however, trade-offs may arise in the use of policy instruments, making gradualism a less risky approach. In general, the *economic* arguments in favor of gradualism are the following:

- **Preexisting distortions**, which cannot be removed at the time the reform program is announced. Such distortions include labor market rigidities, which are often pervasive in developing countries (as noted earlier), capital market imperfections, and a propensity by private agents to overborrow (Edwards and van Wijnbergen, 1986).

- **Imperfect credibility**, which, as stressed by Calvo (1989), is tantamount to a distortion in the intertemporal price of tradable goods. As noted in Chapter 14, if the public wrongly believes that trade liberalization will be reverted in the future, maintaining (or reinforcing) quantitative controls on the capital account may be called for.[8]

- **Congestion externalities**, which may create too much transitional unemployment (relative to the market optimum) after a shock treatment (Gavin, 1996).

- **Weak financial system**. Experience with capital account liberalization in recent years supports the view that, although desirable, financial openness may need to proceed gradually over time. As noted in Chapter 15, premature liberalization can be risky in the absence of adequate prudential regulations of the banking system.

There are also a number of *political economy* arguments for and against gradualism. The fundamental reason why the pace of reform can be heavily influenced by political constraints is because all structural reforms involve (as emphasized in the previous section) some **distributional changes** in favor of some groups and against others, and there are limits to how much such changes can be tolerated. Along these lines, proponents of shock therapy have argued such an approach does not allow time for *opposition* to build up and for *interest groups* to get together to increase their lobbying activities against the reforms. In particular, for a new, reformist government, maintaining the momentum for reform may be difficult beyond a **honeymoon period**; a gradual approach would give the political opposition time to organize itself and gather strength.

There are also, however, political arguments in favor of a gradualist approach to structural reforms. The general idea is that it may help to minimize adjustment costs and limit the distributional burdens on particular groups in the initial phases of reform. Dewatripont and Roland (1992) provided a good example of this type of argument. Following the logic of their analysis, consider a reform-minded government facing an inefficient public sector with workers that are *heterogeneous* in terms of the employment opportunities that they face in the private sector. Improving allocative efficiency requires a shift to higher productivity activities and lay-offs in the public sector. In order to make shock

---

[8]Rodrik (1989), among others, claimed that if imperfect credibility arises because the public is unsure about the true preferences of the government, shock therapy may be preferable to a gradual approach because overshooting can act as a *signaling* device. However, as noted in Chapter 5, if drastic policies are not perceived to be *sustainable*, they may be counterproductive.

therapy *politically acceptable*, all workers in the public sector must be paid the same compensation, which is determined by the income loss of the less productive worker and therefore maximizes the fiscal cost. Hence, shock therapy is costly, and if raising revenue is *distortionary*, a gradual reform (which generates less of a budgetary burden) may be preferable on welfare grounds. However, the argument loses weight if governments can indeed finance compensation cost, for instance through **foreign assistance** (as in the Wyplosz model presented earlier) and by providing a well-targeted **social safety net**. In such conditions, shock therapy may remain preferable.[9]

Another argument in favor of gradualism was proposed by Dewatripont and Roland (1995), who argued that if partial reforms are *unstable*—in the sense that they cannot yield full results unless they are complemented by other reforms—at each stage of the reform process the issue is between accepting the next set of reforms or reversing the previous one. If the previous reforms are deemed successful, people are more willing to accept further (possibly less popular) reforms so as not to lose the gains achieved as a result of the previous set of reforms and to avoid a costly policy reversal. A related argument was presented by Wei (1998), who argued that a gradual approach to reform may allow the building of constituencies for reform.[10] A package of reforms that would have been rejected by majority voting may gain approval if submitted *piecemeal*, thus allowing information about costs to flow and alliances to form. This argument is diametrically opposite to the one conventionally made about shock therapy—the ability to prevent vested interests to get organized and block the reform process. Martinelli and Tommasi (1998), however, criticized Wei's argument on the ground that, in societies with powerful interest groups and characterized by a cobweb of redistributive and distortionary policies, unbundling a reform program may be **time inconsistent**. Winners of early reforms who are hurt by later reforms have an incentive to *stop* the gradual path in its later stages. Knowing that, losers from early reforms will oppose the earlier measures. In such conditions, there may be no alternative to shock therapy.

The implication of the foregoing discussion is that there is no general rule for determining the optimal pace of economic reforms. Initial economic and political conditions facing the reforming economy, and possibly the amount of foreign assistance available, determine the optimal pace of reform. On the one hand, a faster pace of reform may *enhance credibility* in the reform process if the results achieved in the short run are sufficiently favorable to vindicate the reforms and those who implement them, and thereby ensure against reversibility. On the other, shock therapy may impose *high transitional costs* and hence weaken political support for reform. A gradualist approach can generate greater credibility if it avoids unnecessary disruptions in the short run and allows time for those who benefit from the reforms to gather strength and develop a vested interest in their continuation.

---

[9] However, as noted earlier, even a well-designed safety net may not have much effect on the political sustainability of reform programs.

[10] Wei's analytical framework is based on the model developed by Fernández and Rodrik (1991), which emphasizes individual-specific uncertainty (see Chapter 14).

17.5   Summary

- Stabilization and adjustment policies have effects that often operate in the same direction; these **policy complementarities** provide arguments for a *comprehensive approach* to reform, and for **shock therapy**. However, macroeconomic and structural policies may also have *conflicting effects*, particularly in the short run. In such conditions, it may be optimal to adopt a less comprehensive and more gradual program.

- If productive resources could move instantaneously and without cost among alternative uses, and if product and factor prices could adjust immediately to clear all markets, the optimal reform program would entail removing all distortions immediately and simultaneously. In practice, however, productive resources cannot be moved instantaneously and costlessly among contracting and expanding sectors of the economy, and the various markets concerned adjust with different speeds toward their long-run equilibrium in response to various reforms.

- The opening of the *capital account* should occur in general after trade account liberalization and domestic financial reforms. Because large capital flows tend to increase the vulnerability of weak financial systems, an adequate prudential, regulatory, and supervision infrastructure must be put in place before the capital account is liberalized.

- Beyond that, however, there are few general principles on the proper sequencing of reforms. The analytical basis for comparing different sequences for removing structural distortions (including those on *labor markets*) in a **second-best world** is limited. In practice, therefore, the appropriate sequence will depend on characteristics specific to each country.

- Changes associated with the beginning of a process of economic reform almost inevitably give rise to **distributional conflicts**. Such conflicts are particularly likely to emerge in cases in which the winners and losers from reform are difficult to identify *ex ante*. If the political system is fragmented or a large degree of consensus is needed for the continuation of reforms, these conflicts will make it more difficult to sustain politically the reform process. Indeed, they may engender a situation in which the reform process stalls because no sufficient consensus can be gathered for a continuation or reversal of policies—a **status quo bias**.

- There is no general rule for choosing between **shock treatment** and a **gradualist approach** in economic reforms. Initial economic and political conditions, and possibly the level of foreign aid, determine the optimal pace of reform. A faster pace of reform may enhance *credibility* in the adjustment process and reduce the risk of policy reversals if the short-run outcomes are favorable enough to vindicate the initial decisions. On the other, shock therapy may impose *high transitional costs* and hence weaken political support for reform.

Appendix
The Costs of Corruption

Corruption is generally defined as the abuse of public office for private gain (Klitgaard, 1988). Although corruption is a widespread phenomenon, its incidence is particularly pervasive where, as is the case in many developing countries, *large and inefficient bureaucracies* exist, *regulations* lack transparency, *property rights* are not well defined, and *judicial systems* are deficient. More specifically, the incidence of corruption is closely related to **rent-seeking behavior** (as defined in Chapter 12). Such behavior may be exacerbated by the presence of government-induced sources of rents—quantitative restrictions on trade (such as quotas on imports), subsidies (for instance to public enterprises), price controls, foreign exchange allocation schemes, and low wages in the public sector—or factors such as resource endowments and sociological factors (Bardhan, 1997).

Most of the economic literature on corruption uses the **principal-agent framework** to analyze the relationship between the government (the principal) and the bureaucrats (the agents).[11] Corruption is seen as the result of **imperfect monitoring** by the government. Bureaucrats take bribes in the process of buying and selling goods from the private sector on behalf of the government. Such a framework is used to examine the extent to which bribery is affected by alternative sanctions or incentives, monitoring technologies, and the degree of competition among agents and private individuals in providing government goods to the private sector and in selling privately produced goods to the government.

A good example of this type of model is the one developed by Shleifer and Vishny (1993). In the Shleifer-Vishny framework, bureaucrats take bribes from private individuals demanding government-produced goods. Taking this relationship as given, the model attempts to explain both the *incidence* of corruption as well as its *costs*. To explain the incidence of corruption requires assessing the *degree of competition* among bureaucrats and consumers. The model assumes that the private sector needs various complementary government goods as inputs (that is, licenses, permits, and so on) provided through various public agencies—each run by a bureaucrat. With multiple government goods, the market structure, in the provisions of these goods, helps explain the incidence of corruption. Shleifer and Vishny analyzed three types of market structure:

- the different bureaucratic agencies, each supplying one (and only one) of the complementary government goods, collude in *one monopoly*;

---

[11] The use of economic analysis to study corruption (or, rather, crime and law enforcement in general) was pioneered by Becker (1968). Becker showed that the amount of *resources* (spent on police, courts, and so on) and the *punishment* that should be used to enforce the rule of law are determined by minimizing a social loss function—which captures the net cost of crime to society, the cost of apprehension and conviction, and the cost of punishing offenders. He concluded that the probability of apprehension and conviction (which depends on the level of resources spent) and the potential punishment deter offenders at the margin; thus *crime not paying off* (at the margin) is an optimality condition and not a statement about the efficiency of police activities and the judicial system.

- the agencies, each supplying one (and only one) of the complementary government goods, act as *independent monopolists*;

- the agencies, each supplying more than one of the government-produced goods, *compete* in the provision of these goods.

They concluded that the third case (competition) yields the lowest level of bribes, the second (independent monopolists) the highest, and the first (collusion) in between. The total bribe revenue collection, however, is the highest in the first case where the agencies collude, precisely to maximize the total value of bribes.

The *consequences* of corruption are pervasive. Because bribes to corrupt officials act as an implicit tax, they *reduce* the **incentive to invest**—and thus, ultimately, hinder economic growth. It also has an adverse effect on the *allocation of talent* and *skills*, as emphasized by Murphy, Shleifer, and Vishny (1991) and as noted in Chapter 12: in an environment where the return to corruption is high, the more talented and highly educated will be more likely to engage in rent-seeking activities than in productive ones—again, with potentially adverse effects on long-run growth. It also implies a loss of tax revenue (as a result, for instance, of illegal use of tax exemptions), higher public expenditure (through higher subsidies, for instance), and lower quality of public services. Finally, corruption may also reduce the effectiveness of *foreign aid*, by channeling funds to unproductive government expenditures.

Owing to its very nature, corruption is difficult to measure. Various attempts have been made, in recent years, to construct (subjective) indices of the degree of corruption across countries. These indices are subject to a number of limitations; in particular, they typically do not distinguish between *high-level* corruption (involving, say, senior government officials) and *low-level* corruption (involving bureaucrats at the low end of public administrations); these two types of activities are likely to be substantially different in their economic effects. Nevertheless, several studies (based on cross-sectional regressions) have provided evidence suggesting that corruption may have a large, adverse effect on investment and growth. Mauro (1997), in particular, estimates that to a large extent the effects of corruption on growth takes place through investment.

Annex A

Informal Sector and Urban Labor Market

The purpose of this annex is to present an analytical framework that captures some of the main features of the urban labor market in developing countries. A key feature of the model is its emphasis on efficiency considerations along the lines of the **shirking model** developed by Shapiro and Stiglitz (1984).[1] The first section presents the basic framework and focuses on the case where only skilled workers may face unemployment. Section A.2 extends the basic setup to consider unemployment of unskilled workers by introducing a **Harris-Todaro migration mechanism** which generates **wait unemployment** as a result of workers' decisions to queue for jobs in the formal sector. Section A.3 considers the effects of an increase in the minimum wage in the alternative settings presented in the previous sections, and analyzes the behavior of relative wages, unemployment, and the distribution of employment across sectors.

A.1   The Basic Framework

Consider an economy producing two nonstorable goods. The domestic prices of both goods are constant and normalized to unity.[2]

- The first good is produced in the **formal sector**, using capital as well as skilled and unskilled labor. The wage paid to unskilled workers is the *legally binding minimum wage*, whereas the wage paid to skilled work-

---

[1] As discusssed by Agénor (1996), a growing literature supports the existence of efficiency considerations in the modern sector in developing countries. The evidence often takes the form of large interindustry wage differentials for equally-skilled workers. See Gatica, Mizala and Romaguera (1995) for a recent study focusing on Brazil.

[2] The assumption of constant prices can be justified by assuming that both goods are tradables. See Agénor (1999) for a more general treatment, in which relative prices are endogenously determined.

ers (together with the employment level of both categories of labor) are determined by firms' optimization decisions.

- The second good is produced in the **informal sector** using only unskilled labor. In the basic framework considered for the moment, wages in the informal sector adjust instantaneously to clear the labor market.

There are no physical or institutional impediments to mobility across sectors for either category of workers. As a result, skilled workers who are unable to find employment in the formal sector may work as unskilled workers in the informal sector if they so decide. Both categories of workers have infinite lives, and discount future earnings at the constant rate $\rho > 0$. Capital markets do not exist, and neither group may lend or borrow.

Endowments of skilled and unskilled workers—and thus the economy's total labor force—is assumed fixed throughout. The number of firms operating in each production sector is also assumed fixed, and is normalized to unity.

The representative firm in the informal sector produces output Q_I using labor in quantity n_I. Supervision and monitoring of workers' activities are costless, so that employed workers always provide the level of effort required by their employers, e_U. The production technology is characterized by diminishing returns:

$$Q_I = Q_I(n_I), \quad Q_I' > 0, Q_I'' < 0. \tag{A1}$$

The firm takes wages as given and hires labor up to the point where the cost of the marginal unit of labor just offsets its product. The demand for labor in the informal sector is therefore given by

$$n_I^d = n_I^d(w_I), \quad n_I' = 1/Q_I'' < 0, \tag{A2}$$

where w_I denotes the market-clearing wage, which is determined below.

Production in the formal sector is a function of both labor inputs, skilled labor, n_S, and unskilled labor, n_U:

$$Q_F = Q_F(n_S, n_U), \tag{A3}$$

where the function $Q_F(\cdot)$ exhibits positive but decreasing marginal productivity to each labor category. Using a **quadratic approximation** and dropping constant terms yields

$$Q_F = \sigma_1 n_S + \sigma_2 n_U + \sigma_{11} n_S^2/2 + \sigma_{22} n_U^2/2 + \sigma_{12} n_S n_U,$$

where $\sigma_1, \sigma_2 > 0$, and $\sigma_{11}, \sigma_{22} < 0$. Labor inputs are assumed to be **Edgeworth complements**, so that $\sigma_{12} > 0$.[3]

---

[3] Evidence on the degree of substitutability between skilled and unskilled labor in developing countries is reviewed by Agénor (1996). The evidence suggests that skilled and unskilled workers in the modern sector tend to be *Hicks-Allen substitutes*, that is, that the *output-constant cross elasticities* of demand for each category of labor are positive. This, of course, does not preclude the possibility that these two groups of workers be gross complements at the same time.

The minimum wage for unskilled labor in the formal sector is set by the government at the level w_m, and firms comply fully with the legislation. In equilibrium, the minimum wage is assumed to be strictly greater than the informal sector market-clearing wage $(w_m > w_I)$.[4] From the first-order conditions for profit maximization, and normalizing constant terms to zero, the demand functions for unskilled and skilled labor in the formal sector are, respectively,

$$n_U^d = (\sigma_{11} w_m - \sigma_{12} w_S)/\Delta, \qquad (A4)$$

$$n_S^d = (\sigma_{22} w_S - \sigma_{12} w_m)/\Delta, \qquad (A5)$$

where w_S denotes the efficiency wage paid to skilled workers and

$$\Delta = \sigma_{22} \sigma_{11} - \sigma_{12}^2,$$

which is positive as a result of the *second-order conditions* for profit maximization. Equations (A4) and (A5) indicate that both an increase in the wage earned by skilled workers and in the minimum wage reduces the demand for both categories of labor.

Both categories of workers are **risk neutral** and dislike effort. Their instantaneous utility function takes the linear form

$$u(w, e) = w - e,$$

where w is the wage earned in the sector of employment and e the actual level of effort. The effort level provided by unskilled workers in the formal sector and those employed in the informal sector is the same, e_U, and corresponds to the level of effort required by employers. Skilled workers, however, have the *possibility to shirk* because firms in the formal sector cannot monitor perfectly their on-the-job effort. They supply either the level of effort required from them $(e = e_S)$ or a zero level of effort when shirking $(e = 0)$.[5] Firms, in equilibrium, set the wage of skilled workers so as to deter them from shirking and induce them to provide the required level of effort.

The *monitoring technology* is such that there exists a constant probability (per unit time), v, that a skilled worker engaged in shirking is caught. If detected, the worker is fired and faces two options:

- he or she can remain unemployed in the formal sector; or

---

[4] This assumption ensures that unskilled workers will look for job opportunities in the formal sector first, and avoids *corner solutions*. More generally, it could be assumed that employment in the formal sector provides also a nonpecuniary benefit, such as an enhanced social status. As a result of this assumption, the informal sector market-clearing wage could be either higher or lower than the legal minimum wage in equilibrium—but the wage differential would still need to be less than the nonpecuniary benefit.

[5] The assumption that shirking involves a zero level of effort is made for simplicity only. It is straightforward to generalize the analysis to consider the case where even when shirking, workers provide a *minimum* level of effort.

- he or she can seek employment in the informal sector.[6]

In general, the choice between these two options depends on a variety of factors, both noneconomic (such as the perceived *loss of social status*) and economic—for instance, whether informal-sector employment has an **adverse signaling effect** or whether it is easier to seek a job in the formal sector by being unemployed or working in the informal sector. Here the choice is assumed to depend solely on whether the worker's **reservation wage** is higher or lower than the going wage in the informal sector, adjusted for the disutility of effort.

Let τ denote the exogenous turnover rate per unit of time for skilled workers. Following Shapiro and Stiglitz (1984), asset-like equations can be used to derive the wage of skilled workers. Let V_{Fs}^S denote the expected lifetime utility of a skilled worker currently employed in the formal sector who chooses to shirk, and let V_{Fn}^S be the expected utility stream if the employed worker is not shirking. The asset equations are

$$\rho V_{Fs}^S = w_S + (\tau + \upsilon)(V_n^S - V_{Fs}^S), \tag{A6}$$

$$\rho V_{Fn}^S = w_S - e_S + \tau(V_n^S - V_{Fn}^S), \tag{A7}$$

where V_n^S is the expected lifetime utility of a skilled worker who is not employed in the formal sector.[7] Equations (A6) and (A7) can be interpreted as indicating that the interest rate times the asset value equals the flow benefits (dividends) plus the expected capital gain (or loss). For instance, if a skilled worker shirks, he or she obtains the wage w_S without providing any effort but faces a probability $\tau + \upsilon$ of losing his or her job, thus incurring a loss in utility equal to $(V_{Fs}^S - V_n^S)$.

To elicit the appropriate level of effort requires that $V_{Fn}^S \geq V_{Fs}^S$, so that, using Equations (A6) and (A7):

$$w_S \geq \rho V_n^S + \frac{\Lambda e_S}{\upsilon}, \quad \Lambda \equiv \rho + \tau + \upsilon. \tag{A8}$$

---

[6] In principle, a skilled worker who attaches a nonpecuniary benefit to formal sector employment may also be willing to accept an unskilled position in that sector. This case can be excluded by assuming that an employer whose aim is to minimize frictions among its employees would refrain from hiring skilled workers to fill unskilled positions, while at the same time other skilled workers occupy positions consistent with their qualifications.

[7] Consider, for instance, Eq. (A7). Following Shapiro and Stiglitz (1984), the expected utility stream derived within an infinitesimally small time interval $(t, t + dt)$ can be defined as

$$V_{Fn}^S = (w_S - e_S)dt + \exp(-\rho dt)[(1 - \tau dt)V_{Fn}^S + \tau dt V_n^S],$$

because τdt measures the probability of a skilled worker leaving the job during the interval $(t, t + dt)$. Approximating the discount factor by $\exp(-\rho dt) \simeq 1 - \rho dt$ and solving for V_{Fn}^S yields

$$V_{Fn}^S = (w_S - e_S)dt + (1 - \rho dt)\tau dt(V_n^S - V_{Fn}^S)/[1 - (1 - \rho dt)].$$

Taking limits as $dt \to 0$ yields Eq. (A7).

Equation (A8) is the **no-shirking condition** (*NSC*) originally derived by Shapiro and Stiglitz (1984). In equilibrium this condition holds as an equality, and a rational worker will be indifferent between working and not working.

A.2   Equilibrium with Luxury Unemployment

The equilibrium solution of the model requires solving for the informal sector market-clearing wage and calculating V_n^S, the expected lifetime utility of a skilled worker not employed in the formal sector, to determine w_S. As indicated before, whether a skilled worker who is not hired in the formal sector takes up employment in the informal economy or enters the unemployment pool depends on whether utility while employed in the informal sector, $w_I - e_U$, is greater or lower than θ, the **reservation wage**—which can be viewed here as the imputed value (in wage units) of leisure.

Along the lines of Shapiro and Stiglitz (1984), skilled workers perceive the transition probabilities into a formal-sector job out of informal unemployment or unemployment as identical and equal to the exogenous hiring rate (or employment probability), a. The asset equations for a skilled worker who is not employed in the formal sector are therefore equal to

$$\rho V_n^S = \theta + a(V_F^S - V_n^S), \quad w_I - e_U \leq \theta, \tag{A9}$$

$$\rho V_n^S = w_I - e_U + a(V_F^S - V_n^S), \quad w_I - e_U > \theta, \tag{A10}$$

where it is assumed that, in equilibrium, the no-shirking condition (A8) holds with equality so that

$$V_{Fn}^S = V_{Fs}^S = V_F^S.$$

The quantity $a(V_F^S - V_n^S)$ in Equations (A9) and (A10) is equal to the *net expected utility gain* of being employed in the formal sector, times the probability (per unit time) of being hired in that sector.

Solving Equations (A7), (A9) and (A10) simultaneously yields the expected discounted utility of a skilled worker not employed in the formal sector:

$$\rho V_n^S = \frac{\theta(\rho + \tau)}{\Omega} + \frac{a}{\Omega}(w_S - e_S), \quad w_I - e_U \leq \theta, \tag{A11}$$

$$\rho V_n^S = w_I - e_U + \frac{a}{\Omega}[(w_S - e_S) - (w_I - e_U)], \quad w_I - e_U > \theta, \tag{A12}$$

where $\Omega = a + \rho + \tau$.

Substituting these results in (A8) yields

$$w_S = \Omega^{-1}[\theta(\rho + \tau) + a(w_S - e_S)] + \frac{e_S \Lambda}{v}, \quad w_I - e_U \leq \theta, \tag{A13}$$

$$w_S = w_I - e_U + \frac{a}{\Omega}[(w_S - e_S) - (w_I - e_U)] + \frac{e_S \Lambda}{v}. \quad w_I - e_U > 0. \quad \text{(A14)}$$

In a steady-state equilibrium, the flow of skilled workers in and out of employment in the formal sector must be equal. Because all skilled workers who are not currently employed in the formal sector can be hired by firms in that sector, it must be that

$$\tau n_S^d = a(\bar{n}_S - n_S^d), \quad \text{(A15)}$$

where $\bar{L}_S$ denotes the total number of skilled workers available.

Substituting Equation (A15) for a in Equations (A13) and (A14) yields the **steady-state NSC**:

$$w_S = \theta + \frac{e_S}{v}\left\{\Lambda + \frac{\tau n_S^d}{\bar{n}_S - n_S^d}\right\}, \quad w_I - e_U \leq \theta, \quad \text{(A16)}$$

$$w_S - e_S = w_I - e_U + \frac{e_S}{v}\left\{\Lambda + \frac{\tau n_S^d}{\bar{n}_S - n_S^d}\right\}, \quad w_I - e_U > 0. \quad \text{(A17)}$$

Equations (A16) and (A17) indicate that to deter skilled workers from shirking, firms must pay a going wage sufficiently high relative to the opportunity cost of effort. The difference between Equations (A16) and (A17) is that in the first case an increase in the informal sector wage—which is such that the condition $w_I - e_U \leq \theta$ continues to hold—has *no effect* on the efficiency wage, whereas in the second case it raises in the *same proportion* the efficiency wage. The wage differential between skilled and unskilled workers (adjusted for the disutility of effort) for $w_I - e_U > 0$, and the wage level itself for $w_I - e_U \leq \theta$, depend positively on the required level of effort in the formal sector, the turnover rate, and the discount rate (because future losses incurred if caught shirking are less valued), and negatively on the probability v of being caught shirking.

The market-clearing wage in the informal sector depends on whether skilled workers seek employment in the informal economy or not, that is, on whether $w_I - e_U \gtrless \theta$. If skilled workers choose to remain unemployed, the equilibrium wage is determined by

$$n_U^s - n_U^d = n_I^d, \quad w_I - e_U \leq \theta, \quad \text{(A18)}$$

where $n_U^s = n^s - n_S^s$ denotes the total number of unskilled workers, and n^s the size of the labor force. If skilled workers decide to take up employment in the informal sector, by contrast, the equilibrium condition of the informal-sector labor market is

$$n^s - (n_S^d + n_U^d) = n_I^d, \quad w_I - e_U > 0. \quad \text{(A19)}$$

Equations (A18) and (A19) can be solved for w_I as a function of the efficiency wage and the minimum wage, as shown below.

Thus, depending on whether $w_S - e_U \gtrless \theta$, *two equilibria* may emerge in the above framework.

Consider first the case where the informal sector wage—net of the disutility of effort—exceeds the reservation wage ($w_I - e_U > \theta$), so that skilled workers subject to job rationing opt to take unskilled positions in the informal sector. The equilibrium is consequently characterized by **full employment**, and is depicted in Figure A1. In panel A, the demand curves for both skilled and unskilled workers in the formal sector are shown to be inversely related to the efficiency wage. Panel B gives the supply constraint imposed by the given size of the labor force. Using the 45-degree line shown in that quadrant, the demand for unskilled labor in the informal sector can be reported from panel A to panel C. The overall labor supply constraint determines, given the level of employment of skilled workers, the residual supply of labor in both sectors, $n^s - n_S^d$. This quantity is also equal to total demand for unskilled workers, the demand curve of which is also shown in panel C as $n_U^d + n_I^d$. By subtracting vertically from the total demand curve the level of employment of unskilled workers in the formal sector, the demand curve for unskilled labor in the informal sector and the market-clearing wage are obtained. The equilibrium wage for unskilled workers is determined at point C, with total employment in the informal sector measured by the distance CC'. The *NSC* condition, which is shown in panel D as a positive relation between w_S and w_I, is derived by substituting the demand function for skilled workers, Equation (A5), in Equation (A17). Given the informal sector wage (determined at point C), the efficiency wage is determined through the *NSC* curve at point D.[8] Finally, given the *NSC*, the demand for skilled labor is determined at point A.

In the second case, where the informal sector wage (again, adjusted for the disutility of effort) is too low relative to the reservation wage ($w_I - e_U \leq \theta$), rationed workers prefer to remain unemployed rather than work in the informal sector. The **luxury unemployment** equilibrium is illustrated in Figure A2, which is constructed essentially in the same manner as Figure A1. The *NSC*, however, is now *horizontal*—because w_S does not depend on w_I—as shown in panel D of the diagram. The demand for skilled workers is again determined at point A, but skilled unemployment prevails, at the rate $(n_S^s - n_S^d)/n_S^d$.

Thus, in this basic framework, unemployment affects only skilled workers, and can be deemed **quasi-voluntary**. It is *involuntary* in the sense that employment opportunities requiring highly qualified workers are demand constrained, and all skilled workers (given the required level of effort) would prefer to earn the efficiency wage. It is also *voluntary*, however, in the sense that skilled workers could find employment in the informal sector but opt not to work there—because their **reservation wage** (or, equivalently, the opportunity cost of effort) is too high relative to the going wage.

---

[8]Note that when skilled workers elect to seek employment in the informal sector the no-shirking efficiency wage will depend, through w_I, on the level of employment of both categories of workers in the formal economy. Note also that from Eq. (A17), the informal sector wage is always lower than the efficiency wage.

A.3   Unemployment of Unskilled Labor

The assumption of wage flexibility and the absence of barriers to entry in the
informal sector in the basic framework developed above implies that unemployment of unskilled workers cannot emerge in equilibrium. A worker who is unable
to find employment in the formal economy can always be hired in the informal
sector at the going wage. These features of the model, as discussed by Agénor
(1996), are well supported by the evidence: in several developing countries, open
unemployment tends to affect mostly skilled workers, because unskilled workers
(in the absence of any *unemployment benefits*, as discussed in Chapter 14) often
cannot afford to remain unemployed for long. Nevertheless, even where it does
not exist on a massive scale, open unskilled unemployment can be observed in
a number of developing countries.

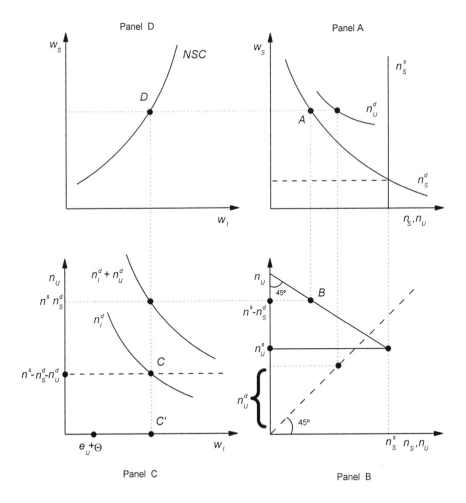

Figure A.1. Equilibrium with Full Employment.

Accordingly, this section extends the basic framework to account for the possibility of unemployment of unskilled workers. The analysis focuses essentially on a mechanism similar to the one underlying the migration model of Harris and Todaro (1970), which provides an explanation for **wait unemployment**, that is, a situation where workers' wage expectations lead them to remain unemployed and queue up for job opportunities in the formal sector.

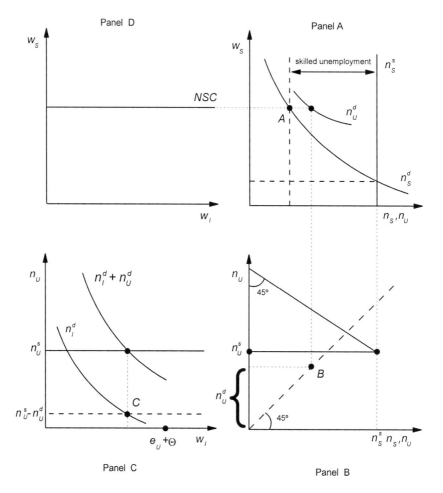

Figure A.2. Equilibrium with Unemployment of Skilled Labor.

Suppose that, as before, on-the-job search is excluded and that employers in the formal sector can hire only out of the pool of unemployed workers. Along the lines of the migration mechanism proposed by Harris and Todaro (1970), unskilled workers may opt not to take a job in the informal sector and instead remain unemployed if the perceived benefit of doing so is higher than the opportunity cost of waiting. To determine these benefits and costs suppose that unskilled workers' reservation wage is θ_U, which is lower than the legal minimum wage (so that unskilled workers are always willing to work in the formal sector) and satisfies $w_I - e_U > \theta_U$.[9]

Let π denote the perceived employment probability (that is, the perceived hiring rate) for unskilled workers in the formal sector. In analogy with Equations (A9) and (A10), the asset equation for an unskilled worker who decides to remain unemployed is given by

$$\rho V_H = \pi(V_F^U - V_H), \tag{A20}$$

where V_F^U measures the discounted utility stream derived by an unskilled worker who works in the formal sector and and V_H the discounted utility stream derived by an unskilled worker who is unemployed. V_F^U is defined by

$$\rho V_F^U = w_m - e_U + \tau_U(V_H - V_F^U), \tag{A21}$$

where τ_U denotes the turnover rate for unskilled workers in the formal sector.

Solving Equations (A20) and (A21) implies

$$\rho V_H = \frac{\pi(w_m - e_U)}{\Gamma}, \quad \Gamma \equiv \tau_U + \rho + \pi. \tag{A22}$$

Along the lines of the Harris-Todaro mechanism, unskilled workers opt to wait for employment in the formal sector as long as the net expected utility stream of queueing is positive. In equilibrium, the expected utility stream associated with queueing (that is, being unemployed), V_H, must be equal to the discounted utility stream associated with employment in the informal sector, V_I. Because employers in the formal sector hire only out of the pool of unemployed workers, the turnover rate in the informal sector is zero in equilibrium. As a result, $V_I = (w_I - e_U)/\rho$. Using Equation (A22), the **migration equilibrium condition**, $V_H = V_I$, can be solved to yield

$$w_I = e_U + \rho V_H = (\rho + \tau_U)e_U + \pi w_m, \tag{A23}$$

which shows that in equilibrium, for a given turnover rate, an increase in the minimum wage leads to a less-than-proportional increase in wages in the informal sector.

In a stationary equilibrium, flows of unskilled workers in and out of employment in the formal sector must be equal. Thus, because formal sector firms hire only unemployed workers, an equilibrium condition similar to Equation (A15) holds:

$$\tau_U n_U^d = \pi(n_U^s - n_U^d - n_I^d), \tag{A24}$$

---

[9] If the informal sector wage (adjusted for the disutility of effort) were lower than the reservation wage ($w_I - e_U \leq \theta_U$), all unskilled workers who are unable to find a job in the formal economy would opt to remain unemployed. This situation would yield an unemployment equilibrium similar to the one described in the previous section. That interpretation is not examined here, where only the case where $w_I - e_U > \theta_U$ is considered. As shown later, however, this condition is not sufficient to prevent the emergence of wait unemployment of unskilled workers.

which can be solved for π:

$$\pi = \frac{\tau_U n_U^d}{n_U^s - n_U^d - n_I^d}.$$

Substituting this result in Equation (A23), and using (A2) and (A4), yields the equilibrium wage in the informal sector:

$$w_I = G(w_S; w_m), \quad G_{w_S} > 0. \tag{A25}$$

Equation (A25) shows that (regardless of whether skilled and unskilled workers are substitutes or complements in the formal sector) there is a *positive relationship* between the skilled wage in the formal sector and wages in the informal economy.

Given the assumed flexibility of wages in the informal sector, firms in that sector must be on their labor demand curve. Combining Equations (A2) and (A25) yields the equilibrium level of employment in the informal sector:

$$n_I^d = n_I^d(w_S; w_m), \quad \partial n_I^d/\partial w_S < 0. \tag{A26}$$

Aggregate unskilled unemployment is thus given by[10]

$$n_U^s - (n_U^d + n_I^d). \tag{A27}$$

The case of **generalized unemployment** is illustrated in Figure A3, using a similar construction process as the one used before. It assumes that $w_I - e_U \le \theta_U$, so that, as discussed in the previous section, skilled workers who are unable to find a job in the formal sector choose to remain unemployed. The *NSC* curve in panel D is thus horizontal, as in Figure A2. Relation (A25) between the efficiency wage and the informal sector wage, denoted *ILC*, is shown also in panel D. The equilibrium wage in the informal sector is determined at the intersection of the *NSC* and *ILC* curves in that panel, at point D. Employment in the informal economy is determined at the intersection between the equilibrium wage, determined at point D in panel D, and the labor demand curve in the informal sector (point C). Given the total demand for unskilled labor (in the formal and informal sectors), unskilled unemployment, $n_U^s - (n_U^d + n_I^d)$, is given by the distance $C'C''$ in panel C.

A.4   Increase in the Minimum Wage

As discussed in Chapter 14, the impact of changes in minimum wages on employment and the distribution of earnings remains controversial. In what follows, the effects of an increase in the minimum wage paid to unskilled workers on wage

---

[10] When skilled workers opt to seek employment in the informal sector, Eq. (A27) holds only if it is assumed that unskilled workers are hired first. This assumption is needed to equate the demand for labor in the informal sector with actual employment of unskilled workers in that sector. In practice, of course, it is not necessarily appropriate.

dispersion, employment allocation, and unemployment in the segmented labor market setting developed in the previous sections are examined. This is done first under the assumption that in the initial position of the economy skilled workers who are unable to find a job in the formal sector choose to work in the informal sector—an outcome that requires, as shown earlier, $w_I - e_U > \theta$.

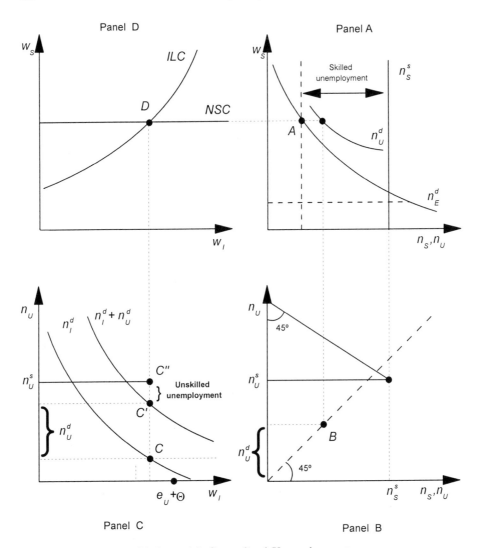

Figure A.3. Equilibrium with Generalized Unemployment.

The appendix to this annex shows that an increase in the minimum wage lowers the informal sector wage, because it reduces the demand for unskilled workers in the formal sector and raises labor supply in the informal economy. The efficiency wage also falls, thereby dampening the direct effect of the increase in the minimum wage on the demand for unskilled labor in the formal economy.

The net effect on the demand for skilled labor is ambiguous; the direct effect is to reduce the demand for that category of labor, but the indirect effect (associated with the reduction in the efficiency wage) is to increase it. The demand for labor in the informal sector also tends to increase, offsetting job losses in the formal sector.[11] Wage dispersion in the formal economy (that is, the skilled wage-minimum wage differential) tends to fall. However, because $w_m > w_I$ in the initial equilibrium, the differential between wages earned by unskilled workers in the formal and informal sectors rises. In addition, because both the skilled workers' wage and the informal sector wage fall, the net effect on the differential between these two wages is ambiguous. An important implication of the above analysis is that it is possible for the informal sector wage to fall so much that the inequality $w_I - e_U > \theta$ is reversed. In that case, skilled workers that were initially employed in the *informal sector* will choose to quit. As can be derived from the results presented in the appendix, the lower the elasticity of the demand for labor in the informal sector, the larger will be the reduction in the market-clearing wage, and thus the more likely it is that skilled unemployment will emerge.

Suppose now that in the initial equilibrium position unskilled workers who are unable to find a job in the formal sector choose to remain unemployed (that is, $w_I - e_U \leq \theta$). Similar conclusions to those obtained in the preceding case can be derived (see the appendix): the increase in the legal minimum wage raises skilled employment and shifts unskilled employment toward the informal sector. Although the skilled wage-minimum wage differential falls, wage disparity between unskilled workers in the formal and informal sectors rises.

Consider now the extended framework in which unemployment of unskilled workers may emerge in equilibrium and suppose that $w_I - e_U > \theta$ initially. Equations (A25), (A26), and (A17), written as $w_S = w_S(w_m)$, yield (see the appendix):

$$dw_I/dw_m \lessgtr 0, \quad dn_I^d/dw_m \lessgtr 0, \tag{A28}$$

which shows that an increase in the minimum wage has, in general, an ambiguous effect on the equilibrium levels of employment and wages in the informal sector.

- The increase in the minimum wage raises, on the one hand, the supply of labor in the informal sector, thus exerting downward pressure on wages there and stimulating the demand for labor.

- The movement in wages (at a given employment rate in the formal sector) on the other hand, leads more workers to queue up for employment in the formal economy. That is, for a given turnover rate in the formal sector, the increase in the minimum wage raises the expected utility

---

[11] Graphically, as can be inferred from Fig. A1, the labor demand curves for both skilled and unskilled workers shift to the left in panel A. The labor demand curves in panel C also shift to the right. The NSC curve in panel D—which depends on the minimum wage as a result of the labor demand curve—shifts downward.

stream associated with waiting in the formal economy. But because the higher legislated wage also lowers labor demand in the formal sector, the employment probability (the hiring rate) falls.

Whether the indirect wage effect is large enough to compensate for the direct effect cannot be determined a priori. If the elasticity of demand for unskilled labor in the formal sector with respect to a change in the minimum wage is less than unity in absolute value (that is, if $\sigma \equiv |w_m h'_U / h_U| < 1$, where the function h_U is defined in the appendix), the wage effect will dominate and the overall impact of an increase in the minimum wage on employment in the informal sector will be negative. By contrast, if the elasticity σ is sufficiently large, employment in the informal sector will increase.

From these results, it can be inferred that an increase in the minimum wage has also an ambiguous effect on the unemployment level of unskilled workers. If the elasticity of the demand for unskilled labor in the formal sector with respect to a change in the minimum wage is sufficiently low, unemployment will unambiguously increase.

Alternatively, consider the case where the initial situation is characterized by generalized unemployment (that is, $w_I - e_U \leq \theta$), so that the skilled workers' wage is independent of w_I. As shown in the appendix, the effect of an increase in the minimum wage on employment and wages in the informal sector remains ambiguous; if the minimum wage is initially very low, the effect is likely to be positive. For the formal sector, the results are

$$\frac{dw_S}{dw_m} > 0, \quad \frac{dn_S^d}{dw_m} > 0, \quad \frac{dn_U^d}{dw_m} < 0, \tag{A29}$$

together with

$$\frac{d(w_S - w_m)}{dw_m} < 0, \quad \frac{d(n_S^d + n_U^d)}{dw_m} < 0. \tag{A30}$$

Thus, an increase in the minimum wage raises wages and labor demand for skilled workers, and lowers employment for unskilled workers in the formal sector. The increase in the skilled wage is less than proportional, implying a reduction in wage dispersion in the formal sector. Also, aggregate employment falls in the formal sector, as the increase in skilled employment is not large enough to offset the reduction in unskilled employment.

Appendix

This Appendix establishes the sign of dw_I/dw_m under alternative assumptions about $w_I - e_U$ and perfect and imperfect mobility of the unskilled labor force.

Consider first the case of perfect mobility, and suppose that initially $w_I - e_U > \theta$. From Equation (A19), we have

$$dn_U^d + dn_S^d + dn_I^d = 0. \tag{A31}$$

From Equation (A2), $dn_I^d = n_I' dw_I$, whereas from Equations (A4) and (A5):

$$dn_U^d = \Delta^{-1}(\sigma_{11} dw_m - \sigma_{12} dw_S), \tag{A32}$$

$$dn_S^d = \Delta^{-1}(\sigma_{22} dw_S - \sigma_{12} dw_m), \tag{A33}$$

where Δ, as defined in the text, is positive. Combining the above results yields

$$\Delta^{-1}[(\sigma_{11} - \sigma_{12}) dw_m + (\sigma_{22} - \sigma_{12}) dw_S] + n_I' dw_I = 0. \tag{A34}$$

From Equation (A17), we have[12]

$$dw_S = dw_I + \gamma dn_S^d, \quad \gamma \equiv \frac{\rho \tau n_S^s}{\nu(n_S^s - \tilde{n}_S^d)^2} > 0,$$

or, using Equation (A33),

$$dw_S = dw_I + \gamma \Delta^{-1}(\sigma_{22} dw_S - \sigma_{12} dw_m). \tag{A35}$$

Equations (A34) and (A35) can be written as

$$\begin{bmatrix} n_I' & \Delta^{-1}(\sigma_{22} - \sigma_{12}) \\ 1 & \gamma\Delta^{-1}\sigma_{22} - 1 \end{bmatrix} \begin{bmatrix} dw_I \\ dw_S \end{bmatrix} = \begin{bmatrix} \Delta^{-1}(\sigma_{11} - \sigma_{12}) \\ \gamma\Delta^{-1}\sigma_{12} \end{bmatrix} dw_m,$$

from which it can be shown that, because $\sigma_{22} - \sigma_{12} < 0$ and $\sigma_{11} - \sigma_{12} < 0$:

$$dw_I/dw_m < 0.$$

Suppose now that initially $w_I - e_U \leq \theta$. From Equation (A16), the efficiency wage w_S is thus independent of w_I. Using the **implicit function theorem**—see, again, Chiang (1984, pp. 206-208)—it can be shown that the minimum wage lowers the efficiency wage; thus, $w_S = w_S(w_m)$, with $w_S' < 0$. Substituting this result in Equation (A4) yields

$$n_U^d = \Delta^{-1}[\sigma_{11} w_m - \sigma_{12} w_S(w_m)] \equiv h_U(w_m), \quad h_U' < 0, \tag{A36}$$

---

[12] In evaluating γ as well as ϕ and the C coefficients later, labor demand functions are valued at initial steady-state levels, which are denoted by '~'.

which indicates that the net effect of an increase in the minimum wage on the demand for unskilled workers in the formal sector is negative. Similarly, using Equation (A5), it can be shown that an increase in the minimum wage has an unambiguously positive effect on the demand for skilled labor.

Solving Equation (A18) using (A2) and (A36) yields

$$w_I = \frac{n_U^s - h_U(w_m)}{n_I^{d'}} \equiv w_I(w_m), \quad w_I' > 0,$$

which shows that an increase in the minimum wage lowers the market-clearing wage in the informal sector.

Consider now the model with the **Harris-Todaro migration mechanism**. Equation (A23) can be rewritten as

$$w_I - e_U - \frac{\pi}{\tau_U + \rho + \pi}(w_m - e_U) = 0. \tag{A37}$$

Substituting (A24) for π in the above equation yields an equation from which it can be shown that

$$\frac{dw_I}{dw_S} = -\frac{(w_m - e_U)\Gamma(\partial\pi/\partial w_S)}{1 - (w_m - e_U)\Gamma(\partial\pi/\partial w_I)}, \quad \Gamma \equiv (\tau_U + \rho)/(\tau_U + \rho + \pi)^2.$$

It can also be shown that

$$\text{sg}(\frac{\partial\pi}{\partial w_I}) = \text{sg}(\frac{dn_I^d}{dw_I}) < 0, \quad \text{sg}(\frac{\partial\pi}{\partial w_S}) = \text{sg}(\frac{\partial n_U^d}{\partial w_S}) = -\text{sg}(\sigma_{12}) > 0,$$

which imply that

$$dw_I/w_S > 0.$$

Consider now the effects of an increase in the minimum wage when $w_I - e_U \le \theta$. From Equations (A5) and (A16),

$$w_S = \theta + \frac{e_S}{\upsilon}\left\{\Lambda + \frac{\tau n_S^d}{\bar{n}_S - n_S^d}\right\},$$

which implies that

$$dw_S = \phi(\sigma_{22}dw_S - \sigma_{12}dw_m),$$

where $\phi \equiv e_S\tau\tilde{n}_S^d/\upsilon(n_S^s - \tilde{n}_S^d)^2\Delta > 0$. Thus

$$\frac{dw_S}{dw_m} = -\frac{\phi\sigma_{12}}{1 - \phi\sigma_{22}} > 0. \tag{A38}$$

Using Equation (A4) yields

$$\frac{dn_U^d}{dw_m} = \Delta^{-1}[\sigma_{11} - \sigma_{12}(\frac{dw_S}{dw_m})],$$

that is, using Equation (A38):

$$\frac{dn_U^d}{dw_m} = -\frac{\phi - \Delta^{-1}\sigma_{11}}{1 - \phi\sigma_{22}} < 0.$$ (A39)

Equation (A38) also implies that

$$\frac{d(w_S - w_m)}{dw_m} = \frac{\phi(\sigma_{22} - \sigma_{12}) - 1}{1 - \phi\sigma_{22}},$$

which is negative because $\sigma_{22} - \sigma_{12} < 0$.

Equation (A5) yields

$$\frac{dn_S^d}{dw_m} = \Delta^{-1}[\sigma_{22}(\frac{dw_S}{dw_m}) - \sigma_{12}],$$

that is, using Equation (A38):

$$\frac{dn_S^d}{dw_m} = -\frac{\Delta^{-1}\sigma_{12}}{1 - \phi\sigma_{22}} > 0.$$ (A40)

Combining Equations (A39) and (A40) yields

$$\frac{d(n_S^d + n_U^d)}{dw_m} = -\frac{\Delta^{-1}(\sigma_{12} - \sigma_{11}) + \phi}{1 - \phi\sigma_{22}},$$

which is negative because $\sigma_{11} - \sigma_{12} < 0$.

To calculate dw_I/dw_m, begin by differentiating (A37) with respect to w_m. This yields

$$\frac{dw_I}{dw_m} - \frac{\pi}{\tau_U + \rho + \pi} - \Gamma(w_m - e_U)\frac{d\pi}{dw_m} = 0.$$ (A41)

From Equation (A24), it can be shown that

$$\frac{d\pi}{dw_m} = -C_1\frac{dw_I}{dw_m} + C_2\frac{dw_S}{dw_m} - C_3,$$ (A42)

where

$$C_1 = -(\frac{dn_I^d}{dw_m})\frac{\pi}{(n_U^s - \tilde{n}_U^d - \tilde{n}_I^d)} > 0, \quad C_2 = -\frac{\sigma_{12}(n_U^s - \tilde{n}_I^d)\pi}{\Delta\tilde{n}_U^d(n_U^s - \tilde{n}_U^d - \tilde{n}_I^d)} > 0,$$

$$C_3 = -\frac{\sigma_{11}(n_U^s - \tilde{n}_I^d)\pi}{\Delta\tilde{n}_U^d(n_U^s - \tilde{n}_U^d - \tilde{n}_I^d)} > 0.$$

Equations (A41) and (A42) imply

$$\frac{dw_I}{dw_m} = (1 + C_1C_4)^{-1}\frac{\pi}{\tau_U + \rho + \pi} - C_4(C_3 - C_2\frac{dw_S}{dw_m}),$$

where $C_4 = \Gamma(w_m - e_U)$. It can be shown that in the general case dw_I/dw_m is ambiguous. For w_m low initially, $w_m - e_U \simeq 0$ and $C_4 \simeq 0$, so that $dw_I/dw_m > 0$.

Annex B

Informal Financial Markets

The macroeconomic role of informal financial markets attracted considerable attention in the 1980s and early 1990s, particularly in the context of a renewed controversy regarding the short- and long-run effects of **financial repression**. While there exists a large consensus on the microeconomic distortions implied by interest rate ceilings (as discussed in Chapter 2), there is widespread disagreement regarding the short- and medium-run macroeconomic effects associated with **interest rate liberalization** (see Chapter 15). Analysts in the tradition of McKinnon (1973) and Shaw (1973) have argued that raising controlled interest rates would lead to a shift in the composition of aggregate demand from consumption to investment, exerting a positive effect on output growth. By contrast, adherents of the **New Structuralist school**, most notably Taylor (1983, 1991) and van Wijnbergen (1983), have emphasized that in the presence of informal loan markets, raising controlled interest rates would draw funds away from these markets—thereby raising interest rates there, reducing aggregate supply, and raising inflation, both in the short and the medium run. The macroeconomic effects of parallel markets for foreign exchange also attracted a great deal of interest, particularly in the context of exchange market reforms (see Chapter 15). The costs associated with these markets are now well understood, and several countries attempted to unify their official and parallel markets for foreign exchange.

This annex begins by reviewing the nature of informal credit and foreign-currency markets. It then discusses their implications for macroeconomic modeling and analysis. The last part analyzes the conduct of monetary policy in a setting in which both types of markets coexist, focusing in particular on a rise in official interest rates, an expansion in the amount of credit allocated by the central bank to commercial banks, and an increase in the required reserve ratio.

B.1   Informal Financial Markets

Because of their very nature, informal financial markets are difficult to monitor or quantify in a meaningful manner. However, the *qualitative features* and *basic structural characteristics* of these markets are relatively well documented.

B.1.1   Informal Loan Markets

Informal credit markets consist of a variety of *unregulated transactions*, which include the lending and borrowing activities of professional and nonprofessional **moneylenders**, private **finance firms**, **indigenous bankers**, **rotating saving and credit associations**, **pawnshops**, traders, landlords, and households. These transactions can be classified into the following four categories, whose importance varies considerably across countries (Agénor and Montiel, 1999):

- **regular moneylending** by individuals or institutions (such as pawnbrokers, indigenous bankers, or finance companies) whose principal activity consists of lending through the use of their own funds or intermediated funds;

- **occasional** or **intermittent lending** by individuals, firms, and institutions with a surplus of funds;

- **tied credit**, that is, lending by those whose main activity lies in markets other than the credit market but who tie credit to transactions in markets where they operate;

- **group finance**, or various forms of cooperative efforts aimed at generating loanable funds for individual credit needs.

Informal credit markets were for a long time an important feature of financial markets in developing countries. The estimates reported by Agénor and Montiel (1999) for a large group of developing countries suggested that the share of informal credit in total credit in developing countries varied from about a third to about three-quarters in the late 1980s. Informal credit accounted for about a third to two-thirds of total credit in Bangladesh and China, about two-fifths in India and Sri Lanka, and two-thirds to three-quarters in Nepal, Pakistan, Thailand, and Malaysia. In Taiwan, the ratio of financial loans to private enterprises from the informal credit market to those from the regulated market averaged nearly 28 percent during the period 1971-88 (Huang, Cheng, Chou, and Lin Shung-Ying, 1992). In some sub-Saharan African countries, the volume of loans transacted through the informal credit market even exceeded the amount of resources lent through formal financial markets (Aryeetey and Hyuha, 1991). However, more recent data suggest that the scope of these markets may have fallen substantially in many developing countries. In particular, in Latin America, the informal credit market was an important source of financial intermediation during the 1970s and early 1980s—a period during which countries faced difficult problems in the regular banking sector. This situation, however, changed significantly during the late 1980s and 1990s, as *financial reform* and *macroeconomic stabilization* led to increased intermediation through formal financial channels. Only in sub-Saharan Africa do informal credit markets continue to be very large.

Interest rates in informal markets are in general substantially higher than those prevailing in official markets.[1] Unofficial credit markets may therefore represent an expensive source of finance for business investment and working capital needs. In the absence of organized securities markets and in the presence of financial repression, the lending rate in the informal credit market represents the relevant *opportunity cost* of holding money for domestic residents. The evidence reported by Agénor and Montiel (1999) suggested that informal interest rates are influenced not only by domestic money-market conditions but also by *arbitrage relationships* with foreign financial variables. In the long run, the size of the differential between official and informal interest rates depends also on *structural factors*, such as the degree of rationing in the official credit market.

The **degree of financial repression** captures the distortion introduced by the existence of a price differential between the official and unofficial markets. Because interest rate ceilings imply an *implicit tax* on depositors and a *subsidy* for creditors, the degree of financial repression can be related to the present value of the subsidy, per unit of bank credit, implied by legal ceilings on interest rates. This subsidy—and thus the degree of financial repression—can, in turn, be approximated by the difference between the official interest rate and the informal rate, divided by the official rate.

The total subsidy received by individuals with access to bank credit can be approximated by the interest rate differential between curb market loans and bank credit times the amount of bank credit extended. Depositors, by contrast, are taxed by an amount approximately equal to the product of the value of bank deposits and the interest rate differential. The sum of these subsidies and taxes—which can be explicitly related to the index of financial repression—is the *net addition* to household income. The **net income effect** of financial repression depends therefore on whether households are *net creditors* or *net debtors* with respect to the banking system.[2] In the presence of large **reserve requirements** (a situation that prevails in countries where large public fiscal deficits are financed through central bank credit) households tend to be net

---

[1] If households are free to hold assets in the formal sector (such as deposits with the banking system) as well as in the informal sector (such as deposits with unregulated finance companies) and allocate their portfolio so as to equalize risk-adjusted rates of return, the implicit tax on bank deposits (discussed later) cannot explain the large interest rate differential between official and unofficial credit markets. Rather, it may reflect the *risk component* assigned to intermediation by informal finance companies, the *informational advantage* of moneylenders, and the *limited alternatives* available to borrowers. It is not necessarily symptomatic of *pure rents* accruing to moneylenders.

[2] In some countries the banking system is dominated by large, loss-making, state-owned banks. In such circumstances the cost of the subsidy to borrowers may be absorbed by banks in the form of *lower profits* and *reduced net worth*, instead of being passed onto depositors in the form of lower deposit rates relative to rates available in the informal market. To the extent that the quasi-fiscal deficit is financed by higher inflation, the *net implicit tax* on borrowers can be positive.

creditors to the banking system. In this case, therefore, the implicit tax imposed on households by interest rate ceilings on deposits exceeds the subsidy received by favored borrowers. Policies that increase (decrease) the degree of financial repression will thus reduce (increase) households' income or financial wealth.

B.1.2   Parallel Markets for Foreign Exchange

Parallel currency markets in developing countries tend to emerge primarily as a result of *foreign trade restrictions* and *capital controls*.[3]

- The imposition of tariffs and regulations (such as licensing procedures, administrative allocations of foreign exchange, and quotas) on trade flows creates incentives to *smuggle* and *fake invoices* (to lower the tariff duties) by creating excess demand for goods at illegal, pre-tax prices.

- Illegal trade creates a demand for illegal currency which, in turn, stimulates its supply and leads to the creation and establishment of a parallel currency market.[4] In some Latin American countries, for instance, the development of the illegal market for dollars has been closely associated with drug-related trade (Melvin and Ladman, 1991).

- To the extent that they lead to **capital flight**, the imposition of capital controls may stimulate the development of a parallel currency market. In countries where *macroeconomic instability* is endemic, parallel currency markets may also be highly developed if restrictions on access to foreign exchange exist, because foreign currency is a hedge against sudden bursts of inflation.

Although illegal, parallel currency markets are often tolerated by governments in developing countries. The size of this market depends on the range of transactions subject to exchange controls, as well as the degree to which restrictions are enforced by the authorities. In countries where large and chronic external deficits force the central bank to ration foreign exchange allocated to the private sector (because government needs are large and must be satisfied in priority), parallel currency markets will typically be well developed, with an exchange rate substantially more depreciated than the official rate. Figure B1 shows the evolution of the **parallel market premium**—the proportion by which the parallel rate exceeds the official rate—in Ecuador, Malawi, Nigeria, and Morocco for the period 1983-93. The figure shows that the premium, which depends in the long run upon *structural factors*—such as the *penalty*

---

[3] The imposition of such restrictions resulted in many cases from the desire to maintain an overvalued exchange rate, either for reasons of national prestige (as happened in several countries that became independent in the 1960s) or for fostering economic development by making imported capital and intermediate goods relatively cheap for domestic producers.

[4] The demand for foreign exchange associated with illegal trade cannot in general be channeled through the central bank, as a result of restrictions on eligible transactions at the official exchange rate—which, together with potential penalties, limit the extent to which importers can cover illegal operations by legal ones.

structure and the amount of resources devoted to apprehension and prosecution of offenders—displays large fluctuations in the short run, a phenomenon often seen as reflecting the *asset-price characteristics* of the parallel exchange rate.[5] In periods characterized by uncertainty over macroeconomic policies, or unstable political and social conditions, parallel market rates tend to react rapidly to expected changes in future economic circumstances.

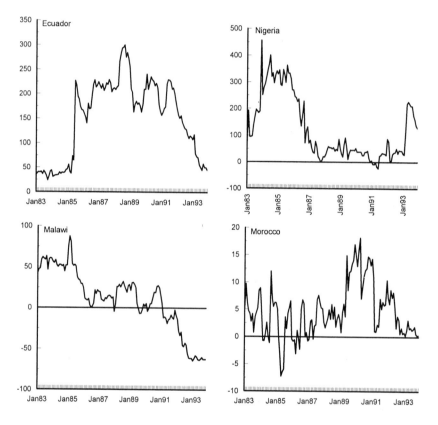

Figure B.1. Parallel Market Premium (In percent).
Source: International Monetary Fund.

The single most important source of foreign-currency *supply* in the parallel market is **underinvoicing of exports**. When there is a *tax* on exports, underinvoicing allows the exporter to avoid the tax and to sell the illegally acquired foreign exchange at a premium; when there is a *subsidy* on exports that is less than the parallel market premium, the sale of foreign exchange in the parallel market may more than compensate for the loss of the subsidy. Thus, for given taxes, the higher the parallel market premium, the higher the propensity to underinvoice exports. The *demand* for foreign currency in the parallel

---

[5] In the long run, as shown formally by De Macedo (1987), the premium can be expressed directly as a function of import tariff rates and export subsidy rates.

market results generally from four main components: imports (legal and illegal), residents traveling abroad, portfolio diversification, and **capital flight**.

B.2 Analytical Implications

Although informal credit markets and parallel markets for foreign exchange have coexisted in many developing economies, the approach followed in the early literature was to consider both types of markets separately. However, several authors attempted subsequently to integrate both types of informal financial markets in a systematic and consistent framework. This section briefly reviews some of these attempts. It is assumed that the menu of financial assets available to agents consists of domestic currency, deposits with the banking system, foreign currency, loans extended through the informal market, land, and physical capital.[6] Holdings of these assets are financed by the individuals' personal net worth or by borrowing both from the banking system or through the informal credit market. Financial repression in this setting is captured by assuming that interest rates on assets and liabilities of the formal banking system are fixed by administrative restrictions, while the price of foreign currency on the parallel market, and that of real assets as well as the interest rate on informal credit market loans, are determined by market conditions.

The existence of large and relatively efficient informal financial markets establishes important new linkages between the financial and real spheres of the economy. Central elements in the analysis of these linkages are the **parallel market premium** and the **degree of financial repression**, as defined earlier. This section examines these various channels of real and financial integration, beginning with those operating through the fiscal and balance-of-payments accounts.

B.2.1 Fiscal and Balance-of-Payments Effects

The fiscal effects of informal credit and foreign-currency markets vary depending on the type of market considered. As discussed in Chapter 2 and in the previous section, financial repression and informal loan markets generate a series of implicit taxes and subsidies on asset holders. The fiscal effects associated with parallel currency markets result from the role of the premium as an *implicit tax on exports* repatriated through official channels—an important consideration, as discussed in Chapter 15, for the analysis of the longer-run effects of **exchange market unification**.

The balance-of-payments and monetary effects associated with informal financial markets result essentially from the role of the premium in affecting the *propensity to underinvoice* exports. A divergence between the official and parallel exchange rates induces in the short run a flow of *arbitrage activity*, the magnitude of which depends on both the costs of evading exchange controls and

---

[6] As indicated in Chapter 2, equity markets remain underdeveloped in most developing countries.

the size of the exchange rate differential. The arbitrage flows tend to alter over time the behavior of foreign reserves held by the central bank, and thus the money supply (see Annex C). The dependence of legal imports on the exchange rate differential as well as income (which, as indicated earlier, depends on the degree of financial repression and on the net asset position of agents with regard to the banking sector) may also alter the evolution of foreign reserves and the money stock.

B.2.2   Income and Wealth Effects

As indicated earlier, net implicit taxes associated with financial repression tend to affect private current income. Changes in the premium may also affect income (because it affects the propensity to underinvoice and thus the flow of income generated through legal and illegal exports) and may generate sizable *wealth effects* associated with changes in the valuation of holdings of foreign exchange in private portfolios. In addition, of course, there is a *pure portfolio effect* associated with both categories of informal financial markets: both the curb market interest rate and the expected rate of depreciation of the parallel exchange rate play a critical role in determining the allocation of wealth among available financial assets.

B.2.3   Expenditure and Intertemporal Effects

Informal credit markets have an expenditure or intertemporal effect to the extent that the informal interest rate, which measures the **marginal cost of funds**, is used by households to evaluate the real cost of borrowing. Spending may also depend on the level of financial wealth, and may thus be affected by the type of wealth effects associated with changes in the parallel exchange rate, as described above.

B.2.4   Price and Output Effects

Parallel currency markets have two types of effects on domestic prices.

- The parallel exchange rate, being the *marginal cost* of foreign exchange, tends to affect the domestic price of imports.

- If exporters have the possibility to smuggle out a portion of their sales abroad, the parallel exchange rate will also affect the *producer price of exportables*. In turn, this will generate a direct supply-side effect.

The informal interest rate may also have a direct *negative effect* on output, if (as in the three-good model of Chapter 8) firms need to finance labor costs and their working capital needs prior to the sale of output. They may also affect domestic prices *directly*, if—as often postulated in the New Structuralist literature—prices are set as a **markup** over financial as well as nonfinancial costs. In models such as the simulation framework presented by Agénor and

Montiel (1999), prices (of nontradable goods) are determined through *general equilibrium interactions*, implying that informal interest rates only have an indirect effect on domestic inflation.

B.3 Monetary Policy Shocks

In practice, the relative importance of the different channels identified above (and thus the relative effects of policy shocks in the presence of informal financial markets) will vary as a result of various factors—including, in particular, the *degree of substitutability* among assets. A relatively high degree of substitutability implies that a large shift in resources would occur from one sector to another in response to a given shock. The real effects would also differ as a result, depending on differences in the use of resources across sectors. In a financially repressed economy, the menu of assets available to private agents is often limited to holding of consumer durables, land and physical capital, domestic and foreign currencies, sight and time deposits in the formal financial sector, and informal market loans. Because of their relative lack of liquidity, real assets are likely to be poorer substitutes for deposits than currency. Curb market loans, real assets, and foreign-currency denominated assets that are traded on parallel markets differ from domestic currency holdings and bank deposits in that the nominal returns from holding the former category of assets are endogenous. These returns consist of any real income derived from them as well as the expected rate of change in the nominal price of the asset. As indicated earlier, changes in the valuation of private sector wealth could occur as a result of relative changes in asset prices.

As discussed in Chapter 2, monetary authorities in financially repressed economies—characterized by the absence of organized primary financial markets (such as credit auctions or government securities auctions) and secondary securities markets—typically have recourse to three non-market-based instruments of monetary policy:

- The level of **administered interest rates** charged by commercial banks;

- The **amount of credit** extended by the central bank to the commercial banking system; and

- The **required reserve ratio**.

In order to understand the transmission process of these policies in the presence of informal financial markets, the effects of changes in all three policy instruments are studied in a setting where the portfolio structure of private agents is as described above, and prices of nontraded goods are determined through general equilibrium interactions, as in the simulation model presented by Agénor and Montiel (1999).[7]

---

[7] Another instrument of monetary policy in a financially repressed economy is the *statutory liquidity ratio*, which could be introduced in the framework described previously by adding

B.3.1   Increase in Administered Interest Rates

Increasing interest rates on bank deposits causes asset holders to reallocate their portfolios by moving funds away from both the informal loan market and foreign-asset holdings into the banking system. The informal market interest rate therefore rises and the parallel exchange rate appreciates. The magnitude of both effects depends, again, on the degree of substitutability among assets held in individual portfolios. As the parallel exchange rate appreciates, the domestic-currency value of financial wealth falls, to an extent that depends on the *relative share* of foreign-currency assets in private portfolios. The reduction in the nominal value of wealth causes a secondary reallocation of portfolios, because the demand for interest-bearing assets depends also on total (noncurrency) financial wealth. Because of this *wealth effect*, the demand for domestic deposits may rise or fall in net terms.

As discussed by Agénor and Montiel (1999), this measure also has a **deflationary effect** as well as a **contractionary effect** on output for a number of reasons.

- The appreciation of the parallel exchange rate reduces the real value of private wealth, which in turn tends to reduce aggregate demand.

- The exchange rate appreciation also reduces the domestic *producer price for exports*, which dampens incentives to the supply of exportable goods.

- To the extent that the proportional increase in administered interest rates exceeds that in the informal market, the degree of financial repression will fall. If households are *net debtors* with respect to the banking system, the implicit subsidy provided by controls on interest rates will also fall on impact, thereby reducing income and aggregate demand.

- The increase in the informal interest rate exerts direct contractionary effects on spending as well.

Consequently, output and domestic prices (that is, prices of nontraded goods) fall when the measure is implemented. Ignoring informal market linkages and wealth effects in the determination of macroeconomic outcomes, as in the analysis of McKinnon and Shaw, would have led to the result that an increase in official interest rates is *unambiguously expansionary*, as a consequence of an increase in bank deposits and an expansion in bank lending (or a reduction in the degree of financial repression), which reduces the intensity of rationing in the official credit market. In New Structuralist models where informal currency markets are absent and where prices are determined as a markup over financial and nonfinancial costs (with no role attributed to aggregate demand)—such as in Taylor (1983, 1991)—the rise in the informal interest rate leads directly to an *unambiguous increase* in prices. In the extended framework considered

---

affect the formal intermediation process in a manner similar to changes in the reserve requirement ratio.

by Agénor and Montiel (1999) in which prices are determined through general equilibrium interactions, however, changes in informal interest rates have only an indirect, downward effect on domestic prices through an increase in the real interest rate and a reduction in private expenditure.

B.3.2   Credit Expansion by the Central Bank

An expansion of credit by the central bank to commercial banks leads to an initial excess supply of domestic monetary assets in private agents' portfolios. Attempts to restore portfolio balance leads to an increased demand for foreign assets and hence to a depreciation of the parallel exchange rate as well as an increase in the domestic price level in order to induce households to absorb the increased supply of money. Given administered interest rates, the increase in the price level implies a fall in the real rate of interest in the formal sector. The private sector's demand for deposits is reduced, causing households to shift assets toward informal market loans, which leads in turn to a fall in the informal market interest rate. The fall in informal interest rates also reduces the real interest rate, which stimulates private expenditure, contributing therefore to the increase in the domestic price level and output. This expansion of demand is somewhat dampened by a reduction in the degree of financial repression, which results from the decline in the implicit subsidy provided by official controls on interest rates.

If the stimulus resulting from the fall in the real interest rate outweighs the adverse effect on aggregate demand resulting from the reduced level of financial wealth, the net effect would be an expansion of private spending, which would stimulate output and raise prices. Net foreign assets of the central bank would fall as a consequence of the higher level of domestic activity (which would raise imports) and the increase in underinvoicing of exports resulting from the higher parallel market premium.

B.3.3   Increase in the Required Reserve Ratio

A rise in the required reserve ratio is equivalent to an increase in the *cost* of deposits and thus, because banks cannot increase loan rates, translates into a *lower deposit rate*. The induced increase in the financial repression tax exerts a *negative income effect* on aggregate demand. Portfolio reallocation results in a substitution toward informal market loans and foreign currency holdings, lowering interest rates in the former and the premium in the latter. Lower informal market interest rates tend to offset the adverse effect of the higher degree of financial repression on domestic economic activity. Nevertheless, the net effect is likely to be a reduction in domestic demand and output, which lowers the demand for imports while the propensity to underinvoice exports falls as a result of the lower premium. The net effect on the stock of foreign assets of the central bank is thus positive. The stock of foreign-currency assets held by the public also rises in the long run.

Annex C

Exchange Market Unification

The purpose of this annex is to complement the discussion of exchange market unification provided in Chapter 14 by presenting a simple macroeconomic model of an economy in which both official and parallel markets for foreign exchange exist, and to study the short-run dynamics of exchange rates, official reserves, and the money supply when the two markets are unified. The first section describes the model, and the second characterizes the pre-reform equilibrium. The postreform regime (which can be either a pure floating exchange rate arrangement or a managed float) is studied in section C. The dynamic adjustment process to exchange market unification is characterized in the last section.

C.1 The Model

Consider a small open economy operating an informal dual exchange rate regime in which an official, pegged exchange rate coexists with a freely determined parallel rate.

- The official rate applies to current account transactions authorized by the central bank.

- The parallel rate is used for capital account transactions and the remainder of current account items.

Agents are endowed with **perfect foresight** and hold domestic- and foreign-currency balances in their portfolios. Domestic firms produce a single good whose output is entirely sold abroad and is taken as exogenous. Agents consume imported goods, the demand for which depends on the level of real money balances. In each period, exporters surrender a given proportion of their foreign exchange earnings at the official exchange rate, and repatriate the remaining proceeds via the parallel market.

Formally, the model is described by the following log-linear equations:

$$m - p = -\alpha \dot{s}, \quad \alpha > 0 \tag{C1}$$

$$m = \eta d + (1 - \eta)R, \quad 0 < \eta < 1 \tag{C2}$$

$$p = s, \tag{C3}$$

$$\dot{R} = -\Phi(s - e) - \kappa(m - p), \quad \Phi, \kappa > 0 \tag{C4}$$

$$\dot{d} = \mu, \quad \mu \geq 0, \tag{C5}$$

where m denotes the nominal money stock, d domestic credit, R the stock of net foreign assets held by the central bank, p the domestic price level, e the official exchange rate, s the parallel exchange rate, and $\dot{x} \equiv dx/dt$. All variables are measured in logarithms.

- Equation (C1) describes *money market equilibrium*.[1]

- Equation (C2) is a *log-linear approximation* that defines the domestic money stock as a weighted average of domestic credit and foreign reserves (see Chapter 7).

- Equation (C3) indicates that the *price level* depends only on the parallel exchange rate, which measures the marginal cost of foreign exchange.[2]

- Equation (C4) describes the behavior of *net foreign assets*. The negative effect of the premium—defined as the difference between the official and parallel exchange rates—on the behavior of reserves results from its impact on **underinvoicing of exports**. The higher the parallel exchange rate is relative to the official rate, the greater will be the incentive to falsify export invoices and to divert export proceeds to the unofficial market (see Kamin, 1993, and Annex B). The demand for imports is taken to be proportional to the stock of real money balances.

- Finally, Equation (C5) indicates that the nominal *stock of credit* grows at a constant rate, which reflects underlying fiscal rigidities.[3]

---

[1] Because the parallel exchange rate can make discrete jumps, s in Eq. (C1) must be interpreted as the right-hand time derivative of s.

[2] Assuming that prices depend also on the *official* exchange rate would only complicate the algebra without affecting qualitatively the results.

[3] This assumption follows the literature on speculative attacks and balance-of-payments crises; see Chapter 5.

Prior to reform, the forward-looking parallel rate s and the predetermined nominal money stock m are endogenous variables, whereas the official exchange rate e is assumed set at e^f by the authorities. Substituting Equations (C3)-(C5) in (C2) yields

$$\dot{m} = \eta\mu - (1-\eta)(s - e^f) - \kappa(1-\eta)(m - s), \tag{C6}$$

from which it can be shown that the net effect of a depreciation of the parallel exchange rate on the rate of money growth is ambiguous.

- It raises, on the one hand, the incentive to underinvoice exports, which tends to lower the rate of accumulation of foreign reserves.

- It lowers, on the other, real money balances, which reduces the demand for imports and tends to increase the rate of growth of official reserves.

The net effect depends on the sign of $\kappa - \Phi$.

Substituting Equation (C3) in (C1) yields, together with (C6):

$$\begin{bmatrix} \dot{s} \\ \dot{m} \end{bmatrix} = \begin{bmatrix} 1/\alpha & -1/\alpha \\ (1-\eta)(\kappa-\Phi) & -\kappa(1-\eta) \end{bmatrix} \begin{bmatrix} s \\ m \end{bmatrix} + \begin{bmatrix} 0 \\ \Theta \end{bmatrix}, \tag{C7}$$

where $\Theta = \eta\mu + \Phi(1-\eta)e^f$.

The determinant of the coefficients matrix is equal to $-\Phi(1-\eta)/\alpha$, which is always *negative*—regardless of the sign of $\kappa - \Phi$. Thus the two characteristic roots of the system (C7) are *real* and have *opposite signs*, which indicates that the long-run equilibrium of the system is a **saddlepoint**.

Let ρ_1 denote the negative root and ρ_2 the positive root of system (C7). Solving for the particular solutions yields

$$s = \tilde{s} + C_1 e^{\rho_1 t} + C_2 e^{\rho_2 t}, \tag{C8}$$

$$m = \tilde{m} + \gamma_1 C_1 e^{\rho_1 t} + \gamma_2 C_2 e^{\rho_2 t}, \tag{C9}$$

where C_1 and C_2 are undetermined coefficients, and

$$\gamma_1 = (1 - \alpha\rho_1) > 0, \quad \gamma_2 = (\alpha\rho_1 - 1) < 0,$$

with the steady-state values of the parallel exchange rate $\tilde{s}$ and the nominal money stock $\tilde{m}$ given by

$$\tilde{s} = \tilde{m} = e^f + \frac{\eta\mu}{\Phi(1-\eta)}.$$

If the dual rate regime lasts forever, stability requires setting $C_2 = 0$ in Equations (C8) and (C9). Using an *initial condition* on the money stock thus allows the determination of C_1. The slope of the saddlepath, SS, in Figure C1 is $1/\gamma_1$.

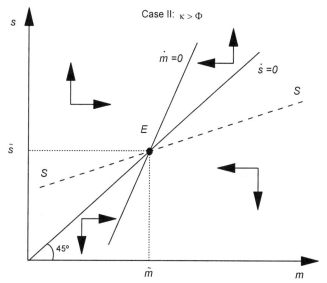

Figure C.1. Steady-State Equilibrium Prior to Reform.

The *saddlepath solution* of system (C15) is given by

$$\varepsilon = \tilde{\varepsilon} + Ce^{\nu_1 t}, \quad t \geq T \tag{C10}$$

$$m = \tilde{\varepsilon} + h_1 Ce^{\nu_1 t}, \quad t \geq T \tag{C11}$$

where $h_1 = -(\alpha \nu_1 - 1) > 0$, and ν_1 is the negative root of system (C16). C is an undetermined coefficient, and

$$\tilde{\varepsilon} = \varepsilon^d + \frac{\eta \mu}{\upsilon(1 - \eta)}.$$

C.2 Pre-reform Equilibrium

Let us first suppose that the existing exchange rate arrangement is expected to *last forever*. Figure C1 illustrates the steady-state solution of the system in the s-m space. The saddlepath SS shown in the figure has a positive slope and is flatter than the locus $[\dot{s} = 0]$, whose slope is unity. The economy's equilibrium path passes through the stationary point E. For any given value of the nominal money stock, rational agents will select the corresponding value of the parallel exchange rate that lies on the stable path. The upper panel of the figure corresponds to the case where $\kappa > \Phi$, and the lower panel to $\kappa < \Phi$. The direction of the arrows depicted in the two panels are determined by the sign of the coefficients appearing in Equations (C7). For instance, in the upper panel, for values of the parallel exchange rate located above (below) the $[\dot{m} = 0]$ locus, the money stock is falling (increasing), as indicated by the arrows pointing west (east). For values of the money stock located to the right (left) of the $[\dot{s} = 0]$ locus, the parallel exchange rate is appreciating (depreciating).

An increase in the rate of growth of domestic credit shifts the $[\dot{m} = 0]$ locus to the right while leaving the $[\dot{s} = 0]$ locus unaffected, and raises in the same proportion the steady-state values of the parallel exchange rate and the nominal money stock. A devaluation of the official exchange rate also translates into a rightward shift of the $[\dot{m} = 0]$ locus and leads in the long run to an equi-proportional depreciation of the parallel exchange rate and the money stock.[4]

C.3 Postreform Regime

Let $T > 0$ denote the *future transition date* announced at period $t = 0$, that is, the initial instant at which the policymakers intend to abandon the informal, dual exchange rate regime. In the postreform regime (which is characterized by a *uniform exchange rate*), the central bank may adopt either a *pure floating rate arrangement* or a *managed float*. A general specification that captures both of these options consists in formulating the change in foreign reserves as

$$R = -\upsilon(\varepsilon - \varepsilon^d), \quad t \geq T, \tag{C12}$$

where ε denotes the unified exchange rate and ε^d the "desired" level of the unified rate.[5] The coefficient $\upsilon \geq 0$ measures the **degree of intervention** in

---

[4]Note that in the steady state foreign reserves fall at a constant rate, which is proportional to the rate of credit growth. In practice, of course, the existence of a *lower bound on reserves* would eventually force the authorities to alter their credit policy to avoid a *currency crisis*, as discussed in Chapter 7.

[5]Factors affecting the desired unified rate include the relative composition of foreign exchange flows and the targeted level of the current account balance.

the foreign exchange market.

- If $v = 0$, the central bank will opt for a purely flexible exchange rate regime in which official reserves remain constant.

- If $v > 0$, the central bank will adjust reserves so as to dampen deviations of the unified exchange rate from its desired value.[6]

In both cases, the demand for foreign exchange induced by private demand for imports is implicitly satisfied through adjustment of the capital account.[7]

Consider first the case of *pure floating* ($v = 0$). Reserves are thus constant beyond $t > T$ at, say, R_T^+. The unified flexible exchange rate is thus determined by setting $s = e = \varepsilon$ in Equations (C1)-(C3), which implies that

$$\dot{\varepsilon} = (\eta\varepsilon - m|_{R=R_T^+})/\alpha, \quad \text{where} \quad m|_{R=R_T^+} = \eta d + (1 - \eta)R_T^+.$$

The solution of this differential equation is given by

$$\varepsilon = Ce^{\eta t/\alpha} + m|_{R=R_T^+}, \tag{C13}$$

which requires setting the constant term C to zero to ensure stability. Using Equation (C5) yields therefore

$$\varepsilon = m|_{R=R_T^+}, \quad t \geq T. \tag{C14}$$

Equation (C14) shows that the post-unification floating exchange rate depends, through the constant stock of reserves, on the *unification date*.

Consider now the case where the postunification regime is a *managed float* ($v > 0$). Setting $s = e = \varepsilon$ in Equations (C2), (C3), and (C5), and using (C12) yields

$$\begin{bmatrix} \dot{\varepsilon} \\ \dot{m} \end{bmatrix} = \begin{bmatrix} 1/\alpha & -1/\alpha \\ -v(1-\eta) & 0 \end{bmatrix} \begin{bmatrix} \varepsilon \\ m \end{bmatrix} + \begin{bmatrix} 0 \\ \eta\mu + v(1-\eta)\varepsilon^d \end{bmatrix}. \tag{C15}$$

The determinant of the matrix of coefficients is equal to $-v(1-\eta)/\alpha$ which is *negative*, thus indicating that the equilibrium of the system is again a saddlepoint. The exact solutions are given in the appendix to this annex.

The long-run equilibrium of the managed float regime is illustrated in Figure C2. The saddlepath AA also has a positive slope. The steady-state value of the unified rate is equal to the desired exchange rate if the rate of growth of

---

[6] The case in which $v \to \infty$ corresponds to the fixed exchange rate case, in which the unified rate is maintained continuously at the level ε^d. Given the limited empirical relevance of this case—despite well-known benefits associated with the use of the exchange rate as a nominal anchor—it will not be discussed any further.

[7] The required movement in the capital account is determined from Eqs. (C4) and (C12). This assumption is particularly relevant if the exchange rate reform is part of a comprehensive and sufficiently credible reform program which attracts (or is supported by) external public financing and private capital inflows. Capital movements of this type are assumed to have no feedback effect on the short-run behavior of the economy.

domestic credit is zero. An increase in the credit growth rate has the same qualitative effects as before: it expands the money stock and depreciates the flexible exchange rate.

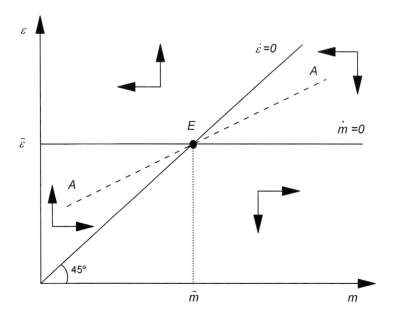

Figure C.2. The Postreform Steady State Under Managed Float.

C.4 Dynamics in Anticipation of Reform

Under perfect foresight, private agents will begin adjusting the composition of their portfolios as soon as the central bank announces its intention to switch to a unified exchange rate regime at a well-defined date in the future.

C.4.1 Pure Float

Consider first the short-run dynamics associated with an expected switch to a pure floating arrangement. To examine graphically the dynamics of unification under this type of arrangement, suppose that the nominal credit stock remains constant over time ($\mu = 0$) at, say, d_0. From Equation (C14), therefore, the postreform exchange rate is *constant* and equal to

$$\varepsilon_T^+ = m_T^+ = \eta d_0 + (1 - \eta)R_T^+, \quad t \geq T. \tag{C16}$$

The complete solution of the system is determined by two conditions that connect the two regimes:

- an initial condition on the money stock;

- a condition that rules out any jump in the parallel exchange rate at the moment the reform is implemented.

These conditions are

$$m_0 \text{ given}, \quad s_T = \varepsilon_T^+. \tag{C17}$$

The exact solutions of the parallel exchange rate and the money stock during the transition period ($0 < t \leq T$), as well as the value of the postunification exchange rate are given in the Appendix to this Annex. In general, the postreform value of the unified exchange rate may be either more depreciated or more appreciated than the initial parallel exchange rate, s_0. Both cases are examined graphically (mathematical details are relegated to the appendix). The focus throughout is on a situation in which the initial value of the premium is *positive* (so that $e^f < s_0$), a realistic case for most countries contemplating reform. From the equation of the pre-reform saddlepath given above, this condition also implies that $m_0 > e^f$.

The relationship between the money stock and the unified exchange rate at time T shown in Equation (C16) defines a **terminal curve**, denoted CC in Figure C3, whose slope is equal to unity—and is thus identical to the slope of the $[\dot{s} = 0]$ locus. The pre-reform saddlepath SS is, by construction, flatter than the terminal curve CC.

The upper panel in Figure C3 illustrates the case where $s_0 < \varepsilon_T^+$, whereas the lower panel corresponds to $s_0 > \varepsilon_T^+$. As assumed above, the position of the economy prior to reform announcement is such that the premium is positive and is located on a point such as A on SS. As shown in the appendix, the position of the unified exchange rate depends on the transition date, T.

- If the reform occurs **overnight**, that is, when $T \to 0^+$, upon announcement the economy moves immediately to its postreform steady state. In both panels, the parallel exchange rate jumps from A to B (located on CC), with no change in the initial—and therefore final—money stock, and a unified exchange rate equal to ε_{0+}.

- If T is positive, at the moment the future reform is announced, the parallel exchange rate depreciates instantaneously (jumping to a point such as D) and continues to depreciate during the transition period toward a point such as B' on curve CC, which is reached—without further jumps—at the moment the reform is implemented, T. In the upper panel of Figure C3 the unified exchange rate is equal to ε_T^+, which is more appreciated than ε_{0+} and more depreciated than s_0.

- If the exchange rate reform is announced to occur in the very distant future (that is, for $T \to \infty$), the announcement will have no effect on the path of the parallel exchange rate and reserves. The economy will remain at the initial position A upon announcement, and then move along the original saddlepath SS toward E.

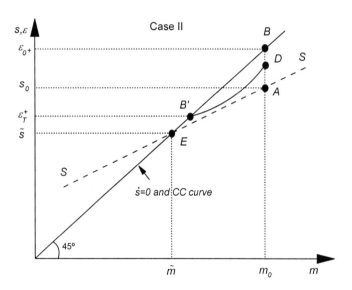

Figure C.3. Unification Dynamics–Pure Float.

There are, therefore, three possible paths for the parallel market exchange associated with unification: it can

- jump instantaneously to a more depreciated equilibrium level;

- jump instantaneously and appreciate along an unstable trajectory during the transition period;

- appreciate continuously with no initial jump toward the unified exchange rate—which, if no reform is ever expected to take place, coincides with the official exchange rate.

In the second and third scenarios, reserves fall continuously.

Alternatively, as illustrated in the lower panel of Figure C3, the parallel exchange rate (after jumping from A to D' upon announcement of the future reform) evolves along DB' during the adjustment period. B' is now characterized by an *appreciated* postunification exchange rate relative to the initial parallel exchange rate ($s_0 > \varepsilon_T^+$). Again, the transition process is characterized by falling reserves and a continuous appreciation of the parallel exchange rate.

C.4.2   Managed Float

Consider now the case of *managed floating*. The assumption of perfect foresight imposes three conditions under a managed float:

- an initial condition on the money stock, m; and

- two conditions that rule out jumps in the parallel exchange rate and the money stock at the moment the reform is implemented.

These conditions are

$$m_0 \text{ given,} \quad s_T = \varepsilon_T, \quad m_T|_{e=e^f} = m_T|_{e=s=\varepsilon}, \qquad \text{(C18)}$$

where $m_T|_{e=e^f}$ is obtained from the solution of Equation (C7), and $m_T|_{e=s=\varepsilon}$ from Equation (C15).

Again, the exact solutions of the parallel exchange rate and the money stock prior to and after reform are given in the appendix to this annex. The focus here is on a graphical presentation of the dynamics associated with the unification process. As before, the analysis assumes that the initial value of the premium is positive ($e^f < s_0 = \tilde{s}$).[8]

Consider first the case where $\kappa < \Phi$. The dynamics of unification in this scenario are illustrated in Figure C4. Two subcases must be considered depending on whether the steady-state value of the unified exchange rate, $\tilde{\varepsilon}$, is higher or lower than the initial steady-state value of the parallel exchange rate, $\tilde{s}$.

The upper panel illustrates the case where $\tilde{\varepsilon} < \tilde{s}$. The position of the economy before the reform announcement is at E, while the position of the steady-state equilibrium in the postunification regime is at E', which is located along the 45-degree line—because in both regimes the flexible exchange rate is equal to the money stock in equilibrium. The transition between E and E', however, depends on how far in the future the reform date T is.

---

[8] As can be inferred from Eqs. (C8) and (C9), this is always the case if $\mu > 0$.

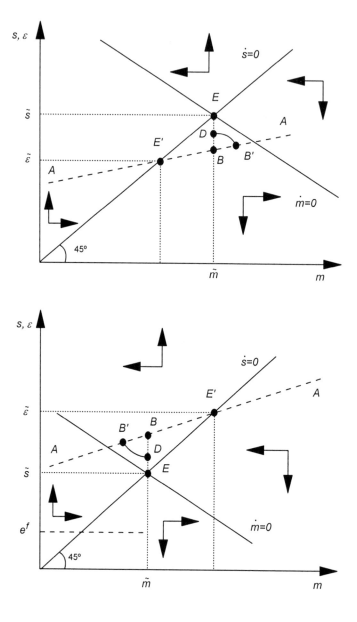

Figure C.4. Unification Dynamics–Managed Float ($\kappa < \Phi$).

- If the reform occurs overnight $(T \to 0^+)$, the parallel exchange rate will appreciate upon announcement, from E to B (located on the postreform saddlepath, AA), with no change in the money stock. From then on, the economy will begin converging toward E', with a continuous appreciation of the parallel exchange rate and a fall in the money stock.

- If T is positive, the parallel exchange rate will also appreciate instantaneously (jumping from E to a point such as D) at the moment the future reform is announced, and will appreciate continuously during the transition period toward point B' located on the postreform saddlepath AA, which is reached—without further jumps—at the moment the reform is implemented, T. Foreign reserves tend to increase during the adjustment period. After T, the parallel exchange rate continues to depreciate and reserves begin falling, until the postreform steady state is reached, at E'.

The lower panel of Figure C4 illustrates the case where $\tilde{\varepsilon} > \tilde{s}$. If the reform occurs overnight, the parallel exchange rate will depreciate immediately and jump from E to B located on the postunification saddlepath AA. If the reform is preannounced, the initial upward jump will be from E to a point such as D, followed by a movement during the transition period along the unique, unstable trajectory DB', which causes the economy to arrive at the unique postunification convergent path AA at period T. In this scenario, thus, the transition process is characterized by falling reserves and a continuous depreciation of the parallel exchange rate. After the reform is implemented, the economy proceeds along the post-reform stable path, with a continued depreciation of the unified exchange rate and an increase in reserves, until the post-reform steady-state equilibrium is reached, at E'.

Figure C5 considers the case where $\kappa > \Phi$. The logic of the analysis is very much the same as before, but the transitional dynamic path is quite different. If the postreform steady-state value of the unified exchange rate is more appreciated than the initial steady-state value of the parallel exchange rate (as shown in the upper panel of the figure), an overnight reform will lead to the same adjustment path as before: an immediate downward jump in the parallel exchange rate, followed by a continuous appreciation and a fall in official reserves. However, if the reform is preannounced, the transition period will be characterized by a fall in the central bank's net foreign assets, instead of an increase as obtained previously. Similarly, if the postreform steady-state value of the flexible exchange rate is more depreciated than the initial equilibrium value of the parallel exchange rate (as shown in the lower panel of the figure), the dynamics associated with a preannounced reform will be characterized by an accumulation of foreign exchange reserves, rather than a continuous reduction in the central bank's net holdings of foreign assets.

In summary, the short-run behavior of official reserves and the parallel exchange rate in anticipation of reform depends on

- the nature of the *post-unification regime;*

- the *state of expectations* about the *timing of reform;*

- the *initial position* of the economy;

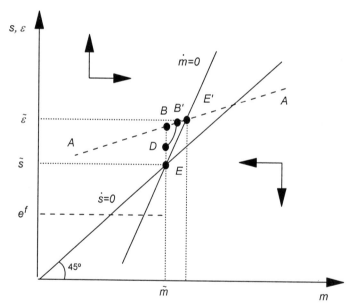

Figure C.5. Unification Dynamics–Managed Float $(\kappa > \Phi)$.

- the *length of the transition* period between announcement and implementation of reform;

- the *macroeconomic policy stance* that agents expect policymakers to adopt in the aftermath of reform.

Under a *pure float*, it was shown that the unified exchange rate may be above or below the initial parallel exchange rate, depending on the length of the transition period and the parameter values.[9] A similar result was obtained under a *managed float*, with the desired level of the exchange rate playing an important role.

Underlying the above analytical results is the intuitive argument that if an exchange rate reform is fully anticipated, agents will—in order to avoid capital losses—adjust their portfolios toward foreign-currency-denominated assets if the post-unification equilibrium floating exchange rate is expected to be more depreciated than the pre-reform equilibrium parallel rate, and toward domestic-currency-denominated assets if it is expected to be more appreciated. As a result of this portfolio adjustment, the parallel market rate will depreciate (or appreciate, under a managed float) *immediately*—at the moment the unification attempt is announced or when expectations are formed—toward the level asset holders expect the postunification floating rate to be. After the initial jump, the parallel market rate may either steadily depreciate or appreciate toward the unified exchange rate. Depending on the postreform regime and the structural parameters of the model, however, foreign assets of the central bank may either increase or fall during the transition process.

---

[9] In practice, the date at which the reform will take place in the future may not be perfectly known by agents. A likely outcome of the introduction of uncertainty about the reform date is that expectations of reform would cause a jump in the parallel exchange rate at the moment the reform is implemented as well as erratic exchange rate movements prior to transition if this type of uncertainty varies over time. In such conditions, it may be particularly difficult to interpret short-run movements in the parallel exchange rate.

Appendix

To study the dynamics associated with reform, consider first the transition to a *pure float*. The solution values for the constant terms C_1 and C_2 are given by, using Equations (C16), (C17), (C8), and (C9), the solution of the following two-equation system:

$$\gamma_1 C_1 + \gamma_2 C_2 = m_0 - \tilde{m},$$

$$\tilde{m} + \gamma_1 C_1 e^{\rho_1 T} + \gamma_2 C_2 e^{\rho_2 T} = \tilde{s} + C_1 e^{\rho_1 T} + C_2 e^{\rho_2 T},$$

where $\tilde{s} = \tilde{m} = e^f$ with $\mu = 0$. Solving this system yields

$$C_1 = (m_0 - e^f)(1 - \gamma_2)e^{\rho_2 T}/\Omega, \tag{C19}$$

$$C_2 = -(m_0 - e^f)(1 - \gamma_1)e^{\rho_1 T}/\Omega, \tag{C20}$$

where

$$\Omega = \gamma_1(1 - \gamma_2)e^{\rho_2 T} - \gamma_2(1 - \gamma_1)e^{\rho_1 T}.$$

Because $\gamma_1 > 1$, whereas $\gamma_2 < 0$, the sign of Ω is in general ambiguous. But it can be verified that for $T \to 0$, or for $T \to \infty$, the condition $\Omega > 0$ holds.

Equations (C8), (C9), (C16), (C19), and (C20) yield the solutions of the parallel exchange rate and the money stock during the transition period ($0 < t \le T$), and the value of the *postunification exchange rate*:

$$s = e^f + \frac{(m_0 - e^f)}{\Omega}\left\{(1 - \gamma_2)e^{\rho_1 t + \rho_2 T} - (1 - \gamma_1)e^{\rho_2 t + \rho_1 T}\right\}, \tag{C21}$$

$$m = e^f + \frac{(m_0 - e^f)}{\Omega}\left\{\gamma_1(1 - \gamma_2)e^{\rho_1 t + \rho_2 T} - \gamma_2(1 - \gamma_1)e^{\rho_2 t + \rho_1 T}\right\}, \tag{C22}$$

$$\varepsilon_T^+ = e^f + \frac{(m_0 - e^f)}{\Omega}\left\{\gamma_1(1 - \gamma_2) - \gamma_2(1 - \gamma_1)\right\}e^{(\rho_1 + \rho_2)T}, \tag{C23}$$

where the expression in brackets in (C23) is equal to $\gamma_1 - \gamma_2 > 0$. The case where (for $T > 0$) the unified exchange rate ε_T^+ is lower than the pre-reform official rate e^f was excluded in the foregoing discussion—an assumption that requires imposing $\Omega > 0$.

The postreform value of the unified exchange rate may be either more depreciated or more appreciated than the initial parallel exchange rate, s_0, obtained by considering the solution of Equations (C8) and (C9) with $C_2 = 0$. Formally, with $\mu = 0$, Equation (C8) yields

$$s_0 = e^f + (1/\gamma_1)(m_0 - e^f),$$

Using this result together with Equation (C23), the condition for $\varepsilon_T^+ < s_0$ can be shown to be

$$\gamma_1 e^{(\rho_1 + \rho_2)T} < \frac{\Omega}{\gamma_1 - \gamma_2},$$

or equivalently,

$$T < \frac{1}{\rho_1 + \rho_2} \ln\left(\frac{\Omega}{\gamma_1 - \gamma_2}\right). \tag{C24}$$

Inequality (C24) is a nonlinear condition on the unification date, and cannot in general be solved analytically.[10] The lower panel in Figure C3 illustrates the case where inequality (C24) holds, whereas the upper panel corresponds to the case where it does not.

To examine, for instance, the effects of an *overnight* reform requires setting $T \to 0$ in solutions (C21)-(C23). This yields $s_{0+} \to \varepsilon_T^+ = m_0$. To verify that the exchange rate jumps upward on impact requires showing that

$$s_{0+} > s_0 = e^f + (m_0 - e^f)/\gamma_1.$$

Using Equation (C21) with $t = 0$ yields

$$(\gamma_2 - \gamma_1)(1 - \gamma_1)e^{\rho_1 T} > 0,$$

which always holds, regardless of the value of T. Thus, the parallel exchange rate always depreciates. Setting $T \to \infty$ in Equations (C21)-(C23) yields the case where the exchange rate reform is announced to occur in the very distant future.

Consider now the case where the postreform regime is a *managed float*. Because private agents are endowed with perfect foresight, the solution values for the constant terms C, C_1, and C_2 appearing in (C8), (C9), (C10) and (C11) are again simultaneously determined by the conditions that connect the two regimes—given in Equation (C18), with $m_T|_{e=s=\varepsilon}$ denoting the postreform solution given by (C11) with $t = T$.

Setting $t = 0$ in Equation (C9), $t = T$ in Equations (C8), (C9), (C10), and (C11) and, using Equation (C18), yields

$$\gamma_1 C_1 + \gamma_2 C_2 = m_0 - \tilde{s}, \tag{C25}$$

$$\tilde{s} + C_1 e^{\rho_1 T} + C_2 e^{\rho_2 T} = \tilde{\varepsilon} + C e^{\nu_1 T}, \tag{C26}$$

$$\tilde{s} + \gamma_1 C_1 e^{\rho_1 T} + \gamma_2 C_2 e^{\rho_2 T} = \tilde{\varepsilon} + h_1 C e^{\nu_1 T}. \tag{C27}$$

Assuming that the initial position is a steady-state equilibrium implies that $m_0 = \tilde{s}$. The required solutions are thus given by

$$C_1 = -\alpha \nu_1 \gamma_2 (\tilde{\varepsilon} - \tilde{s}) e^{\nu_1 T}/\Delta, \tag{C28}$$

$$C_2 = \alpha \nu_1 \gamma_1 (\tilde{\varepsilon} - \tilde{s}) e^{\nu_1 T}/\Delta = -C_1 \gamma_1/\gamma_2, \tag{C29}$$

$$C = (\tilde{\varepsilon} - \tilde{s}) \left\{ \gamma_2(\gamma_1 - 1)e^{\rho_1 T} + \gamma_1(1 - \gamma_2)e^{\rho_1 T} \right\}/\Delta, \tag{C30}$$

where

$$\Delta = \gamma_1(\gamma_2 - h_1)e^{(\nu_1 + \rho_2)T} + \gamma_2(h_1 - \gamma_1)e^{(\nu_1 + \rho_2)T}.$$

Substituting Equations (C28)-(C30) in Equations (C8), (C9), (C10), and (C11) yields the solutions for the parallel exchange rate and the money stock prior to and after reform.

---

[10] Note that the dynamics of unification under a pure float do not depend on the sign of $\kappa - \Phi$. However, this is not the case under a managed float.

References

Abdel-Motaal, Karim, "Capital Flows to the Middle East in the 1990s: Quantifying the Role of Internal and External Factors," unpublished, Harvard University (February 1995).

Abel, Andrew B., "Optimal Investment under Uncertainty," *American Economic Review*, 73 (March 1983), 228-33.

Abraham, Katharine, and Susan Houseman, "Does Employment Protection Inhibit Labor Market Flexibility? Lessons from Germany, France, and Belgium," in *Social Protection versus Economic Flexibility: Is There a Trade-off?* ed. by Rebecca M. Blank, Chicago University Press (Chicago, Il.: 1994).

Adam, Christopher, "Fiscal Adjustment, Financial Liberalization, and the Dynamics of Inflation: Some Evidence from Zambia," *World Development*, 23 (May 1995), 735-50.

Adam, Christopher, and David Bevan, "Costs and Benefits of Incorporating Asset Markets into CGE Models—Evidence and Design Issues," Working Paper No. 202, Institute of Economics and Statistics, University of Oxford (October 1998).

Agénor, Pierre-Richard, "Credibility and Exchange Rate Management in Developing Countries," *Journal of Development Economics*, 45 (August 1994), 1-16.

——, "Credibility Effects of Price Controls in Disinflation Programs," *Journal of Macroeconomics*, 17 (Winter 1995), 161-71.

——, "The Labor Market and Economic Adjustment," *IMF Staff Papers*, 43 (June 1996), 261-335.

——, "Stabilization Policies, Poverty and the Labor Market: Analytical Issues and Empirical Evidence," unpublished, World Bank Institute (January 1999).

Agénor, Pierre-Richard, and Joshua Aizenman, "Contagion and Volatility with Imperfect Credit Markets," *IMF Staff Papers*, 45 (June 1998), 207-35.

——, "Asymmetric Information and the Credit Market in a Small Open Economy," unpublished, World Bank Institute (January 1999).

Agénor, Pierre-Richard, and Robert P. Flood, "Macroeconomic Policy, Speculative Attacks and Balance of Payments Crises," in *The Handbook of International Macroeconomics*, ed. by Frederick Van der Ploeg, Basil Blackwell (Oxford: 1994).

Agénor, Pierre-Richard, and Alexander Hoffmaister, "Money, Wages, and Inflation in Middle-Income Developing Countries," unpublished, International Monetary Fund (October 1997).

Agénor, Pierre-Richard, and Paul R. Masson, "Credibility, Reputation, and the Mexican Peso Crisis," *Journal of Money, Credit, and Banking*, 31 (February 1999) 70-84.

Agénor, Pierre-Richard, C. John McDermott, and Eswar Prasad, "Macroeconomic Fluctuations in Developing Countries: Some Stylized Facts," unpublished, the World Bank (January 1998). Forthcoming, *World Bank Economic Review*.

Agénor, Pierre-Richard, and Peter J. Montiel, *Development Macroeconomics*, Princeton University Press, 2nd ed. (Princeton, New Jersey: 1999).

Agénor, Pierre-Richard, and Mark P. Taylor, "Testing for Credibility Effects," *IMF Staff Papers*, 39 (September 1992), 545-71.

Agénor, Pierre-Richard, C. John McDermott, and E. Murat Ucer, "Fiscal Imbalances, Capital Inflows, and the Real Exchange Rate: Evidence for Turkey," *European Economic Review*, 41 (April 1997), 819-25.

Agénor, Pierre-Richard, and E. Murat Ucer, "Exchange Market Reform, Inflation and Fiscal Deficits," *Journal of Policy Reform*, 3 (March 1999), 81-96.

Agell, Jonas, Lars Calmfors, and Gunnar Jonsson, "Fiscal Policy when Monetary Policy is Tied to the Mast," *European Economic Review*, 40 (August 1996), 1413-40.

Aghion, Philippe, and Peter Howitt, *Endogenous Growth Theory*, the MIT Press (Cambridge, Mass.: 1998).

Aizenman, Joshua, "Inflation, Tariffs and Tax Enforcement Costs," *Journal of International Economic Integration*, 2 (September 1987), 12-28.

Aizenman, Joshua, and Eduardo Borensztein, "Strategic Investment in a Debt Bargaining Framework," *Journal of International Trade and Economic Development* (June 1993), 2:43-63.

Aizenman, Joshua, and Nancy P. Marion, "Policy Uncertainty, Persistence and Growth," *Review of International Economics*, 1 (June 1993), 145-63.

——, "Volatility and Investment: Interpreting Evidence from Developing Countries," *Economica*, 66 (May 1999), 157-79.

Alba, Joseph D., and David H. Papell, "Exchange Rate Determination and Inflation in Southeast Asian Countries," *Journal of Development Economics*, (April 1998), 421-37.

Alba, Pedro, Amar Bhattacharya, Stijn Claessens, Swati Ghosh, and Leonardo Hernandez, "The Role of Macroeconomic and Financial Sector Linkages in East Asia's Financial Crisis," in *Financial Crises: Contagion and Market Volatility*, ed. by Pierre-Richard Agénor, Marcus Miller, David Vines, and Axel Weber (Cambridge University Press: 1999).

Alesina, Alberto, and Allan Drazen, "Why Are Stabilizations Delayed?," *American Economic Review*, 81 (December 1991), 1170-88.

Alesina, Alberto, Vittorio Grilli, and Gian Maria Milesi-Ferretti, "The Political Economy of Capital Controls," in *Capital Mobility: The Impact on Con-*

sumption, Investment, and Growth, ed. by Leonardo Leiderman and Assaf Razin, Cambridge University Press (Cambridge: 1994).

Alesina, Alberto, and Roberto Perotti, "The Political Economy of Growth: A Critical Survey of the Recent Literature," *World Bank Economic Review*, 8 (September 1994), 351-71.

——, "Income Distribution, Political Instability, and Investment," *European Economic Review*, 40 (June 1996), 1203-28.

Alesina, Alberto, and Dani Rodrik, "Redistributive Politics and Economic Growth," *Quarterly Journal of Economics*, 109 (May 1994), 465-90.

Alesina, Alberto, and Guido Tabellini, "External Debt, Capital Flight, and Political Risk," *Journal of International Economics*, 27 (November 1989), 199-20.

——, "Positive Theory of Fiscal Deficits and Government Debt," *Review of Economic Studies*, 57 (July 1990), 403–14.

Alexander, William E., Tomás J. Baliño, and Charles Enoch, *The Adoption of Indirect Instruments of Monetary Policy*, Occasional Paper No. 126, International Monetary Fund (June 1995).

Allignham, Michael G., and Agnar Sandmo, "Income Tax Evasion: A Theoretical Analysis," *Journal of Public Economics*, 1 (November 1972), 323-38.

Amadeo, Edward J., "Bargaining Power, Mark-up Power, and Wage Differentials in Brazil," *Cambridge Journal of Economics*, 18 (June 1994), 313-22.

Anand, Ritu, and Sweder van Wijnbergen, "Inflation and the Financing of Government Expenditure: An Introductory Analysis with an Application to Turkey," *World Bank Economic Review*, 3 (March 1989), 17-38.

Anderson, J. E., "The Theory of Protection," in *Surveys of International Trade*, ed. by David Greenaway and L. Alan Winters, Basil Blackwell (Oxford: 1994).

Ando, Albert, and Franco Modigliani, "The Life-Cycle Hypothesis of Saving: Aggregate Implicatios and Tests," *American Economic Review*, 53 (March 1963), 55–84.

Arcand, Jean-Louis, and Marcel G. Dagenais, "The Empirics of Economic Growth in a Cross Section of Countries: Do Errors in Variables Really Not Matter?," CRDE Discussion Paper No. 4195, University of Montreal (October 1995).

Arestis, Philip, and Panicos Demetriades, "Financial Development and Economic Growth: Assessing the Evidence," *Economic Journal*, 107 (May 1997), 783-99.

Arrow, Kenneth, "The Economic Implications of Learning by Doing," *Review of Economic Studies*, 29 (June 1962), 155-73.

Aspe, Pedro, *Economic Transformation: The Mexican Way*, Cambridge University Press (Cambridge, Mass.: 1993).

Atkinson, Anthony B., and John Mickelwright, "Unemployment Compensation and Labor Market Transitions: A Critical Review," *Journal of Economic Literature*, 29 (December 1991), 1679-727.

Atiyas, Izak, Gerard Jr. Caprio, and James A. Hanson, "An Overview of Financial Reform Episodes," in *Financial Reform: Theory and Experience*, ed.

by Gerard Caprio, Jr., Izak Atiyas, and James A. Hanson, Cambridge University Press (Cambridge: 1994).

Aryeetey, Ernest, and Mukwasanon, Hyuha, "The Informal Financial Sector and Markets in Africa: An Empirical Study," in *Economic Reform in sub-Saharan Africa*, ed. by Ajay Chhibber and Stanley Fischer, the World bank (Washington D.C.: 1991).

Azariadis, Costas, and Allan H. Drazen, "Thresholds in Economic Development," *Quarterly Journal of Economics*, 105 (May 1990), 501-25.

Bacha, Edmar L., "A Three-Gap Model of Foreign Transfers and the GDP Growth Rate in Developing Countries," *Journal of Development Economics*, 32 (April 1990), 279-96.

Bahmani-Oskooee, Mohsen, "Real and Nominal Effective Exchange Rates for 22 LDCs: 1971:1-1990:4," *Applied Economics*, 27 (July 1995), 591-604.

Bailey, Martin J., "The Welfare Cost of Inflationary Finance," *Journal of Political Economy*, 64 (April 1956), 93-110.

Baldwin, Richard, and Anthony Venables, "Regional Economic Integration," in *Handbook of International Economics*, Vol. 3, ed. by Gene M. Grossman and Kenneth Rogoff, North Holland (Amsterdam: 1995).

Barry, Frank, and Michael B. Devereux, "The Macroeconomics of Government Budget Cuts: Can Fiscal Contraction be Contractionary?," in *Deficit Reduction: What Pain, What Gain?*, ed. by William Robson and William Scarth, C. D. Howe Institute (Toronto: 1994).

——, "'Expansionary Fiscal Contraction' Hypothesis: A Neo-Keynesian Analysis," *Oxford Economic Papers*, 47 (April 1995), 249-64.

Bardhan, Pranab, "Corruption and Development: A Review of Issues," *Journal of Economic Literature*, 35 (September 1997), 1320-46.

Baldwin, Richard, and Paul R. Krugman, "Persistent trade Effects of Large Exchange Rate Shocks," *Quarterly Journal of Economics*, 104 (November 1989), 635-54.

Baldwin, Robert E., "Are Economists' Traditional Trade Policy Views still Valid?," *Journal of Economic Literature*, 30 (June 1992), 804-29.

Baliño, Tomás J., amd Charles Enoch, *Currency Board Arrangements: Issues and Experiences*, Occasional Paper No. 151, International Monetary Fund (August 1997).

Bandara, Jayatilleke S., "Computable General Equilibrium Models for Development Policy Analysis in LDCs," *Journal of Economic Surveys*, 5 (January 1991), 3-69.

Bandara, Jayatilleke S., and Mark McGillivray, "Trade Policy Reforms in South Asia," *The World Economy*, 21 (September 1998), 881-96.

Bar-Ilan, Avner, and William C. Strange, "Investment Lags," *American Economic Review*, 86 (June 1996), 610-22.

Barro, Robert J., "Are Government Bonds Net Wealth?," *Journal of Political Economy*, 82 (November 1974), 1095-117.

——, "Inflationary Finance under Discretion and Rules," *Canadian Journal of Economics*, 16 (February 1983), 1-16.

——, "The Ricardian Approach to Budget Deficits," *Journal of Economic Perspectives*, 3 (March 1989), 37-54.

——, "Government Spending in a Simple Model of Endogenous Growth," *Journal of Political Economy*, 98 (October 1990), s103-s25.

——, "Economic Growth in a Cross Section of Countries," *Quarterly Journal of Economics*, 106 (May 1991), 407-43.

——, *Determinants of Economic Growth*, MIT Press (Cambridge, Mass.: 1997).

——, "Notes on Growth Accounting," Working Paper No. 6654, National Bureau of Economic Research (July 1998).

Barro, Robert J., and David B. Gordon, "A Positive Theory of Monetary Policy in a Natural Rate Model," *Journal of Political Economy*, 91 (August 1983), 589-610.

Barro, Robert J., N. Gregory Mankiw, and Xavier Sala-i-Martin, "Capital Mobility in Neoclassical Models of Growth," *American Economic Review*, 85 (March 1995), 103-15.

Barro, Robert J., and Xavier Sala-i-Martin, "Public Finance in Models of Economic Growth," *Review of Economic Studies*, 59 (October 1992), 645-61.

——, *Economic Growth*, McGraw Hill (New York: 1995).

Basu, Kaushik, *Analytical Development Economics*, 2nd ed., MIT Press (Cambridge, Mass.: 1997).

Baumol, William J., "Entrepreneurship: Productive, Unproductive, and Destructive," *Journal of Political Economy*, 98 (October 1990), 893-921.

Beaugrand, Philippe, "Zaïre's Hyperinflation, 1990-96," Working Paper No. 97/50, International Monetary Fund (April 1997).

Becker, Gary, "Crime and Punishment: An Economic Approach," *Journal of Political Economy*, 76 (March/April 1968), 169-217.

Becker, Gary, Kevin Murphy, and Robert Tamura, "Human Capital, Fertility, and Economic Growth," *Journal of Political Economy*, 98 (October 1990), 12-37.

Bell, Linda A., "The Impact of Minimum Wages in Mexico and Colombia," *Journal of Labor Economics*, 15 (July 1997), s102-s35.

Bénabou, Roland, "Inequality and Growth," in *NBER Macroeconomics Annual 1996*, ed. by Ben S. Bernanke and Julio J. Rotemberg, MIT Press (Cambridge, Mass.: 1997).

Bencivenga, Valerie R., and Bruce D. Smith, "Financial Intermediation and Endogenous Growth," *Review of Economic Studies*, 58 (April 1991), 195-209.

——, "Deficits, Inflation, and the Banking System in Developing Countries: The Optimal Degreee of Financial Repression," *Oxford Economic Papers*, 44 (October 1992), 767-90.

Benhabib, Jess, and Mark M. Spiegel, "The Role of Human Capital in Economic Development: Evidence from Aggregate Cross-Country Data," *Journal of Monetary Economics*, 34 (October 1994), 143-73.

Berg, Andrew, and Catherine Pattillo, "Are Currency Crises Predictable? A Test," Working Paper No. 98/154, International Monetary Fund (November 1998).

Bernard, Andrew B., and Steven N. Durlauf, "Interpreting Tests of the Convergence Hypothesis," *Journal of Econometrics*, 71 (March 1996), 161-73.

Bernstein, E. M., "Some Economic Aspects of Multiple Exchange Rates," *IMF Staff Papers*, 2 (September 1950), 224-37.

Bertola, Guiseppe, and Allan H. Drazen, "Trigger Points and Budget Cuts: Explaining the Effects of Fiscal Austerity," *American Economic Review*, 83 (March 1993), 11-26.

Bester, Helmut, "Screening vs. Rationing in Credit Markets with Imperfect Information," *American Economic Review*, 75 (September 1985), 850-55.

Bevilaqua, Afonso S., and Rogério L. Werneck, "Fiscal Impulse in the Brazilian Economy, 1989-96," Working Paper No. 379, Pontificia Universidade de Rio do Janeiro (October 1997).

Bhagwati, Jagdish, and Arvind Panagariya, "Preferential Trading Areas and Multilateralism: Strangers, Friends or Foes?," in *The Economics of Preferential Trade Arrangements*, ed. by Jagdish Bhagwati and Arvind Panagariya, the American Enterprise Institute Press (Washington DC: 1996).

Bhagwati, Jagdish, Arvind Panagariya, and T. N. Srinivasan, *Lectures on International Trade*, 2nd ed., MIT Press (Cambridge: Mass.: 1998).

Bhattacharya, Amar, Peter J. Montiel, and Sunil Sharma, "Private Capital Inflows to Sub-Saharan Africa: An Overview of Trends and Determinants," in *External Finance for Low-Income Countries*, edited by Zubair Iqbal and Ravi Kanbur, the World Bank (Washington, DC: 1997).

Bhattacharya, Prabir, "Rural-Urban Migration in Economic Development," *Journal of Economic Surveys*, (September 1993), 243-81.

Bhattacharya, Sudipto, Arnoud W. Boot, and Anjan V. Thakor, "The Economics of Bank Regulation," *Journal of Money, Credit, and Banking*, 30 (November 1998), 745-70.

Bils, Mark, and Peter J. Klenow, "Does Schooling Cause Growth or the Other Way Around?," Working Paper No. 6393, National Bureau of Economic Research (February 1998).

Blackburn, Keith, and Michael Christensen, "Monetary Policy and Policy Credibility: Theories and Evidence," *Journal of Economic Literature*, 27 (March 1989), 1-45.

Blanchard, Olivier-Jean, "Suggestions for a New Set of Fiscal Indicators," in *The Political Economy of Government Debt*, ed. by H. A. Verbon and F. A. van Winden, Elsevier (Amsterdam: 1993).

Blank, Rebecca M., and Richard B. Freeman, "Evaluating the Connection between Social Protection and Economic Flexibility," in *Social Protection versus Economic Flexibility: Is There a Trade-off?* ed. by Rebecca M. Blank, Chicago University Press (Chicago, Il.: 1994).

Bleaney Michael F., "Macroeconomic Stability, Investment and Growth in Developing Countries," *Journal of Development Economics*, 48 (March 1996), 461-77.

Bleaney Michael F., and David Greenaway, "Long-Run Trends in the Relative Price of Primary Commodities and in the Terms of Trade of Developing Countries," *Oxford Economic Papers*, 45 (July 1993), 349-63.

Blejer, Mario I., and Adrienne Cheasty, "The Measurement of Fiscal Deficits: Analytical and Methodological Issues," *Journal of Economic Literature*, 29 (December 1991), 1644-78.

Blejer, Mario I., and Ke-Young Chu, *Measurement of Fiscal Impact: Methodological Issues*, Occasional Paper No. 59, International Monetary Fund (June 1988).

Blejer, Mario I., and Nissan Liviatan, "Fighting Hyperinflation: Stabilization Strategies in Argentina and Israel," *IMF Staff Papers*, 34 (September 1987), 409-38.

Bliss, Christopher, and Nicholas Stern, "Productivity, Wages, and Nutrition: Part I–The Theory," *Journal of Development Economics*, 5 (December 1978), 331-62.

Boone, Peter, "Politics and the Effectiveness of Foreign Aid," *European Economic Review*, 40 (February 1996), 289-329.

Boot, Arnoud W., and Anjan V. Thakor, "Self-Interested Bank Regulation," *American Economic Review*, 83 (May 1993), 206-12.

Boote, Anthony R., and Kamau Thugge, *Debt Relief for Low-Income Countries: The HIPC Initiative*, IMF Pamphlet Series, No. 51, revised (Washington, D.C.: 1999).

Borensztein, Eduardo, José De Gregorio, and Jong Wha Lee, "How Does Foreign Direct Investment Affect EconomicGrowth?," *Journal of International Economics* 45 (June 1998), 115–35.

Borio, Claudio E. V., "The Implementation of Monetary Policy in Industrial Countries: A Survey," Economic Paper No. 47, Bank for International Settlements (July 1997).

Bourguignon, Francois, Jaime de Melo, and Akiko Suwa, "Modeling the Effects of Adjustment Programs on Income Distribution," *World Development*, 19 (November 1991), 1527-44.

Bowe, Michael, and James W. Dean, *Has the Market Solved the Sovereign-Debt Crisis?*, Princeton Studies in International Finance, No. 83 (August 1997).

Boyd, John H., and Bruce D. Smith, "The Co-Evolution of the Real and Financial Sectors in the Growth Process," *World Bank Economic Review*, 10 (May 1996), 371-96.

Boyle,G. E., and T. G. McCarthy, "A Simple Measure of β-Convergence," *Oxford Bulletin of Economics and Statistics*, 59 (May 1997), 257-64.

Brecher, Richard, and Carlos Díaz-Alejandro, "Tariffs, Foreign Capital, and Immiserizing Growth," *Journal of International Economics*, 7 (November 1977), 317-22.

Brunetti, Aymo, "Political Variables in Cross-Country Growth Analysis," *Journal of Economic Surveys*, 11 (June 1997), 163-90.

Bruno, M, *High Inflation and the Nominal Anchors of an Open Economy*, Princeton Essay in International Finance, No. 183, Princeton University (Princeton; New Jersey: 1991).

Bruno, Michael, and William Easterly, "Inflation Crises and Long-Run Growth," *Journal of Monetary Economics*, 41 (February 1998), 3-26.

Bruno, Michael, and Stanley Fischer, "Seigniorage, Operating Rules, and the High Inflation Trap," *Quarterly Journal of Economics*, 105 (May 1990), 353-74.

Bruno, Michael, Martin Ravallion, and Lyn Squire, "Equity and Growth in Developing Countries: Old and new Perspectives on the Policy Issues," in *Income Distribution and High-Quality Growth*, ed. by Vito Tanzi and Ke-Young Chu, MIT Press (Cambridge, Mass.: 1998).

Bruton, Henry, "Import Substitution," in *Handbook of Development Economics*, II, ed. by Hollis B. Chenery and T.N. Srinivasan, North Holland (Amsterdam: 1989).

Buffie, Edward F., "Devaluation, Investment and Growth in LDCs," *Journal of Development Economics*, 20 (March 1986), 361-79.

Bulir, Ales, "Income Inequality: Does Inflation Matter?," Working Paper No. 98/7, International Monetary Fund (January 1998).

Buiter, Willem H., "Structural and Stabilization Aspects of Fiscal and Financial Policy in the Dependent Economy," *Oxford Economic Papers*, 40 (June 1988), 220-45.

———, "Aspects of Fiscal Performance in Some Transition Economies Under Fund-Supported Programs," Working Paper No. 97/131, International Monetary Fund (April 1997).

Buiter, Willem H., and Urjit R. Patel, "Debt, Deficits and Inflation: An Application to the Public Finances of India," *Journal of Public Economics*, 47 (March 1992), 171-205.

Burgess, Robin, and Nicholas Stern, "Taxation and Development," *Journal of Economic Literature*, 31 (June 1993), 762-830.

Burmeister, Edwin, and A. Rodney Dobell, *Mathematical Theories of Economic Growth*, Mcmilllan (New York: 1970).

Burnside, Craig, and David Dollar, "Aid, Policies, and Growth," PRE Working Paper No. 1777, the World Bank (June 1997).

Buttrick, J., "A Note on Professor Solow's Growth Model," *Quarterly Journal of Economics*, 72 (November 1958), 633–36.

Caballero, Ricardo J., "Consumption Puzzles and Precautionary Savings," *Journal of Monetary Economics*, 25 (January 1990), 113-36.

———, "On the Sign of the Investment-Uncertainty Relationship," *American Economic Review*, 81 (March 1991), 279-88.

Calmfors, Lars, "Centralization of Wage Bargaining and macroeconomic Performance: A Survey," *OECD Economic Studies*, 10 (Winter 1993), 161-91.

Calvo, Guillermo A., "Incredible Reforms," in *Debt, Stabilization and Development*, ed. by Guillermo A. Calvo, Ronald Findlay, Pentti Kouri, and Jorge Braga de Macedo, Basil Blackwell (Oxford: 1989).

———, "The Perils of Sterilization," *IMF Staff Papers*, 38 (December 1991), 921-26.

———, "Varieties of Capital-Market Crises," in *The Debt Burden and its Consequences for Monetary Policy*, ed. by Guillermo A. Calvo and Mervyn King, Macmillan (London: 1998).

Calvo, Guillermo A., Leonardo Leiderman, and Carmen M. Reinhart, "Inflows of Capital to Developing Countries in the 1990s: Causes and Effects," *Journal of Economic Perspectives*, 10 (Spring 1996), 123-39.

Calvo, Guillermo A., and Enrique G. Mendoza, "Rational Herd Behavior and the Globalization of Securities Markets," Working Paper No. 120, Institute for Empirical Macroeconomics (August 1997).

Calvo, Guillermo A., Carmen M. Reinhart, and Carlos A. Végh, "Targeting the Real Exchange Rate: Theory and Evidence," *Journal of Development Economics*, 47 (June 1995), 97-133.

Calvo, Guillermo A., and Carlos A. Végh, "Exchange Rate-Based Stabilization under Imperfect Credibility," in *Open Economy Macroeconomics*, ed. by Helmut Frisch and Andreas Worgotter, St. Martin's Press (New York: 1993).

Calvo, Sara, and Carmen M. Reinhart, "Capital Flows to Latin America: Is There Evidence of Contagion Effects?" in *Private Capital Flows to Emerging Markets after the Mexican Crisis*, ed. by Guillermo A. Calvo, Morris Goldstein, and Eduard Hochreiter, Institute for International Economics (Washington DC: 1996).

Campbell White, Oliver, and Anita Bhatia, *Privatization in Africa*, the World Bank (Washington D.C.: 1998).

Caprio, Gerard, Jr., and Daniela Klingebiel, "Bank Insolvencies: Cross Country Experience," Policy Research Working Paper No. 1620, the World Bank (July 1996).

Cárdenas, Mauricio, and Felipe Barrrera, "On the Effectiveness of Capital Controls: The Experience of Colombia During the 1990s," *Journal of Development Economics*, 54 (October 1997), 27-58.

Cárdenas, Mauricio, and Andrés Escobar, "Saving Determinants in Colombia: 1925-1994," *Journal of Development Economics*, 57 (October 1998), 5-44.

Cardoso, Eliana, and Ilan Goldfajn, "Capital Flows to Brazil: The Endogeneity of Capital Controls," *IMF Staff Papers*, 45 (March 1998), 161-202.

Cardoso, Eliana, R. Paes de Barro, and Andre Urani, "Inflation and Unemployment as Determinants of Income Inequality in Brazil: The 1980s," in *Reform, Recovery, and Growth: Latin America and the Middle East*, ed. by Rudiger Dornbusch and Sebastián Edwards, University of Chicago Press (Chicago, Il.: 1995).

Casella, Alessandra, and Barry Eichengreen, "Can Foreign Aid Accelerate Stabilisation?," *Economic Journal*, 106 (May 1996), 605-19.

Caselli, Francesco, Gerardo Esquivel, and Fernando Lefort, "Reopening the Convergence Debate: A New Look at Cross-Country Growth Empirics," *Journal of Economic Growth*, 1 (September 1996), 363-90.

Cashin, Paul, "Government Spending, Taxes, and Economic Growth," *IMF Staff Papers*, 42 (June 1995), 237-69.

Chand, Sheetal K., "Fiscal Impulse Measures and their Fiscal Impact," in *How to Measure the Fiscal Deficit*, ed. by Mario I. Blejer and Adrienne Cheasty, International Monetary Fund (Washington DC: 1993).

Chang, Roberto, and Andrés Velasco, "Financial Crises in Emerging Markets: A Canonical Model," Working Paper No. 6606, National Bureau of Economic Research (June 1998).

Chenery, Hollis B., and Alan Strout, "Foreign Assistance and Economic Development," *American Economic Review* 56 (September 1966), 679-733.

Chiang, Alpha C., *Fundamental Methods of Mathematical Economics*, Mc-Graw Hill, 3rd edition (New York: 1984).

Chinn, Menzie D., "Before the Fall: Were East Asian Currencies Overvalued?," Working Paper No. 6491, National Bureau of Economic Research (April 1998).

Choudhry, Taufiq, "High Inflation Rates and the Long-Run Money Demand Function: Evidence from Cointegration Tests," *Journal of Macroeconomics*, 17 (Winter 1995), 77-91.

Chuhan, Punam, Gabriel Perez-Quiros, Helen Popper, "International Capital Flows: Do Short-Term Investment and Direct Investment Differ?," PRE Working Paper No. 1669, the World Bank (October 1996).

Claessens, Stijn, "The Debt Laffer Curve: Some Estimates," *World Development*, 18 (December 1990), 1671-77.

Claessens, Stijn, Michael P. Dooley, Andrew Warner, "Portfolio Capital Flows: Hot or Cold?," *World Bank Economic Review*, 9 (January 1995), 153-74.

Clarke, George R., "More Evidence on Income Distribution and Growth," *Journal of Development Economics*, 47 (August 1995), 403-27.

Cline, William R., *International Debt Reexamined*, Institute for International Economics (Washington DC: 1995).

Cnossen, Sijbren, "Design of the Value Added Tax: Lessons from Experience," in *Tax Policy in Developing Countries*, ed. by Javad Khalilzadeh-Shirazi and Anwar Shah, the World Bank (Washington D.C.: 1991).

Coe, David T., Elhanan Helpman, and Alexander W. Hoffmaister, "North-South R&D Spillovers," *Economic Journal*, 107 (January 1997), 134-49.

Cohen, Daniel, " The Sustainability of African Debt," Policy Research Paper No. 1621, International Economics Department, the World Bank (July 1996*a*).

——, "Tests of the Convergence Hypothesis: Some Further Results," *Journal of Economic Growth*, 1 (September 1996*b*), 351-61.

Coles, Melvyn, and Apostolis Philippopoulos, "Are Exchange Rate Bands better than Fixed Exchange Rates? The Imported Credibility Approach," *Journal of International Economics*, 43 (August 1997), 133-53.

Collier, Paul, and Jan W. Gunning, "Policy Toward Commodity Shocks in Developing Countries," Working Paper No. 96/84, International Monetary Fund (August 1996).

Collins, Susan M., "On Becoming more Flexible: Exchange Rate Regimes in Latin America and the Caribbean," *Journal of Development Economics*, 51 (October 1996), 117-38.

Collins, Susan M., and Barry P. Bosworth, "Economic Growth in East Asia: Accumulation versus Assimilation," *Brookings Papers on Economic Activity*, No. 2 (December 1996), 135-203.

Conley, John C., and William F. Maloney, "Optimum Sequencing of Credible Reforms with Uncertain Outcomes," *Journal of Development Economics*, 48 (October 1995), 151-66.

Conlisk, John, 'A Modified Neo-Classical Growth Model with Endogenous Technical Change," *Southern Economic Journal*, 34 (October 1967), 199-208.

Conway, Patrick, "IMF Lending Programs: Participation and Impact," *Journal of Development Economics*, 45 (December 1994), 365-91.

Cooper, Richard N., *Economic Stabilization in Developing Countries*, ICS Press (San Francisco, Cal.: 1991).

Corbo, Vittorio, and Leonardo Hernández, "Macroeconomic Adjustment to Capital Inflows: Lessons from Recent Latin American and East Asian Experience," *World Bank Research Observer*, 11 (February 1996), 61-85.

Corden, W. Max, "Booming Sector and Dutch Disease Economics: Survey and Consolidation," *Oxford Economic Papers*, 36 (November 1984), 359-80.

Cowell, Frank A., *Cheating the Government: The Economics of Evasion*, MIT Press (Cambridge, Mass.: 1990).

Cuddington, John, "Long-Run Trends in 26 Primary Commodity Prices," *Journal of Development Economics*, 39 (October 1992), 207-27.

——, "Analyzing the Sustainability of Fiscal Deficits in Developing Countries," unpublished, Georgetown University (March 1997).

Cukierman, Alex, *Central Bank Strategy, Credibility, and Independence*, MIT Press (Cambridge, Mass.: 1992).

Cukierman, Alex, and Francesco Lippi, "Central Bank Independence, Centralization of Wage Bargaining, Inflation and Unemployment: Theory and Evidence," Discussion Paper No. 1847, Centre for Economic Policy Research (March 1998).

Cukierman, Alex, Miguel A. Kiguel, and Leonardo Leiderman, "Transparency and the Evolution of Exchange Rate Flexibility in the Aftermath of Disinflation," in *Financial Factors in Economic Stabilization and Growth*, ed. by Mario I. Blejer, Zvi Eckstein, Zvi Hercowitz, and Leonardo Leiderman, Cambridge University Press (Cambridge: 1996).

Cumby, Robert E., and Maurice Obstfeld, "Capital Mobility and the Scope for Sterilization: Mexico in the 1970s," in *Financial Policies and the World Capital Market*, ed. by Pedro A. Armella, Rudiger Dornbusch and Maurice Obstfeld, Chicago University Press (Chicago, Il.: 1983).

Currie, Janet, and Ann Harrison, "Sharing the Costs: The Impact of Trade Reform on Capital and Labor in Morocco," *Journal of Labor Economics*, 15 (July 1997), s44-s71.

Dasgupta, Partha, "The Population Problem: Theory and Evidence," *Journal of Economic Literature*, 33 (December 1995), 1879-902.

Dayal-Gulati, Anuradha, and Christian Thimann, "Saving in Southeast Asia and Latin America Compared: Searching for Policy Lessons," in *Macroeconomic Issues Facing ASEAN Countries*, ed. by John Hicklin, David Robinson, and Anoop Singh, International Monetary Fund (Washington DC: 1997).

Deaton, Angus S., *Understanding Consumption*, Oxford University Press (Oxford: 1992).

Benjamin, Dwayne, and Angus Deaton, "Household Welfare and the Pricing of Cocoa and Coffee in Côte d'Ivoire: Lessons from the Living Standards Surveys," *World Bank Economic Review*, 7 (September 1993), 293-318.

Deaton, Angus S., and Ronald I. Miller, *International Commodity Prices, Macroeconomic Performance, and Politics in Sub-Saharan Africa*, Princeton Essays in International Finance No. 79 (Princeton, New Jersey: 1995).

De Gregorio, José, "Economic Growth in Latin America," *Journal of Development Economics*, 39 (July 1992), 59-84.

——, "Inflation, Taxation, and Long-Run Growth," *Journal of Monetary Economics* 31 (June 1993), 271-98.

——, "Borrowing Constraints, Human Capital Accumulation, and Growth," *Journal of Monetary Economics*, 37 (February 1996), 49-72.

De Gregorio, José, Sebastian Edwards, and Rodrigo O. Valdés, "Capital Controls in Chile: An Assessment," unpublished, Central Bank of Chile (March 1999).

De Haan, Jakob, and Dick Zelhorst, "The Impact of Government Deficits on Money Growth in Developing Countries," *Journal of International Money and Finance*, 9 (December 1990), 455-69.

De la Fuente, Angel, "The Empirics of Growth and Convergence: A Selective Review," *Journal of Economic Dynamics and Control*, 21 (January 1997), 23-73.

De Macedo, Jorge Braga, "Currency Inconvertibility, Trade Taxes and Smuggling," *Journal of Development Economics*, 27 (October 1987), 109-25.

Dellas, Harris, and Alan C. Stockman, "Self-Fulfilling Expectations, Speculative Attacks, and Capital Controls," *Journal of Money, Credit, and Banking*, 25 (November 1993), 721-30.

Demetriades, Panicos, and Khaled A. Hussein, "Does Financial Development Cause Economic Growth? Time-Series Evidence from 16 Countries," *Journal of Development Economics*, 51 (December 1996), 387-411.

Demetriades, Panicos, and Kul B. Luintel, "The Direct Costs of Financial Repression: Evidence from India," *Review of Economics and Statistics*, 79 (May 1997), 311-19.

Demirgüç-Kunt, Asli, and Enrica Detragiache, "The Determinants of Banking Crises in Developing Countries," *IMF Staff Papers*, 45 (March 1998a), 81-109.

——, "Financial Liberalization and Financial Fragility," Policy Research Working Paper No. 1917, the World Bank (May 1998b).

Deshpande, Ashwini, "The Debt Overhang and the Disincentive to Invest," *Journal of Development Economics*, 52 (February 1997), 169-87.

Devarajan, Shantayanan, Delfin S. Go, "The Simplest Dynamic General Equilibrium Model of an Open Economy," *Journal of Policy Modeling*, 20 (December 1998), 677-714.

Devarajan, Shantayanan, Delfin S. Go, Jeffrey D. Lewis, Sherman Robinson, and Pekka Sinko, "Simple General Equilibrium Modeling," in Joseph F. Francois and Kenneth A. Reinhert, *Applied Methods for Trade Policy Analysis*, Cambridge University Press (Cambridge: 1997).

Devarajan, Shantayanan, Jeffrey D. Lewis, Sherman Robinson, "Policy Lessons from Trade-Focused, Two-Sector Models," *Journal of Policy Modeling*, 12 (Winter 1990), 625-57.

——, "External Shocks, Purchasing Power Parity and the Equilibrium Real Exchange Rate," *World Bank Economic Review*, 7 (January 1993), 45-63.

Devarajan, Shantarajan, and Dani Rodrik, "Do the Benefits of Fixed Exchange Rates Outweigh their Costs? The Franc Zone in Africa," in *Open Economy Structural Adjustment and Agriculture*, ed. by I. Goldin and L. Alan Winters, Cambridge University Press (Cambridge: 1992).

Devarajan, Shantayanan, Vinaya Swaroop, and Heng-fu Zou, "The Composition of Public Expenditure and Economic Growth," *Journal of Monetary Economics*, 37 (April 1996), 313-44.

Devenow, Andrea, and Ivo Welch, "Rational Herding in Financial Economics," *European Economic Review*, 40 (April 1996), 603-15.

Dewatripont, Mathias, and Gilles Michel, "On Closure Rules, Homogeneity, and Dynamics in Applied General Equilibrium Models," *Journal of Development Economics*, 26 (June 1987), 65-76.

Dewatripont, Mathias, and Gerard Roland, "Economic Reform and Dynamic Political Constraints," *Review of Economic Studies*, 59 (October 1992), 703-30.

——, "The Design of Reform Packages under Uncertainty," *American Economic Review*, 85 (December 1995), 1207-23.

Diamond, Douglas W., and Philip H. Dybvig, "Bank Runs, Deposit Insurance, and Liquidity," *Journal of Political Economy*, 91 (June 1983), 401-19.

Díaz-Alejandro, Carlos, "Good-Bye Financial Repression, Hello Financial Crash," *Journal of Development Economics*, 19 (September 1985), 1-24.

Dixit, Avinash, "Taxation in Open Economies," *Handbook of Public Economics*, Vol. I, ed. by Alan J. Auerbach and Martin S. Feldstein, North Holland (Amsterdam: 1985).

——, "Hysterisis, Import Penetration, and Exchange Rate Pass-through," *Quarterly Journal of Economics*, 104 (May 1989), 205-28.

Dixit, Avinash, and Robert S. Pindyck, *Investment under Uncertainty*, Princeton University Press (Princeton, New Jersey: 1994).

Dollar, David, "Outward-Oriented Developing Economies Really Do Grow More Rapidly: Evidence from 95 LDCs, 1976-1985," *Economic Development and Cultural Change*, 40 (April 1992), 523-44.

Dooley, Michael, "A Survey of the Literature on Controls over International Capital Transactions," *IMF Staff Papers* 43 (December 1996), 639-87.

Dornbusch, Rudiger, and Stanley Fischer, "Stopping Hyperinflations, Past and Present," *Weltwirtschaftliches Archives*, 122 (March 1986), 1-47.

——, "Moderate Inflation," *World Bank Economic Review*, 7 (January 1993), 1-44.

Dornbusch, Rudiger, Federico Sturzenegger, and Holger Wolf, "Extreme Inflation: Dynamics and Stabilization," *Brookings Papers on Economic Activity*, No. 1 (March 1990), 1-84.

Doroodian, Khosrow, "Macroeconomic Performance and Adjustment under Policies Commonly Supported by the International Monetary Fund," *Economic Development and Cultural Change*, 41 (July 1993), 849-64.

Drazen, Allan H., 'The Political Economy of Delayed Reform," *Journal of Policy Reform*, 1 (March 1996), 25-46.

Drazen, Allan H., and Leonardo Bartolini, "Capital Account Liberalization as a Signal," *American Economic Review*, 87 (March 1997), 138-54.

Drazen, Allan H., and Vittorio Grilli, "The Benefits of Crises for Economic Reforms," *American Economic Review*, 83 (June 1993), 598-607.

Drazen, Allan, and Paul R. Masson, "Credibility of Policies versus Credibility of Policymakers," *Quarterly Journal of Economics* 104 (August 1994), 735-54.

Easterly, William, "A Consistency Framework for Macroeconomic Analysis," Working Paper Series No. 234, the World Bank (June 1989).

——, "Endogenous Growth in Developing Countries with Government-Induced Distortions," in *Adjustment Lending Revisited: Policies to Restore Growth*, ed. by Vittorio Corbo, Stanley Fischer, and Steven B. Webb, the World Bank (Washington DC: 1992).

——, "When are Stabilizations Expansionary? Evidence from High Inflation," *Economic Policy*, No. 22 (April 1995), 67-107.

——, "The Ghost of Financing Gap: Testing the Growth Model used in the International Financial Institutions," *Journal of Development Economics*, 60 (December 1999), 423-38.

Easterly, William, Norman Loayza, and Peter J. Montiel, "Has Latin America's Post-Reform Growth been Disappointing?," *Journal of International Economics*, 43 (November 1997), 287-311.

Easterly, William, and Sergio Rebelo, "Fiscal Policy and Economic growth: An Empirical Investigation," *Journal of Monetary Economics*, 32 (December 1993), 417-58.

Easterly, William, and Klaus Schmidt-Hebbel, "The Macroeconomics of Public Sector Deficits: A Synthesis," in *Public Sector Deficits and Macroeconomic Performance*, ed. by William Easterly, Carlos A. Rodríguez, and Klaus Schmidt-Hebbel, Oxford University Press (Oxford: 1994).

Eaton, Jonathan, "Sovereign Debt: A Primer," *World Bank Economic Review*, 7 (May 1993), 137-72.

Edwards, Sebastián, *Real Exchange Rates, Devaluation and Adjustment: Exchange Rate Policies in Developing Countries*, MIT Press (Cambridge, 1989).

——, "Openness, Trade Liberalization, and Growth in Developing Countries," *Journal of Economic Literature*, 31 (September 1993), 1358-93.

——, "Exchange Rates, Inflation and Disinflation: Latin American Experiences," in *Capital Controls, Exchange Rates and Monetary Policy in the World Economy*, ed. by Sebastián Edwards, Cambridge University Press (New York: 1995).

——, "Public Sector Deficits and Macroeconomic Stability in Developing Economies," Working Paper No. 5407, National Bureau of Economic Research (January 1996*a*).

——, "The Determinants of the Choice between Fixed and Flexible Exchange Rate Regimes," Working Paper No. 5756, National Bureau of Economic Research (September 1996*b*).

——, "Openness, Productivity and Growth: What Do We Really Know?," *Economic Journal*, 108 (March 1998*b*), 383-98.

Edwards, Sebastián, and Sweder van Wijnbergen, "The Welfare Effects of Trade and Capital Market Liberalization," *International Economic Review*, 27 (February 1986), 141-48.

Eichengreen, Barry, "Does Mercosur Need a Single Currency?," Working Paper No. c98, University of California (October 1998).

Eichengreen, Barry, and Paul Masson, *Exit Strategies: Policy Options for Countries Seeking Greater Exchange Rate Flexibility*, Occasional Paper No. 168, International Monetary Fund (June 1998).

Eichengreen, Barry, Andrew K. Rose, and Charles Wyplosz, "Contagious Currency Crises," Working Paper No. 5681, National Bureau of Economic Research (July 1996).

Eichengreen, Barry, James Tobin, and Charles Wyplosz, "Two Cases for Sand in the Wheels of International Finance," *Economic Journal*, 105 (January 1995), 162-72.

Elbadawi, Ibrahim A., Benno J. Ndulu, and Njuguna Ndung'u, "Debt Overhang and Economic Growth in sub-Saharan Africa," in *External Finance for Low-Income Countries*, edited by Zubair Iqbal and Ravi Kanbur, the World Bank (Washington, DC: 1997).

Evans, J. L., and George K. Yarrow, "Some Implications of Alternative Expectations Hypotheses in the Monetary Analysis of Hyperinflations," *Oxford Economic Papers* 33 (March 1981), 61-80.

Fallon, Peter R., and Luis A. Riveros, "Adjustment and the Labor Market," PRE Working Paper No. 214, the World Bank (June 1989).

Falvey, Rod, and Cha Dong Kim, "Timing and Sequencing Issues in Trade Liberalisation," *Economic Journal*, 102 (July 1992), 908-24.

Faruqee, Hamid, "Dynamic Capital Mobility in Pacific Basin Developing Countries: Estimation and Policy Implications," *IMF Staff Papers*, 39 (September 1992), 706-17.

Feldman, Robert A., and Rajnish Mehra, "Auctions," *IMF Staff Papers*, 40 (September 1993), 485-511.

Fernández, Raquel, and Dani Rodrik, "Resistance to Reform: Status Quo Bias in the Presence of Individual Specific Uncertainty," *American Economic Review*, 81 (December 1991), 1146-55.

Fernández-Arias, Eduardo, "The New Wave of Private Capital Inflows: Push or Pull?," *Journal of Development Economics*, 48 (March 1996), 389-418.

Fernández-Arias, Eduardo, and Peter J. Montiel, "The Surge in Capital Inflows to Developing Countries: An Analytical Overview," *World Bank Economic Review*, 10 (March 1996), 51-77.

Fields, Gary S., "Changing Labor Market Conditions and Economic Development in Hong Kong, the Republic of Korea, Singapore, and Taiwan," *World Bank Economic Review*, 8 (September 1994), 395-414.

Fields, Gary S., and Henry Wan, Jr., "Wage-Setting Institutions and Economic Growth," *World Development*, 17 (September 1989), 1471-83.

Fischer, Stanley, "Exchange Rate versus Money Targets in Disinflation," in *Indexing, Inflation, and Economic Policy*, MIT Press (Cambridge, Mass.: 1986).

——, "The Role of Macroeconomic Factors in Growth," *Journal of Monetary Economics*, 32 (December 1993), 485-512.

Fischer, Stanley, and Jacob Frenkel, "Economic Growth and the Stages of the Balance of Payments," in *Trade, Stability, and Macroeconomics*, ed. by G. Horwich and Paul Samuelson, Academic Press (New York: 1974).

Fishlow, Albert, "Inequality, Poverty and Growth: Where Do We Stand?," in *Annual World Bank Conference on Development Economics*, ed. by Michael Bruno and Boris Pleskovic, the World Bank (Washington D.C.: 1995).

Flood, Robert P., and Peter M. Garber, "Collapsing Exchange Rate Regimes: Some Linear Examples," *Journal of International Economics*, 17 (August 1984), 1-13.

Flood, Robert P., Peter M. Garber, and Charles Kramer, "Collapsing Exchange Rate Regimes: Another Linear Example," *Journal of International Economics* 41 (November 1996), 223-34.

Flood, Robert P., and Nancy P. Marion, "Perspectives on the Recent Currency Crisis Literature," *International Journal of Finance and Economics*, 4 (January 1999), 1-26.

Forder, James, "Central Bank Independence: Conceptual Clarifications and Interim Assessment," *Oxford Economic Papers*, 50 (July 1998), 307-34.

Frankel, Jeffrey A., and Chudozie Okongwu, "Liberalized Portfolio Capital Inflows in Emerging Markets: Sterilization, Expectations, and the Incompleteness of Interest Rate Convergence," *International Journal of Finance and Economics*, 1 (January 1996), 1-24.

Freeman, Richard B., "Labor Market Institutions in Economic Development," *American Economic Review*, 83 (May 1993), 403-8.

Frenkel, Jacob A., and Assaf Razin, *Fiscal Policies and the World Economy*, MIT Press, 3rd ed. (Cambridge, Mass.: 1995).

Friedman, Milton, *A Theory of the Consumption Function*, Princeton University Press (Princeton, New Jersey: 1957).

Froot, Kenneth A., Paul R. Krugman, "Market-Based Debt Reduction for Developing Countries: Principles and Prospects," in *Analytical Issues in Debt*, ed. by ed. by Jacob A. Frenkel, Michael Dooley, and Peter Wickham, International Monetary Fund (Washington DC: 1989).

Fry, Maxwell J., *Money, Interest and Banking in Economic Development*, Johns Hopkins University Press, 2nd ed. (Baltimore, Md.: 1995).

——, "In Favour of Financial Liberalisation," *Economic Journal*, 107 (May 1997), 754-70.

Fry, Maxwell J., Charles A. E. Goodhart, and A. Almeida, *Central Banking in Developing Countries*, Paul Routledge (London: 1996).

Galor, Oded, and Daniel Tsiddon, "The Distribution of Human Capital and Economic Growth," *Journal of Economic Growth*, 2 (March 1997), 93-124.

Galor, Oded, and Joseph Zeira, "Income Distribution and Macroeconomics," *Review of Economic Studies*, 60 (January 1993), 35-52.

Gandolfo, Giancarlo, *Economic Dynamics*, Springer Verlag (Berlin: 1996).

Garber, Peter, "Issues of Enforcement and Evasion in a Tobin Tax on Foreign Exchange Transactions," in *The Tobin Tax*, ed. by Mahbub Ul Haq, Oxford

University Press (New York: 1996).

——, "Derivatives in International Capital Flows," Working Paper No. No. 6623, National Bureau of Economic Research (June 1998).

Garber, Peter M., and Subir Lall, "Derivative Products in Exchange Rate Crises," in *Managing Capital Flows and Exchange Rates*, ed. by Reuven Glick, Cambridge University Press (Cambridge: 1998).

Garber, Peter M., and Michael G. Spencer, "Dynamic Hedging and the Interest Rate Defense," in *The Microstructure of Foreign Exchange Markets*, ed. by Jeffrey A. Frankel, Giampaolo Galli, and Alberto Giovannini, University of Chicago Press (Chicago, Il.: 1996).

Gatica, Jaime, Alejandra Mizala, and Pilar Romaguera, "Interindustry Wage Differentials in Brazil," *Economic Development and Cultural Change*, 43 (January 1995), 315-31.

Gavin, Michael, "Unemployment and the Economics of Gradualist Policy Reform," *Journal of Policy Reform*, 1 (March 1996), 239-58.

Gersovitz, Mark, "Saving and Development," in *Handbook of Development Economics*, ed. by Hollis B. Chenery and T. N. Srinivasan, North Holland (Amsterdam: 1988).

Gersovitz, Mark, "Saving and Development," in *Handbook of Development Economics*, ed. by Hollis B. Chenery and T. N. Srinivasan, Amsterdam (North Holland: 1988).

Ghartey, Edward E., "Monetary Dynamics in Ghana: Evidence from Cointegration, Error Correction Modelling, and Exogeneity," *Journal of Development Economics*, 57 (October 1998), 473-86.

Ghei, Nita, Miguel A. Kiguel, and Stephen A. O'Connell, "Parallel Exchange Rates in Developing Countries: Lessons from Eight Case Studies," in *Parallel Exchange Rates in Developing Countries*, ed. by Miguel A. Kiguel, J. Saúl Lizondo, and Stephen A. O'Connell, Macmillan (London: 1997).

Ghosh, Atish R., Anne-Marie Gulde, Jonathan D. Ostry, and Holger C. Wolf, "Does the Nominal Exchange Rate Regime Matter?," Working Paper No. 5874, National Bureau of Economic Research (January 1997).

Ghosh, Atish R., Anne-Marie Gulde, and Holger C. Wolf, "Currency Boards—The Better Peg?," Working Paper No. G-97-04, Princeton University (November 1997).

Ghosh, Atish R., and Jonathan Ostry, "Export Instability and the External Balance in Developing Countries," *IMF Staff Papers*, 41 (June 1994), 214-35.

Giovannini, Alberto, and Martha De Melo, "Government Revenue from Financial Repression," *American Economic Review*, 83 (September 1993), 953-63.

Giovannini, Alberto, and Bart Turtelboom, "Currency Substitution," in *The Handbook of International Macroeconomics*, ed. by Frederick van der Ploeg, Basil Blackwell (Oxford: 1994).

Glick, Reuven, Michael Hutchison, and Ramon Moreno, "Is Pegging the Exchange Rate a Cure for Inflation? East Asian Experiences," in *International Trade and Finance: New Frontiers of Research*, ed. by Benjamin Cohen, Cambridge University Press (Cambridge: 1997).

Goldstein, Morris, and Philip Turner, *Banking Crises in Emerging Economies: Origins and Policy Options*, Economic Paper No. 46, Bank for International Settlements (October 1996).

Gould, David M., "Does the Choice of Nominal Anchor Matter?," Working Paper No. 96-11, Federal Reserve Bank of Dallas (October 1996).

Green, John H., "Inflation Targeting: Theory and Policy Implications," *IMF Staff Papers*, 43 (December 1996), 779-95.

Greenaway, David, and Chris Milner, *Trade and Industrial Policy in Developing Countries*, University of Michigan Press (Ann Arbor, Michigan: 1994).

Greenaway, David, Wyn Morgan, and Peter Wright, "Trade Reform, Adjustment and Growth: What Does the Evidence Tell Us?," *Economic Journal*, 108 (September 1998), 1547-61.

Greene, William H., *Econometric Analysis*, 3rd. edition, Prentice Hall (Upper Saddle River, New Jersey: 1997).

Greenwood, Jeremy, and Boyan Jovanovich, "Financial Development, Growth, and the Distribution of Income," *Journal of Political Economy*, 98 (October 1990), 1076-107.

Greenwood, Jeremy, and Bruce D. Smith, "Financial Markets in Development, and the Development of Financial Markets," *Journal of Economic Dynamics and Control*, 21 (January 1997), 145-82.

Grobar, Lisa M., "Effect of Real Exchange Rate Uncertainty on LDC Manufactured Exports," *Journal of Development Economics*, 41 (August 1993), 367-76.

Grosse, Robert, "Jamaica's Foreign Exchange Black Market," *Journal of Development Studies*, 31 (October 1994), 17-43.

Grisanti, Alejandro, Ernesto H. Stein, and Ernesto Talvi, "Institutional Arrangements and Fiscal Performance: The Latin American Experience," Working Paper No. 367, Inter-American Development Bank (January 1998).

Grossman, Gene, ans Elhanan Helpman, *Innovation and Growth in the Global Economy*, MIT Press (Cambridge, Mass.: 1991).

Guidotti, Pablo E., and Carlos A. Rodríguez, "Dollarization in Latin America." *IMF Staff Papers* 39 (September 1992) 518-44.

Gundlach, Erich, "The Role of Human Capital in Economic Growth: New Results and Alternative Interpretations," *Weltwirtschafliches Archives*, 131 (June 1995), 383-402.

Gylfason, Thorvaldur, "Privatization, Efficiency and Economic Growth," Discussion Paper No. 1844, Center for Economic Policy Research (March 1998a).

Gylfason, Thorvaldur, and Michael Schmid, "Does Devaluation Cause Stagflation?" *Canadian Journal of Economics*, 16 (November 1983), 641-54.

Hadjimichael, Michael, and Dhaneshwar Ghura, "Public Policies and Private Savings and Investment in Sub-Saharan Africa," Working Paper No. 95/19, International Monetary Fund (February 1995).

Hall, Robert E., and Charles I. Jones, "Why Do some Countries Produce so much more Output per Worker than Others?" *Quarterly Journal of Economics*, 114 (February 1999), 83-116.

Handy, Howard, and others, *Egypt: Beyond Stabilization, Toward a Dynamic Market Economy*, Occasional Paper No. 163, International Monetary Fund (July 1998).

Hanke, Steven H., and Kurt Schuler, *Currency Boards for Developing Countries*, International Center for Economic Growth, ICS Press (San Francisco, Cal.: 1994).

Harberger, Arnold C., "Currency Depreciation, Income and the Balance of Trade," *Journal of Political Economy*, 53 (February 1950), 47-60.

Harris, John, and Michael P. Todaro, "Migration, Unemployment and Development: A Two-Sector Analysis," *American Economic Review*, 60 (March 1970), 126-43.

Harrison, Ann, "Openness and Growth: A Time-Series, Cross-Country Analysis for Developing Countries," *Journal of Development Economics*, 48 (March 1996), 419-47.

Harrison, Ann, and Gordon Hanson, "Who Gains from Trade Reform? Some Remaining Puzzles," *Journal of Development Economics*, 59 (June 1999), 125-54.

Heller, Peter, Richard Haas, and Ahsan Mansur, "A Review of the Fiscal Impulse Measure," Occasional Paper No. 44, International Monetary Fund (Washington, DC: 1986).

Helpman, Elhanan, "Voluntary Debt Reduction: Incentives and Welfare," *IMF Staff Papers*, 36 (September 1989), 580-611.

Helpman, Elhanan, and Paul R. Krugman, *Market Structure and Foreign Trade*, MIT Press (Cambridge, Mass.: 1985).

Helpman, Elhanan, Leonardo Leiderman, and Gil Bufman, "New Breed of Exchange Rate Bands: Chile, Israel and Mexico," *Economic Policy* 9 (October 1994), 260-306.

Hernández, Leonardo, and Klaus Schmidt-Hebbel, "Capital Controls in Chile: Effective? Efficient? Endurable?," unpublished, Central Bank of Chile (April 1999).

Hoffmaister, Alexander W., and Jorge E. Roldós, "Are Business Cycles Different in Asia and Latin America?," Working Paper No. 97/9, International Monetary Fund (January 1997).

Hoffmaister, Alexander W., Jorge E. Roldós, and Peter Wickham, "Macroeconomic Fluctuations in Sub-Saharan Africa," *IMF Staff Papers*, 45 (March 1998), 132-60.

Holzmann, Robert, "Pension Reform, Financial Market Development, and Economic Growth: Preliminary Evidence from Chile," *IMF Staff Papers*, 44 (June 1997), 149-78.

Hopenhayn, Hugo A., and María E. Muniagurria, "Policy Variability and Economic Growth," *Review of Economic Studies*, 63 (October 1996), 611-25.

Huang, Iiff J., Jen-Chi Cheng, Ching-Sheng Chou, and Charles Lin Shung-Ying, "The Substitutability of Monetary Assets in Taiwan," *Southern Economic Journal*, 58 (April 1992), 975-87.

International Finance Corporation, *Privatization: Principles and Practice*, IFC Lessons of Experience Series No. 1 (Washington D.C.: 1995).

International Monetary Fund, *Theoretical Aspects of the Design of Fund-Supported Programs*, Occasional Paper No. 55, International Monetary Fund (Washington DC: September 1987).

——, *World Economic Outlook*, International Monetary Fund (Washington DC: October 1997*a*).

——, *International Capital Markets: Developments, Prospects, and Key Policy Issues*, International Monetary Fund (Washington DC: November 1997*b*).

Islam, Nazrul, "Growth Empirics: A Panel Data Approach," *Quarterly Journal of Economics*, 110 (November 1995), 1127-70.

Johnston, R. Barry, and Chris Ryan, "The Impact of Controls on Capital Movements on the Private Capital Accounts of Countries' Balance of Payments: Empirical Estimates and Policy Implications," Working Paper No. 94/78 (July 1994).

Jones, Charles I. "Time Series Tests of Endogenous Growth Models," *Quarterly Journal of Economics*, 110 (May 1995), 495-525.

Jones, Larry E., Rodolfo E. Manuelli, "A Convex Model of Equilibrium Growth," *Journal of Political Economy*, 98 (October 1990), 1008-38.

——, "The Sources of Growth," *Journal of Economic Dynamics and Control*, 21 (January 1997), 75-114.

Kahkonen, Juha, "Liberalization Policies and Welfare in a Financially Repressed Economy," *IMF Staff Papers*, 34 (September 1987), 531-47.

Kamas, Linda, "External Disturbances and the Independence of Monetary Policy under the Crawling Peg in Colombia," *Journal of International Economics*, 19 (November 1985), 313-27.

Kamin, Steven B., "Devaluation, Exchange Controls, and Black Markets for Foreign Exchange in Developing Countries," *Journal of Development Economics*, 40 (February 1993), 151-69.

Kaminsky, Graciela, Saul Lizondo, and Carmen M. Reinhart, "Leading Indicators of Currency Crises," *IMF Staff Papers*, 45 (March 1998), 1–48.

Kaminsky, Graciela, and Carmen M. Reinhart, "The Twin Crises: The Causes of Banking and Balance-of-Payments Problems," *American Economic Review*, 89 (June 1999), 473-500.

Karras, Georgios, "Government Spending and Private Consumption: Some International Evidence," *Journal of Money, Credit, and Banking*, 26 (February 1994*a*), 9-22.

——, "Macroeconomic Effects of Budget Deficits: Further International Evidence," *Journal of International Money and Finance*, 13 (April 1994*b*), 190-210.

Kaufman, Martin D., "An Incursion into the Confidence Crisis-Credit Rationing, Real Activity Channel: Evidence from the Argentine 'Tequila' Crisis," unpublished, Central Bank of Argentina (February 1996).

Kawai, Masahiro, and Louis J. Maccini, "Fiscal Policy, Anticipated Switches in Methods of Finance, and the Effects on the Economy," *International Economic Review* 31 (November 1990), 913-34.

Khan, Mohsin S., and Manmohan S. Kumar, "Public and Private Investment and the Growth Process in Developing Countries," *Oxford Bulletin of Economics and Statistics* 59, (February 1997), 69-88.

Khan, Mohsin S., Peter J. Montiel, and Nadeem U. Haque, "Adjustment with Growth: Relating the Analytical Approaches of the IMF and the World Bank," *Journal of Development Economics*, 32 (January 1990), 155-79.

Kiguel, Miguel A., and Leonardo Leiderman, "On the Consequences of Sterilized Intervention in Latin America: The Case of Colombia and Chile," unpublished, Tel-Aviv University (June 1993).

Kiguel, Miguel A., and Nissan Liviatan, "When Do Heterodox Stabilization Programs Work? Lessons from Experience," *World Bank Research Observer*, 7 (January 1992a), 35-57.

——, "The Business Cycle Associated with Exchange Rate Based Stabilization," *World Bank Economic Review*, 6 (May 1992b), 279-305.

Killick, Tony, *IMF Programmes in Developing Countries: Design and Impact*, Paul Routledge (Andover: 1995).

King, Robert G., and Ross Levine, "Finance, Entrepreneurship, and Growth: Theory and Evidence," *Journal of Monetary Economics*, 32 (December 1993), 513-42.

Kletzer, Kenneth, "External Borrowing by LDCs: A Survey of Some Theoretical Issues," in *The State of Development Economics*, ed. by Gustav Ranis and Paul T. Schultz, Basil Blackwell (New York: 1988).

Klitgaard, Robert, *Controlling Corruption*, University of California Press (Berkeley, Cal.: 1988).

Knight, Malcolm, Norman Loayza, and Delano Villanueva, "Testing the Neoclassical Theory of Economic Growth," *IMF Staff Papers*, 40 (September 1993), 512-41.

Koskela, Erkki, "A Note on Progression, Penalty Schemes and Tax Evasion," *Journal of Public Economics*, 22 (October 1983), 127-33.

Kreinin, Mordechai, and Lawrence H. Officer, *The Monetary Approach to the Balance of Payments: A Survey*, Essay in International Finance No. 43, Princeton University (Princeton, New Jersey: 1978).

Krueger, Ann O., The Political Economy of the Rent-Seeking Society," *American Economic Review*, 64 (June 1974), 291-303.

Krugman, Paul, "Pricing to Market when the Exchange Rate Changes," in *Real-Financial Linkages among Open Economies*, ed. by Sven W. Arndt and John D. Richardson, MIT Press (Cambridge, Mass.: 1987).

——, "Financing versus Forgiving a Debt Overhang: Some Analytical Notes," *Journal of Development Economics*, 29 (December 1988), 253-68.

——, "Differences in Income Elasticities and trends in Real Exchange Rates," *European Economic Review*, 33 (May 1989a), 1031-54.

——, "Market-Based Debt Reduction Schemes," in *Analytical Issues in Debt*, ed. by Jacob Frenkel, Michael Dooley, and Peter Wickham, International Monetary Fund (Washington DC: 1989b).

——, "Target Zones and Exchange Rate Dynamics," *Quarterly Journal of Economics*, 106 (November 1991), 669-82.

Labán, Raúl, and Felipe B. Larraín, "Can a Liberalization of Capital Outflows Increase Net Capital Inflows?," *Journal of International Money and Finance*, 21 (June 1997), 415-31.

Larraín B., Felipe, M. Raúl Labán, and Rómulo A. Chumacero, "What Determines Capital Inflows? An Empirical Analysis for Chile," Harvard Institute for International Development, Discussion Paper No. 590 (June 1997).

Laursen, Svend, and Lloyd A. Metzler, "Flexible Exchange Rates and the Theory of Employment," *Review of Economics and Statistics*, 32 (November 1950), 281-99.

Lee, Eric Y., and Michael Szenberg, "Intertemporal Interpretation of the U.S. Current Account Deficit," *International Journal of Finance*, 6 (October 1994), 990-1002.

Lee, Jong-Wha, "International Trade, Distortions and Long-Run Economic Growth," *IMF Staff Papers*, 40 (June 1993), 299-328.

Lee, Kiseok, and Ronald A. Ratti, "On Seigniorage, Operating Rules, and Dual Equilibria," *Quarterly Journal of Economics*, 108 (May 1993), 543-50.

Leiderman, Leonardo, and Gil Bufman, "Searching for Nominal Anchors in Shock-Prone Economies in the 1990s: Inflation Targets and Exchange Rate Bands," in *Securing Stability and Growth in Latin America*, ed. by Ricardo Hausmann and Helmut Reisen, OECD (Paris: 1996).

Leland, H- E., "Saving and Uncertainty: The Precautionary Demand for Saving," *Quarternly Journal of Economics*, 82 (August 1968), 465-73.

Levine, Ross, "Financial Development and Economic Growth: Views and Agenda," *Journal of Economic Literature*, 35 (June 1997), 688-726.

Levine, Ross, and David Renelt, "A Sensitivity Analysis of Cross-Country Growth Regressions," *American Economic Review*, 82 (September 1992), 942-63.

Lienert, Ian, and Jitendra Modi, "A Decade of Civil Service Reform in sub-Saharan Africa," Working Paper No. 97/179, International Monetary Fund (December 1997).

Lindgren, Carl-Johan, Gillian Garcia, and Matthew I. Saal, *Bank Soundness and Macroeconomic Policy*, by International Monetary Fund (Washington D.C.: 1996).

Lipton, Michael, and Martin Ravallion, "Poverty and Policy," in *Handbook of Development Economics*, Vol. III, ed. by Jere Behrman and T. N. Srinivasan, North Holland (Amsterdam: 1995).

Lizondo, J. Saul, "Alternative Dual Exchange Market Regimes," *IMF Staff Papers* 38 (September 1991), 560-81.

――――, "Real Exchange Rate Targeting under Imperfect Asset Substitutability," *IMF Staff Papers*, 40 (December 1993), 829-51.

Loayza, Norman V., "The Economics of the Informal Sector: A Simple Model and Some Empirical Evidence from Latin America," Carnegie-Rochester Conference Series on Public Policy, Vol. 45 (June 1996).

Loayza, Norman V., Klaus Schmidt-Hebbel, and Luis Servén, "What Drives Saving across the World?," in *The Economics of Saving and Growth*, ed. by Klaus Schmidt-Hebbel and Luis Servén, Cambridge University Press (Cambridge: 1999).

Londoño, Juan Luis, and Miguel Székely, "Persistent Poverty and Excess Inequality: Latin America, 1970-1995," Working Paper No. 352, Inter-American

Development Bank (October 1997).

López-Mejía, Alejandro, and Juan R. Ortega, "Private Saving in Colombia," Working Paper No. 98/171 (December 1998).

Lora, Eduardo, and Felipe Barrera, "A Decade of Structural Reform in Latin America: Measurement and Growth Effects," Inter-American Development Bank, unpublished (July 1997).

Lora, Eduardo, and Mauricio Olivera, "Macro Policy and Employment Problems in Latin America," Working Paper No. 372, Inter-American Development Bank (March 1998).

Lucas, Robert E., "On the Mechanics of Economic Development," *Journal of Monetary Economics*, 22 (July 1988), 3-42.

——, "Why Doesn't Capital Flow from Rich to Poor Countries?," *American Economic Review*, 80 (May 1990), 92-96.

Mackenzie, George A., and Peter Stella, *Quasi Fiscal Operations of Public Financial Institutions*, Occasional Paper No. 142, International Monetary Fund (October 1996).

Mackenzie, George A., David W. Orsmond, and Philip R. Gerson, *The Composition of Fiscal Adjustment and Growth*, Occasional Paper No. 149, International Monetary Fund (March 1997).

Maddison, Angus, *Monitoring the World Economy, 1820-1992*, Development Centre Studies, Organisation for Economic Co-operation and Development (Paris: 1995).

Maloney, William F., "Testing Capital Account Liberalization without Forward Rates: Another Look at Chile, 1979-82," *Journal of Development Economics*, 52 (February 1997), 139-68.

Mankiw, N. Gregory, David Romer, and D. Weil, "A Contribution to the Empirics of Economic Growth," *Quarterly Journal of Economics*, 107 (May 1992), 407-37.

Manzocchi, Stefano, "Stages in the Balance of Payments: A Survey of the Neoclassical Theory," *Economic Notes* (September 1990), 397-416.

Márquez, Gustavo, and Carmen Pagés-Serra, "Trade and Employment: Evidence from Latin America and the Caribbean," Working Paper No. 366, Inter-American Development Bank (January 1998).

Marsh, Ian W., and Stephen P. Tokarick, "An Assessment of three Measures of Competitiveness," *Weltwirtschaftliches Archives*, 132 (December 1996), 700-22.

Martinelli Cesar, and Mariano Tommasi, "Sequencing of Economic Reforms in the Presence of Political Constraints," in *The political economy of reform*, ed. by Federico Sturzenegger and Mariano Tommasi, MIT Press (Cambridge, Mass.: 1998).

Masson, Paul R., Tamim Bayoumi, and Hossein Samiei, "Saving Behavior in Industrial and Developing Countries," in *Staff Studies for the World Economic Outlook*, International Monetary Fund (Washington DC: September 1995).

Mathieson, Donald J., and Liliana Rojas-Suárez, *Liberalization of the Capital Account: Experiences and Issues*, Occasional Paper No. 103, International Monetary Fund (March 1993).

Matusz, Steven J., and David Tarr, "Adjusting to Trade Policy Reform," unpublished, the World Bank (May 1999).

Mauro, Paolo, "The Effects of Corruption on Growth, Investment, and Government Expenditure: A Cross-Country Analysis," in *Corruption in the World Economy*, ed. by Fred Bergsten and Kimberly Elliott, Institute for International Economics (Washington DC: 1997).

McCarthy, F. Desmond, J. Peter Neary, and Giovanni Zanalda, "Measuring the Effect of External Shocks and the Policy Response to them: Empirical Methodology Applied to the Philippines," Policy Research Working Paper No. 1271, the World Bank (March 1994).

McDonald, Calvin A., and Yin-Fun Lum, "Operational Issues Related to the Functioning of Interbank Foreign Exchange Markets in Selected African Countries," Working Paper No. 94/48, International Monetary Fund (April 1994).

McKinnon, Ronald I., *Money and Capital in Economic Development*, the Brookings Institution (Washington DC: 1973).

McKinnon, Ronald I., and Huw Pill, "Credible Liberalizations and International Capital Flows: The Overborrowing Syndrome," in *Deregulation and Integration in East Asia*, ed. by Takatoshi Ito and Anne O. Krueger, Chicago University Press (Chicago, Il.: 1996).

McNelis, Paul D., and Liliana Rojas-Suárez, "Currency Substitution as Behavior toward Risk: The Case of Bolivia and Peru," unpublished, Department of Economics, Georgetown University (November 1996).

Mehran, Hassanali, Piero Ugolini, Jean-Philippe Briffaux, George Iden, Tonny Lybek, Stephen Swaray, and Peter Hayward, *Financial Sector Developments in sub-Saharan African Countries*, Occasional Paper No. 169, International Monetary Fund (December 1998).

Menon, Jayant, "Exchange Rate Pass-Through," *Journal of Economic Surveys*, 9 (June 1995), 197-231.

Melvin, Michael, and Jerry Ladman, "Coca Dollars and the Dollarization of South America," *Journal of Money, Credit, and Banking*, 23 (November 1991), 752-63.

Mikić, Mia, *International Trade*, St. Martin's Press (New York: 1998).

Milesi-Ferretti, Gian Maria, and Nouriel Roubini, "Growth Effects of Income and Consumption Taxes," *Journal of Money, Credit, and Banking*, 30 (November 1998), 721-44.

Milesi-Ferretti, Gian Maria, and Assaf Razin, *Current-Account Sustainability*, Princeton Study In International Finance No. 81 (Princeton, New Jersey: 1996).

Mishkin, Frederic, S., *The Economics of Money, Banking, and Financial Markets*, Addison-Wesley (Reading, Mass.: 1998).

Modigliani, Franco, and Richard Brumberg, "Utility Analysis and the Consumption Function: An Interpretation of Cross-Section Data," in *Post-Keynesian Economics*, ed. by Kenneth Kurihara, Rutgers University Press (New Brunswick, New Jersey: 1954).

Mondino, Guillermo, Federico Sturzenegger, and Mariano Tommasi, "Recurrent High Inflation and Stabilization: a Dynamic Game," *International Economic Review*, 37 (November 1996), 981-96.

Montiel, Peter J., Pierre-Richard Agénor, and Nadeem Haque, *Informal Financial Markets in Developing Countries*, Basil Blackwell (Oxford: 1993).

Montiel, Peter J., and Jonathan Ostry, "Macroeconomic Implications of Real Exchange Rate Targeting in Developing Countries," *IMF Staff Papers*, 38 (December 1991), 872-900.

——, "Real Exchange Rate Targeting under Capital Controls," *IMF Staff Papers*, 39 (March 1992), 58-78.

Montiel, Peter J., and Carmen M. Reinhart, "Do Capital Controls and Macroeconomic Policies Influence the Volume and Composition of Capital Flows? Evidence from the 1990s," unpublished, Williamns College (- 1999).

Morris, Stephen, "Inflation Dynamics and the Parallel Market for Foreign Exchange," *Journal of Development Economics*, 46 (April 1995), 295-316.

Moser, Gary G., "The Main Determinants of Inflation in Nigeria," *IMF Staff Papers*, 42 (June 1995), 270-89.

Muellbauer, John, "The Assessment: Consumer Expenditure," *Oxford Review of Economic Policy*, 10 (Summer 1994), 1-41.

Mulligan, Casey B., and Xavier Sala-i-Martin, "Transitional Dynamics in Two-Sector Models of Endogenous Growth," *Quarterly Journal of Economics*, 108 (August 1993), 739-73.

Murphy, Kevin M., Andrei Shleifer, and Robert W. Vishny, "Industrialization and the Big Push," *Journal of Political Economy*, 97 (October 1989), 1003-26.

——, "The Allocation of Talents: Implications for Growth," *Quarterly Journal of Economics*, 106 (May 1991), 503-30.

Muscatelli, Vito A., and Andrew A. Stevenson, "Modeling Aggregate Manufactured Exports for some Asian Newly Industrializing Economies," *Review of Economics and Statistics*, 77 (February 1995), 147-55.

Nashashibi, Karim, and Stefania Bazzoni, "Exchange Rate Strategies and Fiscal Performance in Sub-Saharan Africa," *IMF Staff Papers*, 41 (March 1994), 76-122.

Nelson, Joan M., "Organized Labor, Politics, and Labor Market Flexibility in Developing Countries," in *Labor Markets in an Era of Adjustment*, Vol. I, ed. by Susan Horton, Ravi Kanbur, and Dipak Mazumdar, the World Bank (Washington DC: 1994).

Nelson, Michael A., and Ram D. Singh, "The Deficit-Growth Connection: Some Recent Evidence from Developing Countries," *Economic Development and Cultural Change* 43 (October 1994), 167-91.

Nelson, Richard R. "A Theory of the Low-Level Trap in Underdeveloped Economies," *American Economic Review*, 46 (December 1956), 894–908.

Ng, Francis, and Alexander Yeats, "Open Economies Work Better! Did Africa's Protectionist Policies Cause its Marginalization in World Trade?," *World Development*, 25 (June 1997), 889-904.

North, Douglas C., *Institutions, Institutional Change and Economic Performance*, Cambridge University Press (New York: 1990).

Obstfeld, Maurice, "Aggregate Spending and the Terms of Trade: Is there a Laursen-Metzler Effect?," *Quarterly Journal of Economics*, 47 (May 1982), 251-70.

——, "Capital Flows, the Current Account, and the Real Exchange Rate: Consequences of Liberalization and Stabilization," in *Economic Adjustment and Exchange Rates in Developing Countries*, ed. by Liaqat Ahmed and Sebastián Edwards, University of Chicago Press (Chicago, Il.: 1986).

——, "The Logic of Currency Crises," in *Monetary and Fiscal Policy in an Integrated Europe*, ed. by Barry Eichengreen, Jeffrey Frieden, and Jürgen von Hagen, Springer Verlag (London: 1995).

——, "Risk-Taking, Global Diversification and Growth," *American Economic Review*, 84 (November 1994), 1310-29.

——, "International Capital Mobility in the 1990s," in *Understanding Interdependence: The Macroeconomics of the Open Economy*, ed. by Peter B. Kenen, Princeton University Press (Princeton, New Jersey: 1995).

——, "Models of Currency Crises with Self-Fulfilling Features," *European Economic Review*, 40 (April 1996), 1037-47.

——, "The Global Capital Market: Benefactor or Menace?," Working Paper No. 6559, National Bureau of Economic Research (May 1998).

Obstfeld, Maurice, and Kenneth Rogoff, "The Mirage of Fixed Exchange Rates," *Journal of Economic Perspectives*, 9 (Fall 1995), 73–96.

Ogaki, Masao, Jonathan Ostry, and Carmen M. Reinhart, "Saving Behavior in Low- and Middle-Income Developing Countries: A Comparison," *IMF Staff Papers*, 43 (March 1996), 38-71.

Olson, Mancur, "Big Bills Left on the Sidewalk: Why some Nations are Rich, and Others Poor," *Journal of Economic Perspectives*, 10 (Spring 1996), 3-24.

Önis, Ziya, and Süleyman Ozmucur, "Exchange Rates, Inflation and Money Supply in turkey: Testing the Vicious Circle Hypothesis," *Journal of Development Economics*, 32 (January 1990), 133-54.

Orphanides, Athanasios, "The Timing of Stabilizations," *Journal of Economic Dynamics and Control* 20 (January 1996), 257–79.

Oshikoya, Temitope W., "Macroeconomic Determinants of Domestic Private Investment in Africa," *Economic Development and Cultural Change*, 42 (April 1994), 573-96.

Ostry, Jonathan D., and Carmen M. Reinhart, "Private Saving and Terms-of-Trade Shocks," *IMF Staff Papers*, 39 (September 1992), 495-517.

Ozkan, F. Gulcin, and Alan Sutherland, "Policy Measures to Avoid a Currency Crisis," *Economic Journal*, 105 (March 1995), 510-19.

Ozler, Sule, and Guido E. Tabellini, "External Debt and Political Instability," Working Paper No. 3772, National Bureau of Economic Research (July 1991).

Pack, Howard, and John M. Page, "Accumulation, Exports, and Growth in the High-Performing Asian Economies," Carnegie-Rochester Conference Series on Public Policy, 40 (June 1994), 199-250.

Palokangas, Tapio, "Inflation and Growth in an Open Economy," *Economica*, 64 (August 1997), 509-18.

Panagides, Alexis, and Harry A. Patrinos, "Union-Nonunion Wage Differentiuals in the Developing World: A case Study of Mexico, PRE Working Paper No. 1269, the World Bank (March 1994).

Papageorgiou, Demetris, Armeane M. Choksi, and Michael Michaely, *Liberalizing Foreign Trade in Developing Countries*, the World Bank (Washington, DC: 1990).

Park, Yung Chul, "Financial Repression and Liberalization," in *Liberalization in the Process of Economic Development*, ed. by Lawrence B. Krause and Kim Kihwan, University of California Press (Berkeley, Cal.: 1991).

Parker, Karen, and Steffen Kastner, "A Framework for Assessing Fiscal Sustainability and External Viability, with an Application to India," IMF Working Paper, No. 93/78 (October 1993).

Pattillo, Catherine, "Investment, Uncertainty, and Irreversibility in Ghana," *IMF Staff Papers*, 45 (September 1998), 522-53.

Persson, Torsten, and Guido Tabellini, "Is Inequality Harmful for Growth?," *American Economic Review*, 84 (June 1994), 600-21.

Persson, Torsten, and Sweder van Wijnbergen, "Signalling, Wage Controls, and Monetary Disinflation Policy," *Economic Journal*, 103 (January 1993), 79-97.

Pesaran, M. Hashem, and Ron Smith, "Estimating Long-Run Relationships from Dynamic Heterogeneous Panels," *Journal of Econometrics*, 68 (July 1995), 79-113.

Pill, Huw, and Mahmood Pradhan, "Financial Indicators and Financial Change in Africa and Asia," Working Paper No. 95/123, International Monetary Fund (November 1995).

Pinto, Brian, "Unification of Official and Black Market Exchange Rates in Sub-Saharan Africa," in *Exchange Rate Policies in Developing and Post-Socialist Countries*, ed. by Emil-Maria Claassen, ICS Press (San Francisco, Cal.: 1991).

Polackova, Hana, "Government Contingent Liabilities: A Hidden Risk to Fiscal Stability," Policy Research Working Paper No. 1989, the World Bank (October 1998).

Polak, Jacques J., "Monetary Analysis of Income Formation and Payments Problems," *IMF Staff Papers*, 6 (November 1957), 1-50.

Premchand, A., *Public Expenditure Management*, International Monetary Fund (Washington D.C.: 1993).

Price, Simon, "Demand for Indonesian Narrow Money: Long-Run Equilibrium, Error Correction and Forward-Looking Behaviour," *Journal of International Trade and Economic Development*, 3 (July 1994), 147-63.

Pritchett, Lant, "Divergence, Big Time," *Journal of Economic Perspectives*, 11 (Summer 1997), 3-18.

Psacharopoulos, George, and others, "Poverty and Income Inequality in Latin America During the 1980s," *Review of Income and Wealth*, 41 (September

1995), 245-64.

Pyle, D. J., "The Economics of Taxpayer Compliance," *Journal of Economic Surveys*, 5 (June 1991), 163-98.

Quah, Danny T., "Empirics for Economic Growth and Convergence," *European Economic Review*, 40 (June 1996*a*), 1353-75.

——, "Twin Peaks: Growth and Convergence in Models of Distribution Dynamics," *Economic Journal*, 106 (July 1996*b*), 1045-55.

——, "Empirics for Growth and Distribution: Stratification, Polarization and Convergence Clubs," Discussion Paper No. 324, London School of Economics (January 1997).

Radelet, Steven, and Jeffrey D. Sachs, "The East Asian Crisis: Diagnosis, Remedies, Prospects," *Brookings Papers on Economic Activity*, No. 1 (June 1998), 1-90.

Rama, Martín, "Empirical Investment Equations in Developing Countries," in *Striving for Growth after Adjustment*, ed. by Luis Servén and Andrés Solimano, the World Bank (Washington DC: 1993).

——, "The Labor Market and Trade Reform in Manufacturing," in *The Effects of Protectionism on a Small Country: The Case of Uruguay*, ed. by Michael Connolly and Jaime de Melo, World Bank (Washington DC: 1994).

Rama, Martín, "Do Labor Market Policies and Institutions Matter? The Adjustment Experience in Latin America and the Caribbean," unpublished, the World Bank (May 1995).

——, "Organized Labor and the Political Economy of Product Market Distortions," *World Bank Economic Review*, 11 (May 1997*a*), 327-55.

——, "Efficient Public Sector Downsizing," Policy Research Working Paper No. 1840 (November 1997*b*).

Ravallion, Martin, *Poverty Comparisons*, Harwood Academic Press (Chur: 1994).

Ravallion, Martin, and Shaohua Chen, "What Can New Survey Data Tell Us about Recent Changes in Distribution and Poverty?," *World Bank Economic Review*, 11 (May 1997), 357-82.

Razin, Assaf, and Efraim Sadka, "Efficient Investment Incentives in the Presence of Capital Flight," *Journal of International Economics*, 31 (August 1991), 171-81.

Rebelo, Sergio, "Long-Run Policy Analysis and Long-Run Growth," *Journal of Political Economy*, 99 (June 1991), 500-21.

Rebelo, Sergio, and Carlos A. Végh, "Real Effects of Exchange-Rate Based Stabilization: An Analysis of Competing Theories," *NBER Macroeconomics Annual 1996*, ed. by Ben S. Bernanke and Julio J. Rotemberg, MIT Press (Cambridge, Mass.: 1997).

——, "Devaluation, Relative Prices, and International Trade: Evidence from Developing Countries," *IMF Staff Papers*, 42 (June 1995), 290-312.

Reinhart, Carmen M., and Carlos A. Végh, "Nominal Interest Rates, Consumption Booms, and Lack of Credibility," *Journal of Development Economics*, 46 (April 1995), 357-78.

Revenga, Ana, "Employment and Wage Effects of Trade Liberalization: The Case of Mexican Manufacturing," *Journal of Labor Economics*, 15 (July 1997), s20-s43.

Risager, Ole, "Devaluation, Profitability and Investment," *Scandinavian Journal of Economics*, 90 (June 1988), 125-40.

Rivera-Batiz, Luis, and Paul Romer, "Economic Integration and Endogenous Growth," *Quarterly Journal of Economics*, 106 (May 1991), 531-56.

Robbins, Donald J., "Trade, Trade Liberalization and Inequality in Latin America and East Asia—Synthesis of Seven Country Studies," unpublished, Harvard Institute for International Development (March 1996).

Robinson, Sherman, "Macroeconomics, Financial Variables, and Computable General Equilibrium Models," *World Development*, 19 (November 1991), 1509-25.

Rochet, Jean-Charles, "Capital Requirements and the Behavior of Commercial Banks," *European Economic Review*, 36 (June 1992), 1137-70.

Rodrik, Dani, "Imperfect Competition, Scale Economies, and Trade Policy in Developing Countries," in *Trade Policy Issues and Empirical Analysis*, ed. by Robert E. Baldwin, University of Chicago Press, (Chicago, Il.: 1988).

———, "Credibility of Trade Reforms—A Policymaker's Guide," *World Economy*, 12 (March 1989), 1-16.

———, "Limits of Trade Policy Reform in Developing Countries," *Journal of Economic Perspectives*, 6 (Winter 1992), 87-105.

———, "Trade and Industrial Policy Reform," in *Handbook of Development Economics*, III, ed. by Jere Behrman and T.N. Srinivasan, North Holland (Amsterdam: 1995b).

———, "Political Economy of Trade Policy," in *Handbook of International Economics*, Vol. III, ed. by Gene M. Grossman and Kenneth Rogoff, North Holland (Amsterdam: 1995c).

———, "Understanding Economic Policy Reform," *Journal of Economic Literature*, 34 (March 1996a), 9-41.

———, "Trade Policy and Economic Performance in sub-Saharan Africa," Working Paper No. 6562, National Bureau of Economic Research (May 1998a).

———, "Why Do More Open Economies Have Bigger Governments?," *Journal of Political Economy*, 106 (October 1998b), 997-1032.

Rojas-Suárez, Liliana, and Steven Weisbrod, *Financial Fragilities in Latin America: The 1980s and 1990s*, Occasional Paper No 132, International Monetary Fund (October 1995).

Roldós, Jorge, "Supply-Side Effects of Disinflation Programs," *IMF Staff Papers*, 42 (March 1995), 158-83.

———, "On Gradual Disinflation, the Real Exchange Rate, and the Current Account," *Journal of International Money and Finance*, 16 (February 1997a), 37-54.

———, "Potential Output Growth in Emerging Market Countries: The Case of Chile," Working Paper No. 97/194 (September 1997b).

Romer, David, *Advanced Macroeconomics*, McGraw Hill (New York: 1995).

Romer, Paul, "Increasing Returns and Long-Run Growth," *Journal of Political Economy*, 94 (October 1986), 1002-37.

——, "Capital Accumulation in the Theory of Long-Run Growth," in *Modern Business Cycle Theory*, ed. by Robert Barro, Harvard University Press (Cambridge, Mass.: 1989).

——, "Endogenous Technological Change," *Journal of Political Economy*, 98 (October 1990), s71-s102.

——, "Two Strategies for Economic Development : Using Ideas vs. Producing Ideas, in *World Bank Conference on Development Economics*, the World Bank (Washington DC: 1992).

——, "New Goods, Old Theory, and the Welfare Costs of Trade Restrictions," *Journal of Development Economics*, 43 (February 1994), 5-38.

Rosenstein-Rodan, Paul N., "Notes on the Theory of the 'Big Push,'" in *Economic Development for Latin America*, ed. by Howard S. Ellis and Henry C. Wallich, St. Martin's Press (New York: 1961).

Rossi, Nicola, "Government Spending, the Real Interest Rate, and the Behavior of Liquidity-Constrained Consumers in Developing Countries," *IMF Staff Papers*, 35 (March 1988), 104-40.

Rostow, William W., *The Stages of Economic Growth*, Cambridge University Press (Cambridge: 1960).

Roubini, Nouriel, and Xavier Sala-i-Martin, "A Growth Model of Inflation, Tax Evasion and Financial Repression," *Journal of Monetary Economics*, 35 (April 1995), 275-301.

Sachs, Jeffrey, "The Debt Overhang of Developing Countries," in *Debt, Stabilization and Development*, ed. by Ronald Findlay, Guillermo Calvo, Pentti J. Kouri, and Jorge Braga de Macedo, Basil Blackwell (Oxford: 1989).

Sachs, Jeffrey, Aarón Tornell, and Andrés Velasco, "What Have We Learned from the Mexican Peso Crisis? ," *Economic Policy*, No. 22 (April 1996*a*), 15-63.

——, "Financial Crises in Emerging Markets: The Lessons From 1995," *Brookings Papers in Economic Activity*, No. 1 (June 1996*b*), 147-98.

Sachs, Jeffrey, and Andrew M. Warner, "Fundamental sources of long-run growth," *American Economic Review*, 87 (May 1997*a*), 184-88.

——, "Sources of Slow Growth in African Economies," *Journal of African Economies* (October 1997*b*), 335-76.

Sah, Raaj K., and Joseph E. Stiglitz, *Peasants versus City-Dwellers*, Clarendon Press (Oxford: 1992).

Sandmo, Agnar, "The Effect of Uncertainty on Saving Decisions," *Review of Economic Studies*, 37 (July 1970), 353-60.

Sarel, Michael, "Nonlinear Effects of Inflation on Economic Growth," *IMF Staff Papers*, 43 (March 1996), 199-215.

——, "Growth and Productivity in ASEAN Countries," in *Macroeconomic Issues Facing ASEAN Countries*, ed. by John Hicklin, David Robinson, and Anoop Singh, International Monetary Fund (Washington DC: 1997).

Sato, Ryuzo, "Fiscal Policy in a Neoclassical Growth Model: An Analysis of Time Required for Equilibrating Adjustment," *Review of Economic Studies*, 30 (February 1963), 16-23.

Sawada, Yasuyuki, "Are the Heavily Indebted Countries Solvent? Tests of Intertemporal Borrowing Constraints," *Journal of Development Economics*, 45 (December 1994), 325-37.

Schiff, Maurice, and Alberto Valdés, *The Plundering of Agriculture in Developing Countries*, the World Bank (Washington, DC: 1992).

Schmidt-Hebbel, Klaus, "Does Pension Reform Really Spur Productivity, Saving, and Growth?," unpublished, Central Bank of Chile (January 1999).

Schmidt-Hebbel, Klaus, Luis Servén, and Andrés Solimano, "Saving and Investment: Paradigms, Puzzles, Policies," *World Bank Research Observer*, 11 (February 1996), 87-117.

Seater, John, "Ricardian Equivalence," *Journal of Economic Literature*, 31 (March 1993), 142-90.

Senhadji, Abdelhak, "Time-Series Estimation of Structural Import Demand Equations: A Cross-Country Analysis," *IMF Staff Papers*, 45 (June 1998), 236-68.

Servén, Luis, "Uncertainty, Instability, and Irreversible Investment : Theory, Evidence, and Lessons for Africa," PRE Working Paper No. 1722, the World Bank (February 1997).

——, "Macroeconomic Uncertainty and Private Investment in Developing Countries," PRE Working Paper No. 2035, the World Bank (December 1998).

Shapiro, Carl, and Joseph E. Stiglitz, "Equilibrium Unemployment as a Worker Discipline Device," *American Economic Review*, 74 (June 1984), 433-44.

Sharer, Robert L., Hema R. De Zoysa, and Calvin A. McDonald, *Uganda: Adjustment with Growth*, Occasional Paper No. 121, International Monetary Fund (Washington DC: March 1995).

Shaw, Edward S., *Financial Deepening in Economic Development,* Oxford University Press (New York: 1973).

Sherwood, Joyce, "Revenue Features of Multiple Exchange Rate Systems: Some Case Studies," *IMF Staff Papers*, 5 (February 1956), 74-107.

Shleifer, Andrei, and Robert W. Vishny, "Corruption," *Quarterly Journal of Economics*, 108 (August 1993), 599-618.

Shome, Parthasarathi, Stotsky, Janet G., "Financial Transactions Taxes," *Tax Notes International*, 12 (January 1996), 47-56.

Sikken, Bernd Jan, and Jakob De Haan, "Budget Deficits, Monetization, and Central Bank Independence in Developing Countries," *Oxford Economic Papers*, 50 (July 1998), 493-511.

Södersten, Bo, *International Economics*, 2nd ed., St. Martin's Press (New York: 1980).

Solow, Robert M., "A Contribution to the Theory of Economic Growth," *Quarterly Journal of Economics,* 50 (February 1956), 65-94.

——, "Pespectives on Growth Theory," *Journal of Economic Perspectives*, 8 (Winter 1994), 45-54.

Spahn, Paul B., "International Financial Flows and Transactions Taxes: Survey and Options," Working Paper No. 95/60, International Monetary Fund (June 1995).

Spaventa, Luigi, "The Growth of Public Debt," *IMF Staff Papers*, 34 (June 1987), 374-99.

Spilimbergo, Antonio, Juan Luis Londoño,, and Miguel Székely, "Income Distribution, Factor Endowments, and Trade Openness," *Journal of Development Economics*, 59 (June 1999), 77-101.

Srinivasan, T. N., "Tax Evasion: A Model," *Journal of Public Economics*, 2 (November 1973), 339-46.

Standing, Guy, "Structural Adjustment and Labour market Policies: Towards Social Adjustment?" in *Towards Social Adjustment: Labour Market Issues in Structural Adjustment*, ed. by Guy Standing and Victor Tokman, International Labor Organization (Geneva: 1991).

Stein, Ernesto, "Fiscal Decentralization and Government Size in Latin America," unpublished, Inter-American Development Bank (October 1997).

Stern, Nicholas H., "Optimum Taxation and Tax Policy," *IMF Staff Papers*, 31 (June 1984), 339-78.

——, "The Economics of Development: A Survey," *European Economic Review*, 99 (September 1989), 597-685.

Stiglitz, Joseph E., "Alternative Theories of Wage Determination and Unemployment in LDCs: The Labor Turnover Model," *Quarterly Journal of Economics*, 98 (May 1974), 194-227.

——, "Alternative Theories of Wage Determination and Unemployment: the Efficiency Wage Model," in *The Theory and Experience of Economic Development*, ed. by Mark Gersovitz et al., Allen and Unwin (London: 1982).

Stiglitz, Joseph E., and Andrew Weiss, "Credit Rationing in Markets with Imperfect Information," *American Economic Review*, 53 (June 1981), 393-410.

——, "Asymmetric Information in Credit Markets and its Implications for Macroeconomics," *Oxford Economic Papers*, 44 (October 1992), 694-724.

Stotsky, Janet G., "Summary of IMF Tax Policy Advice," in *Tax Policy Handbook*, ed. by Parthasarathi Shome, International Monetary Fund (Washington, DC: 1995).

Stotsky, Janet G., and Asegedech WoldeMariam, "Tax Effort in Sub-Saharan Africa," Working Paper No. 97/107, International Monetary Fund (September 1997).

Subramanian, Arvind, "The Egyptian Stabilization Experience: An Analytical Retrospective," Working Paper No. 97/105, International Monetary Fund (September 1997).

Svensson, Lars, "Fixed Exchange Rates as a Means to Price Stability: What Have We Learned?," *European Economic Review*, 38 (April 1994), 447-68.

Svensson, Lars, and Assaf Razin, "The Terms of Trade and the Current Account: The Harberger-Laursen-Metlzer Effect," *Journal of Political Economy*, 91 (February 1983), 97-125.

Swan, Trevor W., "Economic Growth and Capital Accumulation," *Economic Record*, 32 (November 1956), 334-61.

Talvi, Ernesto, "Exchange Rate-Based Stabilization with Endogenous Fiscal Response," *Journal of Development Economics*, 54 (October 1997), 59-75.

Tanzi, Vito, Mario I. Blejer, and Mario O. Teijeiro, "Effects of Inflation on Measurement of Fiscal Deficits: Conventional versus Operational Measures," in *How to Measure the Fiscal Deficit: Analytical and Methodological Issues*, ed. by Mario I. Blejer and Adrienne Cheasty, International Monetary Fund (Washington DC: 1993).

Tanzi, Vito, and Howell H. Zee, "Fiscal Policy and Long-Run Growth," *IMF Staff Papers*, 44 (June 1997), 179-209.

Taylor, John B., "Aggregate Dynamics and Staggered Contracts," *Journal of Political Economy*, 88 (February 1980), 1-23.

Taylor, Lance, *Structuralist Macroeconomics*, Basic Books (New York: 1983).

——, *Income Distribution, Inflation and Growth*, MIT Press (Cambridge, Mass.: 1991).

——, "Gap Models," *Journal of Development Economics*, 45 (October 1994), 17-34.

Temple, Jonathan, "The New Growth Evidence," *Journal of Economic Literature*, 37 (March 1999), 112-56.

Ter-Minassian, Teresa, "Decentralizing government," *Finance and Development*, 34 (September 1997), 36-39.

Ter-Minassian, Teresa, and Gerd Schwartz, "The Role of Fiscal Policy in Sustainable Stabilization: Evidence from Latin America," Working Paper No. 97/94, International Monetary Fund (August 1997).

Thirsk, Wayne, "Overview: The Substance and Process of the Reform in Eight Developing Countries," in *Tax Reform in Developing Countries*, ed. by Wayne Thirsk, the World Bank (Washington D.C.: 1997).

Tokman, Victor, "Policies for a Heterogeneous Informal Sector in Latin America," in Beyond Regulation: *The Informal Economy in Latin America*, L. Rienner (Boulder, Col.: 1992).

Tommasi, Mariano, and Andrés Velasco, "Where Are We in the Political Economy of Reform?," *Journal of Policy Reform*, 1 (June 1996), 187-238.

Tornell, Aaron, and Andrés Velasco, "Fiscal Discipline and the Choice of a Nominal Anchor in Stabilization," *Journal of Development Economics*, 46 (October 1998), 1-30.

Tower, Christopher, "Government Contingent Liabilities and the Measurement of Fiscal Impact," in *The Measurement of Fiscal Deficits*, ed. by Mario I. Blejer and Adrienne Cheasty, International Monetary Fund (Washington DC: 1990).

United Nations, *Agricultural Taxation in Developing Countries*, Food and Agriculture Organization (Rome: 1993).

Upadhyay, Mukti P., "Accumulation of Human Capital in LDCs in the Presence of Unemployment," *Economica*, 61 (August 1994), 355-78.

Uribe, Martín, "Exchange-Rate-Based Inflation Stabilization: The Initial Real Effects of Credible Plans," *Journal of Monetary Economics*, 39 (July 1997a), 197-221.

——, "Hysteresis in a Simple Model of Currency Substitution," *Journal of Monetary Economics*, 39 (July 1997b), 197–221.

Van Gompel, J., "Stabilization with Wage Indexation and Exchange Rate Flexibility," *Journal of Economic Surveys*, 8 (September 1994), 252-81.

Van Wijnbergen, Sweder, "Interest Rate Management in LDCs," *Journal of Monetary Economics*, 12 (September 1983), 433-52.

——, "Exchange Rate Management and Stabilization Policies in Developing Countries," *Journal of Development Economics*, 23 (October 1986*b*), 227-47.

Varian, Hal R., *Microeconomic Analysis*, W. W. Norton and Co. (New York: 1992).

Végh, Carlos A., "Stopping High Inflation: an Analytical Overview," *IMF Staff Papers*, 39 (September 1992), 626-95.

Velasco, Andrés, "A Model of Endogenous Fiscal Deficits and Delayed Fiscal Reforms," Working Paper No. 6336, National Bureau of Economic Research (December 1997*b*).

Veidyanathan, Geetha, "Consumption, Liquidity Constraints and Economic Development," *Journal of Macroeconomics*, 15 (Summer 1993), 591-610.

Villanueva, Delano, "Openness, Human Development, and Fiscal Policies: Effects on Economic Growth and Speed of Adjustment," *IMF Staff Papers*, 41 (March 1994), 1-29.

Viner, Jacob, *The Customs Union Issue*, Cargenie Endowment for International Peace (New York: 1950).

Warner, Andrew, "Did the Debt Crisis Cause the Investment Crisis?," *Quarterly Journal of Economics*, 98 (June 1993), 1161-86.

Wei, Shang-Jin, "Gradualism versus Big Bang: Speed and Sustainability of Reforms," in *The political economy of reform*, ed. by Federico Sturzenegger and Mariano Tommasi, MIT Press (Cambridge, Mass.: 1998).

Welch, John H., and Darryl McLeod, "The Costs and Benefits of Fixed Dollar Exchange Rate in Latin America," unpublished, Federal Reserve Bank of Dallas (January 1993).

Wette, Hildegard, "Collateral in Credit Rationing in Markets with Imperfect Information," *American Economic Review*, 73 (June 1983), 442-5.

Williamson, John, and Stephan Haggard, "The Political Conditions for Economic Reform," in *The Political Economy of Economic Reform*, ed. by John Williamson, Institute for International Economics (Washington DC: 1994).

Williamson, John, and Molly Mahar, *A Survey of Financial Liberalization*, Essay in International Finance No. 211, Princeton University (November 1998).

Williamson, Stephen D., "Costly Monitoring, Financial Intermediation, and Equilibrium Credit Rationing," *Journal of Monetary Economics*, 18 (September 1986), 159-79.

Willman, Alpo, "The Collapse of the Fixed Exchange Rate Regime With Sticky Wages and Imperfect Substitutability between Domestic and Foreign Bonds," *European Economic Review* 32 (November 1988), 1817-38.

Wolfson, Michael, "Diverging Inequalities," *American Economic Review*, 84 (May 1994), 353-58.

World Bank, *The East Asian Miracle*, Oxford University Press (Oxford: 1993).

——, *Adjustment in Africa: Reforms, Results, and the Road Ahead*, Ocford University Press (Oxford: 1994).

——, *Private Capital Flows to Developing Countries: The Road to Financial Integration*, Oxford University Press (New York: 1997a).

——, "RMSM-X: User's Guide," unpublished, Development Data Group, the World Bank (July 1997b).

Wyplosz, Charles, "After the Honeymoon: On the Economics and the Politics of Economic Transformation," *European Economic Review*, 37 (April 1993), 379-86.

Yeats, Alexander J., "Does Mercosur's Trade Performance Raise Concerns about the Effects of Regional Trade Arrangements?," PRE Working Paper No. 1729, the World Bank (February 1997).

Yitzhaki, Shlomo, "A Note on Income Tax Evasion: A Theoretical Analysis," *Journal of Public Economics*, 3 (May 1974), 201-02.

Young, Alwyn, "The Tyranny of Numbers: Confronting the Statistical Realities of the East Asian Growth Experience," *Quarterly Journal of Economics*, 110 (August 1995), 641–80.

Zee, Howell, "Sustainability and Optimality of Government Debt," *IMF Staff Papers*, 35 (December 1988), 658-85.

——, "Taxation and Efficiency," in *Tax Policy Handbook*, ed. by Parthasarathi Shome, International Monetary Fund (Washington, DC: 1995).

Zeira, Joseph, "Cost Uncertainty and the Rate of Investment," *Journal of Economic Dynamics and Control*, 14 (February 1990), 53-63.

Zhang, Jie, "Optimal Public Investments in Education and Endogenous Growth," *Scandinavian Journal of Economics*, 98 (September 1996), 387-404.

INDEX